CONTENTS

LEGEND FOR CLUB STADIUM PLANS

- Covered seating
- Covered standing
- Uncovered seating
- Uncovered standing
- Disabled Facilities, wheelchairs access and viewing areas
- Main entrances
- Main exits

LEGEND FOR CLUBS' TEN YEAR LEAGUE RECORD

- Premier Division/S.P.L.
- First Division
- Second Division
- Third Division
- Hatched area indicates where the number of teams in the division have been fewer than 12 or 14. (See below)

FOOTNOTE FOR EACH CLUB'S TEN YEAR PLAYING RECORD

The number of teams playing in each division of The Scottish Football League and The Scottish Premier League has altered on several occasions during the past ten seasons and in order to assist the reader, the following information explains the various formats in operation during the following period:-

SEASON	PREMIER DIVISION	FIRST DIVISION	SECOND DIVISION	THIRD DIVISION
1989/90	10	14	14	N/A
1990/91	10	14	14	N/A
1991/92	12	12	14	N/A
1992/93	12	12	14	N/A
1993/94	12	12	14	N/A
1994/95	10	10	10	10
1995/96	10	10	10	10
1996/97	10	10	10	10
1997/98	10	10	10	10
	S.P.L.	S.F.L. FD	S.F.L. SD	S.F.L. TD
1998/99	10	10	10	10

A VERY WARM WELCOME

Once again, it gives me great pleasure in my capacity as President of The Scottish Football League in extending to all football fans, a very warm welcome to the 1999/2000 edition of The Tennent's Lager Scottish Football Review.

It would be fair to say that this season's Review is somewhat special as it witnesses the 20th edition of this prestigious publication and having recently had the opportunity to look back at some of the earlier editions of the Review, it was fascinating to observe how the events concerning our national game have unfolded together with the many changes that have taken place during this particular period. Indeed, whilst it is important not to dwell too much on the past, our game has been shaped by the events that have taken place over the past twenty years or so and as we approach the end of the 20th Century, we thought that it would be both proper and prudent to devote a couple of articles looking back and acknowledging both the events that have taken place as well as some of the personalities that have enriched our game since the Review was first published back in season 1980/81. Hopefully, both of these particular articles will evoke special memories and remind supporters of some of the great moments that have taken place in Scottish football during the past couple of decades.

However, whilst it is always important to look back with nostalgia at some of the events that have taken place during the past few years, it is also vital that we prepare our game for the undoubted challenges that lie ahead as we approach a new Millennium. As you will note elsewhere in the Review, there is an article which looks at The Scottish Football League's Youth Development Initiative Programme and hopefully, this will give supporters a better insight into the work that is currently being undertaken by the various football authorities as well as by most of the clubs in Scotland in an attempt to ensure the future wellbeing of Scottish football. Although it is not an area that receives too much publicity within the various sectors of the media, we at The Scottish Football League believe that it is vitally important that we have in place, a youth development structure which will encourage clubs to nurture and develop indigenous Scottish talent. There are already signs (albeit only a few at this stage) emerging to prove that the various youth development programmes which have been introduced by The Scottish Football League in recent years will bear fruit in the future.

I would stress that it is vitally important that all clubs, no matter what division they play in, continue to invest not only financially but also in time and effort in the development and training of our raw talent otherwise in a few years time, whoever is writing this introductory article may not be as fortunate as I have been to look back with pride on some of the notable achievements of Scottish football and indeed, the many great players and managers that have helped shape our game during the past twenty years.

It is always customary at this point to look back on the events of the preceding season and once again, Scottish football enjoyed its fair share of excitement and drama. Congratulations must be extended to Rangers for winning the domestic treble and as I write this article, recently qualified for the initial group stages of the Champions League and in this regard, I would take this opportunity in wishing them every success in their quest to do well in Europe's premier club competition. In the First Division, Hibernian, after a nervous start, dominated proceedings and comprehensively won the Championship with several weeks of the season remaining. In the Second Division, Livingston and Inverness Caledonian Thistle ensured that there would be drama right up until the final day of the season and although by this stage, both clubs had secured their places in the First Division, it was not until 4.45p.m. on 8th May, 1999 that Livingston emerged victorious as Champions. Congratulations also go to Ross County for their efforts in so convincingly winning the Third Division Championship together with Stenhousemuir, who pipped Brechin City on the final day.

Following the departure from The Scottish Football League of the Premier clubs, we had to encourage investment in the new thirty club organisation and I am pleased that we were successful in attracting two very well known and established companies to sponsor three of our competitions. First of all, I am especially delighted to welcome the return of our old friends Bell's, with whom we developed an extremely close working relationship for four years during the middle part of this decade and I am sure that I endorse the views of the thirty member clubs in welcoming their decision to once again invest in Scottish football by sponsoring the three divisions of the League Championship and the Challenge Cup competition. Secondly, there was further good news for Scottish football during the summer when we managed to enter into a long term sponsorship deal with CIS Insurance for that company to sponsor the League Cup competition and it is hoped that in the months and years ahead, the SFL, all of the 40 clubs together with CIS Insurance can develop a very good working relationship which will be mutually beneficial to all parties involved.

Talking about sponsorship, we are of course delighted that Tennent's Lager continue to sponsor what is commonly referred to as the "Bible" of Scottish football. This is the fourth year that Tennent Caledonian Breweries have sponsored the Review and together with their sponsorship of the Scottish Cup Competition, their support and commitment to Scottish football is not only appreciated but greatly valued.

As you will no doubt be aware, the SPL has decided to increase its membership to 12 clubs and following their decision to increase its membership by a further two clubs with effect from season 2000/01, member clubs of The Scottish Football League at its Annual General Meeting back in May decided to retain the current League format comprising three divisions of ten clubs. As a result, this particular organisation will lose two clubs at the end of this season and accordingly, we have invited applications from clubs currently playing outwith membership of the SFL to join. We are currently in the process of making inspection visits to all of the applicant clubs during the next couple of months and thereafter, these clubs will have the opportunity to put forward presentations to all of the SFL clubs. It is anticipated that a Special General Meeting will be convened early next year and it certainly will be a busy few months ahead for everyone involved in Scottish football!

Although we have increased the cover price slightly this season to reflect increased printing costs, we have also increased the number of pages to once again improve the content of the book and I am sure that you will agree with me that the Review retains its title as the most authoritative reference book on Scottish football. A tremendous amount of time and effort is required in the preparation of this book and I would like to thank the following:-

David C. Thomson (Editor); all the staff at The Scottish Football League especially Jan Murdoch and Anton Fagan; the 40 clubs of The Scottish Football League and Scottish Premier League; Alan Elliott and Jim Jeffrey; our contributors; the various sectors of the media for their co-operation and assistance; our sponsors, Tennent Caledonian Breweries; Creative Services and in particular, Dave and Nick Kelly and Emma Robinson; Programme Publications, especially Bill Cotton, Ron Vallance and Christine Green.

Finally, as the new Millennium approaches and we celebrate the 20th edition of the Review, let us all hope that future editions of this publication can record both in text and pictures, many more glorious moments that will enhance the reputation of Scottish football worldwide.

ENJOY YOUR FOOTBALL.

JAMES OLIVER
President, The Scottish Football League

A WORD FROM OUR SPONSORS

Last season marked two historic events for Tennent's Lager – the tenth anniversary of the brand's sponsorship of the Cup and the return of the Final to its spiritual home Hampden Park. It was perhaps fitting that the £60 million stadium's opening game was the Tennents Scottish Cup Final. The National Stadium provided a magnificent backdrop for the day which saw Rangers beat Celtic 1-0 to win the tenth Tennents Scottish Cup.

Although Rangers and Celtic may seem to dominate Scottish football, over the past ten seasons seven different clubs have lifted the illustrious trophy. The romance of the Cup has always appealed to Tennent's and every town and city has some association with the tournament. But Tennent's are not the only ones to be inspired by the Cup.

Hollywood legend Robert Duvall recently filmed "The Cup", which was supported by Tennent's Lager and follows the fortunes of Kilnockie, a small town team which makes it to the Millennium Tennents Scottish Cup Final.

Although we know the ending to the Hollywood Final, we will have to wait until May 27th, 2000 before we know which of the 48 teams setting out on the long road to Hampden this season will lift world football's oldest trophy.

Tennent's Lager has had a long association with Scottish football and is again delighted to support the game's "Bible" – *The Tennent's Lager Scottish Football Review*. The following pages are an invaluable guide to Scottish football and will be a handy reference throughout the season.

CALLUM MacKAY
Head of Sponsorship
Tennent Caledonian Breweries

COVER PHOTOGRAPHS
Rangers' captain Lorenzo Amoruso with the Tennents Scottish Cup and the League Cup • Rangers players with the Scottish Premier League trophy • Hibernian players with the First Division trophy • Livingston players with the Second Division trophy • Ross County players with the Third Division trophy • Scotland's Player of the Year, Henrik Larsson (Celtic)

Scottish Football – reassessing the priorities

So what's new in Scottish football? Certainly not the influx of foreign players which, with the new Millennium approaching, showed no sign of abating.

Morton and Dundee United, back in the 1960's, were at the forefront of an initiative to import talent, mostly from Scandinavia and mostly of a high calibre. Erik Sorensen, Kai Johansen, Orjan Persson, Finn Dossing and quite a few more of their fondly remembered ilk helped colour the scene, without ever threatening to monopolise it.

Home-bred players continued to form the huge majority of the old First Division roll and the best of them, along with the top Anglos, comprised a highly talented, if under-achieving, international squad.

But that was then. The situation, so far as Scotland is concerned, has become rather less healthy since the second coming of players from abroad, in conspicuously greater numbers, was signalled early in this decade.

Rangers and Celtic, who could be relied upon beforehand to nurture talent for the national team, were in the vanguard of the new movement, the effect of which has made the native Scot almost an endangered species in their sides. Those with pretensions to keeping abreast of them have sought to emulate their signing policy, albeit on only a relative financial scale but again to the detriment of our indigenous footballers.

Thus, with the 20th Century ending, Scottish football finds itself in conflict, with the needs of the national team under severe threat of being rendered secondary to the interests of top clubs.

Could it be, then, that we have seen the best of Scotland as a team, especially in those memorable years between 1974 and 1998 when they competed in all the World Cup Finals but one?

The question ranks high amongst those which have to be asked of our game in the year 2000 and beyond. Put it another, more emotive way; will we ever see the likes of Denis Law, Jim Baxter and Kenny Dalglish again?

The Scottish Football League, likewise The Scottish Football Association and the infant Scottish Premier League, are pledged in their different ways to promoting the game from within and, in particular, encouraging youth development.

Their efforts, which can be measured in both the investment of substantial sums of money as well as the application of manpower, would appear to argue well for the national team and all of those who follow it.

Yet, despite the promises from club level to create youth academies or centres of excellence, we have yet to see one even in its embryo state, far less gauge how well such a concept actually might work.

Goodness knows, Scotland could have had a whole network of these facilities by now, if only those who had the opportunity to build them had been able to resist channelling still more of their assets into some foreign transfer market. Such a temptation is always going to exist, regardless of how many young Scottish players

Dundee United's Steven Thompson - one of Scottish football's stars of the future

might emerge from the envisaged pipeline, for the reason that today's result is necessarily more important than tomorrow's.

But the medium to long term economic benefits to top Scottish clubs of producing their own players, rather than paying hefty prices to recruit from abroad, are so evident that they hardly need to be stated here. Even the Old Firm seem agreed that this is the way forward although they would be likely to describe as both reactionary and unrealistic anybody who suggested that success in Europe can be attained without outside assistance.

How things have changed in this regard; how they have changed even since The Scottish Football League launched this annual publication back in 1980 with Aberdeen and Dundee United still waiting to show what could be achieved against the continentals with players reared within Scotland. Aberdeen won the European Cup Winners' Cup in 1983 with an all Scottish side while Dundee United, built on the same basis, were to reach the Semi-Finals of the European Cup and Final of the UEFA Cup within the next four years.

The widely-held notion that never again could any Scottish club perform anything like as well with native resources only is waiting to be over-turned; not immediately, right enough, but some time thereafter. Anybody who argues otherwise fails to take cognisance of what has been done lately in countries of comparable size to our own; for example, Norway, where Rosenborg of Trondheim have performed creditably in the Champions League with a squad made up almost entirely of Norwegians.

We have to believe, first of all, that Scotland remains capable of producing good footballers if such a standard is to be emulated. The Scottish Football League evidently do,

Barry Ferguson - product of Rangers' youth programme

having put in place four years ago a Youth Development Initiative which has been embraced by so many clubs.

The Scottish Football Association, too, have worked in parallel towards the same ideal and over the same period, disbursing some £3 million to clubs not just in membership of The Scottish Football League and The Scottish Premier League but also in the Highland and South of Scotland Leagues. Theirs is a broad-based recognition that latent talent still exists everywhere and that, by means of special funding awarded on the basis of merit claims, it should be encouraged to spiral ever upwards.

The advent of such schemes came at a time when, almost without exception, the country's top clubs and a significant number of the lesser ones were still being driven by the demands to improve their stadia or, indeed, move to new ones. They were forced in most cases to re-order their priorities, channelling only minimal amounts into what was happening on the field and rather more towards what was being built up around it.

But a difficult, some would say almost perilous, transition has virtually

been completed, with the result that those most affected can begin devoting much more attention to vital playing matters and, in the process, making up for lost time and opportunity.

It is highly encouraging for the Scottish game that this drive towards higher standards has not been peculiar only to those in membership of The Scottish Premier League which, of course, is now in its second season. Just look at the advances made by the likes of Livingston who, as well as creating a handsome environment for themselves at Almondvale, have embarked on an ascent of the divisions with a place in the highest being their ultimate aim. Inverness Caledonian Thistle and Ross County, near neighbours in the north and the two clubs admitted most recently to The Scottish Football League, have demonstrated similar ambition and resourcefulness which can only be good for the game's growth.

The Scottish Football League began moves earlier this season to accord membership to another two clubs; this because of The Scottish Premier League's avowed intention to increase their numbers from 10 to 12 in time for next term.

So, more than a century on from senior football's beginnings in Scotland and despite gloomy predictions of clubs slipping into extinction, there exists a feeling of vibrancy in many, if not all, quarters. The influx of players from abroad undoubtedly has contributed to it. Who amongst us, after all, has not felt uplifted by watching the likes of Brian Laudrup or Henrik Larsson?

Yet, ultimately, the welfare of Scottish football in the future can only be enhanced by the re-discovery of native skills; with, of course, the national team benefiting in proportion.

By Brian Scott
(Scottish Daily Mail)

Pittodrie Stadium, Pittodrie Street,
Aberdeen, AB24 5QH

CHAIRMAN
Stewart Milne

VICE-CHAIRMAN
Ian R. Donald

DIRECTORS
Gordon A. Buchan,
Richard A. M. Ramsay,
Martin J. Gilbert,
Keith H. Burkinshaw &
William Gilmore

SECRETARY
Richard A. M. Ramsay

OPERATIONS MANAGER
David Johnston (01224) 650433

MANAGER
Ebbe Skovdahl

ASSISTANT MANAGER
Tommy Moller Nielson

RESERVE TEAM/YOUTH COACH
Gardner Spiers

YOUTH DEVELOPMENT MANAGER
Drew Jarvie

FITNESS COACH
Stuart Hogg

KIT MANAGERS
Teddy Scott & Jim Warrender

CLUB DOCTOR
Dr. Derek Gray

PHYSIOTHERAPISTS
David Wylie & John Sharp

S.F.A. COMMUNITY COACH
Chic McLelland

CHIEF SCOUT
John Kelman

**FOOTBALL SAFETY OFFICERS'
ASSOCIATION REPRESENTATIVE**
John Morgan (01224) 650400

GROUNDSMAN
Moray Galbraith

MARKETING & SALES MANAGER
Harvey Smith (01224) 650426

TELEPHONES
Ground/General Enquiries
(01224) 650400
Ticket Office (01224) 632328
Fax (01224) 644173
Dons Clubcall (0891) 121551

E-MAIL & INTERNET ADDRESS
talkback@thedons.co.uk
http://www.afc.co.uk
http://www.thedons.co.uk

CLUB SHOPS
AFC Direct, 23 Bridge Street,
Aberdeen, Tel (01224) 405305
and **Ticket Office**, c/o Aberdeen F.C.,
Pittodrie Stadium, Aberdeen

OFFICIAL SUPPORTERS CLUB
Association Secretary:
Mrs. Susan Scott, 'Aldon',
Wellington Road,
Aberdeen, AB12 4BJ

CLUB CAPTAIN
Jim Leighton

TEAM CAPTAIN
Derek Whyte

SHIRT SPONSOR
Atlantic Telecom Group Plc.

6

LIST OF PLAYERS 1999-2000

SURNAME	FIRST NAME	MIDDLE NAME	DATE OF BIRTH	PLACE OF BIRTH	DATE OF SIGNING	HEIGHT FT INS	WEIGHT ST LBS	POS. ON PITCH	PREVIOUS CLUB
Anderson	Russell		25/10/78	Aberdeen	19/07/96	6 0.0	11 10	Def	Dyce Juniors
Bernard	Paul		30/12/72	Edinburgh	29/09/95	6 0.0	12 10	Mid	Oldham Athletic
Bett	Baldur		12/04/80	Reykjavik	23/10/96	5 8.5	11 7	Mid	Hermes
Bett	Calum		03/10/81	Reykjavik	13/07/98	5 9.5	10 8	Mid	S Form
Buchan	Martin	James	03/04/77	Manchester	26/08/95	5 11.0	12 0	Def	Stonehaven
Clark	Christopher		15/09/80	Aberdeen	16/08/97	5 8.0	10 8	Fwd	Hermes
Dow	Andrew	James	07/02/73	Dundee	06/07/98	5 9.0	11 10	Def/Mid	Hibernian
Duncan	Russell		15/09/80	Aberdeen	28/08/96	5 10.0	11 1	Fwd	Hall Russells
Esson	Ryan		19/03/80	Aberdeen	23/10/96	6 1.0	12 7	Gk	Parkvale
Gillies	Richard	Charles	24/08/76	Glasgow	08/08/97	5 10.0	12 2	Fwd	St. Mirren
Good	Iain	David	09/08/77	Glasgow	14/03/96	6 0.5	11 7	Def	Queen's Park
Hamilton	James		09/02/76	Aberdeen	25/03/99	6 0.0	12 5	Fwd	Heart of Midlothian
Hart	Michael		10/02/80	Bellshill	12/08/97	5 10.0	11 11	Fwd	Stoneywood
Jess	Eoin		13/12/70	Aberdeen	05/07/97	5 10.0	11 9	Mid	Coventry City
Kiriakov	Ilian		04/08/67	Pavlikeni	14/06/96	5 5.0	11 6	Mid	Anorthosis
Leighton	James		24/07/58	Johnstone	12/06/97	6 1.5	13 3	Gk	Hibernian
Lilley	David	William	31/10/77	Bellshill	23/08/99	6 1.0	11 4	Def	Queen of the South
Mackie	Darren	Graham	05/01/82	Inverurie	13/07/98	5 9.0	10 4	Fwd	S Form
Marwick	Steven	Gordon	11/09/81	Aberdeen	13/07/98	5 7.0	10 10	Mid	S Form
Mayer	Andreas		13/09/72	Burgau	29/01/99	5 11.0	12 3	Mid	Rosenborg B.K.
McAllister	James	Reynolds	26/04/78	Glasgow	10/05/99	5 10.0	11 0	Def	Queen of the South
McCaffrey	Stuart	Muir	30/05/79	Glasgow	09/07/98	5 11.5	12 12	Def	Hibernian
McGuire	Philip		04/03/80	Glasgow	19/09/97	5 11.5	11 4	Def	Dyce Juniors
McNaughton	Kevin	Paul	28/08/82	Dundee	20/07/99	5 10.0	10 6	Def	S Form
Michie	Scott	David	22/08/83	Aberdeen	20/07/99	5 10.0	11 1	Fwd	S Form
Milne	Kevin		27/04/81	Edinburgh	16/08/97	5 11.0	12 3	Mid	Hermes
O'Donnoghue	Ross		09/02/83	Glasgow	20/07/99	5 9.0	10 5	Mid	S Form
Peat	Mark		13/03/82	Bellshill	20/07/99	6 1.0	11 13	Gk	S Form
Pepper	Colin	Nigel	25/04/68	Rotherham	26/11/98	5 10.5	12 3	Mid	Bradford City
Perry	Mark	George	07/02/71	Aberdeen	06/07/98	6 1.0	12 11	Def	Dundee United
Preece	David	Douglas	26/08/76	Darlington	30/07/99	6 2.0	12 10	Gk	Darlington
Rowson	David	Andrew	14/09/76	Aberdeen	05/10/94	5 10.5	12 2	Mid	F.C. Stoneywood
Rutkiewicz	Kevin		10/05/80	Glasgow	25/03/98	6 0.5	12 6	Def	Larkhall Thistle
Smith	Gary		25/03/71	Glasgow	14/07/97	6 0.0	12 3	Def	Stade Rennais
Solberg	Thomas		25/01/70	Oslo	26/08/99	6 1.5	12 12	Def	Viking Stavanger
Tiernan	Fergus		03/01/82	Helensburgh	13/07/98	5 10.0	11 1	Mid	S Form
Whyte	Derek		31/08/68	Glasgow	19/12/97	5 11.5	13 2	Def	Middlesbrough
Winters	Robert		04/11/74	East Kilbride	23/09/98	5 10.0	12 3	Fwd	Dundee United
Wyness	Dennis	Middleton	22/03/77	Aberdeen	05/10/94	5 10.5	12 1	Mid	F.C. Stoneywood
Young	Darren		13/10/78	Glasgow	16/09/95	5 9.0	11 11	Mid	Crombie Sports
Young	Derek		27/05/80	Glasgow	22/10/96	5 8.5	10 10	Fwd	Lewis United

Milestones

YEAR OF FORMATION: 1903
MOST CAPPED PLAYER: Alex McLeish
NO. OF CAPS: 77
MOST LEAGUE POINTS IN A SEASON: 64 (Premier Division - Season 1992/93) (44 games)(2 Points for a Win)
MOST LEAGUE GOALS SCORED BY A PLAYER IN A SEASON: Benny Yorston (Season 1929/30)
NO. OF GOALS SCORED: 38
RECORD ATTENDANCE: 45,061 (-v- Heart of Midlothian – 13.3.1954)
RECORD VICTORY: 13-0 (-v- Peterhead – Scottish Cup, 9.2.1923)
RECORD DEFEAT: 0-8 (-v- Celtic - Division 1, 30.1.65)

The Dons' ten year league record

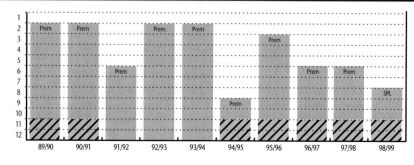

THE DONS' CLUB FACTFILE 1998/99 RESULTS... APPEARANCES... SCORERS

Date	Venue	Opponents	Att.	Res	Leighton J.	Perry M.	Smith G.	Whyte D.	Inglis J.	Anderson R.	Hignett C.	Jess E.	Dodds W.	Kiriakov I.	Newell M.	Rowson D.	Gillies R.	Buchan M.J.	Dow A.	Young Derek	Hart M.	Wyness D.	Winters R.	Young Darren	Bett B.	Pepper N.	Good I.	Stillie D.	Mayer A.	Notman A.	Bernard P.	Hamilton J.	Warner A.
Aug 1	A	Dundee	7,816	2-0	1	2	3	4	5	6	7¹	8¹	9	10	11	12	13																
16	H	Celtic	16,640	3-2†	1	2¹	3	4	5	6	7¹	8	9	10	11			12															
22	A	Heart of Midlothian	14,416	0-2	1	2	3	4	5		7	8	9	12		11		6	10	13													
29	A	Dunfermline Athletic	6,510	1-1	1	2¹		4	5	6	7	8	9	13		10		12	3		11												
Sep 12	H	Motherwell	11,260	1-1	1	2	3	4	5			8¹	9	12	11	7	13	6	10			14											
19	A	St. Johnstone	5,814	0-2	1		3	4	12	2	6	8	9	10	11	7	13	5				14											
23	H	Rangers	17,862	1-1	1	2	3	4	5		7	8¹		12	13	11	14	6	10				9										
27	H	Kilmarnock	13,048	0-0	1	2		4	5	13	7	8		12	10	11		6	3				9										
Oct 4	A	Dundee United	8,933	0-1	1	2	3	4		6	7	8		11	12	10		5					9										
17	H	Dundee	10,004	2-2	1	2	3	4		6		8²		10	13	12	11	5				14	9	7									
24	A	Celtic	59,963	0-2	1	2	3	4		6	7	8		14		11	13	5				12	9	10									
31	A	Motherwell	8,146	2-2	1	2	3	4		6		8		10	11¹	7	12	5	13				9¹										
Nov 7	H	Dunfermline Athletic	10,293	2-1	1	2	3	4		5	6	8²		10	11	7							9										
14	A	Rangers	49,479	1-2	1	2	3	4		5	6	8¹		10	11	7						12	9										
21	H	St. Johnstone	10,044	0-1	1	2	3	4		5		8		10	11	7	13			14		12	9			6							
28	H	Dundee United	11,964	0-3	1	2	3	4				8		10	11	7			5			12	9			6							
Dec 5	A	Kilmarnock	9,785	0-4	1		3	4	5	12		8		13	11			6	2			10	9		7	14							
12	H	Heart of Midlothian	11,137	2-0	1	2	3	4	5			8¹		10	12	11		6					9¹		7								
19	H	Dundee	6,340	2-1	1	2		4	5			8		10		11		6	3				9²		7								
26	A	Dunfermline Athletic	7,873	2-1		2		4	5¹			8¹		10	12	11		6	3				9		7			1					
29	H	Motherwell	15,269	1-1		2		4	5			8¹		10	12	11		6	3		13		9		7			1					
Jan 2	A	St. Johnstone	8,971	1-4		2		4	5			8		10	12	11		6¹	3		13		9		7			1					
30	H	Rangers	19,507	2-4	1	2		4	5			8¹		10	11¹					12			9	6	7								
Feb 6	H	Kilmarnock	9,299	2-1	1	2	3	4	5			8¹		10	11			12			13		9	6					7¹				
20	A	Dundee United	8,309	0-3	1	2	3	4	5			8		10	9			12			11			6					7	13			
	A	Heart of Midlothian	13,957	2-0		2	3	4				8			9				5		12	11¹		6			1		7	10¹			
Mar 14	H	Celtic	16,825	1-5		2	3	4				8		10				6	5		7	11	9¹		12			1	13				
20	A	Motherwell	6,963	1-1		2	3	4				14	8	12					5		13	11	9¹	6			1	7		10			
Apr 3	H	Dunfermline Athletic	11,361	3-1		2	3	4				8		12					5			9³	6				1	7		10	11		
10	A	Kilmarnock	9,048	2-4		2	3	4				8							5		12	9¹	6				1	7		10	11¹		
17	H	Dundee United	11,603	0-4		2	3	4				8							5		12	9	6		13				7		10	11	1
25	A	Rangers	49,145	1-3		2¹	3	4				8							5			9	6						7		10	11	1
May 1	H	St. Johnstone	9,561	1-0			3	4		2		8						6	5		11		9¹		13				7		10	12	1
8	H	Dundee	9,790	1-2			3	4		2		8						6	5	13	12	10	9¹						7		14	11	1
15	A	Celtic	59,138	2-3		4¹	3			2		8						5	12	6	13	9							7¹		10	11	1
23	H	Heart of Midlothian	13,042	2-5		2	3	4		6		8¹						11¹	5	12	10	13	9						7				1
TOTAL FULL APPEARANCES					22	32	30	35	16	13	13	36	6	17	14	18	4	19	22	5	6	28	11	1	7		8	13	8	6	6	
TOTAL SUB APPEARANCES								(1)	(3)				(5)	(9)	(4)	(7)	(4)	(3)	(4)	(9)		(8)			(3)	(1)			(2)	(1)	(1)	
TOTAL GOALS SCORED								4	1		2	14		2			2					1	12						2	1	1	

Small bold figures denote goalscorers.   † denotes opponent's own goal.

Pittodrie Stadium

PITTODRIE STREET
GOLF ROAD

CAPACITY: 22,199 (All Seated)

PITCH DIMENSIONS: 109 yds x 72 yds

FACILITIES FOR DISABLED SUPPORTERS:
Wheelchair section in front of Merkland Stand and in front row of Richard Donald Stand and also front row of Main Stand Section F.
(Please telephone Ticket Office and reserve place(s) in advance).

Team playing kits

How to get there

You can reach Pittodrie Stadium by these routes:

BUSES: The following buses all depart from the city centre to within a hundred yards of the ground: Nos. 1, 2, 3 and 11.

TRAINS: The main Aberdeen station is in the centre of the city and the above buses will then take fans to the ground.

CARS: Motor vehicles coming from the city centre should travel along Union Street, then turn into King Street and the park will be on your right, about half a mile further on.
Parking on Beach Boulevard and Beach Esplanade.

email: sfl@sol.co.uk • website: www.sfl.scottishfootball.com

Celtic Park, Glasgow, G40 3RE

COMPANY DIRECTORS
Frank O'Callaghan (Chairman),
Brian Quinn (Vice-Chairman),
Fergus McCann, Eric J. Riley,
Dermot F. Desmond,
Sir Patrick Sheehy & Kevin Sweeney

CLUB DIRECTORS
David W. Kells, John S. Keane
& Michael A. McDonald

CHIEF EXECUTIVE
Allan MacDonald

COMPANY SECRETARY
Heather-Anne Barton
(0141) 551 4208/4201

DIRECTOR OF FOOTBALL OPERATIONS
Kenny Dalglish

HEAD COACH
John Barnes

ASSISTANT HEAD COACH
Eric Black

HEAD YOUTH COACH
William McStay

DEVELOPMENT COACHES
Kenny McDowall & Tom O'Neill

CLUB DOCTOR
Roddy MacDonald

PHYSIOTHERAPIST
Brian Scott

**FOOTBALL SAFETY OFFICERS'
ASSOCIATION REPRESENTATIVE**
George E. Douglas
(0141) 556 2611/551 4256

GROUNDSMAN
John Hayes

KIT CONTROLLER
John Clark

COMMERCIAL DIRECTOR
David W. Kells
(0141) 556 4246/4207

PUBLIC RELATIONS MANAGER
Peter McLean (0141) 551 4276

**MANAGING DIRECTOR
CELTIC POOLS**
John Maguire (0141) 551 9922

TELEPHONES
Ground (0141) 556 2611
Fax (0141) 551 8106
Ticket Services (0141) 551 4223
Credit Card Hotline (0141) 551 8653/4
Celtic View (0141) 551 8103
Celtic Hotline (0891) 1967 21
Walfrid Restaurant (0141) 551 9955
Mail Order Hotline (0141) 550 1888

CELTIC WORLD WIDE WEB-SITE NO
http://www.celticfc.co.uk

CLUB SHOPS
Superstore, Celtic Park, Glasgow, G40 3RE
Tel (0141) 554 4231
(9.00 a.m. to 6.00 p.m. Mon-Sat,
10.00a.m. to 5.00p.m. Sunday),
40 Dundas Street, Glasgow G1 2AQ
Tel (0141) 332 2727
(9.00 a.m. to 5.00 p.m. Mon-Sat)
and **21 High Street,** Glasgow, G1 1LX
Tel (0141) 552 7630
(9.30 a.m. to 5.30 p.m. Mon-Sat,
11.30 a.m. to 4.30 p.m. Sunday)

OFFICIAL SUPPORTERS CLUB
Celtic Supporters Association,
1524 London Road, Glasgow G40 3RJ
Tel (0141) 556 1882/554 6250/554 6342

TEAM CAPTAIN
Tom Boyd

SHIRT SPONSOR
NTL

Celtic

LIST OF PLAYERS 1999-2000

SURNAME	FIRST NAME	MIDDLE NAME	DATE OF BIRTH	PLACE OF BIRTH	DATE OF SIGNING	HEIGHT FT INS	WEIGHT ST LBS	POS. ON PITCH	PREVIOUS CLUB
Berkovic	Eyal		02/04/72	Israel	20/07/99	5 8.0	10 3	Mid	West Ham United
Blinker	Reginald	Waldi	04/06/69	Surinam	06/08/97	5 8.5	11 7	Mid/For	Sheffield Wednesday
Bonnes	Stephane		26/02/78	France	29/07/99	5 6.0	10 0	Mid	F.C. Mulhouse
Boyd	Thomas		24/11/65	Glasgow	06/02/92	5 11.0	12 4	Def	Chelsea
Brattbakk	Harald	Martin	12/12/97	Norway	01/02/71	5 9.0	11 0	Fwd	Rosenborg B.K.
Burchill	Mark	James	18/08/80	Broxburn	03/06/97	5 8.0	9 9	Fwd	Celtic B.C.
Burley	Craig	William	24/09/71	Ayr	25/07/97	5 11.5	12 13	Mid	Chelsea
Casey	Mark		09/10/82	Glasgow	07/07/99	6 2.0	11 3	Def	Celtic Youth Initiative
Cocozza	Marc	Anthony	08/01/81	Glasgow	03/07/97	5 11.0	11 5	Def	St. Johnstone B.C.
Convery	John		01/04/80	Newtonards	28/03/97	6 1.0	11 9	Def	Glenavon
Corr	Barry	John	13/01/81	Glasgow	03/07/97	6 1.0	12 13	Gk	Celtic B.C.
Cortani	Marco		17/12/79	Rome	14/08/98	5 6.0	9 6	Mid	A.S. Roma
Crainey	Stephen	Danial	22/06/81	Glasgow	03/07/97	5 9.0	9 11	Def	Celtic B.C.
Elliot	Barry	Robert	24/10/78	Carlisle	11/08/95	5 10.0	11 5	Fwd	Celtic B.C.
Fraser	Allan		25/06/81	Aberdeen	10/07/98	5 8.0	10 4	Mid	Celtic B.C.
Fyfe	Graham		07/12/82	Dundee	20/07/99	5 8.0	9 8	Mid	S Form
Gallagher	James		13/02/80	Donegal	30/07/96	6 0.0	12 4	Gk	Glenea United
Goodwin	James		20/11/81	Waterford	25/11/97	5 9.0	12 1	Def	Tramore
Gould	Jonathan		18/07/68	London	01/08/97	6 0.0	13 7	Gk	Bradford City
Healy	Colin		14/03/80	Cork	07/07/98	5 11.0	11 0	Mid	Wilton United
Jack	Steven		09/08/83	Bellshill	20/08/99	5 9.0	11 2	Def	S Form
Johnson	Thomas		15/01/71	Newcastle	31/03/97	5 9.0	12 4	Fwd	Aston Villa
Kennedy	John		18/08/83	Bellshill	20/08/99	6 1.0	12 6	Def	S Form
Keogh	Liam	Michael	06/09/81	Aberdeen	18/09/97	5 7.0	10 6	Fwd	Celtic B.C.
Kerr	James	Stewart Robert	13/11/74	Bellshill	27/05/93	6 2.0	13 0	Gk	Celtic B.C.
Kharine	Dmitri		16/08/68	Moscow	12/07/99	6 2.5	13 9	Gk	Chelsea
Kilmartin	Andrew		18/01/83	Downpatrick	21/07/99	5 10.0	10 0	Mid	Rosario Youth Soccer Club
Lambert	Paul		07/08/69	Paisley	07/11/97	5 11.0	10 6	Mid	BV 09 Borussia Dortmund
Larsson	Henrik		20/09/71	Sweden	29/07/97	5 10.0	11 11	Fwd	Feyenoord
Lynch	Simon	George	19/05/82	Montreal	20/07/99	6 0.0	9 9	Fwd	Celtic Youth Initiative
Mahe	Stephane		23/09/68	Puteaux	31/07/97	5 11.0	11 11	Def	Stade Rennais
Maloney	Shaun	Richard	24/01/83	Malaya	07/07/99	5 6.0	10 0	Fwd	Celtic Youth Initiative
McBride	Kevin		14/06/81	Bellshill	10/07/98	5 6.0	8 3	Mid	Celtic B.C.
McCann	Ryan		21/09/81	Bellshill	10/07/98	5 8.0	11 3	Mid	Celtic B.C.
McColligan	Brian		31/10/80	Glasgow	03/07/97	5 8.5	9 11	Mid	Celtic B.C.
McGovern	Jon	Paul	03/10/80	Glasgow	03/07/97	5 7.0	9 6	Fwd	Celtic B.C.
McKinlay	Thomas	Valley	03/12/64	Glasgow	04/11/94	5 10.0	11 9	Def	Heart of Midlothian
McManus	Stephen		10/09/82	Lanark	10/07/98	6 0.0	9 6	Mid	S Form
McNamara	Jackie		24/10/73	Glasgow	04/10/95	5 8.0	9 7	Mid	Dunfermline Athletic
McParland	Anthony	Patrick	20/09/82	Rutherglen	20/07/99	5 7.0	10 4	Mid	S Form
Miller	Liam	William Peter	13/02/81	Cork	28/10/97	5 7.0	10 6	Mid	Ballincollig AFC
Miller	Stephen		04/10/81	Glasgow	10/07/98		9 9	Def	Celtic B.C.
Mjallby	Johan		09/02/71	Sweden	19/11/98	6 1.0	13 4	Def	AIK Stockholm
Moravcik	Lubomir		22/06/65	Slovakia	30/10/98	5 6.0	11 7	Mid	MSV Duisburg
Moriarty	Tadg	Lee	28/09/80	Edinburgh	01/03/97	5 9.5	9 11	Def	Celtic B.C.
Morrison	Allan	James	31/03/82	Irvine	10/07/98	6 0.0	12 0	Gk	Ayr Boswell
Murphy	David		18/01/83	Dublin	02/09/99	5 11.0	12 0	Fwd	Stella Maris
Petrov	Stilian		05/07/79	Bulgaria	06/08/99	5 9.0	12 1	Mid	F.C. CSKA Sofia
Petta	Bobby	Alfred Manuel	06/08/74	Rotterdam	14/07/99	5 7.0	11 3	Mid	Ipswich Town
Prunty	Bryan		12/01/83	Coatbridge	15/01/99	5 8.0	10 7	Fwd	Celtic B.C.
Rieper	Marc	Jensen	05/06/68	Copenhagen	12/09/97	6 3.5	14 0	Def	West Ham United
Riseth	Vidar		21/04/72	Levanger	22/09/98	6 2.0	12 4	Def	LASK Linz
Sanna	Alessandro		17/12/79	Rome	14/08/98	5 8.0	11 0	Mid	Viterbese Calcio
Smith	James		20/11/80	Alexandria	28/12/96	5 6.5	11 0	Mid/For	Celtic B.C.
Stubbs	Alan		06/10/71	Kirkby	17/07/96	6 1.0	13 7	Def	Bolton Wanderers
Sullivan	Vincent		19/04/81	Waterford	14/10/98	5 9.0	9 6	Fwd	Dungarvan United
Tebily	Olivier		19/12/75	Abidjan	09/07/99	6 0.0	13 4	Def	Sheffield United
Viduka	Mark	Anthony	09/10/75	Australia	02/12/98	6 2.0	13 9	Fwd	NK Croatia Zagreb
Wieghorst	Morten		25/02/71	Glostrup	08/12/95	6 3.0	13 4	Mid	Dundee

Milestones

YEAR OF FORMATION: 1888
MOST CAPPED PLAYER: Paul McStay
NO. OF CAPS: 76
MOST LEAGUE POINTS IN A SEASON: 72 (Premier Division – Season 1987/88) (2 points for a Win)
83 (Premier Division – Season 1995/96) (3 points for a Win)
MOST LEAGUE GOALS SCORED BY A PLAYER IN A SEASON: Jimmy McGrory (Season 1935/36)
NO. OF GOALS SCORED: 50
RECORD ATTENDANCE: 92,000 (-v- Rangers – 1.1.1938)
RECORD VICTORY: 11-0 (-v- Dundee – Division 1, 26.10.1895)
RECORD DEFEAT: 0-8 (-v- Motherwell - Division 1, 30.4.1937)

The Bhoys' ten year league record

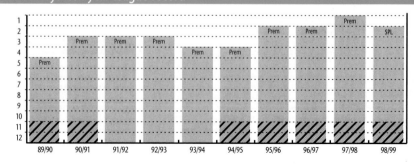

THE BHOYS' CLUB FACTFILE 1998/99 RESULTS... APPEARANCES... SCORERS

Date	Venue	Opponents	Att.	Res	Gould J.	Boyd T.	Mackay M.	McNamara J.	Stubbs A.	Donnelly S.	Lambert P.	Burley C.	Brattbakk H.	Larsson H.	Blinker R.	Jackson D.	Annoni E.	Rieper M.	Mahe S.	McKinlay T.	Burchill M.	O'Donnell P.	Hannah D.	Riseth V.	McConachie A.	Moravcik L.	McBride J.P.	Warner A.	Mjallby J.	Viduka M.	Wieghorst M.	Corr B.	Kerr S.	Marshall S.	Healy C.	Johnson T.
Aug 1	H	Dunfermline Athletic	59,377	5-0	1	2	3¹	4	5	6¹	7	8³	9	10	11	12																				
16	A	Aberdeen	16,640	2-3	1	2			5	6	7	8	12	10²	11	9	3	4																		
22	H	Dundee United	59,133	2-1	1	2			5	11	7	8¹	9	10				4	3	6	12¹															
29	A	Dundee	9,853	1-1	1	2			5	11	7	8¹	12	10	6	9	4	3																		
Sep 12	H	Kilmarnock	58,567	1-1	1	2			5	11	7	8	9	10	6¹	12	4	3	13																	
20	A	Rangers	50,026	0-0	1	2			5	11		8		10	9	13	4	3	12	6	10															
23	H	St. Johnstone	55,745	0-1	1	2			5	6	7	8	9	10	11	12	3	13	14			4														
26	H	Heart of Midlothian	59,283	1-1	1				5	11¹	7	8	9	10			4	3		12			6	2													
Oct 3	A	Motherwell	12,103	2-1	1	2			5	11	7¹	8	9	10			4	3				12	6														
17	A	Dunfermline Athletic	10,968	2-2	1	2			5	11	7	8	9¹	10¹			4		12			6	3														
24	H	Aberdeen	59,963	2-0	1	2		6		11²	7	8	9	10		4			5			13	12	3													
31	A	Kilmarnock	16,695	0-2	1	2		4		11	7	8	9	10			3	6	13	12		5														
Nov 7	H	Dundee	58,974	6-1		4				6¹	7			10³			3	11²		8		5	1	9	12											
14	A	St. Johnstone	9,762	1-2		4				6				10¹			3	12	11	8	10	5		9		1										
21	H	Rangers	59,783	5-1	1	2			5	11	7			10²			3		13¹	8	12	6		9²		1	4									
28	H	Motherwell	59,227	2-0	1	2			5	11	7		14	10¹		12	3		13	8¹		6		9		1	4									
Dec 6	A	Heart of Midlothian	17,334	1-2	1	2			5	11	7			10			3		12	8¹		6		9			4									
12	A	Dundee United	11,612	1-1	1	2			5	11	7			10¹			3		12	8		6		9			4									
19	H	Dunfermline Athletic	59,024	5-0	1	2			5	6	7		14	10²		12	3		11	8		13		9²			4¹									
27	A	Dundee	10,043	3-0	1	2		12	5		7		13	10¹			3		11¹	8		6¹		9			4									
Jan 3	A	Rangers	50,059	2-2	1	2		11	5¹		7			10¹			3			8		6		9			4									
31	H	St. Johnstone	59,746	5-0	1	2			5	14	7		9³	10¹	13		3			8	12	6		11¹			4									
Feb 6	H	Heart of Midlothian	59,844	3-0	1	2			5		7		9	10³	13	12	3		14	8		6		11			4									
17	H	Kilmarnock	59,220	1-0				6			7		9	10	11		3	2				5¹		8			4									
21	A	Motherwell	11,963	7-1	1	2		6			7	12¹	9	10⁴	11		3	13	14¹			5		8¹			4									
27	H	Dundee United	59,902	2-1	1	2		6			7	8¹	9	10¹	11		3					5					4	12								
Mar 14	A	Aberdeen	16,825	5-1	1	2		6			7	8¹		10²	11			3	12			5					4	9²								
21	A	Kilmarnock	14,472	0-0	1	2		6			7	8		10	11			3				5					4	9								
Apr 3	H	Dundee	59,269	5-0	1	2		6			7	8¹	12	10²	11¹			3	14			5					4	9¹	13							
14	A	Heart of Midlothian	16,388	4-2	1	2		6			7	8		10	11¹		4	3				5¹						9²		15						
17	A	Motherwell	59,588	1-0		2					7	8	13	10¹	11		6	3	14			5					4	9	12		1					
24	A	St. Johnstone	10,393	0-1		2		6	13	12	7	8		10			4	3	14			5						9	11		1					
May 2	H	Rangers	59,918	0-3				6	12	7		11	10			4	3				5						9	8		1	2	13			
8	A	Dunfermline Athletic	8,848	2-1				2	6	7		12	10			4			14	8		5					9	3		1	13	5	11²		
15	H	Aberdeen	59,138	3-2	1			2	7			10	11¹			4	6		12¹		5						9	3				8	9¹		
23	A	Dundee United	10,062	2-1	1	2		5			8	11					3	12	7²			10					4	6							9
TOTAL FULL APPEARANCES					28	31	1	15	22	20	33	20	16	35	13	4	9	7	24	11	5	13	5	26	1	14	3	17	8	5	4	1	2	3
TOTAL SUB APPEARANCES								(1)	(1)	(3)		(1)	(8)				(2)	(2)	(5)	(7)	(16)	(2)	(4)	(1)		(1)		(1)	(2)	(1)		(1)	(1)	
TOTAL GOALS SCORED						1		1		5	1	9	5	29	4					9	2		3		6		1	5					3

Small bold figures denote goalscorers. † denotes opponent's own goal.

Celtic Park

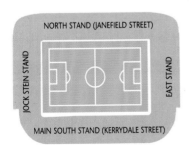

NORTH STAND (JANEFIELD STREET)

JOCK STEIN STAND

EAST STAND

MAIN SOUTH STAND (KERRYDALE STREET)

CAPACITY: 60,506 (All Seated)

PITCH DIMENSIONS: 120 yds x 74 yds

FACILITIES FOR DISABLED SUPPORTERS:
There is provision for 142 wheelchair positions for disabled supporters and their helpers. These are split into 87 in the North Stand, at the front of the lower terracing, 10 in the East Stand, lower terracing and 37 in the South Stand, lower terracing. There is also a provision for 6 away positions in the lower East Stand.

Team playing kits

How to get there

The following routes may be used to reach Celtic Park:
BUSES: The following buses all leave from the city centre and pass within 50 yards of the ground. Nos. 61, 62, and 64.
TRAINS: There is a frequent train service from Glasgow Central Low Level station to Bridgeton Cross Station and this is only a ten minute walk from the ground. There is also a train from Queen Street Station (lower level) to Bellgrove Rail Station, approximately 1¹/₂ miles from the ground.
CARS: From the city centre, motor vehicles should travel along London Road and this will take you to the ground. Parking space is available in front of the Main Stand. On matchdays all car parking is strictly limited and is only available to those in possession of a valid car park pass.

The Bhoys

email: sfl@sol.co.uk • website: www.sfl.scottishfootball.com

Dens Park Stadium,
Sandeman Street, Dundee, DD3 7JY

CHAIRMAN
James M. Marr

DIRECTORS
James Connor & A. Ritchie Robertson

ASSOCIATE BOARD
Dave Forbes, Bob Hynd & Jim Thomson

CHIEF EXECUTIVE
Peter Marr

SECRETARY
A. Ritchie Robertson

MANAGER
John Scott

ASSISTANT MANAGER
James Bone

COACH
Billy Thomson

YOUTH TEAM COACH
Ray Farningham

SPRINT COACH
Harry Hay

CLUB DOCTOR
Dr. Phyllis Windsor, M.D., FRCR

PHYSIOTHERAPIST
John McCreadie, MSST, Dip. ST

FOOTBALL SAFETY OFFICERS'
ASSOCIATION REPRESENTATIVE
James Thomson (01382) 815250

YOUTH DEVELOPMENT
CO-ORDINATOR
Kenny Cameron

STADIUM MANAGER
Jim Thomson

GROUNDSMAN
Brian Robertson

COMMERCIAL MANAGER
Jim Connor Tel (01382) 884450
Fax (01382) 858963

MARKETING &
COMMERCIAL EXECUTIVE
Brian Gray

TELEPHONES
Football/Manager (01382) 826104
Administration/Accounts/
Youth Development (01382) 889966
Commercial/ Marketing
(01382) 884450
Secretary (01382) 826104
Fax (01382) 832284
Commercial Fax (01382) 858963

E-MAIL & INTERNET ADDRESS
dfc@dundeefc.co.uk

CLUB SHOP
Dundee F.C. Shop, Commercial
Street, Dundee. Tel (01382) 205664
Ticket Line (01382) 204777

OFFICIAL SUPPORTERS CLUB
Contact: Norrie Price (01224) 818697

TEAM CAPTAIN
Barry Smith

SHIRT SPONSOR
Ceramic Tile Warehouse

LIST OF PLAYERS 1999-2000

SURNAME	FIRST NAME	MIDDLE NAME	DATE OF BIRTH	PLACE OF BIRTH	DATE OF SIGNING	HEIGHT FT INS	WEIGHT ST LBS	POS. ON PITCH	PREVIOUS CLUB
Annand	Edward		24/03/73	Glasgow	31/03/97	5 11.0	11 1	Fwd	Clyde
Bayne	Graham		22/08/79	Kirkcaldy	18/03/98	6 1.0	12 7	Fwd	Newburgh
Beith	Gavin		07/10/81	Dundee	25/05/99	5 10.0	9 2	Mid	S Form
Boyack	Steven		04/09/76	Edinburgh	25/02/99	5 10.0	10 7	Fwd	Rangers
Boylan	Colin		19/07/83	Glasgow	25/08/99	5 0.0	9 0	Mid	S Form
Clark	Paul		09/03/80	Dundee	08/04/98	5 10.0	10 7	Mid	St. Joseph's
Coyne	Thomas		14/11/62	Glasgow	07/07/98	6 0.0	10 13	Fwd	Motherwell
Douglas	Robert	James	24/04/72	Lanark	01/08/97	6 3.0	14 12	Gk	Livingston
Earlie	James	Joseph	24/04/80	Rutherglen	25/05/99	5 5.0	10 9	Fwd	S Form
Elliott	John		04/07/80	Edinburgh	11/06/97	5 9.0	10 0	Fwd	Whitehill Welfare
Falconer	William	Henry	05/04/66	Aberdeen	07/07/98	6 1.0	13 0	Mid/Fwd	Motherwell
Forbes	Barry		08/09/81	Dundee	25/05/99	6 0.0	10 5	Mid	S Form
Gibson	Keith		01/05/81	Dundee	25/05/99	5 11.0	9 13	Mid	S Form
Gilfillan	Finn		26/01/81	Edinburgh	10/06/99	5 11.0	11 4	Fwd	Carnoustie Juniors
Grady	James		14/03/71	Paisley	27/06/97	5 7.0	10 0	Fwd	Clydebank
Kelly	Jonathan		25/05/82	Perth	25/05/99	5 10.0	10 9	Fwd	S Form
Langfield	James		22/12/79	Paisley	26/12/96	6 4.0	13 0	Gk	Glasgow City B.C.
Mackay	David		02/05/81	Rutherglen	20/08/99	5 5.0	11 0	Def	Benburb Thistle
Maddison	Lee	Robert	05/10/72	Bristol	23/07/97	6 2.0	13 0	Def	Northampton Town
Mair	Lee		09/12/80	Aberdeen	07/06/99	6 0.0	11 3	Mid	Formartine United A
McGuiness	Kieran	Joseph	05/05/82	Motherwell	25/08/99	6 0.0	12 10	Def	Unattached
McSkimming	Shaun	Peter	29/05/70	Stranraer	29/07/98	5 11.0	10 8	Mid	Motherwell
Miller	William	Nisbit	01/11/69	Edinburgh	08/07/98	5 8.0	11 2	Def	Hibernian
Milne	Steven		05/05/80	Dundee	16/10/97	5 7.0	10 0	Fwd	Downfield Jnrs
Montgomery	Richard		19/01/82	Perth	25/05/99	5 8.5	10 0	Mid	X Form
Puras	Roberto	Matute	26/08/72	San Asensio	09/09/99	6 0.0	11 7	Def	Belenenses
Rae	Gavin		28/11/77	Aberdeen	01/09/95	5 11.0	10 4	Def	Hermes Juniors
Raeside	Robert		07/07/72	South Africa	10/07/96	6 0.0	11 10	Def	Raith Rovers
Riley	David		11/12/81	Dundee	25/05/99	5 10.0	9 7	Mid	S Form
Robb	Steven		08/03/82	Perth	25/08/99	5 6.0	9 4	Mid	S Form
Robertson	Hugh	Scott	19/03/75	Aberdeen	08/01/97	5 9.0	13 11	Mid	Aberdeen
Sharp	Lee		22/05/75	Glasgow	03/12/98	5 8.0	11 7	Def	Dumbarton
Slater	Mark	Andrew	02/04/79	Buckie	11/06/97	5 11.0	11 5	Def	Buckie Thistle
Smith	Barry	Martin	19/02/74	Paisley	08/12/95	5 10.0	12 0	Def	Celtic
Soutar	Derek	Robert James	04/06/81	Dundee	25/05/99	6 1.5	12 0	Gk	S Form
Thompson	Jonathan		26/11/81	Dundee	25/05/99	6 2.0	12 0	Def	S Form
Thomson	Graeme	David	23/02/81	Falkirk	25/05/99	5 8.0	10 7	Def	S Form
Tweed	Steven		08/08/72	Edinburgh	18/12/98	6 3.0	15 0	Def	Stoke City
Van Eijs	Frank		02/11/71	Geleen	30/07/99	6 4.0	12 1	Def/Mid	F.C. Vinkenslag
Watson	Steven		29/03/83	Aberdeen	25/08/99	5 11.0	11 3	Def	S Form
Wilkie	Lee		20/04/80	Dundee	08/09/98	6 4.0	13 0	Def	Downfield Juniors
Yates	Michael		07/11/79	Ormskirk	09/07/99	5 10.0	11 0	Fwd	Burscough

Milestones

YEAR OF FORMATION: 1893
MOST CAPPED PLAYER: Alex Hamilton
NO. OF CAPS: 24
MOST LEAGUE POINTS IN A SEASON: 58 (First Division – Season 1991/92) (2 points for a Win)
70 (First Division – Season 1997/98) (3 points for a Win)
MOST LEAGUE GOALS SCORED BY A PLAYER IN A SEASON: Alan Gilzean (Season 1963/64)
NO. OF GOALS SCORED: 32
RECORD ATTENDANCE: 43,024 (-v- Rangers – 1953)
RECORD VICTORY: 10-0 (-v- Fraserburgh, 1931; -v- Alloa, 1947; -v- Dunfermline Athletic, 1947; -v- Queen of the South, 1962)
RECORD DEFEAT: 0-11 (-v- Celtic – Division 1, 26.10.1895)

The Dark Blues' ten year league record

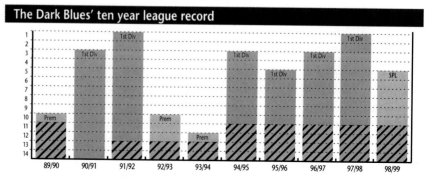

THE DARK BLUES' CLUB FACTFILE 1998/99 RESULTS... APPEARANCES... SCORERS

Small bold figures denote goalscorers. † denotes opponent's own goal.

Date	V	Opponents	Att.	Res	Douglas R.	Miller W.	Smith B.	Irvine B.	McSkimming S.	Maddison L.	Garcin E.	Adamczuk D.	Coyne T.	Grady J.	Falconer W.	Pounewatchy S.	McCormick S.	Magee D.	McInally J.	O'Driscoll J.	Raeside R.	Annand E.	Grant B.	Rae G.	Rogers D.	Anderson I.	Langfield J.	Hunter G.	Fleming D.	Sharp L.	Tweed S.	Robertson H.	Strachan G.	Boyack S.	Bayne G.
Aug 1	H	Aberdeen	7,816	0-2	1	2	3	4	5	6	7	8	9	10	11	12	13	14																	
Aug 15	A	Dunfermline Athletic	5,279	0-2	1	2	13	4	3			8	9	10	11	5			6	7	12														
Aug 23	H	St. Johnstone	3,641	0-1	1	2	3			6	12	8	9	10	11	4			7		5	13													
Aug 29	H	Celtic	9,853	1-1	1	2	3	4		6	7	8		10	9				11		5	14^1		12	13										
Sep 12	A	Heart of Midlothian	13,117	2-0	1	2	3	4	11	6		8^2		10	9						5	12		7	13	14									
Sep 19	H	Dundee United	12,081	2-2	1	2	3	4	11	6		8^1		10	9			14			5	12^1		7	13										
Sep 23	A	Kilmarnock	7,069	1-2	1	2	3	4	10			8			11						5	9^1		7	6	12									
Sep 26	H	Motherwell	5,655	1-0	1	2	3	4^1	10	6		8	13		11						5	9		7	12										
Oct 4	A	Rangers	48,348	0-1	1	2	3	4	10	6		8	12		11						5	9		7	13										
Oct 17	A	Aberdeen	10,004	2-2	1	2	3	4	10			8			11						5	9^2	13	6		12		15							
Oct 28	H	Dunfermline Athletic	4,619	1-0	1	2	3	4	10						11^1							9	8	12	6		7		5						
Oct 31	H	Heart of Midlothian	6,142	†1-0	1	2	3	4	10				12								8	13	9	6		7		5							
Nov 7	A	Celtic	58,974	1-6	1	2	3	4	10						11						8	12	9^1	13	6		7		5						
Nov 14	H	Kilmarnock	4,249	1-1	1		2	4	6			8	14		11						10	5	9^1	13	12	7	1	3							
Nov 22	A	Dundee United	11,230	1-0	1		2	4	6			8	9	12^1							7	5	10	13	3	11									
Dec 12	A	St. Johnstone	6,033	1-1	1		2	12	4	6		8^1	13	10							7	5	9		3	11									
Dec 16	A	Motherwell	5,840	1-2	1		3	4	6			8^1	13	10	9						5		2	12	11			7							
Dec 19	H	Aberdeen	6,340	1-2	1	2	3	4	6			8			11						10	9	7^1	12				14	2	11	13	5			
Dec 27	H	Celtic	10,043	0-3	1		3	4	6			8		10	9						12		14	2	11				13	5					
Dec 30	A	Heart of Midlothian	13,383	2-1	1		3	4	14			8		10	9^1						2	13	7	12				6^1	5	11					
Jan 2	H	Dundee United	11,751	1-3	1		3	4	7^1			8	14	10	12			11			2	9	13					6	5						
Jan 27	H	Rangers	10,043	0-4	1		12	4	14	3		8		10	7						9	2		11				5	6	13					
Jan 30	A	Kilmarnock	7,677	0-0	1		3	4		6		8		10	9			2					12				13	5	7	11					
Feb 6	H	Motherwell	4,187	1-0	1		12	4				8	9	10							14		13	2	11		3	5^1	6	7					
Feb 20	A	Rangers	49,462	1-6	1		3		6	4		8^1	9	10	11						12		13	2				5	7						
Feb 27	H	St. Johnstone	7,245	0-1	1		3		7	4		8	14	10	9						2	13		6	12			5	11						
Mar 13	A	Dunfermline Athletic	6,980	0-2	1	2		4	7	3		8		13	9						10	6		11				5	12						
Mar 20	H	Heart of Midlothian	5,500	2-0	1	2	3	4		6					10						5	9^2	8	12				7	11						
Apr 3	H	Celtic	59,269	0-5	1	2	3	4	7	6					10			8			5	9	11												
Apr 10	A	Motherwell	5,717	2-1	1	2	3	4	14	6			13^1	10^1							5	9		11		12			7					8	
Apr 18	H	Rangers	11,070	1-1	1	2	3	4	7	5			9	10	12							6		11^1										8	
Apr 24	H	Kilmarnock	4,296	2-1	1		3	4	5^1	2			9	10	7						12	6		11^1										8	
May 1	A	Dundee United	12,280	2-0	1	2	3	4^1	7	5			13^1	10							9	6		11								7		8	
May 8	A	Aberdeen	9,790	2-1	1	2	3	4		5	12		13	10							9	6		11^1								7		8^1	
May 15	H	Dunfermline Athletic	4,179	3-1	1	2	3	4^1		5	12	14	9	10^1							6			11								7		8^1	13
May 23	A	St. Johnstone	10,575	0-1	1	2	3	4	13	5			9	10							6			11								7		8	12
TOTAL FULL APPEARANCES					35	26	29	33	25	21	2	24	8	20	31	2		1	14	19	19	23	7	17	1	3	1	4	10	9	4			8	
TOTAL SUB APPEARANCES						(4)		(4)		(1)	(2)	(8)	(6)	(2)	(1)	(1)	(1)	(1)	(2)	(10)	(4)	(7)		(4)	(11)	(1)		(2)			(1)	(2)		(2)
TOTAL GOALS SCORED							3	2				6		3	4							9		1		3				1	1			2	

Dens Park Stadium

Surrounding streets: SANDEMAN STREET, TANNADICE STREET, PROVOST ROAD, DENS ROAD

CAPACITY: 12,085 (All Seated)

PITCH DIMENSIONS: 110 yds x 72 yds

FACILITIES FOR DISABLED SUPPORTERS:
There is provision for disabled supporters in the East Enclosure (Away Support) and West Enclosure (Home Support)

Team playing kits

How to get there

You can reach Dens Park Stadium by the following routes:

BUSES: There is a frequent service of buses from the city centre. Nos. 1A and 1B leave from Albert Square and Nos. 18, 19 and 21 leave from Commercial Street.

TRAINS: Trains from all over the country pass through the mainline Dundee station and fans can then proceed to the ground by the above buses from stops situated close to the station.

CARS: Cars may be parked in the car park and local streets adjacent to the ground.

email: sfl@sol.co.uk • website: www.sfl.scottishfootball.com

Dundee United

LIST OF PLAYERS 1999-2000

SURNAME	FIRST NAME	MIDDLE NAME	DATE OF BIRTH	PLACE OF BIRTH	DATE OF SIGNING	HEIGHT FT INS	WEIGHT ST LBS	POS. ON PITCH	PREVIOUS CLUB
Bruce	James		03/12/82	Rutherglen	05/07/99	6 0.0	12 6	Def	Dundee United B.C.
Byrne	David		14/11/79	Dublin	26/08/99	6 0.5	12 7	Mid	Shelbourne
Combe	Alan		03/04/74	Edinburgh	17/06/98	6 2.0	13 2	Gk	St. Mirrren
Cooper	Marc		24/09/81	Glasgow	30/06/98	5 11.0	11 5	Mid	Dundee United B.C.
Curran	Lee		22/10/82	Lanark	05/07/99	5 9.0	9 11	Mid	Wishaw B.C.
Davidson	Hugh	Norman	03/08/80	Dundee	01/07/97	5 11.5	12 6	Mid	Dundee United B.C.
De Vos	Jason	Richard	02/01/74	Ontario	12/10/98	6 4.0	14 3	Def	Darlington
Delaunay	Jean	Pierre	17/01/66	Harfleur	10/08/99	6 0.0	13 3	Def	Le Havre
Dodds	William		05/02/69	New Cumnock	23/09/98	5 8.0	12 2	Fwd	Aberdeen
Duff	Stuart		23/01/82	Aberdeen	05/07/99	5 11.0	10 3	Mid	Dundee United B.C.
Duffy	John		22/08/81	Paisley	30/06/98	5 11.0	11 12	Def	Dundee United B.C.
Easton	Craig		26/02/79	Bellshill	31/08/95	5 10.0	11 3	Mid	Dundee United B.C.
Fallon	Steven		08/05/79	Paisley	31/08/95	5 8.5	11 10	Def	Dundee United B.C.
Ferraz	Joaquim Miguel	Leitao De Freitas	16/05/74	Parades	25/06/99	6 4.0	12 10	Fwd	CF OS Belenenses
Gallacher	Paul	James	16/08/79	Glasgow	02/09/97	6 0.0	11 11	Gk	Lochee United Juniors
Hannah	David		04/08/73	Coatbridge	05/02/99	5 11.5	11 8	Mid	Celtic
Jarvie	Paul		14/06/82	Aberdeen	25/05/99	6 0.0	12 3	Gk	Stoneywood B.C.
Jenkins	Iain		24/11/72	Whiston	27/03/98	5 10.0	12 0	Def	Chester City
Jonsson	Sigurdur		27/09/66	Arkanes	26/11/97	6 3.0	12 9	Def/Mid	Orebro
Malpas	Maurice	Daniel Robert	03/08/62	Dunfermline	14/08/79	5 8.0	12 0	Def	S Form
Mathie	Alexander		20/12/68	Bathgate	16/10/98	5 10.0	11 7	Fwd	Ipswich Town
McConalogue	Stephen		16/06/81	Glasgow	01/07/97	5 9.0	10 13	Fwd	Dundee United B.C.
McCracken	David		16/10/81	Glasgow	30/06/98	6 2.0	11 6	Def	Dundee United B.C.
McCulloch	Scott	Anderson James	29/11/75	Cumnock	26/02/99	6 0.0	13 4	Def/Mid	Dunfermline Athletic
McCulloch	Stephen	George	03/04/81	Irvine	30/06/98	6 1.0	11 9	Mid	Maybole Amateurs
McCunnie	Jamie		15/04/83	Bellshill	05/07/99	5 10.0	10 3	Def	Dundee United B.C.
McDonald	Kevin		23/01/81	Rutherglen	01/07/97	5 9.0	11 4	Def	Dundee United B.C.
McNally	Mark		10/03/71	Motherwell	14/07/99	5 9.0	11 7	Def	Stoke City
Middleton	Gary		05/03/82	Arbroath	05/07/99	5 9.0	11 0	Fwd	Dundee United B.C.
Partridge	David	William	26/11/78	London	12/03/99	6 1.0	13 8	Def	West Ham United
Pascual	Bernard		10/04/67	Aubervilliers	07/08/98	5 10.5	11 12	Mid	Le Havre
Paterson	James	Lee	25/09/79	Bellshill	03/07/96	5 11.0	12 13	Mid	Dundee United B.C.
Patterson	Darren	James	15/10/69	Belfast	13/07/99	6 1.0	12 8	Def	Luton Town
Reilly	Colin		04/09/82	Bellshill	29/09/98	5 10.0	11 2	Def	Dundee United B.C.
Skoldmark	Magnus		22/09/68	Langsele	19/09/97	6 2.5	12 3	Def	Dalian Wanda
Smith	James	Anthony	28/10/73	Bellshill	02/07/99	5 8.0	11 5	Def/Mid	Airdrieonians
Sturrock	Blair		25/08/81	Dundee	05/07/99	6 0.0	11 1	Fwd	S Form
Telesnikov	Jan		11/12/72	Torinsk	26/08/99	5 7.0	11 12	Mid	Beitar Jerusalem
Thompson	Steven		14/10/78	Paisley	01/07/96	6 2.0	12 10	Fwd	Dundee United B.C.
Venetis	Anastasios		24/03/80	Larissa	19/08/99	6 1.0	11 3	Mid	Larissa
Winters	David		07/03/82	Paisley	05/07/99	5 11.0	10 11	Fwd	Dundee United B.C.
Worrell	David		12/01/78	Dublin	30/03/99	5 10.0	11 7	Def	Blackburn Rovers

Milestones

YEAR OF FORMATION: 1923 (1909 as Dundee Hibs)
MOST CAPPED PLAYER: Maurice Malpas
NO. OF CAPS: 55
MOST LEAGUE POINTS IN A SEASON: 60 (Premier Division - Season 1986/87) (2 Points for a Win)
67 (First Division - Season 1995/96) (3 Points for a Win)
MOST LEAGUE GOALS SCORED BY A PLAYER IN A SEASON: John Coyle (Season 1955/56)
NO. OF GOALS SCORED: 41
RECORD ATTENDANCE: 28,000 (-v- Barcelona – 16.11.1966)
RECORD VICTORY: 14-0 (-v- Nithsdale Wanderers – Scottish Cup, 17.1.1931)
RECORD DEFEAT: 1-12 (-v- Motherwell – Division 2, 23.1.1954)

The Terrors' ten year league record

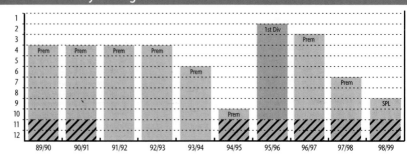

THE TERRORS' CLUB FACTFILE 1998/99 RESULTS... APPEARANCES... SCORERS

Date	Venue	Opponents	Att.	Res	Dijkstra S.	Skoldmark M.	Jenkins I.	Malpas M.	Jonsson S.	Zetterlund L.	Miller J.	Mols T.	Olofsson K.	Easton C.	Boli R.	Valentini J.	Thompson S.	McNally M.	Pascual B.	Patterson D.	McLaren A.	Winters R.	Duffy C.	Paterson J.	McSwegan G.	Dodds W.	Mathie A.	De Vos J.	Combe A.	Dolan J.	Pedersen E.	Hannah D.	Eustace J.	McCulloch S.	McLaughlin B.	Murray N.	Worrall D.	McConalogue S.	Partridge D.
Aug 1	A	Kilmarnock	8,208	0-2	1	2	3	4	5	6	7	8	9	10	11	12	13	14																					
16	H	Heart of Midlothian	9,629	0-0	1		3	4		7	6	10	8	9	12	11		14		2	5	13																	
22	A	Celtic	59,133	1-2	1		7			4	6		8	9	10		13	3	2	5		11¹	12																
30	A	Motherwell	11,201	0-1	1		3	12	4	7	6		8	9	10	11		5	2		13		14																
Sep 12	H	Rangers	12,088	0-0	1	5	3	4		6		8	9							11		2	7	10															
19	A	Dundee	12,081	2-2	1	5	3	4		6		8	9¹	14		12				11	13	2	7	10¹															
23	H	Dunfermline Athletic	6,957	1-1	1		2	4		6		8	9						5	11		3	7	10¹	12														
26	A	St. Johnstone	6,655	3-1	1		3	2	4		6			11	8				7	5				10	9³														
Oct 4	H	Aberdeen	8,933	1-0	1		3		4		6	11			8				2	5	12		7	10¹	9														
17	H	Kilmarnock	8,137	0-2	1			4			6		11	8		13	3		5	12		2	7		9	10	14												
24	A	Heart of Midlothian	13,124	1-0	1		2	4			6	12	11	8					5			7		9¹	10	3													
31	A	Rangers	49,503	1-2	1		3	4	7	6	13		11	8		14		2	5		12			9¹	10														
Nov 7	H	Motherwell	6,616	2-2	1		3	4	7¹	6	12		11	8				2	5					9¹	10														
15	H	Dunfermline Athletic	10,704	1-2	1		3	4	7	6	13		11	8		14		2	5					9	10¹	12													
22	H	Dundee	11,230	0-1				4	5	6	7		12	8				2			11			9	10	3	1												
28	A	Aberdeen	11,964	3-0				4		6	12¹		11¹	8¹				2	5		13			9	10	3	1	7											
Dec 5	H	St. Johnstone	7,293	1-1				4		6	12		11	8		13		2	5					9¹	10	3	1	7											
12	H	Celtic	11,612	1-1		5		4		6¹			11	8				2						9	10	3	1	7											
20	A	Kilmarnock	13,538	0-2						6	13	8	11		12			2	5		14			9	10	3	1	7	4										
26	A	Motherwell	6,001	0-2		14		4		7	13		11	8				2	5					9	10	3	1	12	6										
30	H	Rangers	11,707	1-2				4		7	11		8					2		5				9¹	10	3	1		6										
Jan 2	A	Dundee	11,751	3-1	1	12		4		7	6	11¹	8		10¹		2			5				9¹	13	3													
30	H	Dunfermline Athletic	7,646	1-1	1			4	5	13	7	8	11¹		10		2	14						9	12	3		6											
Feb 6	A	St. Johnstone	5,771	1-2	1	2		4	5		12		11	8		13			14					9	10	3		6	7										
20	H	Aberdeen	8,309	3-0	1			4	13		7		11¹	8			14	2	12		9¹		3		5	10¹	6												
27	A	Celtic	59,902	1-2	1	12		4			7		11	8			13	2	5		9¹	14	3		10	6													
Mar 20	A	Rangers	49,164	1-0	1	5			4				11¹	8			12		2		9	13	3		10	6	7												
Apr 3	H	Motherwell	8,110	0-3	1	5		4			7		11	8				2			9	13	3		10	6	5	12											
6	H	Heart of Midlothian	10,648	1-3	1	5		4	12	13			11	8				2			9¹	14	3		10	6	7												
17	A	Aberdeen	11,603	4-0	1	5		4	2		6¹		11¹	8		13					9²		3		10		7		12										
20	H	St. Johnstone	6,741	1-2	1	5		4			7		11	8		5			14		9	13	3		10	12		6											
24	A	Dunfermline Athletic	6,227	2-2	1	5		4	2		6		11	8		12					9²		3		10	13	7												
May 1	H	Dundee	12,280	0-2	1	5		4			10		11	8			2				9	13	3		6	12	7			14									
8	H	Kilmarnock	7,190	0-0		5					11	8			10			9	3	1			6	7	4	12		2												
15	A	Heart of Midlothian	13,187	1-4				12			10	5			9	13	3	1	6	7¹	4	11	8	2															
23	H	Celtic	10,062	1-2	15	5					11		10		6			9¹	3	1	8	7	4	2	12	13													
TOTAL FULL APPEARANCES					26	22	5	31	12	20	14	11	32	28	3	5	4	16	17	3	1	12	8	5	29	13	23	10	4	6	13	8	9	1	2	3		
TOTAL SUB APPEARANCES					(1)	(3)	(1)		(2)	(1)	(10)		(2)	(2)		(1)	(10)	(1)		(2)	(5)	(2)	(3)	(7)		(1)	(9)	(2)		(1)			(3)		(2)	(1)	(1)	(1)	(1)
TOTAL GOALS SCORED									1	1	2		7	1			1				1			3	17	1						1	1				

Small bold figures denote goalscorers. † denotes opponent's own goal.

Tannadice Park

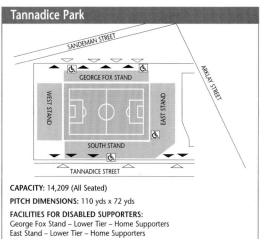

SANDEMAN STREET
GEORGE FOX STAND
WEST STAND · EAST STAND
SOUTH STAND
ARKLAY STREET
TANNADICE STREET

CAPACITY: 14,209 (All Seated)

PITCH DIMENSIONS: 110 yds x 72 yds

FACILITIES FOR DISABLED SUPPORTERS:
George Fox Stand – Lower Tier – Home Supporters
East Stand – Lower Tier – Home Supporters
West Stand – Away Supporters

Team playing kits

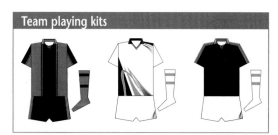

How to get there

Tannadice Park can be reached by the following routes:

BUSES: The following buses leave from the city centre at frequent intervals:- Nos. 18, 19 and 21 from Meadowside and No. 20 from Littlewoods High Street.

TRAINS: Trains from all over the country pass through the main Dundee station and fans can then proceed to the ground by the above bus services from stops situated within walking distance of the station.

CARS: There is parking in the streets adjacent to the ground.

email: sfl@sol.co.uk • website: www.sfl.scottishfootball.com

Heart of Midlothian

Tynecastle Stadium, Gorgie Road,
Edinburgh, EH11 2NL

CHAIRMAN
Douglas A. Smith

DIRECTORS
Leslie G. Deans,
Christopher P. Robinson,
Fraser S. Jackson, Colin G. Wilson,
Stewart Fraser & Brian J. Duffin

CHIEF EXECUTIVE
Christopher P. Robinson

P.A. to CHIEF EXECUTIVE
Irene McPhee (0131) 200 7245

**FINANCE DIRECTOR/
COMPANY SECRETARY**
Stewart Fraser

MANAGER
James Jefferies

ASSISTANT MANAGER
Billy Brown

COACH
Peter Houston

YOUTH COACH
John McGlynn

CLUB DOCTOR
Dr. Dewar Melvin

PHYSIOTHERAPIST
Alan Rae

KIT CONTROLLER
Norrie Gray

S.F.A. COMMUNITY OFFICER
Alan White (0131) 200 7242

CHIEF SCOUT
John Murray

PITCH MAINTENANCE
Souters of Stirling

CLUB SHOP MANAGER
Clare Sargent (0131) 200 7211

**CORPORATE HOSPITALITY/
BANQUETING**
Graeme Pacitti (0131) 200 7240

PUBLIC RELATIONS MANAGER
Douglas Dalgleish (0131) 200 7260

SALES/COMMERCIAL MANAGER
Kenny Wittmann (0131) 200 7205

**FOOTBALL SAFETY OFFICERS'
ASSOCIATION REPRESENTATIVE**
James Johnstone (0370) 578858

STADIUM MANAGER
Brian Mitchell (0131) 200 7254

TICKET MANAGER
Neil Hunter (0131) 200 7201

TELEPHONES
Ground (0131) 200 7200
Fax (0131) 200 7222
Ticket Office (0131) 200 7201
Information Service (0131) 200 7255
Sales & Marketing (0131) 200 7205
Credit Card Bookings (0131) 200 7209

E-MAIL & INTERNET ADDRESS
irene @homplc.co.uk
www.heartsfc.co.uk

CLUB SHOP
Heart of Midlothian Superstore,
Tynecastle Stadium, Gorgie Road,
Edinburgh. Tel (0131) 200 7211.
Open 9.30 a.m. – 5.30 p.m.
Mon. to Sat. and match days.

OFFICIAL SUPPORTERS CLUB
Heart of Midlothian Federation,
John N. Borthwick, 21/9 Festival
Gardens, Edinburgh, EH11 1RB

TEAM CAPTAIN
Colin Cameron

SHIRT SPONSOR
Strongbow

LIST OF PLAYERS 1999-2000

SURNAME	FIRST NAME	MIDDLE NAME	DATE OF BIRTH	PLACE OF BIRTH	DATE OF SIGNING	HEIGHT FT INS	WEIGHT ST LBS	POS. ON PITCH	PREVIOUS CLUB
Adam	Stephane	Lucien	15/05/69	Lille	11/07/97	5 11.0	12 0	Fwd	Metz
Cameron	Colin		23/10/72	Kirkcaldy	31/03/96	5 5.5	9 6	Mid	Raith Rovers
Clyde	Bobby		18/10/79	Edinburgh	05/03/99	6 1.0	11 9	Def	Musselburgh Athletic
Davidson	Ryan	Thomas	22/04/82	Irvine	29/09/98	5 10.0	10 0	Fwd	Heart of Midlothian B.C.
Findlay	Craig		22/09/80	Bangour	29/09/98	6 0.5	12 2	Def	Whitburn Athletic
Flögel	Thomas		07/06/71	Vienna	11/07/97	5 9.5	11 2	Mid/For	Austria Vienna
Fulton	Stephen		10/08/70	Greenock	12/10/95	5 10.0	11 0	Mid	Falkirk
Goldie	Darren		25/02/81	Glasgow	05/08/97	5 9.5	11 8	Def	West Park United
Graham	Alisdair		17/08/80	Lanark	07/08/98	5 10.0	11 0	Mid	Musselburgh Juniors
Holmes	Derek		18/10/78	Lanark	05/01/95	6 0.0	12 2	Fwd	Royal Albert
Horn	Robert	David	03/08/77	Edinburgh	13/05/95	5 9.0	11 0	Def	Edinburgh United
Jackson	Darren		25/07/66	Edinburgh	30/03/99	5 10.0	11 0	Fwd	Celtic
James	Kevin	Francis	03/12/75	Edinburgh	31/03/99	6 7.0	13 10	Def	Falkirk
Janczyk	Neil		07/04/83	Edinburgh	16/07/99	5 10.0	11 0	Mid	Heart of Midlothian Youth
Jenkinson	Leigh		09/07/69	Doncaster	30/12/98	6 2.0	13 0	Mid/For	Wigan Athletic
Kaczan	Paul		03/02/83	Bellshill	19/03/99	5 11.0	10 0	Def	Hibernian B.C.
Kirk	Andrew		29/05/79	Belfast	18/02/99	5 10.0	11 0	Fwd	Glentoran
Leclercq	Fabien	Christain Rene	19/10/72	Lille	20/07/99	5 10.0	9 12	Fwd	Lille Olympic Sporting Club
Locke	Gary		16/06/75	Edinburgh	31/07/92	5 10.0	11 8	Mid	Whitehill Welfare
Makel	Lee	Robert	11/01/73	Sunderland	13/03/98	5 10.0	11 4	Mid	Huddersfield Town
McIlroy	Alan	Stewart	07/04/81	Vale of Leven	14/05/99	5 10.0	11 3	Mid	Musselburgh Athletic
McKenzie	Roderick		08/08/75	Bellshill	30/07/96	6 0.0	12 0	Gk	Stenhousemuir
McKinnon	Robert		31/07/66	Glasgow	15/07/98	5 10.0	11 12	Def	F.C. Twente
McSwegan	Gary	John	24/09/70	Glasgow	09/10/98	5 7.5	12 8	Fwd	Dundee United
Milne	Kenneth		26/08/79	Stirling	02/08/97	6 2.5	12 8	Fwd	Edinburgh United
Murray	Grant	Robert	29/08/75	Edinburgh	02/03/95	5 10.0	12 0	Def	Bonnyrigg Rose
Naysmith	Gary	Andrew	16/11/78	Edinburgh	17/06/96	5 7.0	11 8	Def	Whitehill Welfare Colts
Neilson	Robbie		19/06/80	Paisley	25/10/96	5 8.0	11 0	Mid	Rangers B.C.
O'Donnell	Steven	James	09/08/80	Edinburgh	29/09/98	5 7.0	10 12	Mid	Musselburgh Athletic
O'Neil	Kris		29/09/80	Edinburgh	29/09/98	5 7.0	10 10	Mid	Musselburgh Juniors
Perez	Juanjo	Carricondo	04/05/77	Barcelona	09/10/98	5 8.0	10 0	Fwd	Barcelona
Pressley	Steven	John	11/10/73	Elgin	10/07/98	6 0.0	12 6	Def	Dundee United
Quitongo	Jose	Manuel	18/11/74	Luanda	11/10/97	5 7.5	10 7	Fwd	Hamilton Academical
Ritchie	Paul	Simon	21/08/75	Kirkcaldy	31/07/92	5 11.0	12 0	Def	Links United
Rousset	Gilles		22/08/63	Hyeres	03/11/95	6 5.0	14 7	Gk	Stade Rennes
Salvatori	Stefano		29/12/67	Rome	04/09/96	5 10.0	12 3	Mid	Atalanta
Severin	Scott	Derek	15/02/79	Stirling	22/05/97	5 11.0	12 7	Mid	Musselburgh Athletic
Simmons	Stephen	Christopher	27/02/82	Glasgow	10/09/97	6 0.5	11 10	Mid	Celtic B.C.
Sloan	Robert		14/07/83	Paisley	14/07/99	5 8.0	9 12	Fwd	Heart of Midlothian Youth
Smith	Barry	John	16/03/82	Dublin	10/12/98	5 10.5	11 0	Def	Manortown
Smith	Grant	Gordon	05/05/80	Irvine	19/03/99	6 1.0	12 6	Def	Reading
Strang	Scott		14/03/80	Glasgow	23/09/98	6 1.0	11 12	Gk	Easthouses B.C.
Wales	Gary		04/01/79	East Calder	28/07/99	5 10.0	11 2	Fwd	Hamilton Academical

Milestones

YEAR OF FORMATION: 1874
MOST CAPPED PLAYER: Bobby Walker
NO. OF CAPS: 29
MOST LEAGUE POINTS IN A SEASON: 63 (Premier Division - Season 1991/92)(2 Points for a Win)
67 (Premier Division - Season 1997/98)(3 Points for a Win)
MOST LEAGUE GOALS SCORED BY A PLAYER IN A SEASON: Barney Battles (Season 1930/31)
NO. OF GOALS SCORED: 44
RECORD ATTENDANCE: 53,396 (-v- Rangers – 13.2.1932)
RECORD VICTORY: 21-0 (-v- Anchor – EFA Cup, 1880)
RECORD DEFEAT: 1-8 (-v- Vale of Leven – Scottish Cup, 1883)

The Jam Tarts' ten year league record

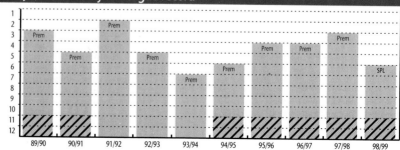

THE JAM TARTS' CLUB FACTFILE 1998/99 RESULTS… APPEARANCES… SCORERS

Date	Venue	Opponents	Att.	Res	Rousset G.	Locke G.	Naysmith G.	Weir D.	Salvatori S.	Ritchie P.	McCann N.	Fulton S.	Adam S.	Hamilton J.	Flögel T.	Murray G.	Pressley S.	McKinnon R.	Quitongo J.	Holmes D.	Makel L.	Murie N.	McKenzie R.	McPherson D.	Guerin V.	McSwegan G.	Carricondo J.	O'Neill K.	Jenkinson L.	Lilley D.	Callaghan S.	Cameron C.	Kirk A.	Berthe M.	Jackson D.	James K.	Severin S.
Aug 2	H	Rangers	15,272	2-1	1	2	3	4	5	6	7	8	9[1]	10[1]	11	12																					
16	A	Dundee United	9,629	0-0	1	2	3	4	5	6	7	8	9	10	11																						
22	H	Aberdeen	14,416	2-0	1	7	3	4	13	6		8[1]	9	10			2[1]	5	11	12	14																
30	A	Kilmarnock	10,376	0-3	1		3			6	7	8	9	10	11		2	5	12	14	13																
Sep 12	H	Dundee	13,117	0-2	1	5	3	4		6	7	8	12		13		2	11						9	10												
20	A	Dunfermline Athletic	5,963	1-1	1		3	4	5	6	7	8	9	10[1]	13		2		11	12																	
23	H	Motherwell	12,323	3-0		8	3	4[1]	5	6	7[2]		9	10			2		11	12			1														
26	A	Celtic	59,283	1-1		8	3	4	5	6	7		9	10[1]			2		11	12			1	13													
Oct 4	H	St. Johnstone	13,121	1-1	1		3	4	5	6			9	10			2	7	11[1]	13				8	12												
17	A	Rangers	49,749	0-3	1		3	4	5	6		8	10	11			2	12						13	9	7	14										
24	A	Dundee United	13,124	0-1	1			4	5	6		8	10				2	3	11					7	9	12	13										
31	A	Dundee	6,142	0-1	1	7	12	4				8	9	13	6		2	3	11					5	14	10											
Nov 7	H	Kilmarnock	14,363	2-1	1	7	3	4				8[1]	9[1]	12	6		2	14						5	11	10	13										
14	A	Motherwell	8,912	2-3	1	7	3	4				8	9	12[1]	6		2	13						5	11[1]	10	14										
21	H	Dunfermline Athletic	13,268	2-1			3	4		6	7[1]	8	9	10	11[1]		2				1	5			12												
Dec 6	H	Celtic	17,334	2-1	1	13	3	4		6		8	9[2]	10	11		2	12					5	7	14												
9	A	St. Johnstone	4,808	1-1	1	7	3	4		6		8	9	10[1]	11		2	13	14				5	12													
12	A	Aberdeen	11,137	0-2	1	14	3	4		6		8	10				2	12		13			5	7													
19	H	Rangers	17,134	2-3	1	7[1]		4		6		8	9	10[1]	11		2	3	14		12		5		13												
26	A	Kilmarnock	10,668	0-1	1	7		4				8	10	11	6		2	3	12	14	13		5	9													
30	H	Dundee	13,383	1-2	1	13		4				8	12	11			2	3		6			5	9	14				7	10[1]							
Jan 2	A	Dunfermline Athletic	9,227	0-0		6						8	10	11	4		2	3		1		5	12						7	9								
30	H	Motherwell	12,821	0-2			3	4	5	6			9	10	11		2	13		1		8							14	7	12						
Feb 6	A	Celtic	59,844	0-3			3	4	5	6		8			11	7	2	12		1		13							9	10							
20	A	St. Johnstone	12,229	0-2			4	3				8	9	10			2	14		1		5	6	13					7	12							
27	A	Aberdeen	13,957	0-2			3	4		6		8	9	10	11		2			1		5	13	12					7	14							
Mar 20	A	Dundee	5,500	0-2	1		4	3		6		8	13	11			2					5	7	9		14								12	10		
Apr 3	H	Kilmarnock	14,689	2-2	1		4			6		8	9				2	3	13			5		10[2]		7								11	12		
6	A	Dundee United	10,648	3-1	1					6		8	9[1]		4		2	3				5	14	10[1]		7[1]								11	12	13	
14	H	Celtic	16,388	2-4	1		4			6		8	9[2]		13		2	3				5	14	10		7								11	12		
17	A	St. Johnstone	6,154	0-0	1		12			6		8	9		4		2	3						10		7								11	5	13	
24	A	Motherwell	8,926	4-0	1		5			6		9[2]			4		2	3				12		10		7[1]	13							11[1]			8
May 3	H	Dunfermline Athletic	15,176	2-0	1		5	12		6		9			4		2	3				13		10		7[2]	14							11			8
9	A	Rangers	49,495	0-0	1		6	5		3		9			4		2					13		10		7	12							11			8
15	H	Dundee United	13,187	4-1			6	5		3[1]		9[1]	12		4		2	1				13		10[1]	14	7[1]								11			8
23	A	Aberdeen	13,042	5-2			5	3		9		8[1]	4		2		12	1				10[3]		14		7[1]								11			6
TOTAL FULL APPEARANCES					26	22	23	23	11	29	8	27	28	20	18		18	29	14	5	1	6		10	17	9	17	1	3	3	2	10		1	9	1	5
TOTAL SUB APPEARANCES						(3)		(3)	(1)		(1)			(5)	(2)	(3)	(1)	(2)	(7)	(5)	(8)	(4)		(1)	(10)	(4)	(9)		(3)	(2)	(1)		(1)	(5)		(3)	(2)
TOTAL GOALS SCORED						1		1		1	3	2	10	6	2		1								1		1	7				1		6		1

Small bold figures denote goalscorers. † *denotes opponent's own goal.*

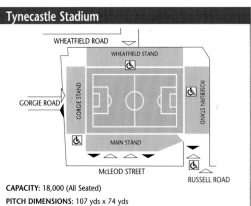

Tynecastle Stadium

WHEATFIELD ROAD

WHEATFIELD STAND

GORGIE ROAD

GORGIE STAND

ROSEBURN STAND

MAIN STAND

McLEOD STREET

RUSSELL ROAD

CAPACITY: 18,000 (All Seated)

PITCH DIMENSIONS: 107 yds x 74 yds

FACILITIES FOR DISABLED SUPPORTERS:
There are 15 spaces for visiting fans at the Roseburn Stand. Regarding facilities for home supporters, see Season Ticket and League Admission Price information.

Team playing kits

How to get there

Tynecastle Stadium can be reached by the following routes:

BUSES: A frequent service of buses leaves from the city centre, Nos. 1, 2, 3, 4, 33, 34, 35 and 44 all pass the ground.

TRAINS: Haymarket Station is about half a mile from the ground.

CARS: Car Parking facilities exist in the adjacent side streets in Robertson Avenue and also the Westfield area.

email: sfl@sol.co.uk • website: www.sfl.scottishfootball.com

Hibernian

Easter Road Stadium,
12 Albion Place,
Edinburgh, EH7 5QG

CHAIRMAN
Malcolm H. McPherson

MANAGING DIRECTOR
Rod M. Petrie

DIRECTORS
Stephen W. Dunn & Erick Davidson

SECRETARY
Mrs. Mary Anne McAdam

MANAGER
Alexander McLeish

ASSISTANT MANAGER
Andy Watson

COACH
Donald Park

CLUB DOCTOR
Dr. Tom Schofield

PHYSIOTHERAPIST
Malcolm Colquhoun

S.F.A. COMMUNITY COACH
Malcolm J. Thomson

**YOUTH DEVELOPMENT
OFFICER/CHIEF SCOUT**
John Park

COMMERCIAL MANAGER
Tommy Dickson

CATERING MANAGER
Craig Samson

**BUSINESS DEVELOPMENT
MANAGER**
Beverley Thorpe

STADIUM MANAGER
Gary O'Hagen

**FOOTBALL SAFETY OFFICERS'
ASSOCIATION REPRESENTATIVE**
Gordon Jackson (0131) 313 0507

HEAD GROUNDSMAN
Tom McCourt

TELEPHONES
Ground/Commercial (0131) 661 2159
Fax (0131) 659 6488/652 1907
Ticket Office (0131) 661 1875
Information Service (0891) 707070

E-MAIL & INTERNET ADDRESS
http://www.hibs.co.uk

CLUB SHOP
26 Albion Place, Edinburgh
Open Tue.-Sat.: 9.00 a.m. - 5.00 p.m.,
Home Match Days: 9.30 a.m. -
3.30 p.m. & 4.30 p.m. - 5.30 p.m.
Away First Team Match Days:
9.00 a.m. - 5.00 p.m.
Tel (0131) 656 7078/7079

OFFICIAL SUPPORTERS CLUB
11 Sunnyside Lane, Off Easter Road,
Edinburgh, EH7

TEAM CAPTAIN
John Hughes

SHIRT SPONSOR
Carlsberg

LIST OF PLAYERS 1999-2000

SURNAME	FIRST NAME	MIDDLE NAME	DATE OF BIRTH	PLACE OF BIRTH	DATE OF SIGNING	HEIGHT FT INS	WEIGHT ST LBS	POS. ON PITCH	PREVIOUS CLUB
Alexander	Daniel	James	05/08/82	Edinburgh	10/08/99	6 1.0	11 0	Def	Stoke City
Bannerman	Scott	John	21/03/79	Edinburgh	18/07/95	5 6.0	10 4	Fwd	Hutchison Vale B.C.
Barr	Richard		27/01/82	Johannesburg	31/12/98	5 10.0	10 4	Fwd	Bishopton United
Beaton	Lloyd	Thomas John	26/11/81	Edinburgh	25/05/96	6 2.0	12 7	Def	Hutchison Vale B.C.
Bottiglieri	Emilio	Hugh	13/04/79	Port Hardy	10/09/97	5 8.0	11 6	Mid	Metro-Ford
Brebner	Grant	Ian	06/12/77	Edinburgh	19/08/99	5 10.0	11 3	Mid	Reading
Brown	Kris	James	28/10/82	Edinburgh	06/01/99	5 10.0	13 2	Def	Hutchison Vale B.C.
Campbell	John	David	06/11/79	Fort William	26/08/98	5 11.5	10 11	Gk	Dunbar United
Colgan	Nick		19/09/73	Drogheda	29/07/99	6 1.0	13 4	Gk	A.F.C. Bournemouth
Collins	Derek	Joseph	15/04/69	Glasgow	12/12/98	5 8.0	11 2	Def	Morton
Cormack	Scott		12/12/82	Edinburgh	06/01/99	5 8.0	10 0	Fwd	Hutchison Vale B.C.
Crawford	Stephen		09/01/74	Dunfermline	21/07/97	5 10.5	12 0	Fwd	Millwall
Dempsie	Allan	Henry	05/11/82	Bellshill	06/01/99	5 10.0	10 0	Def	Hibernian B.C.
Dempsie	Mark	William	19/10/80	Bellshill	25/01/97	5 9.0	10 6	Mid	Hibernian B.C.
Dennis	Shaun		20/12/69	Kirkcaldy	10/01/97	6 1.0	13 7	Def	Raith Rovers
Ewart	Jamie	Ross	10/06/82	Edinburgh	10/07/98	6 0.0	11 9	Def	Hutchison Vale B.C.
Gibson	Craig	McIndewar	06/08/83	Dumbarton	26/05/99	5 10.0	10 0	Fwd	Hibernan Youth
Gottskalksson	Olafur		12/03/68	Keflavik	29/07/97	6 3.0	13 12	Gk	Keflavik
Hartley	Paul		19/10/76	Glasgow	23/12/98	5 8.0	10 7	Fwd	Raith Rovers
Henry	Fabrice		13/02/68	Argenteuil	22/07/99	5 10.0	11 5	Mid	Basel
Hilland	Paul		28/07/83	Glasgow	26/05/99	5 9.0	10 9	Mid	Hibernian Youth
Holsgrove	Paul		26/08/69	Cosford	31/07/98	6 2.0	12 8	Mid	Brighton & Hove Albion
Huggon	Russel	William	20/10/79	Maple Ridge	21/11/96	5 8.0	10 7	Mid	Metro Ford U'21
Hughes	John		09/09/64	Edinburgh	31/10/96	6 0.0	13 7	Def	Celtic
Hughes	Martin		09/05/80	Glasgow	04/06/97	5 9.0	10 12	Mid	S Form
Jack	Matthias		15/02/69	Leipzig	29/07/99	6 3.0	13 6	Def	Fortuna Dusseldorf
Jeffrey	Ross		30/08/81	Bellshill	06/08/98	5 11.0	9 10	Mid	Motherwell
Latapy	Russell	Nigel	02/08/68	Trinidad & Tobago	23/10/98	5 7.0	11 0	Fwd	Aston Villa
Lavety	Barry		21/08/74	Paisley	13/08/96	6 0.0	12 12	Fwd	St. Mirren
Lehmann	Dirk		16/08/71	Aachen	15/07/99	6 1.0	11 6	Fwd	Fulham
Lindsay	Paul	Henry Reid	23/01/81	Coatbridge	27/07/98	5 9.0	11 5	Mid	Hutchison Vale B.C.
Lovell	Stuart		09/01/72	Sydney	03/08/98	5 10.0	12 0	Fwd	Reading
Lovering	Paul	James	25/11/75	Glasgow	31/10/98	5 10.0	11 1	Def	Clydebank
McGinlay	Patrick	David	30/05/67	Glasgow	01/11/94	5 10.0	11 1	Mid	Celtic
McGladrigan	Thomas		29/12/82	Bellshill	01/09/99	6 0.0	11 0	Gk	Dundee United
McManus	Thomas	Kelly	28/02/81	Glasgow	10/07/97	5 9.0	10 2	Fwd	S Form
Miller	Kenneth		23/12/79	Edinburgh	22/05/96	5 9.0	10 9	Fwd	Hutchison Vale B.C.
Morton	Colin		17/01/81	Ashington	10/06/99	5 10.0	11 5	Def	Derby County
Murray	Ian	William	20/03/81	Edinburgh	13/07/99	6 0.0	10 11	Mid	Dundee United
O'Connor	Garry	Lawrence	07/05/83	Edinburgh	14/05/99	6 0.0	10 7	Fwd	Salvesen B.C.
O'Sullivan	Liam		28/10/81	Edinburgh	22/12/97	6 3.0	11 12	Def	Hutchison Vale B.C.
Paatelainen	Mika-Matti	Petteri	03/02/67	Helsinki	11/09/98	6 0.0	14 0	Fwd	Wolverhampton Wanderers
Phillips	Thomas	George	15/03/81	Newcastle	10/06/99	6 0.0	12 8	Gk	Derby County
Reid	Alan		21/10/80	Paisley	06/07/98	5 8.0	10 0	Fwd	Renfrew Victoria
Renwick	Michael		29/02/76	Edinburgh	03/08/92	5 9.0	11 6	Def/Mid	Hutchison Vale B.C.
Riordan	Derek	George	16/01/83	Edinburgh	14/05/99	5 10.0	9 8	Fwd	Hutchison Vale B.C.
Sauzee	Franck	Gaston Henri	28/10/65	Aubenas	17/02/99	6 2.0	14 0	Mid	Montpellier
Smith	Thomas	William	12/10/73	Glasgow	08/01/99	5 8.5	11 7	Mid	Clydebank
Widera	Sean	Forde	18/11/81	Adelaide	15/07/99	5 8.0	10 12	Fwd	South Australian Sports Inst.

Milestones

YEAR OF FORMATION: 1875
MOST CAPPED PLAYER: Lawrie Reilly
NO. OF CAPS: 38
MOST LEAGUE POINTS IN A SEASON: 57 (First Division – Season 1980/81)(2 Points for a Win)
        89 (First Division – Season 1998/99)(3 Points for a Win)
MOST LEAGUE GOALS SCORED BY A PLAYER IN A SEASON: Joe Baker (Season 1959/60)
NO. OF GOALS SCORED: 42
RECORD ATTENDANCE: 65,860 (-v- Heart of Midlothian – 2.1.1950)
RECORD VICTORY: 22-1 (-v- 42nd Highlanders 3.9.1881)
RECORD DEFEAT: 0-10 (-v- Rangers – 24.12.1898)

The Hibees' ten year league record

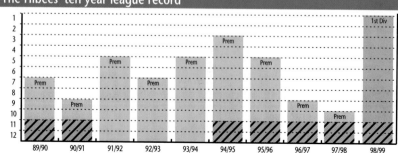

THE HIBEES' CLUB FACTFILE 1998/99 RESULTS... APPEARANCES... SCORERS

Date	Venue	Opponents	Att.	Res	Gottskalksson O.	Renwick M.	Elliot D.	Holsgrove P.	Hughes J.	Dennis S.	Lovell S.	Skinner J.	Crawford S.	Lavety B.	McGinlay P.	Rougier A.	Bannerman S.	Guggi P.	Paton E.	Harper K.	Shannon R.	Tosh P.	Prendeville B.	Dietrich K.	Paatelainen M-M.	Anderson D.	Miller K.	Latapy R.	Lovering P.	Collins D.	Dempsie M.	Hartley P.	Smith T.	Marenkov A.	Sauzee F.	Reid A.	McManus T.	Bottiglieri E.
Aug 4	A	Greenock Morton	5,747	1-0	1	2	3	4	5	6	7	8	9	10¹	11	12	15																				
15	H	Stranraer	9,489	1-2	1	2	3	4	5	6	9	8¹	12	10	11	7		14	15																			
22	A	Falkirk	5,748	1-1	1	2	3	14	5	6¹	12	8	9	10	11	7		4																				
29	H	Ayr United	9,231	4-2	1	2	3	12	5	6	14¹	8	9²	10	11	7		4¹		15																		
Sep 5	A	Clydebank	1,828	2-2			3	15	5	6	10	8	9¹	14	11			4			12¹	2	7															
12	A	St. Mirren	3,638	0-2	1		3		5	6	12	8	9	14	11			4	15			2	7	10														
19	H	Raith Rovers	8,853	3-1	1	7			6	5			12	9²	10	11		4¹	15			2			3	8												
26	H	Hamilton Academical	9,696	0-0	1		3	8	5	15			9	10	11	14		4				2	12	6	7													
Oct 3	A	Airdrieonians	4,301	3-1	1	3		4	5			9	8	12	11²	7						2	10¹	6														
10	A	Stranraer	1,832	1-0	1	3		4	5		9¹		12	10	11	7	15	8				2	10	6														
17	H	Greenock Morton	9,524	2-1	1	3			5		9	8	12		11¹	7	15	4				2¹	10	6														
24	A	Ayr United	4,684	3-3	1	3		5²	14	9	8	12		11	7	15						2	10¹	6		4												
31	H	Clydebank	10,172	2-1	1	3		15	5	6	9	8	12		11¹	7	14					2	10¹			4												
Nov 7	A	Raith Rovers	4,925	3-1	1			4	5	6	12		8¹	15	11¹	7	14					2	9¹			10	3											
21	A	Hamilton Academical	2,288	2-2	1			5	6			4	8		11	7	15					2	9²			10	3											
24	H	St. Mirren	9,153	4-1	1			5	6	10²	4	8	14	11¹	12	7						2¹	9				3											
28	H	Airdrieonians	9,732	1-0	1			5	6	7¹	4	8	12	11								2	9			10	3											
Dec 5	A	Greenock Morton	3,150	3-1	1			5	6	7¹	4	8¹	12	11	14¹							2	9			10	3											
12	H	Falkirk	12,572	2-1	1			5¹	6	7	4	8¹		11	14								9			10	3	2	15									
19	H	Clydebank	9,064	3-0	1			5	6	7	4	8	12	11²		15							9			10¹	3	2											
26	H	Ayr United	14,106	3-0	1			5	6	7	4	8	12	11¹									9²			10	3	2	15	14								
Jan 2	H	Raith Rovers	14,703	†5-1	1			15	5	6	7¹	4	8	12	11²								9			10¹	3	2		14								
9	A	St. Mirren	6,674	2-1	1		3		6	7	4	8	12	11									9¹			10		5	15¹	2								
16	H	Hamilton Academical	10,233	4-0	1			12	6		4		8¹	11¹	15								9²			10	3		5	7	2							
30	A	Airdrieonians	4,809	4-1	1			15	6	7²	4¹	8	12	11									9¹			10	3	2	5	14								
Feb 6	H	Stranraer	8,659	2-0	1			15	6	7	4	8²	12	11									9			10	3	2	5	14								
20	A	Falkirk	6,086	†2-1	1				6		4	9		11									10	3	2	7¹				5	8							
27	A	Ayr United	5,010	3-1	1	12			6		4	9³	7	11		14							10	3	2					5	8							
Mar 13	A	Clydebank	1,695	0-2	1				6	4		7	12										9	11	10	3	2			5	8							
20	H	Airdrieonians	9,991	3-0	1			7¹	6¹	11	8												9	14	10	3¹	2			5	4	15						
Apr 3	H	Hamilton Academical	4,350	2-0	1			7	6	11	8	14											9		10²	3	2			12	5⁴	4						
10	A	Raith Rovers	5,730	3-1	1			12	6¹	7	8	15	11										9		10¹		2		14	5¹	4							
17	H	St. Mirren	8,959	2-1	1	3			6	11	8	12											9	15	10¹		2		7¹	14	5	4						
24	H	Greenock Morton	8,865	2-1	1	3			6	11¹	14												9¹				2	15	7	12	5	4¹						
May 1	A	Stranraer	1,597	4-0	1	3				11¹		8¹	12		10								9¹				2	4	7¹	6	5						14	15
8	H	Falkirk	14,801	2-1	1	3			12	6	11		8	15	14								9		10		2		7¹		5	4¹						
TOTAL FULL APPEARANCES					36	15	8	9	22	29	26	24	28	9	29	10	2	7	1	1	1	13	1	25	6	5	23	17	16	5	6	3	10	9			
TOTAL SUB APPEARANCES						(1)		(9)	(1)	(2)	(5)		(7)	(18)	(1)	(5)	(10)	(1)	(3)	(2)					(1)		(2)			(3)	(7)	(2)		(1)	(1)	(1)
TOTAL GOALS SCORED							1	3	3	11	2	14	2	12	1			2		1				2	12		1	6	1		5		1	2		

Small bold figures denote goalscorers. † denotes opponent's own goal.

Easter Road Stadium

ALBION PLACE

ALBION RD

CAPACITY: 16,032 (All Seated)

PITCH DIMENSIONS: 112 yds x 74 yds

FACILITIES FOR DISABLED SUPPORTERS:
Area in South Seated Enclosure and North Stand.

Team playing kits

How to get there

Easter Road Stadium can be reached by the following routes:

BUSES: The main bus station in the city is served by buses from all over the country and the following local buses departing from Princes Street all stop near the ground:- Nos. 4, 15, 42 and 44.

TRAINS: Edinburgh Waverley Station is served by trains from all parts of the country and the above buses all stop near the ground.

The Hibees

email: sfl@sol.co.uk • website: www.sfl.scottishfootball.com

Kilmarnock

Rugby Park, Rugby Road, Kilmarnock, KA1 2DP

CHAIRMAN
William Costley

VICE-CHAIRMAN
John Paton

DIRECTORS
James T. Moffat,
James H. Clark,
Robert Wyper, Thomas Cairns,
Ian Welsh, MA (Hons), MA, DPSE, FRSA
& Brian J. Sage

CHIEF EXECUTIVE
Ian Welsh, MA (Hons), MA, DPSE, FRSA

SECRETARY
Kevin D. Collins

MANAGER
Robert Williamson

ASSISTANT MANAGERS
Jim Clark & Gerry McCabe

GOALKEEPING COACH
Jim Stewart

YOUTH COACHES
Paul Clarke & Stuart McLean

YOUTH DEVELOPMENT
Alan Robertson

HON. MEDICAL OFFICER
Dr. Masood Zaidi

CROWD DOCTOR
Dr. Brian Syme

PHYSIOTHERAPISTS
Alistair Macfie, B.Sc. (Hons),
M.C.S.P., S.R.P. &
Hugh Allan, M.B.E.

S.F.A. COMMUNITY OFFICER
Eric Young

COMMERCIAL MANAGER/ PRESS OFFICER
Jim McSherry (01563) 545305

COMMERCIAL ASSISTANT
Anne Clark

STADIUM MANAGER
Angus Hollas

FOOTBALL SAFETY OFFICERS' ASSOCIATION REPRESENTATIVES
Kevin D. Collins & Jim Brogan
(01563) 545306

TELEPHONES
Ground (01563) 545300
Fax (01563) 522181
Matchday/Ticket Information
(0891) 633249

E-MAIL & INTERNET ADDRESS
www.kilmarnockfc.co.uk
kfc@sol.co.uk

CLUB SHOP
Killie Sports, JJB Sports Superstore,
Glencairn Retail Park, Kilmarnock.
Tel (01563) 533579.
Open 7 days a week
9.00 a.m. – 5.00 p.m.

OFFICIAL SUPPORTERS CLUB
c/o Rugby Park, Kilmarnock, KA1 2DP

TEAM CAPTAIN
Ian Durrant

SHIRT SPONSOR
JJB Sports

18

LIST OF PLAYERS 1999-2000

SURNAME	FIRST NAME	MIDDLE NAME	DATE OF BIRTH	PLACE OF BIRTH	DATE OF SIGNING	HEIGHT FT INS	WEIGHT ST LBS	POS. ON PITCH	PREVIOUS CLUB
Bagan	David		26/04/77	Irvine	16/11/95	5 6.0	10 10	Fwd	Troon Juniors
Baker	Martin		08/06/74	Govan	06/06/97	6 0.0	11 10	Def	St. Mirren
Beesley	Darren		16/03/81	Rotherham	31/08/99	5 10.5	12 8	Def	Rotherham United
Boyd	Kris		18/08/83	Irvine	25/08/99	5 6.0	12 5	Fwd	S Form
Boyle	Christopher		10/06/82	Irvine	09/06/99	6 0.0	9 4	Def	Kilmarnock Youth
Burke	Alexander		11/11/77	Glasgow	18/08/95	5 7.5	10 12	Fwd	Kilmarnock B.C.
Canero	Peter		18/01/81	Glasgow	25/06/98	5 9.0	11 4	Def	Kilmarnock Youth Team
Davidson	Stuart	William	03/08/79	Glasgow	19/08/97	5 7.0	11 3	Mid	Glasgow City B.C.
Di Giacomo	Paul		30/06/82	Glasgow	08/07/98	5 10.0	10 10	Fwd	Kilmarnock Youth
Dindeleux	Frederic		16/01/74	Lille	24/07/99	5 11.0	11 10	Def	Lille Olympic Sporting Club
Durrant	Ian		29/10/66	Glasgow	08/07/98	5 8.0	11 4	Mid	Rangers
Fowler	James		26/10/80	Stirling	18/10/97	5 9.0	10 11	Def	Gairdoch B.C.
Hay	Garry		07/09/77	Irvine	18/08/95	5 7.5	10 4	Def	Kilmarnock B.C.
Hessey	Sean		19/09/78	Liverpool	31/08/99	6 0.0	12 7	Def	Huddersfield Town
Holt	Gary	James	09/03/73	Irvine	18/08/95	5 11.5	12 8	Mid	Stoke City
Innes	Christopher		13/07/76	Broxburn	13/05/98	6 1.0	13 3	Def	Stenhousemuir
Jeffrey	Michael		11/08/71	Liverpool	14/07/99	5 11.5	11 9	Fwd	Fortuna Sittard
Kerr	Dylan		14/01/67	Malta	11/10/96	5 11.0	12 11	Def	Carlisle United
Lauchlan	James	Harley	02/02/77	Glasgow	20/07/94	6 1.0	12 1	Def	Kilmarnock B.C.
Lundie	James		02/08/82	Irvine	12/02/99	5 10.0	11 4	Def	Kilmarnock U'16s
MacPherson	Angus	Ian	11/10/68	Glasgow	10/06/86	5 11.0	11 12	Def	Rangers
Mahood	Alan	Scott	26/03/73	Kilwinning	09/07/98	5 8.0	11 5	Mid	Morton
Marshall	Gordon	George Banks	19/04/64	Edinburgh	21/01/98	6 4.0	14 5	Gk	Celtic
McCoist	Alistair	Murdoch	24/09/62	Bellshill	06/08/98	5 11.0	13 5	Fwd	Rangers
McCutcheon	Gary	Kyle	08/10/78	Dumfries	18/08/95	5 5.0	11 4	Fwd	Kilmarnock B.C.
McDonald	Gary	Matthew	10/04/82	Irvine	04/06/99	6 0.0	11 6	Fwd	Kilmarnock Youth
McGowne	Kevin		16/12/69	Kilmarnock	02/09/96	6 1.0	14 1	Def	St. Johnstone
McNeill	Kevin	John	20/08/82	Irvine	09/06/99	5 8.0	10 4	Def	Kilmarnock Youth
Meldrum	Colin	George	26/11/75	Kilmarnock	03/09/93	5 10.5	14 3	Gk	Kilwinning Rangers
Mitchell	Alistair	Robert	03/12/68	Kirkcaldy	05/07/91	5 7.0	11 9	Fwd	East Fife
Moffat	Ross	Stuart	17/01/82	Glasgow	08/06/99	5 7.0	10 13	Fwd	Kilmarnock Youth
Reilly	Mark	Francis	30/03/69	Bellshill	06/11/98	5 8.0	11 8	Mid	Reading
Roberts	Mark	Kingsley	29/10/75	Irvine	07/02/92	5 10.5	11 3	Fwd	Bellfield B.C.
Smith	Graeme		03/10/82	Bellshill	09/06/99	5 10.0	11 2	Def	Kilmarnock Youth
Stewart	Colin		10/01/80	Middlesbrough	23/07/99	6 3.0	12 12	Gk	Ipswich Town
Vareille	Jerome		01/06/74	Vernoux	29/07/97	5 11.0	12 8	Fwd	F.C. Mulhouse
Watt	Michael		27/11/70	Aberdeen	06/08/99	6 2.0	14 2	Gk	Norwich City
Williams	David		29/09/81	Glasgow	09/06/99	5 10.0	11 2	Fwd	Kilmarnock Youth
Wright	Paul	Hamilton	17/08/67	East Kilbride	31/03/95	5 8.0	12 3	Fwd	St. Johnstone

Milestones

YEAR OF FORMATION: 1869
MOST CAPPED PLAYER: Joe Nibloe
NO. OF CAPS: 11
MOST LEAGUE POINTS IN A SEASON: 58 (Division 2 - Season 1973/74)
MOST LEAGUE GOALS SCORED BY A PLAYER IN A SEASON: Harry "Peerie" Cunningham (Season 1927/28) and Andy Kerr (Season 1960/61)
NO. OF GOALS SCORED: 34
RECORD ATTENDANCE: 34,246 (-v- Rangers – August, 1963)
RECORD VICTORY: 13-2 (-v- Saltcoats – Scottish Cup, 12.9.1896)
RECORD DEFEAT: 0-8 (-v- Rangers and Hibernian - Division 1)

Killie's ten year league record

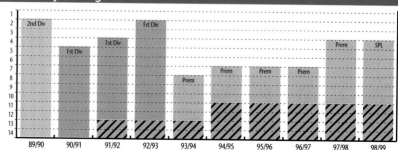

KILLIE'S CLUB FACTFILE 1998/99 RESULTS... APPEARANCES... SCORERS

Date	Venue	Opponents	Att.	Res	Marshall G.	MacPherson A.	Baker M.	Lauchlan J.	McGowne K.	Holt G.	Nevin P.	Mahood A.	Wright P.	Durrant I.	Mitchell A.	Roberts M.	Burke A.	Henry J.	Vareille J.	McCoist A.	Kerr D.	Montgomerie S.R.	Bagan D.	McCutcheon G.	Hamilton S.	Innes C.	Reilly M.
Aug 1	H	Dundee United	8,208	2-0	1	2	3	4	5	6	7[1]	8	9[1]	10	11	12	13	14									
15	A	St. Johnstone	6,210	0-0	1	2	3	4	5	6	11	8	9	10	7				12	13							
22	H	Rangers	17,608	1-3	1	2		4	5	6	14	13	9[1]	10	7	12			11	8	3						
30	H	Heart of Midlothian	10,376	3-0	1	2			5	6		8	9	10		12	13		7	11[3]	3	4	14				
Sep 12	A	Celtic	58,567	1-1	1	2	11		5	6		8	14	10	7	12	13			9[1]	3	4					
19	A	Motherwell	9,063	0-0	1	2	11		5	6		13	9	10	7	12				8	3	4					
23	H	Dundee	7,069	2-1	1	2	11		5[1]	6			9	10	7	12	13			8[1]	3	4					
27	A	Aberdeen	13,048	1-0	1	2			5	6			9[1]	10	7	12	13		11	8	3	4		14			
Oct 3	H	Dunfermline Athletic	8,346	0-0	1	2			5	6		8	9	10	7	12			11		3	4					
17	A	Dundee United	8,137	2-0	1	2	3		5[1]	6		12	9	10	8	11	14		7[1]			4		13			
24	H	St. Johnstone	9,336	2-2†	1		3			6		13	9	10	8	11[1]	12		7			4		14	5	2	
31	H	Celtic	16,695	2-0	1		3		5	6		8	12	10	7[1]				11	9[1]		4		13		2	
Nov 7	A	Heart of Midlothian	14,363	1-2	1		3		5	6		8	13[1]	10	7				11	9		4				2	12
14	H	Dundee	4,249	1-1	1	2	3		5	6		8	9	10	7				11[1]			4					
21	H	Motherwell	10,176	0-0	1	2	3		5	6		14	9	10	7	12			11	8		4		13			
28	A	Dunfermline Athletic	5,608	3-0	1	2	3		5	6[1]		12	9	10[2]	7					8		4		13			11
Dec 5	H	Aberdeen	9,785	4-0	1	2	3		5	6		13	9[1]	10	7[2]				11[1]	12		4		14			8
12	A	Rangers	49,781	0-1	1	2	3		5	6		12	9	10	7				11	13		4		14			8
20	A	Dundee United	13,538	2-0	1	2	3		5	6		14	9[1]	10[1]	7				11	12		4		13			8
26	H	Heart of Midlothian	10,668	1-0	1	2	3		5	6[1]		13	9	10	7				11	12		4		14			8
Jan 1	A	Motherwell	8,532	2-1	1	2	3		5[1]	6			9	10	7				11[1]			4					8
30	H	Dundee	7,677	0-0	1	2	3		5	6		8		10		12			11	9		4					7
Feb 6	A	Aberdeen	9,299	1-2	1	2	3		5			8[1]	14	10		12	13			9		4		11	6		7
17	A	Celtic	59,220	0-1	1	2	3		5	6		9	14	10	12		13		11	8		4					7
28	H	Rangers	16,242	0-5	1		3		5	6		9		10	12		13		11	8		4				2	7
Mar 6	H	Dunfermline Athletic	8,032	1-1	1			4	5	6		8	9	10	12		14		11	13	3					2	7
13	A	St. Johnstone	5,461	1-0	1	2		4	5	6[1]		13	9	10	8				11	12	3						7
21	H	Celtic	14,472	0-0	1	2		4	5	6		14	9	10	8		13		11	12	3						7
Apr 3	A	Heart of Midlothian	14,689	2-2	1	2		4	5	6		8	9	10	14				11	12[1]	3			13[1]			7
10	H	Aberdeen	9,048	4-2	1	2[1]		4		6		8[1]	9	10	14				11	12	3			13[2]	5		7
17	A	Dunfermline Athletic	5,585	6-0	1	2		4		6		8	13	10[1]	12				11[1]	9[1]	3			14[1]	5		7[2]
24	A	Dundee	4,296	1-2	1	2		4		6		8	13	10	12				11	9	3			14	5[1]		7
May 1	H	Motherwell	15,300	0-1	1	2	3	4	5	6		14	9	10	7				11	8				13			
8	A	Dundee United	7,190	0-0	1	2	3	4	5	6				10	11	12			7	9				13			8
15	A	St. Johnstone	15,086	1-1	1	2		4	5	6		8	13	10	12				11[1]	9	3			14			7
23	A	Rangers	48,835	1-1	1	2		4	5[1]	6		8	14	10	12				11	9	3			13			7
TOTAL FULL APPEARANCES					36	31	23	14	32	33	2	16	25	36	27	9	2	7	20	16	16	22	1	2	5	4	17
TOTAL SUB APPEARANCES											(1)	(12)	(8)		(5)	(13)	(17)		(4)	(3)	(10)			(4)	(11)		(1)
TOTAL GOALS SCORED							1		4	3	1	2	6	4	4	3			3	5	7			2			1

Small bold figures denote goalscorers.   † denotes opponent's own goal.

Rugby Park

Diagram labels: DUNDONALD RD, Car Park, RUGBY ROAD, SOUTH HAMILTON STREET

CAPACITY: 18,128 (All Seated)

PITCH DIMENSIONS: 112 yds x 74 yds

FACILITIES FOR DISABLED SUPPORTERS:
Contact: John Toal, Secretary, Persons with a Disability Association, 71B Mill Street, Ayr KA7 1PH. Tel: (01292) 288905

Team playing kits

How to get there

Rugby Park can be reached by the following routes:

BUSES: The main bus station, which is served by buses from all over the country, is ten minutes walk from the ground, but there are three local services which run from here to within a two minute walk of the park. These are the Kilmarnock-Saltcoats, Kilmarnock-Ardrossan and Kilmarnock-Largs.

TRAINS: Kilmarnock station is well served by trains from Glasgow and the West Coast, and the station is only 15 minutes walk from the ground.

CARS: Car parking is available in the club car park by permit only. Entry **ONLY** from Dundonald Road. Visiting supporters enter **ONLY** from Rugby Road Entrance.

Killie

email: sfl@sol.co.uk • website: www.sfl.scottishfootball.com

Chapman Building, Firpark Street, Motherwell, ML1 2QN

HON. LIFE PRESIDENT
James C. Chapman, O.B.E.

CHAIRMAN
John Boyle

DIRECTORS
William H. Dickie, R.I.B.A., A.R.I.A.S,
Alisdair F. Barron, Fiona Boyle,
James H. Chapman, John Swinburne
& Andrew Lapping

PLAYER/CHIEF EXECUTIVE
Patrick Nevin

SECRETARY
Alisdair F. Barron

MANAGER
William Davies

ASSISTANT MANAGER
Jim Griffin

HON. MEDICAL OFFICER
Dr. Robert Liddle

PHYSIOTHERAPIST
John Porteous

S.F.A. COMMUNITY OFFICER
Colin McKinnon

YOUTH DEVELOPMENT OFFICER/ CHIEF SCOUT
Dave McParland

FOOTBALL SAFETY OFFICERS' ASSOCIATION REPRESENTATIVE
Kenneth Davies
(0411) 237800 (Mobile)

GROUNDSMAN
Grant Murdoch

COMMERCIAL MANAGER
Karen Paterson
Tel (01698) 333333

TELEPHONES
Ground/Commercial
(01698) 333333
Fax (01698) 338001
Ticket Office (01698) 333030
Clubcall (09068) 121553

E-MAIL & INTERNET ADDRESS
online@motherwellfc.com

CLUB SHOP
Motherwell Football & Athletic Club,
Firpark Street, Motherwell, ML1 2QN
Tel (01698) 333333. Open Tues,
Thurs & Fri from 10.00 a.m. to
3.00 p.m. Sautrday (Home Match
days), 10.00 a.m. to 3.00 p.m. &
4.30 p.m. to 5.30 p.m. and
Saturday (Away Matches)
10.00 a.m. to 1.00 p.m.

OFFICIAL SUPPORTERS CLUB
c/o Fir Park, Firpark Street,
Motherwell, ML1 2QN.

TEAM CAPTAIN
Andy Goram

SHIRT SPONSOR
Motorola

LIST OF PLAYERS 1999-2000

SURNAME	FIRST NAME	MIDDLE NAME	DATE OF BIRTH	PLACE OF BIRTH	DATE OF SIGNING	HEIGHT FT INS	WEIGHT ST LBS	POS. ON PITCH	PREVIOUS CLUB
Adams	Derek	Watt	25/06/75	Glasgow	15/09/98	5 10.0	11 8	Fwd	Ross County
Brannan	Gerard	Daniel	15/01/72	Liverpool	28/10/98	6 0.0	13 2	Mid	Manchester City
Brown	Michael		07/11/79	Stranraer	26/07/99	6 1.0	12 5	Gk	Manchester City
Callachan	Craig		28/06/81	Bellshill	31/08/99	5 9.0	9 10	Mid	X Form
Clarke	David		22/06/83	Rutherglen	31/08/99	5 11.0	9 2	Mid	S Form
Constable	John		01/12/82	Lanark	31/08/99	5 9.0	10 0	Mid	X Form
Craigan	Stephen	James	29/10/76	Newtonards	07/09/95	6 0.0	12 8	Def	Blantyre Vics
Davies	William	McIntosh	31/05/64	Glasgow	12/03/94	5 6.0	10 9	Mid	Dunfermline Athletic
Dempsie	Brian		04/02/83	Bellshill	31/08/99	6 0.0	11 7	Def	Motherwell B.C.
Denham	Greig	Paterson	05/10/76	Glasgow	19/08/93	6 2.0	13 6	Def	Cumbernauld United
Doesburg	Michel	Johannes	10/08/68	Beverwyk	31/07/98	5 11.0	12 2	Def	AZ Alkmaar
Doherty	David	John	08/05/80	Bellshill	02/08/99	5 10.0	11 2	Mid	Motherwell B.C.
Fallon	John		14/01/82	Bellshill	30/07/99	5 10.0	10 4	Fwd	Calderbraes B.C.
Goodman	Donald	Ralph	09/05/66	Leeds	30/03/99	5 9.5	13 3	Fwd	Hiroshima
Goram	Andrew	Lewis	13/04/64	Bury	13/01/99	5 11.5	14 6	Gk	Sheffield United
Halliday	Stephen		03/05/76	Sunderland	24/07/98	5 10.0	12 7	Fwd	Hartlepool United
Hammell	Steven		18/02/82	Rutherglen	31/08/99	5 10.0	12 1	Def	X Form
Lasley	Keith	William	21/09/79	Glasgow	20/03/99	5 9.5	11 0	Mid	Cathkin United B.C.
Matthaei	Rob		20/09/66	Amsterdam	06/07/98	5 8.5	11 4	Mid	F.C. Volendam
McCulloch	Lee	Henry	14/05/78	Bellshill	17/08/95	6 0.5	13 2	Fwd	Cumbernauld United
McFadden	James		14/04/83	Glasgow	30/07/99	5 10.0	10 10	Mid	Motherwell B.C.
McGowan	Jamie		05/12/70	Morecambe	06/07/98	6 0.0	11 5	Def	Falkirk
McLaughlin	Kevin		11/10/81	Glasgow	31/08/99	5 10.0	10 7	Def	Cathkin United U'18
McMillan	Stephen		19/01/76	Edinburgh	19/08/93	5 10.0	11 12	Def/Mid	Troon Juniors
Miller	Colin		11/01/83	Glasgow	01/09/99	5 8.5	10 3	Fwd	S Form
Nevin	Patrick	Kevin Francis	06/09/63	Glasgow	07/09/98	5 6.5	10 9	Fwd	Kilmarnock
Nicholas	Steven	Arthur	08/07/81	Stirling	17/03/99	5 8.5	10 3	Fwd	Stirling Albion
Ramsay	Douglas		26/04/79	Irvine	03/07/97	5 11.0	11 0	Mid	Bearsden B.C.
Spencer	John		11/09/70	Glasgow	29/01/99	5 6.5	11 11	Fwd	Everton
Teale	Shaun		10/03/64	Southport	07/08/98	6 1.5	14 0	Def	Happy Valley
Thomas	Tony		12/07/71	Liverpool	16/12/98	6 0.5	13 11	Def	Everton
Townsley	Derek		21/03/73	Carlisle	10/06/99	6 5.0	13 0	Mid	Queen of the South
Twaddle	Kevin		31/10/71	Edinburgh	10/06/99	6 3.0	12 2	Mid/For	Morton
Valakari	Simo	Johannes	28/04/73	Helsinki	06/02/97	5 10.5	12 5	Mid	Finn PA
Wilson	Scott	William	20/04/82	Bellshill	31/08/99	6 3.0	10 10	Mid	Ayr United
Woods	Stephen	Gerard	23/02/70	Glasgow	22/07/94	6 2.0	13 5	Gk	Preston North End

Milestones

YEAR OF FORMATION: 1886
MOST CAPPED PLAYER: Tommy Coyne (Republic of Ireland)
NO. OF CAPS: 13
MOST LEAGUE POINTS IN A SEASON: 66 (Division 1 - Season 1931/32)
MOST LEAGUE GOALS SCORED BY A PLAYER IN A SEASON: William McFadyen (Season 1931/32)
NO. OF GOALS SCORED: 52
RECORD ATTENDANCE: 35,632 (-v- Rangers – Scottish Cup, 12.3.1952)
RECORD VICTORY: 12-1 (-v- Dundee United – Division 2, 23.1.1954)
RECORD DEFEAT: 0-8 (-v- Aberdeen - Premier Division, 26.3.1979)

The Well's ten year league record

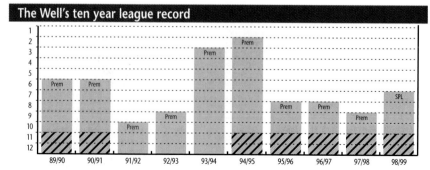

THE WELL'S CLUB FACTFILE 1998/99 RESULTS... APPEARANCES... SCORERS

Date	Venue	Opponents	Att.	Res	Kaven M.	Doesburg M.	McMillan S.	McGowan J.	Stirling J.	Valakari S.	Matthaei R.	Michels J.	Ross I.	McClair B.	Coyle O.	Denham G.	Halliday S.	McCulloch L.	Woods S.	Teale G.	Nyssonen K.	Miller G.	Shivute E.	Nevin P.	Adams D.	Craigan S.	Christie K.	Brannan G.	Spencer J.	May E.	Thomas T.	Goram A.	Bacque H.	Ramsay D.	Gower M.	Nicholas S.	Goodman D.
Aug 1	H	St. Johnstone	5,686	1-0	1	2	3	4	5¹	6	7	8	9	10	11	12	13	14																			
15	A	Rangers	49,275	1-2		2		4	5	6	7	8		10	11¹		13	12	1	3	9																
22	H	Dunfermline Athletic	9,858	0-0	1	2	3	4		6	7	8	10		11			12	5	9	13																
30	H	Dundee United	11,201	1-0	1	2	3	4		6	7		8	10	11			12	5	9¹																	
Sep 12	A	Aberdeen	11,260	1-1	1	2	3	4	13	6	7	8	9	10	11¹				5			12															
19	H	Kilmarnock	9,063	0-0	1	2	3	4		6	7	8	9	10	11		14		5			12	13														
23	A	Heart of Midlothian	12,323	0-3	1	2	3	4		6	7	8	10	14	11		13		5			12	9														
26	A	Dundee	5,655	0-1	1	2	3	4		6	8	14	13	10	11		12		5			7	9														
Oct 3	H	Celtic	12,103	1-2		2	3	4	8	6	7		9	10	11				1	5		12	13¹														
17	A	St. Johnstone	4,062	0-5		2		4	3	8	12		6	10	11		13		1	5		7	9	14													
28	A	Rangers	11,777	1-0	1	2	3	4		8					11				12			13	9			6	7	10¹									
31	H	Aberdeen	8,146	2-2	1	2	3	4¹		8					11		9	14		5		12	13			6	7	10¹									
Nov 7	H	Dundee United	6,616	2-2	1	2	3	4		8				11²			9			5		12	14	13		7	10¹	6									
14	H	Heart of Midlothian	8,912	3-2	1	2	3	4		8		12		11²						5		9	13			7	10¹	6									
21	A	Kilmarnock	10,176	0-0	1	2	3	4		8			12	11						5		9	13			7	10	6									
28	A	Celtic	59,227	0-2	1	2	3	4		8			13	11		9				5		12				7	10	6									
Dec 12	A	Dunfermline Athletic	5,182	1-1	1	2	3			8				11			9		5			12				6	7	10¹	4								
16	H	Dundee	5,840	2-1	1	3¹		4		8		13		11¹			9		5			7	12				2	10		6							
19	H	St. Johnstone	5,686	1-2	1	2	3	4		8		14		11			12					13	9¹				5	10	6	7							
26	H	Dundee United	6,001	2-0		2	3¹			8				11			9	1	5			7	14			12	4¹	10	13	6							
29	A	Aberdeen	15,269	1-1		2	3			8				11			9¹	1	5			12	14			7	4	10	13	6							
Jan 1	H	Kilmarnock	8,532	1-2		2		4		8	10	6		11			9	1				7	12				3¹			5							
30	A	Heart of Midlothian	12,821	2-0		2		4		8	7			11			9¹		5			13¹	12			3	10		6	1							
Feb 6	A	Dundee	4,187	0-1		2		4		8				11			10		5			7	9			3			1	12	13						
21	A	Celtic	11,963	1-7		2		4		8		14		11			9	1	5			12	13	7		3¹	10	6									
27	H	Dunfermline Athletic	7,324	1-1	1	2	3	4		8		13		11			9¹		5			10	12			7		6		1		14					
Mar 13	A	Rangers	49,483	1-2		2	3	4		8	14						9		5	13		12	10	7		6		1				11¹					
20	H	Aberdeen	6,963	1-1		2	3			8									5¹	10		13	14	7	9	6	4	1				11	12				
Apr 3	A	Dundee United	8,110	3-0			3	4		8									5	10				2¹	9²	6	1					7	12	11			
10	H	Dundee	5,717	1-2	12	3	4			8									5	10				2	9¹	6	1					7	13	11			
17	A	Celtic	59,588	0-1		2	3	4		8							9		5	13	12			6	10		1				7	14	11			
24	H	Heart of Midlothian	8,926	0-4		2	3	4		8	13						12		5	14				7	9		6	1				11		10			
May 1	A	Kilmarnock	15,300	1-0			3	4		6										12		7	11	5	2¹	9		1				8	13	10			
8	A	St. Johnstone	4,599	0-0			3	4		8	6						12					7	11	5	2	9		1						10			
15	H	Rangers	11,078	1-5			3	4		8							11					14	6	5	2	9		1				12	7	13¹	10		
23	A	Dunfermline Athletic	3,532	2-1			3	4		8	5						9					7	6	2				1				12¹	13	11	10¹		
TOTAL FULL APPEARANCES					16	29	30	32	4	35	14	7	8	26	2	14	7	29	3	1	14	11	6	4	25	21	10	10	13				8	1	8		
TOTAL SUB APPEARANCES						(1)			(1)		(3)	(3)	(4)	(3)		(1)	(2)	(12)				(3)	(1)	(16)	(15)	(4)	(1)		(2)			(1)	(4)	(1)	(6)	
TOTAL GOALS SCORED						2	1	1						7			3		1	1					3			5	7			1	1	1	1

Small bold figures denote goalscorers.   † denotes opponent's own goal.

Fir Park

DALZELL DRIVE

KNOWETOP AVENUE

Chapman Building

FIRPARK STREET

CAPACITY: 13,742 (All Seated)

PITCH DIMENSIONS: 110 yds x 75 yds

FACILITIES FOR DISABLED SUPPORTERS:
Area between Main Stand and South Stand. Prior arrangement must be made with the Secretary and a ticket obtained.

Team playing kits

How to get there

The following routes can be used to reach Fir Park:

BUSES: Fir Park is less than a quarter of a mile from the main thoroughfare through the town and numerous buses serving Lanarkshire and Glasgow all pass along this road. De-bus at the Civic Centre.

TRAINS: Motherwell Station is a main-line station on the Glasgow–London (Euston) route, and the station is particularly well served by trains running from numerous points throughout the Strathclyde Region. Motherwell Station is a twenty minute walk from Fir Park, while the station at Airbles Road is only ten minutes away. East Coast access is via Motherwell Central Station on the Glasgow–London East Coast line. Travel from West Coast and Glasgow areas is via the low level Glasgow Central line to Airbles and Motherwell Central. This is a regular service on a 30 minute basis (8 mins & 38 mins past).

CARS: Controlled supervised car parking is available in the immediate area of Fir Park. Car park season tickets are available for closest proximity car parks. Away fan car parking is extensive in the grounds of Motherwell College on a day rate basis of £5.00. Access to South Stand is within a maximum of 5 minutes walk.

email: sfl@sol.co.uk • website: www.sfl.scottishfootball.com

Ibrox Stadium,150 Edmiston Drive, Glasgow, G51 2XD

CHAIRMAN
David E. Murray

DIRECTORS
Hugh R. W. Adam, Daniel P. Levy,
James MacDonald, R. Campbell Ogilvie
& Ian B. Skelly

SECRETARY
R. Campbell Ogilvie

MANAGER
Dick Advocaat

ASSISTANT MANAGER
Bert van Lingen

RESERVE COACHES
John McGregor & John Brown

YOUTH COACH
John Chalmers

CHIEF SCOUT
Ewan Chester

CLUB DOCTOR
Dr. Gert Jan Goudswaard

PHYSIOTHERAPIST
Grant Downie

PLAYER LIAISON OFFICER
John Greig, M.B.E.

FINANCIAL CONTROLLER
Douglas Odam

RANGERS HOSPITALITY MANAGER
Peter Kingstone

MARKETING & MEDIA MANAGER
Martin Bain

HEAD OF SALES
Alistair Wilson

HOSPITALITY SALES MANAGER
Scot Gardiner

**CUSTOMER SERVICES
TICKET OPERATIONS MANAGER**
Jim Hannah

**OPERATIONS EXECUTIVE/
FOOTBALL SAFETY OFFICERS'
ASSOCIATION REPRESENTATIVE**
Laurence MacIntyre

PITCH SUPERINTENDENT
David Roxburgh

STADIUM FACILITIES MANAGER
Ken Crawford

TELEPHONES
Main Switch Board (0141) 580 8500
Administration (0141) 580 8609
Fax (0141) 580 8947
Ticket Centre
0870-600 1993 Fax (0141) 580 8504
Customer Services 0870-600 1972
Hospitality 0870-600 1964
Commercial 0870-600 1899
Retail/Mail Order 0990 99 1998
Fax Enquiries 0870-600 1978

E-MAIL & INTERNET ADDRESS
dora_howie@rangers.co.uk
http://www.rangers.co.uk

OFFICIAL SUPPORTERS CLUB
Rangers F.C. Supporters' Association,
250 Edmiston Drive, Glasgow, G51 1YU

TEAM CAPTAIN
Lorenzo Amoruso

SHIRT SPONSOR
NTL

LIST OF PLAYERS 1999-2000

SURNAME	FIRST NAME	MIDDLE NAME	DATE OF BIRTH	PLACE OF BIRTH	DATE OF SIGNING	HEIGHT FT INS	WEIGHT ST LBS	POS. ON PITCH	PREVIOUS CLUB
Adamczuk	Dariusz		20/10/69	Stettin	13/07/99	5 10.0	12 0	Mid	Dundee
Albertz	Jorg		29/01/71	Monchengladbach	16/07/96	6 2.0	13 5	Mid	Hamburger S.V.
Amato	Gabriel	Omar	22/10/70	Mar Del Plata	15/07/98	6 1.5	12 11	Fwd	RCD Mallorca SAD
Amoruso	Lorenzo		28/06/71	Bari	02/06/97	6 2.0	13 6	Def	Fiorentina A.C. SPA
Brown	Mark		28/02/81	Motherwell	01/07/97	6 1.5	13 2	Gk	S Form
Carson	Stephen		06/10/80	Ballymoney	02/07/97	5 10.5	12 0	Mid	Linfield
Chalmers	Iain		26/08/81	Glasgow	08/09/97	5 11.5	11 6	Def	Rangers B.C.
Charbonnier	Lionel		25/10/66	Poitiers	15/07/98	5 11.0	12 9	Gk	A.J. Auxerre
Currie	Ross		01/08/81	Glasgow	14/07/98	6 0.0	11 6	Def	Rangers Youth
Dewar	Gary		02/09/81	Dunfermline	14/07/98	5 9.0	10 2	Fwd	Rangers Youth
Dobbie	Stephen		05/12/82	Glasgow	12/07/99	5 8.5	10 4	Fwd	S Form
Dowie	Andrew	John	25/03/83	Bellshill	12/07/99	6 1.0	11 6	Def	S Form
Durie	Gordon	Scott	06/12/65	Paisley	24/11/93	5 11.0	13 11	Fwd	Tottenham Hotspur
Feeney	Lee		21/03/78	Newry	24/12/98	5 9.5	11 8	Mid	Linfield
Ferguson	Barry		02/02/78	Glasgow	06/07/94	5 10.5	11 9	Mid	Rangers S.A.B.C.
Ferguson	Ian		15/03/67	Glasgow	15/02/88	5 11.0	13 6	Mid	St. Mirren
Fitzgerald	Darren		13/10/78	Belfast	06/07/94	5 8.0	11 0	Fwd	St. Andrews B.C.
Gibson	James		19/02/80	Bellshill	01/07/96	5 7.0	11 6	Mid	S Form
Gibson	William		07/08/81	Bellshill	25/08/97	5 10.5	11 13	Def	S Form
Hendry	Edward	Colin James	07/12/65	Keith	05/08/98	6 2.0	13 0	Def	Blackburn Rovers
Hughes	Stephen		14/11/82	Motherwell	12/07/99	5 11.0	9 6	Mid	S Form
Johansson	Jonatan		16/08/75	Stockholm	13/08/97	6 1.0	12 2	Mid	FC Flora
Kanchelskis	Andrei		23/01/69	Kirovograci	15/07/98	6 0.0	12 13	Mid	A.C. Fiorentina
Kelly	Stuart		01/08/81	Glasgow	14/07/98	5 8.0	9 11	Fwd	Rangers Youth
Klos	Stefan		16/08/71	Dortmund	23/12/98	5 10.5	13 5	Gk	Borussia Dortmund
MacDonald	Peter		17/11/80	Glasgow	01/07/97	5 9.5	11 2	Fwd	S Form
Malcolm	Robert		12/11/80	Glasgow	01/07/97	5 11.5	12 2	Def	S Form
McAdam	Steven		03/05/81	Glasgow	01/07/97	5 11.5	11 1	Fwd	S Form
McCann	Neil	Docherty	11/08/74	Greenock	14/12/98	5 7.5	10 5	Fwd	Heart of Midlothian
McCann	Ryan		15/09/82	Belfast	12/07/99	5 9.0	10 1	Mid	St. Andrews B.C.
McGregor	Allan		31/01/82	Edinburgh	14/07/98	6 0.5	11 12	Gk	Rangers Youth
McHale	Paul		30/09/81	Stirling	14/07/98	5 9.0	10 3	Mid	Rangers Youth
McInnes	Derek	John	05/07/71	Paisley	14/11/95	5 7.0	11 5	Mid	Morton
McKnight	Paul		08/02/77	Belfast	05/08/93	5 7.0	11 8	Fwd	St. Andrews B.C.
McLean	Steven		23/08/82	Edinburgh	17/09/98	5 11.5	11 13	Fwd	Rangers Youth
Miller	Charles		18/03/76	Glasgow	02/07/92	5 8.5	10 8	Mid	Rangers B.C.
Mols	Michael		17/12/70	Amsterdam	13/07/99	5 10.5	12 4	Fwd	F.C. Utrecht
Moore	Craig	Andrew	12/12/75	Canterbury, Australia	31/03/99	5 11.5	12 4	Def	Crystal Palace
Morrison	Kevin		04/05/83	Glasgow	12/07/99	5 9.5	9 8	Mid	S Form
Negri	Marco		27/10/70	Milan	27/06/97	5 11.5	12 10	Fwd	Perugia A.C. SPA
Nicholson	Barry		24/08/78	Dumfries	03/07/95	5 7.5	10 12	Mid	Rangers S.A.B.C.
Niemi	Antti		31/05/72	Oulu	26/06/97	6 1.0	13 11	Gk	F.C. Copenhagen A/S
Numan	Arthur		14/12/69	Heemskerk	09/07/98	5 8.5	12 3	Def	P.S.V. Eindhoven
Porrini	Sergio		08/11/68	Milan	09/07/97	5 11.5	11 9	Def	Juventus F.C. SPA
Prodan	Daniel		23/03/72	Satu Mare	31/07/98	6 2.0	14 1	Def	Club Atletico De Madrid
Reyna	Claudio		20/07/73	Livingston, New Jersey	31/03/99	5 9.0	11 9	Fwd	VFL Wolfsburg
Robb	Richard		24/01/83	Irvine	12/07/99	6 5.0	11 12	Def	S Form
Ross	Maurice		03/02/81	Dundee	01/07/97	6 0.0	11 1	Def	Rangers S.A.B.C.
Russell	Iain	Thomas	14/11/82	Dumfries	12/07/99	5 1.0	9 8	Mid	S Form
Smith	Graeme		08/06/83	Edinburgh	13/07/99	6 1.5	12 4	Gk	S Form
Stensaas	Stale		07/07/71	Trondheim	10/06/97	5 11.0	12 1	Def	Rosenborg B.K.
Stone	Michael		15/01/79	Stirling	03/07/95	6 0.5	13 1	Def	Rangers S.A.B.C.
Van Bronckhorst	Giovanni		05/02/75	Rotterdam	15/07/98	5 8.5	11 1	Mid	Feyenoord
Vidmar	Antony		04/07/70	Adelaide	01/07/97	6 0.5	12 10	Def	NAC Breda
Wallace	Rodney		02/10/69	Lewisham	17/07/98	5 7.0	11 2	Fwd	Leeds United
Willoughby	Kirk		28/01/81	Cambridge	01/07/97	5 11.0	10 12	Def	S Form
Wilson	Scott		19/03/77	Edinburgh	01/07/93	6 2.0	12 8	Def	Rangers B.C.
Young	David		01/03/79	Glasgow	03/07/95	5 9.5	11 0	Mid	Rangers S.A.B.C.

Milestones

YEAR OF FORMATION: 1873
MOST CAPPED PLAYER: Alistair McCoist
NO. OF CAPS: 58
MOST LEAGUE POINTS IN A SEASON: 76 (Division 1 - Season 1920/21) (2 Points for a Win)
87 (Premier Division - Season 1995/96) (3 Points for a Win)
MOST LEAGUE GOALS SCORED BY A PLAYER IN A SEASON: Sam English (Season 1931/32)
NO. OF GOALS SCORED: 44
RECORD ATTENDANCE: 118,567 (-v- Celtic – 2.1.1939)
RECORD VICTORY: 14-2 (-v- Blairgowrie – Scottish Cup, 20.1.1934)
RECORD DEFEAT: 2-10 (-v- Airdrieonians – 1886)

The Gers' ten year league record

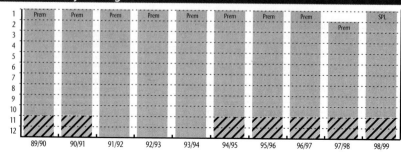

THE GERS' CLUB FACTFILE 1998/99 RESULTS... APPEARANCES... SCORERS

Date	Venue	Opponents	Att.	Res	Niemi A.	Porrini S.	Numan A.	Moore C.	Them J.	Albertz J.	Van Bronckhorst G.	Ferguson I.	Gattuso G.	Durie G.	Wallace R.	Kanchelskis A.	Amato G.	Charbonnier L.	Amoruso L.	Hendry C.	Ferguson B.	Johansson J.	Graham D.	Miller C.	Vidmar A.	Rozental S.	Wilson S.	Guivarc'h S.	Stensaas S.	McCann N.	Klos S.	Nicholson B.	Feeney L.	McInnes D.	Reyna C.	Riccio L.
Aug 2	A	Heart of Midlothian	15,272	1-2	1	2	3	4	5	6	7	8	9	10	11¹	12	13																			
15	H	Motherwell	49,275	2-1		2	3			6¹		8	9		10¹			1	11	4	5	7		12	13												
22	H	Kilmarnock	17,608	3-1		2	3	5		6¹		8			10¹		9	1	11	4		7		12¹													
29	H	St. Johnstone	48,732	4-0		2		5		6¹		8¹	14		10¹		9¹	1	11	4	13	7		12	3												
Sep 12	A	Dundee United	12,088	0-0		2		5			8	6			10		9	1	11	4		7		12	3												
20	H	Celtic	50,026	0-0		3		2		6	8				10		9	1	11	4	5	7	13	12													
23	A	Aberdeen	17,862	1-1		2		5		6	8	13	14		10¹			1	11	4		7	12		9	3											
26	A	Dunfermline Athletic	11,507	2-0		2		5		6	8	12	9		10			1	4		7¹	11¹			3	13	14										
Oct 4	H	Dundee	48,348	1-0		2				6¹	8	14	9		10			1	4	5	7	11	12	3	13												
17	H	Heart of Midlothian	49,749	3-0		2				6	8				10²	9		1	4	5	7	11¹	12	3	13	14											
28	A	Motherwell	11,777	0-1		2	13			6	8	14		12	10	9		1	4	5	7	11		3													
31	H	Dundee United	49,503	2-1		2	12			6	8				10¹	9	11	1	4¹	5	7		13	3													
Nov 8	A	St. Johnstone	9,660	7-0	1		3			6²	8	7			10¹	9¹			4	5	11¹		14	2					12	13²							
14	H	Aberdeen	49,479	2-1	1	2	3			6	8¹	13			10	9¹			5	7	11		4	12													
21	A	Celtic	59,783	1-5	1	2	3			6	8¹	14	12		10	9			5	7		13		4	11												
Dec 5	H	Dunfermline Athletic	47,465	1-1	1	2	3			6	8¹		12		10	9			4	5	7			11													
12	H	Kilmarnock	49,781	1-0	1	2	3			6	8	14	13		10¹	9			4	5	7		12	11													
19	A	Heart of Midlothian	17,134	3-2	1	5				6	8	12			10	9¹			4		7		2	11²	3	13											
26	H	St. Johnstone	49,479	1-0		2¹				6	8				10	9			4	5	7		14	3	13	11	12	1									
30	A	Dundee United	11,707	2-1		2				6	8				10¹	12			4		7	14	13	3	5¹	11	9	1									
Jan 3	H	Celtic	50,059	2-2		2	12				8				10¹	9	11¹		4	5	7	13	3		6	1											
27	A	Dundee	10,043	4-0		2				6					10	9			4	12¹	8²	3	11¹	7	1	5	13										
30	A	Aberdeen	19,507	4-2		2¹				6¹	8				10¹	9¹			4	13	14	3	5	11	7	1	12										
Feb 7	A	Dunfermline Athletic	10,360	3-0		2				6	8				10	9¹			4	7	11²	13	3	12	1	5											
20	H	Dundee	49,462	6-1		2				6³	5¹				10	9	14		4	7	11	13	3	12	8²	1											
28	A	Kilmarnock	16,242	5-0		2				6	5				10³	9			4	12	7	13¹	3	11	8¹	1	14										
Mar 13	H	Motherwell	49,483	2-1		2				6	5				10¹	9	14		4	7	11¹	13	3	8	1	12											
20	H	Dundee United	49,164	0-1		2				7	6				10	9	12		4	11	13	3	5	8	1												
Apr 4	A	St. Johnstone	9,742	1-3		2	5¹			7	6				10	9	12		4	11	3		8	1													
14	H	Dunfermline Athletic	46,220	1-0		2				7	6¹				10	9			4	5	12	3	11	8	1												
18	A	Dundee	11,070	1-1		2				7	6				10	9	12		4	14	11	3¹	8	1	13	5											
25	H	Aberdeen	49,145	3-1		2					7				10¹	9¹	11¹		4	5	14	13	8	1	6	12	3										
May 2	A	Celtic	59,918	3-0		2				7¹	6				10	11			4	5	12	3	8²	1	13	9											
9	H	Heart of Midlothian	49,495	0-0		2				7	6			9	10				4	12	3	5	11	1	14	13	8										
15	A	Motherwell	11,078	5-1		2				7	6¹				10	9¹	11³		4	13	3	8	1	12	5	14											
23	H	Kilmarnock	48,835	1-1		2				7	6				8	9¹			4	10	3	11	12	1	13	5											
TOTAL FULL APPEARANCES					7	35	8	8	1	33	35	4	3	1	34	29	13	11	33	16	23	13	2	26	7	11	1	15	18	3						6
TOTAL SUB APPEARANCES						(2)				(1)		(9)	(2)	(4)		(1)	(7)			(3)		(12)	(3)	(14)	(2)	(3)	(5)	(3)	(4)		(3)	(1)	(7)		(1)
TOTAL GOALS SCORED						2	.	1		11	7				18	8	6		1		1	8		3	1		1	5	5						

Small bold figures denote goalscorers.   † denotes opponent's own goal.

Ibrox Stadium

EDMISTON DRIVE

CAPACITY: 50,403 (All Seated)

PITCH DIMENSIONS: 115yds x 75yds

FACILITIES FOR DISABLED SUPPORTERS:
Special area within stadium and also special toilet facilities provided. The club also have a Rangers Disabled Supporters' Club. Contact: David Milne, Secretary, Disabled Supporters' Club, c/o Ibrox Stadium, Glasgow, G51 2XD. This is free of charge.

Team playing kits

How to get there

You can reach Ibrox Stadium by these routes:

BUSES: The following buses all pass within 300 yards of the Stadium and can be boarded from Glasgow city centre:- Nos. 9A, 23, 23A, 53, 53A, 54A, 54B, 65, 89 and 91.

UNDERGROUND: GGPTE Underground station is Ibrox, which is two minutes walk from the Stadium.

CARS: Motor Vehicles can head for the Stadium from the city centre by joining the M8 Motorway from Waterloo Street. Take the B768 turn-off for Govan. This will then take you to the ground. A limited number of parking spaces will be available in the Albion Car Park.

email: sfl@sol.co.uk • website: www.sfl.scottishfootball.com

St. Johnstone

McDiarmid Park, Crieff Road,
Perth, PH1 2SJ

CHAIRMAN
Geoffrey S. Brown

DIRECTORS
Douglas B. McIntyre,
David F. Sidey &
Henry G. Stewart

HONORARY PRESIDENT
Bruce McDiarmid

MANAGING DIRECTOR/
SECRETARY
A. Stewart M. Duff

MANAGER
Alexander Clark

FIRST TEAM COACH
William Kirkwood

YOUTH COACH
Alastair Stevenson

CLUB DOCTOR
Alistair McCracken

PHYSIOTHERAPIST
Nick Summersgill

S.F.A. COMMUNITY OFFICER
Atholl Henderson

STADIUM MANAGER
Jimmy Hogg

FOOTBALL SAFETY OFFICERS'
ASSOCIATION REPRESENTATIVE
Sandy Drummond (01738) 459090

MARKETING EXECUTIVE
Paul Fraser

SALES EXECUTIVE
Diane Knight
(01738) 459090

LOTTERY MANAGER
Anne Connolly

CATERING MANAGER
Scott Ritchie

TELEPHONES
Ground (01738) 459090
Fax (01738) 625771
Information Service (0891) 121559
Ticket Office (01738) 455000

E-MAIL & INTERNET ADDRESS
www.stjohnstonefc.co.uk

CLUB SHOP
Mon-Fri at Main Reception
at Ground. A shop is also open on
matchdays and is situated at
Ormond (South) Stand

OFFICIAL SUPPORTERS CLUB
c/o McDiarmid Park,
Crieff Road, Perth

TEAM CAPTAIN
Jim Weir

SHIRT SPONSOR
Scottish Hydro-Electric plc

LIST OF PLAYERS 1999-2000

SURNAME	FIRST NAME	MIDDLE NAME	DATE OF BIRTH	PLACE OF BIRTH	DATE OF SIGNING	HEIGHT FT INS	WEIGHT ST LBS	POS. ON PITCH	PREVIOUS CLUB
Bollan	Gary		24/03/73	Dundee	20/02/98	5 11.0	12 12	Def	Rangers
Connolly	Patrick	Martin	25/06/70	Glasgow	14/03/98	5 9.5	11 0	Fwd	Airdrieonians
Conway	Christopher	Thomas	17/07/83	Glasgow	09/07/99	5 11.0	11 2	Def	S Form
Crozier	Brendan	George	07/10/82	Glasgow	10/10/98	5 10.0	8 12	Mid	Busby B.C.
Cuthbert	Kevin	Scott	08/09/82	Perth	21/09/98	5 11.0	10 6	Gk	St. Johnstone B.C.
Dasovic	Nick	Robert	05/12/68	Vancouver	13/11/96	6 1.0	12 4	Mid	Trelleborg F.C.
Dods	Darren		07/06/75	Edinburgh	02/07/98	6 1.0	13 2	Def	Hibernian
Ferguson	Allan	Thomas	21/03/69	Lanark	01/07/98	5 10.5	12 7	Gk	Hamilton Academical
Forsyth	Ross		20/11/82	Glasgow	09/07/99	5 8.0	10 7	Def	Aberdeen B.C.
Fotheringham	Martyn	Fraser	23/03/83	Perth	09/07/99	5 10.0	11 6	Mid	Forfar B.C.
Grant	Roderick	John	16/09/66	Gloucester	29/07/95	5 11.0	12 7	Fwd	Partick Thistle
Griffin	Daniel	Joseph	10/08/77	Belfast	18/02/94	5 10.0	10 12	Def	St. Andrews B.C.
Guy	Kieran	Andrew	16/02/82	Paisley	06/07/98	5 9.0	10 0	Fwd	St. Johnstone B.C.
Kane	Paul	James	20/06/65	Edinburgh	23/07/97	5 9.5	11 0	Mid	Viking Stavanger
Kearney	Darren		16/09/82	Coatbridge	09/07/99	5 8.0	10 8	Mid	Riverside B.C.
Keddie	Alexander		23/01/81	Glasgow	24/11/98	6 1.0	12 4	Def	Leeds United
Kernaghan	Alan	Nigel	25/04/67	Otley	24/12/97	6 2.0	13 7	Def	Manchester City
Lauchlan	Martin	Thomas	01/10/80	Rutherglen	25/05/99	5 10.0	10 7	Fwd	Partick Thistle
Lowndes	Nathan	Peter	02/06/77	Salford	21/08/98	6 0.0	11 0	Fwd	Watford
Main	Alan	David	05/12/67	Elgin	05/01/95	5 11.5	12 13	Gk	Dundee United
Malcolm	Stuart	Ross	20/08/79	Edinburgh	12/07/96	6 1.0	12 5	Def	Hutchison Vale B.C.
McAllister	Steven		17/05/82	Perth	06/07/98	5 8.0	9 7	Mid	St. Johnstone B.C.
McAnespie	Kieran	Liam	11/09/79	Gosport	14/09/95	5 8.0	11 7	Mid/Fwd	St. Johnstone B.C.
McBride	John	Paul	28/11/78	Hamilton	06/02/99	5 10.0	10 2	Mid	Celtic
McClune	David	James	08/02/83	Glasgow	09/08/99	5 7.0	10 4	Def	S Form
McCluskey	Stuart	Campbell	29/10/77	Bellshill	07/07/94	5 11.0	11 7	Def	S Form
McConnell	Nathan	Allum	31/07/82	Lisburn	25/08/99	5 11.0	11 6	Fwd	Linfield
McCulloch	Marc	Raymond	14/03/80	Edinburgh	12/07/96	5 8.0	10 10	Def	Musselburgh Union
McMahon	Gerard	Joseph	29/12/73	Belfast	27/02/98	5 11.0	11 7	Mid	Stoke City
McQuillan	John		20/07/70	Stranraer	04/07/95	5 10.0	11 7	Def	Dundee
O'Boyle	George		14/12/67	Belfast	24/07/94	5 8.0	11 9	Fwd	Dunfermline Athletic
O'Halloran	Keith	James	27/03/77	Dublin	27/03/97	5 9.5	12 5	Mid	Middlesbrough
O'Neil	John	Thomas	06/07/71	Bellshill	04/08/94	5 8.0	11 7	Mid	Dundee United
Parker	Keigan		08/06/82	Livingston	06/07/98	5 7.0	10 5	Fwd	St. Johnstone B.C.
Preston	Allan		16/08/69	Edinburgh	26/03/94	5 10.0	11 7	Def/Mid	Dunfermline Athletic
Robertson	Stephen		16/03/77	Glasgow	16/09/64	5 10.0	11 13	Gk	Ashfield Juniors
Simao	Miguel	Angelo Da Cruz	26/02/73	Oporto	28/08/98	5 8.0	11 4	Mid	Clube Desportivo Das Aves
Smith	Daryn	Andrew Michael	09/10/80	Dundonald	03/07/97	5 7.0	9 7	Mid	Linfield Youth
Stewart	Stephen	William	11/09/82	Glasgow	21/09/98	5 9.0	11 4	Mid	Celtic B.C.
Thomas	Kevin	Roderick	25/04/75	Edinburgh	20/08/99	5 11.0	12 5	Fwd	Morton
Thompson	Barry	Stephen	28/04/83	Falkirk	09/07/99	5 9.0	10 10	Fwd	Riverside B.C.
Weir	James	McIntosh	15/06/69	Motherwell	18/11/94	6 1.0	12 5	Def	Heart of Midlothian
Whiteford	Andrew		22/08/77	Bellshill	09/06/94	5 10.0	11 7	Def	Possil Y.M.C.A.

Milestones

YEAR OF FORMATION: 1884
MOST CAPPED PLAYER: Sandy McLaren
NO. OF CAPS: 5
MOST LEAGUE POINTS IN A SEASON: 59 (Second Division – Season 1987/88)(2 Points for a Win)
80 (First Division – Season 1996/97)(3 Points for a Win)
MOST LEAGUE GOALS SCORED BY A PLAYER IN A SEASON: Jimmy Benson (Season 1931/32)
NO. OF GOALS SCORED: 38
RECORD ATTENDANCE: 29,972 (-v- Dundee 10.2.1951 at Muirton Park)
10,545 (-v- Dundee – SPL, 23.05.1999 at McDiarmid Park)
RECORD VICTORY: 8-1 (-v- Partick Thistle – League Cup, 16.8.1969)
RECORD DEFEAT: 0-12 (-v- Cowdenbeath – Scottish Cup, 21.1.1928)

The Saints' ten year league record

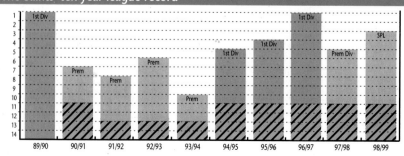

THE SAINTS' CLUB FACTFILE 1998/99 RESULTS... APPEARANCES... SCORERS

Date	Venue	Opponents	Att.	Res	Ferguson A.	McQuillan J.	Dods D.	Preston A.	Griffin D.	McMahon G.	O'Neil J.	Kane P.	McAnespie K.	Dasovic N.	O'Boyle G.	O'Halloran K.	Scott P.	Connolly P.	Main A.	Bollan G.	Grant R.	Simao M.	Lowndes N.	Kernaghan A.	McCluskey S.	Whiteford A.	McBride J.P.	Weir J.	Parker K.
Aug 1	A	Motherwell	5,686	0-1	1	2	3	4	5	6	7	8	9	10	11	12	13	14											
15	H	Kilmarnock	6,210	0-0	1	2	3	4	5	6	7	13	12	10	11		8	9											
23	A	Dundee	3,647	1-0		2	3	4		6	7	8			11	12	10^1		1	5	9								
29	A	Rangers	48,732	0-4		2	3	4			7	8				6	10		1	14	9	11	12						
Sep 12	H	Dunfermline Athletic	5,997	†1-1			3	12	2	6	7			10	11		8		1	5	13	9		4					
19	H	Aberdeen	5,814	2-0			3	13	12	6^1	7	8		10	11				1	5	14	9^1		4	2				
23	A	Celtic	55,745	1-0			3	14	13	6	7	8		10^1	11				1	5	12	9		4	2				
26	H	Dundee United	6,655	1-3			3	12		6	7	8		10	11				1	5	14^1	9		4	2		13		
Oct 4	A	Heart of Midlothian	13,121	1-1		2	3			6^1	7	8		10	11	12			1	5	9	13		4					
17	H	Motherwell	4,062	5-0		2	3^1		6	12	7	8		10	11^2				1	5	9^1	13		4^1					
24	H	Kilmarnock	9,336	2-2		2	3^1		6	13	7	8		10	11				1	5	9	12^1		4					
31	A	Dunfermline Athletic	8,126	1-1		2^1	3		6	12	7	8		10	11				1	5	14	9	13	4					
Nov 8	A	Rangers	9,660	0-7		2	3	12		6	7	8		10	11				1	5	14	9		4			13		
14	H	Celtic	9,762	2-1		2	3			6	7	8		10			12^1		1	5	9	11^1	13	4					
21	A	Aberdeen	10,044	1-0		2	3				7	8	13	10	14	6			1	5	9	11^1	12	4					
Dec 5	A	Dundee United	7,293	1-1		2	3				7	8	13	10		6			1	5	9^1	11	12	4					
9	H	Heart of Midlothian	4,808	1-1		2	3				7	8	13	10		6			1	5	9	11	12	4^1					
12	H	Dundee	6,033	1-1		2	3				7	8		10		6		9	1	5^1		11		4					
19	A	Motherwell	5,686	2-1		2	3		5	6	7	8	13	10				9^1	1		12^1	11		4					
26	A	Rangers	49,479	0-1		2	3			6	7	8		10	11			9	1	5	12	13	14	4					
29	H	Dunfermline Athletic	6,070	1-1		2	3			6	7	8^1	13	10	11				1	5	9	12		4					
Jan 2	H	Aberdeen	8,971	4-1		2	3			6	7^2	8	14	10				9	1	5^1	13	11	12	4^1					
31	A	Celtic	59,746	0-5		2	3	13	9	6	7	8		10			12		1	5		11		4					
Feb 6	H	Dundee United	5,771	1-0		2	3		6	13	7	8		10					1	5^1	9	11	12	4					
20	A	Heart of Midlothian	12,229	2-0		2	3				7	8^1		10				6^1	1	5	9	12	11	4					
27	A	Dundee	7,245	1-0		2	3				7	8		10	12			6	1	5	9^1	13	11	4		14			
Mar 13	A	Kilmarnock	5,461	0-1		2	3		12		7	8		10				6	1	5	9	11	13	4					
20	A	Dunfermline Athletic	5,504	0-1		2	3				7	8		10				6	1	5	9	14	13	4			11	12	
Apr 4	A	Rangers	9,742	3-1			3	13			7	8		10	11^1				1	5	9	12^1	14	4			6		2^1
17	H	Heart of Midlothian	6,154	0-0	15		3			6	7	8		10			12		1	5		11	13	4					2
20	A	Dundee United	6,741	1-0			3	12	4^1	6	7	8		10			13		1	5	9								2
24	A	Celtic	10,393	1-0	12		3	4		6^1	7	8		10	11				1	5	14	9							2
May 1	A	Aberdeen	9,561	0-1			3	14	4	6	7	8		10	11				1	5	13	9	12						2
8	H	Motherwell	4,599	0-0		2	3			6	7	8		10	11		13		1	5	9	12		4					14
15	A	Kilmarnock	15,086	1-1		2				6	7	8	13	10	11				1	5^1	9	11		4	3				12
23	H	Dundee	10,575	1-0		2				6	7	8^1	13	10	11		12		1	5	9	11		4	3				
TOTAL FULL APPEARANCES					2	27	34	8	14	13	33	33	8	31	12	10	14	6	34	32	14	20	12	26	5		2		6
TOTAL SUB APPEARANCES					(1)	(1)		(7)	(5)	(6)		(1)	(10)		(1)	(6)	(2)	(3)		(1)	(11)	(6)	(17)		(2)	(1)	(1)	(1)	(2)
TOTAL GOALS SCORED						1	2	1	1	1	2	3		2	1	2	1	2		1		4	4	4	2		3		1

Small bold figures denote goalscorers. † denotes opponent's own goal.

McDiarmid Park

Diagram labels: ◀ GLASGOW AND EDINBURGH - A9 - INVERNESS ▶ — Car Park — WEST STAND — CRIEFF ROAD — CAR PARK — SOUTH STAND — NORTH STAND — EAST STAND

CAPACITY: 10,673 (All Seated)

PITCH DIMENSIONS: 115 yds x 75 yds

FACILITIES FOR DISABLED SUPPORTERS:
Entrance via south end of West Stand and south end of East Stand. Visiting disabled fans should contact the club in advance. Headphones available in West and North Stands for blind and partially sighted supporters.

Team playing kits

How to get there

The following routes can be used to reach McDiarmid Park:

TRAINS: Perth Station is well served by trains from all parts of the country. The station is about 40 minutes walk from the park.

BUSES: Local services nos. 1 and 2 pass near the ground. Both leave from Mill Street in the town centre.

CARS: The car park at the park holds 1,500 cars and 100 coaches. Vehicles should follow signs A9 to Inverness on Perth City by-pass, then follow "Football Stadium" signs at Inveralmond Roundabout South onto slip road adjacent to McDiarmid Park. Vehicle charges are £2.00 for cars and no charge for coaches.

The Saints

email: sfl@sol.co.uk • website: www.sfl.scottishfootball.com

SCOTTISH PREMIER LEAGUE

Surname	First Name	Middle Name	Squad No.

ABERDEEN

Surname	First Name	Middle Name	Squad No.
Anderson	Russell		15
Bernard	Paul		14
Bett	Baldur		27
Bett	Calum		35
Buchan	Martin	James	16
Clark	Christopher		34
Dow	Andrew	James	12
Duncan	Russell		24
Esson	Ryan		23
Gillies	Richard	Charles	18
Good	Iain	David	28
Hamilton	James		7
Hart	Michael		22
Jess	Eoin		8
Kiriakov	Ilian		11
Leighton	James		1
Lilley	David	William	-
Mackie	Darren	Graham	29
Marwick	Steven	Gordon	36
Mayer	Andreas		10
McAllister	James	Reynolds	30
McCaffrey	Stuart	Muir	25
McGuire	Philip		33
McNaughton	Kevin	Paul	38
Michie	Scott	David	-
Milne	Kevin		32
O'Donnoghue	Ross		-
Peat	Mark		-
Pepper	Colin	Nigel	4
Perry	Mark	George	2
Preece	David	Douglas	40
Rowson	David	Andrew	17
Rutkiewicz	Kevin		37
Smith	Gary		6
Solberg	Thomas		5
Tiernan	Fergus		31
Whyte	Derek		3
Winters	Robert		9
Wyness	Dennis	Middleton	20
Young	Darren		19
Young	Derek		21

CELTIC

Surname	First Name	Middle Name	Squad No.
Berkovic	Eyal		10
Blinker	Reginald	Waldi	20
Bonnes	Stephane		22
Boyd	Thomas		2
Brattbakk	Harald	Martin	9
Burchill	Mark	James	27
Burley	Craig	William	8
Casey	Mark		-
Cocozza	Marc	Anthony	-
Convery	John		-
Corr	Barry	John	38
Cortani	Marco		-
Crainey	Stephen	Danial	-
Elliot	Barry	Robert	28
Fraser	Allan		-
Fyfe	Graham		-
Gallagher	James		-
Goodwin	James		-
Gould	Jonathan		1
Healy	Colin		24
Jack	Steven		-
Johnson	Thomas		12
Kennedy	John		-
Keogh	Liam	Michael	37
Kerr	James	Stewart Robert	21
Kharine	Dmitri		23
Kilmartin	Andrew		-
Lambert	Paul		14
Larsson	Henrik		7
Lynch	Simon	George	-
Mahe	Stephane		3
Maloney	Shaun	Richard	-
McBride	Kevin		-
McCann	Ryan		-
McColligan	Brian		-
McGovern	Jon	Paul	-
McKinlay	Thomas	Valley	18
McManus	Stephen		-
McNamara	Jackie		4
McParland	Anthony	Patrick	-
Miller	Liam	William Peter	-
Miller	Stephen		-
Mjallby	Johan		35
Moravcik	Lubomir		25
Moriarty	Tadg	Lee	-
Morrison	Allan	James	-
Murphy	David		-
Petrov	Stilian		19
Petta	Bobby	Alfred Manuel	15
Prunty	Bryan		-
Rieper	Marc	Jensen	5
Riseth	Vidar		30
Sanna	Alessandro		34
Smith	James		39
Stubbs	Alan		6
Sullivan	Vincent		-
Tebily	Olivier		16
Viduka	Mark	Anthony	36
Wieghorst	Morten		11

DUNDEE

Surname	First Name	Middle Name	Squad No.
Anderson	Iain		-
Annand	Edward		9
Bayne	Graham		22
Beith	Gavin		29
Boyack	Steven		7
Boylan	Colin		-
Clark	Paul		26
Coyne	Thomas		16
Douglas	Robert	James	1
Earlie	James	Joseph	33
Elliott	John		23
Falconer	William	Henry	11
Forbes	Barry		30
Gibson	Keith		32
Gilfillan	Finn		-
Grady	James		10
Kelly	Jonathan		-
Langfield	James		13
Mackay	David		-
Maddison	Lee	Robert	3
Mair	Lee		28
McGuiness	Kieran	Joseph	-
McSkimming	Shaun	Peter	12
Miller	William	Nisbit	4
Milne	Steven		24
Montgomery	Richard		-
Puras	Roberto	Matute	-
Rae	Gavin		8
Raeside	Robert		6
Riley	David		-
Robb	Steven		-
Robertson	Hugh	Scott	14
Sharp	Lee		15
Slater	Mark	Andrew	21
Smith	Barry	Martin	2
Soutar	Derek	Robert James	27
Thompson	Jonathan		-
Thomson	Graeme	David	31
Tweed	Steven		5
Van Eijs	Frank		17
Watson	Steven		-
Wilkie	Lee		20
Yates	Michael		25

DUNDEE UNITED

Surname	First Name	Middle Name	Squad No.
Bruce	James		46
Byrne	David		-
Combe	Alan		1
Cooper	Marc		43
Curran	Lee		48
Davidson	Hugh	Norman	26
De Vos	Jason	Richard	5
Delaunay	Jean	Pierre	-
Dodds	William		14
Duff	Stuart		50
Duffy	John		42
Easton	Craig		7
Fallon	Steven		23
Ferraz	Joaquim	Miguel Leitao De Freitas	10
Gallacher	Paul	James	13
Hannah	David		4
Jarvie	Paul		-
Jenkins	Iain		16
Jonsson	Sigurdur		6
Malpas	Maurice	Daniel Robert	3
Mathie	Alexander		9
McConalogue	Stephen		25
McCracken	David		40
McCulloch	Scott	Anderson James	12
McCulloch	Stephen	George	41
McCunnie	Jamie		47
McDonald	Kevin		39
McNally	Mark		37
Middleton	Gary		45
Partridge	David	William	21
Pascual	Bernard		2
Paterson	James	Lee	18
Patterson	Darren	James	17
Reilly	Colin		38
Skoldmark	Magnus		8
Smith	James	Anthony	11
Sturrock	Blair		44
Telesnikov	Jan		15
Thompson	Steven		19
Venetis	Anastasios		27
Winters	David		49
Worrell	David		20

HEART OF MIDLOTHIAN

Surname	First Name	Middle Name	Squad No.
Adam	Stephane	Lucien	9
Bryson	Gary		-
Cameron	Colin		10
Clyde	Bobby		-
Davidson	Ryan	Thomas	-
Findlay	Craig		-
Flögel	Thomas		14
Fulton	Stephen		8
Goldie	Darren		-
Graham	Alisdair		-
Holmes	Derek		26
Horn	Robert	David	-
Jackson	Darren		11
James	Kevin	Francis	5
Janczyk	Neil		-
Jenkinson	Leigh		19
Kaczan	Paul		-
Kirk	Andrew		24
Leclercq	Fabien	Christain Rene	22
Locke	Gary		4
Makel	Lee	Robert	16
McIlroy	Alan	Stewart	-
McKenzie	Roderick		13
McKinnon	Robert		17
McSwegan	Gary	John	7
Milne	Kenneth		-
Murray	Grant	Robert	12
Naysmith	Gary	Andrew	3
Neilson	Robbie		-
O'Donnell	Steven	James	-
O'Neil	Kris		-
Perez	Juanjo	Carricondo	20
Pressley	Steven	John	2
Quitongo	Jose	Manuel	15
Ritchie	Paul	Simon	6
Rousset	Gilles		1
Salvatori	Stefano		21
Severin	Scott	Derek	27
Simmons	Stephen	Christopher	-
Sloan	Robert		-
Smith	Barry	John	-
Smith	Grant	Gordon	-
Strang	Scott		30
Wales	Gary		23

Surname	First Name	Middle Name	Squad No.
HIBERNIAN			
Alexander	Daniel	James	-
Bannerman	Scott	John	23
Barr	Richard		-
Beaton	Lloyd	Thomas John	-
Bottiglieri	Emilio	Hugh	24
Brebner	Grant	Ian	34
Brown	Kris	James	-
Campbell	John	David	31
Colgan	Nick		13
Collins	Derek	Joseph	2
Cormack	Scott		-
Crawford	Stephen		8
Dempsie	Allan	Henry	-
Dempsie	Mark	William	22
Dennis	Shaun		6
Ewart	Jamie	Ross	-
Gibson	Craig	McIndewar	-
Gottskalksson	Olafur		1
Hartley	Paul		12
Henry	Fabrice		19
Hilland	Paul		-
Holsgrove	Paul		32
Huggon	Russel	William	25
Hughes	John		5
Hughes	Martin		29
Jack	Matthias		21
Jeffrey	Ross		-
Latapy	Russell	Nigel	10
Lavety	Barry		33
Lehmann	Dirk		16
Lindsay	Paul	Henry Reid	-
Lovell	Stuart		7
Lovering	Paul	James	3
McGinlay	Patrick	David	11
McGladrigan	Thomas		-
McManus	Thomas	Kelly	27
Miller	Kenneth		20
Morton	Colin		30
Murray	Ian	William	26
O'Connor	Garry	Lawrence	-
O'Sullivan	Liam		-
Paatelainen	Mika-Matti	Petteri	9
Phillips	Thomas	George	-
Reid	Alan		28
Renwick	Michael		18
Riordan	Derek	George	-
Sauzee	Franck	Gaston Henri	4
Smith	Thomas	William	17
Widera	Sean	Forde	-
KILMARNOCK			
Bagan	David		23
Baker	Martin		16
Beesley	Darren		32
Boyd	Kris		-
Boyle	Christopher		-
Burke	Alexander		25
Canero	Peter		31
Davidson	Stuart	William	28
Di Giacomo	Paul		30
Dindeleux	Frederic		17
Durrant	Ian		10
Fowler	James		26
Hay	Garry		24
Hessey	Sean		18
Holt	Gary	James	8
Innes	Christopher		21
Jeffrey	Michael		4
Kerr	Dylan		3
Lauchlan	James	Harley	22
Lundie	James		-
MacPherson	Angus	Ian	2
Mahood	Alan	Scott	14
Marshall	Gordon	George Banks	1
McCoist	Alistair	Murdoch	13
McCutcheon	Gary	Kyle	27
McDonald	Gary	Matthew	-
McGowne	Kevin		5
McNeill	Kevin	John	-

Surname	First Name	Middle Name	Squad No.
Meldrum	Colin	George	12
Mitchell	Alistair	Robert	11
Moffat	Ross	Stuart	-
Reilly	Mark	Francis	7
Roberts	Mark	Kingsley	19
Smith	Graeme		-
Stewart	Colin		29
Vareille	Jerome		15
Watt	Michael		20
Williams	David		-
Wright	Paul	Hamilton	9
MOTHERWELL			
Adams	Derek	Watt	12
Brannan	Gerard	Daniel	5
Brown	Michael		-
Callachan	Craig		31
Constable	John		34
Clarke	David		36
Craigan	Stephen	James	14
Davies	William	McIntosh	16
Dempsie	Brian		35
Denham	Greig	Paterson	18
Doesburg	Michel	Johannes	2
Doherty	David	John	24
Fallon	John		39
Goodman	Donald	Ralph	10
Goram	Andrew	Lewis	1
Halliday	Stephen		19
Hammell	Steven		25
Lasley	Keith	William	22
Matthaei	Rob		20
McCulloch	Lee	Henry	9
McFadden	James		38
McGowan	Jamie		4
McLaughlin	Kevin		32
McMillan	Stephen		3
Miller	Colin		33
Nevin	Patrick	Kevin Francis	13
Nicholas	Steven	Arthur	11
Ramsay	Douglas		23
Spencer	John		7
Teale	Shaun		6
Thomas	Tony		15
Townsley	Derek		27
Twaddle	Kevin		28
Valakari	Simo	Johannes	8
Wilson	Scott	William	37
Woods	Stephen	Gerard	17
RANGERS			
Adamczuk	Dariusz		17
Albertz	Jorg		11
Amato	Gabriel	Omar	15
Amoruso	Lorenzo		4
Brown	Mark		-
Carson	Stephen		-
Chalmers	Iain		-
Charbonnier	Lionel		22
Currie	Ross		-
Dewar	Gary		-
Dobbie	Stephen		-
Dowie	Andrew	John	-
Durie	Gordon	Scott	24
Feeney	Lee		-
Ferguson	Barry		6
Ferguson	Ian		26
Fitzgerald	Darren		-
Gibson	James		-
Gibson	William		-
Hendry	Edward	Colin James	16
Hughes	Stephen		-
Johansson	Jonatan		20
Kanchelskis	Andrei		7
Kelly	Stuart		-
Klos	Stefan		1
MacDonald	Peter		-
Malcolm	Robert		-
McAdam	Steven		-

Surname	First Name	Middle Name	Squad No.
McCann	Neil	Docherty	18
McCann	Ryan		-
McGregor	Allan		-
McHale	Paul		-
McInnes	Derek	John	-
McKnight	Paul		-
McLean	Steven		-
Miller	Charles		-
Mols	Michael		9
Moore	Craig	Andrew	3
Morrison	Kevin		-
Negri	Marco		21
Nicholson	Barry		23
Niemi	Antti		13
Numan	Arthur		5
Porrini	Sergio		2
Prodan	Daniel		25
Reyna	Claudio		12
Robb	Richard		-
Ross	Maurice		-
Russell	Iain	Thomas	-
Smith	Graeme		-
Stensaas	Stale		-
Stone	Michael		-
Van Bronckhorst	Giovanni		8
Vidmar	Antony		14
Wallace	Rodney		10
Willoughby	Kirk		-
Wilson	Scott		19
Young	David		-
ST. JOHNSTONE			
Bollan	Gary		15
Connolly	Patrick	Martin	14
Conway	Christopher	Thomas	-
Crozier	Brendan	George	30
Cuthbert	Kevin	Scott	-
Dasovic	Nick	Robert	4
Dods	Darren		24
Ferguson	Allan	Thomas	22
Forsyth	Ross		-
Fotheringham	Martyn	Fraser	-
Grant	Roderick	John	9
Griffin	Daniel	Joseph	16
Guy	Kieran	Andrew	-
Kane	Paul	James	11
Kearney	Darren		-
Keddie	Alexander		-
Kernaghan	Alan	Nigel	6
Lauchlan	Martin	Thomas	28
Lowndes	Nathan	Peter	12
Main	Alan	David	1
Malcolm	Stuart	Ross	26
McAllister	Steven		-
McAnespie	Kieran	Liam	23
McBride	John	Paul	20
McClune	David	James	-
McCluskey	Stuart	Campbell	19
McConnell	Nathan	Allum	-
McCulloch	Marc	Raymond	27
McMahon	Gerard	Joseph	25
McQuillan	John		2
O'Boyle	George		10
O'Halloran	Keith	James	17
O'Neil	John	Thomas	8
Parker	Keigan		31
Preston	Allan		3
Robertson	Stephen		18
Simao	Miguel	Angelo Da Cruz	7
Smith	Daryn	Andrew Michael	29
Stewart	Stephen	William	-
Thomas	Kevin	Roderick	32
Thompson	Barry	Stephen	-
Weir	James	McIntosh	5
Whiteford	Andrew		21

ABERDEEN
SEASON TICKET INFORMATION - SEATED

MAIN STAND CENTRE	ADULT	£270
WING STAND	ADULT	£250
SOUTH STAND	ADULT	£200
	OAP	£100
MERKLAND STAND	ADULT	£170
	OAP	£75
	JUVENILE	£60
RICHARD DONALD STAND		£250/240/200

LEAGUE ADMISSION PRICES - SEATED

MAIN STAND CENTRE	ADULT	£20
WING STAND	ADULT	£18
SOUTH STAND HOME SUPPORT	ADULT	£14
	OAP	£8
SOUTH STAND EAST (VISITORS)	ADULT	£14
	JUVENILE/OAP	£8
MERKLAND STAND	ADULT	£13
	JUVENILE/OAP	£7
RICHARD DONALD STAND		£15/17

CELTIC
SEASON TICKET INFORMATION - SEATED

SOUTH STAND REAR	ADULT	£395
	CONCESSION	£225
SOUTH STAND FRONT	ADULT	£339
WEST CORNER STAND	JUVENILE	£145
	PARENT & JUVENILE	£349
NORTH STAND UPPER	ADULT	£379/309/279
NORTH STAND LOWER	ADULT	£395/349/249
	CONCESSION	£225/195/145
JOCK STEIN STAND UPPER	ADULT	£379/309
JOCK STEIN STAND LOWER	ADULT	£449/379/309/279
EAST STAND UPPER	ADULT	£379/309/279/354/284
EAST STAND LOWER	ADULT	£379/309/279/354
	PARENT & JUVENILE	£315
	ADULT	£314
	JUVENILE	£120

LEAGUE ADMISSION PRICES - SEATED

SOUTH STAND REAR	ADULT	£23
	CONCESSION	£9
SOUTH STAND FRONT	ADULT	£21
WEST CORNER STAND	JUVENILE	£10
	PARENT & JUVENILE	£21
NORTH STAND UPPER	ADULT	£23/19/18
	RESTRICTED VIEW	£14
NORTH STAND LOWER	ADULT	£23/16
	CONCESSION	£10
JOCK STEIN STAND UPPER	ADULT	£23/19
JOCK STEIN STAND LOWER	ADULT	£30/23/19/18
EAST STAND UPPER	ADULT	£23/19
EAST STAND LOWER	ADULT	£23/19/18
	PARENT & JUVENILE	£21
	ADULT	£18
	JUVENILE	£10

DUNDEE
SEASON TICKET INFORMATION - SEATED

CENTRE STAND	ADULT	£270
	JUVENILE/OAP	£110
WEST ENCLOSURE	ADULT	£225
	JUVENILE/OAP	£100
WEST ENCLOSURE	ADULT & 1 JUVENILE	£290
(FAMILY)	EACH ADDITIONAL JUVENILE	£90

LEAGUE ADMISSION PRICES - SEATED

CENTRE STAND	ADULT	£15
	JUVENILE/OAP	£7
SOUTH ENCLOSURE (IF OPEN)	ADULT	£13
	JUVENILE/OAP	£6
WEST ENCLOSURE	ADULT	£13
	JUVENILE/OAP	£7
EAST ENCLOSURE	ADULT	£14
	JUVENILE/OAP	£8
FAMILY	ADULT & 1 JUVENILE	£15
	EACH ADDITIONAL JUVENILE	£5

DUNDEE UNITED
SEASON TICKET INFORMATION-SEATED

GEORGE FOX STAND

TOP TIER		ADULT	£265
		JUVENILE/OAP	£150
MIDDLE TIER		ADULT	£323
		JUVENILE/OAP	£160
LOWER TIER		ADULT	£227
		JUVENILE/OAP	£130

EAST STAND

TOP TIER		ADULT	£265
		JUVENILE/OAP	£150
LOWER TIER		ADULT	£227
		JUVENILE/OAP	£130
FAMILY SECTION TOP TIER	1 ADULT & 1 JUVENILE		£378
	SPOUSE		£239
	ADDITIONAL JUVENILE		£139
FAMILY SECTION LOWER TIER	1 ADULT & 1 JUVENILE		£298
	SPOUSE		£188
	ADDITIONAL JUVENILE		£110

LEAGUE ADMISSION PRICES-SEATED

GEORGE FOX STAND

TOP TIER	ADULT	£15
	JUVENILE/OAP	£9
MIDDLE SECTION	ADULT	£17
	JUVENILE/OAP	£10
LOWER TIER	ADULT	£13
	JUVENILE/OAP	£8

EAST STAND

TOP TIER	ADULT	£15
	JUVENILE/OAP	£9
LOWER TIER	ADULT	£13
	JUVENILE/OAP	£8
FAMILY SECTION	1 ADULT & 1 JUVENILE	£21
	EACH ADDITIONAL JUVENILE	£8

SOUTH STAND (AWAY SUPPORTERS)

	ADULT	£15
	JUVENILE/OAP	£9
WEST STAND	ADULT	£13
	JUVENILE/OAP	£8
CATEGORY A MATCHES SUCH AS RANGERS/CELTIC		£17/15

HEART OF MIDLOTHIAN
SEASON TICKET INFORMATION - SEATED

MAIN STAND

ALL SECTIONS	ADULT	£275

WHEATFIELD STAND

UPPER SECTION	ADULT	£320
LOWER SECTION	ADULT	£285

GORGIE STAND

	ADULT & 1 JUVENILE	£395
	ADULT & 2 JUVENILES	£495
	ADULT & 3 JUVENILES	£595
	JUVENILE/SENIOR CITIZENS	£150
	DISABLED/CARER	£150
	STUDENT CLUB	£175

LEAGUE ADMISSION PRICES - SEATED

HOME SUPPORT

CATEGORY A MATCHES (INCLUDES RANGERS, CELTIC, HIBERNIAN & ABERDEEN)		£18
CATEGORY B MATCHES		£16
CATEGORY A&B MATCHES	JUVENILE	£9/8

AWAY SUPPORT - ROSEBURN STAND

CATEGORY A MATCHES (INCLUDES RANGERS, CELTIC, HIBERNIAN & ABERDEEN)		£18
CATEGORY B MATCHES		£16
CATEGORY A&B MATCHES	JUVENILE	£9/8

Tynecastle Stadium, home of Heart of Midlothian

HIBERNIAN
SEASON TICKET INFORMATION - SEATED

		*DISCOUNT SEASON TICKET	SEASON TICKET
WEST CENTRE STAND	ADULT	£260	£320
	JUVENILE/OAP	£175	£220
WEST STAND NORTH UPPER	ADULT	£235	£280
	JUVENILE/OAP	£125	£135
WEST STAND NORTH LOWER	ADULT	£200	£240
	JUVENILE/OAP	£100	£135
FAMOUS FIVE (UPPER & LOWER)	ADULT	£235	£280
	JUVENILE/OAP	£125	£135
FAMOUS FIVE LOWER (FAMILY SECTION)	FAMILY OF 2	£300	N/A
	FAMILY OF 3	£340	N/A
	FAMILY OF 4	£380	N/A
	FAMILY OF 5	£430	N/A
	FAMILY OF 6	£470	N/A
	ADULT & JUVENILE	N/A	£340
	ADDITIONAL PARENT	N/A	£250
	ADDITIONAL JUVENILE	N/A	£90
EAST STAND	ADULT	£200	£240
	JUVENILE/OAP	£100	£135

*Discounted price for existing Season Ticket holders

LEAGUE ADMISSION PRICES - SEATED
Matchday prices for season 1999/2000 will be as follows: Category A, Category B

		A	B
WEST CENTRE STAND	ADULT	£18	£16
WEST STAND NORTH UPPER	ADULT	£17	£15
	JUVENILE/OAP	£8	£8
WEST STAND NORTH LOWER	ADULT	£15	£13
	JUVENILE/OAP	£8	£8
WEST STAND SOUTH	ADULT	£17	£15
	JUVENILE/OAP	£8	£8
FAMOUS FIVE (UPPER & LOWER)	ADULT	£18	£16
	JUVENILE/OAP	£8	£8
EAST STAND	ADULT	£15	£13
	JUVENILE/OAP	£8	£8
SOUTH STAND (UPPER & LOWER)	ADULT	£18	£16
	ADULT	£18	£16
	JUVENILE/OAP	£8	£8

Category A–Rangers, Celtic & Heart of Midlothian
Category B–Aberdeen, Dundee, Dundee United, Kilmarnock, Motherwell & St. Johnstone

KILMARNOCK
SEASON TICKET INFORMATION - SEATED

WEST STAND	ADULT	£220
	OAP	£110
	JUVENILE 13-16	£70
	JUVENILE UNDER 13	£50
EAST STAND & MOFFAT STAND	ADULT	£215
	OAP	£110
	JUVENILE 13-16	£70
	JUVENILE UNDER 13	£50

Juvenile Season Tickets Under 13 on 01/08/99, Under 16 on 01/08/99

LEAGUE ADMISSION PRICES - SEATED
Matchday prices for season 1999-2000 will be as follows: Category A, Category B

		A	B
WEST STAND	ADULT	£15	£12
	OAP/JUVENILE U16	£15	£6
EAST STAND	ADULT	£15	£12
	OAP/JUVENILE U16	£15	£6
MOFFAT STAND	ADULT	£15	£12
	OAP/JUVENILE U16	£15	£6

Category A = Rangers & Celtic.
Category B = Aberdeen, Heart of Midlothian, Dundee United, Motherwell, St. Johnstone, Hibernian & Dundee

MOTHERWELL
SEASON TICKET INFORMATION - SEATED

EAST STAND	ADULT	£160
	JUVENILE	£40
	OAP/STUDENT	£80
	PARKING	£50
DAVID COOPER STAND	ADULT	£210
	PARENT & JUVENILE	£240
	ADDITIONAL JUVENILE	£40
	JUVENILE	£65
	OAP/STUDENT	£120
	COOPER BOX & PARKING	£695
	COOPER BOX	£645
	PARKING	£50
MAIN STAND	ADULT	£240
	JUVENILE	£85
	OAP/STUDENT	£140
	CENTENARY & PARKING	£440
	CENTENARY	£390
	MILLENNIUM & PARKING	£950
	MILLENNIUM	£900
	PARKING	£50
SOUTH STAND	MOTOROLA BOX & PARKING	£1,695
	MOTOROLA BOX	£1,645

LEAGUE ADMISSION PRICES - SEATED

EAST STAND	ADULT	£10/12
	JUVENILE	£2/4
	OAP/STUDENT	£5/7
DAVID COOPER STAND	ADULT	£13/15
	JUVENILE	£4/6
	OAP/STUDENT	£7/9
MAIN STAND	ADULT	£15/17
	JUVENILE	£5/7
	OAP/STUDENT	£8/10
SOUTH STAND (VISITING FANS ONLY)	ADULT	£15/17
	JUVENILE	£5/7
	OAP/STUDENT	£8/10

RANGERS
SEASON TICKET INFORMATION - SEATED

MAIN STAND F/G/O/P	ADULT	£345
	CONCESSIONS/JUVENILE	£245/165
H	ADULT	£490
	CONCESSIONS/JUVENILE	£345/190
J/K/M/N	ADULT	£470
	CONCESSIONS/JUVENILE	£325/190
L (SECTION MLF)	ADULT	£770
	CONCESSIONS	£540
E	ADULT	£450
	CONCESSIONS	£315/190
C/D/Q/R	ADULT	£360
	CONCESSIONS/JUVENILE	£255/165
A/B/S/T	ADULT	£330
	CONCESSIONS/JUVENILE	£225/165
WADDELL SUITE	ADULT	£1,685
	CONCESSIONS	£1,180
WADDELL SUITE (No Car Park Pass)	ADULT	£1,485
	CONCESSIONS	£980
GOVAN REAR 3,4,5	ADULT	£480
	CONCESSIONS/JUVENILE	£335/190
GOVAN REAR 2,6	ADULT	£440
	CONCESSIONS/JUVENILE	£310/190
GOVAN REAR 1,7	ADULT	£405
	CONCESSIONS/JUVENILE	£285/190
GOVAN FRONT 2,3,4,5,6	ADULT	£365
	CONCESSIONS/JUVENILE	£255/165
GOVAN FRONT 1,7/EAST/WEST/ ENCLOSURE SE1,2,3 SW3,4,5	ADULT	£345
	CONCESSIONS/JUVENILE	£245/165
ENCLOSURE SE4,5 SW1,2	ADULT	£355
COPLAND REAR	ADULT	£345
	CONCESSIONS/JUVENILE	£245/165
COPLAND FRONT	ADULT	£335
	CONCESSIONS/JUVENILE	£235/165

LEAGUE ADMISSION PRICES - SEATED

BROOMLOAN REAR/COPLAND REAR/ ENCLOSURE/GOVAN FRONT	ADULT	£18
	CONCESSIONS/JUVENILE	£13/10
BROOMLOAN FRONT/COPLAND FRONT/MAIN STAND REAR	ADULT	£17
	CONCESSIONS/JUVENILE	£13/10
MAIN STAND FRONT & GOVAN REAR	ADULT	£22
	CONCESSIONS/JUVENILE	£15/10

ST. JOHNSTONE
SEASON TICKET INFORMATION - SEATED

WEST STAND	ADULT	£255
	JUVENILE/OAP	£162
EAST STAND	ADULT	£220
	JUVENILE/OAP	£144
SOUTH STAND	ADULT	£185
	FEMALE/JUVENILE/OAP	£90

LEAGUE ADMISSION PRICES - SEATED

WEST STAND	ADULT	£15
	JUVENILE/OAP	£9
EAST STAND	ADULT	£13
	JUVENILE/OAP	£8
NORTH STAND (VISITORS)	ADULT	£13
	JUVENILE/OAP	£8
SOUTH STAND (FAMILY SECTION)	ADULT MALE	£11
	FEMALE/JUVENILE/OAP	£5

Kilmarnock's Rugby Park

A REVIEW OF THE REVIEW – 20 YEARS ON

The Scottish Football League Review is the family album of the game. The book you hold in your hand is the 20th edition and, as always, it is an evocative gathering of photographs and information. This is a vault of precious memories. When you browse through the versions of the publication produced in earlier years there is the fascination of seeing the sport's story vividly unfolding.

The Review first appeared in 1980 and across its centre spread was a shot of the reigning Premier Division Champions. Alex Ferguson stands proudly at the side of his Aberdeen squad. Has much changed since then? He can only be a few pounds heavier in 1999, but some lines have understandably been added to the face, the hair has become grey and Ferguson has certainly stopped wearing flared trousers that completely concealed his shoes.

You still find him in charge of men in red jerseys and there are more trophies than ever in any contemporary picture, with Manchester United currently holding the FA Carling Premiership, the FA Cup and the European Cup. In the context of Scottish football history, his most important achievement came in

Alex Ferguson and Archie Knox celebrate Aberdeen's European Cup Winners' Cup win in 1983

1983 when his Aberdeen team defeated Real Madrid to win the Cup Winners' Cup. Regrettably, the Review has not had the opportunity to celebrate any such European triumph since then.

Dundee United reached the UEFA Cup Final of 1987 and Rangers were unbeaten in the European Cup of season 1992-93, where they came close to a place in the Final, but Scotland's clubs have rarely advanced as far as they had hoped. Europe, on the other hand, has made huge inroads into Scotland. Look at the squads listed in this book and you are

startled by the cosmopolitan kaleidoscope of foreign names.

It was very different back in season 1980/81. Then, there was scarcely a footballer at work here who had not been born in Britain or Ireland. Exotic glamour came with the presence of a certain George Best on Hibernian's books. The information in that season's edition that Dundee United had just signed a player from Witz University in South Africa is so distinctive that it leaps off the page. He is listed simply as Charles Gough. We came to know him better as Richard, the man who captained

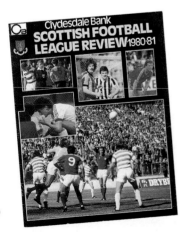

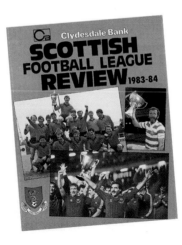

Rangers to a ninth successive Championship in season 1996/97.

The winning of trophies is relished, but perhaps the greatest feat of all lies in the very survival of clubs that have proved surprisingly adaptable as they surmount one difficulty after another. The 38 listed in 1980 are all still in existence, even if Meadowbank Thistle have since turned into Livingston, and two other members, in Inverness Caledonian Thistle and Ross County, have joined.

Football is a durable business. It keeps hundreds of players in full-time employment and hundreds of

George Best playing for Hibernian

thousands of supporters in a state of uproar. Many others have cause to give thanks for the jobs they hold down at clubs, as coaches, groundsmen, administrators, secretaries, catering staff, cleaners and sales assistants, amongst other professions. Then there are the battalions, including turnstile operators and stewards, who find part-time work on match days.

The economic impact has often come as a relief to Scotland's construction industry. In the text and photographs contained within the previous 19 League reviews, one discovers a chronicle of a sport that has transformed its surroundings. Those who enjoy the new comforts of their seats are still dazzled by the speed of change. When Celtic, as recently as season 1994/95, were lodgers at Hampden Park, few could have believed that they would complete the largest club stadium in Britain within four years.

Monumental though Celtic Park is, it is the sheer extent of the work undertaken across the land that really inspires awe. Clubs like St. Johnstone, Clyde, Airdrieonians, Inverness Caledonian Thistle, Stirling Albion and Livingston have moved to entirely new stadia on fresh sites. Heart of

Midlothian, Kilmarnock, Motherwell, Dunfermline Athletic and Dundee United, amongst others, have created almost entirely re-built premises on their familiar addresses. The process has been underway at all levels of the senior game. It is rare to find a club that has not undertaken some major project or other.

At the very least, one can expect to see one modern stand on the skyline when one travels to a game. The shift is not to be measured in architectural terms alone. The very experience of watching football in Scotland has been changed forever. It was not really so long ago that fans at virtually all venues accepted that they might have to stand in the open air, in the rain. At some grounds, they could not be sure of finding a roof over their heads even when they visited the primitive toilets.

The Taylor Report made seating compulsory at the higher echelons of the sport and some still miss the swaying excitement of packed old terraces. Nonetheless, football would have had to reinvent itself in any case. Young people growing up with the luxury of the multiplex cinema developments would not have gone on being charmed by a game that took place against a primitive,

Ibrox Stadium in the 1960s

established itself as a rapid-fire tournament in which penalty shoot-outs ensured a decisive outcome to every match and entertainment was virtually guaranteed. It has always held the element of surprise as well, with Raith Rovers, then in the First Division, lifting the trophy in season 1994/95. There are glowing recollections, to, of some delicious football, particularly in season 1987/88, when Rangers and Aberdeen created an inspiring 3-3 draw in the Final before the Ibrox side won in a penalty shoot-out.

The sponsor's of this very publication, Tennent Caledonian Breweries, have enjoyed an extremely I relationship with Scottish football's oldest competition, the Scottish Cup, and last season's Final between Rangers and Celtic, which also saw the first match played at the impressively refurbished National Stadium at Hampden Park, was the tenth season that they had sponsored

unpleasant backdrop. Sophistication was essential for attendances and the rise in crowds, since the early 1980's, has only been possible because of an increased regard for the needs of customers.

The process has been expensive and there is gratitude to The Football Trust for its grants, but the game has had to develop commercial acumen as well. Looking back, it is almost laughable to realise that there was virtually no television coverage in season 1985/86 as negotiations had stalled because clubs were concerned about the impact which the televising of one live League match would have on attendances. Such a situation is now inconceivable and the wooing of sponsors has also become assiduous.

Since 1985, The Scottish Football League Championship has enjoyed the backing of companies such as Fine Fare, B&Q and Bell's. Indeed, after a brief absence, Bell's are renewing the acquaintance as they once more sponsor The Scottish

Football League, as well as the Challenge Cup. The Scottish Premier League, formed in the restructuring of 1998, is backed by the Bank of Scotland. These commercial concerns become involved because the competitions to which they attach their names are attractive.

The League Cup, variously sponsored by Bell's, Skol and Coca-Cola and now by CIS Insurance,

Ibrox Park as it is today

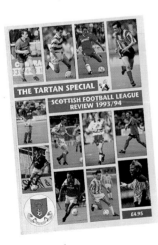

the competition. Whilst last season's Final was contested by Scotland's oldest rivals, the competition has seen seven different winners during Tennents' ten year association with the competition and these statistics hopefully prove that all of the major honours, at least in the cup competitions, are not dominated by the Old Firm.

As every student of football in England and on the continent will agree, it is increasingly difficult to halt the steamroller advance of the bigger clubs in a League Championship. The same effect is felt in Scotland, where the Premier Division and Premier League has been won by either Celtic or Rangers in every season since Aberdeen were triumphant in season 1984/85.

That domination need not always be at the expense of drama. In season 1990/91, Rangers had to beat Aberdeen at Ibrox in the last match to deprive the Pittodrie club of the trophy. Two years ago, Celtic ended Rangers' period of ascendancy, but the outcome was uncertain until the final minutes of the League season when Harald Brattbakk's goal took the trophy to Celtic Park.

It is the nature of sport, wherever it is played, that glory is always for a minority of participants. Football survives, and prospers, only so long as the average person is supplied with enough entertainment by the club he watches, whether or not it actually collects any silverware. Tastes, in some ways, are growing more sophisticated and the introduction of so many players from overseas, for hitherto unimaginable sums, has added to the vibrancy of the scene.

When the incomers possess the gifts of a Brian Laudrup or a Henrik Larsson, their presence is welcome indeed. Nonetheless, there are pleasures that cannot be provided by the holders of foreign passports. A special satisfaction flows from the sight of a home-grown youngster developing to the point where he can acquit himself well.

Since 1974, Scotland has had an extraordinary record of qualifying for the Finals of the World Cup and European Championship, but those

The impressively refurbished National Stadium, Hampden Park

Graeme Armstrong of Stenhousemuir

feats will not be repeated if we stop producing Scottish players of the required standard. There is no sense in denying that the supply of young talent has dwindled and there will be damaging consequences unless development programmes tap new sources. As you will read elsewhere in this book, both The Scottish Football League and The Scottish Football Association have, however, been working extremely hard during the past six or seven years to provide a structure for a new generation of young, talented players from these shores to emerge in the new Millennium.

Despite that, the 20 editions of the Review depict a robust sport that is capable of rising to a challenge. That resilience in the face of a multitude of blows is best encapsulated in the figure of Graeme Armstrong, the Player/Manager of Stenhousemuir, who last season were promoted to the Second Division. At 43, he will be registered to turn out for the team again this season.

His career has a greater span than even the history of this publication. Armstrong's name is to be found in that inaugural edition of the Review in 1980, but, by then, he had already been with Stirling Albion for five years.

KEVIN McCARRA
(The Times)

Excelsior Stadium, Broomfield Park, Craigneuk Avenue, Airdrie, ML6 8QZ

CHAIRMAN
A. McI. Campbell Craig

VICE-CHAIRMAN
Joseph M. Rowan

DIRECTORS
George W. Peat, C.A.,
Anthony D. Kane &
William Tosh

SECRETARY
George W. Peat, C.A.

MANAGER
Gary Mackay

ASSISTANT MANAGER
Walter Kidd

COACHES
Sandy Stewart & Andrew Smith

COMMERCIAL MANAGERS
John Queen & Morna Watkins
(01236) 622000

CLUB DOCTOR
Brian Dunn, M.B.,CLB.,M.R.C.P.(UK)

PHYSIOTHERAPIST
Peter Salila, SF, R.P.

GROUNDSMAN
John McGuire

**FOOTBALL SAFETY OFFICERS'
ASSOCIATION REPRESENTATIVE**
Joseph Rowan (01236) 622000

TELEPHONES
Ground/Ticket Office/Information
Service (01236) 622000
Fax (01236) 626002

CLUB SHOP
93 Graham Street, Airdrie, ML6 6DE.
Tel (01236) 747255. Fax (01236) 756308
Open Mon-Fri. 9.00 a.m. till 1.00 p.m.
and 2.00 p.m. till 5.00 p.m.
Sat 9.00 a.m. – 4.00 p.m.
A club shop is also situated at the stadium
and is open on home matchdays.

OFFICIAL SUPPORTERS CLUB
c/o David Johnstone,
16 Deveron Street, Coatbridge
Tel (01236) 423812

TEAM CAPTAIN
James Sandison

SHIRT SPONSOR
Scotshield Security Systems

34

Airdrieonians

LIST OF PLAYERS 1999-2000

SURNAME	FIRST NAME	MIDDLE NAME	DATE OF BIRTH	PLACE OF BIRTH	DATE OF SIGNING	HEIGHT FT INS	WEIGHT ST LBS	POS. ON PITCH	PREVIOUS CLUB
Conway	Francis	Joseph	29/12/69	Dundee	06/08/99	5 11.0	11 4	Def	Livingston
Dick	James		21/06/72	Bellshill	09/07/99	5 11.0	10 8	Mid	Ayr United
Easton	Stewart		10/10/81	Coatbridge	07/07/99	5 9.0	10 10	Mid	Airdrieonians B.C.
Evans	Gareth	John	14/01/67	Coventry	03/07/98	5 7.5	11 6	Fwd	Partick Thistle
Farrell	David	John	29/10/69	Glasgow	18/12/97	5 9.0	11 4	Def	Partick Thistle
Farrell	Gerard	James	14/06/75	Glasgow	30/07/98	5 8.0	10 10	Mid	Ross County
Forrest	Edward	Alexander	17/12/78	Edinburgh	08/07/99	6 0.0	10 10	Def	Stirling Albion
Ingram	Stuart		07/11/79	Stockton	08/07/99	6 1.0	12 7	Fwd	Sunderland
Jack	Paul	Dunn	15/05/65	Malaya	05/08/89	5 10.0	11 7	Def	Arbroath
Johnston	Forbes	Duthie Stephen	03/08/71	Aberdeen	13/08/96	5 10.0	10 12	Def/Mid	Falkirk
McCann	Henry	Austin	21/01/80	Clydebank	31/07/97	5 9.5	11 13	Def	Wolves B.C.
McClelland	John	Stephen	26/04/77	Glasgow	11/08/95	5 9.0	10 4	Def	Milngavie Wanderers
McCloy	Brian		06/08/79	Pontefract	30/07/97	5 10.5	10 11	Def/Mid	Wolves B.C.
McCormick	Stephen		14/08/69	Dumbarton	12/11/98	6 4.0	11 4	Fwd	Dundee
McGuire	David		27/09/80	Bellshill	07/07/99	5 7.0	10 0	Fwd	Airdrieonians B.C.
McKeown	Stephen	James	17/07/81	Rutherglen	07/07/99	5 9.0	11 10	Fwd	Airdrieonians B.C.
Moore	Allan		25/12/64	Glasgow	04/08/98	5 7.0	10 0	Fwd	Livingston
Neil	Alexander		09/06/81	Coatbridge	08/07/99	5 9.0	11 0	Fwd	Dunfermline Athletic
Sandison	James	William	22/06/65	Edinburgh	27/07/91	5 10.5	10 10	Def	Heart of Midlothian
Stewart	Alexander		14/10/65	Bellshill	14/10/89	5 8.0	11 0	Def/Mid	Kilmarnock
Struthers	William		04/12/81	Bellshill	08/07/99	6 1.0	11 7	Fwd	Airdrieonians B.C.
Taylor	Stuart		26/11/74	Glasgow	07/07/98	6 1.0	11 4	Mid	St. Mirren
Thomson	Scott	Yuill	08/11/66	Edinburgh	29/07/98	6 0.5	12 0	Gk	Hull City

Milestones

YEAR OF FORMATION: 1878
MOST CAPPED PLAYER: Jimmy Crapnell
NO. OF CAPS: 9
MOST LEAGUE POINTS IN A SEASON: 60 (Division 2 - Season 1973/74) (2 Points for a Win)
61 (First Division - Season 1994/95) (3 Points for a Win)
MOST LEAGUE GOALS SCORED BY A PLAYER IN A SEASON: Bert Yarnell (Season 1916/17)
NO. OF GOALS SCORED: 39
RECORD ATTENDANCE: 24,000 (-v- Heart of Midlothian – 8.3.1952 at Broomfield Park)
8,762 (-v- Celtic – 19.8.1998 at Excelsior Stadium)
RECORD VICTORY: 15-1 (-v- Dundee Wanderers – Division 2, 1.12.1894)
RECORD DEFEAT: 1-11 (-v- Hibernian - Division 1, 24.10.1959)

The Diamonds' ten year record

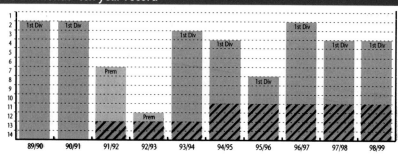

THE DIAMONDS' CLUB FACTFILE 1999/98 RESULTS... APPEARANCES... SCORERS

Date	Venue	Opponents	Att.	Res	Martin J.	Stewart A.	Johnston F.	Sandison J.	Farrell D.	Smith A.	Farrell G.	Wilson M.	Cooper S.	Evans G.	McQuillen P.	Black K.	Taylor S.	McCann H. A.	Jack P.	McCloy B.	Moore A.	Sissoko H.	Mackay G.	McKeown S.	McCormick S.	Thomson S.	McGuire D.	Brady D.	Easton S.	Greacen S.
Aug 4	H	Clydebank	2,716	0-0	1	2	3	4	5	6	7	8	9	10	11	12	14													
15	A	Hamilton Academical	1,137	1-1	1			4	5	11	2	8	9[1]		7	6	10	3	12	14										
22	H	St. Mirren	3,073	1-0	1			4	5	11	12	8			9	6	10	2	3		7	15[1]								
29	H	Raith Rovers	2,297	0-1	1	15	12	4	5	11	14	8			9	6	10	2	3		7									
Sep 5	H	Stranraer	687	2-1	1			14	4	5	10		8	9	15	11	6	12[1]	2	3		7[1]								
12	A	Greenock Morton	2,243	0-1	1	2	12	4			5		8	9	15	6	14	11	3		7									
19	A	Falkirk	4,157	1-0	1	2	5	4			11	14	8	9[1]	10	6		12	3		7									
26	A	Ayr United	2,392	2-1	1	2	5	4	15	10	14	8	9	12[2]	11	6		3			7									
Oct 3	H	Hibernian	4,301	1-3	1	2	3	4	5	11	15	8	9	14	10	6[1]		12			7									
6	H	Hamilton Academical	1,945	3-2	1	2	12	4			5	8	9[2]		10	6[1]		11	3		7		14	15						
17	A	Clydebank	571	1-0	1	2	5	4			14	8	9[1]	10		6		11	3		7			15						
31	A	Stranraer	1,988	3-2	1	2	5	4	12		14	8	9[1]	10		6		11[2]	3		7		15							
Nov 3	A	Raith Rovers	1,406	3-1	1			4	5	15	12	8	9[1]	10		6[1]		11[1]	3		7		14							
7	H	Falkirk	3,570	0-3	1	2		4	12	5		8	9		11	6		10	3		7		14	15						
14	A	Greenock Morton	1,935	0-0	1	2	3	4	5		15	8		10	6			11			7		12		14					
21	H	Ayr United	2,632	0-2	1	2	7	4	5		15		9	10		6		11	3		14		8		12					
28	A	Hibernian	9,732	0-1	1	2	8	4	5				9	12		6		11	3		7				14					
Dec 5	H	Clydebank	1,641	†2-0	1	2	8	4	5		7[1]		9	10	11	6		3			12				14					
12	A	St. Mirren	2,306	5-1	1	2	7	4	5		14	8[1]	9	10[1]	11[1]	6[1]		3[1]			12	15								
19	A	Stranraer	635	2-1	1	2	7	4	5	15		8[1]	9	10	11	6		3			12									
26	H	Raith Rovers	2,077	2-2	1	2	5	4		11		8	9	10[1]	7	6[1]		3			12				15					
Jan 2	A	Falkirk	4,518	1-1	1	2	5	4		15		8	9	10	7	6		11	3		12				14[1]					
16	A	Ayr United	2,387	1-0	1	2	5	4		11				10	12	6			3		7		8	9[1]						
19	H	Greenock Morton	1,801	0-2	1	2	5	4			7	8	12		11	6		14	3		10		15	9						
30	H	Hibernian	4,809	1-4	1	2	7	4		5		8	9	10	12	6[1]		11	3											
Feb 6	A	Hamilton Academical	814	2-0	1	2	5[1]	4		11		8	9	10		6		7[1]					14							
23	A	St. Mirren	1,860	0-3	1	2	5	4	12	11		8		10		6			3		7		15	14	9					
27	A	Raith Rovers	1,896	1-3		2	14	4	5	7		8	9[1]		11	6		3			12		15			1	10			
Mar 13	H	Stranraer	1,341	2-0				5	3			8	9		10	6[1]		11	2	4		7[1]	12			1		14		
20	A	Hibernian	9,991	0-3	5	2	6		11			8	9		12	10		15	3		7				1				4	
Apr 3	H	Ayr United	1,868	0-2	5	2	12		3			8	9			10	14		6			11	15	1		7			4	
10	H	Falkirk	1,957	1-2	2	4	6	3	11			8	15	9		7[1]		5	12			10	1					14		
17	A	Greenock Morton	1,442	2-0	2	7	6	5	11		4	9[1]				8	3				10[1]	15	1					12		
24	A	Clydebank	296	1-0	2	7	6	5	11		4	9				8	3				10[1]	15	1					12		
May 1	H	Hamilton Academical	2,257	1-0	1	2	7	6	5[1]	11	4	9				8	3				10	15			14			12		
8	A	St. Mirren	2,078	0-3		2	7		5	6		9				8	3	4	10	1			14				11	15		
TOTAL FULL APPEARANCES					28	31	26	33	20	23	6	31	25	21	20	30	8	27	21	2	21	4	2	4	8	2	3			
TOTAL SUB APPEARANCES					(1)	(5)	(1)	(4)	(2)	(12)		(2)	(5)	(3)	(1)	(4)	(4)	(1)	(2)	(7)	(1)	(6)	(11)	(8)		(2)	(1)	(4)		(1)
TOTAL GOALS SCORED							1	1			1	2	8	6	1	7	2	4			4	1		1	2					

Small bold figures denote goalscorers. † denotes opponent's own goal.

Excelsior Stadium

CRAIGNEUK AVENUE

CAR PARK | CAR PARK

EAST ♿ STAND

NORTH STAND

SOUTH STAND

JACK DALZIEL STAND

PETERSBURN ROAD

CAR PARK

CAR PARK | CAR PARK

CUMBERNAULD — A73 — NEWHOUSE

CAPACITY: 10,166 (All Seated)

PITCH DIMENSIONS: 115 yds x 74 yds

FACILITIES FOR DISABLED SUPPORTERS: Disabled facilities are provided in the North, East & South Stands

Team playing kits

How to get there

Excelsior Stadium can be reached by the following routes:

BUSES: Nos 260 or 15 from either Airdrie Town Centre or Gartlea Bus Station.

TRAINS: From Glasgow Queen Street to Airdrie there is a train every 15 minutes. From the Station beyond Airdrie, Drumgelloch, there is a train every 30 minutes, then a 10 minute walk to the stadium.

CARS: From Glasgow or Edinburgh leave the M8 at Newhouse junction (A73) and the stadium is 2½ miles north of Newhouse. From Cumbernauld, the stadium is 6 miles south on the A73.

The Diamonds

email: sfl@sol.co.uk • website: www.sfl.scottishfootball.com

Somerset Park, Tryfield Place,
Ayr, KA8 9NB

CHAIRMAN
William J. Barr, O.B.E.,
C. Eng., F.I.C.E., F.C.I.O.B., F.I.Mgt

VICE-CHAIRMAN
Donald R. Cameron B.Sc.

DIRECTORS
George H. Smith,
John E. Eyley, B.A., ACMA,
Kenneth W. MacLeod, M.A.S.I. &
Roy G. Kennedy A.R.I.C.S.

COMPANY SECRETARY
John E. Eyley, B.A., ACMA

ADMINISTRATOR
Brian Caldwell

MANAGER
Gordon Dalziel

COACH
Iain Munro

YOUTH COACH
I. Campbell Money

CLUB DOCTOR
Dr. John A.M. Hannah, B.Sc (Hons)
M.B.Ch.B., M.R.C.G.P., D.R.C.O.G.

PHYSIOTHERAPIST
John Kerr, L.V.M.C. Inst. of H.T.

**FOOTBALL SAFETY OFFICERS'
ASSOCIATION REPRESENTATIVES**
Roy Kennedy & Jim Crombie

GROUNDSMAN
David Harkness

LOTTERY MANAGER
Andrew Downie

TELEPHONES
Ground/Ticket Office
(01292) 263435/6
Fax (01292) 281314
Information Line (09068) 121552

CLUB SHOP
Ayr United Club Shop, Tryfield Place,
Ayr, KA8 9NB. (01292) 263435.
Open 8.30 a.m.-5.30 p.m. Mon-Fri
and 10.00 a.m.-3.00 p.m.
on all first team home matchdays.

OFFICIAL SUPPORTERS CLUB
c/o Ayr United F.C., Somerset Park,
Ayr, KA8 9NB

TEAM CAPTAIN
David Rogers

SHIRT SPONSOR
First Choice Playing Kit: Strachans
Second Choice Playing Kit: Barr Homes

LIST OF PLAYERS 1999-2000

SURNAME	FIRST NAME	MIDDLE NAME	DATE OF BIRTH	PLACE OF BIRTH	DATE OF SIGNING	HEIGHT FT INS	WEIGHT ST LBS	POS. ON PITCH	PREVIOUS CLUB
Armstrong	Gareth	James	31/08/80	Irvine	02/09/99	5 11.0	11 0	Fwd	Glenafton Juniors
Bone	Alexander	Syme Frew	26/12/71	Stirling	28/05/99	5 9.0	10 7	Fwd	Stirling Albion
Bowman	Gary		12/08/74	Glasgow	14/11/97	5 11.0	11 4	Mid/For	St. Johnstone
Bradford	John		15/12/79	Irvine	13/01/98	5 11.0	11 0	Fwd	Dalry Thistle
Burns	Gordon		02/12/78	Glasgow	10/09/97	6 1.0	11 6	Def/Mid	Glenafton Juniors
Campbell	Mark	Thomas	04/02/78	Irvine	26/02/99	6 0.0	10 12	Def	Stranraer
Cooper	Stephen		22/06/64	Birmingham	01/07/99	5 11.0	12 2	Fwd	Airdrieonians
Craig	David	William	11/06/69	Glasgow	16/06/98	6 2.0	13 0	Def	Hamilton Academical
Crilly	Mark		23/05/80	Glasgow	26/09/97	5 10.0	11 0	Mid	Gleniffer Thistle
Davies	John		25/09/66	Glasgow	20/03/98	5 7.0	10 0	Mid	Airdrieonians
Duffy	Cornelius		05/06/67	Glasgow	01/07/99	6 1.0	13 5	Def/Mid	Dundee United
Duthie	Mark	James	19/08/72	Edinburgh	26/01/98	5 8.0	10 0	Fwd	Livingston
Gill	Thomas		16/05/65	Oslo	30/07/99	6 3.0	12 8	Gk	F.C. Copenhagen
Hogg	Keith		27/01/80	Lanark	26/07/97	6 0.0	11 7	Def	Glasgow City
Hurst	Glynn		17/01/76	Barnsley	23/03/98	5 9.0	11 0	Mid	Emley
Jemson	Nigel		10/08/69	Preston	10/09/99	5 11.0	13 0	Fwd	Bury
Kelly	Russell	James	10/08/76	Ballymoney	07/08/98	6 0.0	11 7	Mid	Dundee
Lennon	Daniel	Joseph	06/04/70	Whitburn	04/08/99	5 7.0	10 8	Mid	Raith Rovers
Lindau	Peter		09/12/72	Halmstad	05/08/99	6 1.0	12 2	Fwd	I.S. Halimia
Lyons	Andrew		19/10/66	Blackpool	31/07/98	5 9.0	12 7	Mid	Partick Thistle
Nelson	Craig	Robert	28/05/71	Coatbridge	13/07/98	6 1.0	12 3	Gk	Falkirk
Nolan	John Kenneth	Andrew McBride	30/11/79	Irvine	03/10/97	5 9.0	10 4	Mid	Dalry Thistle
Prenderville	Barry		16/10/76	Dublin	07/06/99	6 0.0	12 8	Def	Coventry City
Reynolds	Michael		19/06/74	Huddersfield	11/12/98	5 5.0	10 7	Mid/For	Emley
Robertson	John		28/03/76	Irvine	24/07/97	6 0.0	11 0	Def	Stranraer
Rogers	David		25/08/75	Liverpool	23/06/99	6 2.0	10 7	Def	Dundee
Scally	Neil		14/08/78	Paisley	16/02/98	5 11.0	12 0	Mid	Glenafton
Teale	Gary		21/07/78	Glasgow	02/10/98	6 0.0	11 4	Fwd	Clydebank
Traynor	John	Francis Campbell	10/12/66	Glasgow	07/11/91	5 10.0	11 0	Def	Clydebank
Wilson	Marvyn		01/12/73	Bellshill	06/07/99	5 7.5	10 0	Mid	Airdrieonians

Milestones

YEAR OF FORMATION: 1910
MOST CAPPED PLAYER: Jim Nisbett
NO. OF CAPS: 3
MOST LEAGUE POINTS IN A SEASON: 61 (Second Division – Season 1987/88)(2 Points for a Win)
77 (Second Division – Season 1996/97)(3 Points for a Win)
MOST LEAGUE GOALS SCORED BY A PLAYER IN A SEASON: Jimmy Smith (Season 1927/28)
NO. OF GOALS SCORED: 66
RECORD ATTENDANCE: 25,225 (-v- Rangers – 13.9.1969)
RECORD VICTORY: 11-1 (-v- Dumbarton – League Cup, 13.8.1952)
RECORD DEFEAT: 0-9 (-v- Rangers, Heart of Midlothian, Third Lanark – Division 1)

The Honest Men's ten year league record

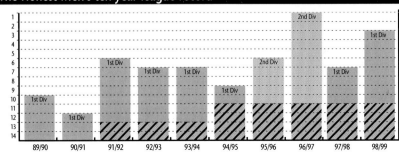

THE HONEST MEN'S CLUB FACTFILE 1998/99 RESULTS... APPEARANCES... SCORERS

Date	Venue	Opponents	Att.	Res	Castilla D.	Robertson J.	Miller C.	Millen A.	Welsh S.	Burns G.	Hurst G.	Agnew P.	Walker A.	Findlay W.	Lyons A.	Traynor J.	Duthie M.	Armstrong G.	Craig D.	Davies J.	Kelly R.	Ferguson I.	Nelson C.	Dick J.	Crilly M.	Teale G.	Winnie D.	Reynolds M.	Horace A.	Scally N.	Barrick D.	Campbell M.	Hamilton B.	Bowman G.	Bradford J.	Stewart D.	Nolan J.
Aug 4	A	Falkirk	3,127	0-1	1	2	3	4	5	6	7	8	9	10	11	12	14	15																			
15	H	Greenock Morton	2,329	1-0	1	2	3	4	5		7		9	10	11	14			6	8^1	12	15															
22	A	Raith Rovers	2,010	0-0	1	2	3	4	5		7		9	10	11				6	8	14																
29	A	Hibernian	9,231	2-4	1	2	3	4	5		7^1		9	10^1	11				6	8	12																
Sep 5	H	Hamilton Academical	1,917	2-3	1	2	14	4	5		7^1		9	10	11				6	8	9				3^1												
12	A	Clydebank	569	1-0		2	12	4	5		7		9^1	10	11				6	8	14	15	1		3												
19	H	Stranraer	1,917	7-1		2^1		4	5		7^1		9^1	10^2	11				6	8	14	12	1		3					15							
26	H	Airdrieonians	2,392	1-2		2		4	5		7		9	10	11				6	8^1		12	1		3												
Oct 3	A	St. Mirren	2,673	2-0		2		4	5		7		9	14	11^1				6	8		12^1	1		3	10				15							
11	A	Greenock Morton	2,156	2-1		2		4	5		7		9	14	11^1				6	8		12	1		3^1	10				15							
17	H	Falkirk	2,731	4-2		2		4	5		7		9^2	14	11				6	8		12	1		3	10^1				15^1							
24	H	Hibernian	4,684	3-3		2		4	5		7^2		9^1		11				6	8		12	1		3	10				15							
31	A	Hamilton Academical	1,267	3-1		2		4^1	5		7		9^1		11				6	8	14	12^1	1		3	10												
Nov 7	A	Stranraer	1,390	1-0		2		4	5		7^1		9		11				6	8		12	1		3	10												
14	H	Clydebank	2,450	4-1		2		4	5		7^2		9^1		11^1				6	8	14	12	1		3	10												
21	A	Airdrieonians	2,632	2-0		2		4	5		7^1		9	14	11				6	8		12	1		3	10^1				15							
28	H	St. Mirren	3,640	1-1		2		4	5		7		9^1	14	11				6	8		12	1		3	10												
Dec 5	A	Falkirk	4,010	0-3		2		4	5		7		9		11				6	8	14	12	1		3	10				15							
12	H	Raith Rovers	2,245	0-2		2		4	5		7		9		11				6	8	14	12	1		3	10				15							
19	H	Hamilton Academical	2,102	5-0	1	2		4	5		7^3		9^2	14					6	8					3	10				15				11	12			
26	A	Hibernian	14,106	0-3	1	2		4	5		7		9	14					6	8					3	10				15				11	12			
Jan 2	H	Stranraer	2,722	4-0	1			4	5		7^2		9^1						6^1	8	14	12			3	10	11		15		2						
16	H	Airdrieonians	2,387	0-1	1	2		4	5		7		9	14					6	8		12			3	10	11		15								
30	A	St. Mirren	2,670	0-1	1	2			5		7		9						6	8	14	12			3	10	11		15								
Feb 6	H	Greenock Morton	2,222	1-0	1	2		4	5		7		9						6^1	8	14	12			3	10	11										
20	A	Raith Rovers	1,873	4-2	1	2		4	5		7		9^1						6^1	8	14				3	10	11^2										
27	H	Hibernian	5,010	1-3	1	2		4	5		7		9^1						6	8	14	12			3	10	11		15								
Mar 20	H	St. Mirren	2,436	2-2		2		4	5		7^1		9						6	8	14	12	1		3	10	11^1		15								
24	A	Hamilton Academical	769	2-0	1	2		4	5		7		9						6	8	14	12			3	10^1	11^1		15								
Apr 3	A	Airdrieonians	1,868	2-0	1			4			7		9^1						6	8	14				3	10^1	11		15	5	2						
10	A	Stranraer	990	2-0	1			4			7^2		9						6	8	14	12			3	10	11		15	5	2						
18	H	Clydebank	2,113	0-0	1			4			7		9						6	8	14	12			3	10	11			5	2						
24	H	Falkirk	2,496	1-2	1			4			7		9^1						6	8	14				3	10	11		15	5	2						
27	A	Clydebank	305	1-2	1			4			7		9						6	8	14				3		11		15	5	2				12	10^1	
May 1	A	Greenock Morton	2,337	4-1	1			4			7^1		9^2						6	8^1		12			3	10	11			5	2				14		15
8	H	Raith Rovers	1,886	1-0	1			4	5		7		9^1						6	8		12			3	10	11				2				14		15
TOTAL FULL APPEARANCES					21	21	4	34	24	4	34	1	31	15	31	22			22	27	7	9	15	1	23	13	11		2	11	9		2		2		
TOTAL SUB APPEARANCES							(2)		(1)	(6)		(2)	(2)	(7)	(1)	(7)	(5)	(2)		(2)	(11)	(13)			(3)	(3)		(7)	(4)				(1)	(4)	(3)	(1)	(1)
TOTAL GOALS SCORED						1		1	1		18		15	2	8	2			3	1		8				4	1									1	

Small bold figures denote goalscorers. † denotes opponent's own goal.

Somerset Park

HOME SUPPORTERS

A77 ►

SOMERSET ROAD

VISITING SUPPORTERS

TRYFIELD PLACE

HOME SUPPORTERS

CAPACITY: 12,178; Seated 1,500, Standing 10,678
PITCH DIMENSIONS: 110 yds x 72 yds
FACILITIES FOR DISABLED SUPPORTERS:
Enclosure and toilet facilities for wheelchairs. Match commentary available for blind persons at all first team matches.

Team playing kits

How to get there

Somerset Park can be reached by the following routes:
TRAINS: There is a half hourly train service from Glasgow to either Ayr or Newton-on-Ayr. The ground is a ten minute walk from both stations.
BUSES: There are several buses from the town centre with a frequency approximately every five minutes. Fans should board buses bound for Dalmilling, Whitletts or any bus passing Ayr Racecourse. The ground is only a ten minute walk from the town centre.
CARS: Car parking facilities are available at Craigie Road, Ayr Racecourse and also at Somerset Road car parks.

email: sfl@sol.co.uk • website: www.sfl.scottishfootball.com

Cappielow Park, Sinclair Street,
Greenock, PA15 2TY

**ALL CORRESPONDENCE
SHOULD BE ADDRESSED TO:**
Billy Hall Esq., Secretary,
Clydebank F.C.,
218 Pentagon Business Centre,
36 Washington Street,
Glasgow, G2 8AZ
OR
Ian McCall, Manager,
Clydebank F.C., c/o West of Scotland
Rugby Club, Burnbrae, Milngavie,
G62 6HX

DIRECTOR
Dr. John McK. Hall

SECRETARY
Billy Hall

PLAYER/MANAGER
Ian McCall

ASSISTANT MANAGER
Stephen Morrison

FIRST TEAM COACH
Fraser Wishart

CLUB DOCTORS
David Pugh, Andrew Renwick
& Daniel McBryan

PHYSIOTHERAPIST
Kevan McLlenan

GROUNDSMAN
Ian Lyle

TELEPHONES
Ground (01475) 723571
(Match Days Only)
Office/Commercial (0141) 955 9048
Fax (0141) 955 9049

E-MAIL & INTERNET ADDRESS
clydebankfc@amazone.com

OFFICIAL SUPPORTERS CLUB
c/o Gordon Robertson,
Clydebank Post,
88 Dumbarton Road, Clydebank

TEAM CAPTAIN
Joe McLaughlin

SHIRT SPONSOR
Bolton Brady

SURNAME	FIRST NAME	MIDDLE NAME	DATE OF BIRTH	PLACE OF BIRTH	DATE OF SIGNING	HEIGHT FT INS	WEIGHT ST LBS	POS. ON PITCH	PREVIOUS CLUB
Cameron	Ian		24/08/66	Glasgow	23/08/99	5 9.0	10 4	Mid	Raith Rovers
Cormack	Peter	Robert	08/06/74	Liverpool	09/08/99	6 0.0	11 5	Def	Stirling Albion
Ewing	Christopher	Gordon	12/10/78	Glasgow	30/07/99	6 4.0	12 2	Fwd	Dumbarton
Gardner	Robert	Lee	11/07/70	Ayr	31/07/98	5 5.0	9 5	Fwd	Albion Rovers
McCall	Ian	Holland	30/09/65	Dumfries	04/08/97	5 9.0	11 7	Mid	Partick Thistle
McIntyre	Paul		18/01/67	Girvan	29/07/99	6 0.0	12 11	Def/Mid	Stranraer
McKelvie	Daniel		06/06/80	Paisley	25/09/98	5 7.0	10 7	Fwd	Beith Juniors
McKinstrey	James		03/07/79	Glasgow	30/10/97	5 9.0	9 10	Def/Mid	Irvine Meadow
McLaughlin	Joseph		02/06/60	Greenock	04/08/97	6 1.0	12 0	Def	Hibernian
McWilliams	Derek		16/01/66	Broxburn	17/10/97	5 10.0	12 0	Mid	AIK Appelbo
Miller	Greg	Allan	01/04/76	Glasgow	09/08/99	5 8.0	10 13	Fwd	Motherwell
Morrison	Stephen		15/08/61	St. Andrews	30/07/99	6 0.0	13 3	Mid	Ardrossan Winton Rovers
Murdoch	Scott	McKenzie	27/02/69	Glasgow	22/10/92	5 7.0	10 7	Mid	St. Rochs
O'Neill	Martin		17/06/75	Glasgow	30/07/99	5 8.0	10 10	Mid	Kilmarnock
Oliver	Neil		11/04/67	Berwick-o-Tweed	26/07/99	5 11.0	12 3	Def	Hamilton Academical
Roddie	Andrew	Robert	04/11/71	Glasgow	03/09/99	5 10.5	11 4	Mid	Carlisle United
Scott	Colin	George	19/05/70	Glasgow	31/07/98	6 2.0	13 10	Gk	Raith Rovers
Stewart	David		14/08/78	Irvine	30/07/99	6 1.0	12 2	Def	Ayr United
Wishart	Fraser		01/03/65	Johnstone	04/08/97	5 8.0	10 7	Def	Motherwell

Milestones

YEAR OF FORMATION: 1965
MOST LEAGUE POINTS IN A SEASON: 58 (Division 1 – Season 1976/77)(2 Points for a Win)
60 (Second Division – Season 1997/98)(3 Points for a Win)
MOST LEAGUE GOALS SCORED BY A PLAYER IN A SEASON: Ken Eadie (Season 1990/91)
NO. OF GOALS SCORED: 29
RECORD ATTENDANCE: 14,900 (-v- Hibernian – 10.2.1965)
RECORD VICTORY: 8-1 (-v- Arbroath – Division 1, 3.1.1977)
RECORD DEFEAT: 1-9 (-v- Gala Fairydean – Scottish Cup, 15.9.1965)

The Bankies' ten year league record

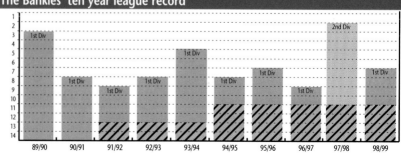

THE BANKIES' CLUB FACTFILE 1998/99 RESULTS... APPEARANCES... SCORERS

Date	Venue	Opponents	Att.	Res	Scott C.	Wishart F.	Lovering P.	Teale G.	McLaughlin J.	Brannigan K.	Nicholls D.	McDonald C.	Taggart C.	Robertson A.	McWilliams D.	Smith T.	Miller S.	Gardner R.L.	Inglis N.	Docherty S.	Brown A.	Murdoch S.	McKelvie D.	Ritchie I.	Dobie S.	Callaghan S.	Anthony M.	Naker R.	McMillan A.	Newland R.	Love G.	Ross S.	McKinstrey J.	Elliot B.	Morrison S.
Aug 4	A	Airdrieonians	2,716	0-0	1	2	3	4	5	6	7	8	9	10	11	12	14	15																	
15	H	Falkirk	928	0-1		2	3	9	5	6	7	8	10		11	4	14	12	1	15															
22	A	Stranraer	570	2-0	1	2	3	12	5	6	7	8	9		11	4^1	15	10^1																	
29	A	Greenock Morton	1,382	2-2	1	2	3	8	5^1	6	7	9	12		11^1	4	14	10																	
Sep 5	H	Hibernian	1,828	2-2	1	2	3	9	5^1	6	7	14	12	8		4^1	11	10																	
12	H	Ayr United	569	0-1	1	2	3	9	5	6	7	12	14	8	15	4	11	10																	
19	A	Hamilton Academical	648	2-1	1	2	3	9^1	5	6	7	12	14	8		4	11^1	10																	
26	H	St. Mirren	1,462	1-0	1	2	3	9^1	5	6	7	12	14	8		4	11	10		15															
Oct 3	A	Raith Rovers	1,661	1-0	1	2	3		5	6	7	9^1	12	8		4	11	10	14	15															
11	A	Falkirk	4,316	2-2	1	2	3		5	6	7	9^2	8			4	11	10		14															
17	A	Airdrieonians	571	0-1	1	2	3		5	6	7	9	8	12		4	11	10		14															
27	A	Greenock Morton	452	2-1	1	2	3		5^1	6	7	9	8^1			4		10		11			14	15											
31	A	Hibernian	10,172	1-2	1	2			5	6	7	9	8	12		4				11	15^1	3	14												
Nov 7	H	Hamilton Academical	451	0-0	1	2			5	6	7	9	8	10		4	12			11	15	3		14											
14	A	Ayr United	2,450	1-4	1	2					7	14	12^1			4	9	10		8		3	15	5		6	11								
21	A	St. Mirren	2,847	0-0	1					6	7	8	14			4^1	9	10		15		2		5	11	3										
28	H	Raith Rovers	417	1-1	1				5	6	7	14	8			4^1	9	10		12		2		15	11	3										
Dec 5	A	Airdrieonians	1,641	0-2	1	2			5	6	7	15	12			4	11	10						9	3	8										
12	H	Stranraer	207	2-1		2			5^1	6	7	12	10			4	11^1			15				9	3	8	1	14								
19	H	Hibernian	9,064	0-3		2			5	6	7		10			4	11	12		14				9		8			1	3						
26	A	Greenock Morton	1,947	1-1		2			5	6	7		9			4	11	12		10^1						8			3	1						
Jan 12	A	Hamilton Academical	651	1-0		2			5	6	7	9^1	14				11	12		10						8			3	1	4					
16	H	St. Mirren	934	2-2		2			5		7^1	9^1	14				11	12		10	15				6	8			3	1	4	11				
30	A	Raith Rovers	1,803	1-2		2			5	6	7	9^1	8					12		10	15					14			3		4	11				
Feb 20	A	Stranraer	452	2-0	1	2			5		7	12	6			11	10				15	4				8^1	3				14	9^1				
Mar 10	H	Falkirk	289	1-2	1	2			5		7	9^1	6			11	10			12	14	4	15			8					3					
13	A	Hibernian	1,695	2-0	1	2			5		7	9	6			11	14			10	15	4				12			3^1			8^1				
20	H	Raith Rovers	300	0-0	1	2			5	6	7	9				11	14			12	15	4				10			3			8				
Apr 3	A	St. Mirren	1,756	1-1	1				5	6	7	9	2			11	8^1			10	15	4		3		12										
10	H	Hamilton Academical	262	0-0	1	2			5	6	7	9	3			11	8			10	15	4				14										
18	A	Ayr United	2,113	0-0	1	2			5	6	7		3			11	8			10	15	4	14									9				
21	H	Greenock Morton	402	1-2	1	2			5	6	7	9^1	3			11	8			10	15		12	4												
24	H	Airdrieonians	296	0-1		2			5	6	7	9	3		15	11	14			10	12	8		4												1
27	H	Ayr United	305	2-1		2				6^1	7		3		14	11^1	8			10	9	15	12	4									5			1
May 1	A	Falkirk	2,737	2-0	1	2				6		9^1	3		14	11	8			10^1	15	7	12	4									5			
8	H	Stranraer	269	1-2	1				5	6		9	3^1		7	11	8			10		2	14	4										12		15
TOTAL FULL APPEARANCES					28	32	12	7	32	31	34	22	25	7	5	20	28	24	1	17	1	13		11	6	5	9	1	1	1	7	3	7	4	2
TOTAL SUB APPEARANCES							(1)					(8)	(10)	(4)	(4)	(1)	(4)	(11)		(11)	(14)	(3)	(9)	(2)			(4)		(1)				(2)		(1)
TOTAL GOALS SCORED								2	3	2	1	9	2	1	1	3	3	2		2		1					1					1		2

Small bold figures denote goalscorers. † denotes opponent's own goal.

Cappielow Park

Limited space – Application only

SINCLAIR STREET

CAPACITY: 8,100; Seated 5,741, Standing 2,359
PITCH DIMENSIONS: 110 yds x 71 yds
FACILITIES FOR DISABLED SUPPORTERS:
Seating facilities below Grandstand.

Team playing kits

How to get there

Cappielow Park can be reached by the following routes:

BUSES: Services from Glasgow stop just outside the park. There are also services from Port Glasgow and Gourock.

TRAINS: The nearest local station is Cartsdyke and it is a five minute walk from here to the ground. There are two to three trains every hour from Glasgow and from Gourock.

CARS: Temporary Car Park adjacent to Stadium.

email: sfl@sol.co.uk • website: www.sfl.scottishfootball.com

East End Park, Halbeath Road,
Dunfermline, Fife, KY12 7RB

CHAIRMAN
John W. Yorkston

DIRECTORS
C. Roy Woodrow, William M. Rennie,
Gavin G. Masterton, C.B.E., F.I.B. (Scot),
Andrew T. Gillies, John Meiklem,
Francis M. McConnell,
W. Brian Robertson &
Graham A. Thomson

SECRETARY/GENERAL MANAGER
Paul A. M. D'Mello

MANAGER
Richard M. Campbell

ASSISTANT MANAGER
James Nicholl

TRAINER
Joe Nelson

CHIEF SCOUT
Robert Paton

CLUB DOCTOR
Dr. Gerry D. Gillespie

PHYSIOTHERAPIST
Philip Yeates, M.C.S.P.

YOUTH DEVELOPMENT MANAGER
John B. Ritchie

FOOTBALL SAFETY OFFICERS' ASSOCIATION REPRESENTATIVE/ SECURITY ADVISOR
David Dickson
Tel: (01383) 725557

STADIUM MANAGER
Brian Gallagher

COMMERCIAL MANAGER
Miss Audrey M. Bastianelli

TELEPHONES
Ground/Commercial/Ticket Office
(01383) 724295/721749
Fax (01383) 723468
Clubcall (0930) 555060

CLUB SHOP
Situated at Ground
Open 9.00 a.m. – 5.00 p.m.
Mon to Sat. Tel: (01383) 724295

OFFICIAL SUPPORTERS CLUB
c/o Mrs. Joan Malcolm, Secretary,
Dunfermline Athletic
Supporters Club,
13 South Knowe,
Crossgates, KY4 8AW

TEAM CAPTAIN
Andrew Tod

SHIRT SPONSOR
Auto Windscreens

LIST OF PLAYERS 1999-2000

SURNAME	FIRST NAME	MIDDLE NAME	DATE OF BIRTH	PLACE OF BIRTH	DATE OF SIGNING	HEIGHT FT INS	WEIGHT ST LBS	POS. ON PITCH	PREVIOUS CLUB
Boyle	Steven	Robert	11/12/80	Edinburgh	05/03/99	5 10.0	10 8	Def	Ratho Colts
Butler	Lee	Simon	30/05/66	Sheffield	14/07/98	6 2.0	15 0	Gk	Wigan Athletic
Coyle	Owen	Columba	14/07/66	Paisley	13/03/99	5 11.0	10 5	Fwd	Motherwell
Dair	Jason		15/06/74	Dunfermline	26/02/99	5 11.0	12 5	Mid/For	Raith Rovers
Dolan	James		22/02/69	Salsburgh	26/02/99	5 9.0	11 9	Mid	Dundee United
French	Hamish	Mackie	07/02/64	Aberdeen	23/10/91	5 10.5	11 7	Mid/For	Dundee United
Graham	David		06/10/78	Edinburgh	15/11/98	5 10.0	11 2	Fwd	Rangers
Huxford	Richard	John	25/07/69	Scunthorpe	17/07/98	5 11.0	12 2	Mid	Burnley
Ireland	Craig		29/11/75	Dundee	12/02/96	6 3.0	13 9	Def	Aberdeen
Martin	Craig		10/11/78	Uphall	30/06/97	6 2.0	11 7	Mid	Links United U'18s
May	Edward	Skillion	30/08/67	Edinburgh	12/07/99	5 8.5	11 7	Def	Motherwell
McGroarty	Christopher	Martin	06/02/81	Bellshill	22/10/98	5 10.0	10 5	Mid/For	Rosyth Recreation U'18s
Moss	David		15/11/68	Doncaster	09/09/99	6 2.0	13 3	Mid	Falkirk
Nish	Colin		07/03/81	Edinburgh	28/07/97	6 3.0	11 8	Fwd	Rosyth Rec Colts U18s
Petrie	Stewart	James John	27/02/70	Dundee	27/08/93	5 10.0	11 11	Fwd	Forfar Athletic
Potter	John	Paul	15/12/79	Dunfermline	06/09/99	6 1.0	13 0	Def	Celtic
Reid	Brian	Robertson	15/06/70	Paisley	07/07/99	6 3.0	13 11	Def	Burnley
Skinner	Justin		30/01/69	London	03/09/99	6 1.0	12 1	Mid	Hibernian
Smith	Andrew	Mark	27/11/68	Aberdeen	21/07/95	6 1.0	12 7	Fwd	Airdrieonians
Squires	James	Alexander	15/11/75	Preston	30/08/99	6 2.0	13 5	Def	York City
Taylor	Russell	Thomas	30/07/80	Dunfermline	06/09/99	6 0.0	11 10	Mid/Fwd	Raith Rovers
Templeman	Christopher		12/01/80	Kirkcaldy	29/07/97	6 4.0	13 2	Fwd	Rosyth Recreation Colts
Thomson	Scott	Munro	29/01/72	Aberdeen	06/07/98	5 10.0	11 4	Fwd	Raith Rovers
Tod	Andrew		04/11/71	Dunfermline	04/11/93	6 3.0	12 6	Def	Kelty Hearts
Westwater	Ian		08/11/63	Loughborough	30/03/94	6 2.0	14 8	Gk	Dundee

Milestones

YEAR OF FORMATION: 1885
MOST CAPPED PLAYER: Istvan Kozma
NO. OF CAPS: Hungary 29 (13 whilst with Dunfermline Athletic)
MOST LEAGUE POINTS IN A SEASON: 65 (First Division – Season 1993/94) (2 Points for a Win)
71 (First Division – Season 1995/96) (3 Points for a Win)
MOST LEAGUE GOALS SCORED BY A PLAYER IN A SEASON: Bobby Skinner (Season 1925/26)
NO. OF GOALS SCORED: 53
RECORD ATTENDANCE: 27,816 (-v- Celtic – 30.4.1968)
RECORD VICTORY: 11-2 (-v- Stenhousemuir – Division 2, 27.9.1930)
RECORD DEFEAT: 0-10 (-v- Dundee – Division 2, 22.3.1947)

The Pars' ten year league record

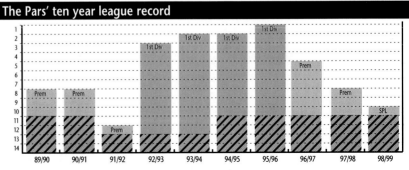

THE PARS' CLUB FACTFILE 1998/99 RESULTS... APPEARANCES... SCORERS

Date	Venue	Opponents	Att.	Res	Westwater I.	Linighan D.	Ireland C.	Shields G.	Tod A.	Huxford R.	Millar M.	French H.	Smith A.	Shaw G.	Thomson S.	Faulconbridge C.	Den Bieman I.	Ferguson D.	Butler L.	Squires J.	Johnson G.	Fraser J.	Templeman C.	Britton G.	McCulloch S.	Petrie S.	Amaral Neto E.	Graham D.	Martin C.	Macdonald W.	McGroarty C.	Nish C.	Dolan J.	Dair J.	Coyle O.	Boyle S.
Aug 1	A	Celtic	59,377	0-5	1	2	3	4	5	6	7	8	9	10	11	12	13	14																		
15	H	Dundee	5,279	2-0			6	4	5				12	9[1]	10[1]		13		8	1	2	3	7	11	14											
22	A	Motherwell	9,858	0-0			6	4	5	12			13	9	10	14			8	1	2		7	11			3									
29	H	Aberdeen	6,510	1-1			5	4		7	12	14[1]	9	13	8				1	2	6		11	10			3									
Sep 12	A	St. Johnstone	5,997	1-1			5	4		7		13	9[1]	14	11			8	1	2	6		10			3	12									
20	H	Heart of Midlothian	5,963	1-1			5	4		7	13	8	9[1]	11	14			6	1	2			10			3	12									
23	A	Dundee United	6,957	1-1			5	4		7		8	9	11				6	1	2[1]			10			3	12									
26	H	Rangers	11,507	0-2			5	4		7	12	8	9	11	14			6	1	2			10			3	13									
Oct 3	A	Kilmarnock	8,346	0-0			5	4	3			8	9	12	10	14		6	1	2		7	13			11										
17	H	Celtic	10,968	2-2			6	4	13	7	14	8[1]	9		12				1	2	3		10[1]	5	11											
28	A	Dundee	4,619	0-1			6	4	5	7	14	8	13	9				12	1	2		10			3	11										
31	H	St. Johnstone	8,126	1-1			6	4	5	13	7		9[1]	8				14	1	2		11	10			3	12									
Nov 7	A	Aberdeen	10,293	1-2			6	4	5	8	12		9					10	1	2[1]	3	14	13	7		11										
15	H	Dundee United	10,704	2-1			6	4	5[1]	13			9					10	1	2	3	14		7[1]	12	8	11									
21	A	Heart of Midlothian	13,268	1-2			6	4	5			13	9					10	1	2	3		7	12	8[1]	11										
28	H	Kilmarnock	5,608	0-3			6	4	5			12	9					10	1	2	3		7	13	8	11										
Dec 5	A	Rangers	47,465	1-1				4	5	6	12	8	9					10	1		3	14	2	13[1]	7	11										
12	H	Motherwell	5,182	1-1				4	5	6	12	8	9[1]					10	1		3		14	2	7	13	11									
19	A	Celtic	59,024	0-5				4		3		8	9	12				10	1	2			13		5	7	6	11	14							
26	H	Aberdeen	7,873	1-2			5	4		6		8	9	11[1]					1	2			10			3	7	12								
29	A	St. Johnstone	6,070	1-1				4	3			8	9[1]	6				10	1			11	2	7			12	5								
Jan 2	H	Heart of Midlothian	9,227	0-0				4	5	3		8	9	6					1			10	2	7	12	11		13								
30	A	Dundee United	7,646	1-1				4	5	6		8	9[1]	10					1	2	3	14	13			12	11			7						
Feb 7	H	Rangers	10,360	0-3				4	5	2		8	9	10				7	1		3	13			11						6	12				
27	A	Motherwell	7,324	1-1				4	5	2		9		7				6	1		3	12[1]	13		11								8	10		
Mar 6	A	Kilmarnock	8,032	0-0				4	5	2		13		7				6	1		3	9	10		14								8	12	11	
13	H	Dundee	6,980	2-0				4	5	2		13		7[1]					1		3	14	9		10	12[1]							8	6	11	
20	H	St. Johnstone	5,504	1-0				4	5	3		12		7					1	2		13	14	10[1]	9								8	6	11	
Apr 3	A	Aberdeen	11,361	1-3				4		3		9	14	7					1	2		12	13	10	8[1]								5	6	11	
14	A	Rangers	46,220	0-1				4	5	2	3	12		7					1			10		9									8	6	11	
17	H	Kilmarnock	5,585	0-6			12	4	5	2	3	12		7				1	14			10		9								13	8	6	11	
24	H	Dundee United	6,227	2-2			12	4	5		3[1]		9[1]	13	7				1			10	14	2									8	6	11	
May 1	A	Heart of Midlothian	15,176	0-2			2	4	5	3		9	13	7					1			10			12								8	6	11	
8	H	Celtic	8,848	1-2			2	4	5	8	6	9	13	7					1			12		10									3		11[1]	
15	H	Dundee	4,179	1-3			2	5	4	6		9	10	7[1]					1	3		14		8			13		12						11	
23	H	Motherwell	3,532	1-2			2	4		5		9		7					1	12	3	13		14			10		8					11	6[1]
TOTAL FULL APPEARANCES					1	1	21	36	24	22	13	15	29	10	20	1		18	35	19	18	2	5	13	19	19	5	14	2		3	10	9	11	11	1
TOTAL SUB APPEARANCES							(2)		(1)	(3)	(8)	(6)	(6)	(8)	(1)	(5)	(2)	(3)		(2)		(4)	(7)	(8)		(11)	(4)	(7)	(1)	(1)	(1)	(2)		(1)	
TOTAL GOALS SCORED							1			1	2	8	2	2				2						2	1	2	1	2						1	1

Small bold figures denote goalscorers. † denotes opponent's own goal.

East End Park

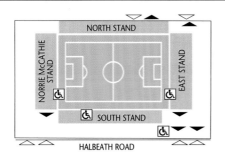

NORTH STAND
NORRIE McCATHIE STAND
EAST STAND
SOUTH STAND
HALBEATH ROAD

CAPACITY: 12,565 (All Seated)

PITCH DIMENSIONS: 115 yds x 70 yds

FACILITIES FOR DISABLED SUPPORTERS:
12 spaces in East Stand for Away Supporters. 12 spaces in West Stand for Home Supporters. 24 seats for helpers.

Team playing kits

How to get there

East End Park may be reached by the following routes:

TRAINS: Dunfermline Station is served by trains from both Glasgow and Edinburgh and the ground is a 15 minute walk from here.

BUSES: Buses destined for Kelty, Perth, St. Andrews and Kirkcaldy all pass close to East End Park.

CARS: Car Parking is available in a large car park adjoining the east end of the ground and there are also facilities in various side streets. Multi-storey car parking approximately 10 minutes walk from the ground.

The Pars

41

email: sfl@sol.co.uk • website: www.sfl.scottishfootball.com

FALKIRK

Brockville Park, Hope Street,
Falkirk, FK1 5AX

CHAIRMAN
W. Martin Ritchie

VICE-CHAIRMAN
Colin Liddell

DIRECTORS
Douglas J. McIntyre, Ann M. Joyce,
E. William Moffat, Colin McLachlan
& Campbell Christie, C.B.E.

SECRETARY
Alexander Blackwood

**DIRECTOR OF
CUSTOMER RELATIONS**
Stephen Joyce

OPERATIONS MANAGER
James Hendry

GENERAL MANAGER
Crawford B. Baptie

MANAGER
Alexander Totten

PLAYER/ASSISTANT MANAGER
Kevin McAllister

CLUB DOCTORS
Dr. R. Gillies Sinclair &
Dr. Ivan Brenkel

PHYSIOTHERAPIST
Alexander MacQueen

**COMMUNITY/YOUTH
DEVELOPMENT OFFICERS**
Ian McIntyre & Fraser Cooper

COMMERCIAL MANAGER
Sarah Scott

**FOOTBALL SAFETY OFFICERS'
ASSOCIATION REPRESENTATIVES**
James Hendry
(01324) 624121

CHIEF SCOUT
Bill Parker

GROUNDSMAN
James Dawson

TELEPHONES
Ground/Commercial/
Ticket Office/Information Service
(01324) 624121
Fax (01324) 612418

E-MAIL & INTERNET ADDRESS
post@falkirkfc.co.uk
www.falkirkfc.co.uk

CLUB SHOP
47 Glebe Street, Falkirk, FK1 1HX
Tel (01324) 639366
Open Mon. – Sat. 9.30 a.m. –
12 Noon and 1.00 p.m. – 5.00 p.m.
(Closed Wed)

OFFICIAL SUPPORTERS CLUB
Association of Falkirk F.C. Supporters
Clubs–Chairman: Gordon McFarlane
Tel (01324) 638104

TEAM CAPTAIN
Scott Crabbe

SHIRT SPONSOR
John R. Weir
Mercedes-Benz Dealer

Falkirk

LIST OF PLAYERS 1999-2000

SURNAME	FIRST NAME	MIDDLE NAME	DATE OF BIRTH	PLACE OF BIRTH	DATE OF SIGNING	HEIGHT FT INS	WEIGHT ST LBS	POS. ON PITCH	PREVIOUS CLUB
Boyle	Joseph		16/05/83	Glasgow	11/08/99	6 0.0	11 8	Mid	Westfield B.C.
Carswell	Allan		26/04/82	Falkirk	13/07/99	5 9.0	12 2	Def	S Form
Christie	Kevin		01/04/76	Aberdeen	28/04/99	6 1.0	12 3	Def	Motherwell
Crabbe	Scott		12/08/68	Edinburgh	17/01/97	5 8.0	11 5	Fwd	Dundee United
Deuchar	Kenneth	Robert John	06/07/80	Stirling	26/08/99	6 3.0	13 0	Fwd	Camelon Juniors
Gray	Alan		14/01/82	Glasgow	03/07/98	6 1.0	10 7	Def	Falkirk B.C.
Hagen	David		05/05/73	Edinburgh	13/10/95	5 11.0	13 0	Fwd	Heart of Midlothian
Henry	John		31/12/71	Vale of Leven	09/09/99	5 10.0	11 0	Mid	Kilmarnock
Hill	Darren		03/12/81	Falkirk	07/07/98	6 1.0	10 6	Gk	Falkirk B.C.
Hogarth	Myles		30/03/75	Falkirk	31/03/99	6 2.5	11 11	Gk	Heart of Midlothian
Hutchison	Gareth	William McKay	04/06/72	Edinburgh	19/08/98	5 10.0	12 0	Fwd	Stenhousemuir
Jones	Allan		27/10/82	Stirling	03/12/98	5 6.0	10 11	Mid	Grangemouth B.C.
Kerr	Mark		02/03/82	Bellshill	03/07/98	5 11.5	10 11	Mid	Falkirk B.C.
Lawrie	Andrew		24/11/78	Galashiels	18/06/96	6 0.0	12 1	Def	Falkirk U'16s
McAllister	Kevin		08/11/62	Falkirk	08/01/97	5 5.0	11 0	Fwd	Hibernian
McDonald	Colin		10/04/74	Edinburgh	05/06/99	5 7.0	10 8	Fwd	Clydebank
McKenzie	Scott		07/07/70	Glasgow	08/09/90	5 9.0	10 5	Mid	Musselburgh Athletic
McLean	Scott	Thomas	27/10/81	Glasgow	07/07/98	5 8.0	9 12	Def	Denny B.C.
McQuilken	James	Charles	03/10/74	Glasgow	14/07/98	5 9.0	10 7	Def	Hibernian
McStay	Garry		21/11/79	Bellshill	06/11/98	5 10.5	11 2	Mid	Bonnybridge Juniors
Morris	Ian		28/08/81	Edinburgh	01/07/98	6 0.5	11 11	Fwd	Rangers B.C.
Nicholls	David	Clarkson	05/04/72	Bellshill	25/05/99	5 8.0	12 6	Mid	Clydebank
Nimmo	Scott		07/04/82	Falkirk	13/07/99	5 10.0	11 9	Mid	S Form
O'Hara	Gerard		29/09/77	Broxburn	25/08/98	5 9.0	10 8	Fwd	Fauldhouse Jnrs
Pearson	Charles		21/04/82	Falkirk	03/07/98	5 7.5	10 5	Fwd	Falkirk B.C.
Rennie	Steven		03/08/81	Stirling	19/07/97	6 2.0	10 12	Def	Hutchison Vale U'15s
Richardson	Grant		15/03/82	Glasgow	26/01/99	5 11.0	10 9	Mid	S Form
Seaton	Andrew	Murray	16/09/77	Edinburgh	18/04/96	5 10.0	11 6	Def	Stoneyburn Juniors
Sinclair	David		06/10/69	Dunfermline	14/10/98	5 11.0	12 12	Def	Dundee United
Thomson	Mark		19/03/83	Glasgow	26/08/99	6 1.0	11 2	Def	Zeneca
Tweedie	Paul		07/06/82	Glasgow	03/07/98	6 0.0	11 0	Fwd	Falkirk B.C.
Waddell	Richard		04/02/81	Falkirk	14/11/97	5 9.0	10 12	Fwd	Stenhousemuir

Milestones

YEAR OF FORMATION: 1876
MOST CAPPED PLAYER: Alex H. Parker
NO. OF CAPS: 14
MOST LEAGUE POINTS IN A SEASON: 66 (First Division – Season 1993/94)(2 Points for a Win) and
66 (First Division – Season 1998/99)(3 Points for a Win)
MOST LEAGUE GOALS SCORED BY A PLAYER IN A SEASON: Evelyn Morrison (Season 1928/29)
NO. OF GOALS SCORED: 43
RECORD ATTENDANCE: 23,100 (-v- Celtic – 21.2.1953)
RECORD VICTORY: 12-1 (-v- Laurieston – Scottish Cup, 23.3.1893)
RECORD DEFEAT: 1-11 (-v- Airdrieonians – Division 1, 28.4.1951)

The Bairns' ten year league record

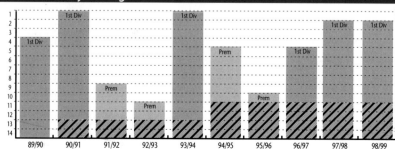

THE BAIRNS' CLUB FACTFILE 1998/99 RESULTS... APPEARANCES... SCORERS

Date	Venue	Opponents	Att.	Res	Mathers P.	Corrigan M.	McQuilken J.	Oliver N.	McCart C.	Hagen D.	McAllister K.	Hamilton B.	Crabbe S.	Keith M.	McKee C.	James K.	Seaton A.	McKenzie S.	Hutchison G.	Duffield P.	O'Hara G.	Henry J.	McStay G.	Sinclair D.	Den Bieman I.	Moss D.	Morrison S.	Hogarth M.	Rennie S.	Kerr M.
Aug 4	H	Ayr United	3,127	1-0	1	2	3	4	5	6	7	8	9[1]	10	11															
15	A	Clydebank	928	1-0	1	2	3	4		6	7	8	9	10[1]	11	5	12	15												
22	H	Hibernian	5,748	1-1	1	2	3	4	5	6	7	14	9	10[1]	15		12	8	11											
29	H	Stranraer	2,741	1-0	1	2	3	4	5		7	14	9	8[1]	15			6	11	10										
Sep 5	A	St. Mirren	2,390	2-0	1	2	3	4	5		7	10	9	8[1]			12	6[1]	15	11										
12	A	Raith Rovers	3,072	1-1	1	2	3		5	11	7		9	8			12	6	14	10[1]	4									
19	H	Airdrieonians	4,157	0-1	1	2	3	4	5	11	7	14	9	8				6	15	10										
26	H	Greenock Morton	3,047	2-1	1	2			5	11	7	14	9[1]	8[1]			3	4	10	15		6								
Oct 3	A	Hamilton Academical	1,427	1-2	1	2			5	11	7	4	9	8			3	12	15	10	6[1]									
11	H	Clydebank	4,316	2-2	1		2[1]		5	11	7		9				3	8	10[1]	15	4	6	14							
17	A	Ayr United	2,731	2-4	1			4		11	7[1]		9	10[1]			3	2	6	8			5							
28	A	Stranraer	502	2-1	1						7	6	9[1]	10[1]			3	2	11	8		14		4	5					
31	H	St. Mirren	3,848	1-1	1						7	6	9	10			3	2	11[1]			8		4	5					
Nov 7	A	Airdrieonians	3,570	3-0	1					14	7	6	9	10[2]			3	2	11	15[1]		8		4	5					
14	H	Raith Rovers	3,611	1-1	1					14	7	6	9	10[1]			3	2	11	15		8		4	5					
21	A	Greenock Morton	1,843	3-0	1	15						6[1]	9	10			3	2	7	11[1]		8[1]		4	5					
28	H	Hamilton Academical	3,325	2-1	1						7	6	9			12	3	2	11[1]	10		8[1]		4	5					
Dec 5	H	Ayr United	4,010	3-0	1		3				7	6[1]	9					2	11[1]	10		8[1]		4	5	15				
12	H	Hibernian	12,572	1-2	1		3				7	6	9			12		2	11	15		8		4	5	10				
19	A	St. Mirren	2,137	3-0	1		2	12	6		7[1]		9[1]				3	8				11[1]		4	5	10				
26	H	Stranraer	3,260	3-2	1		11				7		9	8[2]		5	3	2	14[1]	15				4	6	10				
Jan 2	H	Airdrieonians	4,518	1-1	1						7		9	8		5	3	2	11	15				4	6	10[1]				
9	A	Raith Rovers	3,390	1-2	1		2	14			7		9[1]			5	3	8	11					4	6	10				
16	H	Greenock Morton	2,824	1-2	1		14	6			7		9	8[1]		5	3	2	11					4		10	15			
30	A	Hamilton Academical	1,106	2-0	1		15	2			7		9	8[1]		5		2	11					4	6	10[1]				
Feb 20	H	Hibernian	6,086	1-2	1						7		9	8		5	3	10	11	15				4	6					
27	A	Stranraer	709	1-0	1		2	3	12		7		9	8[1]		5		10	11	15				4	6					
Mar 10	A	Clydebank	289	2-1	1		2	3			7		9	8		5	14		11	15[1]				4	6	10[1]				
13	H	St. Mirren	3,237	1-0	1		2[1]	3	12		7		9	15		5	14	4	11			8			6	10				
20	H	Hamilton Academical	2,206	6-1	1		2	3			7[2]		9[1]	8		5	12		11	15			14[1]	4	6	10[2]				
Apr 3	A	Greenock Morton	1,914	2-3	1		2	3	5[1]		7		9[1]	8				4	11				14		6	10				
10	A	Airdrieonians	1,957	2-1			2[1]	3			7		9	8[1]				4	11				14		6	10		1	5	
17	H	Raith Rovers	2,532	1-0			2	3			7		9[1]	8			14	4	15			11		5	6	10		1		
24	A	Ayr United	2,496	2-1			2	3			7[2]		9	8				4	15			11		5	6	10		1		
May 1	H	Clydebank	2,737	0-2			3				7		9	15				4	11					5	6	10		1	2	8
8	A	Hibernian	14,801	1-2				3	15		7		9[1]					4	11			8		5	6	10		1	2	14
TOTAL FULL APPEARANCES					31	21	21	7	12	9	35	12	36	27	2	11	16	33	24	10	2	11	4	23	24	16		5	3	1
TOTAL SUB APPEARANCES						(3)	(1)	(1)	(2)	(3)		(4)			(2)	(2)	(2)			(8)	(2)	(9)	(7)		(1)	(6)	(1)		(1)	(1)
TOTAL GOALS SCORED							3		1		6	2	10	17				1	6	3				5	1	5				

Small bold figures denote goalscorers.   † denotes opponent's own goal.

Brockville Park

WATSON STREET   HOPE STREET

COOPERAGE LANE

CAPACITY: 7,576; Seated 1,700 Standing 5,876

PITCH DIMENSIONS: 110 yds x 71 yds

FACILITIES FOR DISABLED SUPPORTERS:
Disabled Enclosure opposite Main Stand – takes seven disabled fans in wheelchairs plus one helper each.

Team playing kits

How to get there

Brockville Park can be reached by the following routes:

TRAINS: The main Edinburgh-Glasgow railway line passes by the ground and passengers can alight at Grahamston Station. They will then have a walk of 100 yards to the ground.

BUSES: All buses departing from the city centre pass by Brockville.

CARS: Car parking facilities are available in the Meeks Road car park for coaches and cars and also in a local shopping car park which can hold 500 cars. Supporters coaches and cars will be directed to the appropriate parking area by the police on duty.

Inverness Caledonian Thistle

LIST OF PLAYERS 1999-2000

SURNAME	FIRST NAME	MIDDLE NAME	DATE OF BIRTH	PLACE OF BIRTH	DATE OF SIGNING	HEIGHT FT INS	WEIGHT ST LBS	POS. ON PITCH	PREVIOUS CLUB
Allan	Andrew	Joseph	05/11/80	Inverness	03/12/97	6 1.0	12 7	Def	S Form
Bavidge	Martin		30/04/80	Aberdeen	24/07/99	6 1.0	13 0	Fwd	Forres Mechanics
Byers	Kevin		23/08/79	Kirkcaldy	09/08/99	5 10.0	9 2	Mid	Raith Rovers
Calder	James	Evan	29/07/60	Grantown-on-Spey	29/06/94	5 11.0	13 4	Gk	Inverness Thistle
Cherry	Paul	Robert	14/10/64	Derby	07/07/96	6 0.0	11 6	Mid	St. Johnstone
Christie	Charles		30/03/66	Inverness	05/08/94	5 8.5	11 2	Mid/For	Caledonian
Craig	David	Alexander MacLean	22/01/80	Inverness	24/08/98	5 8.0	11 7	Fwd	Unattached
Farquhar	Gary	Robert	23/02/71	Wick	26/03/99	5 7.0	11 4	Mid	Clachnacuddin
Fridge	Leslie	Francis	27/08/68	Inverness	23/05/97	5 11.0	11 10	Gk	Dundalk
Glancy	Martin	Paul	24/03/76	Glasgow	18/02/99	5 8.0	10 0	Fwd	Dumbarton
Golabek	Stuart		05/11/74	Inverness	27/05/99	5 10.0	11 0	Fwd	Ross County
Hastings	Richard	Corey	18/05/77	Prince George, B.C.	19/07/95	6 0.0	11 8	Def	S Form
Hind	David	Scott	15/02/82	Inverness	24/08/98	6 0.0	11 0	Mid	S Form
Kellacher	Scott	MacKenzie	05/12/80	Inverness	15/05/99	5 7.0	10 12	Mid	Celtic
MacArthur	Iain		18/10/67	Elgin	10/08/95	5 11.0	12 10	Def	Elgin City
MacDonald	Jordan		07/09/82	Inverness	27/07/99	5 9.0	11 12	Mid	Fort William
MacDonald	Neil		08/01/83	Isle of Lewis	24/07/99	5 8.0	10 5	Fwd	S Form
Mann	Robert	Alexander	11/01/74	Dundee	05/02/99	6 3.0	13 7	Def	Forfar Athletic
McCulloch	Mark	Ross	19/05/75	Inverness	22/08/97	5 11.0	12 0	Def	Dunfermline Athletic
McLean	Scott	James	17/06/76	East Kilbride	06/03/98	5 11.5	12 5	Fwd	Clachnacuddin
Munro	Grant	John	15/09/80	Inverness	03/06/99	6 0.0	12 7	Def	Fort William
Newlands	Michael	John	11/08/77	Dufftown	28/07/98	6 2.5	12 10	Def	Aberdeen
Robson	Barry	Gordon George	07/11/78	Aberdeen	15/10/97	5 11.0	12 0	Mid/Fwd	Rangers
Ridgers	Alexander	Trevor	30/06/82	Inverness	24/07/99	6 1.0	10 8	Gk	Inverness Cal. Th. B.C.
Shearer	Duncan	Nicol	28/08/62	Fort William	11/09/97	6 0.0	13 8	Fwd	Aberdeen
Sheerin	Paul	George	28/08/74	Edinburgh	27/01/98	5 10.0	10 4	Def/Mid	Alloa Athletic
Stewart	Graeme		02/04/82	Aberdeen	24/07/99	6 0.0	10 5	Mid	Lewis United
Stewart	Iain	Angus	23/10/69	Dundee	09/06/95	5 7.0	9 12	Fwd	Lossiemouth
Teasdale	Michael	Joseph	28/07/69	Elgin	08/12/95	6 0.0	13 0	Def	Dundee
Tokely	Ross	Norman	08/03/79	Aberdeen	03/06/96	6 3.0	12 0	Mid	Huntly
Wilson	Barry	John	16/02/72	Kirkcaldy	20/07/96	5 11.0	12 4	Fwd	Raith Rovers
Xausa	Davide	Antonio	10/03/76	Vancouver	10/09/99	6 0.0	13 3	Fwd	Dordrecht 90

Milestones

YEAR OF FORMATION: 1994
MOST LEAGUE POINTS IN A SEASON: 76 (Third Division – Season 1996/97) (3 Points for a Win)
MOST LEAGUE GOALS SCORED BY A PLAYER IN A SEASON: Iain Stewart (Season 1996/97)
NO. OF GOALS SCORED: 27
RECORD ATTENDANCE: 4,931 (-v- Ross County – 23.1.1996 - at Telford Street Park)
5,821 (-v- Dundee United – 18.2.1998 - at Caledonian Stadium)
RECORD VICTORY: 8-1 (-v- Annan Athletic – Scottish Cup, 24.1.1998)
RECORD DEFEAT: 0-4 (-v- Queen's Park – Third Division, 20.8.1994)
(-v- Montrose – Third Division, 14.2.1995)
(-v- Forfar Athletic – Third Division, 3.5.1997)

Caley Thistle's ten year league record

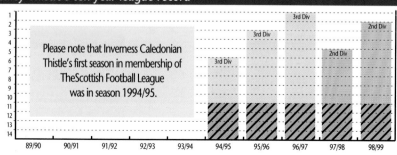

Please note that Inverness Caledonian Thistle's first season in membership of The Scottish Football League was in season 1994/95.

CALEY THISTLE'S CLUB FACTFILE 1998/99 RESULTS... APPEARANCES... SCORERS

Small bold figures denote goalscorers. † denotes opponent's own goal.

Date	Venue	Opponents	Att.	Res	Calder J.	Cherry P.	Sheerin P.	McCulloch M.	Teasdale M.	Farquhar G.	Wilson B.	Shearer D.	McLean S.	Christie C.	Robson B.	Bavidge M.	Hastings R.	Tokely R.	MacArthur I.	Allan A.	Stewart I.	Robertson H.	Addicoat W.	Fridge L.	Glancy M.	Craig D.	Mann R.	Nicol G.
Aug 4	A	Partick Thistle	1,905	1-0	1	2	3	4	5	6	7[1]	8	9	10	11	14												
15	H	Livingston	1,897	2-1	1	2	11	4	5	6	7[1]	8[1]	9	10		14	3											
22	A	Alloa Athletic	616	1-1	1		11	4	2	6	7	8	9	10	14	15	3	5[1]										
29	A	East Fife	814	5-1	1	6[1]	11[1]	4	2[1]		7	8[1]	9	10		14[1]	3	5	12	15								
Sep 5	H	Arbroath	1,836	†2-1	1	6	11	4	10		7	8[1]	9				3	5	2									
12	H	Queen of the South	1,812	3-2	1	6	11[1]	4	2		7[1]	8	9[1]	10	14		3	5	12									
19	A	Stirling Albion	915	1-0	1	6	11	4	2		7	8[1]	9	10	15		3	5				12						
26	A	Clyde	969	1-4	1	6[1]	11	4	2		7		9	10	8		3	5	14			12						
Oct 3	H	Forfar Athletic	1,925	2-2	1	6	11	4	2		7[1]		9[1]	10				5		8		3	15					
10	A	Livingston	4,100	1-2	1	6	11	4	2	14	7		9[1]	10				5		3	8							
17	H	Partick Thistle	2,598	3-2	1	6	11[1]	4	2		7	8	9[2]	10				5		3								
24	H	East Fife	1,547	4-2	1	6	11[1]	4	2		7	8[1]	9[1]	10[1]				5		3								
31	A	Arbroath	934	1-0	1	6[1]	11	4	2	14			9	10				5		3	8							
Nov 7	H	Stirling Albion	2,026	3-1	1	6	11	4			7[1]		9[2]	10	12			5		3	8							
14	A	Queen of the South	1,021	2-2	1	2	11[1]	4	6		7		9[1]	10	12			5		3	8							
21	H	Clyde	2,268	1-1	1	2	11	4	6		7[1]	15	9	10	12	14		5		3	8							
28	A	Forfar Athletic	511	2-2	1	6	11	12	4	8	7	10[1]	9[1]					2		5	3	15						
Dec 16	H	Alloa Athletic	1,323	3-2	1	6	11	2[1]	5	14	7	8	9[1]	10	12			4			3[1]							
19	A	Partick Thistle	2,141	1-2	1	12	2		5	6	7[1]	8	9	10	11			15		4	3							
27	A	East Fife	1,101	2-3	1	6	11	4	2[1]		7	8	9[1]	10				5		12	3	15						
Jan 9	H	Arbroath	1,795	2-0		2	11[1]	6	5		7[1]	12	9	10	14		3	4						1	8			
16	A	Clyde	1,105	1-1			11	6	5		7	12	9	10			3	4	2					1	8[1]	14		
30	H	Forfar Athletic	2,018	2-0	1		11	6	4		7[1]	12	9	10[1]			3	5	2					1	8			
Feb 6	A	Stirling Albion	890	5-1			11[1]	6[1]	4[1]		7	12	9	10	14		3	2						1	8[2]		5	
13	H	Queen of the South	2,204	†1-0			11	6	4		7	8	9	10	12		3	2						1			5	
20	A	Alloa Athletic	595	4-1		12	11	6	4		7[1]	9[2]		10[1]	14		3	2						1	8		5	
27	H	Livingston	3,279	3-1		12	11	6	4		7[1]	8[1]	9[1]	10	15		3	2						1			5	
Mar 6	A	Arbroath	705	1-3		12	11	6	4		7	8	9[1]	10	15		3	2						1		14	5	
13	H	East Fife	1,797	4-0			12[1]	6	4[1]		7[1]	14	9[1]	10	11		3	2		15				1	8		5	
20	A	Forfar Athletic	504	3-0		2	6[1]	7	4	14	12	9[2]	10		11		3							1	8		5	
Apr 3	H	Clyde	3,019	3-0		2	11[1]	6	4		7[1]	12[1]	9	10			3							1	8		5	14
10	H	Stirling Albion	1,778	2-2		2	11	6	4		7	12[2]	9	10			3							1	8		5	14
17	A	Queen of the South	1,214	1-1		2	11	6	4	10	7[1]	9	14	12			3							1			5	8
24	H	Partick Thistle	3,246	3-2		2	11	6[1]	4		7	8	9[2]	10			3					14		1			5	15
May 1	A	Livingston	5,316	3-4			11	6	4		7	8	9	10[1]			3	2				14[1]		1	12		5	
8	H	Alloa Athletic	2,662	1-1			11	6	4		7	8	9	10			3	2				15	14[1]	1	12		5	
TOTAL FULL APPEARANCES					22	24	34	32	36	9	35	21	34	33	4	1	23	23	1	9	1	12	5	14	9		13	1
TOTAL SUB APPEARANCES					(3)	(2)	(1)			(3)		(1)	(9)	(1)	(1)	(11)	(7)		(1)	(3)	(4)	(5)		(4)		(4)	(1)
TOTAL GOALS SCORED						3	10	4	4		14	12	19	4	1			1				1			2		1	3

Caledonian Stadium

MORAY FIRTH

HOME | AWAY

HOME CAR PARK | AWAY SUPPORT CAR PARK

KESSOCK BRIDGE — NORTH — A9 — SOUTH — PERTH
HARBOUR

CAPACITY: 5,580; Seated 2,280, Standing 3,300
PITCH DIMENSIONS: 115 yds x 75 yds
FACILITIES FOR DISABLED SUPPORTERS:
By prior arrangement with the Secretary

Team playing kits

How to get there

The following routes can be used to reach Caledonian Stadium:
TRAINS: Nearest Railway Station is Inverness which is approximately one mile from the ground.
BUSES: Local services available from Union Street situated in Inverness Town Centre opposite the Railway Station.
CARS: The Ground is located on the North side of the A9 Perth/Inverness trunk road and fans should access off the roundabout (first after Perth) before Kessock Bridge. Parking available at stadium.

email: sfl@sol.co.uk • website: www.sfl.scottishfootball.com

Livingston

LIST OF PLAYERS 1999-2000

SURNAME	FIRST NAME	MIDDLE NAME	DATE OF BIRTH	PLACE OF BIRTH	DATE OF SIGNING	HEIGHT FT INS	WEIGHT ST LBS	POS. ON PITCH	PREVIOUS CLUB
Alexander	Neil		10/03/78	Edinburgh	22/08/98	6 1.0	11 7	Gk	Stenhousemuir
Allison	Colin	James	01/07/81	Falkirk	10/08/98	5 7.0	10 7	Fwd	I.C.I. Juveniles
Bennett	John	Neil	22/08/71	Falkirk	06/07/98	5 7.0	10 0	Def/Mid	Stirling Albion
Bingham	David	Thomas	03/09/70	Dunfermline	06/07/98	5 10.0	10 7	Fwd	Dunfermline Athletic
Britton	Gerard	Joseph	20/10/70	Glasgow	14/07/99	6 0.0	11 0	Fwd	Dunfermline Athletic
Clark	Sean	Patrick	10/12/80	Coatbridge	02/10/98	6 1.0	12 0	Def	Albion Rovers
Coughlan	Graham		18/11/74	Dublin	29/03/99	6 2.0	13 5	Fwd	Blackburn Rovers
Courts	Thomas		10/08/81	Kirkcaldy	28/07/98	6 0.0	11 4	Def	Milton Green
Deas	Paul	Andrew	22/02/72	Perth	25/06/98	5 11.0	11 7	Def	Stirling Albion
Fairbairn	Brian		07/04/83	Broxburn	24/08/99	5 8.0	9 9	Fwd	S Form
Fairgrieve	Brydon	Gordon	29/07/83	Edinburgh	24/08/99	5 6.0	9 1	Def	Livingston B.C.
Feroz	Craig		24/10/77	Aberdeen	22/07/98	5 8.0	10 7	Fwd	Brechin City
Fleming	Derek	Adam	05/12/73	Falkirk	20/11/98	5 7.0	10 2	Def/Mid	Dundee
Haggart	Denis	Mochan	14/08/83	Falkirk	24/08/99	5 9.0	11 11	Fwd	Gairdoch B.C.
Keith	Marino		16/12/74	Peterhead	30/07/99	5 10.0	12 12	Fwd	Falkirk
Kelly	Patrick		04/02/68	Paisley	05/07/99	5 7.0	11 0	Def	Newcastle United
King	Charles	Alexander	15/11/79	Edinburgh	07/12/98	5 7.0	10 2	Fwd	St. Johnstone
Little	Ian	James	10/12/73	Edinburgh	25/06/98	5 6.0	8 12	Mid/Fwd	Stenhousemuir
Love	Christopher		04/01/83	Edinburgh	22/01/99	5 9.0	12 0	Fwd	S Form
McCaldon	Ian		14/09/74	Liverpool	21/12/96	6 3.0	12 4	Gk	Glenafton Athletic
McCormick	Mark	Thomas	11/07/79	Bellshill	24/09/97	6 1.0	10 7	Fwd	Harthill Juniors
McEwan	David		26/02/82	Lanark	28/07/98	6 0.0	12 0	Gk	Shotts Bon Accord
McManus	Allan	William	17/11/74	Paisley	23/10/98	6 0.0	12 0	Def	Heart of Midlothian
McPhee	Brian		23/10/70	Glasgow	06/07/98	5 10.0	11 4	Fwd	Airdrieonians
Millar	John		08/12/66	Bellshill	06/07/98	5 10.0	11 10	Mid	Raith Rovers
Millar	Marc		10/04/69	Dundee	14/07/99	5 9.0	10 12	Mid	Dunfermline Athletic
Moffat	Adam		07/05/83	Kirkcaldy	24/08/99	5 10.0	11 0	Mid	S Form
Robertson	John	Grant	02/10/64	Edinburgh	06/07/98	5 6.0	11 4	Fwd	Heart of Midlothian
Santi	Carlo		28/01/84	Glasgow	10/09/99	5 7.0	10 2	Fwd	Celtic South B.C.
Sharp	Alan		16/01/83	Falkirk	24/08/99	5 5.0	8 8	Def	S Form
Sherry	James	Cunningham	09/09/73	Glasgow	26/06/98	5 8.0	12 6	Mid	Hamilton Academical
Sweeney	Sean	Brian	17/08/69	Glasgow	06/07/98	6 0.0	11 0	Def	Airdrieonians
Watson	Gregg		21/09/70	Glasgow	06/07/98	5 9.5	10 9	Def	Partick Thistle
Wilson	Peter	Edward Kirk	06/03/83	Stirling	24/08/99	5 8.0	9 13	Mid	Gairdoch B.C.

Milestones

YEAR OF FORMATION: 1974 (From Seasons 1974/75 to 1994/95 known as Meadowbank Thistle F.C.)
MOST LEAGUE POINTS IN A SEASON: 55 (Second Division – Season 1986/87)(2 Points for a Win)
77 (Third Division – Season 1998/99)(3 Points for a Win)
MOST LEAGUE GOALS SCORED BY A PLAYER IN A SEASON: John McGachie (Season 1986/87)
NO. OF GOALS SCORED: 21
RECORD ATTENDANCE: 2,818 (-v- Albion Rovers, 10.8.1974 at Meadowbank Stadium)
5,316 (-v- Inverness Caledonian Thistle, 1.5.99 at West Lothian Courier Stadium)
RECORD VICTORY: 6-0 (-v- Raith Rovers – Second Division, 9.11.1985)
RECORD DEFEAT: 0-8 (-v- Hamilton Academical – Division 2, 14.12.1974)

Livvy's Lions' ten year league record

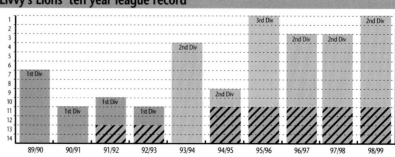

LIVVY'S LIONS' CLUB FACTFILE 1998/99 RESULTS... APPEARANCES... SCORERS

Date	Venue	Opponents	Att.	Res	McCaldon I.	Boyle J.	Deas P.	Conway F.	Watson G.	Millar J.	Rajamaki M.	Bennett J.N.	Bingham D.	Robertson J.	McCormick M.	Little I.	Feroz C.	McManus A.	Sherry J.	McPhee B.	Magee K.	Sweeney S.	King C.	Alexander N.	McMartin G.	Forrest G.	Fleming D.	Harvey P.	Courts T.	Macdonald W.	Coughlan G.	Ferguson I.
Aug 4	H	Stirling Albion	1,496	1-1	1	2	3	4	5	6	7	8	9	10	11¹	12		14														
15	A	Inverness Cal. Th.	1,897	1-2	1	7	3	2	5	8¹	10	6	10	9	14	12	15	4														
22	H	Forfar Athletic	1,193	1-1	1	2	3	6	5		7		10	11¹	9	8		12	4													
29	A	Queen of the South	1,281	1-0	1	2	3	6	5		7	11	12	10	9¹	14		8	4		15											
Sep 5	H	East Fife	3,002	3-1	1	2	3	6	5		7		12	11²	9¹			4	8	10	14											
12	H	Arbroath	2,725	2-1	1		3	4			7	14	11		9	15		2	8¹	10¹	6	5										
19	A	Clyde	1,044	1-1	1		3	4			7	14	12	11¹	9	15		2	8	10	6	5										
26	A	Alloa Athletic	978	4-3	1	2	3¹		6				10	11	9¹	15		4	8²	14		5	7									
Oct 3	A	Partick Thistle	5,200	1-0		2	3¹		6				10	11	9	15		4	8	14		5	7	1	12							
10	H	Inverness Cal. Th.	4,100	2-1		2	3		6				10	11	9¹	15		4	8	14¹		5	7	1	12							
17	A	Stirling Albion	909	3-1		2	3		6				10	11¹	9¹	15		4¹	8	14		5	7	1	12							
24	H	Queen of the South	2,005	2-0		2	3		6				10	11²	9			4		14		5	7	1	12	8						
31	A	East Fife	1,008	3-2		2	3		6				10	11¹	9¹	15¹		4	8	14		5	7	1								
Nov 7	H	Clyde	2,556	2-0		2	3¹		15¹	6			10	11	9	14		4	8	12		5	7	1								
14	A	Arbroath	810	2-2		2	3¹	15	4	6			10	11¹	9	14			8	12		5	7	1								
21	H	Alloa Athletic	1,992	2-1		2	3		5	6¹			10	11	9	12		4	8			7¹	1			15						
28	A	Partick Thistle	2,341	3-1		2	3		5	6			9¹	12		15		4	8¹	11		7	1			10¹						
Dec 12	A	Forfar Athletic	502	2-1		2	3		5	6			11¹	9	14			4	8	12		7¹	1			10						
19	H	Stirling Albion	1,996	0-0		2	3		5	6			11	9	12			4	8			7	1			10						
27	A	Queen of the South	1,221	2-1		2	3	8	5	6¹			11¹	9	14	12		4	14	15		7	1			10						
Jan 16	A	Alloa Athletic	774	3-1		2	3	5		6			11	9¹	10	14¹		4	8	12¹		7	1			15						
20	H	East Fife	1,554	1-0		2	3		5	6¹			11	12		9		14	4	8		10	7	1								
30	H	Partick Thistle	3,293	1-1		2	3		5	6			9	10	14			4	8	12¹		7	1			15	11					
Feb 6	A	Clyde	1,366	3-0		2	3		5				9¹	14	11			4		12¹		7¹	1			8	10	6	15			
16	H	Arbroath	888	1-0		2	3		5	6			9	10				4	8	12		7	1			11¹						
20	H	Forfar Athletic	1,534	5-0		2	3		5	6			9²	10¹	14			4	8	12		7²	1			11	15					
27	A	Inverness Cal. Th.	3,279	1-3		2	3	8	5	6			9	10¹				14	4	12		7	1			11	15					
Mar 6	A	East Fife	995	1-1		2			5	6			9	10	11	14		4	8	12		7	1			15	3¹					
13	H	Queen of the South	2,300	1-2		2¹	3		5	6		8	12	9				14	4		10		7	1			11	15					
20	A	Partick Thistle	2,112	1-1	1	2	3	15	5				10	9	12	8¹	14	4					7				11			6		
Apr 3	A	Alloa Athletic	1,892	1-0	1	2	3		5			15	11	10		6				12¹			7							8	4	9
10	H	Clyde	1,925	2-0	1	2	3		5			14	11	15	12	8				10¹			7¹							6	4	9
17	A	Arbroath	977	1-1	1	2	3		5			6	11	15¹	10	14				12			7							8	4	15
24	A	Stirling Albion	1,404	0-0	1	2	3		5				11	9	14	10		6		12			7							8	4	15
May 1	H	Inverness Cal. Th.	5,316	4-3	1	2	3¹		5	8		15	9	14	12			6		10¹			7²				11				4	
8	A	Forfar Athletic	1,395	2-1	1	2	3		5	8		15	9	14	12			6		10¹			7¹				11				4	
TOTAL FULL APPEARANCES					15	34	35	10	26	30	3	13	29	30	10	7	1	31	20	9	2	10	29	21	2	14	1			5	6	3
TOTAL SUB APPEARANCES								(2)	(1)		(2)	(7)			(6)	(22)	(7)	(10)		(2)	(19)	(1)			(4)	(3)	(1)	(3)	(1)			(1)
TOTAL GOALS SCORED						1	5		1	4			11	12	4	1	1	1	4	9			9			3					

Small bold figures denote goalscorers.   † denotes opponent's own goal.

West Lothian Courier Stadium

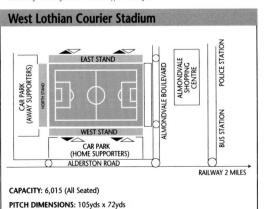

EAST STAND · WEST STAND · NORTH STAND · CAR PARK (AWAY SUPPORTERS) · CAR PARK (HOME SUPPORTERS) · ALMONDVALE BOULEVARD · ALMONDVALE SHOPPING CENTRE · POLICE STATION · BUS STATION · ALDERSTON ROAD · RAILWAY 2 MILES

CAPACITY: 6,015 (All Seated)

PITCH DIMENSIONS: 105yds x 72yds

FACILITIES FOR DISABLED SUPPORTERS:
By prior arrangement with Secretary.

Team playing kits

How to get there

West Lothian Courier Stadium can be reached by the following routes:

BUSES: By bus to terminus at Almondvale Shopping Centre. Follow direction signs for St. John's Hospital or West Lothian Courier Stadium and it is a short 5 minute walk.

TRAINS: To either Livingston North or South Stations, and by taxi to stadium. Approximate cost is £2.00.

CARS: Leave M8 at Livingston Junction (East). Follow signs for St. John's Hospital or West Lothian Courier Stadium.

email: sfl@sol.co.uk • website: www.sfl.scottishfootball.com

Livvy's Lions

Morton

Cappielow Park, Sinclair Street,
Greenock, PA15 2TY

CHAIRMAN
Hugh Scott

DIRECTORS
Mrs Elizabeth A. Scott,
William P. Hunter,
James McCallion &
Gary W. Miller

CHIEF EXECUTIVE
Steve Morgon

SECRETARY
Gary W. Miller

MANAGER
William Stark

HEAD OF YOUTH DEVELOPMENT
Peter Weir

COACH
Frank Connor

BUSINESS DEVELOPMENT MANAGER
Joe Harper

CLUB DOCTOR
Dr. R. Craig Speirs

CROWD DOCTOR
Dr. Fraser Gray

PHYSIOTHERAPIST
Ian Cardle

CHIEF SCOUT
Tom Bell

GROUNDSMAN
Ian Lyle

FOOTBALL SAFETY OFFICERS' ASSOCIATION REPRESENTATIVES
Michael King
Mobile (0385) 380921

KIT MANAGER
Andrew Bryan

STADIUM MANAGER
Alex Renfrew

TELEPHONES
Ground/Ticket Office
(01475) 723571
Fax (01475) 781084

E-MAIL & INTERNET ADDRESS
www.mortonfootballclub.co.uk

CLUB SHOP
Greenock Morton F.C. Enterprises,
85 Cathcart Street, Greenock, PA15 1DE
Tel (01475) 888812
Fax (01475) 785855
Open 9.00 a.m. - 5.30 p.m. Mon - Sat.

OFFICIAL SUPPORTERS CLUB
Greenock Morton Supporters Club,
Regent Street, Greenock

TEAM CAPTAIN
Owen Archdeacon

SHIRT SPONSOR

48

LIST OF PLAYERS 1999-2000

SURNAME	FIRST NAME	MIDDLE NAME	DATE OF BIRTH	PLACE OF BIRTH	DATE OF SIGNING	HEIGHT FT INS	WEIGHT ST LBS	POS. ON PITCH	PREVIOUS CLUB
Aitken	Christopher		31/03/81	Glasgow	03/08/99	5 9.0	10 8	Mid	Erskine B.C.
Aitken	Stephen	Smith	25/09/76	Glasgow	05/12/95	5 6.0	9 7	Mid	Beith Juniors
Anderson	Derek	Christopher	15/05/72	Paisley	24/12/98	6 0.0	11 0	Def	Hartlepool United
Anderson	John	Patton	02/10/72	Greenock	25/01/94	6 2.0	12 2	Def	Gourock Y.A.C.
Archdeacon	Owen		04/03/66	Greenock	21/11/97	5 9.0	10 8	Def/Mid	Carlisle United
Carlin	Andrew		06/01/81	Glasgow	23/02/99	6 1.0	13 4	Gk	Ayr Boswell
Curran	Henry		09/10/66	Glasgow	13/03/98	5 8.0	11 8	Mid	Dunfermline Athletic
Fenwick	Paul	Joseph	25/08/69	London	24/07/98	6 2.0	12 7	Def	St. Mirren
Ferguson	Ian		05/08/68	Dunfermline	29/06/99	6 1.0	13 2	Fwd	Livingston
Hamill	Paul		27/03/81	Greenock	27/08/99	5 8.0	11 0	Def/Mid	S Form
Hart	Michael	John	01/09/80	Rutherglen	03/08/99	5 11.0	10 0	Fwd	Lenzie Youth Club
Hawke	Warren	Robert	20/09/70	Durham	28/07/95	5 10.5	11 4	Fwd	Berwick Rangers
Kerr	Brian		30/10/81	Ayr	23/02/99	5 10.0	11 11	Mid/For	Ayr Boswell
MacDonald	Stuart		15/05/81	Glasgow	03/08/99	5 11.0	10 7	Def	Erskine B.C.
Matheson	Ross		15/11/77	Greenock	02/07/96	5 6.0	9 10	Mid	Rangers
Maxwell	Alastair	Espie	16/02/65	Hamilton	18/09/98	5 10.0	12 13	Gk	Dundee United
McDonald	Paul	Thomas	20/04/68	Motherwell	14/07/99	5 6.5	9 7	Fwd	Partick Thistle
McGregor	David		09/06/81	Greenock	26/08/99	5 11.0	11 7	Def	S Form
McPherson	Craig		27/03/71	Greenock	07/10/94	5 9.0	11 3	Mid	Gourock Amateurs
Millen	Andrew	Frank	10/06/65	Glasgow	01/06/99	5 11.0	11 2	Def	Ayr United
Murie	David		02/08/76	Edinburgh	29/03/99	5 8.0	10 4	Def	Heart of Midlothian
Reid	Stephen		20/01/81	Irvine	26/08/99	5 4.0	10 0	Fwd	Ardeer Thistle
Robb	Ross		09/03/81	Glasgow	03/08/99	5 11.0	11 6	Def	Hillington B.C.
Slavin	Bryan		23/09/77	Irvine	22/10/97	5 9.0	11 1	Def	Dalry Thistle
Tweedie	Garry		02/01/81	Ayr	23/02/99	5 11.0	12 0	Def/Mid	Ayr Boswell
Whalen	Stephen		03/05/82	Irvine	23/02/99	5 8.0	11 1	Fwd	Ayr Boswell
Wright	Keith	Arthur	17/05/65	Edinburgh	20/11/98	5 11.0	12 6	Fwd	Raith Rovers

Milestones

YEAR OF FORMATION: 1874
MOST CAPPED PLAYER: Jimmy Cowan
NO. OF CAPS: 25
MOST LEAGUE POINTS IN A SEASON: 69 (Division 2 – Season 1966/67)
MOST LEAGUE GOALS SCORED BY A PLAYER IN A SEASON: Allan McGraw (Season 1963/64)
NO. OF GOALS SCORED: 58
RECORD ATTENDANCE: 23,500 (-v- Celtic – 1922)
RECORD VICTORY: 11-0 (-v- Carfin Shamrock – Scottish Cup, 13.11.1886)
RECORD DEFEAT: 1-10 (-v- Port Glasgow Athletic, 5.5.1884)

The Ton's ten year league record

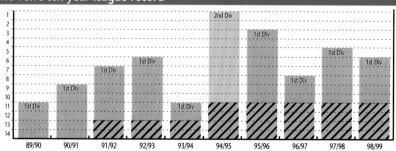

THE TON'S CLUB FACTFILE 1998/99 RESULTS... APPEARANCES... SCORERS

Small bold figures denote goalscorers. † denotes opponent's own goal.

Date	V	Opponents	Att.	Res	Wylie D.	Collins D.	Archdeacon O.	Curran H.	Anderson J.	Fenwick P.	George M.	Matheson R.	Hawke W.	Duffield P.	Twaddle K.	Blaikie A.	Blair P.	Aitken S.	Foster M.	Morrow J.	McPherson C.	Juttla J.	Maxwell A.	McCormick S.	Thomas K.	Wright K.	Slavin B.	Tweedie G.	Anderson D.	Whalen S.	Murie D.	McDonald S.
Aug 4	H	Hibernian	5,747	0-1	1	2	3	4	5	6	7	8	9	10	11	14	16															
15	A	Ayr United	2,329	0-1	1	2	3	4	5	6			9	10	11				7	8	14											
22	H	Hamilton Academical	1,691	1-2	1	2	3	4	5	6[1]			9	16	11	12			7	8		10										
29	H	Clydebank	1,382	2-2	1	2	3	4[1]	5[1]	6			9		11				8	7		10										
Sep 5	A	Raith Rovers	1,880	0-0	1	2	3	4	5	6			9		11				8	7	14	10										
12	A	Airdrieonians	2,243	1-0	1	2	3	4	5	6			9[1]		11	14			8	7	12	10										
19	H	St. Mirren	4,108	0-1		2	3		5	6		16	9		11	12		4	8	7	10		1									
26	A	Falkirk	3,047	1-2		2	3	4	5	6[1]		7	9		11				8		10	14	1									
Oct 3	H	Stranraer	1,444	3-0		2	3	4	5	6		7[1]	9		11[1]	14[1]			8		10		1									
11	H	Ayr United	2,156	1-2		2	3	4	5	6		7	9[1]		11				8		14		1		10							
17	A	Hibernian	9,524	1-2		2	3	4	5	6		7	9		11				8		10		1	12								
27	H	Clydebank	452	1-2		2	3	4	5	6[1]		7	9		11	16			8		10		1	12								
31	H	Raith Rovers	1,468	2-0		2	3	4	5	6		7	9[1]		11			12	8		14		1		10[1]							
Nov 7	A	St. Mirren	4,776	0-1		2	3	4	5	6		7	9	16	11				8		14		1		10							
14	H	Airdrieonians	1,935	0-0		2	3	4	5	6		7	9		11			12	8		14		1		10							
21	H	Falkirk	1,843	0-3		2	3	4	5	6		7			11	16		12	8		14		1		10			9				
28	A	Stranraer	795	3-2		2	3	4	5[1]	6[1]		14	9		11[1]			7	8		12		1	8	10							
Dec 5	H	Hibernian	3,150	1-3		2	3		5	6[1]		14	9		11			4	7				1	8	10							
12	A	Hamilton Academical	1,012	0-0		2	3		5	6		12	9		11			4	7				1	8	10							
19	A	Raith Rovers	2,721	3-1		2	3	4[2]	5	6		14	9		11			12	8	7			1	16	10[1]							
26	H	Clydebank	1,947	1-1		2	3	4	5[1]	6		14	9		11				8	7			1	16	10							
Jan 5	H	St. Mirren	2,936	0-0		2	3	4	5	6		14	9		11			12	8	7			1		10							
16	A	Falkirk	2,824	2-1		2	3	8	5	6		7	9		11[1]			12					1		10[1]		14		4			
19	A	Airdrieonians	1,801	†2-0		2	3	4	5	6		8[1]	9		11			12	7				1		10		14			16		
30	H	Stranraer	1,581	1-0		2	3	4	5	6		8[1]	9		11			12	7				1		10		14			16		
Feb 6	A	Ayr United	2,222	0-1		2	3		5	6		8	9		11			12	7				1		10		14		4	16		
20	H	Hamilton Academical	1,914	3-0		2	3	8[1]	5	6			9		11			12	7				1		10		14[2]		4	16		
Mar 13	H	Raith Rovers	1,795	1-1		2	3	8	5	6					11				7				1		10[1]	9	14		4			16
20	A	Stranraer	563	1-0		2	3	8	5	6					11				7				1		10[1]	9	14		4			
Apr 3	H	Falkirk	1,914	3-2		2	3	8[1]	5[1]	6					11			12	7				1		10	9[1]	14		4	16		
10	A	St. Mirren	3,538	5-1		2	3	8	5	6					11				7				1		10[3]	9[2]	14		4	16	5	
17	H	Airdrieonians	1,442	0-2		2	3	8		6					11			12	7				1		10	9	14		4	16	5	
21	A	Clydebank	402	2-1		2	3	8	5[1]	6			9		11			12	7				1		10[1]		14		4	16		
24	H	Hibernian	8,865	1-2		2	3	8	5	6					11			12	7				1		10	9	14		4[1]	16		
May 1	H	Ayr United	2,337	1-4		2	3	8	5[1]	6					11			12	7				1		10	9			4			
8	A	Hamilton Academical	744	2-0		2	3	8	5	6						14		12	7				1		10[1]	9[1]			4			16
TOTAL FULL APPEARANCES					6	18	33	33	33	31	1	17	27	2	31	3		19	14	4	20	4	30	3	22	10	11	2	16	6		
TOTAL SUB APPEARANCES											(3)	(14)		(4)	(1)			(9)	(2)	(4)	(5)	(1)		(13)	(4)	(2)	(6)	(4)	(1)	(1)	(1)
TOTAL GOALS SCORED								5	6	5		1	3		5	1									1	9	6		1		

Cappielow Park

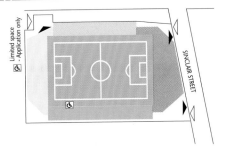

Limited space - Application only

SINCLAIR STREET

CAPACITY: 8,100; Seating 5,741, Standing 2,359
PITCH DIMENSIONS: 110 yds x 71 yds
FACILITIES FOR DISABLED SUPPORTERS:
Seating facilities below Grandstand.

Team playing kits

How to get there

Cappielow Park may be reached by the following routes:
BUSES: Services from Glasgow stop just outside the park. There are also services from Port Glasgow and Gourock.
TRAINS: The nearest local station is Cartsdyke and it is a five minute walk from here to the ground. There are two to three trains every hour from Glasgow and from Gourock.
CARS: Temporary Car Park adjacent to Stadium.

email: sfl@sol.co.uk • website: www.sfl.scottishfootball.com

RAITH ROVERS FOOTBALL CLUB

Stark's Park, Pratt Street,
Kirkcaldy, Fife, KY1 1SA

CHAIRMAN
William Gray

DIRECTORS
James White, Mario Caira,
Daniel Smith & Colin C. McGowan

PRESIDENT
John Urquhart

COMPANY SECRETARY
Eric Drysdale

OFFICE MANAGER
William McPhee

MANAGER
John McVeigh

ASSISTANT MANAGER
Peter Hetherston

YOUTH COACHES
Kenny Black & David Kirkwood

CLUB DOCTOR
Nicol Street/St. Brycedale Surgery

PHYSIOTHERAPIST
John Cooper

**FOOTBALL SAFETY OFFICERS'
ASSOCIATION REPRESENTATIVE**
Brian Murray (01592) 263514

GROUNDSMAN
John Murray

KIT MANAGER
John Valente

COMMERCIAL MANAGER
Pat McAuley

COMMERCIAL EXECUTIVE
Jennifer Tottenham

TELEPHONES
Ground (01592) 263514
Fax (01592) 642833

E-MAIL & INTERNET ADDRESS
www.raithrovers.com

CLUB SHOP
South Stand Shop situated within
stand. Open home matchdays
only 2.00 p.m. to 5.00 p.m.

OFFICIAL SUPPORTERS CLUB
c/o Fraser Hamilton,
22 Tower Terrace, Kirkcaldy, Fife

TEAM CAPTAIN
Guido Van De Kamp

SHIRT SPONSOR
Fife Fabrications

LIST OF PLAYERS 1999-2000

SURNAME	FIRST NAME	MIDDLE NAME	DATE OF BIRTH	PLACE OF BIRTH	DATE OF SIGNING	HEIGHT FT INS	WEIGHT ST LBS	POS. ON PITCH	PREVIOUS CLUB
Agathe	Didier		16/08/75	Saint Pierre	31/08/99	6 1.0	12 7	Fwd	Montpellier Herault S.C.
Agnew	Paul		28/06/72	Coatbridge	08/07/99	5 7.0	10 10	Mid	Ayr United
Andrews	Marvin	Anthony	22/12/75	Trinidad & Tobago	11/02/98	6 2.0	13 0	Def	Carib
Black	Kenneth	George	29/11/63	Stenhousemuir	02/07/99	5 9.0	11 10	Mid	Airdrieonians
Browne	Paul	Gerard	17/02/75	Glasgow	03/07/96	6 2.0	12 6	Def	Aston Villa
Burns	Alexander		04/08/73	Bellshill	06/07/99	5 8.0	10 6	Mid	Southend United
Clark	Andrew	Alexander	21/04/80	Stirling	01/07/98	5 10.0	10 12	Fwd	Hutchison Vale B.C.
Coyle	Craig	Robert	06/09/80	Edinburgh	01/07/98	5 10.0	10 7	Gk	Salvesen B.C.
Craig	Steven		05/02/81	Blackburn	02/07/98	5 10.0	11 0	Fwd	Hutchison Vale B.C.
Dargo	Craig	Peter	03/01/78	Edinburgh	11/10/95	5 6.0	10 1	Fwd	Links United
Ellis	Laurence		07/11/79	Edinburgh	02/07/98	5 11.0	10 7	Def	Links United
Fotheringham	George	Thomas	13/03/81	Glasgow	01/07/98	5 11.0	11 0	Mid	Cathkin United
Gaughan	Kevin		06/03/78	Glasgow	02/07/99	6 1.0	12 2	Def	Partick Thistle
Hamilton	Steven	James	19/03/75	Baillieston	13/07/99	5 9.0	12 10	Def	Kilmarnock
Hampshire	Paul	Christopher	20/09/81	Edinburgh	02/07/98	5 11.0	10 7	Mid	Hutchison Vale
Hetherston	Brian		23/11/76	Bellshill	20/07/99	6 0.0	10 6	Mid	Sligo Rovers
Hughes	James		30/08/82	Falkirk	03/08/99	6 0.0	12 0	Gk	Gairdoch United B.C.
Kirkwood	David	Stewart	27/08/67	St. Andrews	18/07/97	6 0.0	12 7	Mid	Airdrieonians
Maughan	Roderick	Edward Alexander	18/12/80	Edinburgh	01/07/00	5 10.0	10 8	Mid	Granton B.C.
McCulloch	Greig		18/04/76	Girvan	24/02/96	5 8.0	10 7	Def	Aberdeen
McEwan	Craig	George	03/10/77	Glasgow	16/07/97	5 8.5	11 0	Def	Clyde
McInally	David		03/03/81	Glasgow	01/07/98	5 6.0	9 7	Fwd	Cathkin United
McKenzie	James		29/11/80	Bellshill	08/07/99	5 7.5	10 7	Mid	Partick Thistle
McLeish	Kevin	Michael	03/12/80	Edinburgh	01/07/00	5 10.0	10 8	Mid	Edina Hibs
McManus	Scott		18/06/82	Perth	13/07/99	5 6.0	9 0	Mid	Rosyth Recreation
Mill	Christopher		16/02/80	Kirkcaldy	29/05/98	5 9.0	11 0	Def	Kelty Hearts
Morrison	Stuart		23/12/80	Falkirk	02/07/98	6 2.0	13 0	Def	Hutchison Vale B.C.
Nicol	Kevin	Andrew	19/01/82	Kirkcaldy	01/07/98	5 8.0	11 2	Mid	Hill O' Beath
Penman	George	Strachan Beveradge	14/01/82	Dunfermline	29/05/98	5 9.0	10 8	Def	Rosyth Recreation
Rushford	John		09/02/82	Dunfermline	13/07/99	5 11.0	10 7	Mid	Rosyth Recreation
Shields	Dene		16/09/82	Edinburgh	14/07/99	5 9.0	12 0	Fwd	Granton B.C.
Shields	Paul	Martin	15/08/81	Dunfermline	02/06/98	5 11.0	12 0	Fwd	Milton Green
Smart	Craig		26/11/78	Kirkcaldy	25/08/97	5 9.0	12 0	Fwd	Glenrothes Juniors
Stein	Jay		13/01/79	Dunfermline	11/10/95	5 7.5	10 7	Mid	Inverkeithing United
Stewart	Allan		14/04/81	Glasgow	01/07/98	5 10.0	10 8	Fwd	Cathkin United
Tosh	Paul	James	18/10/73	Arbroath	02/07/99	6 0.0	11 1	Fwd	Hibernian
Tosh	Steven	William	27/04/73	Kirkcaldy	31/03/98	5 11.0	11 7	Mid	St. Johnstone
Van De Kamp	Guido		08/02/64	's-Hertogenbosch	01/07/97	6 2.5	12 12	Gk	Dunfermline Athletic
Venables	Ross	Adam	22/03/79	Dartford	02/09/97	5 10.0	10 7	Mid	Millwall
Waldie	Colin		06/02/81	Lanark	13/01/99	5 7.5	10 3	Mid	Motherwell
Webster	Kevin	Peter	09/06/81	Kirkcaldy	29/05/98	5 5.0	9 0	Def	Milton Green

Milestones

YEAR OF FORMATION: 1883
MOST CAPPED PLAYER: David Morris
NO. OF CAPS: 6
MOST LEAGUE POINTS IN A SEASON: 65 (First Division - Season 1992/93)(2 Points for a Win)
69 (First Division - Season 1994/95)(3 Points for a Win)
MOST LEAGUE GOALS SCORED BY A PLAYER IN A SEASON: Norman Heywood (Season 1937/38)
NO. OF GOALS SCORED: 42
RECORD ATTENDANCE: 31,306 (-v- Heart of Midlothian – Scottish Cup, 7.2.1953)
RECORD VICTORY: 10-1 (-v- Coldstream – Scottish Cup, 13.2.1954)
RECORD DEFEAT: 2-11 (-v- Morton – Division 2, 18.3.1936)

The Rovers' ten year league record

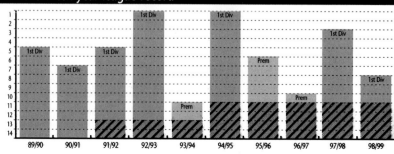

THE ROVERS' CLUB FACTFILE 1998/99 RESULTS... APPEARANCES... SCORERS

Date	Venue	Opponents	Att.	Res	Van De Kamp G.	McEwan C.	McPherson D.	McCulloch G.	Browne P.	Fotheringham K.	Hartley P.	Bowman D.	Wright K.	Tosh S.	Dair J.	Dair L.	Stein J.	Venables R.	Cameron I.	Smart C.	Shields P.	Robertson G.	Dargo C.	Andrews M.	Lennon D.	Byers K.	Fotheringham C.	Britton G.	Ellis L.	Brownlie P.	Holmes D.	Kirkwood D.	McKeown M.	Cormack P.	McQuade J.	McLeish K.	Maughan R.	Nicol K.	McInally D.	Clark A.
Aug 4	H	Hamilton Academical	2,316	0-2	1	2	3	4	5	6	7	8	9	10	11			14		16																				
15	A	St. Mirren	2,106	1-2	1		3	12	5		6	7	8		9	10	2	16	4	11[1]	14																			
22	H	Ayr United	2,010	0-0	1	2		12	5		6	7	4		9	10	3		11	16	8	14																		
29	A	Airdrieonians	2,297	1-0	1	2		12	5		6	7[1]	8		10	3			4	11		14	9																	
Sep 5	H	Greenock Morton	1,880	0-0	1			2	5	6	7	8	12	10	3		16		11		9	4																		
12	H	Falkirk	3,072	1-1	1	2		8	12	5	6	7	4		10	3			11		16	14	9[1]																	
19	A	Hibernian	8,853	1-3	1	2			4	5		7	8	12[1]	10	3			11		16		9	6																
26	A	Stranraer	618	2-2	1	2			5	4	7[1]	8	9	10	3[1]			11	16				6	14																
Oct 3	H	Clydebank	1,661	0-1	1	2		16	4	6	7	8	14	12	3			11				9	5	10																
11	H	St. Mirren	1,963	1-0	1			2	5	6	7		9[1]		3		11		10			12	4	8	16															
17	A	Hamilton Academical	790	2-3	1	12		2	6		7	4	9	8[2]	3		16					10	5	11																
31	A	Greenock Morton	1,468	0-2	1			2	5		7	4		10	3			12	8	16		9	6	4	14	16														
Nov 3	H	Airdrieonians	1,406	1-3	1			12	5		7	2	8	10	3			11[1]				9	6	4	14	16														
7	H	Hibernian	4,925	1-3	1	2			5	6	7	8	12		3		16	11			9[1]	14	10	4																
14	A	Falkirk	3,611	1-1	1	2		12	5	6			11	8	3		14	10			9[1]		7	4																
21	H	Stranraer	1,938	2-0	1			2	5	6	7[1]			12	3			11			9[1]		8	4	10															
28	A	Clydebank	417	1-1	1			12	2		6	7[1]			4	3		14	11			5	8	10	9															
Dec 8	H	Hamilton Academical	1,929	1-1	1	14			2		6	7			4	3			11			9	5	8	12	10[1]														
12	A	Ayr United	2,245	†2-0	1	2			4	5	6	7	10		3[1]		12					8	11	9																
19	H	Greenock Morton	2,721	1-3	1	2		5		6		10			3		12	11[1]	7	16		8	4		9	14														
26	A	Airdrieonians	2,077	2-2	1	2			6	5			4		3		12[1]	11[1]		10	16	9	8	7		14														
Jan 2	A	Hibernian	14,703	1-5	1	2			4	5					3			11		10	12	6	9[1]	8	7		16	14												
9	H	Falkirk	3,390	2-1	1	2			4	6		7		11	3		12[1]					9	5	8			16	10[1]	14												
16	A	Stranraer	575	0-2	1	2		12	6			4			3			11				9	5	8			14	10	7											
30	H	Clydebank	1,803	2-1		2			6	8		4		7[1]	3[1]		14	11	9			5	12		16			10		1										
Feb 6	A	St. Mirren	1,621	1-3		2				6		4		7	3		11	10	9			5[1]			16		14	12	8		1									
20	A	Ayr United	1,873	2-4					5	11		7		4	2		10		16		9	6	12				14	8[2]			1	3								
27	A	Airdrieonians	1,896	0-1	1	2			6	12	3			4			16	11		9	14	5	8				7	10												
Mar 13	A	Greenock Morton	1,795	1-1	1	2			4	5	3			7	8		16	11			9[1]	6	12				10	14												
20	A	Clydebank	300	0-0	1	2			4	5	3			7	8		11	10	16		6						9												
Apr 3	H	Stranraer	1,883	3-2	1	12			7	4	3[1]			2			11	6			9[1]	5	8				10					16[1]							
10	H	Hibernian	5,730	1-3	1	2			7	5	3			4			11				9	6	8				14	10[1]				12	16						
17	A	Falkirk	2,532	0-1	1	2			7	5	6										9	12	8	14			3	16	10	4		11							
24	A	Hamilton Academical	1,398	2-1	1	2			7	5	6				16						9[1]	12	8	14			3	10[1]	4			11							
May 1	H	St. Mirren	2,380	1-1	1				6	5					11						9	14					3	16	10[1]	4		12	8	2	7				
8	A	Ayr United	1,886	0-1	1	2			6						12						5		8	7			3	10	4		9					14	11	16
TOTAL FULL APPEARANCES					33	23	3	23	31	26	18	23	8	23	27		6	2	26	3	6	3	21	19	21	10	1	5	4	2	13	5	3	1	3	1	1	1	1
TOTAL SUB APPEARANCES					(3)	(1)	(8)	(1)			(4)	(2)			(2)	(14)			(2)	(3)	(8)	(3)	(1)	(5)	(4)	(5)	(4)		(5)	(7)	(1)	(1)		(3)	(1)		(1)		(1)
TOTAL GOALS SCORED									1	4			2	3	3		1		5				8	1				1			6				1			

Small bold figures denote goalscorers. † denotes opponent's own goal.

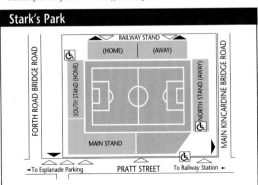

Stark's Park

FORTH ROAD BRIDGE ROAD — SOUTH STAND (HOME) — RAILWAY STAND (HOME) (AWAY) — NORTH STAND (AWAY) — MAIN KINCARDINE BRIDGE ROAD — MAIN STAND — ◄ To Esplanade Parking — PRATT STREET — To Railway Station ►

CAPACITY: 10,271 (All Seated)

PITCH DIMENSIONS: 113 yds x 70 yds

FACILITIES FOR DISABLED SUPPORTERS:
By prior arrangement with the Secretary.
North Stand – Away Supporters. South Stand – Home Supporters.

Team playing kits

How to get there

The following routes may be used to reach Stark's Park:
TRAINS: Kirkcaldy railway station is served by trains from Dundee, Edinburgh and Glasgow (via Edinburgh) and the ground is within walking distance of the station.
BUSES: The main bus station in Kirkcaldy is also within 15 minutes walking distance of the ground, but the Edinburgh, Dunfermline and Leven services pass close by the park.
CARS: Car parking is available in the Esplanade, which is on the south side of the ground, in Beveridge Park, which is on the north side of Stark's Road, and in ground adjacent to the railway station.

email: sfl@sol.co.uk • website: www.sfl.scottishfootball.com

St. Mirren Park, Love Street,
Paisley, PA3 2EJ

CHAIRMAN
Stewart G. Gilmour

VICE-CHAIRMAN
George P. Campbell

DIRECTORS
Bryan A. McAusland,
Mrs Jill Lucas &
Mrs Helen McGeoch

HON. PRESIDENT
William Todd, M.B.E., J.P.

SECRETARY
Allan W. Marshall, LL.B.

MANAGER
Thomas Hendrie

ASSISTANT MANAGER
John Coughlin

**CHIEF SCOUT/YOUTH
DEVELOPMENT OFFICER**
Joe Hughes

PHYSIOTHERAPIST
Colin Brow, B.Sc.(Hons), M.C.S.P.

CLUB DOCTOR
Stewart McCormick, M.B., Ch.B.

GROUNDSMAN
Tom Docherty

COMMERCIAL MANAGER
Campbell Kennedy
(0141) 840 1337

LOTTERY CO-ORDINATOR
Jim Crawford

CATERING MANAGERESS
Mrs. Sally A. MacDonald

SPORTS COMPLEX MANAGER
Jack Copland

**FOOTBALL SAFETY OFFICERS'
ASSOCIATION REPRESENTATIVE**
Peter Copland
(0141) 889 2558

PROGRAMME EDITOR
Alastair MacLachlan

COMMUNITY COACH
Matt Kerr

TELEPHONES
Ground (0141) 889 2558/840 1337
Enquiries (0141) 849 0611
Sports Leisure Complex
(0141) 849 0609
Fax (0141) 848 6444

CLUB SHOP
Situated in Sports Complex
Open 7.30 a.m. – 10.00 p.m.
Seven days a week.

OFFICIAL SUPPORTERS CLUB
St. Mirren Supporters' Club,
11 Knox Street, Paisley

TEAM CAPTAIN
Thomas Turner

SHIRT SPONSOR
CETCO

52

LIST OF PLAYERS 1999-2000

SURNAME	FIRST NAME	MIDDLE NAME	DATE OF BIRTH	PLACE OF BIRTH	DATE OF SIGNING	HEIGHT FT INS	WEIGHT ST LBS	POS. ON PITCH	PREVIOUS CLUB
Baltacha	Sergei	Sergeevich	28/07/79	Kiev	16/01/99	6 5.0	12 0	Def	Kinnoul Juniors
Brown	Thomas	Heron	01/04/68	Glasgow	04/06/97	5 7.0	10 10	Fwd	Kilmarnock
Drew	Colin		05/05/79	Paisley	31/07/97	5 9.0	11 3	Def	Giffnock North
Gallacher	Stephen		29/07/81	Glasgow	05/07/99	6 0.0	11 3	Def	St. Mirren B.C.
Gallagher	Kieran		25/05/81	Bellshill	26/04/99	5 7.0	10 1	Fwd	St. Mirren B.C.
Kerr	Christopher		06/09/78	Paisley	31/07/97	6 0.0	11 2	Def	St. Mirren B.C.
McGarry	Steven		28/09/79	Paisley	21/01/97	5 9.0	11 0	Fwd	Giffnock North
McLaughlin	Barry	John	19/04/73	Paisley	01/08/91	6 1.0	13 1	Def	St. Mirren B.C.
McQuilter	Ronald		24/12/70	Glasgow	11/06/98	6 1.0	12 7	Def	Dundalk
McWhirter	Norman		04/09/69	Johnstone	16/09/85	5 10.0	11 10	Def	Linwood Rangers B.C.
Mendes	Junior	Albert	15/09/76	London	30/04/96	5 10.0	11 12	Fwd	Chelsea
Murray	Hugh		08/01/79	Bellshill	21/01/97	5 10.0	11 0	Midfield	Giffnock North
Nicolson	Iain		13/10/76	Glasgow	30/07/98	5 10.0	11 1	Midfield	Partick Thistle
Robinson	Ryan	Robert Kennedy	30/08/80	Paisley	21/04/99	5 10.0	10 2	Def/Mid	St. Mirren B.C.
Ross	Ian		27/08/74	Broxburn	11/07/99	5 10.0	11 10	Midfield	Motherwell
Roy	Ludovic		18/08/77	Tours	05/09/98	6 1.0	12 3	Gk	La Berrichonne de Chateauroux
Rudden	Paul		10/08/80	Glasgow	18/06/98	5 8.0	10 8	Def	St. Mirren B.C.
Scrimgour	Derek		29/03/78	Glasgow	06/09/95	6 3.0	14 2	Gk	Largs Thistle
Turner	Thomas	Gibson	11/10/63	Johnstone	09/01/97	5 10.0	10 7	Midfield	Partick Thistle
Walker	Scott	Edward	05/03/75	Glasgow	21/05/99	6 1.0	13 9	Def	East Stirlingshire
Yardley	Mark		14/09/69	Livingston	22/09/95	6 2.0	13 1	Fwd	Cowdenbeath

Milestones

YEAR OF FORMATION: 1877
MOST CAPPED PLAYERS: Iain Munro & Billy Thomson
NO. OF CAPS: 7
MOST LEAGUE POINTS IN A SEASON: 62 (Division 2 – Season 1967/68)
MOST LEAGUE GOALS SCORED BY A PLAYER IN A SEASON: Dunky Walker (Season 1921/22)
NO. OF GOALS SCORED: 45
RECORD ATTENDANCE: 47,438 (-v- Celtic 7.3.1925)
RECORD VICTORY: 15-0 (-v- Glasgow University – Scottish Cup, 30.1.1960)
RECORD DEFEAT: 0-9 (-v- Rangers – Division 1, 4.12.1897)

The Buddies' ten year league record

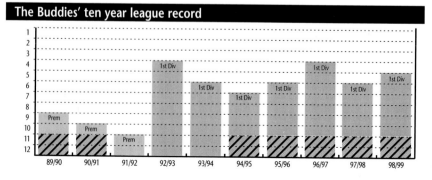

THE BUDDIES' CLUB FACTFILE 1998/99 RESULTS... APPEARANCES... SCORERS

Date	Venue	Opponents	Att.	Res	Scrimgour D.	McNamee D.	Nicolson I.	Rudden P.	McQuilter R.	McLaughlin B.	Murray H.	Drew C.	McCarry S.	Mendes J.	Brown T.	Yardley M.	Prentice A.	Milne D.	McWhirter N.	Kerr C.	O'Brien B.	Turner T.	Creaney G.	Roy L.	Walker P.	Innes C.	Cameron D.	Robinson R.
Aug 5	A	Stranraer	1,058	1-0	1	2	3¹	4	5	6	7	8	9	10	11	14	15											
15	H	Raith Rovers	2,106	2-1	1	3	8¹	6	5	2	7	4	9	14	11¹	12				10								
22	A	Airdrieonians	3,073	0-1	1	3	8	6	5	2	7	4	9	14	11	12				10								
29	A	Hamilton Academical	1,575	0-0	1	3	8	6	5	2	7		9	14	11	12				10	4	15						
Sep 5	H	Falkirk	2,390	0-2	1	3	8	6	5	2	7		9	14		12				11	4	15	10					
12	H	Hibernian	3,638	2-0	1	2	12¹	6	5	8	7		9			11¹				10	4	3	14	15				
19	A	Greenock Morton	4,108	1-0	1	2	10	6	5	8	7		9¹			11					4	3	14					
26	A	Clydebank	1,462	0-1	1	2	10	6	5	8	7		9			11					4	3	14					
Oct 3	A	Ayr United	2,673	0-2	1	2		6	5		7	11	14	10	9	12		15		4	3		8					
11	H	Raith Rovers	1,963	0-1	1	2	10	6	5	8	7		9		14	11		7		4		15						
17	H	Stranraer	2,884	1-0	1	3	6	2	5	7	12	8	9	14	11	15¹				4			10					
24	H	Hamilton Academical	2,312	3-2	1	2	11	12	5	6	7	8	14¹		9	15				4	3		10²					
31	A	Falkirk	3,848	1-1	1	2	7	3	5	6		8	9		14	11	15¹			4	12		10					
Nov 7	H	Greenock Morton	4,776	1-0	1	2		12	5	6	7	8	9¹	14	11	15				4	3		10					
21	H	Clydebank	2,847	0-0	1		12	6	5	2	7	8	9		11	15	14			4	3		10					
24	A	Hibernian	9,153	1-4	1	3	12	6	5	2	7	8	14		15	11¹		9		4			10					
28	A	Ayr United	3,640	1-1	1		2		5	6	7		14		9	11¹	8	12		4	3		10					
Dec 5	A	Stranraer	890	2-1	1		8		5	6	15	2	9¹		7¹	11				4	3		10					
12	H	Airdrieonians	2,306	1-5	12	3	2	5	6	7	4		9		8	11		14				15	10¹					
19	H	Falkirk	2,137	0-3	2	8			5	6	7		9							4	3	14	10	1				
26	H	Hamilton Academical	1,450	0-0	2	8			5	6	7		9					14		4	3	11	10	1		12		
Jan 5	A	Greenock Morton	2,936	0-0	2		12			6	7	5	9	10		11					3	8	4	1				
9	A	Hibernian	6,674	1-2	2	12			5				9	10	15	11					3¹	8	4	14	1		6	
16	A	Clydebank	934	†2-2	2								15	10	9¹	11					3	8	4		1		6	
30	H	Ayr United	2,670	1-0	3		12	5			7	2	15	10¹	9	11						8	4		1		6	
Feb 6	H	Raith Rovers	1,621	3-1	2					6¹	7	14	12¹	10	9	11¹					3	8	4	1			5	15
23	A	Airdrieonians	1,860	3-0	2	14			5		7		9¹	10¹		11				4		8	3		1		6	12¹
27	H	Hamilton Academical	2,130	1-0	2	7			5				9	10		11					3	8¹	4		1		6	14
Mar 13	A	Falkirk	3,237	0-1	2	12			5		7		9	10	15	11				4	3	8			1		6	14
20	A	Ayr United	2,436	2-2		2		14	5		7				10¹	11¹				4	3	8			1		6	9
Apr 3	H	Clydebank	1,756	1-0		2		14	5		7		9	10		11				4	3¹	8			1		6	12
10	H	Greenock Morton	3,538	1-5	3	2	14				7		9	10		11¹	15			4	5	8	6		1		12	
17	A	Hibernian	8,959	1-2	3	2	7						9¹	10	11	15				4	5	8	6		1		12	14
24	H	Stranraer	2,210	†5-1	3	2	12				7		9¹	15¹	10	11²				4	5	8	6		1		14	
May 1	A	Raith Rovers	2,380	1-1	3	2	5						9	10¹	7		14			6	8	4			1		11	
8	H	Airdrieonians	2,078	3-0	7	2¹	5						10	3	11¹					6	8	4			1		9¹	
TOTAL FULL APPEARANCES					19	30	24	18	29	23	27	15	27	13	23	22	1	7		24	24	17	13	11	17		9	3
TOTAL SUB APPEARANCES						(1)	(6)	(8)		(2)	(1)	(7)	(9)	(3)	(13)	(5)	(2)	(1)		(4)	(5)	(1)	(1)		(1)		(8)	(1)
TOTAL GOALS SCORED							4		1				8	4	4	11					2	1	3				2	

Small bold figures denote goalscorers. † denotes opponent's own goal.

St. Mirren Park

LOVE STREET

ALBION STREET

CAPACITY: 14,935; Seated 8,935, Standing 6,000
PITCH DIMENSIONS: 112 yds x 74 yds
FACILITIES FOR DISABLED SUPPORTERS:
Full wheelchair facilities available for visiting supporters in the Caledonia Stand.

Team playing kits

How to get there

St. Mirren Park can be reached by the following routes:

TRAINS: There is a frequent train service from Glasgow Central Station and all coastal routes pass through Gilmour Street. The ground is about 400 yards from the station.

BUSES: All SMT coastal services, plus buses to Johnstone and Kilbarchan, pass within 300 yards of the ground.

CARS: The only facilities for car parking are in the streets surrounding the ground.

email: sfl@sol.co.uk • website: www.sfl.scottishfootball.com

AIRDRIEONIANS
SEASON TICKET INFORMATION - SEATED

ADULT	£205
JUVENILE/OAP	£115
HUSBAND & WIFE	£355
PARENT & JUVENILE	£295

LEAGUE ADMISSION PRICES -SEATED

ADULT	£12
JUVENILE/OAP	£7
PARENT & JUVENILE	£18

AYR UNITED
SEASON TICKET INFORMATION
SEATED

CENTRE STAND	ADULT	£190
	OAP	£155
WING STAND	ADULT	£165
	JUVENILE/OAP	£140
FAMILY STAND	ADULT/JUVENILE	£165
	ADDITIONAL JUVENILE	£40

STANDING

GROUND/ENCLOSURE	ADULT	£130
	JUVENILE/OAP	£65
	ADULT & JUVENILE	£165

LEAGUE ADMISSION PRICES
SEATED

MAIN STAND (Centre)	ADULT	£14
MAIN STAND (Wing)	ADULT	£13
	CONCESSION	£11
FAMILY STAND	ADULT/JUVENILE	£12

(Plus £5.00 for each additional Juvenile)

STANDING

ENCLOSURE	ADULT	£10.50
GROUND	ADULT	£10
	JUVENILE/OAP	£5

CLYDEBANK
SEASON TICKET INFORMATION
SEATED

ADULT	£220
JUVENILE/OAP	£150

STANDING

ADULT	£180
OAP	£75
JUVENILES 15-U18	£85
JUVENILES 14 & UNDER	£20

LEAGUE ADMISSION PRICES
SEATED

ADULT	£13
JUVENILE/OAP	£9
PARENT & JUVENILE	£17

STANDING

ADULT	£11
JUVENILE/OAP	£7
PARENT & JUVENILE	£13

DUNFERMLINE ATHLETIC
SEASON TICKET INFORMATION - SEATED

AREA	SEASON TICKET PRICES UP TO 31.07.99	SEASON TICKET PRICES AFTER 01.08.99
SOUTH MAIN STAND		
ADULT	£180	£195
CONCESSION	£90	£98
SOUTH WEST STAND		
ADULT	£180	£195
CONCESSION	£90	£98
NORRIE McCATHIE STAND		
ADULT	£165	£180
CONCESSION	£75	£83
NORTH WEST STAND		
ADULT	£165	£180
CONCESSION	£75	£83
NORRIE McCATHIE STAND FAMILY AREA		
PARENT AND JUVENILE*	£165 plus £55	£180 plus £65
EXTRA PARENT	£165	£180
EXTRA JUVENILE	£55	£65

* Juvenile must be 14 years or under and accompanied by parent.

LEAGUE ADMISSION PRICES

	ADULT	CONCESSION
SOUTH MAIN STAND	£12	£6
ALL OTHER STANDS	£11	£5

FALKIRK
SEASON TICKET INFORMATION
SEATED

ADULT	£220/£205
JUVENILE/OAP (Wing Stand)	£145/£105
HUSBAND & WIFE	£380

STANDING

SOUTH ENCLOSURE		
	ADULT	£190
	JUVENILE/OAP	£100
GROUND		
	ADULT	£175
	JUVENILE/OAP	£90

LEAGUE ADMISSION PRICES
SEATED

ADULT	£15/£13.50
JUVENILE/OAP (Wing Stand)	£6.50

STANDING

ENCLOSURE		
	ADULT	£11.50
	JUVENILE/OAP	£5.50
GROUND		
	ADULT	£10
	JUVENILE/OAP	£5

Airdrieonians' Excelsior Stadium

INVERNESS CALEDONIAN THISTLE

SEASON TICKET INFORMATION

SEATED	ADULT	£165
	JUVENILE/OAP	£100
STANDING	ADULT	£120
	JUVENILE/OAP	£75

LEAGUE ADMISSION PRICES

SEATED	ADULT	£11
	JUVENILE/OAP	£6
STANDING	ADULT	£9
	JUVENILE/OAP	£5

RAITH ROVERS
SEASON TICKET INFORMATION - SEATED

MAIN STAND/RAILWAY STAND/SOUTH STAND

ADULT	£180
JUVENILE/OAP	£90
PARENT & JUVENILE	£250
PARENT & 2 JUVENILES	£325

LEAGUE ADMISSION PRICES - SEATED
MAIN STAND/ RAILWAY STAND/SOUTH STAND/NORTH STAND

ADULT	£11
JUVENILE/OAP	£6

LIVINGSTON

SEASON TICKET INFORMATION - SEATED

ADULT	£150
PARENT & JUVENILE	£180
PARENT & 2 JUVENILES	£210
2 PARENTS & 2 JUVENILE	£350
OAP & JUVENILE	£70

LEAGUE ADMISSION PRICES - SEATED

ADULT	£8
JUVENILE/OAP	£4

The West Lothian Courier Stadium - home of Livingston

MORTON
SEASON TICKET INFORMATION
SEATED

ADULT	£220
JUVENILE/OAP	£150

STANDING

ADULT	£180
OAP	£75
JUVENILES 15-U18	£85
JUVENILES 14 & UNDER	£20

LEAGUE ADMISSION PRICES
SEATED

ADULT	£13
JUVENILE/OAP	£9
PARENT & JUVENILE	£17

STANDING

ADULT	£11
JUVENILE/OAP	£7
PARENT & JUVENILE	£13

ST. MIRREN
SEASON TICKET INFORMATION
SEATED

MAIN STAND	ADULT	£195
	JUVENILE/OAP	£120
NORTH STAND	ADULT	£170
	JUVENILE/OAP	£110
ENCLOSURE	ADULT	£170
	JUVENILE/OAP	£110

LEAGUE ADMISSION PRICES
SEATED

MAIN STAND	ADULT	£11
	JUVENILE/OAP	£5.50
LOWER ENCLOSURE	ADULT	£10
	JUVENILE/OAP	£5
NORTH STAND	ADULT	£10
	JUVENILE/OAP	£5
	1 PARENT & 1 JUVENILE	£12

STANDING

ADULT	£9
JUVENILE/OAP	£5

THE PAST REVISITED

Throughout the past two decades, rapt readers of The Scottish Football League Review have come to ask themselves the question that has been applied through the 20th Century to the telephone, the motor car, the aeroplane, the radio, the television, the refrigerator, the washing machine and the computer... how on earth did we manage without it?

As an indispensable appendage to the everyday lives of those with a passionate interest in the old game, this remarkable volume has competed with the best that technology can offer since the day it was launched back in 1980.

With impeccable appropriateness,

the twentieth edition takes us through the close of the century and into the first season of the next Millennium. The life of the book has, with almost spooky timing, coincided precisely with the most significant period of upheaval in the history of a sport which had been (the scrapping of the players' maximum wage in 1960 excepted) untouched since its beginnings.

But it is no coincidence that the Review has, since its birth, contained in text and pictures details of many of the extraordinary people who have been involved with the evolutionary - in some cases, revolutionary - process through the past 20 years.

Looking through the first issue, you rediscover that history has a starting

Alex Totten, manager of Alloa Athletic in 1980 (above) and urging on his Falkirk team during the 1997 Tennents Scottish Cup Final (below).

point, in some cases clearly delineated. In many instances, sadly, it also comes to an abrupt end. George Best, for example, is in that first Review, the first name on the list of registered players of a Hibernian side who had just been relegated from the Premier Division.

Best, relatively soon after, would quit the game he had enriched for ten years at Manchester United. But, in the matter of drifting off, he had plenty of company. Of the 38 managers of clubs in membership of The Scottish Football League in that summer of 1980, only three are still doing the job.

One of them is now a knight and in charge of the biggest club in the world, another is an OBE and manages Scotland's national team and the third is Alex Totten. If Alex Ferguson and Craig Brown represent what it is possible to achieve in a game as democratic as football, Totten's work during the same period has been no less heroic.

In his address to the English Professional Footballers Association Player of the Year Dinner last season, Howard Wilkinson paid a handsome and deserved tribute to men whose endeavours, like those of anonymous philanthropists, pass unseen and unheralded.

"There are great managers who will never see a trophy," said Wilkinson, the Technical Director of The Football Association. "Down in those lower Leagues with clubs of extremely limited income, there are very capable and resourceful men for whom merely surviving at their own level is a huge achievement."

Totten is one of those unsung managers who has been delivering that kind of work for these 20 years and more, his occasional arrival in a Cup Final or Semi-Final reminding the public of his abilities under almost intolerable restrictions.

Alex Ferguson himself began in such circumstances, but his talents at East Stirlingshire and St. Mirren did

not go unnoticed and, by the time of publication of the inaugural Review, he had just led Aberdeen to the first of the three League Championships they would win in his care.

Of all the characters who featured in the first edition, Ferguson would make the greatest impact, taking the Pittodrie side to four Scottish Cups, one League Cup, the European Cup Winners' Cup and the European Super Cup before, in 1986, being lured to Old Trafford and the unparalleled success he would produce in England.

Craig Brown, manager of Clyde in 1980 (above) and Scotland Coach in 1999 (below)

Craig Brown was then in charge of Clyde, doing the kind of work with which Totten has been familiar throughout his managerial career. The thanklessness of that kind of job was captured by an incident one day at Shawfield, where Clyde then resided, soon after Brown had been made a Director of the club.

As he emerged from the tunnel behind his team for a match, one long suffering supporter shouted, "Hey, Broon! Noo ye're a Director, dae ye think ye could find us a decent manager?"

If Brown's subsequent elevation to Scotland manager and his achievements in taking the national team to the Finals of major championships would have been virtually impossible to predict from a look at his situation in 1980, there were similarities to be found in the route taken by Tony Higgins.

Higgins is pictured on the front cover, playing for Partick Thistle under the management of Bertie Auld...........and in the Premier Division. Then 26, the towering midfielder/striker would still be claiming at 30, with a giggle, that he had yet to fulfil his potential.

His destiny in the game lay in a non-playing, non-coaching capacity,

Alex Ferguson, manager of Aberdeen in 1980 (above) and manager of European Champions League winners, Manchester United in 1999

as full-time Secretary of The Scottish Professional Footballers Association. This development would come as no surprise to anyone who knew the Higgins family background on the north side of Glasgow.

The 'wean' among the six children produced by Mary and Danny Higgins, Tony was influenced by brothers who, when the conversation turned political, gave the impression they regarded Lenin as a fascist. During his tenure at the Players' Union, Higgins has helped to steer his members through great changes such as Bosman and has been the prime mover behind many innovations such as welfare schemes, academic and business courses for players and the pursuit of a share of the revenue generated by television and sponsorship.

Back on the field of play, how could anyone have foreseen what would become of a young midfielder,

not yet 18 and looking like a mop-top refugee from the 1960's, whose head and shoulders picture appeared along with those of other teammates at St. Johnstone?

The Perth side were in the First Division then and Ally McCoist had still to endure an unproductive two years at Sunderland before being lassoed by John Greig and hauled back to Scotland to begin a career that would make him the most prolific scorer of League goals in Rangers' history.

McCoist, of course, did not confine his exploits to club football. He managed to transfer his talent to the international arena, where a series of important goals helped Scotland to reach World Cup and European Championship Finals, making him the most productive striker to have graced the national side since Kenny Dalglish.

The upheaval in the Scottish game

Ally McCoist playing for Kilmarnock in 1999

through the years spanned by the Review is not, of course, restricted to legislation, litigation and administration. A look at the League tables shows a Premier Division which includes Airdrieonians, Morton, Partick Thistle and St. Mirren, all of whom are regarded nowadays as middle-order clubs.

The First Division, in contrast, contains Hibernian, Dundee, Motherwell and St. Johnstone, a quartet now with expectations of maintaining their Premier status for the foreseeable future.

But perhaps the fluctuations of fate have been most pronounced in the career of the man who wrote the very first forward and welcoming message in The Scottish Football League Review. That was Jim Farry, then Secretary of The Scottish Football League and, later, an always quotable Chief Executive of The Scottish Football Association.

Farry's removal earlier this year from what had always been considered a job for life is arguably the most convincing evidence that, in football, nothing remains constant. Apart, of course, from the indispensability of The Scottish Football League Review.

GLENN GIBBONS
(The Scotsman)

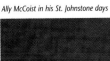

Ally McCoist in his St. Johnstone days

Alloa Athletic

LIST OF PLAYERS 1999-2000

SURNAME	FIRST NAME	MIDDLE NAME	DATE OF BIRTH	PLACE OF BIRTH	DATE OF SIGNING	HEIGHT FT INS	WEIGHT ST LBS	POS. ON PITCH	PREVIOUS CLUB
Aitken	Duncan		10/10/81	Falkirk	13/07/99	6 2.0	10 7	Def	East Stirlingshire
Allan	Gilbert	Chapman	21/02/73	St. Andrews	19/03/99	6 0.0	11 0	Def/Mid	East Fife
Baird	James		25/05/83	Bangour	17/08/99	5 9.0	10 0	Gk	Tynecastle B.C.
Barnes	Steven		11/05/82	Glasgow	17/08/99	5 11.0	12 0	Def	Bo'ness, Linlithgow B.C.
Beaton	David	Robert	08/08/67	Bridge of Allan	30/03/99	5 11.0	11 4	Def	Berwick Rangers
Bovill	Stewart		23/05/80	Bellshill	22/06/99	5 10.0	10 12	Mid	East Kilbride U'18s
Boyle	James	Thomson	19/02/67	Glasgow	29/07/99	5 6.0	11 2	Def/Mid	Livingston
Cairns	Mark	Henry	25/09/69	Edinburgh	05/07/97	6 0.0	13 2	Gk	Partick Thistle
Cameron	Martin	George William	16/06/78	Dunfermline	11/10/97	6 1.0	12 12	Fwd	Craigmillar Thistle
Christie	Martin	Peter	07/11/71	Edinburgh	14/09/99	5 6.0	10 4	Mid	Spartans
Clark	Derek	Grant	24/08/76	Stirling	15/07/98	5 6.0	10 0	Mid	China Fortune
Clark	Gary		13/09/64	Glasgow	06/08/99	5 10.0	11 10	Mid/Fwd	Hamilton Academical
Cowan	Mark		16/01/71	Edinburgh	17/06/96	6 0.0	12 7	Def	Berwick Rangers
Donaghy	Mark		29/08/72	Glasgow	07/11/98	5 8.0	9 13	Mid	Partick Thistle
Duncan	Ross		19/07/82	Kirkcaldy	13/07/99	5 10.0	10 8	Mid	Glenrothes Strollers U'21
Irvine	William		28/12/63	Stirling	31/05/96	5 10.0	11 3	Mid/Fwd	Berwick Rangers
Jarvis	Craig		18/05/83	Stirling	13/07/99	5 9.0	9 0	Mid	Riverside Athletic
Keir	Derek		04/10/81	Falkirk	17/08/99	6 1.0	10 7	Def	I.C.I. Juveniles
McAneny	Paul	James	11/11/73	Glasgow	07/10/95	5 11.0	12 1	Def	Stirling Albion
McArthur	Stuart		06/02/82	Falkirk	28/08/99	5 11.0	11 0	Fwd	I.C.I. Grangemouth
McKechnie	Gregor	Alistair	04/06/74	Stirling	12/03/98	5 10.0	11 11	Fwd	Stirling Albion
McMillan	David		03/10/83	Stirling	17/08/99	5 6.0	8 0	Mid	Riverstone Athletic
Menelaws	David		14/04/78	Chorley	12/06/99	5 7.0	10 4	Fwd	Shotts Bon Accord
Muir	Gary		19/08/82	Stirling	13/07/99	5 10.0	9 7	Def	Falkirk U'16s
Nelson	Mark		09/08/69	Bellshill	01/03/94	5 11.0	11 0	Def	Dumbarton
Parkyn	Martin		05/05/81	Lisburn	04/09/99	6 2.0	11 2	Gk	Dunfermline Athletic
Sharp	Raymond		16/11/69	Stirling	13/11/98	5 11.0	12 5	Def	Forfar Athletic
Taylor	Colin		20/09/81	Falkirk	13/07/99	5 8.0	9 5	Fwd	Unattached
Todd	Jamie	Alexander	16/07/82	Stirling	17/08/99	5 10.0	11 5	Def	Sauchie B.C.
Valentine	Craig		16/07/70	Edinburgh	20/07/96	5 8.0	11 0	Def	Berwick Rangers
Veitch	Stephen	David	03/01/82	Falkirk	17/08/99	5 10.0	10 7	Mid	Bo'ness, Linlithgow B.C.
Wilson	Lee		01/10/81	Stirling	13/07/99	5 10.0	10 7	Mid	Zeneca
Wilson	Mark		31/07/74	Dechmont	04/01/97	5 11.0	10 8	Mid	Berwick Rangers

Milestones

YEAR OF FORMATION: 1883
MOST CAPPED PLAYER: Jock Hepburn
NO. OF CAPS: 1
MOST LEAGUE POINTS IN A SEASON: 60 (Division 2 – Season 1921/22)(2 Points for a Win)
76 (Third Division – Season 1997/98)(3 Points for a Win)
MOST LEAGUE GOALS SCORED BY A PLAYER IN A SEASON: William Crilley (Season 1921/22)
NO. OF GOALS SCORED: 49
RECORD ATTENDANCE: 13,000 (-v- Dunfermline Athletic – 26.2.1939)
RECORD VICTORY: 9-2 (-v- Forfar Athletic – Division 2, 18.3.1933)
RECORD DEFEAT: 0-10 (-v- Dundee – Division 2 and Third Lanark – League Cup)

The Wasps' ten year league record

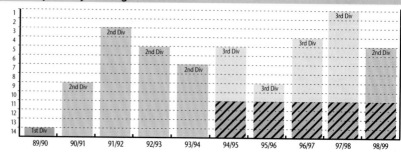

THE WASPS' CLUB FACTFILE 1998/99 RESULTS... APPEARANCES... SCORERS

Date	Venue	Opponents	Att.	Res	Cairns M.	Valentine C.	Nelson M.	McAnery P.	McCulloch K.	Pew D.	Wilson M.	Wilson S.	Simpson P.	Irvine W.	McKechnie G.	Ramsay S.	McLeod K.	Cowan M.	Cameron M.	Mackay S.	Gilmour J.	Haddow L.	Donaghy M.	Sharp R.	Clark D.	Duthie M.	Armstrong G.	Allan G.	Beaton D.
Aug 4	H	Forfar Athletic	495	1-2	1	2	3	4	5	6	7	8	9[1]	10	11	12	15												
15	A	East Fife	737	2-2	1	2	3	4		6		7	9	10[1]	11[1]	8		5	12	14									
22	H	Inverness Cal. Th.	616	1-1	1	2	3	4		6	7		9[1]	10	11	8		5	12	14	15								
29	H	Stirling Albion	1,272	7-0	1	2	3	4		6[1]		7	9[1]	10[1]	11[2]	8		5[1]	12	15[1]									
Sep 5	A	Partick Thistle	1,655	0-1	1	2	3	4		6		7	9	10	11	8		5	12	15		14							
12	H	Clyde	755	3-0	1	2		4		6	16	7	9	10[1]	11	8[1]		5[1]	12				3						
19	A	Arbroath	687	2-0	1	2	15	4		11		7	8	9[1]	10[1]	6		5	12		16		3						
26	H	Livingston	978	3-4	1	2	7	4		11		6	9[1]	10[2]		8		5	12				3						
Oct 3	A	Queen of the South	1,038	1-2	1	2	12	4		6		7	9	10[1]		8	16	5	11		15		3						
10	H	East Fife	526	5-1	1	2	7	4		12		8	9[1]	10[2]		6		5	11[2]				3						
17	H	Forfar Athletic	401	2-1	1	2	7	4[1]		6		8	9	10				5	11[1]				3						
24	H	Stirling Albion	1,085	2-4	1	2	7	4		12	15[1]	8	9[1]	10	16			5	11				3	6					
31	H	Partick Thistle	1,469	3-1	1	2	7	4		12	15	8	9[1]	10[1]	16			5	11[1]				3	6					
Nov 7	H	Arbroath	653	1-1	1	2	7	4		12		8		10	11			5	9[1]		15		3	6					
14	A	Clyde	908	1-2	1	2	7			6		8	9	10	11	16		5		15[1]			3		4				
21	A	Livingston	1,992	1-2	1	2	15					7	9	10[1]	12	6		5	11	8			3	14	4				
28	H	Queen of the South	592	2-1	1	2	7	4		15			9	10	12[1]	6		5	11[1]	8			3						
Dec 16	A	Inverness Cal. Th.	1,323	2-3	1	2	15	4		8		7	12	10	9	6		5[1]	11[1]				3						
19	H	Forfar Athletic	466	3-1	1	2	7	4		6		8	15	10[1]	9[2]	16		5	11				3						
29	H	Stirling Albion	971	2-2	1			5		6		4	2	12	10	11	7		9[2]		8			3	14				
Jan 13	A	Partick Thistle	1,502	1-2	1	2		4		6	7	8	5	10	11	14			9[1]		12			3	15				
16	H	Livingston	774	1-3	1	2		4		6		5	9[1]	10	12	7			11		8			3	15				
30	A	Queen of the South	1,201	0-0	1	2		4	5	12	7	8	11	10		6			9					3					
Feb 6	A	Arbroath	603	2-1	1	2		4[1]	5	6	7	8	12	10	11[1]				9	15				3					
16	H	Clyde	508	1-0	1	2	16	4	5	6	7	8	12	10	11[1]				9	15				3					
20	H	Inverness Cal. Th.	595	1-4	1	2	5	4		6	7	8		10	11[1]				9						16		3		
27	A	East Fife	708	4-0	1	2	5	4		6	7		12	10[1]	11				9[3]	14			8		3				
Mar 6	H	Partick Thistle	996	0-1	1	2	5			6	7	4	11	10					15			8		3	12	9			
13	A	Stirling Albion	1,225	1-1	1	2	3	4	5	15	7	6	16	10								8			11	9[1]			
20	H	Queen of the South	523	3-5	1	2	16	4	5			6							9[2]			8		3	11[1]	10	12	7	
Apr 3	A	Livingston	1,892	0-1	1	2		5			7	6	12						9		3	8			11	10			4
10	H	Arbroath	505	1-2	1	2		5		12	7	6			11[1]				9	15		8		3		10			4
17	A	Clyde	800	1-0	1	2					7	6[1]	8	10					9					3		11	12		
24	A	Forfar Athletic	440	1-3	1	2	16	5			7	6	8	10					9					3		11	12[1]	15	4
May 1	H	East Fife	806	3-1	1	2	16	5			7	6	8	10[1]	9[1]					3						11	12		4[1]
8	A	Inverness Cal. Th.	2,662	1-1	1		3	5			7		12	10	9					8				6	15	11[1]	2		4
TOTAL FULL APPEARANCES					36	34	19	33	6	21	22	27	25	33	20	15		18	21	6	12	10	15	9	5	1	2		6
TOTAL SUB APPEARANCES						(7)	(1)			(8)	(3)	(1)	(8)		(5)	(4)	(2)		(7)	(13)	(1)	(1)	(1)	(2)	(5)	(3)	(1)	(1)	
TOTAL GOALS SCORED							2			1	1	1	10	15	9	1		3	15	2					2	2			1

Small bold figures denote goalscorers. † denotes opponent's own goal.

Recreation Park

CLACKMANNAN ROAD

HILTON ROAD

CAPACITY: 3,142; Seated 414, Standing 2,728

PITCH DIMENSIONS: 110 yds x 75 yds

FACILITIES FOR DISABLED SUPPORTERS:
Accommodation for wheelchairs and invalid carriages in front of Stand. Disabled toilets are also available.

Team playing kits

How to get there

Recreation Park can be reached by the following routes:

TRAINS: The nearest railway station is Stirling, which is seven miles away. Fans would have to connect with an inter-linking bus service to reach the ground from here.

BUSES: There are three main services which stop outside the ground. These are the Dunfermline-Stirling, Stirling-Clackmannan and Falkirk-Alloa buses.

CARS: Car Parking is available in the car park adjacent to the ground and this can hold 175 vehicles.

The Wasps

email: sfl@sol.co.uk • website: www.sfl.scottishfootball.com

Gayfield Park,
Arbroath, Angus, DD11 1QB

PRESIDENT
John D. Christison

VICE-PRESIDENT
Charles W. Kinnear

COMMITTEE
R. Alan Ripley (Treasurer),
William J. Thomson,
George Johnson,
Michael Caird,
Alexander G. F. Law,
David G. Hodgens &
Michael J. Leonard

SECRETARY
Charles W. Kinnear

MANAGER
David A. Baikie

ASSISTANT MANAGER
Graeme Irons

**FIRST TEAM COACH/
CHIEF SCOUT**
John Martin

YOUTH COACHES
Jake Shaw, Ray McWalter,
Steve Bourke & John Welsh

CLUB DOCTOR
Dr. Dick Spiers

PHYSIOTHERAPIST
Alan Anderson

CHIROPODIST
Alex McKinnon

**FOOTBALL SAFETY OFFICERS'
ASSOCIATION REPRESENTATIVE**
Charles Kinnear

GROUNDSMAN
Iain Gunn

KIT SUPERVISOR
Peter Nicoll

COMMERCIAL MANAGER
Bruce McLean
Bus. (01382) 907111

TELEPHONES
Ground/Fax/Ticket Office/Club Shop
(01241) 872157
Sec. Home (01241) 876640
Sec. Bus. (01382) 424336

CLUB SHOP
Gayfield Park, Arbroath, DD11 1QB.
Open on home matchdays.
Premier Sports, West Port, Arbroath,
DD11 1RF. Open Mon. to Sat.

TEAM CAPTAIN
John McAulay

SHIRT SPONSOR
Abbeyfruit

62

LIST OF PLAYERS 1999-2000

SURNAME	FIRST NAME	MIDDLE NAME	DATE OF BIRTH	PLACE OF BIRTH	DATE OF SIGNING	HEIGHT FT INS	WEIGHT ST LBS	POS. ON PITCH	PREVIOUS CLUB
Anderson	Mark		26/06/82	Dundee	07/08/99	6 4.0	11 4	Gk	Dundee
Anderson	Robert		04/02/82	Dundee	30/07/99	5 7.0	11 5	Def	S Form
Arbuckle	David		12/08/73	Bellshill	21/05/98	5 10.0	11 5	Mid	Queen's Park
Brownlie	Paul	Jack	30/08/77	Falkirk	31/07/99	5 9.0	10 8	Fwd	Raith Rovers
Bryce	Thomas	Charles	27/01/60	Johnstone	16/06/99	5 8.0	11 10	Mid/Fwd	Queen of the South
Butler	David	Patrick	31/01/81	Glasgow	13/08/97	5 11.0	11 7	Fwd	Arbroath Sporting Club
Campbell	Stephen		11/03/82	Perth	30/07/99	5 6.0	10 9	Def	Dundee
Carlin	James		25/07/81	Dundee	21/07/99	5 8.0	10 7	Mid	Dundee
Cooper	Craig		17/01/73	Arbroath	08/08/97	5 10.0	10 13	Mid	Montrose
Crawford	Jonathan		14/10/69	Johnstone	31/03/95	6 1.0	12 7	Def	Arthurlie Juniors
Deswarte	Frederic		09/12/72	Malo-Les-Bains	09/08/99	5 10.0	12 8	Fwd	F.C Loon-Plage
Devine	Christopher		21/02/79	Bellshill	31/03/99	5 6.0	11 1	Fwd	Dundee United
Evans	David	Charles	07/12/81	Dundee	30/07/99	5 8.0	10 4	Fwd	S Form
Flight	Blair		18/03/82	Dundee	21/07/99	6 1.0	12 6	Def	S Form
Florence	Steven		28/10/71	Dundee	20/05/88	5 6.0	11 5	Mid	Arbroath Lads Club
Gallagher	John		02/06/69	Glasgow	25/10/96	5 9.0	10 10	Mid	Albion Rovers
Heenan	Kevin	Alexander	07/03/82	Dundee	30/07/99	5 9.0	10 8	Fwd	S Form
Hinchcliffe	Craig	Peter	05/05/72	Glasgow	04/08/95	5 11.0	13 0	Gk	Elgin City
Houston	Steven	James	15/03/82	Dundee	30/07/99	5 8.0	11 4	Fwd	S Form
McAulay	John		28/04/72	Glasgow	04/07/95	5 9.0	11 7	Def	Clyde
McGlashan	Colin	James	17/03/64	Perth	10/10/98	5 7.0	10 12	Fwd	Montrose
McWalter	Mark	Nicoll	20/06/68	Arbroath	02/08/96	5 11.0	13 2	Fwd	Ballymena United
Mercer	James		30/07/74	Glasgow	18/07/98	6 5.0	13 7	Mid/Fwd	Queen's Park
Mitchell	Brian	Charles	29/02/68	Arbroath	04/02/99	5 8.0	13 0	Def	Brechin City
Peters	Scott		09/12/72	Dundee	29/07/97	5 11.0	11 7	Mid	Hill O'Beath
Peters	Scott	John	01/08/81	Dundee	30/07/99	5 10.0	10 12	Def	Dundee
Sellars	Barry	Michael	06/12/75	Arbroath	06/02/98	6 1.0	12 10	Mid	Forfar West End
Spink	Darren		08/01/81	Arbroath	05/11/98	5 10.0	11 4	Mid	Forfar Albion
Steele	Kevin		11/10/81	Dundee	30/07/99	5 10.0	11 0	Fwd	Dundee
Thomson	James		15/05/71	Stirling	05/06/99	6 1.0	12 7	Def	Queen of the South
Thomson	Neil		21/10/69	East Kilbride	09/08/97	5 6.0	10 10	Mid	Montrose
Tindal	Kevin	Douglas	11/04/71	Arbroath	09/01/97	5 9.0	12 7	Mid	Montrose
Wares	Colin	Scott	05/02/81	Dundee	24/10/98	5 9.0	11 1	Mid/Fwd	Forfar Albion
Webster	Andrew	Neil	23/04/82	Dundee	02/09/99	6 0.0	10 0	Def	S Form
Wight	Craig	MacDonald	24/07/78	Glasgow	09/10/97	5 11.0	11 10	Gk	Hibernian

Milestones

YEAR OF FORMATION: 1878
MOST CAPPED PLAYER: Ned Doig
NO. OF CAPS: 2
MOST LEAGUE POINTS IN A SEASON: 57 (Division 2 – Season 1966/67)(2 Points for a Win)
68 (Third Division – Season 1997/98)(3 Points for a Win)
MOST LEAGUE GOALS SCORED BY A PLAYER IN A SEASON: David Easson (Season 1958/59)
NO. OF GOALS SCORED: 45
RECORD ATTENDANCE: 13,510 (-v- Rangers – Scottish Cup, 23.2.1952)
RECORD VICTORY: 36-0 (-v- Bon Accord – Scottish Cup, 12.9.1885)
RECORD DEFEAT: 1-9 (-v- Celtic – League Cup, 25.8.1993)

The Red Lichties' ten year league record

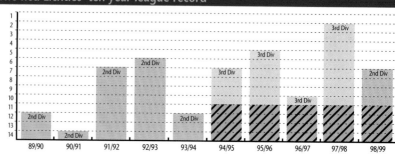

THE RED LICHTIES' CLUB FACTFILE 1998/99 RESULTS... APPEARANCES... SCORERS

Date	Venue	Opponents	Att.	Res	Hinchcliffe C.	Mitchell B.	Tindal K.	McAulay J.	Jones K.	Crawford J.	Cooper C.	Thomson N.	Grant B.	Spence W.	Scott W.D.	Mercer J.	Florence S.	Sellars B.	McWalter M.	Gallagher J.	Peters S.	Scott S.	Burns K.	Wight C.	O'Driscoll J.	McClashan J.	Arbuckle D.	McGlashan C.	Elliott J.	Devine C.	Donachie B.
Aug 4	H	East Fife	807	0-2	1	2	3	4	5	6	7	8	9	10	11	12															
15	A	Queen of the South	1,104	0-0	1	5	2	4		6			8	12	9	11	10	3		7	14										
22	H	Stirling Albion	805	0-3	1		7	4		6			8	12		11	9	2	10		3	5	14	15							
29	H	Forfar Athletic	905	†2-1		12		4	5	6	7^{1}		14		2	9	3	8						1		10	11				
Sep 5	A	Inverness Cal. Th.	1,836	1-2		12		4		6		14	9		11		2	7		3^{1}	5			1		10	8				
12	A	Livingston	2,725	1-2		12		4	15	6			7		11	14	2			3	5^{1}	9		1		10	8				
19	H	Alloa Athletic	687	0-2	1	8		4	5	6		12	9			10	7			3	2	15		1		11					
26	H	Partick Thistle	2,006	0-2	1	2		4	5	6	7	14	9			10	3			11						8					
Oct 3	H	Clyde	710	0-0	1	2		4	5	6	7	15	9		11	10			12	3						8	14				
10	H	Queen of the South	603	2-1	1	2		4	5	6	7					10	3	14		11			15			8^{1}	12	9^{1}			
17	A	East Fife	719	3-0	1	2		4	5	6	7	15				10	3	14		11^{2}						8	12	9^{1}			
26	A	Forfar Athletic	800	3-1	1	2		4	5	6		12			10^{1}		3	14		11^{1}						8	7	9^{1}			
31	H	Inverness Cal. Th.	934	0-1	1	2		4	5	6					10		3	14		11						8	7	9			
Nov 7	A	Alloa Athletic	653	1-1	1	14		4	5	6		12			10		3	2^{1}		11						8	7	9			
14	H	Livingston	810	2-2	1			4		6	7	12		15	10		3	2		11						8^{1}	5^{1}	9			
21	H	Partick Thistle	1,121	1-0	1			4		6	7				10		3	2^{1}		11						8	5	9			
28	A	Clyde	918	0-3	1	12		4	5	6	7	14					3	2		11						8	10	9			
Dec 12	A	Stirling Albion	824	1-0	1	12			5	6		7		15	3	10	2	4		11	15					8		9^{1}			
19	H	East Fife	701	2-1	1	12	14		5	6	15	7			3	10	2	4^{2}		11						8		9			
Jan 9	A	Inverness Cal. Th.	1,795	0-2	1			4	5	6	7			15	3	10	2									8		9			
16	H	Partick Thistle	2,105	0-0	1	2		4		6	5			15	10		3	7		11						8		9			
19	H	Forfar Athletic	767	2-2	1	12^{1}		4		6	7	5		15	10		3	2		11						8^{1}		9			
30	H	Clyde	777	0-3	1	11		4	5		7	6	14		10		2	8		3						12		9			
Feb 6	H	Alloa Athletic	603	1-2	1	3		4	5	6				15	10		2	11		12						8		9^{1}	7		
16	A	Livingston	888	0-1	1			4	2	5	6	14			10		3	12		11						8		9	7		
20	H	Stirling Albion	610	1-0	1			4	2	5	6	7			12		3			11						8		9^{1}	10		
27	A	Queen of the South	1,020	0-3	1	8			2	5	6	7	15		3			14		11						4		9	10		
Mar 6	H	Inverness Cal. Th.	705	3-1				4^{1}	2	5	6	15			12		3	14		7	10	3		1		8		9^{2}	11		
13	A	Forfar Athletic	864	2-5				4^{1}	2	5	6				12		3	14		7	10	3		1		8		9^{1}	11		
20	A	Clyde	694	1-1				4	2	6	7	14			8	11				10	3	5				15		9	12		
Apr 3	H	Partick Thistle	1,301	2-1	1	8			2	5	6^{1}	7			11					10	3	12				4^{1}		9			15
10	A	Alloa Athletic	505	2-1	1	8		4		6	7			15	11					12^{1}	3	2				5^{1}		9	14	10	
17	H	Livingston	977	1-1	1	8		4		6^{1}					12					7	3	2			1	5		9	11	10	14
24	A	East Fife	837	2-1				4		6		15			14	11				7	3	2			1	5		9^{1}	12	10^{1}	8
May 1	H	Queen of the South	976	0-2				4		6					14					7	3	2			1	5		9	11	10	8
8	A	Stirling Albion	1,005	1-2		8		4		6		11			3					7	15	2			1	5		9^{1}	11	10	8
TOTAL FULL APPEARANCES					25	2	23	34	22	35	13	14	2	5	15	22	24	22	3	31	10	1		11	3	14	23	27	8	5	2
TOTAL SUB APPEARANCES						(8)	(1)	(1)		(4)	(9)	(6)	(6)	(5)	(7)		(8)	(2)	(1)	(2)	(2)	(1)		(1)		(5)		(3)	(1)	(1)
TOTAL GOALS SCORED							3			2	1				1		5		4	1						2	4	12			1

Small bold figures denote goalscorers. † denotes opponent's own goal.

Gayfield Park

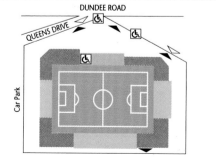

DUNDEE ROAD
QUEENS DRIVE
Car Park

CAPACITY: 6,488; Seated 715, Standing 5,773

PITCH DIMENSIONS: 115 yds x 71 yds

FACILITIES FOR DISABLED SUPPORTERS:
Enclosure at west end of Stand with wide steps to take a wheelchair. Toilet facilities are also available.

Team playing kits

How to get there

The following routes may be used to reach Gayfield Park:

BUSES: Arbroath is on the main route from both Glasgow and Edinburgh to Aberdeen. Buses from these three cities, plus Stirling, Dundee and Perth all stop at Arbroath Bus Station at hourly intervals. There is also a local service between Dundee-Arbroath and Montrose and this service is half hourly until 7.00 p.m. Between 7.00 p.m. and 10.45 p.m. the service is hourly. The bus station is 10 minutes walk from the ground.

TRAINS: Arbroath is on the Inter-City 125 route from London to Aberdeen and there are frequent local services between Arbroath, Dundee and Edinburgh. Trains also travel north from Glasgow, Stirling and Perth. The station is a 15 minute walk from the ground.

CARS: There is free parking for 500 cars just next to the ground in Queen's Drive.

email: sfl@sol.co.uk • website: www.sfl.scottishfootball.com

Broadwood Stadium,
Cumbernauld, G68 9NE

CHAIRMAN
William B. Carmichael

DIRECTORS
John F. McBeth, F.R.I.C.S.,
Gerard W. Dunn, M.A.,
Ronnie MacDonald,
Harry McCall, B.A., C.Eng., M.I.C.E.
& John D. Taylor, A.I.B.

SECRETARY
John D. Taylor, A.I.B.
(Bus) 0141-248 4078

OFFICE ADMINISTRATION
Mrs. Lynn Calder &
Mrs. Molly Stallan

CHIEF EXECUTIVE
Ronnie MacDonald

FIRST TEAM MANAGER
Allan Maitland

RESERVE TEAM MANAGER
/ASSISTANT COACH
Denis McDaid

HEAD OF YOUTH DEVELOPMENT
Douglas McBean

HEAD COACH
Bill Munro

YOUTH TEAM COACHES
John Reilly, Sam Millar,
Robert Ferguson & Billy Reid

CLUB DOCTOR
John A. MacLean

FIRST TEAM PHYSIOTHERAPIST
John Watson

FITNESS COACH
Paul Caton

CHIEF SCOUT
Stevie Campbell

FOOTBALL SAFETY OFFICERS'
ASSOCIATION REPRESENTATIVE
Ronald McCammick
Bus (0141) 445 2351

KIT MAN
Douglas Fraser

CLUB CHAPLAIN
Pastor George Barr

TELEPHONES
Ground (01236) 451511
Fax (01236) 733490

E-MAIL & INTERNET ADDRESS
http://www.clydefc.co.uk

CLUB SHOP
Situated at Ground
Open on Home Match Days 2 hours
before and for 1 hour after match

OFFICIAL SUPPORTERS CLUB
180 Main Street, Rutherglen

TEAM CAPTAIN
Ian Spittal

SHIRT SPONSOR
OKI

Clyde

LIST OF PLAYERS 1999-2000

SURNAME	FIRST NAME	MIDDLE NAME	DATE OF BIRTH	PLACE OF BIRTH	DATE OF SIGNING	HEIGHT FT INS	WEIGHT ST LBS	POS. ON PITCH	PREVIOUS CLUB
Barrett	John	Patrick	18/04/71	Glasgow	31/07/98	6 1.0	11 12	Fwd	Pollok
Carrigan	Brian		26/09/79	Glasgow	21/12/96	5 8.0	10 7	Fwd	Kilsyth Rangers
Convery	Steven		27/10/72	Glasgow	31/07/98	5 11.0	11 6	Fwd	Arthurlie
Cranmer	Craig	Hamilton	21/02/68	Johnstone	31/07/98	6 2.0	12 12	Def	Pollok
Farrell	Terence	John	11/07/72	Glasgow	02/07/99	6 0.0	11 5	Def	Maryhill Juniors
Grant	Allan		01/07/73	Glasgow	31/07/98	5 10.0	11 0	Fwd	Maryhill
Hay	Paul		14/11/80	Glasgow	16/07/97	5 8.0	10 4	Def/Mid	West Park B.C.
Keogh	Patrick	Sebastian	07/05/76	Redlands	04/08/98	6 2.0	12 10	Def	Maryhill
McClay	Andrew		26/11/72	Glasgow	31/07/98	5 6.0	9 12	Mid	Maryhill
McCusker	Richard		24/08/70	Glasgow	31/07/98	6 0.0	12 0	Mid	Maryhill
McDonald	Ian		07/03/78	Newcastle	11/12/98	6 0.0	12 13	Def	Hibernian
McGhee	Graham	Henry	24/09/81	Coatbridge	02/10/97	6 1.0	12 6	Def	Albion Rovers B.C.
McGraw	Mark	Robertson	05/01/71	Rutherglen	14/03/98	5 11.5	11 2	Fwd	Morton
McIntyre	Gordon		15/11/74	Alexandria	31/07/98	6 2.0	12 4	Gk	Maryhill
McLauchlan	Martin	James	02/01/70	Bellshill	02/07/99	6 0.0	12 13	Fwd	Forfar Athletic
McLaughlin	Mark		02/12/75	Greenock	28/07/99	6 2.0	13 5	Def	Arthurlie
Mitchell	Jamie		06/01/76	Glasgow	05/03/99	5 7.0	10 0	Mid	Scarborough
Murray	Darren	Thomas	25/01/74	Glasgow	31/07/98	6 1.0	11 10	Def	Maryhill
Ross	John	James	05/06/76	Falkirk	02/07/99	6 1.0	11 5	Mid	Camelon
Smith	Bryan	James	21/08/70	Clydebank	31/07/98	5 10.0	11 0	Def	Petershill
Spittal	John	Ian	14/02/65	Glasgow	31/07/98	6 1.0	12 0	Def	Pollok
Woods	Thomas		17/04/71	Glasgow	26/05/99	5 10.0	12 5	Fwd	Maryhill Juniors
Wylie	David		04/04/66	Johnstone	18/09/98	6 0.0	13 0	Gk	Morton

Milestones

YEAR OF FORMATION: 1878
MOST CAPPED PLAYER: Tommy Ring
NO. OF CAPS: 12
MOST LEAGUE POINTS IN A SEASON: 64 (Division 2 – Season 1956/57)
MOST LEAGUE GOALS SCORED BY A PLAYER IN A SEASON: Bill Boyd (Season 1932/33)
NO. OF GOALS SCORED: 32
RECORD ATTENDANCE: 52,000 (-v- Rangers – 21.11.1908 – at Shawfield Stadium)
　　　　　　　　　　　7,382 (-v- Celtic – 14.8.1996 (Coca-Cola Cup) – at Broadwood Stadium)
RECORD VICTORY: 11-1 (-v- Cowdenbeath – Division 2, 6.10.1951)
RECORD DEFEAT: 0-11 (-v- Dumbarton and Rangers, Scottish Cup)

The Bully Wee's ten year league record

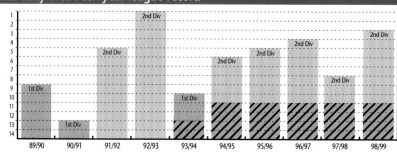

THE BULLY WEE'S CLUB FACTFILE 1998/99 RESULTS... APPEARANCES... SCORERS

Date	Venue	Opponents	Att.	Res	McIntyre G.	Smith B.	Cranmer C.	Spittal J.	Murray D.	McCusker R.	Convery S.	Keogh P.	McGraw M.	Rice B.	Grant A.	McHarg S.	O'Brien A.	Sexton D.	Campbell P.	Balfour R.	McLay A.	McMillan A.	Carrigan B.	Barrett J.	Dillon J.	Wylie D.	Peters S.	McPhee Gary	Brownlie P.	McDonald I.	Hay P.	Mitchell J.	McPhee Graham
Aug 4	H	Queen of the South	631	2-0	1	2	3	4	5	6	7	8	9¹	10	11	12	15¹																	
	15	A	Stirling Albion	1,059	2-1		5	3	4	2	6	7	8	9¹	10	14	11	12¹	1	15														
	22	H	East Fife	806	0-0		5	3	4	2	6	7	8	9		15	11	12	14	1	10													
	29	H	Partick Thistle	2,621	1-2	1	5	3	4	2	6	9	8			12	11¹	7	14		10														
Sep 5	A	Forfar Athletic	494	2-2		5	3	4¹	2	10	9¹	8			11		14			1	7	6	15											
	12	A	Alloa Athletic	755	0-3		5	3	4	2	10	7	8			11			14	1		6	12	9	15										
	19	H	Livingston	1,044	1-1		5	15	4	2	6¹	7	10				12					8		9	11	14	1	3							
	26	H	Inverness Cal. Th.	969	4-1		5	3	4	2	10¹	7¹	15			11¹		14				8	6	12	9¹		1								
Oct 3	A	Arbroath	710	0-0		5	3	4	2	10	7	14			11	15					8	6	9			1	12							
	10	A	Stirling Albion	1,008	2-1		5		4	2	10	7²	3			11	15					8	6	12	9		1								
	17	A	Queen of the South	1,139	1-2		5	3	4	2	10	7	11			14	15¹					8	6	12	9		1								
	24	A	Partick Thistle	2,627	2-0		5	14	4	2	10¹	7	3¹	15	11	9						8	6	12			1								
	31	H	Forfar Athletic	918	3-1			14	4	2	10²	7¹	5	3	11	9						8	6	12	15		1								
Nov 7	A	Livingston	2,556	0-2		5		4	2	10	7	3			11						8	6	15	9		1								
	14	A	Alloa Athletic	908	2-1		5	3	1		10¹	7¹	2		6	11	15					8		9	14		12	4	15						
	21	A	Inverness Cal. Th.	2,268	1-1		5	3	4	2	10¹	7	6		12	11	15					8		9	14		1								
	28	H	Arbroath	918	3-0		5		4	2	10¹	9¹	6		3	11	14					8		7¹			1								
Dec 12	H	East Fife	804	0-0		5	3	4		10	7	2		6	11		15				8		9	14		1						12		
	19	H	Queen of the South	794	2-1		5		4	2	10	7¹	6		3	11	15					8		9¹	14		1						12		
	26	H	Partick Thistle	2,673	0-1		5		4	2	10	7	8		12	11	14							6	9		1						3		
Jan 16	H	Inverness Cal. Th.	1,105	1-1		5		4	2	10	7¹	6		12	11	14					8		15	9		1						3		
	30	A	Arbroath	777	3-0		5	15	4	2	10	7¹	6¹		12	11	9					8¹		14			1						3		
Feb 2	A	Forfar Athletic	419	1-3		5		4	2	10¹	7	6		12	11	9					8		14	15		1						3		
	6	H	Livingston	1,366	0-3		5	14	4	2	10	7	6		12	11	15					8		9			1						3		
	16	A	Alloa Athletic	508	0-1		5	2	4		10	7	6		12	11	14					8		9			1						3	15	
	20	H	East Fife	768	1-0		5	4		10	7	2			11	14¹						8		9			1						3	6	15
	27	A	Stirling Albion	888	3-2		5	2	4		10	7²	9		12	14						8		11¹			1						3	6	
Mar 6	H	Forfar Athletic	815	1-0		5	2	4	15	10	7	9¹		12	8	14					11					1						3	6	
	13	A	Partick Thistle	3,342	1-0		5	2	4	6	10	7	9¹			11						8					1						3	12	
	20	A	Arbroath	694	1-1		5	2¹	4		7	10		9	14	11	15					8		6			1						3	12	
Apr 3	A	Inverness Cal. Th.	3,019	0-3		5	2	4	14	10		11	9		7						8		6			1						3	12	15
	10	A	Livingston	1,925	0-2		5	2	4	7	10		3			14	15					8		11	9							12	6		
	17	H	Alloa Athletic	800	0-1		5	2	4	12	10		9			15						8		7	11		1						3	6	14
	24	A	Queen of the South	1,218	1-2		5		4	2	10		8			11						7		9	15¹		1		14				3	6	12
May 1	H	Stirling Albion	1,107	4-1		5	2	4	15	10¹		3¹			11¹						8		9¹			1		6				12	14	7
	8	A	East Fife	845	1-2		5	3	4		10		2¹		6	11						8		15	9		1		14					7	12
TOTAL FULL APPEARANCES					2	35	23	35	25	35	30	34	5	8	28	7	1	1		3	29	9	19	13	29		1	2	14	6	2		
TOTAL SUB APPEARANCES							(5)		(4)		(2)		(10)	(6)	(9)	(15)			(4)				(12)	(7)	(2)	(1)	(1)	(2)	(1)	(4)	(5)	(4)	(1)
TOTAL GOALS SCORED							1	1		10	12	6	2		2	2	3				1		3	3								

Small bold figures denote goalscorers. † denotes opponent's own goal.

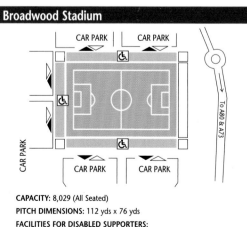

CAR PARK | CAR PARK
CAR PARK
CAR PARK | CAR PARK
To A80 & A73

CAPACITY: 8,029 (All Seated)
PITCH DIMENSIONS: 112 yds x 76 yds
FACILITIES FOR DISABLED SUPPORTERS:
Facilities available in Home, Away and New Stands.

Team playing kits

How to get there

The following routes may be used to reach Broadwood Stadium:

BUSES: From Buchanan Street Bus Station in Glasgow, fans should board Bus No. 36A (Glasgow to Westfield).

TRAINS: There are regular trains from Queen Street Station, Glasgow to Croy Station. The Stadium is a 15 minute walk from here.

CARS: From Glasgow City Centre, fans should take the Stepps By-Pass joining the A80 towards Stirling. Take Broadwood turn-off to Stadium.

Hamilton Academical

Firhill Stadium, 80 Firhill Road,
Glasgow, G20 7AL

OFFICE ADDRESS
Enable Building, Prospect House,
New Park Street, Hamilton, ML3 0BN

CHIEF EXECUTIVE/DIRECTOR
William Sherry

SECRETARY
Scott A. Struthers, B.A. (Hons)

OFFICE SECRETARY
Mrs Margaret Montgomery

HON. LIFE PRESIDENT
Dr. Alexander A. Wilson

MANAGER
Alistair Dawson

HON. MEDICAL OFFICER
Dr. Brian Lynas

PHYSIOTHERAPIST/COACH
Jim Fallon

COMMUNITY SCHEME ASSISTANT
Mark Nelson

**FOOTBALL SAFETY OFFICERS'
ASSOCIATION REPRESENTATIVE**
Scott A. Struthers, B.A. (Hons)
(01698) 286103

GROUNDSMAN
Partick Thistle FC Groundsman -
George Furze

TELEPHONES
Office/Commercial (01698) 286103
Ground (0141) 579 1971
(Matchdays Only)
Fax-Office (01698) 285422
Information Service
(09068) 666492

CLUB SHOP
"The Acciesshop",
Hamilton Academical F.C.,
Enable Building, Prospect House,
New Park Street, Hamilton, ML3 0BN

OFFICIAL SUPPORTERS CLUB
The Stand Club,
c/o Hamilton Academical F.C.,
Enable Building, Prospect House,
New Park Street, Hamilton, ML3 0BN

TEAM CAPTAIN
Steven Thomson

SHIRT SPONSOR
M.J. Gleeson Group Plc.

LIST OF PLAYERS 1999-2000

SURNAME	FIRST NAME	MIDDLE NAME	DATE OF BIRTH	PLACE OF BIRTH	DATE OF SIGNING	HEIGHT FT INS	WEIGHT ST LBS	POS. ON PITCH	PREVIOUS CLUB
Bonnar	Martin	Michael	12/01/79	Bellshill	02/07/97	5 7.0	9 4	Mid	X Form
Cunnington	Edward		12/11/69	Bellshill	28/03/97	5 7.5	12 0	Def	Coleraine
Davidson	William	Andrew	01/12/77	Bellshill	08/08/96	5 10.0	11 0	Fwd	X Form
Gaughan	Paul		27/09/80	Glasgow	04/09/97	6 2.0	13 0	Def	West Park United B.C.
Henderson	Darren		12/10/66	Kilmarnock	04/06/98	5 11.0	12 0	Mid	Ayr United
Henderson	Nicholas	Sinclair	08/02/69	Edinburgh	10/07/98	6 0.0	11 11	Mid	Partick Thistle
Hillcoat	Christopher	Patrick	03/10/69	Glasgow	19/05/87	5 10.0	12 0	Def	St. Bridget's B.G.
Hunter	Gordon		03/05/67	Wallyford	08/09/99	6 0.0	12 0	Def	Viking U.R.
Kelly	Ryan	William	07/08/80	Rutherglen	05/07/99	5 10.0	11 3	Def/Mid	Rutherglen Thistle
Lynn	Gary		16/12/80	Glasgow	30/03/99	5 10.5	10 6	Def	Scarborough
MacFarlane	Ian		05/12/68	Bellshill	06/03/99	6 2.0	13 7	Gk	Glenafton Athletic
MacLaren	Ross	Stewart	09/07/81	Bellshill	25/08/97	6 1.0	12 0	Def	S Form
Martin	Michael	Benjamin	23/05/81	Glasgow	22/10/98	5 8.0	10 7	Def	Preston North End B.C.
McAulay	Ian	Mackay	06/06/74	Glasgow	15/07/98	5 6.0	11 0	Mid	Stranraer
McCormick	Steven	Walter	10/11/75	Bellshill	02/06/94	5 6.0	10 0	Fwd	Mill United B.C.
McCreadie	Iain	Hugh	20/01/82	Kilmarnock	04/09/99	5 8.5	10 0	Mid	Kello Rovers
McFarlane	David	Thomas Muir	10/04/79	Glasgow	06/08/96	5 11.0	12 0	Fwd	S Form
Moore	Michael	Jordan	24/03/81	Paisley	16/12/98	6 1.0	11 7	Mid/Fwd	Unattached
Muir	Dean		21/02/81	Bellshill	02/06/99	5 8.0	10 5	Mid/Fwd	Hamilton Academical B.C.
Reid	Christopher	Thomas	04/11/71	Edinburgh	31/07/98	6 2.0	13 10	Gk	Hibernian
Renicks	Steven	John	28/11/75	Bellshill	01/06/94	5 8.5	10 8	Def	Hamilton Academical B.C.
Russell	Allan	John	13/12/80	Glasgow	02/07/99	6 0.0	12 1	Mid	Hibernian
Thomson	Steven	William	19/04/73	Glasgow	06/01/95	6 2.0	12 0	Def/Mid	Kirkintilloch Rob Roy

Milestones

YEAR OF FORMATION: 1874
MOST CAPPED PLAYER: Colin Miller (Canada)
NO. OF CAPS: 29
MOST LEAGUE POINTS IN A SEASON: 57 (First Division – Season 1991/92)(2 Points for a Win)
74 (Second Division – Season 1996/97)(3 Points for a Win)
MOST LEAGUE GOALS SCORED BY A PLAYER IN A SEASON: David Wilson (Season 1936/37)
NO. OF GOALS SCORED: 35
RECORD ATTENDANCE: 28,690 (-v- Heart of Midlothian – Scottish Cup 3.3.1937)
RECORD VICTORY: 10-2 (-v- Cowdenbeath – Division 1, 15.10.1932)
RECORD DEFEAT: 1-11 (-v- Hibernian – Division 1, 6.11.1965)

The Accies' ten year league record

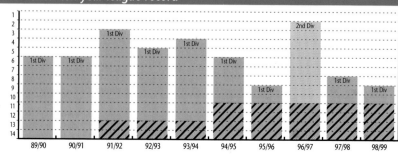

THE ACCIES' CLUB FACTFILE 1998/99 RESULTS... APPEARANCES... SCORERS

Date	Venue	Opponents	Att.	Res	Reid C.	Renicks S.	Cunningham E.	Hillcoat C.	Berry N.	Thomson S.	McAulay I.	Tait T.	Geraghty M.	Wales G.	Henderson N.	McFarlane D.	Clark G.	MacLaren R.	MacFarlane I.	McKenzie P.	Henderson D.	Robertson S.	McCormick S.	Miller C.	Krivokapic M.	Moore M.	McGill D.	Hillcoat J.	Bonnar M.	Davidson W.	Rajamaki M.	Martin M.	Kerr A.	Oliver N.	Lynn G.	Kelly R.	Muir D.
Aug 4	A	Raith Rovers	2,316	2-0	1	2	3	4	5	6	7	8	9¹	10¹	11	12	14	15																				
15	H	Airdrieonians	1,137	1-1		2	3	4	5	6	7	8	9¹	10	11	12				1																		
22	A	Greenock Morton	1,691	2-1		2	3	4	5	6		8	9	10²	11	12	7			1	14																	
29	H	St. Mirren	1,575	0-0		2	3	4	5	6	7	8	9	10	11	12				1																		
Sep 5	A	Ayr United	1,917	3-2		2	3	4	5	6	7	8	9²	10¹		12		15	1		11																	
12	A	Stranraer	666	1-2		2¹	3		5	6	7	8	9	10			4				11	1	15															
19	A	Clydebank	648	1-2		2	3¹	4		6	7	8	9	10			14	5		12	11	1	15															
26	A	Hibernian	9,696	0-0		2	3	4		6		8	9	10	15		7			5	11	1	12															
Oct 3	H	Falkirk	1,427	2-1		2	3	4		6	12		9¹	10¹	8		7			5	11	1	14															
6	A	Airdrieonians	1,945	2-3		2	3	4		6	12			10¹	8	14	7			5	11¹	1	9															
17	H	Raith Rovers	790	3-2			3	4		6	2			10¹	8	9	7			5	11	1	12²															
24	A	St. Mirren	2,312	2-3		2	3	4		6	14			10²	8	12	7		1	5	11		9															
31	H	Ayr United	1,267	1-3		2	3			6	7			10¹	8	14		4	1	5	11		9															
Nov 7	A	Clydebank	451	0-0		2	3	4		6	7	5		10	8	15	12		1		11		9															
14	H	Stranraer	609	1-2		2		4		6	7	5		10	8	9¹	12		1		11			15	3													
21	H	Hibernian	2,288	2-2		2		4		6	7	5			8	10	12		1		11¹		9		3	14	15¹											
28	A	Falkirk	3,325	1-2		2	3	4		6	7	8		12	10	9		1	5		11¹					14												
Dec 8	A	Raith Rovers	1,929	1-1			3	4	14	6	7	8¹	12	10	15	9		1	5		11			2														
12	H	Greenock Morton	1,012	0-0		7	3	4	5	6		8	9		14	12		1			11			2			10											
19	A	Ayr United	2,102	0-5		2		4	5	6		8	9			7		1			11			12	3		10											
26	A	St. Mirren	1,450	0-0		2	3	4	5	6		8	9			7				12		14					10	1										
Jan 9	A	Stranraer	565	2-2		2	3	4	5¹	6		8	9	15	11		7				14		10¹							1	12							
12	A	Clydebank	651	0-1		2	3	4	5			8	9	15	11		14				6		10							1		7						
16	A	Hibernian	10,233	0-4		2	3	4	5		7	8		9	11		12				6					14				1		10						
30	H	Falkirk	1,106	0-2		2	3	4	5	14		8	9		11		7				6			10		12				1		15						
Feb 6	H	Airdrieonians	814	0-2		2	3	4		6		12	9	10	11		7	5		8			14			15				1								
20	A	Greenock Morton	1,914	0-3		2	3	4	5	6			10						8		9	7		14		1				11								
27	A	St. Mirren	2,130	0-1		2	3			5		6	15	9		12	4		11				7			10		1		8								
Mar 20	A	Falkirk	2,206	1-6			3			6	4		12	10¹	14		15	5		8	11					9		1		7		2						
24	H	Ayr United	769	0-2			3			5	4		12	9	7		14	1		6	10									8		11	2	15				
Apr 3	H	Hibernian	4,350	0-2		2	3			6	8			9	10		5	1	15	11						12				14			7	4				
10	A	Clydebank	262	0-0	1	2	3			6	8		9	10	7		5			11						12				14				4				
17	H	Stranraer	525	1-0	1	2	3			6¹	8			10	7		5			11	9									15				4				
24	H	Raith Rovers	1,398	1-2	1	2	3			6	8			10	7		14	5		11	9¹													4				
May 1	A	Airdrieonians	2,257	0-1	1	2	3			6	8			15	10	7		11	5					9	12		14							4				
8	H	Greenock Morton	744	0-2	1	2	3			6				9	10			7	5					8						14				4		11	12	15
TOTAL FULL APPEARANCES					6	32	33	25	14	33	21	21	18	28	24	5	14	12	15	13	25	6	12	7		3	3	9		3	4	2	1	6	1		
TOTAL SUB APPEARANCES						(1)	(1)	(3)	(1)	(5)	(2)	(4)	(10)	(11)	(3)		(5)			(9)	(1)	(1)	(9)		(1)	(1)	(3)		(1)	(1)					(1)	(1)
TOTAL GOALS SCORED						1	1		1	1		1	5	11	1						3		4	1												

Small bold figures denote goalscorers. † denotes opponent's own goal.

Firhill Stadium

Please Note: Only the Jackie Husband (East) Stand is used for Hamilton Academical Matches

Jackie Husband (East) Stand
Main (West) Stand
FIRHILL ROAD

CAPACITY: 14,538; Seated 8,397, Standing 6,141

PITCH DIMENSIONS: 110 yds x 75 yds

FACILITIES FOR DISABLED SUPPORTERS:
Covered places are available for 17 disabled supporters in front of the Main Stand (North area). Telephone call in advance to Office Secretary for arrangements.

Team playing kits

How to get there

The following routes may be used to reach Firhill Stadium:
TRAINS: The nearest railway stations are Glasgow Queen Street and Glasgow Central and buses from the centre of the city pass within 100 yards of the ground.
BUSES: The following buses from the city centre all pass near the ground: No's. 18, 56, 61, 71, 118, 119 and 120 and the frequency of the buses is just under 10 minutes from Hope Street.
UNDERGROUND: The nearest Strathclyde PTE Underground station is St.George's Cross and supporters walking from here should pass through Cromwell Street into Maryhill Road and then walk up this road as far as Firhill Street. The ground is then on the right. The Kelvinbridge Underground Station is also not far from the ground and supporters from here should walk along Great Western Road as far as Napiershill Street and then follow this into Maryhill Road.
CARS: Street parking in the vicinity of the ground is somewhat limited.

The Accies

email: sfl@sol.co.uk • website: www.sfl.scottishfootball.com

18 76

Firhill Stadium, 80 Firhill Road, Glasgow, G20 7AL

CHAIRMAN
T. Brown McMaster

VICE-CHAIRMAN
Thomas Hughes

DIRECTORS
Allan Cowan,
James Oliver,
Edward Prentice,
Norman Springford &
Margaret W.G. Forsyth

PRESIDENT
James R. Aitken

HON. VICE-PRESIDENT/ ASSOCIATE DIRECTOR
Robert W. Reid

ASSOCIATE DIRECTOR
Les Hope

CHIEF EXECUTIVE/SECRETARY
Alan C. Dick

MANAGER
John Lambie

ASSISTANT MANAGER
Gerry Collins

PLAYER/COACH
Kenneth Brannigan

YOUTH COACH
Alan Morgan

HONORARY MEDICAL OFFICER
Dr Alan W. Robertson

PHYSIOTHERAPIST
Walter Cannon

YOUTH DEVELOPMENT OFFICER/ CHIEF SCOUT
Robert Dinnie, M.B.E.

STADIUM MANAGER
Alan C. Dick

CHIEF OF SECURITY
Alan C. Dick

FOOTBALL SAFETY OFFICERS' ASSOCIATION REPRESENTATIVE
Alan C. Dick (0141) 579 1971

GROUNDSMAN
George Furze

COMMERCIAL/MARKETING/SALES
George Carson & Amanda Stark
(0141) 579 1971

LOTTERY MANAGER
Bobby Briggs

TELEPHONES
Ground/Ticket Office/Commercial
(0141) 579 1971
Fax (0141) 945 1525
JAGSLINE (09068) 666474

CLUB SHOP
80 Firhill Road, Glasgow, G20 7AL
Tel (0141) 579 1971.
Open Matchdays and every
Wednesday from
12.30p.m. - 4.30p.m.

OFFICIAL SUPPORTERS CLUB
Ms. Morag McHaffie,
c/o Firhill Stadium, 80 Firhill Road,
Glasgow, G20 7AL

TEAM CAPTAIN
Kenneth Brannigan

SHIRT SPONSOR
D.H. Morris Group

LIST OF PLAYERS 1999-2000

SURNAME	FIRST NAME	MIDDLE NAME	DATE OF BIRTH	PLACE OF BIRTH	DATE OF SIGNING	HEIGHT FT INS	WEIGHT ST LBS	POS. ON PITCH	PREVIOUS CLUB
Archibald	Alan	Maxwell	13/12/77	Glasgow	19/09/96	6 0.0	11 7	Def	Kilwinning Rangers
Arthur	Kenneth		07/12/78	Bellshill	01/06/97	6 3.0	13 8	Gk	Possilpark Y.M.C.A.
Bonar	Steven	Andrew	20/05/79	Glasgow	28/08/98	5 9.5	10 0	Mid	Ayr United
Brannigan	Kenneth		08/06/65	Glasgow	02/06/99	6 0.0	12 4	Def	Clydebank
Budinauckas	Kevin		16/09/74	Bellshill	20/07/99	5 10.0	11 0	Gk	Baillieston Juniors
Callaghan	Thomas		28/08/69	Glasgow	30/07/98	5 10.0	11 4	Mid	Finn Harps
Craig	Albert	Hughes	03/01/62	Glasgow	20/07/99	5 8.0	11 4	Mid	Stenhousemuir
Dallas	Stephen		02/11/74	Glasgow	05/07/99	5 7.0	10 4	Fwd	Baillieston Juniors
Docherty	Stephen		18/02/76	Glasgow	20/07/99	5 8.0	10 10	Mid/Fwd	Clydebank
Duncan	Gavin		07/08/73	Glasgow	05/07/99	5 10.0	10 7	Def	Arthurlie Juniors
Dunn	Robert		28/06/79	Glasgow	27/06/97	5 10.0	10 5	Fwd	Possilpark Y.M.C.A.
Elliot	David		13/11/69	Glasgow	20/08/99	5 9.0	11 0	Fwd	Hibernian
English	Isaac		12/11/71	Paisley	26/07/99	5 9.0	10 11	Mid/Fwd	Coleraine
Frame	Andrew	Robert	17/10/78	Lanark	01/10/98	5 8.0	10 0	Mid	Hibernian
Howie	William		09/07/82	Rutherglen	21/05/99	5 8.0	10 1	Mid	Partick Thistle B.C.
Jacobs	Quinton		22/01/79	Windhoek	02/09/99	5 11.0	11 12	Mid/Fwd	Black Africa
McAllister	Thomas	James	21/02/72	Glasgow	05/07/99	6 0.0	12 6	Mid	Maryhill Juniors
McCann	Kevin		17/12/80	Bellshill	01/10/98	5 11.0	12 3	Def	Partick Thistle B.C.
McGuinness	Edward	Thomas	17/05/69	Bellshill	05/07/99	6 0.0	13 4	Mid	Lesmahagow Juniors
McKeown	Desmond	Michael	18/01/70	Glasgow	11/06/98	5 11.0	11 0	Def	Queen of the South
Miller	Scott	Kerr	04/05/75	Glasgow	07/07/99	5 9.0	10 5	Fwd	Clydebank
Montgomerie	Samuel	Raymond	17/04/61	Irvine	14/07/99	5 8.0	11 12	Def	Kilmarnock
Morgan	Andrew	Alan	10/12/74	Glasgow	05/09/97	5 9.0	10 12	Fwd	Forfar Athletic
Newall	Richard		29/03/78	Glasgow	05/07/99	5 11.0	11 8	Mid	Ayr United
Paton	Eric	John	01/08/78	Glasgow	05/07/99	5 8.5	11 11	Mid	Hibernian
Walker	Andrew	Francis	06/04/65	Glasgow	10/09/99	5 8.0	10 7	Fwd	Carlisle United

Milestones

YEAR OF FORMATION: 1876
MOST CAPPED PLAYER: Alan Rough
NO. OF CAPS: 53
MOST LEAGUE POINTS IN A SEASON: 57 (First Division - Season 1991/92)
MOST LEAGUE GOALS SCORED BY A PLAYER IN A SEASON: Alec Hair (Season 1926/27)
NO. OF GOALS SCORED: 41
RECORD ATTENDANCE: 49,838 (-v- Rangers – 18.2.1922)
RECORD VICTORY: 16-0 (-v- Royal Albert – Scottish Cup, 17.1.1931)
RECORD DEFEAT: 0-10 (-v- Queen's Park - Scottish Cup, 3.12.1881)

The Jags' ten year league record

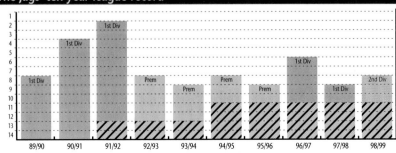

THE JAGS' CLUB FACTFILE 1998/99 RESULTS... APPEARANCES... SCORERS

Date	Venue	Opponents	Att.	Res	Arthur K.	Kennedy D.	McArthur S.	Jamieson W.	Archibald A.	Connell G.	Lauchlan M.	Bryce T.	Morgan A.	Callaghan T.	Donaghy M.	Johnston S.	Dunn R.	Martin A.	Callaghan W.	Gaughan K.	McDonald P.	McKeown D.	Ross S.	McKenzie J.	Flannigan C.	Bonar S.	Tosh P.	Dair I.	Frame A.	Hood G.	McHarg S.	Houston S.	Burns G.	Avdiu K.	McCann K.	Howie W.
Aug 4	H	Inverness Cal. Th.	1,905	0-1	1	2	3	4	5	6	7	8	9	10	11	12	14																			
15	A	Forfar Athletic	1,053	1-0	1	2	3	4	5	6	7^1		9	10	11		8		14																		
22	H	Queen of the South	1,963	2-2	1	2	3	4	5	6	7	8	9^1		11	12^1	10		14																		
29	A	Clyde	2,621	2-1	1	2	3	4	5	6	7	8	9^2		11	12	10	14	15																		
Sep 5	H	Alloa Athletic	1,655	1-0	1	2	3			6	7	8	9^1			14	10		12	4	11	5															
12	H	Stirling Albion	1,998	1-0	1	2			5	6	7	8^1	9			12	10		14	4	11	3															
19	A	East Fife	1,314	3-1		2			5	6	7^1	8	9			14	10^2		12	4	11	3	1														
26	H	Arbroath	2,006	2-0		2			5	6	7	8^1	9^1			12	10		15	4	11	3	1														
Oct 3	A	Livingston	5,200	0-1		2			5	6	7	8	9			12	10		15	4	11	3	1														
11	H	Forfar Athletic	2,870	2-0		2			5	6	7	8^1	9^1				10			4	11	3	1														
17	A	Inverness Cal. Th.	2,598	2-3		2			5^1	6		8	9	7			10		12	4	11^1	3	1	15													
24	A	Clyde	2,627	0-2		2			5	6	7	8	9			12	10		14	4	11	3	1	15													
31	A	Alloa Athletic	1,469	1-3		2			5	6		8		7		14		12	9	4	11	3	1				10^1										
Nov 7	H	East Fife	1,870	0-1				4	5	6		8	12	7			14	15	9	2	11	3	1				10										
14	A	Stirling Albion	1,513	0-2				4	5	6		8				14	15	12	10	2	11	3	1		7	9											
21	A	Arbroath	1,121	0-1				4	5	6		8				14		12	10		11	3	1	2	9	7											
28	H	Livingston	2,341	1-3	1	2		4	5		7					14	15		10^1	6	11	3			8		12		9								
Dec 12	A	Queen of the South	1,731	0-0	1	2		4	5		7								10	6	11	3			8		12		9								
19	H	Inverness Cal. Th.	2,141	2-1	1	2		4	5		7^1								10	6	11	3			8		12	14	9^1	15							
26	H	Clyde	2,673	1-0	1	2		4	5		7							15	10	6	11^1	3			8		12	14	9								
Jan 13	H	Alloa Athletic	1,502	†2-1	1	2		4	5		7	15							10^1	6	11	3			8		11	14	9								
16	H	Arbroath	2,105	0-0	1	2		4	5		7	14							10	6	11	3			8		15		9								
30	A	Livingston	3,293	1-1	1	2		4	5			12							10^1	6	11	3				7			9								
Feb 6	A	East Fife	1,241	0-1	1	2		4			7	12						15	10	5	11	3			8	6			9								
17	H	Stirling Albion	1,203	0-1	1	2		4	5	6		8	9								11	3			15	10	12		14								
20	H	Queen of the South	1,510	1-3	1			4	5		7	8	9^1					15			11	3			12	10	6		14	2							
27	A	Forfar Athletic	662	1-2	1			4	5^1	6	7	8	9			12					11			2					3	10							
Mar 6	A	Alloa Athletic	996	1-0	1	2		4		6	7^1	8	9	10							11	3			12	15			5	14							
13	H	Clyde	3,342	0-1	1	2			5	6		8	9	11					15	4	10				7	3			14	12							
20	H	Livingston	2,112	1-1	1		3		5	6	2	11							8		10^1				7	4	14		9						12		
Apr 3	A	Arbroath	1,301	1-2	1		3		5	6	4	7				14		15	9^1		11				12				2					8	10		
10	H	East Fife	1,811	2-2	1				5	6		8							9	15	11	3			2				12^1					4	10^1		
17	A	Stirling Albion	1,664	0-3	1				5	6	2	14					7	9		4	11	3			15									8	10		
24	A	Inverness Cal. Th.	3,246	2-3	1				5^1			8	7			12	9^1			6	11	3			2									4	10		
May 1	H	Forfar Athletic	2,539	1-0	1				5		14	7		4		12	9			6	11^1	3			15				2					8	10		
8	A	Queen of the South	2,335	2-2	1		3		5	6	8	7^2				15					11				9				2	10				4			14
TOTAL FULL APPEARANCES					26	24	8	25	33	32	22	18	12	14	1	4	26		7	22	29	30	10	3	8	7	10	1	4	6	1		6	6	1	
TOTAL SUB APPEARANCES							(1)			(1)	(5)	(1)	(1)	(11)		(11)	(8)		(1)	(6)	(4)	(2)		(4)	(8)	(7)		(3)		(1)	(2)					(1)
TOTAL GOALS SCORED									2	1	1	5	3	6			10				3				1	1						1		1	

Small bold figures denote goalscorers.   † denotes opponent's own goal.

Firhill Stadium

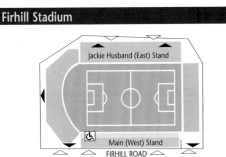

Jackie Husband (East) Stand

Main (West) Stand
FIRHILL ROAD

CAPACITY: 14,538; Seated 8,397 Standing 6,141

PITCH DIMENSIONS: 110 yds x 75 yds

FACILITIES FOR DISABLED SUPPORTERS:
Covered places are available for 17 disabled supporters in front of the Main Stand (North area). Prior arrangement must be made with the Secretary and a ticket obtained.

Team playing kits

How to get there

The following routes may be used to reach Firhill Stadium:
TRAINS: The nearest railway stations are Glasgow Queen Street and Glasgow Central and buses from the centre of the city pass within 100 yards of the ground.
BUSES: The following buses from the city centre all pass near the ground: No's. 18, 56, 61, 71, 118, 119 and 120 and the frequency of the buses is just under 10 minutes from Hope Street.
UNDERGROUND: The nearest Strathclyde PTE Underground station is St.George's Cross and supporters walking from here should pass through Cromwell Street into Maryhill Road and then walk up this road as far as Firhill Street. The ground is then on the right. The Kelvinbridge Underground Station is also not far from the ground and supporters from here should walk along Great Western Road as far as Napiershill Street and then follow this into Maryhill Road.
CARS: Street parking in the vicinity of the ground is somewhat limited.

email: sfl@sol.co.uk • website: www.sfl.scottishfootball.com

Queen of the South

Palmerston Park, Terregles Street,
Dumfries, DG2 9BA

CHAIRMAN
Norman G. Blount

VICE-CHAIRMAN
Ronald Bradford

DIRECTORS
Thomas G. Harkness
& Keith M. Houliston

COMPANY SECRETARY
Richard Shaw, M.B.E.

FIRST TEAM COACHES
George Rowe & Kenneth Eadie

CLUB COACHES
Trevor Wilson, Whitehead Moffat,
John McCaig, Ian Bell, Ian Mundell,
Steve Swailes & Kevin Hetherington

YOUTH DEVELOPMENT OFFICER
Walter MacAdam

MATCH ANALYST
Iain McChesney

CLUB DOCTORS
Dr. Phil Clayton & Dr. Steven Morris

ORTHOPAEDIC SURGEON
Mr. Clark Dreghorn

PHYSIOTHERAPISTS
Marion Hamilton & George Hannah

FOOTBALL SAFETY OFFICERS'
ASSOCIATION REPRESENTATIVE
George Galbraith (01387) 254853

GROUNDSMAN
Kevin McCormick

COMMERCIAL MANAGER
Robert McKinnell
(01387) 254853

TELEPHONES
Ground/Ticket Office/
Information Service
(01387) 254853
Football Office Only (01387) 251666
Restaurant (01387) 252241
Fax (01387) 254853
Hotline: (09066) 555 983

E-MAIL & INTERNET ADDRESS
mail@qosfc.co.uk
www.qosfc.co.uk

CLUB SHOP
Palmerston Park, Terregles Street,
Dumfries, DG2 9BA (01387) 254853
Open 9.00 a.m. – 4.00 p.m. Mon. to
Fri. and 1.30 p.m. – 5.00 p.m.
on home match days.

OFFICIAL SUPPORTERS CLUB
c/o Palmerston Park, Terregles Street,
Dumfries, DG2 9BA

TEAM CAPTAIN
Steven Leslie

SHIRT SPONSOR
Alex Wilson TV-VIDEO-HI-FI

70

LIST OF PLAYERS 1999-2000

SURNAME	FIRST NAME	MIDDLE NAME	DATE OF BIRTH	PLACE OF BIRTH	DATE OF SIGNING	HEIGHT FT INS	WEIGHT ST LBS	POS. ON PITCH	PREVIOUS CLUB
Adams	Charles	Stuart Scarlett	21/03/76	Irvine	24/07/98	5 10.0	11 5	Fwd	Clydebank
Aitken	Andrew	Robert	02/02/78	Dumfries	10/07/96	6 1.0	12 7	Def	Annan Athletic
Bailey	Lee		10/07/72	Edinburgh	24/07/98	5 6.0	10 0	Fwd	Livingston
Boyle	Denis	Patrick	24/04/81	Letterkenny	30/09/97	5 7.0	10 1	Mid	Keadue Youths
Brown	Alastair		05/02/82	Irvine	30/07/99	5 10.0	10 7	Mid	Ayr United
Caldwell	Bryan Robert Andrew James		20/03/81	Glasgow	27/07/98	5 7.0	9 0	Fwd	Queen of the South B.C.
Cleeland	Marc		15/12/75	Whitehaven	30/07/98	5 8.0	10 4	Mid	Unattached
Dowie	Scott		06/07/75	Edinburgh	16/06/99	6 1.0	12 5	Gk	West Calder Jnrs
Eadie	Kenneth	William	26/02/61	Paisley	18/07/97	5 10.0	11 8	Fwd	Airdrieonians
Findlay	William	McCall	29/08/70	Kilmarnock	30/07/99	5 10.0	12 13	Mid	Ayr United
Finlayson	Raymond		29/07/79	Glasgow	28/07/99	5 10.0	11 4	Fwd	Queen's Park
Harvey	Paul	Edward	28/08/68	Glasgow	30/07/99	5 9.0	11 2	Mid	Raith Rovers
Hillcoat	John	George	16/12/70	Paisley	29/07/99	5 11.5	12 12	Gk	Hamilton Academical
Kerr	Alan	Thomas	07/05/76	Irvine	30/07/99	5 8.0	11 7	Mid	Thor
Leslie	Steven		06/02/76	Dumfries	30/07/98	5 5.5	10 0	Mid	Annan Athletic
Mallan	Stephen	Patrick	30/08/67	Glasgow	03/08/93	5 11.0	12 4	Fwd	Clyde
Mathieson	David	James	18/01/78	Dumfries	02/08/96	5 11.0	10 13	Gk	St. Johnstone
McCaig	John	George	19/11/82	Ayr	13/05/99	6 1.0	12 6	Fwd	S Form
McGuffie	Russel		05/09/81	Dumfries	13/05/99	5 11.0	11 7	Def	S Form
Moffat	Adam	James	31/01/81	Lanark	10/09/98	5 9.0	11 8	Def	S Form
Muirhead	Thomas		03/10/81	Dumfries	10/09/98	5 10.0	11 8	Gk	S Form
Paterson	Geoffrey	Samson	10/03/82	Dumfries	28/07/99	5 8.0	10 5	Mid	S Form
Robison	Kevin	Richard	26/10/80	Dumfries	28/07/99	5 11.0	11 0	Def	Rangers
Rowe	John	George	23/08/68	Glasgow	26/08/92	6 0.0	11 7	Def	Clydebank
Stewart	Paul		01/08/79	Glasgow	28/07/99	5 10.0	10 0	Mid	Clyde
Strain	Christopher	Robert	25/03/80	Irvine	01/07/99	5 10.0	10 7	Fwd	Kilmarnock
Weir	Mark	John	30/03/80	Lanark	10/07/97	5 8.0	10 10	Mid	Forth Wanderers

Milestones

YEAR OF FORMATION: 1919
MOST CAPPED PLAYER: William Houliston
NO. OF CAPS: 3
MOST LEAGUE POINTS IN A SEASON: 55 (Division 2 – Season 1985/86)
MOST LEAGUE GOALS SCORED BY A PLAYER IN A SEASON: Jimmy Gray (Season 1927/28)
NO. OF GOALS SCORED: 37
RECORD ATTENDANCE: 24,500 (-v- Heart of Midlothian – Scottish Cup, 23.2.1952)
RECORD VICTORY: 11-1 (-v- Stranraer – Scottish Cup, 16.1.1932)
RECORD DEFEAT: 2-10 (-v- Dundee – Division 1, 1.12.1962)

The Doonhamers' ten year league record

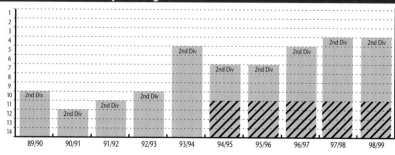

THE DOONHAMERS' CLUB FACTFILE 1998/99 RESULTS... APPEARANCES... SCORERS

Date	Venue	Opponents	Att	Res	Mathieson D.	Milligan R.	Love G.	Rowe J.G.	Thomson J.	Cleeland M.	McAllister J.	Leslie S.	Eadie K.	Nesovic A.	Bailey L.	Mallan S.	Boyle D.	Lilley D.	Townsley D.	Potts C.	Aitken A.	Doig K.	Adams C.	MacLeod J.	Caldwell B.	Weir M.	McKee C.	Turner T.	Armstrong G.	Russell G.	McCaig J.	Bryce T.	Moffat A.	McGuffie R.
Aug 4	A	Clyde	631	0-2	1	2	3	4	5	6	7	8	9	10	11	12	14																		
15	H	Arbroath	1,104	0-0	1		3	4	5	6		8	10	15		9	14	2	7	11	12													
22	A	Partick Thistle	1,963	2-2	1		3	4	5			8	9^{1}	10	11			2	7^{1}			6	14											
29	H	Livingston	1,281	0-1	1		3	4	5		15	8	9	10	11			2	12	7		6												
Sep 5	A	Stirling Albion	640	0-1	1		3	4	5	2		8	9	10	11				12	7		6	14											
12	A	Inverness Cal. Th.	1,812	2-3	1			6^{1}	5		12		14	10	8	9^{1}			7	11	3	4	15	2										
19	H	Forfar Athletic	916	3-0	1		3	6	5	2	11		12^{1}	10		9	15		7^{2}			4	8											
27	A	East Fife	803	0-2	1		3	6	5	2	11		12	10		9			7			4	8	15										
Oct 3	H	Alloa Athletic	1,038	2-1	1		3		5	6	11		10			12	9^{1}	2	8^{1}	15	4	7												
10	A	Arbroath	603	1-2	1		3	14	5	6	11		10	15	12	9^{1}		2	8		4	7												
17	H	Clyde	1,139	2-1	1			4	5	6		15	9^{1}	10	8	14^{1}		2	12		3	7				11								
24	A	Livingston	2,005	0-2	1			4	5	6			10	8	9			2	12		3	7				15	11							
31	H	Stirling Albion	1,128	2-3	1			5		4	8		10^{1}	14	12			2	6^{1}		3	7				11	9							
Nov 7	A	Forfar Athletic	389	0-1	1				4	3	8		10		9	11	2	15		6	5					7								
14	H	Inverness Cal. Th.	1,021	2-2	1			5	6	11	8	9^{1}	10	7^{1}	15			4		3			2	14	12									
21	H	East Fife	937	0-0	1			5	4	11	8	9		10	12			6		3			2	14		7								
28	A	Alloa Athletic	592	1-2	1			12	5	6	11	8		10	9^{1}			4		3			2	14		7								
Dec 12	H	Partick Thistle	1,731	0-0	1			4	5			6	12	10	14	9		2		3			8	11	7									
19	A	Clyde	794	1-2	1			4^{1}	5			6	9	10	12	15	14	2		3				11	7	8								
27	H	Livingston	1,221	2-2	1			5		3		9^{1}	10	6	14^{1}	11		2		4	15				7	8								
Jan 17	A	East Fife	797	1-0	1			4		3		10^{1}	6	9	14	2		5	15				11		7	8								
26	A	Stirling Albion	643	3-1	1			4	12	3		10^{1}	7	9		2		5		6		14^{1}	11		15^{1}	8								
30	H	Alloa Athletic	1,201	0-0	1			4		3		10	7	9		2		5		6		14	11		15	8								
Feb 6	H	Forfar Athletic	968	0-3	1			4	11	3	7		10	6	9	2	12	5				15			14	8								
13	A	Inverness Cal. Th.	2,204	0-1	1			4	5	12	3		15		11	9		2	7		6	14			10	8								
20	A	Partick Thistle	1,510	3-1	1			4^{1}		8	3	6	9		10^{2}	11		2	7		5	14												
27	H	Arbroath	1,020	3-0	1			4		6	3	8^{1}	9		10			2	7^{2}		5	12			11									
Mar 6	H	Stirling Albion	1,014	3-0	1			4		6^{1}	3	8	9	14	12			2	7^{1}		5	10^{1}			15	11								
13	A	Livingston	2,300	2-1	1			4		6	3	8		9	12			2	7^{1}		5	10^{1}			14	11			15					
20	A	Alloa Athletic	523	5-3	1			4^{1}		6	3	8			10^{2}				7^{1}		5	9^{1}			11				2	15				
Apr 3	H	East Fife	1,411	2-0	1			4^{1}		6	3	8		12	10			2	7		5	9^{1}			11				15	14				
10	A	Forfar Athletic	416	1-2	1			4^{1}		6	3	8			10			2	7		5	9			15	11				7				
17	H	Inverness Cal. Th.	1,214	1-1	1			4^{1}		6	3	8			10			2			5	9			14	11				7				
24	H	Clyde	1,218	2-1	1			4		6	3				10^{2}	8		2	7		5	9			14	11					12			
May 1	A	Arbroath	976	2-0	1					6	3				15	10^{2}	8	2	7		5	9			14	11					12	4		
8	H	Partick Thistle	2,335	2-2	1					6					14	10^{1}	8	2	7^{1}		5	9			11	15					12	4	3	
TOTAL FULL APPEARANCES					36	1	9	28	18	26	25	21	15	20	16	24	6	27	21	5	27	9	18	4	2	17	2	5	4	5	1	1	2	1
TOTAL SUB APPEARANCES						(2)		(2)	(2)	(1)	(5)		(3)	(10)	(7)	(5)		(6)		(2)		(9)			(13)	(2)			(3)	(1)	(1)		(5)
TOTAL GOALS SCORED								7	1		1	5	3		1	15		10	1			4			1				1				

Small bold figures denote goalscorers. † denotes opponent's own goal.

Palmerston Park

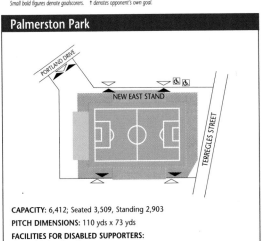

PORTLAND DRIVE • NEW EAST STAND • TERREGLES STREET

CAPACITY: 6,412; Seated 3,509, Standing 2,903
PITCH DIMENSIONS: 110 yds x 73 yds
FACILITIES FOR DISABLED SUPPORTERS: Situated in East Stand.

Team playing kits

How to get there

Palmerston Park can be reached by the following routes:

TRAINS: There is a reasonable service to Dumfries Station from Glasgow on Saturdays, but the service is more limited in midweek. The station is about 3/4 mile from the ground.

BUSES: Buses from Glasgow, Edinburgh, Ayr and Stranraer all pass within a short distance of the park.

CARS: The car park may be reached from Portland Drive or King Street and has a capacity for approximately 174 cars.

Detailed Plan on the Internet

email: sfl@sol.co.uk • website: www.sfl.scottishfootball.com

Ross County

LIST OF PLAYERS 1999-2000

SURNAME	FIRST NAME	MIDDLE NAME	DATE OF BIRTH	PLACE OF BIRTH	DATE OF SIGNING	HEIGHT FT INS	WEIGHT ST LBS	POS. ON PITCH	PREVIOUS CLUB
Campbell	Connor		26/01/80	Inverness	19/02/99	5 4.0	9 0	Mid/Fwd	Brora Rangers
Canning	Martin		03/12/81	Glasgow	28/07/99	6 2.0	11 11	Mid	Clydebank
Cooper	Neale	James	24/11/63	Darjeeling	02/08/96	6 0.0	12 7	Def	Dunfermline Athletic
Dlugonski	Bryan		18/10/82	Banff	13/09/99	6 0.0	11 0	Mid	Ross County B.C.
Escalon	Franck		27/07/73	Paris	23/12/97	5 10.0	10 9	Mid/Fwd	Berwick Rangers
Ewing	Garry		10/01/82	Inverness	19/02/99	5 9.0	9 0	Def	Nairn County
Ferguson	Steven		18/05/77	Edinburgh	22/11/96	5 8.0	11 6	Mid	Dunfermline Athletic
Finlayson	Kevin		07/12/79	Glasgow	28/07/99	5 9.0	10 0	Fwd	Queen's Park
Fraser	John		17/01/78	Dunfermline	29/07/99	5 10.0	11 4	Mid/Fwd	Dunfermline Athletic
Geraghty	Michael	John	30/10/70	Glasgow	29/07/99	5 11.0	11 7	Fwd	Hamilton Academical
Gilbert	Kenneth	Robert	08/03/75	Aberdeen	11/02/97	5 6.5	11 4	Mid	Hull City
Hamilton	Garry		28/01/81	Tullibody	29/07/99	5 11.0	10 10	Gk	St. Mirren
Irvine	Brian	Alexander	24/05/65	Bellshill	27/07/99	6 2.5	13 7	Def	Dundee
Kinnaird	Paul		11/11/66	Glasgow	27/07/99	5 8.0	11 11	Mid	Stranraer
Mackay	David		17/09/75	Dingwall	16/09/94	5 11.0	12 1	Def	Ross County B.C.
Mackay	Steven		26/06/81	Invergordon	19/02/99	5 11.0	10 5	Mid/Fwd	Nairn County
MacLeod	Brian		12/05/81	Inverness	19/02/99	5 9.0	11 0	Mid	Nairn County
Maxwell	Ian		02/05/75	Glasgow	12/06/98	6 3.0	12 5	Def	Queen's Park
McBain	Roy	Adam	07/11/74	Aberdeen	18/10/96	5 11.0	11 5	Fwd	Dundee
McGlashan	John		03/06/67	Dundee	11/12/98	6 1.0	12 0	Mid	Dundee
Nicol	Gary		07/09/80	Inverness	27/07/99	5 9.0	10 1	Fwd	Celtic
Ross	David	William	30/06/70	Inverness	12/06/98	6 2.0	12 7	Fwd	Inverness Caledonian Thistle
Shaw	George		10/02/69	Glasgow	29/07/99	5 7.0	11 0	Fwd	Dunfermline Athletic
Tully	Craig		07/01/76	Stirling	19/02/99	5 11.0	11 0	Def	Dundee
Walker	Joseph	Nicol	29/09/62	Aberdeen	19/12/97	6 2.0	12 7	Gk	Aberdeen
Wood	Garry	Pringle Gillan	18/09/76	Edinburgh	22/03/97	5 11.0	12 7	Fwd	Cowdenbeath

Milestones

YEAR OF FORMATION: 1929
MOST LEAGUE POINTS IN A SEASON: 77 (Third Division – Season 1998/99) (3 Points for a Win)
MOST LEAGUE GOALS SCORED BY A PLAYER IN A SEASON: Derek Adams (Season 1996/97)
NO. OF GOALS SCORED: 22
RECORD ATTENDANCE: 8,000 (-v- Rangers – Scottish Cup, 28.2.66)
RECORD VICTORY: 11-0 (-v- St. Cuthbert Wanderers – Scottish Cup, 1994)
RECORD DEFEAT: 1-10 (-v- Inverness Thistle – Highland League)

The County's ten year league record

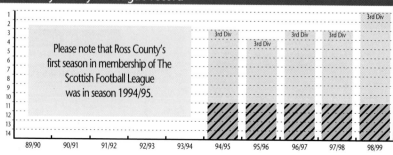

Please note that Ross County's first season in membership of The Scottish Football League was in season 1994/95.

72

THE COUNTY'S CLUB FACTFILE 1998/99 RESULTS... APPEARANCES... SCORERS

Date		Venue	Opponents	Att.	Res	Walker J.N.	Mackay D.	McBain R.	Furphy W.	Maxwell I.	Gilbert K.	Escalon F.	Adams D.	Tarrant N.	Taylor A.	Ross D.	Hunter M.	Ferguson S.	Campbell C.	Herd W.	Wood G.	Hart R.	Golabek S.	Den Bieman I.	Ferries K.	Higgins G.	Haro M.	Matheson D.	Williamson R.	McClashan J.	Meldrum C.	Tully C.	McKee C.	Kinnaird P.	Mackay S.	Ewing G.	MacLeod B.	Stewart G.	Munro G.
Aug	4	H	East Stirlingshire	1,021	1-0	1	2	3[1]	4	5	6	7	8	9	10	11	14																						
	15	A	Albion Rovers	302	8-0	1	2	3[1]	4	5	6	7[1]		9[3]	10	11[1]	14	8[2]	12	15																			
	22	H	Montrose	1,266	†3-1	1	2	3		5	6	7	8	9	10	15		11[1]	12	4	14[1]																		
	29	H	Cowdenbeath	1,553	2-0	1	2	3		5	6	7	8[1]	9	10	14		11[1]		4	15																		
Sep	5	A	Berwick Rangers	453	2-0	1		3		5	6	10	8[2]	9	12	11	15	7		4	2																		
	12	A	Queen's Park	688	2-4	1		3	8	5	6	10		14[2]	11	2	9	7	12	4	15																		
	19	H	Stenhousemuir	2,105	0-1	1		3	12	5	6	2		9	10			7	14	4	15	8	11																
	26	H	Brechin City	1,512	0-1	1		3	4	5	6	10		11	14		9	7				2	8	12															
Oct	3	A	Dumbarton	538	2-1	1		3[1]	4	5	6			12	10		9	7	15	14		2	8[1]	11															
	10	H	Albion Rovers	1,385	1-2	1		3	2	5	6	15		12	11		8	10		9[1]			7	4															
	17	A	Montrose	339	6-3	1		3[1]		4	6	10		14	12		8[1]			9[4]		11	7	5	2	15													
	28	A	Cowdenbeath	212	2-1	1		3		5	6	10		12	14		8			9[2]		11	7	4		2													
	31	H	Berwick Rangers	1,546	3-1	1		3		5	6	10		12[1]	14		8[2]			9		11	7	4	2	15													
Nov	7	A	Stenhousemuir	510	4-2	1		3		5	6			9	10[1]	14	8[3]					11	7	4	2														
	14	H	Queen's Park	1,433	5-1	1		3		5	6			9[3]	10	14	8[1]					11	7[1]	12	4	2													
	21	A	Brechin City	826	1-0	1		3		5	6			9[1]	10	14	8					11	7	4	2														
	28	H	Dumbarton	1,759	2-0	1		3		5	6			9	10[1]	12	8[1]	15				11	7	4	2														
Dec	12	A	East Stirlingshire	338	2-2	1	14	3		5	6			9	10	15	8	12				11[1]	7	2			4[1]												
	19	H	Montrose	1,571	3-0	1	2	3		5	6			9[1]	10[1]	15				12		11	7[1]	4			8												
	26	H	Cowdenbeath	1,842	1-0	1	2	3		5	6			9	10	7				15		11[1]	12	4			8												
Jan	27	H	Berwick Rangers	319	2-2	1	2	3[1]		5	6			9			8[1]			15		11	7	4			10												
	30	A	Dumbarton	400	0-0	1	2	3		5	6	11		9		7	8			15	14	12		4			10												
Feb	6	H	Stenhousemuir	1,837	2-2	1	2	3		5[1]	6	10		9		15	8			12		11	7	4			14[1]												
	13	A	Queen's Park	581	†3-0	1	2	3		5[1]		10		9	12	7	8			6		11	14[1]	4															
	27	A	Albion Rovers	432	†3-3	2	3			5				9	7	7	6[1]			8[1]		11	14	4			10	1											
Mar	2	H	East Stirlingshire	1,021	4-2		3			5				9[1]	10	7	6[2]			11[1]		14		4			8	1	2	12									
	6	A	Berwick Rangers	1,732	6-0	1	15	3		5				9[2]	10[1]	7[1]	6			12		14		4			8[2]	2		11									
	9	H	Brechin City	1,537	2-1	1		3		5				9[1]	10	7	6[1]			12		14		4			8	2		11									
	13	A	Cowdenbeath	316	†3-2	1		3		5[1]				9[1]	10	7	6			14		15		4			8	2		11									
	20	H	Dumbarton	2,374	1-2	1	14			5	6			9[1]	10	7				12	3			4			8	2		11	15								
Apr	3	A	Brechin City	698	1-0	1	3			5	6	10		9	12	11				14			7	4[1]	2		8			15									
	10	A	Stenhousemuir	492	2-3		2			5		10		11	8	1				9[1]	3			4			6			7[1]		15							
	17	H	Queen's Park	3,758	1-2		2	3		5		10		9	14	7				15	6	12		4			8[1]			11			1						
	24	H	Montrose	394	3-2		2	3	14	5				10	7[2]					9		12		4			6[1]	1		8	11	15							
May	1	H	Albion Rovers	1,837	2-0	1	15	3	14	5				10	7[2]					9		12		4			6	2		8	11								
	8	A	East Stirlingshire	356	2-1	1	2	3	12	5				10	7[1]					9[1]				8		4	11	15	14			6							
TOTAL FULL APPEARANCES						31	16	33	6	36	25	17	4	27	24	19	3	26	1	5	12	1	18	2	15	1	26	7	1	16	2	8		10		1	1	1	1
TOTAL SUB APPEARANCES						(4)		(4)		(1)		(6)	(8)	(9)	(3)		(7)	(2)	(15)		(5)		(7)	(2)			(2)	(1)			(1)			(2)	(2)	(2)	
TOTAL GOALS SCORED							5		3			1	3	17	4	7		17			12		2		4	1		6			1						

Small bold figures denote goalscorers.   † denotes opponent's own goal.

Victoria Park Stadium

JUBILEE ROAD

CAPACITY: 5,320, Seated 1,520, Standing 3,800
PITCH DIMENSIONS: 110 yds x 75 yds
FACILITIES FOR DISABLED SUPPORTERS:
Areas in Main Stand and Terracing. Toilet facilities are also available.

Team playing kits

How to get there

The following routes may be used to reach Victoria Park Stadium:

TRAINS: The nearest mainline station is Inverness and fans travelling from the south should alight and board a train that takes them direct to Dingwall Station.

BUSES: Regular buses on a daily basis from Glasgow, Edinburgh and Perth.

CARS: The major trunk roads, A9 and A96, connect Dingwall with the North, the South and the East.

Stenhousemuir

LIST OF PLAYERS 1999-2000

SURNAME	FIRST NAME	MIDDLE NAME	DATE OF BIRTH	PLACE OF BIRTH	DATE OF SIGNING	HEIGHT FT INS	WEIGHT ST LBS	POS. ON PITCH	PREVIOUS CLUB
Armstrong	Graeme	John	23/06/56	Edinburgh	31/10/92	5 9.0	10 12	Def	Meadowbank Thistle
Banks	Alan		25/02/70	Edinburgh	29/05/96	5 11.0	11 0	Def	Berwick Rangers
Brown	Scott		05/03/80	Edinburgh	15/12/98	5 5.0	10 0	Mid	Haddington Juniors
Carlow	Ross		14/09/80	Falkirk	29/06/99	6 0.0	11 7	Def	Gairdoch United
Croly	Stewart		10/03/82	Glasgow	08/07/99	5 10.0	10 0	Def	Preston North End B.C.
Cummings	Aaron		20/12/79	Edinburgh	29/06/99	5 9.0	12 0	Mid	Edinburgh City
Davidson	Graeme		18/01/68	Edinburgh	21/08/98	5 10.0	11 0	Def	Livingston
Fisher	James		14/10/67	Bridge of Allan	18/01/92	5 10.0	10 11	Mid	Bo'ness United
Gibson	John		20/04/67	Blantyre	22/06/98	5 10.0	10 5	Mid	Stirling Albion
Graham	Thomas		12/05/68	Edinburgh	22/06/98	6 0.0	13 0	Def	Livingston
Hall	Michael		11/12/74	Edinburgh	02/02/98	6 1.0	12 5	Def	Edinburgh United
Hamilton	Lindsay		11/08/62	Bellshill	22/07/98	6 2.0	13 4	Gk	Queen's Park
Hamilton	Ross		17/06/80	Falkirk	08/08/98	5 10.0	11 0	Fwd	Grahamston B.C.
Kerr	Paul		17/09/81	Glasgow	08/07/99	6 1.0	12 0	Mid	Preston North End B.C.
Lawrence	Alan		19/08/62	Edinburgh	22/06/98	5 7.0	10 0	Fwd	Partick Thistle
Lorimer	David	James	26/01/74	Bellshill	26/06/99	5 9.0	11 5	Mid/Fwd	Albion Rovers
McGurk	Ryan		06/06/81	Edinburgh	28/08/99	6 3.0	12 0	Gk	Falkirk
McKinnon	Colin	Graham	29/08/69	Glasgow	13/03/99	6 0.0	11 7	Mid/Fwd	Dumbarton
Miller	Paul		14/05/83	Falkirk	26/06/99	5 9.0	10 4	Fwd	Gairdoch United
Mooney	Martin	James	25/09/70	Alexandria	31/07/99	5 7.5	11 0	Fwd	Dumbarton
Perriss	Richard	Elliott	26/03/82	Glasgow	08/07/99	5 6.0	9 0	Fwd	Preston North End B.C.
Stronach	Grant	William	25/10/81	Falkirk	08/07/99	6 1.0	11 0	Fwd	Riverside B.C.
Watters	William	Devlin	05/06/64	Bellshill	28/07/98	5 10.0	12 2	Fwd	Albion Rovers
Wood	David	Wilson	30/12/75	Broxburn	04/03/99	5 9.5	11 2	Fwd	Whitburn Juniors

Milestones

YEAR OF FORMATION: 1884
MOST LEAGUE POINTS IN A SEASON: 50 (Division 2 – Season 1960/61) (2 Points for a Win)
64 (Third Division – Season 1998/99) (3 Points for a Win)
MOST LEAGUE GOALS SCORED BY A PLAYER IN A SEASON Evelyn Morrison (Season 1927/28) and
Robert Murray (Season 1936/37)
NO. OF GOALS SCORED: 31
RECORD ATTENDANCE: 12,500 (-v- East Fife – 11.3.1950)
RECORD VICTORY: 9-2 (-v- Dundee United – Division 2, 16.4.1937)
RECORD DEFEAT: 2-11 (-v- Dunfermline Athletic – Division 2, 27.9.1930)

The Warriors' ten year league record

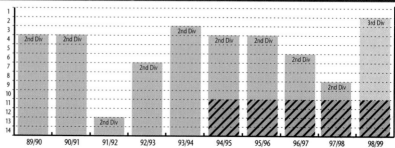

THE WARRIORS' CLUB FACTFILE 1998/99 RESULTS... APPEARANCES... SCORERS

Date	Venue	Opponents	Att.	Res	Hamilton L.	Sprott A.	Banks A.	Armstrong G.	Graham T.	Baptie C.	Kane K.	Lansdowne A.	Watters W.	Hutchison G.	Gibson J.	Brown S.	Middlemist R.	Fisher J.	Hamilton R.	Davidson G.	Craig A.	Lawrence A.	Budinauckas K.	Hall M.	Hunter P.	Miller K.	Christie M.	Huggon R.	McKinnon C.	Wood D.
Aug 4	A	Brechin City	286	0-1	1	2	3	4	5	6	7	8	9	10	11	14	15													
15	H	Cowdenbeath	306	1-2	1	2	15	4	5	6	12	7	9	10	3			8	11[1]											
22	A	Dumbarton	378	2-0	1		3	4		5	11	6	9		12			8	7[2]	2	10									
29	H	East Stirlingshire	357	1-0	1	11[1]	3	4	14	5		6	12		15			8	7	2	10	9								
Sep 5	A	Queen's Park	499	0-0	1	11	3	4	15	5		14	12		6			8	7	2	10	9								
12	H	Montrose	283	4-0	1	11	3	4	6[2]	5			12					8	7	2	10[2]	9								
19	A	Ross County	2,105	1-0	1	11	3	4	6[1]	5								8	7	2	10	9								
26	A	Berwick Rangers	358	2-1	1	11	3	4	6	5			12[1]					8	7	2	10	9[1]								
Oct 3	H	Albion Rovers	410	4-1	1	11		4	6	5		3	12					8	7	2	10[1]	9[3]								
9	A	Cowdenbeath	320	2-0	1	11[1]		4	6	5		3						8	7[1]	2	10	9								
17	H	Dumbarton	456	0-3	1	11		4	6	5	14	3	12					8	7	2	10	9								
26	A	East Stirlingshire	387	1-1	1	11	3	4	6	5	14		12					8	7	2	10[1]	9	1	15						
31	H	Queen's Park	387	2-1	1	11	3	4	6	5		8	12						7[1]	2	10	9[1]		15						
Nov 7	H	Ross County	510	2-4	1	11	3	4	6	5			14					8	7[1]	2	10	9[1]								
14	A	Montrose	271	0-0	1		3	4	2	5			8		11			6	7		10	9		15	14					
21	H	Berwick Rangers	389	1-2	1		3	4[1]	6	5	12		14		11			8	7	2	10	9								
28	A	Albion Rovers	337	3-1	1			4[1]		5	6		14		3			8	7	2	10	9				11[2]				
Dec 15	A	Brechin City	294	0-1	1	14		4		5	6				3			8	7	2		9				12	11	10		
19	A	Dumbarton	283	4-1	1			4		5[1]	12				3[1]				7[1]	2	10	9				11		8	6[1]	
26	H	East Stirlingshire	979	2-2	1		15	4							3			8	7	2	10	9		5		11[2]	6			
Jan 16	A	Berwick Rangers	349	1-2	1		15	4		5			14[1]		6			8	7	2	10	9		3		11				
26	A	Queen's Park	333	1-4		3	15	4		5	12		14[1]		6			8	7	2	10	9	1			11				
30	H	Albion Rovers	382	1-2	1	14	3	4		5	6		7[1]					8	12		10	9		2		11				
Feb 6	A	Ross County	1,837	2-2	1		15	3	4	5			9		14[1]			8	6		10	7[1]		2		11				
20	A	Brechin City	265	2-0	1		15	3	4	5			9		12			8	6		10	7		2		11[2]				
23	H	Montrose	276	3-1	1		15	3	4				9[1]					8	6	5	10	7		2		11[2]				
27	A	Cowdenbeath	361	4-1	1	14		4		5			9[1]		8			3	6[1]		10[2]	7		2		11				
Mar 6	H	Queen's Park	425	4-1	1	11[1]	3	4	5			15	9[1]					8	6[2]		10	7		2					12	
13	A	East Stirlingshire	391	1-1	1	11	3	4	5				9						6	12	10	7		2					8[1]	14
20	A	Albion Rovers	326	2-1	1	11	12	4	5				9		3				6		10	7		2				14[1]	8[1]	15
Apr 3	A	Berwick Rangers	424	1-1	1	14	15	4	5				9[1]		3			11	6		10	7		2					8	12
10	H	Ross County	492	3-2	1		15	12[1]		5	14		9[1]		8[1]			3	6	4	10	7		2						11
17	H	Montrose	354	2-1	1		12	4		5[1]			9		3				6	2	10	7[1]							8	11
24	A	Dumbarton	629	0-2	1		12	4		5	15		9						6	2		7							8	11
May 1	A	Cowdenbeath	300	2-0	1		15	12	4	5			9		14			10	7		6[1]			2		3			8	11[1]
8	H	Brechin City	1,654	1-0	1		14	8	4	5			9					10	7[1]		6			2		3			15	11
TOTAL FULL APPEARANCES					34	17	20	35	22	25	3	10	18	2	17			29	34	23	32	33	2	15		11	3		6	5
TOTAL SUB APPEARANCES						(13)	(7)		(2)	(2)	(3)	(7)	(11)		(5)	(1)	(1)		(1)	(1)				(3)	(2)			(2)	(1)	(3)
TOTAL GOALS SCORED						3	1	2	4	1			9		3				11		7	8				8	1	1	2	1

Small bold figures denote goalscorers. † denotes opponent's own goal.

Ochilview Park

TRYST ROAD
GLADSTONE ROAD

CAPACITY: 2,354; Seated 626, Standing 1,728
PITCH DIMENSIONS: 110 yds x 72 yds
FACILITIES FOR DISABLED SUPPORTERS:
Accommodation for disabled in new Stand. Toilet facilities also provided.

Team playing kits

How to get there

Ochilview Park can be reached by the following routes:

TRAINS: The nearest station is Larbert, which is about half a mile away from the ground.

BUSES: There are regular bus services from Falkirk.

CARS: There is a large car park on the north side of the ground.

email: sfl@sol.co.uk • website: www.sfl.scottishfootball.com

Forthbank Stadium, Springkerse, Stirling, FK7 7UJ

CHAIRMAN
Peter McKenzie

VICE-CHAIRMAN
Peter Gardiner, C.A.

DIRECTORS
Duncan B. McGregor
& John L. Smith

SECRETARY
Mrs. Marlyn Hallam

PLAYER/COACH
John Philliben

YOUTH DEVELOPMENT OFFICER
Raymond Ross

CLUB DOCTOR
Dr. Duncan B. McGregor

PHYSIOTHERAPIST
George Cameron

**FOOTBALL SAFETY OFFICERS'
ASSOCIATION REPRESENTATIVE**
Nick Sabo (01786) 443322

GROUND MAINTENANCE
Souters of Stirling

COMMERCIAL MANAGER
Mrs. Marlyn Hallam
Tel (01786) 450399

TELEPHONES
Ground/Ticket Office
(01786) 450399
Fax (01786) 448592

CLUB SHOP
Situated at Forthbank Stadium.
Open Mon. – Fri. and
Home Match Days.

OFFICIAL SUPPORTERS CLUB
Stephen Torrance, Secretary,
Forthbank Stadium, Springkerse,
Stirling, FK7 7UJ

TEAM CAPTAIN
Craig Taggart

SHIRT SPONSOR
McKenzie Trailers

LIST OF PLAYERS 1999-2000

SURNAME	FIRST NAME	MIDDLE NAME	DATE OF BIRTH	PLACE OF BIRTH	DATE OF SIGNING	HEIGHT FT INS	WEIGHT ST LBS	POS. ON PITCH	PREVIOUS CLUB
Aitken	Alan	Alexander	04/09/82	Stirling	26/02/99	5 7.0	10 8	Fwd	Sauchie B.C.
Bell	David		24/07/79	Bellshill	10/06/98	5 10.0	9 12	Fwd	Motherwell
Clark	Patrick	John	13/03/74	Bellshill	31/07/98	5 11.0	11 1	Def	Arbroath
Dennehy	Brian		25/04/82	Stirling	24/08/99	5 10.5	10 13	Fwd	Riverside B.C.
Donald	Graeme	Still	14/04/74	Stirling	15/07/98	6 0.0	12 4	Def	Hibernian
Donald	Ross		27/09/81	Stirling	24/08/99	5 10.0	11 8	Mid	Riverside B.C.
Eales	Simon		09/09/82	Paisley	24/08/99	5 10.5	11 2	Mid	Largs Thistle
Gardiner	Jason	Stanley	30/10/73	Edinburgh	09/08/99	6 0.0	13 5	Gk	Hibernian
Gardner	James		27/09/67	Dunfermline	28/07/99	5 11.0	11 10	Mid	Exeter City
Gow	Garry	Paul	24/06/77	Glasgow	15/07/98	5 11.0	11 12	Gk	Motherwell
Graham	Alastair	Slowey	11/08/66	Glasgow	29/10/98	6 3.0	12 7	Fwd	T.P.V. Tampere
Greenwell	Lee		20/03/82	Glasgow	24/08/99	5 9.0	10 7	Def	Cumbernauld Hearts
Harley	Douglas		15/04/81	Stirling	24/08/99	6 0.0	11 8	Def	Riverside B.C.
Kelly	Gary		01/09/81	Falkirk	24/08/99	5 11.0	10 7	Mid	Riverside B.C.
Martin	Brian		24/02/63	Bellshill	15/07/98	6 0.0	13 0	Def	Motherwell
McCallion	Kevin		23/07/82	Bellshill	31/07/98	5 8.0	9 10	Mid	Mill United B.C.
McCallum	David	John	07/09/77	Bellshill	15/07/98	5 11.0	10 12	Def	Motherwell
McGrillen	Paul	Alexander	19/08/71	Glasgow	03/09/99	5 8.5	10 12	Fwd	East Fife
McQuade	John		08/07/70	Glasgow	23/07/99	5 10.0	11 7	Fwd	Raith Rovers
Mortimer	Paul		14/02/80	Falkirk	20/07/96	5 11.0	10 9	Mid	Denny F.C. U'16s
Munro	Gareth	Ross	13/10/82	Stirling	05/07/99	5 9.0	10 8	Mid	Cumbernauld Hearts B.C.
Paterson	Andrew		05/05/72	Glasgow	26/08/94	5 9.0	11 3	Def	St. Mirren
Philliben	John		14/03/64	Stirling	15/07/98	5 11.5	12 7	Def	Motherwell
Sinclair	Scott	Ralph	08/05/83	Stirling	05/07/99	5 11.0	11 4	Def	Riverside B.C.
Stuart	William	Gibb	28/01/83	Paisley	05/07/99	5 6.0	8 13	Def	West Park United
Taggart	Craig		17/01/73	Glasgow	07/07/99	5 9.0	11 8	Mid	Clydebank
Tortolano	Joseph		06/04/66	Stirling	23/07/99	5 9.5	12 0	Def	I.R. Iceland
Williams	Alexander	Boyd	15/01/83	Glasgow	27/08/99	5 10.5	10 7	Fwd	West Park U'15
Wilson	Mark		11/04/81	Stirling	24/08/99	5 11.0	11 3	Mid	Riverside B.C.
Wood	Christopher Alan		29/09/79	Stirling	25/09/98	5 10.0	11 7	Mid	Gairdoch United

Milestones

YEAR OF FORMATION: 1945
MOST LEAGUE POINTS IN A SEASON: 59 (Division 2 – Season 1964/65)(2 Points for a Win)
81 (Second Division – Season 1995/96)(3 Points for a Win)
MOST LEAGUE GOALS SCORED BY A PLAYER IN A SEASON: Joe Hughes (Season 1969/70)
NO. OF GOALS SCORED: 26
RECORD ATTENDANCE: 26,400 (-v- Celtic – Scottish Cup, 11.3.1959)
RECORD VICTORY: 20-0 (-v- Selkirk – Scottish Cup, 8.12.1984)
RECORD DEFEAT: 0-9 (-v- Dundee United – Division 1, 30.12.1967)

The Albion's ten year league record

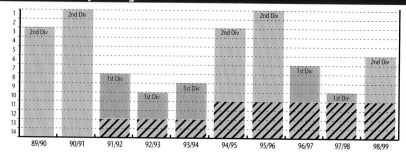

THE ALBION'S CLUB FACTFILE 1998/99 RESULTS... APPEARANCES... SCORERS

Date	Venue	Opponents	Att.	Res	McGeown M.	Paterson A.	McCallum D.	Clark P.	Martin B.	Philliben J.	Bone A.	Donald G.	Price G.	Mortimer P.	Nicholas S.	Bell D.	Hendry J.	Forrest E.	Bradley M.	Provan A.	McCallion K.	Wood C.	Jackson C.	Gow G.	Graham A.	Grant B.	Aitken A.	McKee C.	Cormack P.	Jaffa G.
Aug 4	A	Livingston	1,496	1-1	1	2	3	4	5	6	7	8[1]	9	10	11	12														
15	H	Clyde	1,059	1-2	1	2	3	4	5	6	7[1]	8	9	10	11		16													
22	A	Arbroath	805	3-0	1	2	3	4	5	6	7[1]	8		10	11	12	9[2]													
29	A	Alloa Athletic	1,272	0-7	1	2		4	5	6	7	8		11	10	9	3	12	14											
Sep 5	H	Queen of the South	640	1-0	1	2	6	4	5		7		9	10	11[1]	12	8	3	14	15										
12	H	Partick Thistle	1,998	0-1	1	2	9	4	5	6				11	12	10	3	8	7	14	16									
19	H	Inverness Cal. Th.	915	0-1	1	2	14	4	5	6	7			11			8	3	12	9		10								
26	A	Forfar Athletic	427	2-1	1	2	10	4	5[1]	6	7[1]			11			8	3	9			14								
Oct 3	H	East Fife	748	3-2	1	2	3	4	5	6	7[2]			11	12			9				10[1]	8							
10	A	Clyde	1,008	1-2		2	3	4	5	6	7			11[1]			16	9				10	8	1						
17	A	Livingston	909	1-3		2	3[1]	4	5		7	8		14	11	12	6		16			10	9	1						
24	H	Alloa Athletic	1,085	4-2		2	3	4	5		7[3]	12		10	11[1]		6					16	8	1	9					
31	A	Queen of the South	1,128	3-2		2[1]	3	4	5		7[1]	12		10	11[1]	16	6					14	8	1	9					
Nov 7	A	Inverness Cal. Th.	2,026	1-3		2	3	4	5	14	7	12		10	11		6					16	8	1	9[1]					
14	H	Partick Thistle	1,513	2-0		2	12	4	5	3	7[1]	6		10	11		16						8	1	9[1]					
21	H	Forfar Athletic	731	3-1		2	3	4	5		7[2]	6		10	11[1]	16	12					14	8	1	9					
28	A	East Fife	1,003	3-2		2	10	4	5		7[3]	6	16	12	11		3					14	8	1	9					
Dec 12	H	Arbroath	824	0-1		2	10	4	5		7	6	12	14		15	3		11				8	1	9					
19	A	Livingston	1,996	0-0		2	10	4	5		7	6	12		11		3						8	1	9					
29	A	Alloa Athletic	971	2-2		2	10	4		14	7[1]	6	12	5	11		3		16				8	1	9[1]					
Jan 16	A	Forfar Athletic	445	†3-3		2			5	7[1]	6	10	4	11	12		3					16	8[1]	1	9					
26	H	Queen of the South	643	1-3		2	10	12	5	4	7			11	16		3		14			6	8	1	9[1]					
30	H	East Fife	806	0-1		2	10	6	5		7						3		14	16	11	8	1	9	4					
Feb 6	H	Inverness Cal. Th.	890	1-5		2	10	12	5	6	7			11			3		16		14[1]	8	1	9	4					
17	A	Partick Thistle	1,203	0-1		2[1]	10	6	5			7	16	11	12		3		14			8	1	9	4					
20	A	Arbroath	610	0-1		2	10	6	5		9	15	11	12		3		7			8	1		4					
27	H	Clyde	888	2-3		2	10	8	5		9[2]	7	11	12		3		14			6		1		4	15			
Mar 6	A	Queen of the South	1,014	0-3		2		6		5	12	16	7	8	11	14	3					10		1	9	4				
13	H	Alloa Athletic	1,225	1-1		2		5			7	6	10	8	11		3							1	9	4[1]		16		
20	A	East Fife	641	0-1		2	12	5	4		6		7		14		3		15			11	8	1	9		10			
Apr 3	A	Forfar Athletic	820	2-2		2[1]	10		5			4[1]	8	12			3		7			16		1	9				6	11
10	A	Inverness Cal. Th.	1,778	2-2		2	11	4	5	6	7[2]	8	10									15		1	9		3			
17	H	Partick Thistle	1,664	3-0		2	11	4	5	6	7[1]	8[1]		16					10[1]			14		1	9		3		12	
24	H	Livingston	1,404	0-0		2	11	4	5	6	7	8							10			16	14	1	9		3		12	
May 1	A	Clyde	1,107	1-4		2	11	4	5	6	7		14[1]	15					10			12	8	1	9		3			
8	H	Arbroath	1,005	2-1		2		4	5	6	7[1]		10									11	8	1	9[1]		3			
TOTAL FULL APPEARANCES					9	36	28	30	33	20	27	18	14	15	27	1	6	24	4	8		10	21	27	23	7		1	6	1
TOTAL SUB APPEARANCES						(2)	(3)		(2)	(1)	(4)	(5)	(8)		(16)	(1)	(3)		(3)	(10)	(2)	(14)	(1)			(1)	(1)		(2)
TOTAL GOALS SCORED						3	1		1		21	3	3		5			2			1		2	1	5	1				

Small bold figures denote goalscorers. † denotes opponent's own goal.

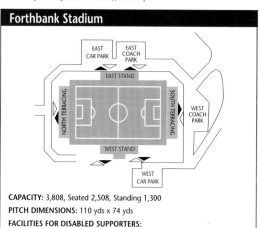

Forthbank Stadium

CAPACITY: 3,808, Seated 2,508, Standing 1,300

PITCH DIMENSIONS: 110 yds x 74 yds

FACILITIES FOR DISABLED SUPPORTERS:
Disabled access, toilets and spaces for 36.

Team playing kits

How to get there

Forthbank Stadium can be reached by the following routes:

TRAINS: The nearest station is Stirling Railway Station, which is approximately 2 miles from the ground. A bus service from Goosecroft Road travels to the stadium (buses run every 25 minutes from 1.50 p.m. – 2.40 p.m. and returns to town at 4.50 p.m.).

BUSES: To Goosecroft Bus Station, Stirling, and bus to stadium from Goosecroft Road (outside Bus Station) Service No 101 operates every 25 minutes from 1.50 p.m. – 2.40 p.m. and returns to town at 4.50 p.m.

CARS: Follow signs for A91 St. Andrews/Alloa. Car Parking is available in the club car park. Home support in West Car Park and visiting support in East Car Park.

email: sfl@sol.co.uk • website: www.sfl.scottishfootball.com

1870

Stair Park, London Road,
Stranraer, DG9 8BS

CHAIRMAN
James Hannah

VICE-CHAIRMAN
Robert J. Clanachan

COMMITTEE
James T. Robertson,
George F. Compton (Treasurer),
Thomas Rice,
James Bark,
Leo R. Sprott,
Alexander McKie,
Nigel C. Redhead,
Thomas L. Sutherland &
R. A. Graham Rodgers

SECRETARY
R. A. Graham Rodgers

MATCH SECRETARY
James T. Robertson

MANAGER
William McLaren

**ASSISTANT MANAGER/
PHYSIOTHERAPIST**
James Denny

GOALKEEPER COACH
John Taylor

**FOOTBALL SAFETY OFFICERS'
ASSOCIATION REPRESENTATIVES**
Leo R. Sprott
(01776) 703271 (Matchdays Only)

GROUNDSMAN
Wilson Hamilton

KIT MAN
William Milliken, M.B.E.

COMMERCIAL MANAGER
Thomas L. Sutherland
(01776) 703271

TELEPHONES
Ground (01776) 703271
Sec. Home/Ticket Office/
Information Service (01776) 702194
Fax (01776) 702194

CLUB SHOP
Situated at Ground.
Open 2.30 p.m. – 3.00 p.m.
and at half-time on home matchdays

TEAM CAPTAIN
Keith Knox

SHIRT SPONSOR
Stena Line

LIST OF PLAYERS 1999-2000

SURNAME	FIRST NAME	MIDDLE NAME	DATE OF BIRTH	PLACE OF BIRTH	DATE OF SIGNING	HEIGHT FT INS	WEIGHT ST LBS	POS. ON PITCH	PREVIOUS CLUB
Abbott	Steven	James	04/04/81	Bellshill	12/05/99	5 9.0	10 0	Def	S Form
Adams	Mark	James	09/08/75	Dumfries	30/07/99	6 0.0	11 0	Fwd	Threave Rovers
Bell	Robert		11/03/76	Glasgow	27/07/98	5 9.5	10 12	Mid	Derry City
Black	Thomas		11/10/62	Lanark	24/07/96	5 11.5	13 0	Def	Kilmarnock
Blaikie	Alan		25/08/72	Greenock	31/03/99	6 1.0	12 0	Fwd	Morton
Bruce	Gordon		10/07/75	Edinburgh	27/05/98	5 11.0	11 12	Gk	Queen's Park
Cahoon	Derek	Alexander	29/09/78	Glasgow	23/05/99	5 9.0	11 0	Mid	Calton Athletic
Furphy	William		07/05/66	London	30/07/99	5 11.0	11 7	Def	Ross County
George	Duncan	Henry	04/12/67	Paisley	01/08/97	5 10.0	10 7	Mid	Ayr United
Harty	Ian	McGuinness	08/04/78	Bellshill	02/07/98	5 8.0	10 7	Fwd	Albion Rovers
Jenkins	Allan	David	07/10/81	Stranraer	03/09/98	5 11.0	11 0	Mid	Ayr Boswell
Johnstone	Douglas	Iain	12/03/69	Irvine	30/01/98	6 2.0	12 8	Def	Morton
Knox	Keith		06/08/64	Stranraer	10/07/97	5 10.0	12 2	Def	Clyde
McGeown	Mark		10/05/70	Paisley	30/07/99	5 10.5	11 6	Gk	Stirling Albion
McGuire	James		10/02/79	Paisley	02/09/99	5 9.0	10 0	Fwd	St. Mirren
McMartin	Grant	Thomas	31/12/70	Linlithgow	04/12/98	5 10.0	10 5	Fwd	Livingston
Mitchell	Allan	Duncan	17/02/79	Glasgow	23/05/99	5 11.0	10 12	Def	Calton Athletic
O'Neill	Stephen		30/06/75	Paisley	30/07/99	6 0.0	13 0	Gk	Renfrew Juniors
Ronald	Paul		19/07/71	Glasgow	30/07/98	6 2.0	12 7	Fwd	East Fife
Smith	James		11/07/78	Glasgow	31/03/99	6 2.0	12 11	Def	East Stirlingshire
Walker	Paul		20/08/77	Kilwinning	17/03/99	5 5.5	9 13	Fwd	St. Mirren
Watson	Paul		16/07/68	Bellshill	14/11/97	6 0.0	12 6	Def	Ayr United
Watt	David		25/03/78	Paisley	14/09/99	5 10.0	11 7	Def	Unattached
Wright	Fraser		23/12/79	East Kilbride	03/09/98	5 10.0	11 10	Def	St. Mirren B.C.
Young	Jason	Anthony	01/03/72	Edinburgh	13/07/98	5 7.0	10 0	Fwd	Livingston

Milestones

YEAR OF FORMATION: 1870
MOST LEAGUE POINTS IN A SEASON: 56 (Second Division – 1993/94)(2 Points for a Win)
61 (Second Division – 1997/98)(3 Points for a Win)
MOST LEAGUE GOALS SCORED BY A PLAYER IN A SEASON: Derrick Frye (Season 1977/78)
NO. OF GOALS SCORED: 27
RECORD ATTENDANCE: 6,500 (-v- Rangers – 24.1.1948)
RECORD VICTORY: 7-0 (-v- Brechin City – Division 2, 6.2.1965)
RECORD DEFEAT: 1-11 (-v- Queen of the South – Scottish Cup, 16.1.1932)

The Blues' ten year league record

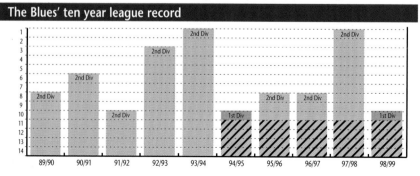

THE BLUES' CLUB FACTFILE 1998/99 RESULTS... APPEARANCES... SCORERS

Date	Venue	Opponents	Att.	Res	Matthews G.	Knox K.	Black T.	Archdeacon P.	Campbell M.	Johnstone D.	Watson P.	McIntyre P.	Young G.	Young J.	Skilling M.	Galloway G.	Bell R.	Harty I.	Jenkins A.	Ronald P.	Wright F.	Brownlie P.	Friels G.	George D.	Kinnaird P.	Meldrum C.	McMartin G.	Adams M.	Bruce G.	Hamilton B.	O'Neill M.	Walker P.	Abbott S.	Blakie A.	Smith J.
Aug 5	H	St. Mirren	1,058	0-1	1	2	3	4	5	6	7	8	9	10	11	12	14	15																	
15	A	Hibernian	9,489	2-1	1		3¹	8	5		6	2	15	10¹	4		11	7	9	12															
22	H	Clydebank	570	0-2	1		3		5		6	2	15	10	7	12			9	8				4	11										
29	A	Falkirk	2,741	0-1	1		3	10	5		6	4	9	2	11			7		8				15											
Sep 5	A	Airdrieonians	687	1-2	1		3	10	5		6	4	9	2	12			7		8¹		11	15	14											
12	H	Hamilton Academical	666	2-1	1		3		5		6	8	15	9	2	11		14		10¹			7	4¹											
19	A	Ayr United	1,917	1-7	1		3		5		6	8	10	2	11	12		14	9				7¹	4											
26	H	Raith Rovers	618	2-2	1		3		5¹	6	7	2	9¹				14	10					8	4	11											
Oct 3	A	Greenock Morton	1,444	0-3	1		3		5	6	7	2	9				14	8	10				15	4	11											
10	H	Hibernian	1,832	0-1	1		3		5	6	7	2	15	9				10					8	4	11											
17	H	St. Mirren	2,884	0-1	1	1	12	3	5	6	7	2	15	9				10					8	4	11											
28	A	Falkirk	502	1-2	1	8	3		5	6	7	2	10¹	9		12							15	4	11											
31	A	Airdrieonians	1,988	2-3		2	3¹		5	6	7	8	10	9									4¹		11	1									
Nov 7	H	Ayr United	1,390	0-1			3		5	6	7	2	10	15	12		8	9		14				4	11	1									
14	A	Hamilton Academical	609	2-1		8	3		5	6	7	10¹	15	2			9¹			14				4	11	1									
21	A	Raith Rovers	1,938	0-2		8	3		5	6	7	10		2			9			12				4	11	1									
28	H	Greenock Morton	795	2-3		2	3		5		6	10		8¹			9	7¹		14				4	11	1									
Dec 5	H	St. Mirren	890	1-2		2	3		5¹		6	9		8			14			10¹				4	11	1					7				
12	A	Clydebank	207	1-2		2	3		5	12	6	9		8			14			10¹				4	11						7	15			
19	H	Airdrieonians	635	1-2		2	3		5¹	6	7			12			8			9			15	4	11	1	10					7				
26	H	Falkirk	3,260	2-3		2	3		5	6	10		15	8			4¹			9¹					11						7				
Jan 2	A	Ayr United	2,722	0-4	1	2	3		5	6		15		8			4	14	12	9			10		11						7				
9	H	Hamilton Academical	565	2-2		2	3		5	12	6	9¹		8			4	14	10				15		11¹						7		1			
16	H	Raith Rovers	575	2-0		2	3		5		6	9²		8			4		14	10					11						7		1			
30	A	Greenock Morton	1,581	0-1		2	3		5	12	6	8	9				4	14	10						11						7		1			
Feb 6	H	Hibernian	8,659	0-2		2			5		6	10	9		3		4	14	15						11						7		1	8		
20	H	Clydebank	452	0-2		2			5	10	6			8	3	14	9	12					15	4	11						7		1			
27	H	Falkirk	709	0-1		6			5	3			2				9	4	11					7	15	1					8	10	12			
Mar 13	A	Airdrieonians	1,341	0-2	1	6			5	3		15		2			10	14	4	9			8								7		11			
20	H	Greenock Morton	563	0-1	1	6			5	3	12	9		2			4	15	14	10			8								7		11			
Apr 3	A	Raith Rovers	1,883	2-3	1	6¹			5	3	4	10		2			12	11¹	14	8			15								7		9			
10	A	Ayr United	990	0-2		6			5	3	2	15		12			8	11	4	10	14							1			7		9			
17	A	Hamilton Academical	525	0-1		4	3		2		10			14	11	7	8											1			15	6	9			5
24	A	St. Mirren	2,210	1-5		6¹	3		2		10	4		8	11	14												1			7		9			5
May 1	H	Hibernian	1,597	0-4		4	6		3	2	15	10	12	14	11	9												1			7	8				5
8	A	Clydebank	269	2-1		4	3		6	10	2	11		8¹	9		15											1			7¹	12	14			5
TOTAL FULL APPEARANCES					18	25	26	4	26	21	36	22	17	13	25	4	12	13	9	25	2	9	17	21	7	13		11	1	1	8	2	4	4	4
TOTAL SUB APPEARANCES						(1)			(3)		(1)	(10)	(2)	(3)	(4)	(8)	(8)	(10)	(4)	(2)		(10)	(1)			(2)				(1)	(2)	(1)		
TOTAL GOALS SCORED							2	2	3				5	2	1		1	2	1	5			1	2	1					1				

Small bold figures denote goalscorers. † denotes opponent's own goal.

Stair Park

LONDON ROAD — ENTRY FOR VISITING SUPPORTERS
NORTH STAND
SOUTH STAND
ENTRY TO SOUTH STAND FOR VISITING SUPPORTERS

CAPACITY: 5,600; Seated 1,830, Standing 3,770

PITCH DIMENSIONS: 110 yds x 70 yds

FACILITIES FOR DISABLED SUPPORTERS:
By prior arrangement with Club Secretary.

Team playing kits

How to get there

Stair Park can be reached by the following routes:

TRAINS: There is a regular service of trains from Ayr and the station is only 1 mile from the ground.

BUSES: Two services pass the park. These are the buses from Glenluce to Portroadie and the Dumfries-Stranraer service.

CARS: Car parking is available in the Public Park at the ground, where there is space for approximately 50 vehicles and also in the side streets around the park. Signs for away supporters will be displayed and parking situated at Stranraer Academy, McMasters Road.

email: sfl@sol.co.uk • website: www.sfl.scottishfootball.com

ALLOA ATHLETIC
SEASON TICKET INFORMATION

SEATED	ADULT	£130
	JUVENILE/OAP	£70
STANDING	ADULT	£120
	JUVENILE/OAP	£60

LEAGUE ADMISSION PRICES

SEATED	ADULT	£9
	JUVENILE/OAP	£5
STANDING	ADULT	£8
	JUVENILE/OAP	£4

HAMILTON ACADEMICAL
SEASON TICKET INFORMATION
SEATED

ADULT	£165
JUVENILE /OAP	£85
JUVENILE (U-14)	£35
16-18 YRS AND/OR REGISTERED STUDENT UNDER 21	£125

LEAGUE ADMISSION PRICES
SEATED

ADULT	£10
U-16/SENIOR CITIZEN	£5

ARBROATH
SEASON TICKET INFORMATION

SEATED	ADULT	£150
	JUVENILE/OAP	£75
STANDING	ADULT	£130
	JUVENILE/OAP	£75
	JUVENILES UNDER 12 YEARS	£25

LEAGUE ADMISSION PRICES

SEATED	ADULT	£9
	JUVENILE/OAP	£5
STANDING	ADULT	£8
	JUVENILE/OAP/	
	UNEMPLOYED (WITH UB40)	£4

PARTICK THISTLE
SEASON TICKET INFORMATION
SEATED

ADULT	£165
OAP/UNDER 16/STUDENT	£80
UNDER 12	£35

LEAGUE ADMISSION PRICES
SEATED

ADULT	£10
OAP/UNDER 16/STUDENT	£5
UNDER 12	£3

STANDING (Overspill only)

ADULT	£9
OAP/UNDER 16/STUDENT	£4
UNDER 12	£3

CLYDE
SEASON TICKET INFORMATION

SEATED	ADULT	£160
	JUVENILE/OAP	£25

LEAGUE ADMISSION PRICES

SEATED	ADULT	£9
	JUVENILE/OAP	£1
	PARENT & JUVENILE	£10

QUEEN OF THE SOUTH
SEASON TICKET INFORMATION

SEATED	ADULT	£120
	JUVENILE (EAST STAND)	£30
	JUVENILE (WEST STAND)	£70
	OAP	£90
STANDING	ADULT	£120
	OAP	£90
	SCHOOL CHILDREN	£30

LEAGUE ADMISSION PRICES

SEATED	ADULT	£8
	SCHOOL CHILDREN/OAP	£6
STANDING	ADULT	£8
	UNEMPLOYED/OAP/UB40'S/	
	FAMILY SUPPLEMENT	£6
	SCHOOL CHILDREN	£3

ROSS COUNTY

SEASON TICKET INFORMATION
SEATED

ADULT	£115
JUVENILE/OAP	£65

STANDING

ADULT	£100
JUVENILE	£50

LEAGUE ADMISSION PRICES
SEATED

ADULT	£8
JUVENILE	£4.50

STANDING

ADULT	£7
JUVENILE/OAP	£3.50

STIRLING ALBION

SEASON TICKET INFORMATION

SEATED

ADULT	£160
JUVENILE/OAP	£85

LEAGUE ADMISSION PRICES
SEATED

ADULT	£9
JUVENILE	£5

STANDING

ADULT	£8
JUVENILE/OAP	£4

STENHOUSEMUIR

SEASON TICKET INFORMATION
SEATED

ADULT	£100
JUVENILE/OAP	£65
FAMILY FLEX - PER ADDITIONAL FAMILY MEMBER	£30

STANDING

ADULT	£100
JUVENILE/OAP	£50

LEAGUE ADMISSIONS PRICES
SEATED

ADULT	£9
JUVENILE/OAP	£5

STANDING

ADULT	£8
JUVENILE/OAP	£4

STRANRAER

SEASON TICKET INFORMATION
SEATED

ADULT	£140
JUVENILE/OAP	£70
FAMILY	£38

STANDING

ADULT	£112
JUVENILE/OAP	£56
FAMILY	£32

LEAGUE ADMISSION PRICES

SEATED

ADULT	£10
JUVENILE	£6

STANDING

ADULT	£8
JUVENILE/OAP	£4

Partick Thistle's Firhill Stadium

YOUTH DEVELOPMENT – IT'S KID'S PLAY

Alan Hansen has been told often enough by now that he got it badly wrong. It was the remark destined to haunt him, the line disproved within months by Alex Ferguson. Try telling those now pumping millions into youth development in Scotland that "you don't win anything with kids".

From Ross County to Rangers, Scotland's senior clubs have in fact decided that nurturing home-grown talent will provide the most satisfying success of all. A quiet revolution is underway in the rearing of our best young footballers. Forget eager and enthusiastic but misguided parents bawling instructions at their boys from the touchline. Forget blaize

pitches. Forget exhausting, 100 games a season schedules. Who knows, one day we might even forget expensive foreign imports forcing young Scots on to the sidelines.

For years, youth development was the issue in which every club in the land talked a good game. Such was the lip service paid to youth policies - to every club it was a "priority" - that the facts became obscured. Actually, most clubs had no dedicated facilities, inadequate scouting networks, and an insufficient coaching staff at youth level. Exciting young players emerged almost in spite of some clubs' efforts.

It took the Bosman Rule to shake Boardrooms throughout Scotland. Overnight the backbone of many

clubs' income - compensation fees for out-of-contract players - was removed. Funds for signings were wiped away. Clubs realised steps had to be taken to restart what once had been conveyor belts of young players. Crucially, the governing bodies also awoke to the need for an overhaul of ineffectual national strategies.

Four years ago, The Scottish Football League introduced a ground breaking scheme which removed the overbearing competitive edge which had come to dominate much of youth football. This minor revolution was a bold sidestep away from the prevailing attitude which demanded victory at all costs. Suddenly, "matches" at Under-16, Under-15 and Under-14 levels were non-

Scotland captain Colin Hendry and Scotland Coach Craig Brown with the youngsters

competitive with the Youth Development Initiative emphasising the need to encourage and develop the skill and technique of teenagers rather than swamping them with winners and runners-up medals. Games need not be held over 90 minutes, they were played in a deliberately relaxed environment, and there were no league tables, cups or medals. The Initiative has proved so successful and popular that from this season, the age range has been lowered to include an Under-13 bracket. A series of coaching days, with high profile visiting guests, will be run throughout this season with some of the most promising young referees in the country also becoming involved in the Initiative.

New, too, is the need to sign a Form "D", a registration document tying each youngster to a single club for the entire season. The paperwork will ensure greater continuity in the coaching of the country's best young players.

Already, players signed to professional clubs can no longer turn out for boy's clubs, and involvement in schools football is also being reviewed by clubs to limit the number of games boys must play. A relaxed football environment to both teach and learn, and coaching from a single source, are the Initiative's twin aims.

Only in the Under-18 Youth Division are youngsters in a competitive environment with a tangible trophy at stake.

"The Scottish Football League deserves a pat on the back for what it's done," said Celtic Youth Coach, Willie McStay. "I have seen big, big changes in the last five years. Now most clubs see the need for youth development and hopefully, we are moving towards what they do in England. Maybe only Celtic and Rangers have the resources to build full-scale academies but others

are doing as much as they can."

Rangers' Youth Coach, John Chalmers, who has worked at Ibrox for 15 years, believes overdue progress has been made since the Youth Development Initiative was introduced. Chalmers, who nurtured Barry Ferguson, Scott Wilson and Barry Nicholson towards Rangers' first team, said: "I think the standard of young player is as good as it ever was, there's just not the same number coming through. For too long we thought talented kids would come through automatically. We should

have done more, and it's only in the last few years that real progress has been made."

The Old Firm, criticised for squandering money on massive transfer fees while failing to invest in youth, both now plan to build a dedicated complex for training and youth development. The proposals are ambitious. Ideally such a facility would involve six training pitches, a mini stadium for Under-21 or youth matches, a full size all-weather pitch, dedicated goalkeeping and specialised coaching areas, a full sized indoor

Form "D" registration document

THIS COPY TO THE SCOTTISH FOOTBALL LEAGUE

THE SCOTTISH FOOTBALL LEAGUE YOUTH DEVELOPMENT INITIATIVE

FORM 'D' REGISTRATION

UNDER-13 AGE LEVEL

FOR PLAYERS WISHING TO BE REGISTERED TO PARTICIPATE IN THE SCOTTISH FOOTBALL LEAGUE YOUTH DEVELOPMENT INITIATIVE. A PLAYER SIGNING THIS REGISTRATION FORM SHALL BE SUBJECT TO THE TERMS OF REFERENCE AND PRINCIPLES OF THE SCOTTISH FOOTBALL LEAGUE YOUTH DEVELOPMENT INITIATIVE, THE RULES OF THE SCOTTISH FOOTBALL LEAGUE OR THE SCOTTISH PREMIER LEAGUE, WHICHEVER IS APPLICABLE, AND THE ARTICLES OF ASSOCIATION OF THE SCOTTISH FOOTBALL ASSOCIATION.

Player's Surname ....

Player's Full Christian Name(s) ....

Present Postal Address ....

Name of Previous Club for which you were Registered .... Postcode ....

Name of Last Club for which you Played ....

Date of Birth .... Place of Birth ....

We, the undersigned parties, agree to the above named player being registered for

.... F.C. in The Scottish Football League

Youth Development Initiative at Under-13 age level for season 19 ..../..........

Player's Signature ....

Signature of Parent or Guardian ....

Address of Parent or Guardian ....

....

.... Postcode ....

Date of Signing ....

Signature of Duly Authorised Club Official ....

Signature of Witness ....

Address of Witness ....

....

.... Postcode ....

PLEASE NOTE:

1. A player or his Parent or Guardian **MUST** receive a copy of the Terms of Reference and Principles of The Scottish Football League Youth Development Initiative before signing a form 'D' and by signing this form, the player or his Parent or Guardian acknowledge that they have received a copy.

2. A club is not permitted to offer and a Youth Development Initiative player registered by means of form 'D' is not permitted to accept any wages whatsoever. A club may reimburse a player registered by form 'D' in respect of necessary hotel and travelling expenses actually incurred. The player may not receive any other payment.

Willie McStay

pitch, and a residential centre where boys would eat, sleep, and do school lessons. The price? No change from £10 million.

The Old Firm's input goes further. Rangers' Assistant Manager, Bert van Lingen, and Celtic First Team Coach, Eric Black, are among those who have worked with SFA Youth Programme Director, Jim Sinclair, to devise the ideal strategy for developing young players and Sinclair has been told to leave no expense spared in formulating his strategy. The Scottish Football Association has always concentrated primarily on broad, community and fun-based coaching rather than on developing excellence. It has invested around £3m into youth development in the last four years but found it difficult to monitor how much of that was ending up directly in the hands of senior clubs. As a result, a more direct input was

introduced via Gold, silver and Bronze Awards for those clubs who could demonstrate a commitment to rearing their own youngsters. More than 60 clubs - from the SPL, SFL, Highland and South of Scotland Leagues - successfully applied for the three graded awards, worth £30,000, £20,000 and £10,000 respectively after submitting their development plans to Park Gardens.

"Maybe I'm deluding myself but I feel we are embarking on one of the most exciting periods for Scottish football," said Sinclair. "If we have managed to improve coaching staff and facilities, I think we are well down the right road. We have made major strides.

"I feel we are at last moving away from parents barking instructions at their kids from the touchline. That's down to money. Whenever the chance of meaningful investment

Kids play

comes along, people will jump through hoops, do whatever it takes, to get it. I think the raw talent is still there but we have to work harder to get it to the top. The coaching must make the most of what is coming through. There used to be a freedom and expression in kids' football that's maybe not there now. We need to get that back and flourishing again.

"Because of that I think we are at a crossroads. We must act together quickly and spend what money is available the best way we can to build on what we are doing. My hope is that within five or six years we start to see the fruits coming through for our clubs and the Scotland team."

New initiatives continue. From this season, the SFA will finance visits from English and European coaches to help broaden the experience of those Scottish coaches involved in the Youth Development Initiative. The quality of the coaching that youngsters are exposed to is vital, so a new development registration form has also been introduced. Essentially, a teenager who currently may be coached by Aberdeen one night, Dundee United the next, will have to choose one professional club for the season. The form will also diminish the input from boys' clubs and school teams, all to minimise the number of games Scotland's most promising children are playing and the variety of coaches with access to them. Working with one quality coach three times a week is of more benefit than learning from three different coaches who may give conflicting instructions.

The number of clubs participating from Under-13 right through to Under-18 age level is also extremely encouraging. On the competitive front, a total of 30 clubs will participate in the Under-18 Youth Division with the set-up split into three sections of ten clubs each. The four age levels of the non-competitive

Young Scotland star, Mark Burchill

Youth Development Initiative also sees an encouraging number of clubs participating this season. There are 26 clubs involved at Under-16 level, 15 clubs at Under-15, 22 clubs taking part at Under-14 level, with the new Under-13 age level attracting 16 clubs in its first season.

Consequently, The Scottish Football League will organise and administer in the region of 1,400 youth matches at the five age levels during the course of the 1999/2000 season, with match officials being appointed centrally by the League to all of these matches. In addition, the introduction of the new Form "D" Registration Form will also see in the region of 1,500 players requiring to be registered at the various age levels of the Youth Development Initiative as well as a substantial number of Apprentices being registered by clubs for the Under-18 Youth Division.

"We have gone a long way forward from where we were five or six years ago," said St. Johnstone Youth Coach, Alastair Stevenson. St. Johnstone, with Queen of the South, Ross County, St. Mirren and Stirling Albion, are some of the clubs whose commitments to youth development has been outstanding. "We've made progress but there's still a long way to go," continued Stevenson. "We are only starting with kids aged 12. You would like them at 10 or 11, although in England they have them even younger than that. But England has the resources. We have to work within our means, but I like what's happening."

If what Stevenson and others are doing achieves the ultimate goal, in four or five years' time, the Tartan Army should like it too.

MICHAEL GRANT
(Sunday Herald)

Cliftonhill Stadium, Main Street, Coatbridge, ML5 3RB

CHAIRMAN
Andrew Dick, M.Sc., B.Sc., C.Eng.

VICE-CHAIRMAN
David T. Shanks, B.Sc.

DIRECTORS
Edward P. Hagerty,
Alan M. Brown
& Robert Watt

GENERAL MANAGER
John Reynolds

SECRETARY
David T. Shanks, B.Sc.

MANAGER
Mark Shanks

ASSISTANT MANAGER
Jimmy Lindsay

PROFESSIONAL YOUTH TEAM COACH
Jimmy Lindsay

YOUTH TEAM COACH
John Bell

PHYSIOTHERAPIST
Derek Kelly

CHIEF SCOUT
Robert Watt

STADIUM DIRECTOR
Andrew Dick, M.Sc., B.Sc., C.Eng.

FOOTBALL SAFETY OFFICERS' ASSOCIATION REPRESENTATIVE
Edward P. Hagerty (01236) 427671

GROUNDSMAN
Hugh McBride

COMMERCIAL MANAGER
Dennis Newall
Mobile (07957) 847388

TELEPHONES
Ground (01236) 606334/607041
Telefax (01236) 606334
Sec. Home (01236) 421686
Sec. Bus. (01236) 762775

CLUB SHOP
Cliftonhill Stadium, Main Street,
Coatbridge, ML5 3RB. Open one
hour prior to kick-off at first team
home matches.

OFFICIAL SUPPORTERS CLUB
John Smith, 45 Blair Road,
Coatbridge (01236) 420417

TEAM CAPTAIN
John McStay

SHIRT SPONSOR
Airdrie & Coatbridge Advertiser
– The Voice of Monklands

Albion Rovers

LIST OF PLAYERS 1999-2000

SURNAME	FIRST NAME	MIDDLE NAME	DATE OF BIRTH	PLACE OF BIRTH	DATE OF SIGNING	HEIGHT FT INS	WEIGHT ST LBS	POS. ON PITCH	PREVIOUS CLUB
Coulter	James		29/01/83	Bellshill	13/05/99	6 0.0	11 0	Mid	S Form
Coulter	Kevin		05/08/81	Bellshill	28/08/99	5 11.0	10 0	Def	Hibernian
Diack	Ian	Gordon	17/02/81	Glasgow	21/10/98	5 11.0	10 8	Fwd	Celtic B.C.
Dobbins	Ian	Alexander	24/08/83	Bellshill	14/07/99	6 0.0	10 5	Mid	S Form
Donnelly	Chris		03/07/82	Australia	25/08/99	5 9.0	9 7	Mid	Unattached
Duncan	Graham		02/02/69	Glasgow	25/07/97	5 11.0	11 6	Mid	Stranraer
Flannigan	Craig	Alexander	11/02/73	Dumfries	29/07/99	5 7.0	10 4	Fwd	Partick Thistle
Greenock	Robert		04/01/80	Coatbridge	12/07/97	5 8.0	10 0	Def	St. Johnstone
Hamilton	James	Michael	09/12/66	Duntocher	16/10/98	5 9.0	11 0	Def	Forfar Athletic
Harty	Martin	John	11/07/82	Bellshill	21/10/98	5 11.0	10 8	Fwd	Albion Rovers B.C.
Johnston	Steven		27/01/83	Livingston	06/09/99	5 8.0	9 0	Mid	Livingston
Lannigan	Martin	Neil	04/12/82	Bellshill	18/05/99	5 10.0	11 0	Mid	Heart of Midlothian
Lumsden	Todd		06/02/78	Consett	10/08/99	6 0.0	12 8	Def	Stirling Albion
McArthur	Scott		18/02/82	Glasgow	15/04/99	5 5.0	9 0	Fwd	Ayr United
McBride	Kevin		12/04/80	Glasgow	15/04/99	5 9.0	10 6	Def	Tower Hearts Juveniles
McCarroll	James		09/09/82	Bellshill	09/08/99	6 2.0	11 0	Def	Albion Rovers B.C.
McIntyre	John		03/08/83	Rutherglen	18/05/99	5 8.0	9 8	Mid	Rangers
McLean	Mark	Andrew	30/03/72	Paisley	31/07/98	6 1.0	13 0	Gk	Clyde
McLees	James	Edward	30/08/80	Coatbridge	21/10/98	5 7.0	10 2	Mid	Lenzie Youth Club
McMillan	Ryan		26/11/81	Glasgow	18/05/99	5 7.0	9 0	Mid	Dundee United
McMullen	Stephen		30/04/82	Bellshill	26/04/99	5 7.0	9 0	Fwd	Dundee United
McStay	John		24/12/65	Larkhall	05/09/98	5 11.0	12 4	Def	Clyde
Nesovic	Alexander		10/11/72	Bradford	07/07/99	6 1.0	12 10	Fwd	Queen of the South
Rae	Derek	Parlane	02/08/74	Glasgow	29/07/99	5 10.0	10 10	Mid	Largs Thistle
Reid	Robert		09/02/82	Rutherglen	18/05/99	5 9.0	11 0	Gk	X Form
Robertson	Graeme	Wm.Thomas	04/06/62	Dumfries	13/08/99	5 7.0	10 5	Def	Ayr United
Russell	Gary	Alexander	18/05/80	Glasgow	29/07/99	5 9.0	10 13	Mid	Queen of the South
Scanlan	Gary		09/06/82	Glasgow	18/05/99	5 8.0	9 5	Fwd	Albion Rovers B.C.
Shaw	Martin	Paul	03/08/80	Glasgow	06/11/98	5 11.0	11 2	Mid	Kirkintilloch Rangers
Silvestro	Christopher		16/03/79	Bellshill	15/04/99	5 7.0	10 4	Mid	Glenboig
Smith	Jordan		02/02/82	Bellshill	29/07/99	6 2.0	12 0	Def	S Form
Sutherland	David		21/08/82	Glasgow	18/05/99	6 0.0	10 5	Def	X Form
Tait	Thomas		08/09/67	Ayr	29/07/99	5 11.0	12 4	Mid	Hamilton Academical

Milestones

YEAR OF FORMATION: 1882
MOST CAPPED PLAYER: John White
NO. OF CAPS: 1
MOST LEAGUE POINTS IN A SEASON: 54 (Division 2 – Season 1929/30)
MOST LEAGUE GOALS SCORED BY A PLAYER IN A SEASON: John Renwick (Season 1932/33)
NO. OF GOALS SCORED: 41
RECORD ATTENDANCE: 27,381 (-v- Rangers 8.2.1936)
RECORD VICTORY: 12-0 (-v- Airdriehill – Scottish Cup, 3.9.1887)
RECORD DEFEAT: 1-11 (-v- Partick Thistle – League Cup, 11.8.1993)

The Wee Rovers' ten year league record

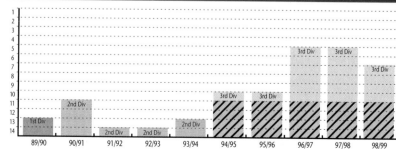

THE WEE ROVERS' CLUB FACTFILE 1998/99 RESULTS... APPEARANCES... SCORERS

Date	Venue	Opponents	Att.	Res	McLean M.	Greenock R.	McGowan N.	Melvin M.	Shaw M.	Docherty R.	Sinclair C.	Ross A.	Bruce D.	Harty M.	Donaldson E.	Lorimer D.	McLees J.	Duncan G.	Mitchell C.	McIlhatton L.	McColm R.	McStay J.	Limond W.	McGowan C.	Diack I.	Goldie G.	Sturrock G.	Hamilton J.	McQuade K.	McBride M.	McBride K.	Botiglieri E.	Murphy J.	Blair P.	Silvestro C.	Smith J.
Aug 4	A	Dumbarton	291	0-2	1	2	3	4	5	6	7	8	9	10	11	12		14																			
15	H	Ross County	302	0-8	1		3		5	7	6	11		12	9	10	8	2	4	15																	
22	A	Berwick Rangers	374	1-2	1		2	3	8[1]		7		12		10	9	11	6	5	15	1	4															
29	H	Queen's Park	419	2-1	1		3	2	7[1]		10	14	9		6[1]	8						4	11														
Sep 5	A	Montrose	244	2-1	1	14	3	2	7		10		9[1]	12	6	8[1]						4	11														
12	A	East Stirlingshire	237	1-0	1		3	2	7		10		9	12	6	8[1]						4	11														
19	H	Brechin City	507	1-4	1	2	3	5		10			9	11	6	8	7					4[1]	12	14	15												
26	H	Cowdenbeath	403	0-1	1	2	3	5	7		9		10	6	8	12						4	14	11	15												
Oct 3	A	Stenhousemuir	410	1-4	1		3	5	12		9[1]		7	11	8	6	2					4	15	10													
10	A	Ross County	1,385	2-1	1	2	3	8		9		12	11	6[1]	7	5						4			10[1]												
17	H	Berwick Rangers	360	1-1	1	2	3	6		9		15	11	8	7	5						4			10[1]			14									
27	A	Queen's Park	336	0-0	1	2	3	7					14	11	8							4	15		9		10	2									
31	H	Montrose	302	4-1	1		7	3	6[2]			9	11[1]	12	8	2						4			14[1]		10	5									
Nov 7	A	Brechin City	307	0-1	1		7	3	5	15		14	11	12	8	2						4			9		10	6									
14	H	East Stirlingshire	304	3-1	1		3	8	14			12	7	9	6[1]	2						4[1]			10[1]		11	5									
21	A	Cowdenbeath	161	3-2	1		3	8	12			11	9[1]	6[2]	2							4			10		7	5									
28	H	Stenhousemuir	337	1-3	1	15	3	8	12			11	10[1]	6	2							4			9		7	5	14								
Dec 12	H	Dumbarton	324	0-2	1		4	3	5	7		12	11	8	6	2									9		10						14	15			
19	A	Berwick Rangers	307	1-1	1	12		4	3	8[1]		11	10	6	2							4			9		15	5							7		
26	H	Queen's Park	322	1-0	1			3	8[1]		15	11	10	6	2							4			9			5							7		
Jan 9	A	Montrose	342	†3-2	1	12		3	8	14		11	10[1]	6	2							4			5										7	9[1]	
30	A	Stenhousemuir	382	2-1	1	12		3	8			11	10	6[1]	2							4			14			5							7	9[1]	
Feb 6	H	Brechin City	259	4-1	1		8	3		12	15	11[1]	10[2]	6	2							4						5	14						7[1]	9	
16	A	East Stirlingshire	244	1-4	1		5	3	8	12		11	10	6[1]	2							4						14							7	9	
23	H	Cowdenbeath	240	1-1	1		3	8				11	12[1]	6	2							4			14			5						7	9	10	
27	H	Ross County	432	3-3	1		6					11[2]	10	3	2							4[1]		14	12			5						7	9	8	
Mar 9	A	Dumbarton	230	1-1	1		3		14			11	8	6	2							4			10			5					7	12	9[1]	15	
13	A	Queen's Park	492	0-0	1		3	2	14			11	8	6								4			12			5					7	10	9		
16	H	Montrose	258	0-0	1		3	7				9	10	6	2							4		14	11			5						12	8		
20	H	Stenhousemuir	326	1-2	1	15	3	7				11	12	6[1]	2							4			9			14	5					10	8		
Apr 3	A	Cowdenbeath	161	2-0	1	12	3	8			14	11	10[1]	6	2							4			9			5			15				7[1]		
10	A	Brechin City	291	1-3	1	2	3	6				12	11	10	8							4						5[1]						9	7		
17	H	East Stirlingshire	304	0-2	1			3	6			9	11	10	5							4		14	2			12					7	8		
24	H	Berwick Rangers	308	0-3	1			2	14			15	12	9	6							4			11			5			3		8	7	10	
May 1	A	Ross County	1,837	0-2	1		3	2				11	9	8								4	15		12			5			14		10	7	6	
8	H	Dumbarton	256	0-2	1	2	3	12				11	9	8								4			15			6					7	10	5	
TOTAL FULL APPEARANCES					35	15	33	33	9	6	2	5	6	8	35	31	29	26	1		1	32	3		14		10	23			1	10	11	12	4	1
TOTAL SUB APPEARANCES						(7)		(1)	(12)		(2)		(1)	(13)	(1)	(5)	(2)				(2)		(2)	(2)	(5)	(1)	(11)	(2)	(1)		(3)	(3)		(1)	
TOTAL GOALS SCORED								5	1			1	1		5	10	6					3			4			1					1	2	2	

Small bold figures denote goalscorers. † denotes opponent's own goal.

Cliftonhill Stadium

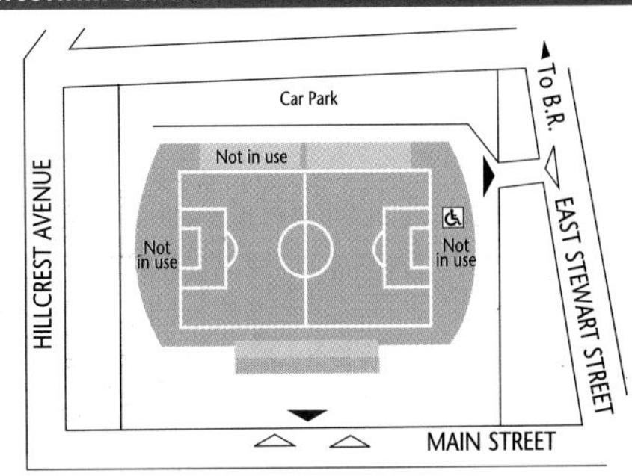

[Stadium diagram: Hillcrest Avenue (left), Car Park and "Not in use" stand (top), pitch with "Not in use" sections, East Stewart Street leading "To B.R.", Main Street (bottom)]

CAPACITY: 2,496; Seated 538, Standing 1,958
PITCH DIMENSIONS: 110 yds x 72 yds
FACILITIES FOR DISABLED SUPPORTERS:
Access from East Stewart Street with toilet facilities and space for wheelchairs, cars etc. Advanced contact with club advised – this area is uncovered.

Team playing kits

How to get there

The following routes can be used to reach Cliftonhill Stadium:
BUSES: The ground is conveniently situated on the main Glasgow-Airdrie bus route and there is a stop near the ground. Local buses serving most areas of Coatbridge and Airdrie pass by the stadium every few minutes.
TRAINS: The nearest railway station is Coatdyke on the Glasgow-Airdrie line and the ground is a ten minute walk from there. The frequency of service is 15 minutes.
CARS: Vehicles may park in Hillcrest Avenue, Albion Street and East Stewart Street, which are all adjacent to the ground.

The Wee Rovers

email: sfl@sol.co.uk • website: www.sfl.scottishfootball.com

Berwick Rangers

LIST OF PLAYERS 1999-2000

SURNAME	FIRST NAME	MIDDLE NAME	DATE OF BIRTH	PLACE OF BIRTH	DATE OF SIGNING	HEIGHT FT INS	WEIGHT ST LBS	POS. ON PITCH	PREVIOUS CLUB
Anthony	Marc		28/03/78	Edinburgh	24/07/99	5 6.0	10 3	Fwd	Celtic
Baigrie	John	Norman	03/12/79	Edinburgh	31/08/99	5 8.0	10 7	Mid	Dalkeith Thistle
Buglass	Kenneth	Colin	08/10/81	Edinburgh	28/08/98	6 1.0	11 0	Def	Hutchison Vale B.C.
Burrell	David		29/12/81	Edinburgh	25/08/99	5 9.0	10 0	Mid	Berwick Rangers Colts
Campbell	Colin	James	05/01/70	Edinburgh	25/06/98	5 11.0	11 0	Def	East Stirlingshire
Clark	John	Brown	25/09/64	Edinburgh	01/08/97	6 0.0	14 1	Def	F.C. Mulhouse
Dixon	Mark		08/08/82	Blackburn	25/08/99	5 6.0	9 5	Mid	Hibernian
Forrester	Paul		03/11/72	Edinburgh	30/03/94	5 9.0	12 8	Fwd	Middlesbrough
Fraser	Graeme	William	07/08/73	Edinburgh	31/03/94	5 11.0	11 8	Def	Dunfermline Athletic
Gallagher	Graham		27/08/81	Edinburgh	25/08/99	5 11.0	11 0	Def	Tynecastle B.C.
Haddow	Lloyd	Simon	21/01/71	Lanark	07/06/99	6 1.0	11 6	Mid	Alloa Athletic
Harvey	Johnny		15/09/82	Glasgow	12/09/99	6 0.0	10 10	Fwd	Whitehill Welfare U'18
Humphreys	Martin	Jay	16/03/76	Dunfermline	28/07/99	6 0.0	13 0	Def/Mid	Cowdenbeath
Hunter	Murray	Russell	08/01/71	Edinburgh	30/12/98	6 1.0	12 0	Mid/Fwd	Ross County
Kerr	William		04/11/81	Edinburgh	25/08/99	5 10.0	10 7	Fwd	Berwick Rangers Colts
Larter	David		18/03/60	Edinburgh	30/07/99	5 10.5	11 4	Gk	Montrose
Leask	Moray	Stuart	02/10/79	Edinburgh	10/09/98	5 9.0	10 12	Fwd	Berwick Rangers Colts
MacWalter	John		03/02/82	Edinburgh	25/08/99	6 1.0	12 0	Mid	Salvesen B.C.
Magee	Kevin		10/04/71	Livingston	21/06/99	5 10.0	11 1	Mid	Montrose
McNicoll	Grant		07/09/77	Edinburgh	30/07/97	5 11.0	11 1	Def	Heart of Midlothian
Moonie	Darren	Dalglish	04/09/81	Edinburgh	25/08/98	5 11.0	10 0	Mid	Tynecastle B.C.
Murray	Gavin		21/05/81	Glasgow	28/08/98	6 2.0	11 8	Def	Berwick Rangers Colts
Neil	Martin		16/04/70	Ashington	17/11/94	5 8.0	11 7	Mid	Bolton Wanderers
Neill	Alan	John	13/12/70	Baillieston	25/06/98	6 1.0	12 7	Def	East Stirlingshire
O'Connor	Gary		07/04/74	Newtongrange	12/09/97	6 3.0	13 7	Gk	Partick Thistle
Patterson	Paul	Joseph	30/07/75	Glasgow	30/07/99	5 10.0	9 1	Fwd	East Stirlingshire
Porteous	Andrew	Grant	13/09/79	Edinburgh	23/08/99	5 11.0	12 0	Fwd	Manchester City
Rafferty	Kenneth		02/04/78	Edinburgh	30/07/97	5 10.0	11 10	Mid	Heart of Midlothian
Ritchie	Innes		24/08/73	Edinburgh	25/06/98	6 0.0	12 7	Def	Clydebank
Scott	Dean		22/09/82	Edinburgh	25/08/99	5 6.0	9 7	Fwd	Granton Sports B.C.
Shankland	Kris		18/04/82	Irvine	25/08/99	5 8.0	10 0	Mid	Dunfermline Athletic Colts
Shaw	Gregory		15/02/70	Dumfries	21/07/98	6 0.0	10 12	Fwd	Clydebank
Sinclair	Craig		19/07/72	Edinburgh	03/03/99	5 11.0	12 0	Mid	Edinburgh City
Smith	Darren		04/06/80	Edinburgh	16/10/98	5 7.0	10 2	Mid	Berwick Rangers Colts
Watt	David		05/03/67	Edinburgh	25/06/98	5 7.0	11 6	Mid	East Stirlingshire

Milestones

YEAR OF FORMATION: 1881
MOST LEAGUE POINTS IN A SEASON: 54 (Second Division – Season 1978/79) (2 Points for a Win)
60 (Second Division – Season 1995/96) (3 Points for a Win)
MOST LEAGUE GOALS SCORED BY A PLAYER IN A SEASON: Ken Bowron (Season 1963/64)
NO. OF GOALS SCORED: 38
RECORD ATTENDANCE: 13,365 (-v- Rangers – 28.1.1967)
RECORD VICTORY: 8-1 (-v- Forfar Athletic (H) – Division 2, 25.12.1965)
8-1 (-v- Vale of Leithen – Scottish Cup at Innerleithen 17.12.1966)
RECORD DEFEAT: 1-9 (-v- Hamilton Academical – First Division, 9.8.1980)

The Borderers' ten year league record

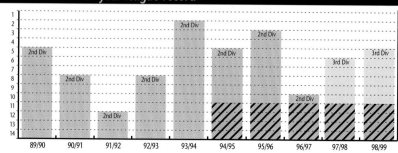

TENNENT'S LAGER · SINCE 1885 · T · J.R. Tennent.

THE BORDERERS' CLUB FACTFILE 1998/99 RESULTS... APPEARANCES... SCORERS

Date	Venue	Opponents	Att.	Res	O'Connor G.	Cunningham T.	Neill A.	Clark J.	Beaton D.	Campbell C.	Rafferty K.	Watt D.	Laidlaw S.	Forrester P.	Ramage I.	Shaw G.	Fraser G.	Baigrie J.	McNicoll G.	Irvine N.	Smith S.	McLeod J.	Dixon A.	Ritchie I.	Seaton S.	Neil M.	Leask M.	Quinn B.	Burgess M.	Smith D.	Hunter M.	Haddow L.	Sinclair C.	Reilly D.	Buglass K.	McCole D.
Aug 4	H	Queen's Park	448	0-3	1	2	3	4	5	6	7	8	9	10	11	12	14	15																	
15	A	Montrose	269	1-1	1		3		5	4		7	12	10	11	9[1]	8		2	6																
22	H	Albion Rovers	374	2-1	1		3		5	6	12	7	10		11	9[1]	4	2[1]	8	14																
29	A	Dumbarton	303	0-0	1		3		5	4	6	7		10	15	9	8	2		12	11	14														
Sep 5	H	Ross County	453	0-2	1		3	4	5	6		7	14	10		9	12	2			11	15	6													
12	A	Cowdenbeath	242	1-1	1		3		5	4	8		10[1]		9		2				11	15	6	7												
19	H	East Stirlingshire	328	1-2	1		3		5	8	2[1]		10						14	11	15	6	4	7	9											
26	H	Stenhousemuir	358	1-2	1		3		5	4	12[1]	11	10		9	8	2		14		6			7	15											
Oct 3	A	Brechin City	404	1-1	1		11		5	4	6[1]	12	10		14	3	2			8			7	9												
11	H	Montrose	921	1-1	1		11		5	4	6	12	10		14	3	2			8			7[1]	9												
17	H	Albion Rovers	360	1-1	1		11[1]		3		6	4		9	12		5	2			8	15	7	10	14											
24	H	Dumbarton	303	3-1	1		3		5		7	8		10[1]			4	15	2		11		6	12		9[2]	14									
31	A	Ross County	1,546	1-3	1		3		5		7	8	15[1]	10		4	2				11		6		12	9	14									
Nov 7	A	East Stirlingshire	277	0-0			3		5		8	6	10	11		4	2		9				7	12			1									
14	H	Cowdenbeath	296	3-1	1		3		5		8	6	9[2]	11		4	2			15	7[1]	10														
21	A	Stenhousemuir	389	2-1	1		3		5		8	6[1]	9	11		4	2				7	10[1]	15		14											
28	H	Brechin City	344	3-0	1		3		5	12	8	6[1]	9[1]	11		4	2			15	7	10[1]			14											
Dec 12	A	Queen's Park	389	1-1	1		3		5		8	6	9[1]	11		4	2			15	7	10			14											
19	H	Albion Rovers	307	1-1	1		3		5		8	6	9	11		4	2				7	10[1]			14	12										
Jan 16	H	Stenhousemuir	349	2-1	1		3		5	8	12	6[1]	10[1]	11		4	2				7	14			9											
27	H	Ross County	319	2-2	1		3		5	8	11	6[1]	9			4	2				7	14			10[1]											
30	A	Brechin City	273	3-0	1		3		5	8	11	6[2]	9[1]	12		4	2				7	14			15	10										
Feb 2	A	Dumbarton	242	1-1	1		3		5		11	6[1]	9	8		4	12	2			7	14			10											
6	A	East Stirlingshire	351	1-2	1		3		5	8	11	6	9	12		4	2				7	10[1]	15		14											
13	H	Cowdenbeath	328	2-1	1		3		5	8	12	6	9	14	15	4	2				7	11[1]			10[1]											
20	H	Queen's Park	330	0-2	1		3			8	5	6		11	12	4	2				7	9	14			10										
27	A	Montrose	301	3-0	1		5			8	12			14	15	4	2				6	7	10[2]			11[1]	9	3								
Mar 6	A	Ross County	1,732	0-6	1		3		5	8	12			14	15	4	2				7		9			11	10		6							
13	H	Dumbarton	321	0-1	1		3		5	8	4		15	14	9						7					11	10	6								
20	H	Brechin City	256	2-3	1				5	8		7		10	14[1]	9	4	15[1]	2				11				12	3	6							
Apr 3	A	Stenhousemuir	424	1-1	1		3			4		6		7	11	9[1]		14	2				10	12		8	5									
10	A	East Stirlingshire	252	3-3	1		3			4	14	6		9	11	7			2				8[1]	12		10[2]	5									
18	H	Cowdenbeath	404	2-1	1		3			4	12	6		9	11	7[1]			2				8[1]	15		10	5									
24	A	Albion Rovers	308	3-0	1		3			4	5[2]	6		9[1]	11	7		12	2				8	14		10								15		
May 1	H	Montrose	606	4-1	1		3			4	5	6		9	11	7	14	15	2				8[1]			10[3]	12									
8	A	Queen's Park	473	1-1	1		3			5				11	9	4	6	2				8	12	10[1]										7	14	15
TOTAL FULL APPEARANCES					35	1	35	2	28	25	24	28	2	28	20	14	26	1	34	2		7		9	4	19	24		1	9	12	3	2	1
TOTAL SUB APPEARANCES						(1)	(8)	(2)	(2)	(2)	(9)	(7)	(3)	(7)					(3)	(1)	(4)		(5)	(1)	(6)	(11)		(6)	(3)		(1)	(1)	(1)
TOTAL GOALS SCORED					1				5	7		9	2	4			1	1							2	12			7	2			

Small bold figures denote goalscorers. † denotes opponent's own goal.

Shielfield Park

To Berwick by-pass (North and South)

Turnstiles B (ALSO ACCESS TO STANDS)

Offices

E NORTH STAND AND ALSO CENTRE/SOUTH STANDS

SHIELFIELD TERRACE

Turnstiles A — Town Centre and Edinburgh North

CAPACITY: 4,131; Seated 1,366, Standing 2,765

PITCH DIMENSIONS: 110 yds x 70 yds

FACILITIES FOR DISABLED SUPPORTERS:
Supporters should enter via gate adjacent to ground turnstiles (see ground plan above) or via official entrance

Team playing kits

How to get there

Shielfield Park can be reached by the following routes:
The ground is approximately 1 1/2 miles south of Berwick town centre and is situated in Shielfield Terrace, Tweedmouth. (Signposted).

BUSES: The local bus route from the town centre is the Prior Park service and the nearest stop to the ground is in Shielfield Terrace. The bus stop is only yards away from the ground.

TRAINS: The only railway station is Berwick, which is situated on the East Coast line and a frequent service operates at various stages during the day. The ground is approximately 1 1/2 miles from the station and a taxi service operates from there or alternatively, fans can take the local bus service as detailed above.

CARS: There is a large car park at the rear of the ground. (Nominal charge).

email: sfl@sol.co.uk • website: www.sfl.scottishfootball.com

Brechin City

Glebe Park, Trinity Road,
Brechin, Angus, DD9 6BJ

CHAIRMAN
David H. Birse

VICE-CHAIRMAN
Hugh A. Campbell Adamson

DIRECTORS
Martin Smith (Treasurer),
I. Michael Holland
(Assistant Treasurer),
David H. Will,
Calum I. McK. Brown,
Kenneth W. Ferguson
& James Dean

SECRETARY
Kenneth W. Ferguson

MANAGER
John Young

ASSISTANT MANAGER
Jake Ferrier

YOUTH DEVELOPMENT OFFICER
Eddie Wolecki

**ASSISTANT YOUTH
DEVELOPMENT OFFICER**
George Shields

CLUB DOCTOR
Dr. Archie McInnes

SPORTS THERAPIST
Tom Gilmartin

**FOOTBALL SAFETY OFFICERS'
ASSOCIATION REPRESENTATIVE**
Calum Brown (01307) 461222

GROUNDSMAN
Alex Laing

COMMERCIAL CONTACT
James Dean (01674) 672606

TELEPHONES
Ground (01356) 622856
Fax (01356) 625667
Sec. Home (01356) 625691
Sec. Bus. (01356) 625285/
(01674) 678910
Sec. Bus. Fax (01356) 625524

E-MAIL & INTERNET ADDRESS
kenny@glebepk.demon.co.uk.
http://www.brechincity.co.uk

CLUB SHOP
Glebe Park, Brechin, Angus, DD9 6BJ
Open during home match days.

OFFICIAL SUPPORTERS CLUB
c/o Glebe Park, Brechin,
Angus, DD9 6BJ

TEAM CAPTAIN
Harry Cairney

SHIRT SPONSOR
A.P. Jess Food Group Ltd.

LIST OF PLAYERS 1999-2000

SURNAME	FIRST NAME	MIDDLE NAME	DATE OF BIRTH	PLACE OF BIRTH	DATE OF SIGNING	HEIGHT FT INS	WEIGHT ST LBS	POS. ON PITCH	PREVIOUS CLUB
Bain	Kevin		19/09/72	Kirkcaldy	29/07/98	6 0.0	11 9	Def	Stirling Albion
Black	Roddy		22/02/78	Dundee	10/09/95	5 9.0	11 0	Mid	Carnoustie Panmure
Boylan	Paul		04/12/80	Dundee	05/03/99	5 10.0	10 2	Def	Dundee United
Brown	Robert		04/08/79	Aberdeen	10/07/98	5 11.0	11 12	Def	Aberdeen
Buick	Garry	Robert	12/01/75	Arbroath	25/11/94	5 5.5	10 4	Mid	Keith
Cairney	Henry		01/09/61	Holytown	12/02/92	5 7.0	10 8	Def	Stenhousemuir
Campbell	Stephen		20/11/67	Dundee	01/08/97	5 7.0	11 0	Def/Mid	Livingston
Christie	Graeme		01/01/71	Dundee	04/08/93	6 1.0	11 0	Def	Carnoustie Panmure
Coulston	Douglas		12/08/71	Glasgow	30/06/99	5 10.0	11 0	Mid /Fwd	Montrose
Dailly	Marcus	Graham	01/10/75	Dundee	31/03/97	5 9.0	11 6	Mid	Exeter City
Davidson	Peter	Forbes	25/03/81	Aberdeen	10/09/99	5 8.0	10 5	Mid	Forfar Albion
Dickson	John	Duke	23/12/69	Glasgow	07/08/98	5 5.0	9 7	Mid/Fwd	Albion Rovers
Durie	Jonathan	Andrew Kennedy	04/05/74	Middlesbrough	30/07/99	5 4.0	9 5	Mid	Carnoustie Panmure
Geddes	Alexander	Robert	12/08/60	Inverness	29/07/99	6 0.0	12 8	Gk	Linfield
Hirons	Kevin	Barry	25/08/82	Dundee	10/09/99	5 6.0	9 8	Def	Forfar Albion
Hood	Gavin		06/05/82	Dundee	10/09/99	5 7.0	9 4	Def	Forfar Albion
Hutcheon	Andrew	John	16/05/79	Aberdeen	19/06/97	5 8.0	9 7	Fwd	Stonehaven U'18s
Kerrigan	Steven	Paul	29/09/70	Wolverhampton	01/02/96	5 9.0	10 0	Fwd	Kirriemuir Thistle
McKellar	James	Robert	29/12/76	Bellshill	26/07/94	5 6.0	10 4	Fwd	Arbroath Lads Club
Riley	Paul	John	07/08/75	Edinburgh	31/03/99	5 7.0	10 6	Mid	Hibernian
Smith	Greig	Robert	26/03/76	Aberdeen	21/12/94	5 9.0	10 12	Def	Culter Juniors
Sorbie	Stuart	Graham	07/09/63	Glasgow	16/02/96	5 9.5	10 5	Mid/Fwd	Livingston
Williamson	Karl		09/11/79	Aberdeen	29/07/98	5 7.5	10 9	Def	Aberdeen

Milestones

YEAR OF FORMATION: 1906
MOST LEAGUE POINTS IN A SEASON: 55 (Second Division – Season 1982/83)(2 Points for a Win)
63 (Third Division – Season 1995/96)(3 Points for a Win)
MOST LEAGUE GOALS SCORED BY A PLAYER IN A SEASON: Ronald McIntosh (Season 1959/60)
NO. OF GOALS SCORED: 26
RECORD ATTENDANCE: 8,122 (-v- Aberdeen – 3.2.1973)
RECORD VICTORY: 12-1 (-v- Thornhill – Scottish Cup, 28.1.1926)
RECORD DEFEAT: 0-10 (-v- Airdrieonians, Albion Rovers and Cowdenbeath – Division 2, 1937/38)

The City's ten year league record

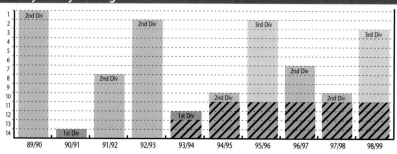

THE CITY'S CLUB FACTFILE 1998/99 RESULTS... APPEARANCES... SCORERS

Date	Venue	Opponents	Att.	Res	Garden S.	Smith C.	Black R.	Cairney H.	Brown R.	Bain K.	Hutcheon A.	Smart C.	Sorbie S.	Dailly M.	Campbell S.	Kerrigan S.	Dickson J.	Williamson K.	Buick G.	McKellar J.	MacLeod I.	Christie G.	Laing K.	Butter J.	Riley P.	Boyle S.	Boylan P.
Aug 4	H	Stenhousemuir	286	1-0	1	2	3	4	5	6	7¹	8	9	10	11	12	14	15									
15	A	East Stirlingshire	263	1-1	1	6	3	4	16	5	7	2¹			8	10	9	11	12	14							
22	H	Queen's Park	300	2-2	1	6	3	4	5		14	8		10¹	9	12	7¹	2		11	16						
29	H	Montrose	452	3-0	1	6	3	4	12	5¹	10	8			11	14	9²	2		7							
Sep 5	A	Cowdenbeath	206	1-0	1	6	3	4	2	5	10	8			11	16	12	9¹	14	7							
12	H	Dumbarton	355	0-0	1	6	3	4		5	14	2	9	8	11		10			7		16					
19	A	Albion Rovers	507	4-1	1	6	10¹	4		5		2	9¹	8	11	12	7²					14	3				
26	A	Ross County	1,512	1-0	1	6	10	4		5		2	9	8	11¹	12	7						3	1			
Oct 3	H	Berwick Rangers	404	1-1	1	6	10	4			12	2	9	8	11		7¹			16		5	3				
10	H	East Stirlingshire	364	0-0	1	6	10	4	16		12	2	9	14		3	7		8	11		5					
17	A	Queen's Park	446	1-1	1	6	10	4		5			9	8		3	7¹	2	14	11							
27	A	Montrose	340	2-1	1	6	10¹	4		5			9¹			3	7	2	8	11							
31	A	Cowdenbeath	291	2-1	1	6	10	4		5			9¹	14¹		3	7	2	8	11		12					
Nov 7	H	Albion Rovers	307	1-0	1	6	10	4		5			9¹			3	7	2		11						8	
14	A	Dumbarton	357	2-1	1	5	6	4	16				9¹	8		3	7¹	14	2	11						10	
21	H	Ross County	826	0-1	1	6	10	4		5	12		9			3	7	2		11						8	
28	A	Berwick Rangers	344	0-3	1	6	10	4		5	12		9			3	7	2		11						8	
Dec 15	A	Stenhousemuir	294	1-0	1	6	10	4		5			9¹		11	3	7	2								8	
19	H	Queen's Park	328	1-0	1	6	10	4		5¹	12	16	9		11	3	7	2								8	
Jan 26	A	Cowdenbeath	117	2-0	1	6	10	4		5		16	9¹		11¹		7	2	14				3			8	
30	H	Berwick Rangers	273	0-3	1	6	10		14				9	16	11		7	2	4	12		5	3			8	
Feb 6	A	Albion Rovers	259	1-4	1	6	10	4		5			9	16	11	3¹	7	2	14			12				8	
13	H	Dumbarton	360	3-3	1	2	10	4	6	5		8¹	9		11¹	3	7¹			12							
16	H	Montrose	317	2-3	1	6	10	4	16	5		8²	9		11	3	7		2	14							
20	H	Stenhousemuir	265	0-2	1	6	10	4		5	11	2	9			3	14	7		16		12				8	
27	A	East Stirlingshire	219	1-4	1	2	10	4	6	5	12	8	9¹	16	11	3	7	14									
Mar 6	A	Cowdenbeath		1-1	1	6	10	4		5		16	9	8	12	3	14¹	7	2							11	
9	A	Ross County	1,537	1-2	1	6	3			5	14	8	9		10	12	7	2	4¹							11	
13	A	Montrose	404	3-1	1		3	4		5	12	8²	9	10	11¹		7	2				6					
20	A	Berwick Rangers	256	3-2	1		3¹	4		5		8²	9	10			7	2				6				11	
Apr 3	H	Ross County	698	0-1	1	6	3	4		5		8	9	10		12	7							1		11	2
10	H	Albion Rovers	291	3-1	1	6	3	4		5²		8	9	10		12	7¹							1		11	2
17	A	Dumbarton	562	0-2	1			4	16	5		8	9			3	7	14				6			10	11	2
24	A	Queen's Park	503	2-0	1			4		5	12	8	9			3	7¹		16	14¹		6			10	11	2
May 1	H	East Stirlingshire	344	1-0	1			4		5¹		8	9			3	7					6			10	11	2
8	A	Stenhousemuir	1,654	0-1	1			4		5	12	8	9			3	7					6			10	11	2
TOTAL FULL APPEARANCES					33	26	32	34	13	31	6	11	31	10	27	14	34	12	15	22		11	5	3	12	8	6
TOTAL SUB APPEARANCES						(1)			(3)		(15)	(1)		(6)	(1)	(12)		(2)	(1)	(7)	(7)	(3)	(5)				
TOTAL GOALS SCORED							1	2		5	1	1	12	1	2	4	15					2	1				

Small bold figures denote goalscorers.   † denotes opponent's own goal.

Glebe Park

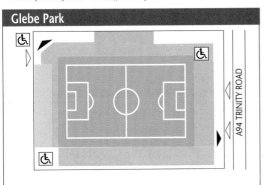

A94 TRINITY ROAD

CAPACITY: 3,960; Seated 1,519, Standing 2,441
PITCH DIMENSIONS: 110 yds x 67 yds
FACILITIES FOR DISABLED SUPPORTERS:
Section of Terracing designated for disabled supporters.

Team playing kits

How to get there

The following routes may be used to reach Glebe Park:

TRAINS: The nearest railway station is Montrose, which is eight miles away. There is a regular Inter-City service from all parts of the country and fans alighting at Montrose can then catch a connecting bus service to Brechin.

BUSES: Brechin bus station is only a few hundred yards from the ground and buses on the Aberdeen-Dundee and Montrose-Edzell routes stop here.

CARS: Car parking is available in the Brechin City car park, which is capable of holding 50 vehicles. There are also a number of side streets which may be used for this purpose.

email: sfl@sol.co.uk • website: www.sfl.scottishfootball.com

Central Park, High Street, Cowdenbeath, KY4 9QQ

CHAIRMAN
Gordon McDougall

VICE-CHAIRMAN
Eric Mitchell

DIRECTORS
James M. Stevenson,
Albert Tait,
Ian Fraser,
Brian Watson,
Dr. Robert Brownlie
& Edward Baigan

GENERAL/COMMERCIAL MANAGER
Joe Macnamara

SECRETARY
Thomas Ogilvie

MANAGER
Craig Levein

ASSISTANT MANAGER
Gary Kirk

YOUTH TEAM COACHES
Tom Milne, Ross Hamilton,
Neil Berry, Paul Armour
& Graham Buckley

SPRINT COACH
Tom Ritchie

CLUB DOCTOR
Dr. Robert Brownlie

PHYSIOTHERAPISTS
Wendy McDonald, Lindsay Peterson
& Gordon Clark

FOOTBALL SAFETY OFFICERS' ASSOCIATION REPRESENTATIVE
David Jones
Home (01383) 872074

GROUNDSMAN
Gordon McDougall Jnr.

KITMAN
James Baxter

TELEPHONES
Ground/Ticket Office/
Information Service
(01383) 610166
Sec. Home (01383) 513013
Sec. Bus (01383) 313400
Fax (01383) 512132

E-MAIL & INTERNET ADDRESS
www.bluebrazil37.freeserve.co.uk
cfc@bluebrazil37.freeserve.co.uk

CLUB SHOP
Situated at Stadium.
Open 10.00 a.m. – 3.00 p.m.
and on Home Match Days

OFFICIAL SUPPORTERS CLUB
Central Park,
Cowdenbeath, KY4 9QQ

TEAM CAPTAIN
Craig Winter

SHIRT SPONSOR
Bernard Hunter Crane Hire

Cowdenbeath

LIST OF PLAYERS 1999-2000

SURNAME	FIRST NAME	MIDDLE NAME	DATE OF BIRTH	PLACE OF BIRTH	DATE OF SIGNING	HEIGHT FT INS	WEIGHT ST LBS	POS. ON PITCH	PREVIOUS CLUB
Bannatyne	Peter		13/08/82	Edinburgh	29/03/99	5 8.0	10 10	Fwd	Heart of Midlothian
Berry	Neil		06/04/63	Edinburgh	09/06/99	6 0.0	13 2	Def	Hamilton Academical
Bradley	Mark		10/08/76	Glasgow	18/12/98	5 6.0	9 7	Mid	Stirling Albion
Brown	Graeme	Robert	08/11/80	Johannesburg	19/08/97	5 11.0	11 0	Fwd	Broomhall Saints B.C.
Burns	John	Paul	11/03/78	Kirkcaldy	02/08/98	5 6.0	10 9	Fwd	Heart of Midlothian
Carnie	Grant		16/10/81	Edinburgh	03/07/98	5 10.5	11 0	Mid	Tynecastle B.C.
Clark	Robert		12/11/80	Edinburgh	26/06/99	5 9.0	10 0	Mid	Vale of Leithen
Cuthbert	Lee	James	28/02/70	Edinburgh	03/07/98	5 8.0	11 0	Def	Bonnyrigg Rose
Daly	Ryan		03/07/81	Dunfermline	26/07/99	5 11.0	10 10	Def	Milton Green U'18
Dinse	Ryan	Pennycook	05/07/79	Kirkcaldy	20/11/98	5 6.0	10 12	Mid	Kelty Hearts
Findlay	Graeme	Douglas	01/12/81	Dunfermline	01/09/99	6 0.0	12 0	Mid	Dundonald Bluebell
Godfrey	Ross		21/01/77	Edinburgh	07/10/98	5 11.0	10 12	Gk	Thornton Hibs
Grieve	Stuart		23/09/81	Dunfermline	14/05/99	5 11.0	11 1	Mid	Kelty Hearts
Hamilton	Alistair	Strathern	12/11/75	Irvine	29/04/95	5 7.0	10 7	Def/Mid	Musselburgh Athletic
Hutchison	Stephen		18/09/70	Glasgow	01/11/97	5 11.5	12 10	Gk	Ross County
Hutt	Kevin	Peter Chastell	02/10/80	Kirkcaldy	08/06/99	5 10.0	11 10	Mid	Glenrothes Strollers
Johnston	Derek		12/06/77	Falkirk	26/06/99	5 9.0	11 10	Mid	Bonnybridge U'21
Johnston	Ross		12/10/82	Edinburgh	17/02/99	5 10.0	10 11	Def	Musselburgh Windsor B.C.
King	Shaun		03/09/81	Kirkcaldy	29/03/99	5 4.0	8 0	Mid/Fwd	Benarty Juniors
Kirkcaldy	Christopher		08/01/82	Edinburgh	26/06/99	5 11.0	11 0	Fwd	Musselburgh Windsor U'16
Letham	Alan		11/08/77	Glasgow	26/06/99	6 0.0	11 7	Fwd	Bonnybridge U'21
McCulloch	Keith	George	27/05/67	Edinburgh	08/06/99	5 10.0	12 0	Def	Alloa Athletic
McDowell	Murray	John Lauden	17/02/78	Dundee	26/06/99	5 11.0	11 9	Fwd	Carnoustie Panmure
McMillan	Craig		04/12/81	Dunfermline	03/07/98	5 10.0	11 0	Mid	Hill of Beath Swifts
Melvin	Adam	George	24/02/80	Dunfermline	07/09/98	5 8.0	11 0	Mid/Fwd	Lochore Miners Welfare
Miah	Jabed	Ul Rahman	04/09/81	Glasgow	11/07/99	5 9.0	11 8	Mid	Milton Green U'18s
Millar	Paul	Eric	04/08/80	Edinburgh	18/09/97	5 11.0	12 3	Mid	Tynecastle B.C.
Mitchell	Wesley	Dean	03/03/82	Edinburgh	28/11/98	6 2.0	12 0	Def	Heart of Midlothian B.C.
Paver	David		09/01/81	Edinburgh	17/07/97	5 11.0	11 7	Def	Musselburgh Windsor B.C.
Perry	Michael	Andrew	30/11/77	Edinburgh	09/07/99	5 10.0	11 10	Mid	Easthouses U'21
Robertson	Malcolm	James	05/05/78	Edinburgh	06/03/98	5 10.0	10 0	Mid	Tollcross United
Simpson	Paul		09/08/68	St. Andrews	25/07/99	6 6.0	14 7	Fwd	Alloa Athletic
Smith	Peter	David Meldrum	11/08/81	Edinburgh	31/03/99	6 3.0	12 3	Def/Mid	St. Johnstone
Snedden	Scott		07/12/71	Dechmont	16/02/98	6 2.0	11 4	Def	East Stirlingshire
Stewart	William	Paul	16/04/77	Glasgow	28/08/95	5 10.0	10 0	Fwd	Thorniewood United
Thomson	Richard	James	11/08/77	Perth	21/10/98	6 0.0	12 0	Def	Dundee United
Urquhart	Murray	Henderson	31/01/79	Kirkcaldy	08/09/99	5 10.0	11 8	Def/Mid	Newburgh Jnrs
Ward	Martin		24/02/81	Dunfermline	12/00/99	5 7.0	10 0	Fwd	Dundonald Bluebell
White	David	William	09/08/79	Edinburgh	09/07/99	6 1.5	11 12	Def	Motherwell
Wilson	William	Stewart	19/08/72	Glasgow	23/07/99	5 8.0	9 12	Mid	Dumbarton
Winter	Craig	John	30/06/76	Dunfermline	19/07/94	5 9.0	10 0	Mid/Fwd	Raith Rovers
Young	Craig		02/12/81	Edinburgh	03/07/98	5 2.0	8 0	Fwd	Tynecastle B.C.

Milestones

YEAR OF FORMATION: 1881
MOST CAPPED PLAYER: Jim Paterson
NO. OF CAPS: 3
MOST LEAGUE POINTS IN A SEASON: 60 (Division 2 – Season 1938/39)
MOST LEAGUE GOALS SCORED BY A PLAYER IN A SEASON: Willie Devlin (Season 1925/26)
NO. OF GOALS SCORED: 40
RECORD ATTENDANCE: 25,586 (-v- Rangers – 21.9.1949)
RECORD VICTORY: 12-0 (-v- Johnstone – Scottish Cup, 21.1.1928)
RECORD DEFEAT: 1-11 (-v- Clyde – Division 2, 6.10.1951)

The Blue Brazil's ten year league record

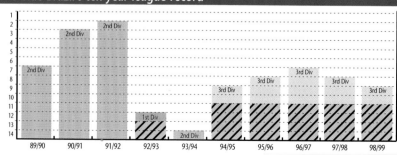

THE BLUE BRAZIL'S CLUB FACTFILE 1998/99 RESULTS... APPEARANCES... SCORERS

Date	Venue	Opponents	Att.	Res	Hutchison S.	Urquhart M.	Cuthbert L.	Bowsher C.	Snedden S.	Hamilton A.	Winter C.	Robertson M.	Burns J.P.	Brown G.	Stewart W.	Graham C.	Ritchie A.	Murray D.	Humphreys M.	Pryde D.	Paterson G.	Welsh B.	Lynch J.	Blair D.	Milne K.	Dair L.	Melvin A.	Thomson R.	McKenzie J.	Godfrey M.	Malcolm S.	Findlay G.	Hunter C.	Bradley M.	Martin A.	Mitchell W.	Millar P.	McMillan C.	Bruno P.	Horn R.	McMillan A.	Carnie G.	Dinse R.	Lackie J.	Ward M.	Bannatyne P.	Smith P.
Aug 4	H	Montrose	161	4-1	1	2	3	4	5^1	6	7	8	9	10^2	11^1																																
15	A	Stenhousemuir	306	2-1	1	2	3	4	5	8	7^1	6	9	10	11					15^1																											
22	H	East Stirlingshire	220	2-1	1	2	3	4	5	8	7	6^1	11	9^1	10	12																															
29	A	Ross County	1,553	0-2	1	2		4	5	8	7	6	11	9	10	3	12	14	15																												
Sep 5	H	Brechin City	206	0-1	1	2	3		5	6	7	8	10	9	11	14	12	12	15			4																									
12	H	Berwick Rangers	242	1-1	1	2			5	8	7	6	11	10^1	9	3	4	14				15																									
19	A	Dumbarton	348	0-5	1	2			5	10		11	14	7	9	12	3	4	6									8	15																		
26	A	Albion Rovers	403	1-0	1			4	5	7		8	10	12	9	11	3			6^1	2																										
Oct 3	H	Queen's Park	280	0-3	1			4	5	7		11	12	14	9	10	3	15	6	8	2																										
9	H	Stenhousemuir	320	0-2	1	2			5	8	7	6	14	9	11	4	12											3	10	15																	
17	A	East Stirlingshire	230	1-1	1				5	7	10	8	9	15	11	4												3	6^1	2																	
28	H	Ross County	212	1-2	1		3	12^1	5		7	8	11	15	9	4												10		6	2																
31	A	Brechin City	291	1-2			6	5	3	7	10	14	11	9		2		15										12	4^1	8	1																
Nov 7	H	Dumbarton	228	0-2	2		12	7	8	6	14	9	10	3				15										5	11	1	4																
14	A	Berwick Rangers	296	1-3	2			7^1	6	14	10	9	5		8													12	4	11	1	3															
21	H	Albion Rovers	161	2-3	15			8	7	6	9	10	12^1	5	14	3^1												2	11	1	4																
28	A	Queen's Park	439	0-2	1			4	14	8	15	9	12	10	11	7	3											2		5	6																
Dec 12	A	Montrose	324	1-1	1				5	7	9	10	6	14		3												2	8	4^1	11																
19	H	East Stirlingshire	108	3-2	1				5	12	7	11	9	2	14	3^1												6^1	8	4	10^1																
26	A	Ross County	1,842	0-1	1				4	2	7	14	9	10	3	15	12											11	8	6	5																
Jan 26	H	Brechin City	117	0-2	1				4	6	7	9	14	10	11	3												2	5	8	12	15															
30	H	Queen's Park	198	0-0	1				5	8	7	10	9	11		3	15	2										6	4																		
Feb 13	H	Berwick Rangers	328	1-2	1	12	6	5		7	11	10	9			3^1												2	8	4	14																
20	H	Montrose	234	1-0	1	8	6	5	2	7	12	9	10			3^1												11	4	15																	
23	A	Albion Rovers	240	1-1	1	11		5	2	7	7^1	12	10	9		3				6								8	4	15	14																
27	A	Stenhousemuir	361	1-4	1	6		5	12	7	14	9	10			3												11^1	4	8	15																
Mar 6	A	Brechin City	269	1-1	1	3		5	8	14	9	10^1				11	12	2										6	4	7																	
13	H	Ross County	316	2-3	1	14			12	9^1	10^1	15				3												8	4	2	5	6	7	11												
20	A	Queen's Park	336	1-2	1	4		5	15^1	14	9	11	12			3												10	6	2	8	7														
Apr 3	H	Albion Rovers	161	0-2	1			5	7	8	11	15	10	9		3												2	6	12	14	4														
5	A	Dumbarton	650	1-6	15			5	2		14^1		9			3												7	1	6	4	12	11	8	10											
10	A	Dumbarton	245	2-1				5	8		11	9				3^1												15	10	6	2	4	7													
18	A	Berwick Rangers	404	1-2					7		11	9^1				3												14	6	1	10	5	2	4	8											
24	A	East Stirlingshire	208	0-0	3						9	10				8													1	6	4	7					5	11	2	12	15					
May 1	H	Stenhousemuir	300	0-2	4						9	11				3^1												8	1	10	6	2	5	7						12	15	14				
8	A	Montrose	293	2-1	1			4	8^1		9	10	11			3^1												2		7		12	6	5								14				
TOTAL FULL APPEARANCES					27	11	15	7	29	22	25	13	23	23	26	11	4	7	10	2	1	4	1	2	23	3		21	5	9	4	5	2	19	13	1	7	1	8	1	8	2	1				
TOTAL SUB APPEARANCES					(2)	(2)	(1)	(1)	(4)		(4)	(4)	(12)	(3)	(4)	(3)	(1)	(3)	(3)			(8)		(1)			(6)	(1)					(1)	(2)	(2)	(6)						(2)	(3)	(1)	
TOTAL GOALS SCORED							1	2	2	2	1		5	7	1							1			6	1		2					1	2											

Small bold figures denote goalscorers.   † denotes opponent's own goal.

Central Park

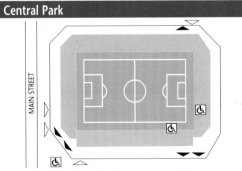

CAPACITY: 4,370; Seated 1,431, Standing 2,939

PITCH DIMENSIONS: 107 yds x 64 yds

FACILITIES FOR DISABLED SUPPORTERS:
Direct access from car park into designated area within ground. Toilet and catering facilities also provided.

Team playing kits

How to get there

You can get to Central Park by the following routes:

TRAINS: There is a regular service of trains from Edinburgh and Glasgow (via Edinburgh) which call at Cowdenbeath and the station is only 400 yards from the ground.

BUSES: A limited Edinburgh-Cowdenbeath service stops just outside the ground on matchdays and a frequent service of Dunfermline-Ballingry buses also stop outside the ground, as does the Edinburgh-Glenrothes service.

CARS: Car parking facilities are available in the public car park adjacent to the ground for 190 cars. There are also another 300 spaces at the Stenhouse Street car park, which is 200 yards from the ground.

The Blue Brazil

email: sfl@sol.co.uk • website: www.sfl.scottishfootball.com

Boghead Park, Miller Street,
Dumbarton, G82 2JA

CHAIRMAN
Douglas S. Dalgleish, M.A., LL.B.

MANAGING DIRECTOR
Neil Rankine

DIRECTORS
David Wright,
G. James Innes
& David O. Stark

HON. PRESIDENTS
Ian A. Bell, J.P. &
R. Campbell Ward, C.A.

CLUB SECRETARY
Colin J. Hosie

ASSISTANT CLUB SECRETARY
J. David Prophet

MANAGER
Jimmy Brown

ASSISTANT MANAGER
Tom Carson

CLUB DOCTORS
James Goldie &
Neil MacKay, MBC, HB

PHYSIOTHERAPIST
David Stobie, B.Sc. (Hons), MCSP

CHIEF SCOUT
Robert Gallie

GROUNDSMAN
Eddie McCreadie

KIT MAN
Jim Cunningham

ADMINISTRATION MANAGER
Andrew Stames

PUBLIC RELATIONS EXECUTIVE
Ian MacFarlane

COMMERCIAL MANAGER
Julie Gilchrist

**FOOTBALL SAFETY OFFICER'S
ASSOCIATION REPRESENTATIVES**
Neil Rankine/David Douglas

TELEPHONES
Ground (01389) 762569/767864
Sec. Bus. (0141) 941 1940
Sec. Home (01389) 841996
Sec. Mobile (0370) 831490
Fax (01389) 762629

E-MAIL & INTERNET ADDRESS
sonsview@aol.com

CLUB SHOP
Situated in ground –
open on home matchdays and
10.00 a.m. – 4.00 p.m. Mon-Fri

OFFICIAL SUPPORTERS CLUB
c/o Boghead Park, Miller Street,
Dumbarton G82 2JA

TEAM CAPTAIN
Thomas King

SHIRT SPONSOR
Methode Electronics Europe

94

LIST OF PLAYERS 1999-2000

SURNAME	FIRST NAME	MIDDLE NAME	DATE OF BIRTH	PLACE OF BIRTH	DATE OF SIGNING	HEIGHT FT INS	WEIGHT ST LBS	POS. ON PITCH	PREVIOUS CLUB
Barnes	Alan	Norman	26/10/81	Greenock	14/05/99	5 7.0	8 9	Mid	Gourock Y.A.C.
Barnes	Derek		20/09/77	Glasgow	31/03/99	6 0.0	11 3	Gk	Cumnock Juniors
Brittain	Craig		10/01/74	Glasgow	14/06/97	5 5.0	9 7	Def	Ashfield Juniors
Brooks	Daniel	Shaw	03/01/82	Vale of Leven	04/09/98	5 6.0	9 2	Mid	Yoker Athletic
Brown	Alan		26/06/82	Alexandria	04/09/98	5 8.0	11 3	Mid	Yoker Athletic
Brown	Andrew		11/10/76	Edinburgh	21/07/99	6 4.0	14 0	Forward	Clydebank
Bruce	Jamie	Ross	29/08/76	East Kilbride	01/02/99	6 0.0	11 4	Def	East Kilbride Thistle
Chang	Richard		30/12/82	Glasgow	14/05/99	5 2.0	8 6	Fwd	Old Kilpatrick U'16s
Cudahy	Robert	Thomas	10/03/82	Vale of Leven	14/05/99	5 8.0	9 5	Fwd	Renton Craigandro U'16s
Dalrymple	Christopher	James	10/04/79	Vale of Leven	04/09/98	5 11.0	10 7	Def	Yoker Athletic
Dennison	Peter	David Turnbull	01/07/78	Edinburgh	17/08/98	6 0.0	11 7	Gk	Vale of Leven
Dickie	Michael	John	05/05/79	Vale of Leven	11/06/99	5 8.0	10 0	Def	Dundee
Dillon	John	Peter	16/12/78	Vale of Leven	30/07/99	5 7.0	10 0	Mid	Clyde
Docherty	Mark		11/02/82	Glasgow	20/11/98	5 5.0	8 10	Def	Bosco Juniors
Finnigan	Paul	John	14/08/79	Glasgow	31/03/99	5 5.0	9 2	Def	Ashfield Juniors
Flannery	Patrick		23/07/76	Glasgow	27/12/97	5 11.0	10 12	Fwd	Morton
Grace	Alexander		20/03/74	Vale of Leven	25/07/97	5 6.0	10 4	Mid	Vale of Leven
Jack	Stephen	John	27/03/71	Bellshill	25/02/98	5 11.0	10 0	Mid	Cowdenbeath
Kilpatrick	Andrew		17/03/82	Dumbarton	04/09/98	5 9.0	10 9	Def	Yoker Athletic
King	Thomas	David	23/01/70	Dumbarton	10/08/98	5 9.0	11 3	Mid	Clyde
Lindsay	David	James	09/07/80	Greenock	14/05/99	6 3.0	12 0	Def	Yoker Athletic
Marner	Sean	Thomas	02/03/81	Paisley	14/05/99	5 9.0	8 12	Fwd	Glenvale "B" U'18
McCormack	John	Thomas	22/07/65	Stirling	30/07/99	5 9.0	10 0	Def	Alloa Athletic
McHarg	Scott	James	16/06/74	Glasgow	23/06/99	5 8.0	10 7	Fwd	Blantyre Victoria
Meechan	David		23/11/81	Vale of Leven	08/06/99	5 10.0	11 0	Fwd	Dumbarton U'21
Meechan	Kenneth		16/02/72	Greenock	04/12/95	6 0.0	12 8	Gk	Greenock Juniors
Melvin	Martin		12/06/77	Glasgow	31/07/98	5 7.0	9 8	Mid/Fwd	Possil Y.M.
Melvin	William	John	12/06/77	Glasgow	27/03/98	5 7.0	9 7	Mid/Fwd	Clydebank
Millar	Keith		29/07/80	Alexandria	04/09/98	5 8.0	10 2	Fwd	Yoker Athletic
Paterson	Ritchie	Campbell	04/08/82	Germany	14/05/99	5 11.0	10 7	Gk	Renton Craigandro U'16s
Robertson	Joseph		12/04/77	Glasgow	14/08/98	5 8.0	11 5	Fwd	Clydebank
Smith	Christopher	James	20/12/76	Glasgow	19/01/99	5 11.0	11 7	Fwd	Rutherglen Glencairn
Ward	Hugh		09/03/70	Dumbarton	26/05/99	5 8.0	9 12	Fwd	East Stirlingshire
Wilkinson	Barry	John	09/05/77	Vale of Leven	31/03/99	6 1.0	12 0	Def	Cumnock Juniors

Milestones

YEAR OF FORMATION: 1872
MOST CAPPED PLAYERS: J. Lindsay and J. McAulay
NO. OF CAPS: 8 each
MOST LEAGUE POINTS IN A SEASON: 53 (First Division – Season 1986/87) (2 Points for a Win)
60 (Second Division – Season 1993/94) (3 Points for a Win)
MOST LEAGUE GOALS SCORED BY A PLAYER IN A SEASON: Kenneth Wilson (Season 1971/72)
NO. OF GOALS SCORED: 38
RECORD ATTENDANCE: 18,001 (-v- Raith Rovers – 2.3.1957)
RECORD VICTORY: 13-2 (-v- Kirkintilloch – Scottish Cup)
RECORD DEFEAT: 1-11 (-v- Ayr United/Albion Rovers)

The Sons' ten year league record

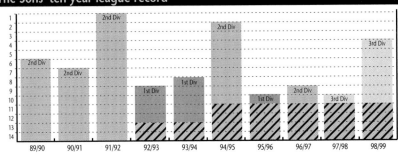

THE SONS' CLUB FACTFILE 1998/99 RESULTS... APPEARANCES... SCORERS

Date	Venue	Opponents	Att.	Res	Dennison P.	Wilson W.	Brittain C.	Sharp L.	Reid D.	Jack S.	Melvin W.	McKinnon C.	Clancy M.	Flannery P.	Grace A.	Melvin M.	Brown A.	Meechan K.	King T.	Mooney M.	Gow S.	Robertson J.	Smith C.	Harvey P.	Wilkinson B.	Millar K.	Barnes D.	Stewart D.	Bruce I.	Bradford J.	Finnigan P.
Aug 4	H	Albion Rovers	291	2-0	1	2	3	4	5	6	7	8[1]	9	10[1]	11			14	15												
15	A	Queen's Park	656	1-0		2	3	4[1]	5	6	7	8	9	10		15		1	11	12											
22	A	Stenhousemuir	378	0-2		2	3	4	5	6	7	8	9	10		15		1	11	12	14										
29	H	Berwick Rangers	303	0-0		2	3	4		6	7		9	15				1	8	10	5	11	12								
Sep 5	A	East Stirlingshire	217	2-1		2	3	4	14	5	11	7		10				1	6[1]	8		9[1]	15								
12	A	Brechin City	355	0-0		2		4	3	5	11	7		10				1	6	8		9	12								
19	H	Cowdenbeath	348	5-0		2		4[1]	3	5	11[2]	7[1]	15	10[1]				1	6	8		9									
26	A	Montrose	318	1-1		2		4	3	5	11	7		10[1]	14			1	6	8		9									
Oct 3	H	Ross County	538	1-2		2		4	3	5	11	7	14	10[1]				1	6	8	12	9									
10	A	Queen's Park	343	1-0		2		4	3	6	7	8		9[1]	14			1		10	5		12								
17	H	Stenhousemuir	456	3-0		2		4	3	5	7	8	11[1]	9[1]				1		10[1]				6	15						
24	A	Berwick Rangers	303	1-3		2		4		5	7	8	11	9				1	3	10		12[1]		6	15						
31	H	East Stirlingshire	309	2-2		2		4		5	12	8	14	9[1]				1	6	10		11[1]		7	3						
Nov 7	A	Cowdenbeath	228	2-0		2		4		5		8		9[2]				1	6	10		11		7	3						
14	H	Brechin City	357	1-2		2		4		5	12	8	15	9[1]	14			1	6	10		11		7	3						
25	H	Montrose	240	0-2		2		4		5		8		9	7		14	1	6	10		11		3	15						
28	A	Ross County	1,759	0-2		2	3	4		5		8		9	11			1	6	7		14	15	10							
Dec 12	A	Albion Rovers	324	2-0		2	3			5	11	7		9[1]				1	6	10[1]		4		8							
19	H	Stenhousemuir	283	1-4		2[1]	3			5	11	7		9	12			1	6	10		4		14	8						
Jan 16	A	Montrose	326	2-4		2				6	11	8		9[2]	7			1		10	5							14	3	4	
26	A	East Stirlingshire	204	2-1		2	11[1]			5	7[1]	10		9				1	6			8							3	4	
30	H	Ross County	400	0-0		2	11			5		8		9	7	15		1	6	10	12								3	4	
Feb 2	H	Berwick Rangers	242	1-1		2	3			5	11	8		9[1]				1	6	10			15							4	
13	A	Brechin City	360	3-3		2	3			5		8		9	11[1]	12	14	1	6	10[1]		7[1]	15							4	
27	A	Queen's Park	516	1-1		2	11			5	12	8		7	10			1	6				15						3	4	9[1]
Mar 6	H	East Stirlingshire	246	0-2		2	3			5	11	8		9	7	12		1	6	10			15							4	
9	H	Albion Rovers	230	1-1		2	3			5	11	8[1]	9	9	7			1	6	12									10	4	
13	A	Berwick Rangers	321	1-0		2	3			5	12	8		9[1]	7			1	6	11									10	4	
20	A	Ross County	2,374	2-1		2	3			5		8		9	7			1	6	11[1]		14							10[1]	4	15
Apr 3	H	Montrose	541	2-1		2	3			5		8		9	7			1	6	10								12	11[2]	4	
5	H	Cowdenbeath	650	6-1	1	2	3			5[1]		8		9[1]	7				6[2]	12		11			4			15	14[1]	10[1]	
10	A	Cowdenbeath	245	1-2		2	3			5		8		9	7			1	6	11							15[1]	10	4	
17	H	Brechin City	562	2-0		2	3			5		9	8	9	7	15		1	6	11[1]					4			14	3	10[1]	
24	A	Stenhousemuir	629	2-0		2	12		14	5		9[1]	8	9	7[1]			1	6	11					4			15	3	10	
May 1	H	Queen's Park	762	0-1		2			14	5		9	8	9	7			1	6	11					4				3	10	2
8	A	Albion Rovers	256	2-0		2	3			5	10	9	8	9	7	14	15	1	6	11[1]								12		4[1]	
TOTAL FULL APPEARANCES					2	35	22	17	9	35	24	27	5	33	18	2	2	33	29	28	6	21	3	7	4	2	1	9	17	4	1
TOTAL SUB APPEARANCES								(1)	(1)		(6)	(5)			(2)	(9)	(5)				(4)	(3)	(5)	(6)	(2)	(2)	(7)		(1)		(2)
TOTAL GOALS SCORED						1	1	2		1	3	3	1	17	1				3	4	1	8	3					1	1	2	

Small bold figures denote goalscorers.   † denotes opponent's own goal.

Boghead Park

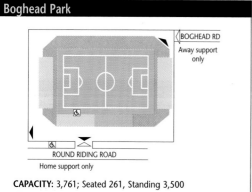

BOGHEAD RD
Away support only

ROUND RIDING ROAD
Home support only

CAPACITY: 3,761; Seated 261, Standing 3,500
PITCH DIMENSIONS: 110 yds x 72 yds
FACILITIES FOR DISABLED SUPPORTERS:
Wheelchairs are accommodated on the track.

Team playing kits

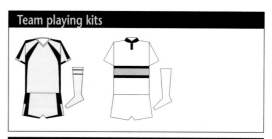

How to get there

Boghead Park can be reached by the following routes:
TRAINS: The train service from Glasgow Queen Street and Glasgow Central Low Level both pass through Dumbarton East Station (away fans best choice) and Dumbarton Central Station, both of which are situated just under a ten minute walk from the ground.
BUSES: There are two main services which pass close to the ground. These are bound for Helensburgh and Balloch from Glasgow.
CARS: Car parking is available in certain side streets around the ground. Supporters buses should follow Police signposts to designated parking area.

FOOTBALL CLUB

Bayview Stadium, Harbour View,
Methil, Leven, Fife, KY8 3RW

CHAIRMAN
Julian S. Danskin

VICE-CHAIRMAN
Gordon Dow

DIRECTORS
Kenneth R. MacKay,
James B. Stewart, James Taylor,
Robert L. Stevenson, David Hamilton,
Alexander R. Lindsay
& Robert Moreland

HONORARY VICE-PRESIDENTS
James Baxter & John Fleming

**DIRECTOR (ADMINISTRATION)/
STADIUM MANAGER**
Jai Paragreen

OFFICE SECRETARY
Mrs Leona Walker

PLAYER/MANAGER
Stephen Kirk

ASSISTANT MANAGERS
David Clark & David Gorman

CLUB DOCTORS
Dr. William McCrossan
& Dr. Robert Dunn

SURGEON
Ivan Brenkell, M.B., Ch.B., F.R.C.S.

PHYSIOTHERAPIST
Neil Bryson

**YOUTH DEVELOPMENT
COACH/CHIEF SCOUT**
Danny Hendry

**FOOTBALL SAFETY OFFICERS'
ASSOCIATION REPRESENTATIVE**
James Dick (01333) 424094

GROUNDSMAN
Ernie McGarr

ASSISTANT GROUNDSMEN
John Burns & Andrew Redpath

KIT MAN
David Wight

COMMERCIAL MANAGER
Stephen Kirk (01333) 426323

COMMERCIAL ASSISTANT
James Baxter

CATERING DIRECTOR
Hugh Malcolm

TELEPHONES
Ground/Commercial (01333) 426323
Fax (01333) 426376

E-MAIL AND INTERNET ADDRESS
east@fife.fsbusiness.co.uk

CLUB SHOP
A Supporters' Club Shop is situated
within the Ground

OFFICIAL SUPPORTERS CLUB
Levenmouth: Mr. Michael McCoull,
60 Rothes Road, Glenrothes, Fife.
(01592) 757249.
East Neuk O'Fife: Mr. Ian Anderson,
1 East Shore, Pittenweem, Fife.
(01334) 310080

TEAM CAPTAIN
Robert Shannon

SHIRT SPONSOR
R. S. Nicol & Sons

LIST OF PLAYERS 1999-2000

SURNAME	FIRST NAME	MIDDLE NAME	DATE OF BIRTH	PLACE OF BIRTH	DATE OF SIGNING	HEIGHT FT INS	WEIGHT ST LBS	POS. ON PITCH	PREVIOUS CLUB
Agostini	Damiano	Pietro	22/11/78	Irvine	28/07/99	5 11.0	12 9	Def	Queen's Park
Cusick	John	James	16/01/75	Kirkcaldy	18/03/94	5 8.0	11 0	Def/Mid	Dundonald Bluebell
Dignan	Ryan		21/03/79	Edinburgh	09/06/99	5 9.0	10 5	Def	Musselburgh Athletic
Gibb	Richard		22/04/65	Bangour	17/09/93	5 7.0	11 0	Def/Mid	Armadale Thistle
Grattan	Kieran		29/05/75	Dunfermline	23/06/99	5 10.0	11 3	Mid	Roysth J.F.C.
Hay	David	Alexander	27/06/80	Edinburgh	05/07/99	6 2.0	13 2	Def	Dunfermline Athletic
Herd	William	David	03/09/65	Buckhaven	22/07/99	5 11.0	12 0	Def	Ross County
Honeyman	Ben		14/02/77	Adelaide	20/03/99	5 9.0	10 3	Fwd	Forfar Athletic
Kirk	Stephen	David	03/01/63	Kirkcaldy	14/01/98	5 11.0	12 6	Fwd	Raith Rovers
Logan	Raymond		20/09/78	Bellshill	07/06/99	5 11.0	11 6	Mid	Whitburn Juniors
Love	Graeme		07/12/73	Bathgate	30/07/99	5 10.0	12 7	Def	Clydebank
Mackay	Stuart	John	03/03/75	Inverness	02/07/99	5 8.0	12 6	Mid	Alloa Athletic
McCulloch	William		02/04/73	Baillieston	07/08/97	6 6.0	12 6	Gk	Ayr United
McIntosh	Scott		13/06/80	Kirkcaldy	11/01/99	5 10.0	11 4	Mid	St. Andrews United
McPherson	Grant		20/12/79	Glasgow	26/06/99	5 8.0	10 2	Mid	Glenrothes Juniors
Moffat	Barrie		27/12/72	Bangour	31/12/96	5 8.0	11 0	Fwd	Alloa Athletic
Mooney	Ryan		16/04/80	Edinburgh	10/03/99	5 10.0	10 8	Fwd	Hill of Beath Juniors
Munro	Kenneth	Neil	08/08/77	Edinburgh	20/09/97	5 10.0	11 0	Def/Mid	Cowdenbeath
Ramsay	Steven		13/04/67	Germiston	20/03/99	5 9.0	11 0	Mid	Alloa Athletic
Robertson	Graham	Stuart	02/11/76	Edinburgh	05/03/99	5 11.0	10 10	Mid	Raith Rovers
Shannon	Robert		20/04/66	Bellshill	10/08/99	5 11.0	12 4	Def	Newcastle Breakers
Stewart	Andrew	Thomas	02/01/78	Dumfries	16/02/99	6 2.0	12 13	Gk	Dundee United
Tinley	Gavin		22/02/79	Dundee	08/09/98	5 9.0	11 1	Mid	Carnoustie Panmure
Wright	Darren	James	22/09/78	Edinburgh	28/07/99	5 10.0	10 12	Fwd	Rosyth Recreation

Milestones

YEAR OF FORMATION: 1903
MOST CAPPED PLAYER: George Aitken
NO. OF CAPS: 5
MOST LEAGUE POINTS IN A SEASON: 57 (Division 2 – Season 1929/30)(2 Points for a Win)
67 (Second Division – Season 1995/96)(3 Points for a Win)
MOST LEAGUE GOALS SCORED BY A PLAYER IN A SEASON: Henry Morris (Season 1947/48)
NO. OF GOALS SCORED: 41
RECORD ATTENDANCE: 22,515 (-v- Raith Rovers – 2.1.1950 at Bayview Park – old Stadium)
1,462 (-v- Forfar Athletic – 14.11.1998 at Bayview Stadium – new Stadium)
RECORD VICTORY: 13-2 (-v- Edinburgh City – Division 2, 11.12.1937)
RECORD DEFEAT: 0-9 (-v- Heart of Midlothian – Division 1, 5.10.1957)

The Fifers' ten year league record

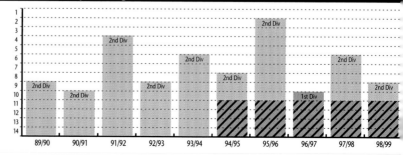

THE FIFERS' CLUB FACTFILE 1998/99 RESULTS... APPEARANCES... SCORERS

Date	Venue	Opponents	Att.	Res	McCulloch W.	Strathdee J.	Gibb R.	Cusick J.	Johnston G.	Coyle R.	Munro K.	Brown G.	Martin J.	Moffat B.	Allan G.	Kirk S.	McNeil J.	Abercromby M.	Fisher D.	Gartshore P.	MacFarlane C.	Butter J.	McPherson G.	Dyer M.	Dixon A.	Findlay M.	Skeldon K.	Dair L.	Harrison T.	Peters S.	Venables S.	Archibald E.	Lawrie A.	Robertson G.	Ramsay S.	Honeyman B.	Mooney R.
Aug 4	A	Arbroath	807	2-0	1	2	3	4	5	6	7	8¹	9	10	11¹																						
15	H	Alloa Athletic	737	2-2	1		3	4	5	6	7	8	9	10¹	11¹	2	14	15																			
22	A	Clyde	806	0-0	1	2	3	4	5	6	7	8	9	10	11		14	12																			
29	H	Inverness Cal. Th.	814	1-5	1	2	3	4	5	6	7	8			11		9	10	12	14¹	15																
Sep 5	A	Livingston	3,002	1-3	1		3	4	5	6	2	8		10¹	11	9	7	12		14																	
12	A	Forfar Athletic	451	2-1			3	4	5	6	2	8¹		10	11	9¹	12	7		14		1	15															
19	A	Partick Thistle	1,314	1-3			3	4¹	5	6	2	12		10	11	9	15	8		14		1		7														
27	H	Queen of the South	803	2-0	1		3	4	5	6	2	14		10¹	11	15¹	12	8				9	7															
Oct 3	A	Stirling Albion	748	2-3	1		3	4	5	6	2	14		10¹	11	15¹	7	8				9	12															
10	A	Alloa Athletic	526	1-5	1		3	5		6	4	2		10		9¹	12	8				7	11															
17	H	Arbroath	719	0-3	1			5		6	2	4		10	11	9	7	8	15					3	12													
24	A	Inverness Cal. Th.	1,547	2-4	1		3	4		6	7	2	15	10¹	11	5		14				9¹		8														
31	H	Livingston	1,008	†2-3	1		3	4		6	2	9¹		10	11	5						15	12	8	7													
Nov 7	A	Partick Thistle	1,870	1-0	1		3	4	5	6	2	9	12	10	11	5		14						8	7¹													
14	H	Forfar Athletic	1,462	1-0	1		3	4	5	6	2	9	14	10¹	11	15		12						8	7													
21	A	Queen of the South	937	0-0	1	14	3	4	5	6	2	7	9	10	11	15								8														
28	H	Stirling Albion	1,003	2-3	1	7	3¹	4	5	6	2		9¹	10	11	15		14						8	12													
Dec 12	H	Clyde	804	0-0	1	2	3	4	5		7	14	9	10	11	15								8	12	6												
19	A	Arbroath	701	1-2	1	14	3	4			2		9¹	10	11	8								12	7	6	5											
27	H	Inverness Cal. Th.	1,101	3-2	1		3	4	5		2		9¹	10	11¹	15		14						7	12¹	6	8											
Jan 17	A	Queen of the South	797	0-1	1			5	6	2		9	10			15		3			4		14		11	8	7										
20	A	Livingston	1,554	0-1	1	3		5	6	2		9	10			15								12	11	4	8	7										
30	A	Stirling Albion	806	1-0	1	2	3		6		14	10	11	5									7	9¹	4		8	12									
Feb 6	H	Partick Thistle	1,241	1-0	1	15	11	6			3		10¹	8	5									7	9	4				2								
16	A	Forfar Athletic	420	4-2	1		11	2		6	3		10³		9									7	8¹	4		12	14	5								
20	A	Clyde	768	0-1	1	14	11	2		6	3		10											7	9	8		4		5								
27	H	Alloa Athletic	708	0-4	1		9	2		6	3	14	10	12										7	8	4		11		5								
Mar 6	A	Livingston	995	1-1	1		2		4	3		10		6									9	11¹	8		7		5								
13	A	Inverness Cal. Th.	1,797	0-4	1		15	2		3		10	12	6									9	11	8		7		5	4							
20	A	Stirling Albion	641	1-0	1			4		2		10¹		6									7	11	8				5	9	3	12	15				
Apr 3	A	Queen of the South	1,411	0-2	1		14	2		3		10		6									8		4	15		5	7	11		9				
10	A	Partick Thistle	1,811	2-2	1		12	2		3	14	10	15¹										11			4	6	5	7¹	9		8				
17	H	Forfar Athletic	605	2-1	1		11	2		6	3	12	10¹	15												14	7	5	9	4¹		8				
24	H	Arbroath	837	1-2	1		3	6		2		12	10¹	9									8		7	5	11	4								
May 1	A	Alloa Athletic	806	1-3	1		3	6		12	2	9	10	15									4		7	5¹			8	11	14					
8	H	Clyde	845	2-1	1		3			6	2	12	10										4		7	5	8	11	9²								
TOTAL FULL APPEARANCES					34	7	28	32	17	25	36	13	11	35	21	17	4	7	1		2	3	4	1	1	18	13	17	5	12		13	7	7	2	3	
TOTAL SUB APPEARANCES						(4)	(3)		(1)		(4)	(9)		(2)	(10)	(7)	(3)	(3)		(5)	(1)		(6)	(2)		(4)	(3)		(2)	(1)	(2)				(1)	(2)	
TOTAL GOALS SCORED						1	1			3	3	13	3	5				1			1			5					1	1	1	2					

Small bold figures denote goalscorers.   † denotes opponent's own goal.

Bayview Stadium

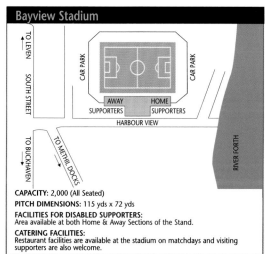

TO LEVEN · SOUTH STREET · CAR PARK · CAR PARK · AWAY SUPPORTERS · HOME SUPPORTERS · HARBOUR VIEW · TO BUCKHAVEN · TO METHIL DOCKS · RIVER FORTH

CAPACITY: 2,000 (All Seated)
PITCH DIMENSIONS: 115 yds x 72 yds
FACILITIES FOR DISABLED SUPPORTERS:
Area available at both Home & Away Sections of the Stand.
CATERING FACILITIES:
Restaurant facilities are available at the stadium on matchdays and visiting supporters are also welcome.

Team playing kits

How to get there

Bayview Stadium can be reached by the following routes:

TRAINS: The nearest railway station is Kirkcaldy (8 miles away), and fans will have to catch an inter-linking bus service from just outside the station to the ground.

BUSES: A regular service from Kirkcaldy to Leven passes close to the ground, as does the Leven to Dunfermline service. The Leven bus terminus is approximately ²/₃ mile from the ground (5 minutes walk).

CARS: There are Car Parking facilities available for both Home and Away fans at the ground.

email: sfl@sol.co.uk • website: www.sfl.scottishfootball.com

EST. 1881

Firs Park, Firs Street,
Falkirk, FK2 7AY

CHAIRMAN
George H. Ronald

VICE-CHAIRMAN
G. Ross A. Strang

DIRECTORS
Peter A. Crawford,
Campbell Crawford
& Ian B. Crozier

SECRETARY
George H. Ronald

MANAGER
Hugh McCann

**YOUTH DEVELOPMENT
DIRECTOR**
Campbell Crawford

CLUB DOCTOR
Dr. Thomas Barr

PHYSIOTHERAPIST
Paul Green

**FOOTBALL SAFETY OFFICERS'
ASSOCIATION REPRESENTATIVE**
Alan Conner

CHIEF SCOUT
Bobby Hill

**STADIUM DIRECTOR/
GROUNDSMAN**
Peter Crawford

KITMAN
Jim Wilson

COMMERCIAL DIRECTOR
Jim Docherty

TELEPHONES
Ground (01324) 623583
Fax (01324) 637862
(Sec. Home/Fax) (01324) 883359
(Sec. Bus/Fax) (01324) 632869

E-MAIL AND INTERNET ADDRESS
georgeh@shire1881freeserve.co.uk

CLUB SHOP
Situated at ground.
Open on all home matchdays or by
telephone appointment

TEAM CAPTAIN
David Muirhead

SHIRT SPONSOR
Euro Environmental Contracts Ltd

LIST OF PLAYERS 1999-2000

SURNAME	FIRST NAME	MIDDLE NAME	DATE OF BIRTH	PLACE OF BIRTH	DATE OF SIGNING	HEIGHT FT INS	WEIGHT ST LBS	POS. ON PITCH	PREVIOUS CLUB
Abdulrahman	Khalid		10/01/81	Falkirk	14/07/99	6 1.0	11 12	Mid	I.C.I. Juveniles
Barr	Anthony		11/09/77	Bellshill	02/08/97	5 9.0	10 1	Mid	Heart of Midlothian
Bowsher	Colin		11/06/73	Musselburgh	02/06/99	6 2.0	13 10	Mid	Cowdenbeath
Brown	Murray	Croft	31/01/80	Edinburgh	29/07/98	6 0.0	11 7	Def	West Bromwich Albion
Butter	James	Ross	14/12/66	Dundee	26/07/99	6 1.0	13 0	Gk	Brechin City
Donnelly	Patrick		26/11/82	Falkirk	14/07/99	5 7.0	9 0	Def	Bonnybridge U'16
Donnelly	Scott	Iain	04/06/79	Glasgow	30/07/99	5 11.0	11 4	Def	St. Mungo's U'21
Elliott	Anthony		07/10/80	Bellshill	26/07/99	5 11.0	11 0	Def	Kilmarnock
Ferguson	Brown		04/06/81	Falkirk	26/07/99	5 10.0	11 8	Mid	S Form
Gordon	Kevin	Mervyn	01/05/77	Tranent	14/07/99	5 9.0	10 0		Easthouses U'21
Hamilton	John		28/01/81	Stirling	14/07/99	5 10.0	11 12	Fwd	Riverside B.C.
Hardie	Martin		22/04/76	Alexandria	12/06/98	5 11.0	11 0	Mid/Fwd	Queen's Park
Hendry	David		26/08/81	Falkirk	14/07/99	5 7.0	10 8	Fwd	Dundee United
Higgins	Gary		15/09/72	Stirling	02/06/99	5 11.0	12 0	Mid/Fwd	Ross County
Jaffa	Stewart	Andrew	05/02/81	Falkirk	14/07/99	5 6.0	8 0	Mid	Hillington B.C.
Laidlaw	Steven	James	17/06/73	Edinburgh	25/01/99	6 0.0	12 0	Fwd	Berwick Rangers
Lynes	Craig		07/02/81	Edinburgh	14/07/99	6 3.0	11 7	Mid/Fwd	Hutchison Vale U'21
MacMillan	Gary	Donald	24/02/81	Stirling	14/07/99	6 2.0	11 7	Def	Tullibody Hearts U'16
McDonald	Gary		08/04/81	Stirling	26/07/99	6 1.0	11 0	Fwd	Kilmarnock
McNeill	William	John	12/03/67	Toronto	31/07/98	5 9.0	11 0	Mid	Brechin City
Morrison	Scott	John	22/10/81	Glasgow	28/07/99	6 1.0	12 3	Gk	Hutchison Vale U'21
Muirhead	David		16/02/78	Stirling	04/01/96	5 11.0	13 4	Mid	Bonnybridge Juniors
Ramage	Neil		22/11/81	Stirling	14/07/99	5 10.0	10 8	Def	S Form
Ross	Brian		15/08/67	Stirling	31/03/91	5 11.0	11 7	Def	Ayr United
Russell	Gordon	Alan	03/03/68	Falkirk	23/09/95	5 9.5	10 0	Def	Stenhousemuir
Scott	Andrew	McKean	11/03/81	Glasgow	14/07/99	5 9.0	10 0	Fwd	S Form
Smith	Richard		08/05/81	Falkirk	14/07/99	5 11.0	11 6	Fwd	Riverside B.C.
Storrar	Andrew	David	06/10/77	Stirling	12/01/98	5 5.0	10 6	Def	Stirling Albion
Stuart	Barry		25/05/81	Falkirk	14/07/99	6 0.0	12 6	Def	Unattached

Milestones

YEAR OF FORMATION: 1881
MOST CAPPED PLAYER: Humphrey Jones
NO. OF CAPS: 5 (for Wales)
MOST LEAGUE POINTS IN A SEASON: 55 (Division 2 – Season 1931/32) (2 Points for a Win)
59 (Third Division – Season 1994/95) (3 Points for a Win)
MOST LEAGUE GOALS SCORED BY A PLAYER IN A SEASON: Malcolm Morrison (Season 1938/39)
NO. OF GOALS SCORED: 36
RECORD ATTENDANCE: 11,500 (-v- Hibernian – 10.2.1969)
RECORD VICTORY: 10-1 (-v- Stenhousemuir – Scottish Cup, 1.9.1888)
RECORD DEFEAT: 1-12 (-v- Dundee United – Division 2, 13.4.1936)

The Shire's ten year league record

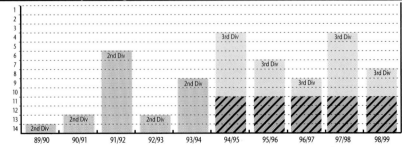

THE SHIRE'S CLUB FACTFILE 1998/99 RESULTS... APPEARANCES... SCORERS

Date	Venue	Opponents	Att.	Res	McDougall G.	Barr A.	Millar D.	Ross B.	Smith J.	Walker S.	Ferguson B.	Muirhead D.	McNeill W.	Patterson P.	McGoldrick K.	McBeth P.	Sime A.	Brown M.	Hardie M.	Hoxley P.	Storrar A.	Ward H.	Hunter S.	Russell G.	Kennedy K.	Bruce G.	Thompson B.	Laidlaw S.	Lepper N.	Scott A.	Abdulrahman K.
Aug 4	A	Ross County	1,021	0-1	1	2	3	4	5	6	7	8	9	10	11	12	15														
15	H	Brechin City	263	1-1	1			4	5	6	2	8	9^1	10	11	12		3	7	14											
22	A	Cowdenbeath	220	1-2	1			4	5	6	2	8	9^1	10	11		15	3	7		14										
29	A	Stenhousemuir	357	0-1	1		7	4	5	6	2	8	9	10	11			3			14										
Sep 5	H	Dumbarton	217	1-2	1		11	4	5	6	2	8	9^1	10	3				7			12	14								
12	H	Albion Rovers	237	0-1	1				2	5	4	7	6		9	11	12	3				15	8	10	14						
19	A	Berwick Rangers	328	2-1	1	8		4	5^1			6	9^1	7	11		12	3			2		10	15							
26	A	Queen's Park	526	4-0	1	8		4	5			6	9^1	7	11^2		12	3			2		10^1	14							
Oct 3	H	Montrose	243	3-1	1	8		4	5			6^1	9^1	7^1	11			3			2		10								
10	A	Brechin City	364	0-0	1	8		4	5		2	6	9	7	11			3					10								
17	A	Cowdenbeath	230	1-1	1	8		4	5		2	6	9^1	7	11			3	14				10	15							
26	H	Stenhousemuir	387	1-1	1	8^1		4	5		2	6	9	7	11			3					10								
31	A	Dumbarton	309	†2-2	1	12		4	5		2	6^1	9	7	11			3	8		14		10				15				
Nov 7	H	Berwick Rangers	277	0-0		8		4	5			6	9	7	11			3			2		10				14	1			
14	A	Albion Rovers	304	1-3		8^1		4	5			6	9	7	11			3			2		10				12	1			
21	H	Queen's Park	247	1-1		8		4	5			6	9	7^1	11			3	14		2		10				15	1			
28	A	Montrose	271	0-2				4	5		12	6	9	7	11			3	8		2		10				15	1			
Dec 12	H	Ross County	338	2-2		10		4	5	8^1		6		7	11			3			2	12	14		9^1		1				
19	A	Cowdenbeath	108	†2-3		10		4	5	8^1		6	14	7	11			3			2	12			9		1				
26	A	Stenhousemuir	979	2-2		2^1		4	5	3^1		6	9	7	12			11	8		14	10			15		1				
Jan 16	H	Queen's Park	224	1-1				4	5^1	6		11	10	7				3	8		2	12			9		1				
26	H	Dumbarton	204	1-2				4	5	6		8^1		10				3	11		2	12			7		1	9			
30	H	Montrose	209	2-1				4	5	6	2	8	14	7					11			10^1		3	12		1	9^1			
Feb 6	H	Berwick Rangers	351	2-1		12		4	5	6	2	8		7					11^1			10		3			1	9^1			
16	H	Albion Rovers	244	4-1		8			5	4	2	6^1		7			15		11^1		14	10^1		3	12		1	9^1			
27	H	Brechin City	219	4-1		8			5^1	4		6	15	7					11		2	10^1		3	12^1		1	9			
Mar 2	A	Ross County	1,021	2-4		8			5	4	15	6^1	14^1	7					11		2	10		3	12		1	9			
6	A	Dumbarton	246	2-0		12			5	4	2	6^1	14	7^1					11			10		3	8		1	9			
13	H	Stenhousemuir	391	1-1		2			5		4	6		7					11		12	10		3	8^1		1	9			
20	A	Montrose	249	0-1		7			5		4		11					12	6		2	10		3	8		1	9			
Apr 3	A	Queen's Park	455	1-2		8			5		4		12	7				3	6	11	2	10^1					1	9	14	15	
10	H	Berwick Rangers	252	3-3					5	4^1	6	8	7^1						11		2	10		3			1	9^1			
17	A	Albion Rovers	304	2-0				4	5	6	8	7					14	11^1			2	10		3			1	9			
24	A	Cowdenbeath	208	0-0				4	5	6	8	7					14	11			2	10		3	12		1	9		15	
May 1	H	Brechin City	344	0-1		8		5	4	2	6	9	11				12				7	10		3			1			14	15
8	H	Ross County	356	1-2		11		4		6	2	8	10^1				15				7			3			1	9	5	12	
TOTAL FULL APPEARANCES					13	23	1	32	28	25	16	34	22	36	19		21	20	1	21	26		13	7	4	19	14	4	19	14	1
TOTAL SUB APPEARANCES						(3)					(2)		(6)		(1)	(3)	(4)	(6)	(2)	(2)	(7)	(5)	(4)	(1)	(11)	(1)	(4)		(1)	(4)	(1)
TOTAL GOALS SCORED						3			3	4		6	8	5	2			3			5				3				6	

Small bold figures denote goalscorers. † denotes opponent's own goal.

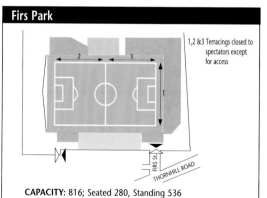

Firs Park

1,2 &3 Terracings closed to spectators except for access

FIRS St.
THORNHILL ROAD

CAPACITY: 816; Seated 280, Standing 536
PITCH DIMENSIONS: 108 yds x 72 yds
FACILITIES FOR DISABLED SUPPORTERS:
By prior arrangement with Secretary.

Team playing kits

How to get there

The following routes may be used to reach Firs Park:

TRAINS: Passengers should alight at Grahamston Station and the ground is then five minutes walk.

BUSES: All buses running from the town centre pass close by the ground. The Grangemouth via Burnbank Road and Tamfourhill via Kennard Street services both stop almost outside the ground.

CARS: Car parking is available in the adjacent side streets. There are also spaces available in the car park adjacent to the major stores around the ground.

Station Park, Carseview Road,
Forfar, DD8 3BT

CHAIRMAN
David McGregor

VICE-CHAIRMAN
Neill McK. Wilson

DIRECTORS
Alastair S. Nicoll,
Michael S. McEwan,
Gordon Menmuir (Treasurer)
& Ronald Blair

HONORARY PATRON
Rt. Hon. Lord Lyell of Kinnordy

SECRETARY
David McGregor

MANAGER
Ian McPhee

ASSISTANT MANAGER
Billy Bennett

COACHING STAFF
Jim Moffat, Malcolm Lowe,
Donald Ritchie, Eric Fleming
& Ally Taylor

PHYSIOTHERAPIST
Jim Peacock

**FOOTBALL SAFETY OFFICERS'
ASSOCIATION REPRESENTATIVE**
Thomas R. Aitken
Home (01307) 468220

GROUNDSMAN/KIT SUPERVISOR
Martin Gray

TELEPHONES
Ground (01307) 463576/462259
Sec. Home (01307) 464924
Sec. Bus. (01307) 475519
Sec. Bus. Fax (01307) 466956

OFFICIAL SUPPORTERS CLUB
c/o Mrs. Yvonne Nicoll,
24 Turfbeg Drive, Forfar

TEAM CAPTAIN
Andy Cargill

SHIRT SPONSOR
Webster Contracts Ltd.

LIST OF PLAYERS 1999-2000

SURNAME	FIRST NAME	MIDDLE NAME	DATE OF BIRTH	PLACE OF BIRTH	DATE OF SIGNING	HEIGHT FT INS	WEIGHT ST LBS	POS. ON PITCH	PREVIOUS CLUB
Brand	Ralph		17/07/70	Dundee	14/07/98	5 9.0	10 3	Fwd	Brechin City
Cargill	Andrew		02/09/75	Dundee	11/01/97	5 6.5	10 8	Mid	Dundee
Catto	Paul	Andrew	29/05/81	Leeds	04/12/98	5 9.0	10 2	Def	S Form
Christie	Sean		15/07/80	Dundee	31/08/98	5 9.0	10 7	Fwd	Carnoustie Panmure
Craig	Douglas	Ewing	30/01/71	London	05/11/94	5 10.0	12 9	Def	Forfar Albion
Donaldson	Euan	Gordon	20/08/75	Falkirk	30/07/99	5 10.0	10 7	Def	Albion Rovers
Ferguson	Graeme	William	03/03/71	Stirling	28/08/97	5 10.0	11 10	Def	Clyde
Ferguson	Stuart		09/11/80	Bangour	29/07/99	5 10.0	10 5	Def/Mid	Forfar West End
Ferrie	Neal		23/11/81	Dundee	11/07/99	5 10.0	10 0	Gk	Dundee United
Garden	Stuart	Robertson	10/02/72	Dundee	04/08/99	5 11.5	12 3	Gk	Brechin City
Glennie	Stuart	Philip	07/10/75	Torphins	14/09/93	6 0.0	13 0	Def	Banchory St. Ternan
Harrow	Andrew	John	26/01/81	Kirkcaldy	18/07/98	5 11.0	10 0	Def/Mid	Rangers
Johnston	George	Michael	09/11/73	Dunfermline	30/03/99	6 2.0	13 2	Def	East Fife
Kiddie	Ross		16/09/80	Dundee	29/07/99	5 10.0	11 10	Def	Forfar West End
Lammie	Scott	Thomas	12/06/83	Uphall	07/07/99	5 8.0	10 0	Mid	Comrie Colts
Lowe	Bradley		16/07/81	Dundee	16/05/99	5 11.0	10 7	Mid	S Form
MacDonald	Innes	James	19/10/62	Inverness	11/07/99	5 10.0	11 3	Mid	Montrose
McCheyne	Graeme		21/12/73	Bellshill	18/07/97	6 1.0	11 3	Def	Clyde
McIllravey	Paul	James	11/04/79	Dundee	04/12/98	5 11.0	12 0	Fwd	Dundee United
McLean	Barry		06/04/78	Blairgowrie	19/03/97	5 11.0	11 4	Fwd	Coupar Angus
McPhee	Gary		01/10/79	Glasgow	17/07/99	5 9.0	10 0	Mid	Clyde
Milne	Craig	David	01/04/81	Perth	16/05/99	5 10.0	11 0	Fwd	S Form
Mitchell	Jonathan	Andrew	22/06/81	Dundee	16/05/99	5 10.0	10 4	Fwd	S Form
Moffat	James		27/01/60	Dunfermline	04/09/98	6 0.0	12 0	Gk	Cowdenbeath
Morris	Roberto		11/02/80	Dundee	30/07/99	6 1.0	10 0	Def	Dundee United Social Club
Nairn	James		25/08/72	Kirkcaldy	21/03/97	5 10.0	10 10	Mid	Newburgh Juniors
Rattray	Alan	Raymond	08/06/79	Dundee	16/11/96	5 10.0	11 0	Def	Dundee Violet
Russell	Craig		25/01/82	Aberdeen	04/09/98	5 3.0	9 0	Fwd	Aberdeen Albion B.C.
Taylor	Alexander		13/06/62	Baillieston	30/07/99	5 9.5	11 7	Mid	Ross County
Taylor	Sean	Peter	24/01/83	Aberdeen	16/06/99	5 9.0	10 0	Fwd	Bank's O Dee

Milestones

YEAR OF FORMATION: 1885
MOST LEAGUE POINTS IN A SEASON: 63 (Second Division – Season 1983/84) (2 Points for a Win)
80 (Third Division – Season 1994/95) (3 Points for a Win)
MOST LEAGUE GOALS SCORED BY A PLAYER IN A SEASON: Dave Kilgour (Season 1929/30)
NO. OF GOALS SCORED: 45
RECORD ATTENDANCE: 10,800 (-v- Rangers – 7.2.1970)
RECORD VICTORY: 14-1 (-v- Lindertis – Scottish Cup, 1.9.1888)
RECORD DEFEAT: 2-12 (-v- King's Park – Division 2, 2.1.1930)

The Loons' ten year league record

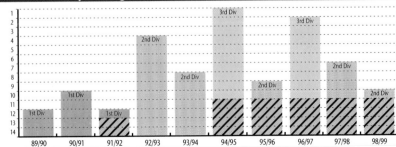

THE LOONS' CLUB FACTFILE 1998/99 RESULTS... APPEARANCES... SCORERS

Date	Venue	Opponents	Att.	Res	Robertson D.	McCheyne G.	Ferguson G.	Hamilton J.	Mann R.	Raynes S.	Gibson A.	Gillies K.	Brand R.	Honeyman B.	Cargill A.	Allison J.	McLauchlan M.	Gray A.	Watson G.	Moffat J.	Sharp R.	Bowes M.	McLean B.	Nairn J.	Craig D.	Rattray A.	McIlravey P.	Tully C.	Christie S.	Johnston G.	Glennie S.
Aug 4	A	Alloa Athletic	495	2-1	1	2	3	4	5	6	7	8	9	10^2	11	12	14	15													
15	H	Partick Thistle	1,053	0-1	1	2	3	4	5	11	8		9	10	7		14		6													
22	A	Livingston	1,193	1-1	1	2	6		4	5	11	7	15	12^1	10	8		9	14	3												
29	A	Arbroath	905	1-2	1	2	6		4	5^1	11	8	7	14	10	12		9		3												
Sep 5	H	Clyde	494	2-2	1	2	6		4	5^1	11	9	8	15^1	10	7	12	14			1	3										
12	H	East Fife	451	1-2	1	2	6			5	12	10^1	8	9		11	7	4		3												
19	A	Queen of the South	916	0-3	1	2	6			5	9	10	8		12	11	7	4		3		14	15								
26	H	Stirling Albion	427	1-2	1		6			5	11	8	7	9	10^1	15	12	2		3		14	4								
Oct 3	A	Inverness Cal. Th.	1,925	2-2	1		6			5	11		7	9^1	10^1	14	8	2		3		4	15								
11	A	Partick Thistle	2,870	0-2	1	15				5	11		7	9	10	14	8	12		2		3	4	6							
17	H	Alloa Athletic	401	1-2	1	2				5	11		7	9	10^1	8		3				14	4	6							
26	H	Arbroath	800	1-3	1	2				5	11	15	7	9^1	10		14	3				4	6								
31	A	Clyde	918	1-3	1					11			7	9	10		12	2		3		14^1	4	6	5						
Nov 7	H	Queen of the South	389	1-0	1	2				5	11		7	9	8	12	10					4^1	3	6							
14	A	East Fife	1,462	0-1	1					5	11		9	12	8	2	10	7				14	4	3	6						
21	A	Stirling Albion	731	1-3	1	2				5	11		9^1		8		10	7				4	3	6							
28	H	Inverness Cal. Th.	511	2-2	1		6			5	11		9	10	8^2	4	7	2				12	3								
Dec 12	H	Livingston	502	1-2	1	2	6			5	11		9		10	8	7	4				12	3^1		15						
19	A	Alloa Athletic	466	1-3	1	2	6			5	11		12	9	10	8	7	3				15^1	4	14							
Jan 16	A	Stirling Albion	445	3-3							14	9	10	11	2	7^2	4	1				12	8	3	6^1	5					
19	A	Arbroath	767	2-2	1					12	14	10	11	2	7^1	4					9^1	8	3	6	5						
30	A	Inverness Cal. Th.	2,018	0-2	1	2				11	8	14	12	10	7	4					9	3	6	5							
Feb 2	H	Clyde	419	3-1	1					11	8	14^1	12	10	2	7	6				3	4^1	9^1	5	15						
6	A	Queen of the South	968	3-0	1					11	8	14	10^2	2	7	6					3	4	9^1	5	12						
16	H	East Fife	420	2-4	1	6	4			11	8	12	14	2	7^1				3	9	5^1										
20	A	Livingston	1,534	0-5	1	2	5			11	8	14	12	10	7	9			6	3	4										
27	H	Partick Thistle	662	2-1	1	2	5			9^1	11^1	10	7		8	6	3	4	14												
Mar 6	A	Clyde	815	0-1		2	5			12	9	11	10	14	7	1	8	6	3	4											
13	H	Arbroath	864	5-2		2^1	5			12	9^2	11	10^1	15	7^1	1	8	6	3	4											
20	H	Inverness Cal. Th.	504	0-3		2	5			11	9	10	12	7	1	8	6	3	4	14											
Apr 3	A	Stirling Albion	820	2-2		2^1	5			11	9^1	10	6	8	1	7	3	4	14												
10	H	Queen of the South	416	2-1		2				11	9	10	8	1	7^1	6^1	3	4	5												
17	A	East Fife	605	1-2		2	5			6	9	10	14	15	1	7^1	8	3	4	11	12										
24	H	Alloa Athletic	440	3-1		2						10^2	8	11	1	7^1	6	3	4	9	12	5									
May 1	H	Partick Thistle	2,539	0-1		2				12		15	10	8	1	7	6	3	4	9	5										
8	H	Livingston	1,395	1-2		2				14		11	10	8	12^1	1	7	6	3	4	9	5	15								
TOTAL FULL APPEARANCES					25	27	19	5	18	27	8	17	24	17	30	19	24	19	11	9	12	22	26	20	6	6	1	4			
TOTAL SUB APPEARANCES						(1)				(5)	(1)	(4)	(10)	(6)	(3)	(8)	(9)	(2)				(1)	(9)		(2)		(3)		(3)	(2)	(1)
TOTAL GOALS SCORED						2			2	1			10	6	7		6							6	2	1	2	2	1	

Small bold figures denote goalscorers. † *denotes opponent's own goal.*

Station Park

CARSEVIEW ROAD

CAPACITY: 8,732; Seated 739, Standing 7,993
PITCH DIMENSIONS: 115 yds x 69 yds
FACILITIES FOR DISABLED SUPPORTERS:
Ramp entrance via Main Stand.

Team playing kits

How to get there

Station Park can be reached by the following routes:

BUSES: There is a regular service of buses departing from Dundee City Centre into Forfar. The bus station in the town is about half a mile from the ground. There is also a local service.

TRAINS: The nearest railway station is Dundee (14 miles away) and fans who travel to here should then board a bus for Forfar from the city centre. Arbroath station is also about 14 miles away.

CARS: There are car parking facilities in adjacent streets to the ground and also in the Market Muir car park.

email: sfl@sol.co.uk • website: www.sfl.scottishfootball.com

Links Park Stadium,
Wellington Street,
Montrose, DD10 8QD

ALL CORRESPONDENCE
SHOULD BE ADDRESSED TO:
Malcolm J. Watters Esq.,
133 Murray Street, Montrose, DD10 8JQ

CHAIRMAN
John F. Paton

VICE-CHAIRMAN
Malcolm J. Watters

DIRECTORS
John D. Crawford, John Archbold
& David I. Tait

HONORARY PRESIDENT
William Johnston, M.B.E., J.P.

SECRETARY
Malcolm J. Watters

ASSISTANT SECRETARY
Andrew Stephen

MATCH DAY SECRETARY
Iain Gordon

MANAGER
Kevin Drinkell

ASSISTANT MANAGER
John Sheran

YOUTH COACH
Alan Smart

COMMERCIAL EXECUTIVE
Glynis Crawford (01674) 673758

CLUB DOCTOR
Dr. Douglas Walker

PHYSIOTHERAPIST
Allan Borthwick

KIT MANAGER
Brian Leiper

FOOTBALL SAFETY OFFICERS'
ASSOCIATION REPRESENTATIVE
Lyndsay Nicoll (01674) 674474

GROUNDSMAN
Ron Marquis

TELEPHONES
Ground/Commercial (01674) 673200
Sec. Home (01674) 674838
Sec. Bus. (01674) 674941
Sec. Fax (01674) 677830
Ground Fax (01674) 677311

CLUB SHOP
Situated at Stadium (01674) 674941.
Open 10.30 a.m. – 5.00 p.m. Fri.
and on home matchdays

OFFICIAL SUPPORTERS CLUB
c/o Links Park, Wellington Street,
Montrose, DD10 8QD

TEAM CAPTAIN
Gary Paterson

SHIRT SPONSOR
The Bervie Chipper

LIST OF PLAYERS 1999-2000

SURNAME	FIRST NAME	MIDDLE NAME	DATE OF BIRTH	PLACE OF BIRTH	DATE OF SIGNING	HEIGHT FT INS	WEIGHT ST LBS	POS. ON PITCH	PREVIOUS CLUB
Collie	Christopher	Andrew	22/04/81	Aberdeen	15/03/99	6 0.0	11 10	Def	Parkvale Juniors
Craib	Mark		08/02/70	St. Andrews	17/07/92	5 10.0	11 12	Def	Dundee
Craib	Stephen	Thomas	14/01/72	Dundee	03/09/99	5 10.0	9 0	Mid	Clyde
Craig	Michael	John	20/09/77	Glasgow	24/12/98	5 9.0	9 12	Fwd	Aberdeen
Duffy	Kenneth		01/01/79	Bellshill	29/07/99	5 10.0	11 6	Mid	Livingston
Farnan	Craig		07/04/71	Dundee	30/07/98	5 10.0	13 3	Mid	Brechin City
Fitzpatrick	Frazer	Thomas	03/10/70	Dundee	31/07/98	5 11.0	11 7	Gk	St. Josephs J.F.C.
Harrison	Thomas	Edward	22/01/74	Edinburgh	03/09/99	5 9.0	11 8	Mid	East Fife
Mailer	Craig	James	27/09/67	Perth	20/02/95	5 11.0	11 7	Def	Kinnoull Juniors
McGlynn	Gary	Dominic	24/11/77	Falkirk	30/07/99	5 11.0	12 5	Gk	Dundee
McHattie	Keith		23/12/80	Aberdeen	15/03/99	5 10.0	10 8	Mid	Parkvale Juniors
McWilliam	Ross	John	13/03/81	Aberdeen	29/08/98	5 10.0	11 7	Mid	Parkvale Juniors
Meldrum	Graham	Ian	27/02/73	Bangour	30/07/98	5 8.0	10 7	Def	Cowdenbeath
Murray	Mark	John	19/12/77	Dundee	06/12/97	5 10.0	11 0	Gk	Jeanfield Swifts
Niddrie	Kristopher		22/01/80	Aberdeen	29/08/98	6 0.0	11 12	Def	Glentanner Juniors
O'Driscoll	Jerry	William	04/04/78	Aberdeen	07/07/99	6 0.0	11 9	Fwd	Dundee
Paterson	Gary		10/11/69	Dunfermline	18/12/98	6 5.0	15 1	Def	Lochore Welfare
Robertson	Stuart		09/03/78	Aberdeen	30/07/99	5 7.0	9 11	Mid	Stonehaven
Scott	Walter	Douglas	01/01/64	Dundee	17/07/99	5 9.0	10 7	Mid	Arbroath
Shand	Martin	Graham	27/06/80	Aberdeen	19/11/98	5 11.0	11 10	Fwd	Stonehaven Juniors
Stevenson	Craig	Thomas	24/03/79	Lanark	15/03/99	6 1.0	11 7	Mid	St. Josephs
Taylor	Scott	Andrew	23/01/77	Forfar	02/08/95	5 9.0	10 0	Fwd	Dundee United

Milestones

YEAR OF FORMATION: 1879
MOST CAPPED PLAYER: Sandy Keiller
NO. OF CAPS: 6 (2 whilst with Montrose)
MOST LEAGUE POINTS IN A SEASON: 53 (Division 2 – 1974/75 and Second Division 1984/85) (2 Points for a Win)
67 (Third Division – Season 1994/95) (3 Points for a Win)
RECORD ATTENDANCE: 8,983 (-v- Dundee – 17.3.1973)
RECORD VICTORY: 12-0 (-v- Vale of Leithen – Scottish Cup, 4.1.1975)
RECORD DEFEAT: 0-13 (-v- Aberdeen, 17.3.1951)

The Gable Endies' ten year league record

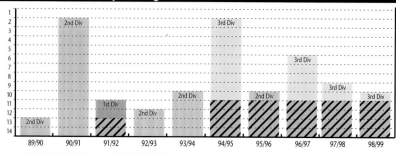

THE GABLE ENDIES' CLUB FACTFILE 1998/99 RESULTS... APPEARANCES... SCORERS

Date	Venue	Opponents	Att.	Res	Murray M.	Mailer C.	Watt J.	Craib M.	Wylie R.	Meldrum G.	Andrew B.	Farnan C.	McGlashan C.	Higgins G.	Loney J.	Taylor S.	Henry J.	Winiarski S.	McWilliam R.	Niddrie K.	Hutton D.	Coulston D.	Irvine B.	Lyon M.	Fitzpatrick F.	Duffy K.	Paterson G.	Shand M.	Craig M.	Magee K.	O'Driscoll J.	Steveson C.
Aug 4	A	Cowdenbeath	161	1-4	1	2	3	4	5	6	7	8	9	10[1]	11	12	14															
15	H	Berwick Rangers	269	1-1	1	5	6	4		3	12	2	9	10	11	7[1]	8															
22	A	Ross County	1,266	1-3	1	5		4		3		2	9	10[1]	11	7	8	6														
29	A	Brechin City	452	0-3	1	5	14	4	6	3	12	8		10	11	9	7	2														
Sep 5	H	Albion Rovers	244	1-2	1			4	6	3	12	8[1]	9	10	11	7		2														
12	A	Stenhousemuir	283	0-4	1	5	14	4	6	3	2	8	9	10	11	7																
19	H	Queen's Park	310	1-0	1	5		4	14	3	12	8[1]	9	10	11	7			2	6												
26	H	Dumbarton	318	1-1	1	5	14	4			12	8	9		11	7			2	6	3	10[1]										
Oct 3	A	East Stirlingshire	243	1-3	1	5	3	4		6	2	8	9[1]		11	7			14		10											
11	A	Berwick Rangers	921	1-1	1	2	6	4		3	11	8			9[1]				7	5	12	10	14									
17	H	Ross County	339	3-6	1	2	6	4		3	10[1]	8[1]			11	9	12		14	5[1]		7										
27	H	Brechin City	340	1-2	1	2		4	6	3	10[1]	8			11	9	12		14	5	15	7										
31	A	Albion Rovers	302	1-4	1	2		4	6	3	10	8			11	9	14		12	5	15	7[1]										
Nov 7	A	Queen's Park	385	0-3	1	2		4	6	3		8				9	14		12	5	11	7		10								
14	H	Stenhousemuir	271	0-0		2		4	6	3		11				9		14		5		7		10	1	8						
25	A	Dumbarton	240	2-0		4	2			3		11				9		14		5[1]		7		10	1	8	6[1]					
28	H	East Stirlingshire	271	2-0		4	2			3		11			10[1]	9[1]				5		7			1	8	6					
Dec 12	H	Cowdenbeath	324	1-1		2	4		6	3		11			10	9[1]				5		7		14	1	8						
19	A	Ross County	1,571	0-3		2	4			3		11			12	9				5		7		10	1	8	6					
Jan 9	A	Albion Rovers	342	2-3			12	6		3		2				9			14	5		4		15[1]	1	8		7[1]	10	11		
16	H	Dumbarton	326	4-2		2				3		4				9				5		7		14[1]	1	8[1]	6	12	10[2]	11		
30	A	East Stirlingshire	209	1-2				4		3		2							12	5		7		9	1	8	6[1]	14	10	11		
Feb 6	H	Queen's Park	260	3-0		2				3		4							14[1]			7		10	1	8	5		9[1]	11[1]		
16	A	Brechin City	317	3-2		6	2			3		4			10[1]				12			8[1]			1		5	7	9	11[1]		
20	A	Cowdenbeath	234	0-1		6	2			3	12	4			10						14	8			1	11	5	7	9			
23	A	Stenhousemuir	276	1-3		6	2			3	12	11			10						6	7			1	8	5[1]	7	9			
27	H	Berwick Rangers	301	0-3			15	4		3	12	11			10			14		5					1	8	6	7	9			
Mar 13	H	Brechin City	404	1-3		2		6		3	14	4			10		12								1	8	5		9[1]	11	7	
16	A	Albion Rovers	258	0-0		2		6		3	14				10		4								1	8	5	12	9	11	7	
20	H	East Stirlingshire	249	1-0		2				3	14				10						6				1	8	5[1]	4	9	11	7	
Apr 3	A	Dumbarton	541	1-2		2				3	10	6						4	12						1	8	5	11	9[1]		7	
10	A	Queen's Park	363	2-1		2[1]				3	10	6							12	5					1	8		7	9	11[1]	4	14
17	H	Stenhousemuir	354	1-2		2				3	10	6							12	5					1	8		7	9	11[1]	4	15
24	H	Ross County	394	2-3		2		6		3	10				7[1]					5					1	8			9	11[1]	4	14
May 1	A	Berwick Rangers	606	1-4		2		6		3	9				10[1]				12	5					1	8		7		11	4	14
8	H	Cowdenbeath	293	1-2	1		4		5	3	7[1]				9				2						21	8		12		11	6	10
TOTAL FULL APPEARANCES					15	32	13	31	4	35	13	30	8	7	14	30	3	5	4	21	3	19		6	21	21	14	9	15	13	9	1
TOTAL SUB APPEARANCES						(5)		(1)		(11)	(1)				(2)	(2)	(5)	(2)	(13)	(1)	(3)			(1)	(3)	(1)		(4)			(4)
TOTAL GOALS SCORED					1					3	3	1	2	1		7				1	1	1		3		2	1	4	1	5	5

Small bold figures denote goalscorers. † denotes opponent's own goal.

Links Park Stadium

WELLINGTON PARK

WELLINGTON STREET

UNION ROW

CAPACITY: 4,338; Seated 1,338, Standing 3,000

PITCH DIMENSIONS: 113 yds x 70 yds

FACILITIES FOR DISABLED SUPPORTERS:
Area set aside for wheelchairs and designated area in new stand.

Team playing kits

How to get there

Links Park can be reached by the following routes:

TRAINS: Montrose is on the Inter-City 125 route from London to Aberdeen and also on the Glasgow-Aberdeen route. There is a regular service and the station is about 15 minutes walk from the ground.

BUSES: An hourly service of buses from Aberdeen and Dundee stop in the town centre and it is a 15 minute walk from here to the ground.

CARS: Car parking is available in the car park at the ground and there are numerous side streets all round the park which can be used if necessary.

email: sfl@sol.co.uk • website: www.sfl.scottishfootball.com

The National Stadium,
Hampden Park, Letherby Drive,
Mount Florida, Glasgow, G42 9BA

PRESIDENT
James Nicholson

COMMITTEE
James C. Rutherford (Treasurer),
Malcolm D. Mackay,
Peter G. Buchanan ,
Austin Reilly,
A. Kenneth C. Harvey,
David Gordon, B.Acc., A.C.M.A.,
David McNeil, Garry M. Templeman
& H. Gordon Wilson

SECRETARY
Alistair MacKay

OFFICE STAFF
Mrs. Janice Balmain
& Mrs. Margaret Dunlop

TEAM COACH
John McCormack

RESERVE TEAM COACH
David Hunter

YOUTH DEVELOPMENT OFFICER
Frank Reilly

CLUB DOCTOR
Alan S. Hutchison

PHYSIOTHERAPIST
Robert C. Findlay

CHIEF SCOUT
Jack Jolly

FOOTBALL SAFETY OFFICERS'
ASSOCIATION REPRESENTATIVE
Alistair MacKay (0141) 632 1275

KIT MANAGER
William Neil

COMMERCIAL DIRECTOR
A. Kenneth C. Harvey
(0141) 632 1275

TELEPHONES
Office (0141) 632 1275
Stadium Operations (0141) 620 4000
Fax (0141) 636 1612

E-MAIL & INTERNET ADDRESS
www.queensparkfc.co.uk

CLUB SHOP
Home matches only – Hampden Park
(Kiosk within BT Scotland Stand).
Open 2.15 p.m. – 3.00 p.m. and
4.45 p.m. – 5.00 p.m. on home
match days. Mail Orders may be
obtained through the Secretary of the
Official Supporters Club.

OFFICIAL SUPPORTERS CLUB
c/o Secretary, Keith McAllister,
58 Brunton Street,
Glasgow, G44 3NQ

CLUB CAPTAIN
David Graham

SHIRT SPONSOR
Barr Irn Bru - Original and Best

LIST OF PLAYERS 1999-2000

SURNAME	FIRST NAME	MIDDLE NAME	DATE OF BIRTH	PLACE OF BIRTH	DATE OF SIGNING	HEIGHT FT INS	WEIGHT ST LBS	POS. ON PITCH	PREVIOUS CLUB
Alexander	David		05/05/79	Vale of Leven	13/07/99	6 0.0	11 10	Def	Knightswood Juveniles
Borland	Paul	Joseph	28/06/79	Rutherglen	27/08/99	5 9.0	9 4	Def	Celtic
Brown	James	Paul	24/09/77	Greenock	26/11/98	5 11.0	12 7	Mid	Gourock Y.A.C.
Carmichael	Derek		03/01/79	Rutherglen	18/09/98	5 10.0	11 6	Fwd	Queen's Park B.C.
Caven	Ross		04/08/65	Glasgow	12/08/82	6 0.0	12 0	Def/Mid	Possil Y.M.C.A.
Connaghan	Denis		09/01/76	Glasgow	05/07/99	5 11.0	11 10	Def	Clydebank
Connell	Graham		31/10/74	Glasgow	21/07/99	5 11.0	11 10	Mid	Partick Thistle
Edgar	Scott		10/06/76	Glasgow	27/07/94	6 4.0	13 0	Fwd	Milngavie Wanderers
Elder	Graeme	John	21/11/61	Glasgow	08/07/86	6 1.0	13 0	Def	Drumchapel Y.M.C.A.
Ferguson	Paul		10/09/73	Glasgow	25/03/94	6 0.0	10 7	Def	Wolves B.C.
Ferry	Daniel		31/01/77	Glasgow	23/06/95	5 7.0	11 4	Mid/Fwd	Queen's Park U'18s
Gallagher	Mark	Andrew	06/12/74	Irvine	23/06/99	6 2.0	11 6	Fwd	Knockentiber A.F.C.
Geoghegan	Joseph		28/11/77	Ontario	30/06/99	5 7.0	11 7	Def	Knightswood A.F.C.
Graham	David	Neil Ramsay	27/01/71	Bellshill	25/07/91	5 10.0	10 8	Def/Mid	Queen's Park Youth
Inglis	Neil	David	10/09/74	Glasgow	16/07/99	6 1.0	12 2	Gk	Linfield
Little	Thomas	Francis	13/02/78	Glasgow	06/08/99	5 4.0	9 8	Mid/Fwd	Neilston Juniors
MacFarlane	Neil		10/10/77	Dunoon	13/07/99	6 1.0	12 8	Mid	Glasgow Amateurs U'21
Martin	Paul	John	08/03/65	Bellshill	28/07/98	6 2.0	13 0	Mid/Fwd	Albion Rovers
McColl	Barry		04/08/79	Glasgow	20/06/98	5 5.0	10 11	Mid	Queen's Park B.C.
McFadyen	Martin		21/01/77	Glasgow	05/06/99	5 11.0	10 8	Gk	Knightswood U'21s
McGhee	David		30/10/81	Glasgow	05/09/98	5 10.0	10 8	Def	Hillington B.C.
McGoldrick	Kevin		12/05/72	Glasgow	05/06/99	5 10.0	12 0	Mid/Fwd	East Stirlingshire
Orr	Stewart	John	05/11/80	Glasgow	05/06/99	5 11.5	11 7	Mid	St. Johnstone
Paterson	Alan		13/03/78	Bellshill	23/06/99	6 0.0	11 1	Mid	East Kilbride Thistle
Reid	Alan		19/01/75	Glasgow	17/10/98	5 7.0	10 0	Mid	Armadale Thistle
Reid	Nicholas	Paul	18/04/78	Belfast	26/06/99	6 1.0	11 7	Fwd	Glasgow University
Rossiter	Barry	Maurice	16/01/72	Glasgow	14/08/98	5 9.0	10 0	Def	Rutherglen Glencairn
Smith	Allan	John	04/08/81	Glasgow	05/06/99	6 0.0	11 8	Gk	Giffnock North A.F.C.
Travers	Mark		07/02/77	Glasgow	23/06/99	5 7.0	9 0	Def	Possil Y.M.
Tyrrell	Paul		11/04/80	Stirling	19/09/98	5 9.0	12 0	Mid	Kilsyth B.C.
Whelan	Jonathan		10/10/72	Liverpool	13/03/99	6 0.0	12 3	Mid	Total Network Solutions

Milestones

YEAR OF FORMATION: 1867
MOST CAPPED PLAYER: Walter Arnott
NO. OF CAPS: 14
MOST LEAGUE POINTS IN A SEASON: 57 (Division 2 – Season 1922/23)
MOST LEAGUE GOALS SCORED BY A PLAYER IN A SEASON: William Martin (Season 1937/38)
NO. OF GOALS SCORED: 30
RECORD ATTENDANCE: 149,547 (Scotland v England – 17.4.1937)
RECORD VICTORY: 16-0 (-v- St. Peters – Scottish Cup, 29.8.1885)
RECORD DEFEAT: 0-9 (-v- Motherwell – Division 1, 29.4.1930)

The Spiders' ten year league record

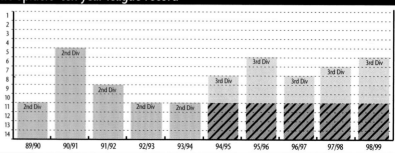

THE SPIDERS' CLUB FACTFILE 1998/99 RESULTS... APPEARANCES... SCORERS

Date	Venue	Opponents	Att.	Res	Monaghan M.	Alexander D.	Connaghan D.	Ferguson P.	Martin P.	Caven R.	Ferry D.	Graham D.	Edgar S.	Parks G.	Little T.	Finlayson K.	Rossiter B.	Cook B.	Agostini D.	Hamilton W.	Orr G.	Inglis N.	McGill D.	Carmichael D.	McGhee D.	Elder G.	Reid A.	McColl B.	Tyrrell P.	Chalmers J.	Finlayson R.	Brown J.	McGuffie R.	Martin A.	Whelan J.	Reid N.
Aug 4	A	Berwick Rangers	448	3-0	1	2	3	4	5	6	7	8^2	9	10	11^1	12																				
15	H	Dumbarton	656	0-1	1	4				2	5	6	7	8	9	10	11	12	3																	
22	A	Brechin City	300	†2-2		4	3	6	5			7	9	10	11	12	8	1	2		14	15^1														
29	A	Albion Rovers	419	1-2	10		3	6	4	2		8	9^1		7	5		1			15	14														
Sep 5	H	Stenhousemuir	499	0-0		2	3		5		7	8	9		11	12	6				14	15	4	1		10										
12	H	Ross County	688	4-2		4	3	14	5^1	6^1		8	9^1		11	15			2			12	7	1		10^1										
19	A	Montrose	310	0-1		2	3		5	6	14	8	9			11	4					12	7	1	15	10										
26	H	East Stirlingshire	526	0-4		2	3		5	6	14	8	9	15		12	4						7	1		10	11									
Oct 3	A	Cowdenbeath	280	3-0		2	3		5^1	6	7	8	9	14		11	4							1		10^2										
10	A	Dumbarton	343	0-1		2	3		5	6	7	8	9	15	16	11	4							1		10	12									
17	A	Brechin City	446	1-1		2	3		5	6		15	9^1			11	12						4	1		10		8	7							
27	H	Albion Rovers	336	0-0		2	3		5		7		9	14		11	4					12		1		10		8	6							
31	A	Stenhousemuir	387	1-2		2	3		5		7		9		12	11	4					15		1		10^1			6	8		14				
Nov 7	H	Montrose	385	3-0		2	3	15	5		7		9^1	12	14	11^1	4							1		10			6^1	8						
14	A	Ross County	1,433	1-5		2	3	15	5		7		9	12	14	11	4							1		10^1			6	8						
21	A	East Stirlingshire	247	1-1		2	3		5		7		9			11	4							1		10^1			6	8						
28	H	Cowdenbeath	439	2-0		15	3		5	2	7		9	14^1		11	4					12		1		10^1			6	8						
Dec 12	H	Berwick Rangers	389	1-1			3		5	2	7	15	9^1	14		11	4					12		1		10			6	8						
19	A	Brechin City	328	0-1		15	3		5	2	7		9			11	4					12		1		10		14	6	8						
26	A	Albion Rovers	322	0-1		2	3				7		9			11	4					12		1		10		15	6	8						
Jan 16	A	East Stirlingshire	224	1-1		2	3	14	5^1		7		9			11	4							1		10			6	8		15				
26	H	Stenhousemuir	333	4-1			3		5	2	7^1		9^2		12	11	4							1		10^1			6	8		15		14		
30	A	Cowdenbeath	198	0-0			3		5	2	7		9		12	11	4							1		10			6	8		15	14			
Feb 6	H	Montrose	260	0-3			3		5	2	7^1		9		12	11	4							1		10			6	8		14				
13	H	Ross County	581	0-3					5	2	7		9		12	11	4		3							10			6	8		14	15			
20	H	Berwick Rangers	330	†2-0					5^1	2	7		12			4			3					1		10			6	8		11	15	14	9	
27	H	Dumbarton	516	1-1		15			5^1	2	7		12				4		3					1		10			6	8		11		14	9	
Mar 6	A	Stenhousemuir	425	1-4		2	3	14	5^1		7		9				4					1				10			6	8		11	15	14	12	
13	H	Albion Rovers	492	0-0			3		5	2	7		9				4					1				10			6	8		11	15	14	12	
20	H	Cowdenbeath	336	2-1			3		5	2	7^1		9				4					1				10^1			6	8		11	15	14	12	
Apr 3	H	East Stirlingshire	455	2-1			3		5^1	2	7^1		12				4					1				10			6	8		11	15	14	9	
10	H	Montrose	363	1-2			3		5	2	7^1		12				4									10			6	8		11	15	14	9	
17	A	Ross County	3,758	2-1			3		5	2	7^1		9				4					1				10^1			6	8		11	15	14	12	
24	H	Brechin City	503	0-2			3		5	2	7		9				4					1				10			6	8		11	15	14	12	
May 1	A	Dumbarton	762	1-0	12		3		5	2	7		9				4					1				10			6	8		11	15^1	14		
8	H	Berwick Rangers	473	1-1			3		5	2	7		9				4					1				10			6^1	8		11	15	14	12	
TOTAL FULL APPEARANCES					2	24	26	11	28	27	31	19	29	7	12	27	26	6	5		4	11	4	12	2	12	6	2	15	17		13	5	4	8	1
TOTAL SUB APPEARANCES					(2)	(4)	(3)		(4)	(1)	(7)	(13)	(9)	(9)	(1)	(4)	(3)		(2)			(1)			(2)	(1)	(9)	(4)			(1)	(1)	(6)	(5)	(2)
TOTAL GOALS SCORED									6	1	1	2	7	1	1	6	1		1						6			1	3		1	1		1	

Small bold figures denote goalscorers.   † denotes opponent's own goal.

The National Stadium, Hampden Park

SOMERVILLE DRIVE

CARMUNNOCK ROAD · Lesser Hampden · WEST STAND · C NORTH STAND D · EAST STAND · AIKENHEAD ROAD

BT SCOTLAND STAND

Letherby Drive · Exit 46 (West Roadway) · MAIN ENTRANCE · Exit 33 (East Roadway) · Kingham Drive

MOUNT ANNAN DRIVE

CAPACITY: 52,046 (All Seated)
PITCH DIMENSIONS: 115 yds x 75 yds
FACILITIES FOR DISABLED SUPPORTERS:
Disabled facilities are situated in the BT Scotland Stand as follows:
West Front (44 places & 44 helpers), West Section A (21 places & 21 helpers)
Ambulant/Blind (55 places), East Front (44 places & 44 helpers)
East Section G (21 places & 21 helpers), Ambulant/Blind (55 places)

Team playing kits

How to get there

The following routes may be used to reach The National Stadium, Hampden Park:

TRAINS: There are two stations within five minutes walk of the ground. Mount Florida Station, on the Cathcart Circle, and King's Park Station. A 15 minute service runs from Glasgow Central.

BUSES: Services to approach Mount Florida end of Stadium: From City Centre: 5, 5A, 5B, M5, M14, 31, 37, 66, 66A, 66B, 66C; From Govan Cross; 34; From Drumchapel: 96, 97, Circular Service: 89, 90; G.C.T. Service: 1; Services to approach King's Park end of Stadium; From City Centre: 12, 12A, 74; Circular Service: 89, 90; G.C.T. Service: 19.

CARS: Car and Coach parking facilities are available in the car park in Letherby Drive, which is capable of holding 200 vehicles. Side streets can also be used.

The Spiders

105

email: sfl@sol.co.uk • website: www.sfl.scottishfootball.com

ALBION ROVERS
SEASON TICKET INFORMATION

SEATED	ADULT	£80
	OAP/UNEMPLOYED	£40
	12-16 YEARS	£20
	UNDER 12'S	£10
STANDING	ADULT	£80

LEAGUE ADMISSION PRICES

SEATED	ADULT	£7
	JUVENILE/OAP	£4
STANDING	ADULT	£6
	JUVENILE/OAP	£3

COWDENBEATH
SEASON TICKET INFORMATION

SEATED	ADULT	£100
	JUVENILE/OAP	£50
STANDING	ADULT	£100
	JUVENILE/OAP	£50

LEAGUE ADMISSION PRICES

SEATED	ADULT	£8
	JUVENILE/OAP	£3.50
STANDING	ADULT	£7
	JUVENILE/OAP	£3

BERWICK RANGERS
SEASON TICKET INFORMATION

SEATED AND STANDING	
ADULT	£105
CONCESSIONS	£45
(Includes Juvenile/OAP/Unemployed with UB40/Registered Disabled)	
JUVENILE (U-16)	£25
FAMILY TICKET (1 ADULT/1JUVENILE)	£120
PLUS £20 FOR EACH ADDITIONAL JUVENILE	

LEAGUE ADMISSION PRICES

SEATED AND STANDING	
ADULT	£7
CONCESSIONS	£3
PRESIDENT'S BOX	
PRICES ON APPLICATION	

N.B. All fans for Stand enter via either Ground 'B' or North Stand Gate 'E'.

DUMBARTON
SEASON TICKET INFORMATION

SEATED		
PRESIDENT'S CLUB	ADULT/JUVENILE/OAP	£250
STAND	ADULT	£150
	JUVENILE/OAP	£100
STANDING	ADULT	£100
	JUVENILE/OAP	£45

LEAGUE ADMISSION PRICES

SEATED	ADULT	£10
	JUVENILE/OAP	£6.50
STANDING	ADULT	£7
	JUVENILE/OAP	£3.50

BRECHIN CITY
SEASON TICKET INFORMATION

SEATED	ADULT	£90
	PARENT & JUVENILE (UNDER 12)	£110
	OAP	£55
	JUVENILE	£35

LEAGUE ADMISSION PRICES

SEATED	ADULT	£5.00
	JUVENILE/OAP	£2.50
ENCLOSURE	ADULT	£5.00
	JUVENILE/OAP	£2.50
STANDING	ADULT	£5.00
	JUVENILE/OAP	£2.50

EAST FIFE
SEASON TICKET INFORMATION

SEATED	ADULT	£140
	JUVENILE/OAP	£70
	PARENT & JUVENILE	£200

LEAGUE ADMISSION PRICES

SEATED	ADULT	£8.50
	JUVENILE/OAP	£4

EAST STIRLINGSHIRE
SEASON TICKET INFORMATION

SEATED	ADULT	£90
OR STANDING	CONCESSIONS*	£45
	FAMILY TICKET	£110

LEAGUE ADMISSION PRICES

SEATED	ADULT	£7
	JUVENILE/OAP	£3.50
STANDING	ADULT	£6
	CONCESSIONS*	£3.50

* Concessionary tickets allow OAPs, Juveniles, UB40 holders, Students and people with long term illness to be admitted to ground at the stated concessionary price. Production of DSS Benefit book or similar documentary proof required.

MONTROSE
SEASON TICKET INFORMATION

SEATED	ADULT	£105
OR STANDING	JUVENILE/OAP	£55
	FAMILY-	
	(1 ADULT & 1 JUVENILE)	£125

LEAGUE ADMISSION PRICES

STANDING	ADULT	£7
	JUVENILE/OAP	£3.50
	STAND TRANSFER	50p

FORFAR ATHLETIC
SEASON TICKET INFORMATION

SEATED	ADULT	£110
	JUVENILE/OAP	£55
STANDING	ADULT	£105
	JUVENILE/OAP	£48

LEAGUE ADMISSION PRICES

SEATED	ADULT	£7.50
	JUVENILE/OAP	£3.50
STANDING	ADULT	£7
	JUVENILE/OAP	£3

QUEEN'S PARK
SEASON TICKET INFORMATION - SEATED

BT SCOTLAND	ADULT	£80
STAND	JUVENILE/OAP	£40
	PARENT & JUVENILE	£90
	FOR EACH ADDITIONAL JUVENILE	£6

LEAGUE ADMISSION PRICES - SEATED

BT SCOTLAND	ADULT	£7
STAND	JUVENILE/OAP	£3
	PARENT & JUVENILE	£7
	FOR EACH ADDITIONAL JUVENILE	£1

Hampden Park, home to Queen's Park, hosted the 1999 Tennents Scottish Cup Final.

Women in Football

Has anyone ever come up with a reasonable argument as to why they believe women shouldn't play football, or be involved in the sport in some capacity, other than the standard 'Cos you're a woman' (or if you're from the West of Scotland 'burd'!) reply? The short answer is that not one person, male or female, has come up with a logical explanation yet.

A woman may not have the physical strength of a man but she can be as equally skilful, if not more so, with a ball at her feet. Due to circumstances beyond her control, she may never have had the chance to play the game but she can both understand it and form opinions on it. As we go into the Millennium, women's football is the fastest growing sport in the world, particularly in Scotland where independent research has shown that 17,000 girls between the ages of 8 and 18 are playing for teams at least fortnightly not to mention the 6,000 or so professional females registered with The Scottish Women's Football Association.

Last summer's Women's World Cup did wonders for the sport and it may surprise people to learn that the Final outsold the men's equivalent in France 1998 by two to one. Organisers had expected to sell 250,000 tickets for the entire tournament but such was the demand that the final figure of briefs sold was almost three times that at 680,000.

Yet still many scoff at the idea of women playing football.

When at the age of 13, I informed my family of my intention to become a sports journalist, the announcement was met with derisory comments that it wasn't the right kind of job for a girl.

It has been reported that Vera Pauw, the National Coach and

Vera Pauw

Technical Director of Girls'/Women's Football in Scotland, met the same opposition as a young girl. Upon seeing her kicking a ball about the streets of her hometown in Holland as a youngster, one of her father's friends commented that it was a shame such skill had been bestowed upon a girl. Vera had the last laugh. As well as being one of the most decorated Dutch footballers, she is the most capped international player - male or female - in Holland, she went on to become one of the most

respected figures in the Dutch F.A. and when the SFA heard she was moving to Scotland they immediately took steps to get her on board as the female equivalent of Craig Brown.

It is doing her a professional disservice to merely refer to her as the wife of Rangers' Assistant Manager, Bert van Lingen, as many sectors of the media often do. Since she started the job, now almost a year ago, she has been working tirelessly to change the face of women's football in Scotland and how it is perceived. She has been working on setting out a clear structure for developing women in the sport whereby young girls playing for their various teams across the country can develop to club level once they reach the correct age. One part of that plan is to get the women's teams affiliated to Premier League teams, a venture which Aberdeen, Heart of Midlothian, Hibernian and Kilmarnock have already embraced.

Vera has also come up with an initiative to introduce mixed football, males and females playing together, outside of primary school, the only area where it currently takes place.

During her reign, the Scotland Women's Under 18's, coached by Tony Gervaise, have qualified for the Semi-Final section of the European Under 18 Championships. The full women's team, her own charges, kicked off their European Championship qualifying campaign at the beginning of October and, if reports are correct, are in with a good chance of making the Play-Offs.

The ranking system for the women's international teams differs from that of their male counterparts with the Scots girls currently in Europe's Group B (rankings 17-32). However, should they finish first or second in their group, they will have a chance to progress to Group A which would see them as hopefuls to make it to the Finals of the next Women's World Cup.

Things obviously won't happen overnight but Maureen McGonigle, who has been Secretary of The Scottish Women's Football Association for almost a decade , has noticed changes.

She said: "The drastic changes I've noticed is in the amount of financial backing from the SFA and the number of male clubs taking an interest which I must say surprised me because I thought they would just pay it lip service. However, four

Premier League teams have taken it very seriously and have feeder teams as well as working at grass roots level.

"The Women's World Cup helped as well because people who before didn't think that women could play football tuned in and were pleasantly surprised at what they saw. I'm not saying Scotland are at that standard yet but I think we'll reach the Play-Off stage for entry to Group A and it will then depend on who we play.

"The teams are coming together as a well organised and talented side because they're getting the opportunity now to learn and play together.

"I'm in no doubt that the sport is growing because domestically we've got more girls wanting to play the game. We've got initiatives with Sport Scotland who have just re-appointed their co-ordinator for Women's football and her remit will be to increase the number of girls playing football in schools so I think it is going to be a huge participant sport for girls in the next three to five years.

"With the involvement of the SFA, there will be changes to come but I'm not sure how radical and accepted they will be. We have to be realistic and say that football as a sport is struggling. There are currently 78 teams in the SFA and a lot of them are finding it difficult to get by on a day to day basis so it's not easy for them to take on a women's team."

It should also be noted that Maureen is the first and only women to be admitted to the inner sanctum of the game's governing body, the SFA Council.

Although it is now over 10 years since I shocked my family with my career choice, on the whole, their attitudes have changed considerably and while some male relatives still find it a little peculiar that they can have an informed conversation with a girl about football, they now accept that I have a knowledge of the game.

Much the same can be said about the attitude of clubs, managers and players. In my five years as a sports

Girls playing at the new Stepford Centre in Easterhouse

The Scotland Under 16 girls team prepare to play England

journalist, covering everything from Junior football to the Premier League, I have never encountered any opposition, asides from the odd and usually flattering sexist remark, at club level but that's the kind of thing you just have to learn to deal with. Wendy McDonald, one of three female physiotherapists in Scottish football, had to learn to deal with a lot more than mere sexist comments. She works with Third Division

The Scotland's Under 16 girls team

Cowdenbeath and her job requires her to be in the changing room before the match, at half-time and afterwards. She admits it took the players a while to adjust to her presence.

"I've been very lucky because the players have treated me very well. They were a bit funny to start with but now they just treat me as one of them. I don't know of any women physio who is full-time in football and

I think it would be difficult for that to happen probably just because it would be a woman," says Wendy.

"It's only at the part-time smaller clubs that it seems to happen and I don't see it happening at any of the bigger clubs. I have a friend who went to work with one of the Premier Clubs' Youth Teams and she had a few problems being accepted mainly because it was a big club."

From my own point of view, perhaps ironically, the greatest opposition I have faced as a sports journalist has been from my own colleagues. Last year, I became the first ever female to be admitted to The Scottish Football Writers Association but not without a major fight. The condition of my being allowed to join was that neither I, or any other member, would be permitted to bring any female guests along to the annual Player of the Year Awards Dinner, the event that the association invite their contacts within the sport to as a means of thanking them for their help throughout the season.

As this article goes to print, the next stage of the battle is to admit

female guests and hereby recognise the role that women play in Scottish football today both on the frontline and behind the scenes. However, when you consider that some of them are still adamant on finding a way of ejecting me, it's safe to assume that the admittance of any other females isn't something they'll take lying down. There will come a time, however, when even the SFWA (it's rather ironic that if you change the letters around it reads SWFA the acronym for the Scottish Womens Football Association!) will have to be dragged, albeit kicking and screaming, into the 21st Century.

Women may only have come to the forefront of Scottish football in the past few years, however, behind the scenes they've been a mute force for at least four decades. The longest serving lady on the sidelines is Molly Stallan, who was with Partick Thistle for an amazing 38 years and is more legendary at Firhill than the 1971 League Cup win. Such is her love of the game that since her retirement from the Jags six years ago, she has been working two days a week in the offices of Second Division rivals Clyde.

"I wasn't particularly conscious that there weren't many women around when I started at Thistle because I didn't really get to go to many other grounds and there was always quite a few ladies who came to our matches. Things have obviously changed now at clubs and you even have female referees. Women are now getting the chance to do things where they never had before," says Molly.

Running a close second to Molly for her years in Scottish football is The Scottish Football League's Maureen Cooper who deals with the vitally important task of appointing referees for matches from The Scottish Premier League right down to the Under-13 Youth Development Initiative. In her 37 years with The Scottish Football League, she has seen many changes and is very much at the heart of, and a supporter of, the latest move to introduce female match officials. Indeed, England's Nationwide Conference set a

Scotland's Colin Cameron with the female Assistant Referee who officiated in the Scotland v Faroe Isles Euro 2000 qualifier

precedent this season when for the first time ever in world football, it appointed three women officials to oversee one of it's matches. Not to be outdone by our friends in the south, the SFL can boast having female officials on its own register.

"Football is becoming more tolerant of females coming into the various aspects of the game," said Maureeen. "It's something they can't ignore.

"Female referees and officials is something that would have been laughed at before but there are actually a considerable number of young girls now interested.

"There was a group of girls in Aberdeen who were actively encouraged by the local Referees Association to go through the training. It has taken a long while for female officials to break through but it's happening more and more. In days to come, female officials will

definitely come into the forefront and I am certain that a woman will officiate a senior match within the next few years.

"When I'm appointing referees for Youth Development Initiative games, I don't take into account whether they're male or female. All referees are treated on merit irrespective of their sex."

With that heartening view in mind and taking into account that football has changed dramatically during the past few years particularly with the increasing number of women now actively participating at all levels of the game, here's hoping that as we approach the 21st Century, all sectors connected with our national game will welcome and indeed, accept our involvement.

MICHELLE EVANS
(Freelance)

BANK OF SCOTLAND SCOTTISH PREMIER LEAGUE

	P	W	L	D	F	A	Pts
RANGERS	36	23	5	8	78	31	77
CELTIC	36	21	7	8	84	35	71
ST. JOHNSTONE	36	15	9	12	39	38	57
KILMARNOCK	36	14	8	14	47	29	56
DUNDEE	36	13	16	7	36	56	46
HEART OF MIDLOTHIAN	36	11	16	9	44	50	42
MOTHERWELL	36	10	15	11	35	54	41
ABERDEEN	36	10	19	7	43	71	37
DUNDEE UNITED	36	8	18	10	37	48	34
DUNFERMLINE ATHLETIC	36	4	16	16	28	59	28

S.F.L. FIRST DIVISION

	P	W	L	D	F	A	PTS
HIBERNIAN	36	28	3	5	84	33	89
FALKIRK	36	20	10	6	60	38	66
AYR UNITED	36	19	12	5	66	42	62
AIRDRIEONIANS	36	18	13	5	42	43	59
ST. MIRREN	36	14	12	10	42	43	52
GREENOCK MORTON	36	14	15	7	45	41	49
CLYDEBANK	36	11	12	13	36	38	46
RAITH ROVERS	36	8	17	11	37	57	35
HAMILTON ACADEMICAL	36	6	20	10	30	62	28
STRANRAER	36	5	29	2	29	74	17

S.F.L. SECOND DIVISION

	P	W	L	D	F	A	PTS
LIVINGSTON	36	22	3	11	66	35	77
INVERNESS CAL. THISTLE	36	21	6	9	80	48	72
CLYDE	36	15	13	8	46	42	53
QUEEN OF THE SOUTH	36	13	14	9	50	45	48
ALLOA ATHLETIC	36	13	16	7	65	56	46
STIRLING ALBION	36	12	16	8	50	63	44
ARBROATH	36	12	16	8	37	52	44
PARTICK THISTLE	36	12	17	7	36	45	43
EAST FIFE	36	12	18	6	42	64	42
FORFAR ATHLETIC	36	8	21	7	48	70	31

S.F.L. THIRD DIVISION

	P	W	L	D	F	A	PTS
ROSS COUNTY	36	24	7	5	87	42	77
STENHOUSEMUIR	36	19	10	7	62	42	64
BRECHIN CITY	36	17	11	8	47	43	59
DUMBARTON	36	16	11	9	53	40	57
BERWICK RANGERS	36	12	10	14	53	49	50
QUEEN'S PARK	36	11	14	11	41	46	44
ALBION ROVERS	36	12	16	8	43	63	44
EAST STIRLINGSHIRE	36	9	14	13	50	48	40
COWDENBEATH	36	8	21	7	34	65	31
MONTROSE	36	8	22	6	42	74	30

S.P.L. UNDER 21 LEAGUE

	P	W	L	D	F	A	Pts
ST. JOHNSTONE	27	17	5	5	42	31	56
RANGERS	27	13	8	6	45	35	45
DUNDEE UNITED	27	12	7	8	28	18	44
HEART OF MIDLOTHIAN	27	12	8	7	34	24	43
ABERDEEN	27	10	11	6	38	36	36
CELTIC	27	9	10	8	34	37	35
DUNFERMLINE ATHLETIC	27	7	10	10	28	26	31
KILMARNOCK	27	8	13	6	31	40	30
MOTHERWELL	27	6	13	8	34	44	26
DUNDEE	27	6	15	6	21	35	24

RESERVE LEAGUE EAST

	P	W	L	D	F	A	Pts
RAITH ROVERS	15	11	1	3	44	15	36
ARBROATH	15	9	4	2	34	25	29
FORFAR ATHLETIC	15	8	4	3	36	24	27
COWDENBEATH	15	4	7	4	27	34	16
BRECHIN CITY	15	2	9	4	20	42	10
MONTROSE	15	2	11	2	16	37	8

RESERVE LEAGUE WEST

	P	W	L	D	F	A	Pts
GREENOCK MORTON	20	15	1	4	57	21	49
AYR UNITED	20	14	2	4	59	26	46
HAMILTON ACADEMICAL	20	11	4	5	48	30	38
ST. MIRREN	20	11	7	2	50	31	35
STRANRAER	20	10	6	4	51	35	34
PARTICK THISTLE	20	7	8	5	36	34	26
ALLOA ATHLETIC	20	7	11	2	37	69	23
CLYDE	20	5	10	5	30	37	20
AIRDRIEONIANS	20	5	11	4	28	32	19
QUEEN'S PARK	20	5	12	3	39	48	18
ALBION ROVERS	20	0	18	2	11	83	2

YOUTH DIVISION A

	P	W	L	D	F	A	Pts
ABERDEEN	18	13	3	2	49	23	41
CELTIC	18	13	3	2	34	14	41
RANGERS	18	12	4	2	38	16	38
HEART OF MIDLOTHIAN	18	8	6	4	35	24	28
DUNDEE	18	8	8	2	33	33	26
DUNFERMLINE ATHLETIC	18	5	8	5	31	42	20
HIBERNIAN	18	5	10	3	27	37	18
KILMARNOCK	18	4	11	3	19	39	15
DUNDEE UNITED	18	3	10	5	27	41	14
ST. JOHNSTONE	18	4	12	2	15	39	14

YOUTH DIVISION B

	P	W	L	D	F	A	Pts
FALKIRK	20	15	2	3	60	20	48
GREENOCK MORTON	20	12	7	1	54	32	37
PARTICK THISTLE	20	10	5	5	32	33	35
RAITH ROVERS	20	10	6	4	47	23	34
FORFAR ATHLETIC	20	7	6	7	28	26	28
LIVINGSTON	20	9	10	1	30	29	28
BERWICK RANGERS	20	7	8	5	34	47	26
QUEEN OF THE SOUTH	20	7	9	4	39	49	25
COWDENBEATH	20	6	8	6	41	42	24
EAST STIRLINGSHIRE	20	4	14	2	20	50	14
STENHOUSEMUIR	20	1	13	6	20	54	9

League Challenge Cup Final
Results Since 1990/91

(In Season 1990/91 known as The B&Q Centenary Cup; In Seasons 1991/92 to 1994/95 known as The B&Q Cup)

SEASON 1990/91
Sunday, 11th November, 1990 at Fir Park, Motherwell;
Attendance 11,506, Referee: K. J. Hope (Clarkston)

AYR UNITED 2	DUNDEE 3

(AET - 2-2 After 90 Minutes)

D. Smyth, I. McAllister   W. Dodds (3)

SEASON 1991/92
Sunday, 8th December, 1991 at Fir Park, Motherwell;
Attendance 9,663, Referee: L.W. Mottram (Forth)

HAMILTON ACADEMICAL 1	AYR UNITED 0

C. Harris

SEASON 1992/93
Sunday, 13th December, 1992 at St. Mirren Park, Paisley;
Attendance 7,391, Referee: J.J. Timmons (Kilwinning)

MORTON 2	HAMILTON ACADEMICAL 3

R. Alexander (2)   C. Hillcoat, G. Clark (2)

SEASON 1993/94
Sunday, 12th December, 1993 at Fir Park, Motherwell;
Attendance 13,763, Referee: D.D. Hope (Erskine)

FALKIRK 3	ST. MIRREN 0

C. Duffy, J. Hughes, R. Cadette

SEASON 1994/95
Sunday, 6th November, 1994 at McDiarmid Park, Perth;
Attendance 8,844, Referee: H.F. Williamson (Renfrew)

DUNDEE 2	AIRDRIEONIANS 3

(AET - 2-2 After 90 Minutes)

G. Britton, G. Hay (o.g.)   P. Harvey, J. Boyle, Andrew Smith

SEASON 1995/96
Sunday, 5th November, 1995 at McDiarmid Park, Perth;
Attendance 7,856, Referee: J. Rowbotham (Kirkcaldy)

STENHOUSEMUIR 0	DUNDEE UNITED 0 (A.E.T.)

Stenhousemuir won 5-4 on Kicks from the Penalty Mark

SEASON 1996/97
Sunday, 3rd November, 1996 at Broadwood Stadium, Cumbernauld;
Attendance 5,522, Referee: K.W. Clark (Paisley)

STRANRAER 1	ST. JOHNSTONE 0

T. Sloan

SEASON 1997/98
Sunday, 2nd November, 1997 at Fir Park, Motherwell;
Attendance 9,735, Referee: R.T. Tait (East Kilbride)

FALKIRK 1	QUEEN OF THE SOUTH 0

D. Hagen

SEASON 1998/99
No Competition

Reserve League Cup – Season 1998/99

PRELIMINARY ROUND
8th September, 1998

GREENOCK MORTON 3	ALLOA ATHLETIC 0

FIRST ROUND
12th August, 1998

STRANRAER 4	QUEEN'S PARK 0

31st August, 1998

ARBROATH 1	COWDENBEATH 2

3rd September, 1998

PARTICK THISTLE 3	CLYDE 2

21st September, 1998

BRECHIN CITY 4	ALBION ROVERS 2

FORFAR ATHLETIC 2	RAITH ROVERS 0

30th September, 1998

LIVINGSTON 1	HAMILTON ACADEMICAL 0

15th December, 1998

GREENOCK MORTON 1	ST. MIRREN 2

17th March, 1999

AIRDRIEONIANS 0	AYR UNITED 3

SECOND ROUND
8th October, 1998

PARTICK THISTLE 6	STRANRAER 3

19th October, 1998

COWDENBEATH 0	FORFAR ATHLETIC 1 (AET)

9th November, 1998

LIVINGSTON 3	BRECHIN CITY 1

(AET - 1-1 After 90 Minutes)

29th March, 1999

AYR UNITED 3	ST. MIRREN 1

SEMI-FINALS
12th April, 1999

FORFAR ATHLETIC 3	AYR UNITED 5
PARTICK THISTLE 1	LIVINGSTON 2

FINAL

Sunday, 25th April, 1999, Somerset Park, Ayr

AYR UNITED 0	LIVINGSTON 1

Ayr United: A. Sadler, J. Carruth, P. Bonar, J. Nolan, S. Welsh, G. Bowman, M. Crilly, A. Horace, G. Armstrong, J. Bradford, R. Kelly

Substitutes not used: L. Duncan, A. Lurinsky, D. Clapperton

Livingston: N. Alexander, S. Clark, (C. Allison), D. Fleming, F. Conway, S. Sweeney, J. Millar, C. Feroz, (T. Courts), G. Forrest, M. McCormick, B. McPhee, N. Bennett

Substitute not used: M. Lyons

Scorer: Livingston: G. Forrest

Referee: Ian Frickleton (Stirling)

Attendance: 735

Scottish League

SEASON	DIVISION ONE	POINTS	DIVISION TWO	POINTS
1890/91	Dumbarton/Rangers	29	(No Competition)	
1891/92	Dumbarton	37	(No Competition)	
1892/93	Celtic	29	(No Competition)	
1893/94	Celtic	29	Hibernian	29
1894/95	Heart of Midlothian	31	Hibernian	30
1895/96	Celtic	30	Abercorn	27
1896/97	Heart of Midlothian	28	Partick Thistle	31
1897/98	Celtic	33	Kilmarnock	29
1898/99	Rangers	36	Kilmarnock	32
1899-1900	Rangers	32	Partick Thistle	29
1900/01	Rangers	35	St. Bernards	25
1901/02	Rangers	28	Port Glasgow	32
1902/03	Hibernian	37	Airdrieonians	35
1903/04	Third Lanark	43	Hamilton Academical	37
1904/05	Celtic (after play-off)	41	Clyde	32
1905/06	Celtic	49	Leith Athletic	34
1906/07	Celtic	55	St. Bernards	32
1907/08	Celtic	55	Raith Rovers	30
1908/09	Celtic	51	Abercorn	31
1909/10	Celtic	54	Leith Athletic	33
1910/11	Rangers	52	Dumbarton	31
1911/12	Rangers	51	Ayr United	35
1912/13	Rangers	53	Ayr United	34
1913/14	Celtic	65	Cowdenbeath	31
1914/15	Celtic	65	Cowdenbeath	37
1915/16	Celtic	67	(No Competition)	
1916/17	Celtic	64	(No Competition)	
1917/18	Rangers	56	(No Competition)	
1918/19	Celtic	58	(No Competition)	
1919/20	Rangers	71	(No Competition)	
1920/21	Rangers	76	(No Competition)	
1921/22	Celtic	67	Alloa	60
1922/23	Rangers	55	Queen's Park	57
1923/24	Rangers	59	St. Johnstone	56
1924/25	Rangers	60	Dundee United	50
1925/26	Celtic	58	Dunfermline Athletic	59
1926/27	Rangers	56	Bo'ness	56
1927/28	Rangers	60	Ayr United	54
1928/29	Rangers	67	Dundee United	51
1929/30	Rangers	60	Leith Athletic*	57
1930/31	Rangers	60	Third Lanark	61
1931/32	Motherwell	66	East Stirlingshire*	55
1932/33	Rangers	62	Hibernian	54
1933/34	Rangers	66	Albion Rovers	45
1934/35	Rangers	55	Third Lanark	52
1935/36	Celtic	66	Falkirk	59
1936/37	Rangers	61	Ayr United	54
1937/38	Celtic	61	Raith Rovers	59
1938/39	Rangers	59	Cowdenbeath	60
Seasons 1939/40 to 1945/46 - (No Competition)				
1946/47	Rangers	46	Dundee	45
1947/48	Hibernian	48	East Fife	53
1948/49	Rangers	46	Raith Rovers*	42
1949/50	Rangers	50	Morton	47

4

Champions since 1890

SEASON	DIVISION ONE	POINTS	DIVISION TWO	POINTS
1950/51	Hibernian	48	Queen of the South*	45
1951/52	Hibernian	45	Clyde	44
1952/53	Rangers*	43	Stirling Albion	44
1953/54	Celtic	43	Motherwell	45
1954/55	Aberdeen	49	Airdrieonians	46
1955/56	Rangers	52	Queen's Park	54
1956/57	Rangers	55	Clyde	64
1957/58	Heart of Midlothian	62	Stirling Albion	55
1958/59	Rangers	50	Ayr United	60
1959/60	Heart of Midlothian	54	St. Johnstone	53
1960/61	Rangers	51	Stirling Albion	55
1961/62	Dundee	54	Clyde	54
1962/63	Rangers	57	St. Johnstone	55
1963/64	Rangers	55	Morton	67
1964/65	Kilmarnock*	50	Stirling Albion	59
1965/66	Celtic	57	Ayr United	53
1966/67	Celtic	58	Morton	69
1967/68	Celtic	63	St. Mirren	62
1968/69	Celtic	54	Motherwell	64
1969/70	Celtic	57	Falkirk	56
1970/71	Celtic	56	Partick Thistle	56
1971/72	Celtic	60	Dumbarton¥	52
1972/73	Celtic	57	Clyde	56
1973/74	Celtic	53	Airdrieonians	60
1974/75	Rangers	56	Falkirk	54

SEASON	PREMIER DIVISION	POINTS	FIRST DIVISION	POINTS	SECOND DIVISION	POINTS	THIRD DIVISION	POINTS
1975/76	Rangers	54	Partick Thistle	41	Clydebank¥	40		
1976/77	Celtic	55	St. Mirren	62	Stirling Albion	55		
1977/78	Rangers	55	Morton¥	58	Clyde¥	53		
1978/79	Celtic	48	Dundee	55	Berwick Rangers	54		
1979/80	Aberdeen	48	Heart of Midlothian	53	Falkirk	50		
1980/81	Celtic	56	Hibernian	57	Queen's Park	50		
1981/82	Celtic	55	Motherwell	61	Clyde	59		
1982/83	Dundee United	56	St. Johnstone	55	Brechin City	55		
1983/84	Aberdeen	57	Morton	54	Forfar Athletic	63		
1984/85	Aberdeen	59	Motherwell	50	Montrose	53		
1985/86•	Celtic¥	50	Hamilton Academical	56	Dunfermline Athletic	57		
1986/87•	Rangers	69	Morton	57	Meadowbank Thistle	55		
1987/88•	Celtic	72	Hamilton Academical	56	Ayr United	61		
1988/89§	Rangers	56	Dunfermline Athletic	54	Albion Rovers	50		
1989/90§	Rangers	51	St. Johnstone	58	Brechin City	49		
1990/91§	Rangers	55	Falkirk	54	Stirling Albion	54		
1991/92§	Rangers	72	Dundee	58	Dumbarton	52		
1992/93	Rangers	73	Raith Rovers	65	Clyde	54		
1993/94	Rangers	58	Falkirk	66	Stranraer	56		
1994/95†	Rangers	69	Raith Rovers	69	Greenock Morton	64	Forfar Athletic	80
1995/96†	Rangers	87	Dunfermline Athletic	71	Stirling Albion	81	Livingston	72
1996/97†	Rangers	80	St. Johnstone	80	Ayr United	77	Inverness Caledonian Thistle	76
1997/98†	Celtic	74	Dundee	70	Stranraer	61	Alloa Athletic	76
SCOTTISH PREMIER LEAGUE			**S.F.L. FIRST DIVISION**		**S.F.L. SECOND DIVISION**		**S.F.L. THIRD DIVISION**	
1998/99	Rangers	77	Hibernian	89	Livingston	77	Ross County	77

Champions on goal average.   • Competition known as Fine Fare League.   † Competition known as Bell's League Championship.
¥ Champions on goal difference.   § Competition known as B&Q League.

S·F·L FIRST ROUND

Saturday, 1st August, 1998

ROSS COUNTY 4   **MONTROSE 1**
D. Adams (3),   B. Andrew
N. Tarrant

Ross County: J. N. Walker, D. Mackay, R. McBain, W. Furphy, I. Maxwell, K. Gilbert, F. Escalon, (W. Herd), D. Adams, N. Tarrant, (M. Hunter), A. Taylor, D. Ross, (K. Ferries)
Montrose: M. Murray, C. Mailer, J. Watt, M. Craib, R. Wylie, G. Meldrum, B. Andrew, C. Farnan, (J. Henry), C. McGlashan, G. Higgins, (S. Taylor), J. Loney
Substitute not used: F. Fitzpatrick
Referee: Steven Kaney (Perth)
Attendance: 923

QUEEN'S PARK 1   **AYR UNITED 3**
D. Graham   S. Welsh, J. Davies, G. Armstrong

Queen's Park: M. Monaghan, D. Alexander, D. Connaghan, G. Elder, P. Martin, R. Caven, D. Ferry, D. Graham, (P. Ferguson), S. Edgar, G. Parks, (D. Agostini), T. Little
Substitute not used: B. Cook
Ayr United: D. Castilla, J. Traynor, (J. Robertson), C. Miller, A. Millen, S. Welsh, A. Lyons, G. Hurst, J. Davies, (P. Agnew), G. Armstrong, (G. Burns), W. Findlay, M. Duthie
Referee: Bobby Orr (Kilbarchan)
Attendance: 1,016

DUMBARTON 0   **ALLOA ATHLETIC 4**
    M. Wilson, P. Simpson,
    G. McKechnie, M. Cameron

Dumbarton: K. Meechan, W. Wilson, C. Brittain, S. Gow, T. Currie, L. Sharp, A. Grace, (D. Reid), S. Jack, C. Smith, (A. Brown), C. McKinnon, W. Melvin, (M. Melvin)
Alloa Athletic: M. Cairns, C. Valentine, M. Nelson, P. McAneny, K. McCulloch, S. Ramsay, (D. Pew), M. Wilson, S. Wilson, P. Simpson, (M. Cameron), W. Irvine, (L. Haddow), G. McKechnie
Referee: Eric Martindale (Glasgow)
Attendance: 352

QUEEN OF THE SOUTH 1   **INVERNESS CALEDONIAN THISTLE 4**
K. Eadie   P. Cherry, D. Shearer,
    S. McLean, P. Sheerin

Queen of the South: D. Mathieson, M. Cleeland, G. Love, G. Rowe, J. Thomson, D. Boyle, (A. Aitken), M. Weir, S. Leslie, S. Mallan, C. Adams, (A. Nesovic), L. Bailey, (K. Eadie)
Inverness Caledonian Thistle: J. Calder, M. Teasdale, R. Hastings, (B. Robson), M. McCulloch, R. Tokely, P. Cherry, B. Wilson, (G. Farquhar), D. Shearer, (M. Bavidge), S. McLean, C. Christie, P. Sheerin
Referee: Cammy Melville (Gourock)
Attendance: 1,227

STRANRAER 1   **ALBION ROVERS 1**
(AET - 1-1 After 90 Minutes)
P. Ronald   E. Donaldson
Stranraer won 3-2 on Kicks from the Penalty Mark
Stranraer: G. Matthews, K. Knox, T. Black, D. George, M. Campbell, D. Johnstone, P. Watson, P. McIntyre, P. Ronald, (G. Young), J. Young, (I. Harty), M. Skilling, (R. Bell)
Albion Rovers: M. McLean, C. Mitchell, (D. Bruce), N. McGowan, M. Melvin, G. Duncan, (J. McAlees), R. Docherty, C. Sinclair, M. Shaw, M. Harty, (R. Greenock), A. Ross, E. Donaldson
Referee: Dougie Smith (Troon)
Attendance: 516

COWDENBEATH 0   **LIVINGSTON 2**
    J. Millar, D. Bingham

Cowdenbeath: S. Hutchison, M. Urquhart, L. Cuthbert, C. Bowsher, S. Snedden, M. Robertson, C. Winter, A. Ritchie, (G. Brown), W. Stewart, C. Graham, A. Hamilton
Substitutes not used: M. Humphreys, B. Welsh
Livingston: I. McCaldon, J. Boyle, P. Deas, S. Sweeney, G. Watson, N. Bennett, J. Millar, D. Bingham, J. Robertson, B. McPhee, (M. McCormick), M. Rajamaki, (I. Little)
Substitute not used: F. Conway
Referee: Kevin Toner (Gourock)
Attendance: 507

FORFAR ATHLETIC 0   **STIRLING ALBION 1**
    G. Price

Forfar Athletic: D. Robertson, G. McCheyne, G. Ferguson, J. Hamilton, R. Mann, S. Raynes, A. Gibson, K. Gillies, (J. Allison), R. Brand, M. McLauchlan, (B. Honeyman), A. Cargill, (G. Watson)

Stirling Albion: M. McGeown, G. Donald, D. McCallum, P. Clark, B. Martin, J. Philliben, A. Bone, D. Bell, (G. Price), S. Nicholas, (K. McCallion), P. Mortimer, I. Angus
Substitute not used: E. Forrest
Referee: Kevin Bissett (Inverness)
Attendance: 524

CLYDE 1   **BERWICK RANGERS 1**
(AET - 1-1 After 90 Minutes)
G. McPhee   S. Laidlaw
Berwick Rangers won 4-3 on Kicks from the Penalty Mark
Clyde: G. McIntyre, B. Smith, C. Cranmer, I. Spittal, D. Murray, (J. Dillon), B. Carrigan, S. Convery, (G. McPhee), R. McCusker, S. McHarg, P. Brownlie, (M. McGraw), A. Grant
Berwick Rangers: G. O'Connor, T. Cunningham, (S. Laidlaw), A. Neill, J. Clark, D. Beaton, C. Campbell, M. Neil, D. Watt, G. Shaw, (K. Rafferty), P. Forrester, I. Ramage, (S. Smith)
Referee: John Underhill (Edinburgh)
Attendance: 594

ARBROATH 0   **CLYDEBANK 1**
    C. McDonald

Arbroath: C. Hinchliffe, B. Mitchell, (B. Sellars), J. Gallagher, J. McAulay, K. Jones, J. Crawford, C. Cooper, K. Tindal, B. Grant, (J. Mercer), W. Spence, N. Thomson, (D. Scott)
Clydebank: C. Scott, F. Wishart, P. Lovering, T. Smith, (G. Teale), J. McLaughlin, K. Brannigan, D. Nicholls, C. McDonald, (S. Miller), C. Taggart, A. Robertson, D. McWilliams, (L. Gardner)
Referee: Ian Elmslie (Portlethen)
Attendance: 649

STENHOUSEMUIR 1   **EAST STIRLINGSHIRE 0**
W. Watters

Stenhousemuir: L. Hamilton, A. Sprott, M. Hall, G. Armstrong, T. Graham, A. Lansdowne, K. Kane, J. Fisher, A. Lawrence, (W. Watters), G. Hutchison, J. Gibson
Substitutes not used: A. Banks, J. McBride
East Stirlingshire: G. McDougall, A. Barr, M. Brown, (P. Hoxley), B. Ross, J. Smith, S. Walker, M. Hardie, D. Muirhead, W. McNeill, (A. Sime), P. Patterson, K. McGoldrick
Substitute not used: P. McBeth
Referee: Tom Brown (Edinburgh)
Attendance: 348

BRECHIN CITY 2   **HAMILTON ACADEMICAL 2**
(AET - 1-1 After 90 Minutes)
A. Hutcheon (2)   S. Renicks, M. Geraghty
Hamilton Academical won 3-2 on Kicks from the Penalty Mark
Brechin City: S. Garden, G. Smith, (K. Williamson), G. Christie, (R. Brown), H. Cairney, K. Bain, R. Black, A. Hutcheon, C. Smart, S. Sorbie, M. Dailly, (S. Kerrigan), S. Campbell
Hamilton Academical: I. MacFarlane, S. Renicks, E. Cunnington, T. Tait, N. Berry, S. Thomson, N. Henderson, (G. Clark), I. McAulay, M. Geraghty, G. Wales, (D. McFarlane), D. Henderson
Substitute not used: C. Hillcoat
Referee: John Rowbotham (Kirkcaldy)
Attendance: 349

EAST FIFE 3   **PARTICK THISTLE 2**
(AET - 2-2 After 90 Minutes)
J. Cusick, R. Coyle, S. Kirk   M. Lauchlan, A. Morgan
East Fife: W. McCulloch, J. Strathdee, R. Gibb, J. Cusick, (P. Gartshore), G. Johnston, R. Coyle, K. Munro, D. Fisher, (G. Brown), J. Martin, B. Moffat, (S. Kirk), G. Allan
Partick Thistle: K. Arthur, D. Kennedy, S. McArthur, W. Jamieson, A. Archibald, G. Connell, M. Lauchlan, T. Bryce, (M. Donaghy), A. Morgan, W. Callaghan, (R. Dunn), S. Johnston, (T. Callaghan)
Referee: Garry Mitchell (Arbroath)
Attendance: 1,231

SECOND ROUND

Saturday, 8th August, 1998

DUNDEE 0   **ALLOA ATHLETIC 1**
    G. McKechnie

Dundee: R. Douglas, B. Smith, S. Pounewatchy, D. Adamczuk, B. Irvine, W. Falconer, W. Miller, E. Garcin, E. Annand, (S. McCormick), T. Coyne, S. McSkimming, (J. Grady)
Substitute not used: J. McInally
Alloa Athletic: M. Cairns, C. Valentine, M. Nelson, P. McAneny, K. McCulloch, D. Pew, (S. Ramsay), M. Wilson, S. Wilson, P. Simpson, W. Irvine, G. McKechnie, (M. Cameron)
Substitute not used: L. Haddow
Referee: Jim Herald (Newton Mearns)
Attendance: 2,057

INVERNESS CALEDONIAN THISTLE 0   ABERDEEN 3

W. Dodds (3)

Inverness Caledonian Thistle: J. Calder, M. Teasdale, R. Hastings, M. McCulloch, R. Tokely, G. Farquhar, B. Wilson, (M. Bavidge), D. Shearer, (I. MacArthur), S. McLean, C. Christie, P. Sheerin

Substitute not used: B. Robson

Aberdeen: J. Leighton, M. Perry, D. Whyte, R. Anderson, (R. Gillies), J. Inglis, G. Smith, C. Hignett, E. Jess, Derek Young, (D. Rowson), W. Dodds, I. Kiriakov, (A. Dow)

Referee: Michael McCurry (Glasgow)

Attendance: 5,164

ST. JOHNSTONE 3   STRANRAER 0

G. O'Boyle, P. Connolly, K. O'Halloran

St. Johnstone: A. Ferguson, J. McQuillan, D. Dods, (A. Whiteford), D. Griffin, G. Bollan, N. Dasovic, J. O'Neil, G. McMahon, G. O'Boyle, P. Connolly, K. O'Halloran,

Substitutes not used: A. Preston, K. McAnespie

Stranraer: G. Matthews, P. McIntyre, T. Black, D. George, M. Campbell, P. Watson, M. Skilling, J. Young, P. Ronald, P. Archdeacon, G. Galloway, (I. Harty)

Substitutes not used: R. Bell, G. Young

Referee: George Simpson (Westhill)

Attendance: 2,679

HAMILTON ACADEMICAL 1   HIBERNIAN 2

D. McFarlane   J. Skinner, S. Lovell

Hamilton Academical: I. MacFarlane, S. Renicks, E. Cunnington, C. Hillcoat, N. Berry, S. Thomson, I. McAulay, T. Tait, M. Geraghty, (D. McFarlane), G. Wales, N. Henderson

Substitutes not used: D. Henderson, R. MacLaren

Hibernian: O. Gottskalksson, M. Renwick, D. Elliot, P. Holsgrove, J. Hughes, S. Dennis, A. Rougier, (K. Harper), J. Skinner, S. Crawford, (S. Lovell), B. Lavety, P. McGinlay

Substitute not used: P. Guggi

Referee: Alan Freeland (Aberdeen)

Attendance: 3,063

GREENOCK MORTON 0   ROSS COUNTY 1

N. Tarrant

Greenock Morton: D. Wylie, D. Collins, O. Archdeacon, H. Curran, J. Anderson, P. Fenwick, M. George, (J. Morrow), P. Blair, (A. Blaikie), W. Hawke, P. Duffield, K. Twaddle

Substitute not used: J. Juttla

Ross County: J.N. Walker, D. Mackay, R. McBain, W. Furphy, (W. Herd), I. Maxwell, K. Gilbert, F. Escalon, (S. Ferguson), D. Adams, N. Tarrant, (M. Hunter), A. Taylor, D. Ross

Referee: Alan Gemmill (Linlithgow)

Attendance: 1,619

EAST FIFE 0   MOTHERWELL 1 (AET)

S. Halliday

East Fife: W. McCulloch, J. Strathdee, R. Gibb, J. Cusick, (D. Fisher), G. Johnston, R. Coyle, K. Munro, G. Brown, J. Martin, (P. Gartshore), B. Moffat, (S. Kirk), G. Allan

Motherwell: M. Kaven, J. McGowan, S. Valakari, S. Halliday, B. McClair, (E. Shivute), L. McCulloch, M. Doesburg, R. Matthaei, J. Stirling, S. Teale, K. Nyyssonen, (G. Miller)

Substitute not used: G. Denham

Referee: George Clyde (Bearsden)

Attendance: 1,592

DUNDEE UNITED 2   STIRLING ALBION 2

(AET - 2-2 After 90 Minutes)

R. Boli, G. McSwegan   A. Bone (2)

Dundee United won 3-0 on Kicks from the Penalty Mark

Dundee United: S. Dijkstra, I. Jenkins, M. Malpas, T. Mols, (J. Dolan), M. McNally, (M. Skoldmark), B. Pascual, K. Olofsson, L. Zetterlund, R. Boli, G. McSwegan, J. Miller, (A. McLaren)

Stirling Albion: M. McGeown, A. Paterson, D. McCallum, P. Clark, B. Martin, J. Philliben, A. Bone, G. Donald, G. Price, P. Mortimer, (D. Bell), S. Nicholas

Substitutes not used: E. Forrest, K. McCallion

Referee: Jim McCluskey (Stewarton)

Attendance: 4,957

STENHOUSEMUIR 0   AIRDRIEONIANS 2

A. Moore (2)

Stenhousemuir: L. Hamilton, A. Sprott, M. Hall, (K. Kane), G. Armstrong, T. Graham, C. Baptie, A. Lansdowne, J. Fisher, W. Watters, G. Hutchison, J. Gibson, (R. Hamilton)

Substitute not used: A. Banks

Airdrieonians: J. Martin, A. Stewart, (K. Black), F. Johnston, (A. McCann), J. Sandison, D. Farrell, A. Smith, G. Farrell, M. Wilson, S. Cooper, A. Moore, P. McGrillen, (S. Taylor)

Referee: John Fleming (Glasgow)

Attendance: 801

RAITH ROVERS 2   CLYDEBANK 0

K. Wright, J. Dair

Raith Rovers: G. Van De Kamp, C. McEwan, D. McPherson, R. Venables, P. Browne, K. Fotheringham, P. Hartley, D. Bowman, K. Wright, (G. Robertson), S. Tosh, J. Dair, (C. Smart)

Substitute not used: K. Byers

Clydebank: C. Scott, (T. Smith), F. Wishart, P. Lovering, G. Teale, J. McLaughlin, K. Brannigan, D. Nicholls, (A. Brown), C. McDonald, C. Taggart, L. Gardner, (S. Miller), D. McWilliams

Referee: Hugh Dallas (Motherwell)

Attendance: 1,556

LIVINGSTON 1   DUNFERMLINE ATHLETIC 0

(AET)

J. Robertson

Livingston: I. McCaldon, F. Conway, P. Deas, S. Sweeney, G. Watson, N. Bennett, M. Rajamaki, (C. Feroz), J. Millar, (I. Little), J. Robertson, B. McPhee, D. Bingham, (M. McCormick)

Dunfermline Athletic: L. Butler, G. Shields, S. McCulloch, A. Tod, D. Linighan, (G. Shaw), M. Millar, H. French, (C. Faulconbridge), R. Huxford, A. Smith, D. Ferguson, S. Thomson, (C. Ireland)

Referee: Kenny Clark (Paisley)

Attendance: 3,038

ST. MIRREN 1   AYR UNITED 3

T. Brown   G. Hurst, A. Walker, A. Lyons

St. Mirren: D. Scrimgour, D. McNamee, (A. Prentice), I. Nicolson, P. Rudden, (M. Yardley), R. McQuilter, B. McLaughlin, H. Murray, C. Drew, S. McGarry, (N. McWhirter), J. Mendes, T. Brown

Ayr United: D. Castilla, J. Robertson, C. Miller, A. Millen, (J. Traynor), S. Welsh, D. Craig, G. Hurst, J. Davies, A. Walker, (G. Armstrong), R. Kelly, (W. Findlay), A. Lyons

Referee: Willie Young (Clarkston)

Attendance: 2,556

BERWICK RANGERS 1   FALKIRK 5

P. Forrester   N. Oliver, S. Crabbe, M. Keith, C. McKee (2)

Berwick Rangers: G. O'Connor, G. McNicoll, (I. Ramage), A. Neill, C. Campbell, D. Beaton, K. Rafferty, (J. Baigrie), M. Neil, (J. Clark), G. Fraser, P. Forrester, D. Watt, S. Laidlaw

Falkirk: P. Mathers, M. Corrigan, A. Seaton, N. Oliver, K. James, (C. McCart), D. Hagen, (J. McQuilken), K. McAllister, (G. McStay), B. Hamilton, S. Crabbe, M. Keith, C. McKee

Referee: Stuart Dougal (Glasgow)

Attendance: 1,015

THIRD ROUND

Tuesday, 18th August, 1998

KILMARNOCK 3   LIVINGSTON 1

(AET - 1-1 After 90 Minutes)

P. Wright (2), A. McCoist   D. Bingham

Kilmarnock: G. Marshall, A. MacPherson, D. Kerr, K. McGowne, J. Lauchlan, G. Holt, P. Nevin, (A. McCoist), I. Durrant, A. Mahood, (J. Vareille), P. Wright, A. Mitchell, (A. Burke)

Livingston: I. McCaldon, J. Boyle, P. Deas, S. Sweeney, G. Watson, F. Conway, (M. Rajamaki), J. Millar, I. Little, (C. Feroz), J. Robertson, B. McPhee, (M. McCormick), D. Bingham

Referee: Eric Martindale (Glasgow)

Attendance: 6,565

MOTHERWELL 0   AYR UNITED 2

G. Hurst, S. Teale (o.g.)

Motherwell: S. Woods, E. May, G. Denham, (J. Stirling), S. Halliday, B. McClair, O. Coyle, J. Michels, K. Christie, W. Davies, (G. Miller), L. McCulloch, (S. Craigan), S. Teale

Ayr United: D. Castilla, J. Robertson, C. Miller, A. Millen, S. Welsh, D. Craig, G. Hurst, (J. Traynor), J. Davies, A. Walker, W. Findlay, A. Lyons

Substitutes not used: R. Kelly, G. Armstrong

Referee: Jim Herald (Newton Mearns)

Attendance: 4,893

FALKIRK 0   ST. JOHNSTONE 1
P. Kane

Falkirk: P. Mathers, M. Corrigan, J. McQuilken, N. Oliver, K. James, D. Hagen, (A. Seaton), K. McAllister, B. Hamilton, S. Crabbe, M. Keith, C. McKee, (S. McKenzie)
Substitute not used: C. McCart
St. Johnstone: A. Main, J. McQuillan, A. Preston, D. Dods, D. Griffin, N. Dasovic, J. O'Neil, P. Kane, R. Grant, G. O'Boyle, G. McMahon, (K. O'Halloran)
Substitutes not used: P. Connolly, A. Whiteford
Referee: Jim McCluskey (Stewarton)
Attendance: 3,749

RANGERS 4   ALLOA ATHLETIC 0
L. Amoruso, B. Ferguson,
J. Albertz (2)

Rangers: L. Charbonnier, S. Porrini, A. Numan, L. Amoruso, C. Hendry, (C. Moore), J. Albertz, G. Van Bronckhorst, B. Ferguson, G. Gattuso, R. Wallace, (C. Miller), G. Amato
Substitute not used: I. Ferguson
Alloa Athletic: M. Cairns, C. Valentine, M. Nelson, P. McAneny, K. McCulloch, (L. Haddow), D. Pew, S. Wilson, S. Ramsay, (S. Mackay), P. Simpson, W. Irvine, G. McKechnie, (M. Cameron)
Referee: John Rowbotham (Kirkcaldy)
Attendance: 42,368

Wednesday, 19th August, 1998

ROSS COUNTY 2   DUNDEE UNITED 0 (AET)
D. Adams (2)

Ross County: J.N. Walker, D. Mackay, R. McBain, W. Furphy, (W. Herd), I. Maxwell, K. Gilbert, F. Escalon, (M. Hunter), S. Ferguson, N. Tarrant, A. Taylor, (D. Adams), D. Ross
Dundee United: S. Dijkstra, B. Pascual, M. Malpas, J. Dolan, D. Patterson, M. Skoldmark, R. Winters, (K. Olofsson), C. Easton, R. Boli, (G. McSwegan), T. Mols, J. Miller
Substitute not used: M. McNally
Referee: George Simpson (Westhill)
Attendance: 3,206

HEART OF MIDLOTHIAN 4   RAITH ROVERS 2
(AET - 2-2 After 90 Minutes)
S. Fulton, S. Adam,   P. Hartley, P. Shields
J. Hamilton, R. McKinnon

Heart of Midlothian: G. Rousset, G. Locke, (T. Flögel), G. Naysmith, D. Weir, S. Salvatori, (R. McKinnon), S. Pressley, N. McCann, S. Fulton, S. Adam, (J. Quitongo), L. Makel, J. Hamilton
Raith Rovers: G. Van De Kamp, C. McEwan, (G. McCulloch), J. Dair, D. Bowman, P. Browne, K. Fotheringham, P. Hartley, P. Shields, (G. Robertson), K. Wright, S. Tosh, (R. Venables), I. Cameron
Referee: Willie Young (Clarkston)
Attendance: 11,653

HIBERNIAN 1   ABERDEEN 0
S. Crawford

Hibernian: O. Gottskalksson, M. Renwick, D. Elliot, P. Guggi, J. Hughes, S. Dennis, A. Rougier, J. Skinner, S. Crawford, B. Lavety, (S. Lovell), P. McGinlay
Substitutes not used: P. Holsgrove, K. Harper
Aberdeen: J. Leighton, M. Perry, (A. Dow), D. Whyte, R. Anderson, J. Inglis, G. Smith, C. Hignett, E. Jess, D. Rowson, W. Dodds, I. Kiriakov, (R. Gillies)
Referee: Stuart Dougal (Glasgow)
Attendance: 8,020

AIRDRIEONIANS 1   CELTIC 0
M. Wilson

Airdrieonians: J. Martin, A. Stewart, (K. Black), P. Jack, J. Sandison, D. Farrell, A. Smith, A. Moore, M. Wilson, S. Cooper, (P. McGrillen), S. Taylor, A. McCann
Substitute not used: G. Farrell
Celtic: J. Gould, T. Boyd, S. Mahe, J. McNamara, (E. Annoni), M. Mackay, P. Lambert, P. O'Donnell, (T. McKinlay), C. Burley, S. Donnelly, D. Jackson, R. Blinker, (M. Burchill)
Referee: Hugh Dallas (Motherwell)
Attendance: 8,762

FOURTH ROUND
Tuesday, 8th September, 1998

AYR UNITED 0   RANGERS 2
G. Amato, C. Miller

Ayr United: C. Nelson, J. Robertson, C. Miller, A. Millen, S. Welsh, D. Craig, G. Hurst, J. Davies, A. Walker, (I. Ferguson), W. Findlay, A. Lyons
Substitutes not used: J. Traynor, R. Kelly

Rangers: L. Charbonnier, S. Porrini, A. Vidmar, L. Amoruso, C. Moore, (C. Hendry), J. Albertz, (C. Miller), B. Ferguson, G. Van Bronckhorst, J. Johansson, R. Wallace, G. Amato, (I. Ferguson)
Referee: Michael McCurry (Glasgow)
Attendance: 11,198

KILMARNOCK 0   AIRDRIEONIANS 1 (AET)
M. Wilson

Kilmarnock: G. Marshall, A. MacPherson, D. Kerr, R. Montgomerie, K. McGowne, G. Holt, P. Wright, I. Durrant, (A. Mitchell), A. McCoist, (M. Roberts), A. Mahood, J. Vareille
Substitute not used: M. Baker
Airdrieonians: J. Martin, A. Stewart, P. Jack, J. Sandison, F. Johnston, (S. Taylor), K. Black, A. Moore, (G. Farrell), M. Wilson, S. Cooper, P. McGrillen, A. McCann
Substitute not used: G. Evans
Referee: John Rowbotham (Kirkcaldy)
Attendance: 7,835

ST. JOHNSTONE 4   HIBERNIAN 0
J. O'Neil, G. McMahon,
N. Lowndes (2)

St. Johnstone: A. Main, J. McQuillan, (D. Griffin), D. Dods, A. Kernaghan, G. Bollan, G. McMahon, J. O'Neil, P. Kane, G. O'Boyle, (R. Grant), N. Dasovic, (A. Preston), N. Lowndes
Hibernian: O. Gottskalksson, M. Renwick, D. Elliot, P. Guggi, J. Hughes, S. Dennis, A. Rougier, (C. Dietrich), P. Holsgrove, (P. Tosh), S. Crawford, S. Lovell, (K. Miller), P. McGinlay
Referee: Willie Young (Clarkston)
Attendance: 8,165

Wednesday, 9th September, 1998

HEART OF MIDLOTHIAN 1   ROSS COUNTY 1
(AET - 1-1 After 90 Minutes)
D. Holmes   R. McBain
Heart of Midlothian won 3-0 on Kicks from the Penalty Mark
Heart of Midlothian: G. Rousset, G. Naysmith, S. Pressley, D. Weir, P. Ritchie, G. Locke, N. McCann, (L. Makel), S. Fulton, S. Adam, J. Hamilton, (D. Holmes), T. Flögel, (J. Quitongo)
Ross County: J.N. Walker, S. Golabek, (C. Campbell), R. McBain, W. Herd, I. Maxwell, K. Gilbert, S. Ferguson, D. Adams, N. Tarrant, (G. Wood), A. Taylor, (D. Ross), F. Escalon
Referee: Kenny Clark (Paisley)
Attendance: 11,672

SEMI-FINALS
Sunday, 25th October, 1998
Celtic Park, Glasgow

RANGERS 5   AIRDRIEONIANS 0
R. Wallace (2), J. Johansson,
I. Ferguson, G. Durie

Rangers: L. Charbonnier, S. Porrini, A. Vidmar, S. Wilson, C. Hendry, J. Albertz, (I. Ferguson), B. Ferguson, G. Van Bronckhorst, (A. Numan), A. Kanchelskis, R. Wallace, J. Johansson, (G. Durie)
Airdrieonians: J. Martin, A. Stewart, P. Jack, (G. Evans), J. Sandison, A. Smith, K. Black, A. Moore, (F. Johnston), M. Wilson, S. Cooper, A. McCann, P. McGrillen
Substitute not used: D. Farrell,
Referee: Kenny Clark (Paisley)
Attendance: 21,171

Tuesday, 27th October, 1998
Easter Road Stadium, Edinburgh

ST. JOHNSTONE 3   HEART OF MIDLOTHIAN 0
A. Preston, N. Dasovic,
G. O'Boyle

St. Johnstone: A. Main, J. McQuillan, D. Dods, A. Kernaghan, G. Bollan, A. Preston, (G. McMahon), J. O'Neil, P. Kane, G. O'Boyle, (R. Grant), N. Dasovic, M. Simao, (N. Lowndes)
Heart of Midlothian: G. Rousset, R. McKinnon, D. McPherson, D. Weir, S. Salvatori, (T. Flögel), P. Ritchie, S. Fulton, G. Locke, S. Adam, J. Hamilton, V. Guerin, (J. Quitongo)
Substitute not used: S. Pressley
Referee: Willie Young (Clarkston)
Attendance: 12,027

FINAL

Sunday, 29th November, 1998

Celtic Park, Glasgow

RANGERS 2   ST. JOHNSTONE 1

Rangers: A. Niemi, S. Porrini, A. Numan, L. Amoruso, C. Hendry, J. Albertz, (I. Ferguson), B. Ferguson, G. Van Bronckhorst, A. Kanchelskis, R. Wallace, S. Guivarc'h, (G. Durie)
Substitute not used: A. Vidmar

St. Johnstone: A. Main, J. McQuillan, D. Dods, A. Kernaghan, G. Bollan, P. Scott, J. O'Neil, (A. Preston), P. Kane, G. O'Boyle, (N. Lowndes), N. Dasovic, M. Simao, (R. Grant)

Scorers: Rangers: S. Guivarc'h, J. Albertz
St. Johnstone: N. Dasovic

Referee: Hugh Dallas (Motherwell)

Attendance: 45,533

THE SCOTTISH FOOTBALL LEAGUE CUP SEASON 1998/99

ROUND BY ROUND GOALS ANALYSIS

	No. of Goals Scored	Ties Played	Average Per Game
First Round	36	12	3
Second Round	31	12	2.6
Third Round	21	8	2.6
Fourth Round	9	4	2.25
Semi-Finals	8	2	4
Final	3	1	3
Total No. of Goals Scored:	108		
Total No. of Ties Played	39		
Average Goals per Game:	2.8		

Jorg Albertz scores Rangers' winning goal

Rangers scorers Stephane Guivarc'h and Jorg Albertz parade the trophy.

SEASON 1946/47

5th April, 1947 at Hampden Park;
Attendance 82,584; Referee: Mr R. Calder (Rutherglen)

RANGERS 4	ABERDEEN 0
Gillick, Williamson, Duncanson (2)	

SEASON 1947/48

25th October, 1947 at Hampden Park;
Attendance 52,781; Referee: Mr P. Craigmyle (Aberdeen)

EAST FIFE 0	FALKIRK 0
After Extra Time	

REPLAY
1st November, 1947 at Hampden Park;
Attendance 30,664; Referee: Mr. P. Craigmyle (Aberdeen)

EAST FIFE 4	FALKIRK 1
Duncan (3), Adams	Aikman

SEASON 1948/49

12th March, 1949 at Hampden Park; Attendance 53,359;
Referee: Mr W. G. Livingstone (Glasgow)

RANGERS 2	RAITH ROVERS 0
Gillick, Paton	

SEASON 1949/50

29th October, 1949 at Hampden Park;
Attendance 38,897; Referee: Mr W. Webb (Glasgow)

EAST FIFE 3	DUNFERMLINE ATHLETIC 0
Fleming, Duncan, Morris	

SEASON 1950/51

28th October, 1950 at Hampden Park;
Attendance 63,074; Referee: Mr J. A. Mowat (Glasgow)

MOTHERWELL 3	HIBERNIAN 0
Kelly, Forrest, Watters	

SEASON 1951/52

27th October, 1951 at Hampden Park;
Attendance 91,075; Referee: Mr J. A. Mowat (Glasgow)

DUNDEE 3	RANGERS 2
Flavell, Pattillo, Boyd	Findlay, Thornton

SEASON 1952/53

25th October, 1952 at Hampden Park;
Attendance 51,830; Referee: Mr J. A. Mowat (Glasgow)

DUNDEE 2	KILMARNOCK 0
Flavell (2)	

SEASON 1953/54

24th October, 1953 at Hampden Park;
Attendance 88,529; Referee: Mr J. S. Cox (Rutherglen)

EAST FIFE 3	PARTICK THISTLE 2
Gardiner, Fleming, Christie	Walker, McKenzie

SEASON 1954/55

23rd October, 1954 at Hampden Park;
Attendance 55,640; Referee: Mr J. A. Mowat (Glasgow)

HEART OF MIDLOTHIAN 4	MOTHERWELL 2
Bauld (3), Wardhaugh	Redpath (pen), Bain

SEASON 1955/56

22nd October, 1955 at Hampden Park;
Attendance 44,103; Referee: Mr H. Phillips (Wishaw)

ABERDEEN 2	ST. MIRREN 1
Mallan (og), Leggat	Holmes

SEASON 1956/57

27th October, 1956 at Hampden Park;
Attendance 58,973; Referee: Mr J. A. Mowat (Glasgow)

CELTIC 0	PARTICK THISTLE 0

REPLAY
31st October, 1956 at Hampden Park;
Attendance 31,126; Referee: Mr J. A. Mowat (Glasgow)

CELTIC 3	PARTICK THISTLE 0
McPhail (2), Collins	

SEASON 1957/58

19th October, 1957 at Hampden Park;
Attendance 82,293; Referee: Mr J. A. Mowat (Glasgow)

CELTIC 7	RANGERS 1
Mochan (2), McPhail (3), Wilson, Fernie (pen)	Simpson

SEASON 1958/59

25th October, 1958 at Hampden Park;
Attendance 59,960; Referee: Mr R. H. Davidson (Airdrie)

HEART OF MIDLOTHIAN 5	PARTICK THISTLE 1
Murray (2), Bauld (2), Hamilton	Smith

SEASON 1959/60

24th October, 1959 at Hampden Park;
Attendance 57,974; Referee: Mr R. H. Davidson (Airdrie)

HEART OF MIDLOTHIAN 2	THIRD LANARK 1
Hamilton, Young	Gray

SEASON 1960/61

29th October, 1960 at Hampden Park;
Attendance 82,063; Referee: Mr T. Wharton (Glasgow)

RANGERS 2	KILMARNOCK 0
Brand, Scott	

SEASON 1961/62

28th October, 1961 at Hampden Park;
Attendance 88,635; Referee: Mr R. H. Davidson (Airdrie)

RANGERS 1	HEART OF MIDLOTHIAN 1
Millar	Cumming (pen)

REPLAY
18th December, 1961 at Hampden Park;
Attendance 47,552; Referee: Mr R. H. Davidson (Airdrie)

RANGERS 3	HEART OF MIDLOTHIAN 1
Millar, Brand, McMillan	Davidson

SEASON 1962/63

27th October, 1962 at Hampden Park;
Attendance 51,280; Referee: Mr T. Wharton (Glasgow)

HEART OF MIDLOTHIAN 1	KILMARNOCK 0
Davidson	

SEASON 1963/64

26th October, 1963 at Hampden Park;
Attendance 105,907; Referee: Mr H. Phillips (Wishaw)

RANGERS 5	MORTON 0
Forrest (4), Willoughby	

SEASON 1964/65

24th October, 1964 at Hampden Park;
Attendance 91,000; Referee: Mr H. Phillips (Wishaw)

RANGERS 2	CELTIC 1
Forrest (2)	Johnstone

SEASON 1965/66

23rd October, 1965 at Hampden Park;
Attendance 107,609; Referee: Mr H. Phillips (Wishaw)

CELTIC 2	RANGERS 1
Hughes (2 (2 pen))	Young (o.g.)

SEASON 1966/67

29th October, 1966 at Hampden Park;
Attendance 94,532; Referee: Mr T. Wharton (Glasgow)

CELTIC 1	RANGERS 0
Lennox	

SEASON 1967/68

28th October, 1967 at Hampden Park;
Attendance 66,660; Referee: Mr R. H. Davidson (Airdrie)

CELTIC 5
Chalmers (2), Hughes,
Wallace, Lennox

DUNDEE 3
G. McLean (2), J. McLean

SEASON 1968/69

5th April, 1969 at Hampden Park;
Attendance 74,000; Referee: Mr W. M. M. Syme (Airdrie)

CELTIC 6
Lennox (3), Wallace, Auld, Craig

HIBERNIAN 2
O'Rourke, Stevenson

SEASON 1969/70

25th October, 1969 at Hampden Park;
Attendance 73,067; Referee: Mr J. W. Paterson (Bothwell)

CELTIC 1
Auld

ST. JOHNSTONE 0

SEASON 1970/71

24th October, 1970 at Hampden Park;
Attendance 106,263; Referee: Mr T. Wharton (Glasgow)

RANGERS 1
Johnstone

CELTIC 0

SEASON 1971/72

23rd October, 1971 at Hampden Park;
Attendance 62,740; Referee: Mr W. J. Mullan (Dalkeith)

PARTICK THISTLE 4
Rae, Lawrie, McQuade, Bone

CELTIC 1
Dalglish

SEASON 1972/73

9th December, 1972 at Hampden Park;
Attendance 71,696; Referee: Mr A. MacKenzie (Larbert)

HIBERNIAN 2
Stanton, O'Rourke

CELTIC 1
Dalglish

SEASON 1973/74

15th December, 1973 at Hampden Park;
Attendance 27,974; Referee: Mr R. H. Davidson (Airdrie)

DUNDEE 1
Wallace

CELTIC 0

SEASON 1974/75

26th October, 1974 at Hampden Park;
Attendance 53,848;
Referee: Mr J. R. P. Gordon (Newport on Tay)

CELTIC 6
Johnstone, Deans (3), Wilson, Murray

HIBERNIAN 3
Harper (3)

SEASON 1975/76

25th October, 1975 at Hampden Park;
Attendance 58,806; Referee: Mr W. Anderson (East Kilbride)

RANGERS 1
MacDonald

CELTIC 0

SEASON 1976/77

6th November, 1976 at Hampden Park;
Attendance 69,268; Referee: Mr J. W. Paterson (Bothwell)

ABERDEEN 2
Jarvie, Robb
After extra-time – 1-1 After 90 Minutes

CELTIC 1
Dalglish (pen.)

SEASON 1977/78

18th March, 1978 at Hampden Park;
Attendance 60,168; Referee: Mr D. F. T. Syme (Rutherglen)

RANGERS 2
Cooper, Smith
After extra-time – 1-1 After 90 Minutes

CELTIC 1
Edvaldsson

SEASON 1978/79

31st March, 1979 at Hampden Park;
Attendance 54,000; Referee: Mr I. M. D. Foote (Glasgow)

RANGERS 2
McMaster (o.g.), Jackson

ABERDEEN 1
Davidson

SEASON 1979/80 –
BELL'S LEAGUE CUP

8th December, 1979 at Hampden Park;
Attendance 27,299; Referee: Mr B. R. McGinlay (Balfron)

DUNDEE UNITED 0
After extra-time

ABERDEEN 0

REPLAY

12th December, 1979 at Dens Park;
Attendance 28,984; Referee: Mr B. R. McGinlay (Balfron)

DUNDEE UNITED 3
Pettigrew (2), Sturrock

ABERDEEN 0

SEASON 1980/81 –
BELL'S LEAGUE CUP

6th December, 1980 at Dens Park;
Attendance 24,466; Referee: Mr R. B. Valentine (Dundee)

DUNDEE UNITED 3
Dodds, Sturrock (2)

DUNDEE 0

SEASON 1981/82

28th November, 1981 at Hampden Park;
Attendance 53,795;
Referee: Mr E. H. Pringle (Edinburgh)

RANGERS 2
Cooper, Redford

DUNDEE UNITED 1
Milne

SEASON 1982/83

4th December, 1982 at Hampden Park;
Attendance 55,372; Referee: Mr K. J. Hope (Clarkston)

CELTIC 2
Nicholas, MacLeod

RANGERS 1
Bett

SEASON 1983/84

25th March, 1984 at Hampden Park;
Attendance 66,369; Referee: Mr R. B. Valentine (Dundee)

RANGERS 3
McCoist 3 (1 pen)
After extra-time – 2-2 After 90 Minutes

CELTIC 2
McClair, Reid (pen)

SEASON 1984/85 – SKOL CUP

28th October, 1984 at Hampden Park;
Attendance 44,698; Referee: Mr B. R. McGinlay (Balfron)

RANGERS 1
Ferguson

DUNDEE UNITED 0

SEASON 1985/86 – SKOL CUP

27th October, 1985 at Hampden Park;
Attendance 40,065; Referee: Mr R. B. Valentine (Dundee)

ABERDEEN 3
Black (2), Stark

HIBERNIAN 0

SEASON 1986/87 – SKOL CUP

26th October, 1986 at Hampden Park;
Attendance 74,219; Referee: Mr D. F. T. Syme (Rutherglen)

RANGERS 2
Durrant, Cooper (pen)

CELTIC 1
McClair

SEASON 1987/88 – SKOL CUP

25th October, 1987 at Hampden Park;
© *Attendance 71,961; Referee: Mr R. B. Valentine (Dundee)*

RANGERS 3   **ABERDEEN 3**
Cooper, Durrant, Fleck   Bett, Falconer, Hewitt
After extra-time – 3-3 After 90 Minutes
Rangers won 5-3 on Kicks from the Penalty Mark

SEASON 1988/89 – SKOL CUP

23rd October, 1988 at Hampden Park;
Attendance 72,122; Referee: Mr G. B. Smith (Edinburgh)

RANGERS 3   **ABERDEEN 2**
McCoist (2), I. Ferguson   Dodds (2)

SEASON 1989/90 – SKOL CUP

22nd October, 1989 at Hampden Park;
Attendance 61,190; Referee: Mr G. B. Smith (Edinburgh)

ABERDEEN 2   **RANGERS 1**
Mason (2)   Walters (pen)
After extra-time – 1-1 after 90 minutes

SEASON 1990/91 – SKOL CUP

28th October, 1990 at Hampden Park;
Attendance 62,817; Referee: Mr J. McCluskey (Stewarton)

RANGERS 2   **CELTIC 1**
Walters, Gough   Elliott

SEASON 1991/92 – SKOL CUP

27th October, 1991 at Hampden Park;
Attendance 40,377; Referee: Mr B. R. McGinlay (Balfron)

HIBERNIAN 2   **DUNFERMLINE ATHLETIC 0**
McIntyre (pen), Wright

SEASON 1992/93 – SKOL CUP

25th October, 1992 at Hampden Park;
Attendance 45,298; Referee: Mr D. D. Hope (Erskine)

RANGERS 2   **ABERDEEN 1**
McCall, Smith (o.g.)   Shearer
After extra-time – 1-1 after 90 minutes

SEASON 1993/94

24th October, 1993 at Celtic Park;
Attendance 47,632; Referee: Mr J. McCluskey (Stewarton)

RANGERS 2   **HIBERNIAN 1**
Durrant, McCoist   McPherson (o.g.)

SEASON 1994/95 – COCA-COLA CUP

27th November, 1994 at Ibrox Stadium;
Attendance 45,384; Referee: Mr J. McCluskey (Stewarton)

RAITH ROVERS 2   **CELTIC 2**
S. Crawford, G. Dalziel   C. Nicholas, A. Walker
After extra-time – 2-2 after 90 minutes

Raith Rovers won 6-5 on Kicks from the Penalty Mark

SEASON 1995/96 – COCA-COLA CUP

26th November, 1995 at Hampden Park;
Attendance 33,099; Referee: Mr L.W. Mottram (Forth)

ABERDEEN 2   **DUNDEE 0**
D. Shearer, W. Dodds

SEASON 1996/97 – COCA-COLA CUP

24th November, 1996 at Celtic Park;
Attendance 48,559; Referee: Mr H. Dallas (Motherwell)

RANGERS 4   **HEART OF MIDLOTHIAN 3**
P. Gascoigne (2),A. McCoist (2)   D. Weir, S. Fulton, J. Robertson

SEASON 1997/98 – COCA-COLA CUP

30th November, 1997 at Ibrox Stadium, Glasgow;
Attendance 49,305; Referee: Mr J. McCluskey (Stewarton)

CELTIC 3   **DUNDEE UNITED 0**
M. Rieper, H. Larsson, C. Burley

SEASON 1998/99

29th November, 1998 at Celtic Park, Glasgow;
Attendance 45,533; Referee: Mr H. Dallas (Motherwell)

RANGERS 2   **ST. JOHNSTONE 1**
S. Guivarc'h, J. Albertz   N. Dasovic

WINNERS AT A GLANCE	
RANGERS	21
CELTIC	10
ABERDEEN	5
HEART OF MIDLOTHIAN	4
DUNDEE	3
EAST FIFE	3
DUNDEE UNITED	2
HIBERNIAN	2
MOTHERWELL	1
PARTICK THISTLE	1
RAITH ROVERS	1

APPEARANCES IN FINALS	
(Figures do not include replays)	
RANGERS	27
CELTIC	22
ABERDEEN	11
HIBERNIAN	7
DUNDEE	6
HEART OF MIDLOTHIAN	6
DUNDEE UNITED	5
PARTICK THISTLE	4
EAST FIFE	3
KILMARNOCK	3
DUNFERMLINE ATHLETIC	2
MOTHERWELL	2
RAITH ROVERS	2
ST. JOHNSTONE	2
FALKIRK	1
MORTON	1
ST. MIRREN	1
THIRD LANARK	1

FIRST ROUND

Saturday, 5th December, 1998

ARBROATH 1   **PARTICK THISTLE 2**
Gallagher   Tosh, Dunn
Arbroath: Hinchcliffe, Florence, (Tindal), Gallagher, Sellars, © Jones, Crawford, Cooper, Arbuckle, C. McGlashan, Mercer, D. Scott
Substitutes not used: N. Thomson, Peters
Partick Thistle: Arthur, Kennedy, D. McKeown, Jamieson, Archibald, Gaughan, Connell, McKenzie, Tosh, Dunn, (Flannigan), McDonald
Substitutes not used: Bonar, Frame
Referee: Bobby Orr (Kilbarchan)
Attendance: 1,333

STENHOUSEMUIR 1   **ALLOA ATHLETIC 1**
Craig   Cameron
Stenhousemuir: L. Hamilton, Davidson, Gibson, Armstrong, Baptie, Lansdowne, R. Hamilton, Fisher, Lawrence, Craig, Sprott
Substitutes not used: Watters, Banks, Christie
Alloa Athletic: Cairns, Valentine, Nelson, McAneny, Cowan, Ramsay, S. Wilson, Mackay, (Pew), Simpson, Irvine, Cameron, (McKechnie)
Substitute not used: Gilmour
Referee: Brian Cassidy (Carmunnock)
Attendance: 566

DUMBARTON 1   **LIVINGSTON 1**
Flannery   Miller
Dumbarton: Barnes, Wilson, Brittain, Gow, Jack, King, Harvey, McKinnon, Flannery, Miller, (W. Melvin), Grace, (J. Robertson)
Substitute not used: Wilkinson
Livingston: Alexander, Boyle, Deas, McManus, Watson, Millar, Little, (Conway), Sherry, J. Robertson, (McPhee), Fleming, Bingham, (McCormick)
Referee: John Fleming (Glasgow)
Attendance: 530

QUEEN'S PARK 2   **BERWICK RANGERS 0**
Parks, Edgar
Queen's Park: Cook, Caven, Connaghan, Ferguson, P. Martin, Elder, Ferry, Tyrell, Edgar, Carmichael, (Little), K. Finlayson, (Parks)
Substitute not used: Alexander
Berwick Rangers: O'Connor, McNicoll, A. Neill, Fraser, Beaton, Watt, M. Neil, Rafferty, Forrester, Leask, Ramage, (Quinn)
Substitutes not used: Campbell, Smith
Referee: Steven Kaney (Perth)
Attendance: 559

FIRST ROUND REPLAYS

Tuesday, 8th December, 1998

LIVINGSTON 3   **DUMBARTON 0**
Wilson (o.g.), Fleming, Bingham
Livingston: Alexander, Boyle, Deas, McManus, Watson, Millar, Conway, McCormick, (Little), Robertson, (McPhee), Fleming, (Bennett), Bingham
Dumbarton: Barnes, Wilson, Brittain, Gow, (Wilkinson), Jack, King, Millar, (Robertson), McKinnon, Flannery, Grace, (W. Melvin), Harvey
Referee: John Fleming (Glasgow)
Attendance: 1,449

Saturday, 12th December, 1998

ALLOA ATHLETIC 0   **STENHOUSEMUIR 2**
    M. Hall, W Watters
Alloa Athletic: Cairns, Valentine, Sharpe, McAneny, Cowan, Pew, M. Wilson, S. Wilson, (Mackay), Simpson, Irvine, McKechnie, (Cameron)
Substitute not used: Nelson
Stenhousemuir: L. Hamilton, Davidson, Gibson, Armstrong, Baptie, Lansdowne, R. Hamilton, Fisher, (Watters), Lawrence, Christie, Hall, (Sprott)
Substitute not used: Craig
Referee: Brian Cassidy (Carmunnock)
Attendance: 643

SECOND ROUND

Saturday, 2nd January, 1999

CIVIL SERVICE STROLLERS 0   **ALBION ROVERS 3**
    Hamilton, Melvin, Diack
Civil Service Strollers: P. Tomassi, Weatherston, Hemmingway, Wood, Dallas, Wright, (Lynch), Given, (Davies), Scott, Smith, Temple, (M. Tomassi), Curran
Albion Rovers: McLean, Duncan, N. McGowan, McStay, Hamilton, McLees, Bottiglieri, Melvin, Diack, (Harty), Lorimer, Donaldson
Substitutes not used: Greenock, Sturrock
Referee: Colin Hardie (Glasgow)
Attendance: 322

MONTROSE 0   **STIRLING ALBION 0**
Montrose: Fitzpatrick, Craib, Meldrum, Mailer, Niddrie, Paterson, Shand, (McWilliam), Duffy, Taylor, Loney, (Lyon), Farnan
Substitute not used: Watt
Stirling Albion: Gow, Paterson, Forrest, Clark, Mortimer, Donald, Bone, Jackson, Graham, (Price), McCallum, (Philliben), Nicholas, (Bell)
Referee: Tom Brown (Edinburgh)
Attendance: 633

WHITEHILL WELFARE 1   **STENHOUSEMUIR 1**
Jardine   Craig
Whitehill Welfare: Cantley, McLaren, (Manson), Gowrie, Purvis, Martin, Bennett, Jardine, (Bird), Samuel, Cameron, McGovern, (Millar), Thorburn
Stenhousemuir: L. Hamilton, Davidson, Gibson, Armstrong, Baptie, Christie, R. Hamilton, Fisher, (Watters), Lawrence, Craig, Hall, (Sprott)
Substitute not used: Lansdowne
Referee: Alan Gemmill (Linlithgow)
Attendance: 901

KEITH 0   **BRECHIN CITY 0**
Keith: Thain, M. McKenzie, Paterson, Murray, Watt, K. McKenzie, Still, Brown, McRitchie, (Hendry), Nichol, Simmers, (Maver)
Substitute not used: Campbell
Brechin City: Garden, Buick, Campbell, Cairney, Bain, Smith, Dickson, Riley, Sorbie, Black, Kerrigan, (McKellar)
Substitutes not used: Williamson, Hutcheon
Referee: Ian Elmslie (Portlethen)
Attendance: 539

DALBEATTIE STAR 1   **EAST STIRLINGSHIRE 2**
Glendinning   Walker (2)
Dalbeattie Star: McKinnon, McMinn, D. Campbell, Aitchison, A. Campbell, Glendinning, (Wykes), Pearson, McMillan, (McGaw), Johnston, Black, (Burns), Rogerson
East Stirlingshire: Thompson, Barr, Walker, B. Ross, Smith, Muirhead, Patterson, Hardie, Kennedy, (Storrar), Ward, (McNeill), Brown, (McGoldrick)
Referee: Graeme Alison (Dumfries)
Attendance: 1,268

INVERNESS CALEDONIAN THISTLE 1   **LIVINGSTON 2**
McManus (o.g.)   Bingham, McCormick
Inverness Caledonian Thistle: Calder, Teasdale, Sheerin, Allan, Tokely, McCulloch, Wilson, Shearer, (Munro), McLean, (Addicoat), Christie, Robson, (Craig)
Livingston: Alexander, Boyle, Deas, McManus, Watson, Millar, King, (Robertson), Conway, McCormick, Fleming, (Feroz), Bingham, (Forrest)
Referee: Steven Kaney (Perth)
Attendance: 3,367

HUNTLY 3   **PETERHEAD 0**
B. Grant (2), Whyte
Huntly: Morgan, Black, Allan, Murphy, Paterson, (McRonald), Morland, De Barros, (Smith), Copland, B. Grant, Whyte, (Wolecki), Wilson
Peterhead: Pirie, S. Clark, Morrison, King, Simpson, Yule, (G. Clark), Yates, Smith, (Paterson), Milne, Brown, Livingston
Substitute not used: Watson
Referee: Alan Freeland (Aberdeen)
Attendance: 1,137

PARTICK THISTLE 5   **COWDENBEATH 2**
Tosh (3), Dunn (2)   Burns, Snedden
Partick Thistle: Arthur, Bonar, McDonald, Archibald, Jamieson, Gaughan, Connell, Frame, (T. Callaghan), Tosh, Dunn, Flannigan
Substitutes not used: Johnston, Bryce
Cowdenbeath: Hutchison, Hamilton, Milne, Hunter, Snedden, Bradley, Winter, Welsh, Stewart, Humphreys, (Graham), Burns
Substitutes not used: Brown, Findlay
Referee: David Somers (Cumbernauld)
Attendance: 3,019

SPARTANS 1   **CLYDE 1**
Hobbins   McCusker
Spartans: Oliver, P. Cowie, (Burns), Munro, Findlay, Thomson, McKeating, Bannon, Ettles, Hobbins, (S. Cowie), Johnston, Middlemist, (Knowles)
Clyde: Wylie, Murray, (Rice), McDonald, Spittal, Smith, Keogh, Convery, McLay, McHarg, McCusker, Grant
Substitutes not used: Carrigan, Cranmer
Referee: John Underhill (Edinburgh)
Attendance: 737

FORFAR ATHLETIC 2   **EAST FIFE 2**
Craig, Brand   Coyle, Moffat
Forfar Athletic: Robertson, Watson, Craig, McCheyne, Mann, Nairn, Gillies, (McLauchlan), Allison, Brand, Cargill, McLean, (Honeyman)
Substitute not used: Rattray
East Fife: McCulloch, K. Munro, Gibb, (Kirk), Cusick, (Skeldon), Johnston, Coyle, Dair, Peters, Martin, Moffat, Allan
Substitute not used: McPherson
Referee: Douglas McDonald (Edinburgh)
Attendance: 657

Saturday, 9th January, 1999

QUEEN OF THE SOUTH 1   **ROSS COUNTY 3**
Nesovic   Tarrant (3)
Queen of the South: Mathieson, Lilley, Aitken, Rowe, Thomson, (Townsley), Leslie, Bailey, Armstrong, Adams, (Mallan), Nesovic, Boyle, (Weir)
Ross County: Walker, Mackay, McBain, Haro, Maxwell, Gilbert, Ferries, Ferguson, Tarrant, McGlashan, Golabek, (Wood)
Substitutes not used: Taylor, Escalon
Referee: Eric Martindale (Glasgow)
Attendance: 1,194

Monday, 18th January, 1999

QUEEN'S PARK 1   **CLACHNACUDDIN (1990) 1**
Edgar   MacPherson
Queen's Park: Chalmers, Alexander, (Parks), Connaghan, Rossiter, Martin, Elder, (Ferguson), Ferry, Tyrrell, Edgar, Little, K. Finlayson
Substitute not used: McColl
Clachnacuddin: Rae, Skinner, Douglas, Bennett, Sinclair, Mackay, (Holmes) Brennan, Lewis, MacPherson, (Hercher), McCraw, Richardson
Substitute not used: McCuish
Referee: Ian Fyfe (Linlithgow)
Attendance: 441

SECOND ROUND REPLAYS

Wednesday, 6th January, 1999

CLYDE 5   **SPARTANS 0**
McHarg, Convery, McLay, Carrigan, Grant
Clyde: Wylie, Murray, (Cranmer), McDonald, (Rice), Spittal, Smith, Keogh, Convery, McLay, McHarg, (Carrigan), McCusker, Grant
Spartans: Oliver, P. Cowie, (McClory), Ettles, Findlay, Thomson, McKeating, Bannon, (Burns), Knox, Hobbins, (Nott), Johnston, Middlemist
Referee: John Underhill (Edinburgh)
Attendance: 939

Saturday, 9th January, 1999

STENHOUSEMUIR 2   **WHITEHILL WELFARE 0**
Miller (2)
Stenhousemuir: L. Hamilton, Davidson, Gibson, Armstrong, Baptie, Christie, (Sprott), R. Hamilton, (Watters), Fisher, Lawrence, Craig, Miller
Substitute not used: Lansdowne
Whitehill Welfare: Cantley, McLaren, (Tulloch), Bird, Purvis, Millar, (McGovern), Gowrie, Thorburn, Samuel, Cameron, Jardine, Manson, (Steel)
Referee: Alan Gemmill (Linlithgow)
Attendance: 1,066

BRECHIN CITY 3   **KEITH 1**
Sorbie, Dickson, Kerrigan   Still
Brechin City: Garden, Buick, Campbell, Cairney, Bain, Smith, Dickson, Riley, Sorbie, Black, (McKellar), Kerrigan, (Hutcheon)
Substitute not used: Williamson
Keith: Thain, M. McKenzie, (Simmers), Paterson, Murray, (Maver), Watt, K. McKenzie, Still, Brown, (Hendry), McRitchie, Nichol, McPherson
Referee: Ian Elmslie (Portlethen)
Attendance: 688

EAST FIFE 0   **FORFAR ATHLETIC 1**
                          Brand
East Fife: McCulloch, Munro, Gibb, Brown, (MacPherson), Johnston, Coyle, L. Dair, Peters, (Skeldon), Martin, Moffat, Allan, (McNeil)
Forfar Athletic: Moffat, McCheyne, (McLean), Craig, Watson, Mann, Rattray, McLauchlan, Nairn, Brand, Honeyman, Cargill
Substitutes not used: Christie, McIlravey
Referee: Douglas McDonald (Edinburgh)
Attendance: 860

TENNENTS SCOTTISH CUP

Monday, 18th January, 1999

STIRLING ALBION 2   **MONTROSE 1**
Graham (2)   Taylor
Stirling Albion: Gow, Paterson, Forrest, Clark, Philliben, Mortimer, (Wood), Bone, Jackson, Graham, Price, Nicholas
Substitutes not used: Provan, Bell
Montrose: Fitzpatrick, Craib, Meldrum, Mailer, Niddrie, Paterson, Shand, (Coulston), Duffy, Taylor, (Loney), Lyon, (Watt), Farnan
Referee: Tom Brown (Edinburgh)
Attendance: 625

Saturday, 23rd January, 1999

CLACHNACUDDIN (1990) 2   **QUEEN'S PARK 3**
Bennett, Sinclair   Graham, Brown, K. Finlayson
Clachnacuddin: Rae, Skinner, Douglas, (Hercher), Bennett, Sinclair, Mackay, (McCuish), Brennan, Holmes, MacPherson, (Keddie), McCraw, Richardson
Queen's Park: Chalmers, Caven, Ferguson, (Tyrrell), Rossiter, P. Martin, Ferry, K. Finlayson, Alexander, Edgar, Graham, Little, (Parks)
Substitute not used: Brown
Referee: Ian Fyfe (Linlithgow)
Attendance: 1,129

THIRD ROUND

Saturday, 23rd January, 1999

GREENOCK MORTON 2   **DUNDEE 1**
Archdeacon, Matheson   Annand
Greenock Morton: Maxwell, Slavin, Archdeacon, D. Anderson, J. Anderson, Fenwick, Matheson, (Twaddle), Curran, Hawke, Thomas, (Aitken), McPherson, (Wright)
Dundee: Douglas, Smith, (Grady), Miller, Tweed, Raeside, Maddison, Robertson, Adamczuk, Annand, Falconer, Grant, (Anderson)
Substitute not used: Rae
Referee: Tom Brown (Edinburgh)
Attendance: 2,823

AYR UNITED 3   **KILMARNOCK 0**
Lyons, Walker (2)
Ayr United: Castilla, Robertson, Winnie, Millen, Traynor, Craig, Hurst, Davies, Walker, Teale, Lyons, (Reynolds)
Substitutes not used: Welsh, Ferguson
Kilmarnock: Marshall, MacPherson, Baker, Montgomerie, McGowne, Roberts, Reilly, Holt, (Mahood), McCoist, Durrant, Mitchell
Substitutes not used: Henry, Lauchlan
Referee: Willie Young (Glasgow)
Attendance: 10,153

STRANRAER 1   **EAST STIRLINGSHIRE 0**
Knox
Stranraer: Bruce, Knox, Black, George, Campbell, Watson, McMartin, Bell, (Jenkins), G. Young, Ronald, (McIntyre), Harty, (Friels)
East Stirlingshire: Thompson, Storrar, Brown, Ross, Smith, Walker, Patterson, (Ferguson), Hardie, Kennedy, Muirhead, Ward, (McNeill)
Substitute not used: Hunter
Referee: John Underhill (Edinburgh)
Attendance: 579

FALKIRK 3   **HUNTLY 0**
Patterson (o.g), Crabbe, McAllister
Falkirk: Mathers, Corrigan, McQuilken, Sinclair, James, Den Bieman, McAllister, Keith, Crabbe, McKenzie, Hutchison
Substitutes not used: McCart, Seaton, Morrison
Huntly: Morgan, Black, Allan, Murphy, Paterson, Morland, Wilson, (N. Grant), Copland, B. Grant, (Wolecki), Whyte, McRonald, (Stewart)
Referee: Garry Mitchell (Arbroath)
Attendance: 3,018

BRECHIN CITY 1   **ALBION ROVERS 1**
Sorbie   Lorimer
Brechin City: Garden, Williamson, Laing, Cairney, Bain, Smith, (McKellar), Dickson, Buick, (Hutcheon), Sorbie, Black, Kerrigan
Substitute not used: Dailly
Albion Rovers: McLean, Duncan, N. McGowan, McStay, Hamilton, (Greenock), McLees, Bottiglieri, Melvin, Murphy, Lorimer, (Sturrock), Donaldson
Substitute not used: Diack
Referee: Robert Orr (Kilbarchan)
Attendance: 463

HIBERNIAN 1
Lovering

STIRLING ALBION 1
Nicholas

Hibernian: Gottskalksson, Smith, (Lovell), Lovering, Skinner, Dempsie, Dennis, Hartley, Lavety, (Crawford), Paatelainen, Latapy, McGinlay
Substitute not used: Holsgrove
Referee: George Simpson (Westhill)
Attendance: 9,306

PARTICK THISTLE 1
Dunn

DUNFERMLINE ATHLETIC 2
Smith (2)

Partick Thistle: Arthur, Kennedy, McKeown, Archibald, Gaughan, Connell, Bonar, T. Callaghan, (Frame), Tosh, Dunn, Flannigan, (Lauchlan)
Substitute not used: McKenzie
Dunfermline Athletic: Butler, Shields, McCulloch, (Johnson), Tod, Shaw, Millar, French, Huxford, Smith, Graham, (Amaral Neto), Petrie
Substitute not used: Squires
Referee: Stuart Dougal (Glasgow)
Attendance: 4,650

ST. JOHNSTONE 1
O'Neil

FORFAR ATHLETIC 0

St. Johnstone: Main, McQuillan, Griffin, Dods, Bollan, O'Halloran, O'Neil, Kane, McMahon, (McAnespie), Connolly, (Grant), Simao, (Preston)
Forfar Athletic: Robertson, Watson, (Raynes), Craig, Tully, Mann, Rattray, Nairn, McCheyne, Brand, Honeyman, (McLean), Cargill
Substitute not used: Allison
Referee: Alan Freeland (Aberdeen)
Attendance: 3,717

RAITH ROVERS 0

CLYDE 4
Convery, McCusker, McHarg, Carrigan

Raith Rovers: Van De Kamp, McEwan, J. Dair, Bowman, Browne, K. Fotheringham, Byers, (Andrews), Lennon, (McCulloch), Dargo, Robertson, (Stein), Cameron
Clyde: Wylie, Murray, McDonald, Spittal, Smith, Keogh, Convery, (Carrigan), McLay, McHarg, (Rice), McCusker, Grant, (Barrett)
Referee: Jim McCluskey (Stewarton)
Attendance: 2,581

ST. MIRREN 1
Mendes

HAMILTON ACADEMICAL 1
Clark

St. Mirren: Roy, Drew, Nicolson, Turner, McLaughlin, McQuilter, Murray, (Rudden), O'Brien, Brown, (McGarry), Mendes, Yardley
Substitute not used: McWhirter
Hamilton Academical: J. Hillcoat, Renicks, Cunnington, C. Hillcoat, Berry, (MacLaren), McKenzie, Davidson, (McCormick), Tait, (Clark), Geraghty, D. Henderson, N. Henderson
Referee: Dougie Smith (Troon)
Attendance: 2,361

CELTIC 3
Larsson, Stewart (o.g.), O'Donnell

AIRDRIEONIANS 1
Cooper

Celtic: Gould, Boyd, Mahe, Stubbs, Mjallby, (Hannah), Riseth, Lambert, O'Donnell, Larsson, Moravcik, (Blinker), Donnelly, (Burchill)
Airdrieonians: Martin, Stewart, McCann, Sandison, Johnston, Black, Jack, Wilson, Cooper, Evans, (Moore), Smith, (McGrillen)
Substitute not used: Mackay
Referee: Kenny Clark (Paisley)
Attendance: 43,609

RANGERS 2
Guivarc'h, Wallace

STENHOUSEMUIR 0

Rangers: Klos, Porrini, Vidmar, Wilson, Hendry, Albertz, (Van Bronckhorst), McCann, (B. Ferguson), Miller, Kanchelskis, Wallace, Guivarc'h, (Amato)
Stenhousemuir: L. Hamilton, Davidson, Sprott, (Banks), Armstrong, Baptie, Gibson, (Lansdowne), R. Hamilton, Fisher, Lawrence, Craig, Miller, (Watters)
Referee: Martin Clark (Edinburgh)
Attendance: 37,759

ABERDEEN 0

LIVINGSTON 1
Robertson

Aberdeen: Stillie, Perry, Dow, Whyte, Smith, Hart, (Inglis), Rowson, (Buchan), Jess, Winters, Kiriakov, Newell
Substitute not used: Esson
Livingston: Alexander, Boyle, Deas, McManus, Watson, Millar, King, Sherry, Robertson, (McPhee), McCormick, (Forrest), Bingham, (Little)
Referee: Eric Martindale (Glasgow)
Attendance: 10,311

MOTHERWELL 3
Brannan, Coyle, Thomas

HEART OF MIDLOTHIAN 1
Hamilton

Motherwell: Goram, Doesburg, McMillan, Brannan, Teale, Thomas, Valakari, Nevin, (Adams), Spencer, McCulloch, (Matthaei), Coyle
Substitute not used: Woods
Heart of Midlothian: Rousset, Pressley, Naysmith, Weir, Locke, (Makel), Ritchie, Lilley, (McSwegan), Fulton, (Jenkinson), Adam, Hamilton, Flögel
Referee: Michael McCurry (Glasgow)
Attendance: 9,372

Tuesday, 2nd February, 1999

QUEEN'S PARK 0
Match Played at Excelsior Stadium, Airdrie

DUNDEE UNITED 0

Queen's Park: Chalmers, Caven, Connaghan, Rossiter, Martin, Graham, K. Finlayson, Ferry, (Alexander), Edgar, Brown, (Tyrrell), Little, (Parks)
Dundee United: Dijkstra, De Vos, Jonsson, Malpas, Duffy, (Skoldmark), Pedersen, Zetterlund, J. Paterson, (Olofsson), Dodds, Mathie, Thompson, (Miller)
Referee: John Rowbotham (Kirkcaldy)
Attendance: 1,953

Wednesday, 3rd February, 1999

CLYDEBANK 1
Nicholls

ROSS COUNTY 1
Tarrant

Clydebank: Scott, Wishart, McMillan, McKinstrey, (Gardner), McLaughlin, Ritchie, Nicholls, Anthony, McDonald, Docherty, (Taggart), Brown
Substitute not used: McCall
Ross County: Walker, Mackay, McBain, Haro, Maxwell, Gilbert, Ross, Ferguson, Tarrant, (Wood), Escalon, (Ferries), Golabek
Substitute not used: Matheson
Referee: Dougie McDonald (Edinburgh)
Attendance: 420

THIRD ROUND REPLAYS

Tuesday, 2nd February, 1999

ALBION ROVERS 3
Murphy (2), Lorimer

BRECHIN CITY 1
Dickson

Albion Rovers: McLean, Duncan, N. McGowan, McStay, Hamilton, McLees, Bottiglieri, Greenock, Murphy, Lorimer, Donaldson
Substitutes not used: Sturrock, McQuade, Shaw
Brechin City: Garden, Williamson, Laing, (McLeod), Campbell, Christie, Black, Dickson, Buick, McKellar, Riley, Kerrigan, (Dailly)
Substitute not used: Butter
Referee: Robert Orr (Kilbarchan)
Attendance: 457

HAMILTON ACADEMICAL 1
Wales

ST. MIRREN 0

Hamilton Academical: J. Hillcoat, Renicks, Cunnington, C. Hillcoat, MacLaren, Thomson, Clark, (McAulay), D. Henderson, Geraghty, (Moore), Wales, N. Henderson
Substitute not used: McCormick
St. Mirren: Roy, McNamee, (Drew), Kerr, Turner, Innes, McLaughlin, Murray, O'Brien, Brown, (McGarry), Mendes, Yardley
Substitute not used: McQuilter
Referee: Dougie Smith (Troon)
Attendance: 3,050

STIRLING ALBION 2
McCallum, Jackson

HIBERNIAN 1
Latapy

Stirling Albion: Gow, Paterson, Forrest, Philliben, Martin, Wood, Bone, Jackson, Price, McCallum, Nicholas
Substitutes not used: Clark, Provan, Bell
Hibernian: Gottskalksson, Collins, (Hartley), Lovering, Skinner, Dempsie, Dennis, Lovell, Crawford, Paatelainen, Latapy, McGinlay
Substitutes not used: Lavety, Holsgrove
Referee: George Simpson (Westhill)
Attendance: 3,643

Tuesday, 9th February, 1999

DUNDEE UNITED 1
Dodds

QUEEN'S PARK 0

Dundee United: Dijkstra, De Vos, Jonsson, Malpas, Pedersen, Dolan, Miller, Mathie, (Thompson), (J. Paterson), Dodds, Olofsson, Easton
Substitute not used: Skoldmark
Queen's Park: Chalmers, Caven, Connaghan, Rossiter, Alexander, Ferguson, (Tyrrell), K. Finlayson, Ferry, Edgar, Brown, (Agostini), Parks, Little
Referee: John Rowbotham (Kirkcaldy)
Attendance: 4,973

125

ROSS COUNTY 2   **CLYDEBANK 3**
Tarrant, McBain   Nicholls, Ritchie, McMillan
Ross County: Walker, Mackay, McBain, Haro, Maxwell, Ross, Ferries, (Escalon), (Taylor), Ferguson, Tarrant, McGlashan, Golabek
Substitute not used: Matheson
Clydebank: Scott, Wishart, Ritchie, McKinstrey, (McMillan), McLaughlin, Brannigan, Nicholls, Anthony, (Taggart), McDonald, (Miller), Gardner, Brown
Referee: Dougie McDonald (Edinburgh)
Attendance: 1,391

FOURTH ROUND

Saturday, 13th February, 1999

AYR UNITED 1   **ALBION ROVERS 0**
Teale
Ayr United: Castilla, Robertson, Winnie, Millen, Traynor, (Reynolds), Craig, Hurst, Davies, Walker, (Ferguson), Teale, Lyons
Substitute not used: Nelson
Albion Rovers: McLean, Duncan, N. McGowan, McStay, Hamilton, (Sturrock), McLees, Greenock, Melvin, Murphy, (Shaw), Lorimer, Donaldson
Substitute not used: McQuade
Referee: John Rowbotham (Kirkcaldy)
Attendance: 3,229

MOTHERWELL 2   **STIRLING ALBION 0**
McCulloch, Forrest (o.g.)
Motherwell: Goram, Doesburg, McGowan, Teale, McMillan, (Craigan), Valakari, Brannan, Nevin, Spencer, McCulloch, (Adams), Coyle
Substitute not used: Ramsay
Stirling Albion: Gow, Paterson, (Bell), Forrest, Clark, Martin, Philliben, Bone, Jackson, Graham, McCallum, Nicholas
Substitutes not used: Provan, Mortimer
Referee: Robert Orr (Kilbarchan)
Attendance: 7,244

GREENOCK MORTON 6   **CLYDE 1**
Rice (o.g.), Thomas (2),   McCusker
Archdeacon, Twaddle (2)
Greenock Morton: Maxwell, Slavin, (Aitken), Archdeacon, D. Anderson, J. Anderson, Fenwick, Twaddle, (Matheson), Curran, Hawke, (Wright), Thomas, McPherson
Clyde: Wylie, Murray, McDonald, (Cranmer), Spittal, Smith, Rice, Convery, (Carrigan), McLay, Keogh, McCusker, Grant
Substitute not used: O'Brien
Referee: Willie Young (Clarkston)
Attendance: 3,005

STRANRAER 1   **FALKIRK 2**
Friels   Moss (2)
Stranraer: Bruce, Knox, Skilling, George, Campbell, Watson, McMartin, McIntyre, Bell, (Jenkins), Ronald, (Friels), Kinnaird
Substitute not used: Johnstone
Falkirk: Mathers, McKenzie, McQuilken, Sinclair, James, Den Bieman, McAllister, Keith, Crabbe, Moss, Hutchison, (Seaton)
Substitutes not used: Corrigan, McCart
Referee: Jim McCluskey (Stewarton)
Attendance: 1,757

LIVINGSTON 1   **ST. JOHNSTONE 3**
Robertson   Grant (2), Scott
Livingston: Alexander, Boyle, (McCormick), Deas, McManus, Watson, Millar, King, Conway, (Forrest), Robertson, McPhee, (Little), Fleming
St. Johnstone: Main, McQuillan, Dods, Bollan, Kernaghan, Scott, O'Neil, (McMahon), Kane, Grant, Dasovic, (Griffin), Lowndes, (Simao)
Referee: Stuart Dougal (Glasgow)
Attendance: 5,788

CELTIC 4   **DUNFERMLINE ATHLETIC 0**
Larsson (3), Brattbakk
Celtic: Gould, McKinlay, Mahe, Riseth, Mjallby, McNamara, Lambert, O'Donnell, (Blinker), Brattbakk, Larsson, (Burchill), Moravcik
Substitute not used: Kerr
Dunfermline Athletic: Butler, Millar, (McGroarty), Shaw, (Nish), Shields, Tod, French, Ferguson, (Huxford), Graham, Smith, Thomson, Petrie
Referee: Eric Martindale (Newlands)
Attendance: 46,887

HAMILTON ACADEMICAL 0   **RANGERS 6**
   Johansson (2), Albertz, Vidmar,
   Kanchelskis, McCann
Hamilton Academical: J. Hillcoat, Renicks, Cunnington, C. Hillcoat, Berry, Thomson, McAulay, (Clark), N. Henderson, (Moore), McCormick, Wales, D. Henderson, (McKenzie)
Rangers: Klos, Porrini, Vidmar, (Wilson), Amoruso, Van Bronckhorst, Albertz, (Miller), B. Ferguson, McCann, Kanchelskis, Wallace, (Guivarc'h), Johansson
Referee: Michael McCurry
Attendance: 7,339

Wednesday, 3rd March, 1999

CLYDEBANK 2   **DUNDEE UNITED 2**
Nicholls, Gardner   Olofsson, D. Patterson
Match Played at Forthbank Stadium, Stirling
Clydebank: Scott, Wishart, Love, Ritchie, McLaughlin, Brannigan, Nicholls, (Docherty), Anthony, (Taggart), McDonald, (Brown), Gardner, Miller
Dundee United: Dijkstra, D. Patterson, J. Paterson, Mols, De Vos, Duffy, Miller, (Skoldmark), Zetterlund, (Mathie), Dodds, Easton, Olofsson
Substitute not used: McLaren
Referee: Kenny Clark (Paisley)
Attendance: 1,299

FOURTH ROUND REPLAY

Saturday, 6th March, 1999

DUNDEE UNITED 3   **CLYDEBANK 0**
Duffy, Olofsson (2)
Dundee United: Dijkstra, D. Patterson, J. Paterson, Mols, De Vos, Duffy, Miller, (Skoldmark), Mathie, Dodds, (Thompson), Easton, Olofsson, (McLaren)
Clydebank: Scott, Wishart, Love, (Murdoch), Ritchie, Taggart, Brannigan, Nicholls, Anthony, McDonald, (Brown),Gardner, (Docherty), Miller
Referee: Kenny Clark (Paisley)
Attendance: 5,570

FIFTH ROUND

Saturday, 6th March, 1999

MOTHERWELL 0   **ST. JOHNSTONE 2**
   Dods, Simao
Motherwell: Goram, Doesburg, (May), McMillan, McGowan, Teale, Brannan, Valakari, Ross, (Nevin), Adams, McCulloch, Spencer
Substitute not used: Craigan
St. Johnstone: Main, McQuillan, Dods, Bollan, Kernaghan, Griffin, (O'Halloran), Kane, Dasovic, Grant, (McBride), Scott, Lowndes, (Simao)
Referee: Michael McCurry (Glasgow)
Attendance: 7,660

Sunday, 7th March, 1999

RANGERS 2   **FALKIRK 1**
McCann, Amoruso   Moss
Rangers: Klos, Porrini, Vidmar, (Amato), Amoruso, Van Bronckhorst, Albertz, B. Ferguson, McCann, (Wilson), Kanchelskis, Wallace, Guivarc'h, (Johansson)
Falkirk: Mathers, Corrigan, McQuilken, Sinclair, James, Den Bieman, McAllister, Keith, Crabbe, (Hutchison), Moss, McKenzie
Substitutes not used: McCart, Seaton
Referee: John Rowbotham (Kirkcaldy)
Attendance: 39,250

Monday, 8th March, 1999

GREENOCK MORTON 0   **CELTIC 3**
   Viduka (2), Larsson
Greenock Morton: Maxwell, Aitken, Archdeacon, D. Anderson, J. Anderson, Fenwick, Twaddle, (Wright), Curran, Matheson, Thomas, McPherson
Substitutes not used: Slavin, Blaikie
Celtic: Gould, Boyd, Mahe, (McKinlay), Mjallby, Stubbs, Riseth, Lambert, Burley, Viduka, (Brattbakk), Larsson, Blinker
Substitute not used: Kerr
Referee: Kenny Clark (Paisley)
Attendance: 12,062

Saturday, 13th March, 1999

AYR UNITED 0   **DUNDEE UNITED 0**
Ayr United: Castilla, Robertson, Barrick, Millen, Traynor, Craig, Hurst, Davies, (Ferguson), Walker, Teale, Lyons
Substitutes not used: Reynolds, Nelson
Dundee United: Dijkstra, D. Patterson, J. Paterson, (Skoldmark), Mols, De Vos, Duffy, Miller, (McLaren), Eustace, Olofsson, (Mathie), Dodds, Easton
Referee: Stuart Dougal (Glasgow)
Attendance: 5,508

FIFTH ROUND REPLAY

Tuesday, 16th March, 1999

DUNDEE UNITED 2   **AYR UNITED 1**
Murray, Skoldmark   Walker

Dundee United: Dijkstra, Skoldmark, Malpas, Murray, Duffy, Jonsson, Miller, (McLaren), Eustace, Olofsson, Dodds, Easton
Substitutes not used: Mathie, McNally

Ayr United: Castilla, Robertson, Barrick, Millen, Traynor, (Reynolds), Craig, Hurst, Davies, Walker, Teale, Lyons, (Ferguson)
Substitute not used: Nelson

Referee: Stuart Dougal (Glasgow)
Attendance: 7,313

SEMI-FINALS

Saturday, 10th April, 1999

Ibrox Stadium, Glasgow

CELTIC 2   **DUNDEE UNITED 0**
Blinker, Viduka

Celtic: Gould, Boyd, Mahe, (Wieghorst), McNamara, Annoni, McKinlay, Lambert, Burley, Viduka, (Donnelly), Larsson, Blinker
Substitute not used: Kerr

Dundee United: Dijkstra, Skoldmark, Malpas, Murray, De Vos, Jonsson, Miller, Easton, Mathie, (Thompson), Dodds, Olofsson,
Substitutes not used: D. Patterson, Duffy

Referee: Willie Young (Clarkston)
Attendance: 43,491

Sunday, 11th April, 1999

Celtic Park, Glasgow

ST. JOHNSTONE 0   **RANGERS 4**
Wallace, Van Bronckhorst, Johansson, McCann

St. Johnstone: Main, Weir, Dods, Kernaghan, Bollan, O'Halloran, McBride, (Simao), Kane, Grant, (Lowndes), Dasovic, (Griffin), McAnespie

Rangers: Klos, Porrini, Vidmar, Amoruso, Hendry, (Wilson), Van Bronckhorst, Albertz, McCann, Kanchelskis, (McInnes), Wallace, Guivarc'h, (Johansson)

Referee: Jim McCluskey (Stewarton)
Attendance: 20,664

FINAL

Saturday, 29th May, 1999

The National Stadium, Hampden Park, Glasgow

CELTIC 0   **RANGERS 1**

Celtic: Gould, Boyd, Mahe, (O'Donnell), Mjallby, Stubbs, Annoni, (Johnson), Lambert, Wieghorst, Moravcik, Larsson, Blinker

Substitute not used: Kerr

Rangers: Klos, Porrini, (Kanchelskis), Amoruso, Hendry, Vidmar, McCann, (I. Ferguson), McInnes, Van Bronckhorst, Amato, (Wilson), Wallace, Albertz

Scorer: Rangers : Wallace

Referee: Hugh Dallas (Motherwell)

Attendance: 51,746

Rod Wallace scores Rangers' winning goal in last season's Tennents Scottish Cup Final

TENNENTS SCOTTISH CUP WINNERS SEASON 1998/99

SEASON 1919/20

17th April, 1920 at Hampden Park; Attendance 95,000;
Referee: Mr W. Bell (Hamilton)

KILMARNOCK 3　　　　　　**ALBION ROVERS 2**
Culley, Shortt, J. Smith　　　Watson, Hillhouse

SEASON 1920/21

16th April, 1921 at Celtic Park; Attendance 28,294;
Referee: Mr H. Humphreys (Greenock)

PARTICK THISTLE 1　　　　**RANGERS 0**
Blair

SEASON 1921/22

15th April, 1922 at Hampden Park; Attendance 75,000
Referee: Mr T. Dougray (Bellshill)

MORTON 1　　　　　　　　**RANGERS 0**
Gourlay

SEASON 1922/23

31th March, 1923 at Hampden Park;
Attendance 80,100; Referee: Mr T. Dougray (Bellshill)

CELTIC 1　　　　　　　　　**HIBERNIAN 0**
Cassidy

SEASON 1923/24

19th April, 1924 at Ibrox Stadium; Attendance 59,218;
Referee: Mr T. Dougray (Bellshill)

AIRDRIEONIANS 2　　　　　**HIBERNIAN 0**
Russell (2)

SEASON 1924/25

11th April, 1925 at Hampden Park;
Attendance 75,137; Referee: Mr T. Dougray (Bellshill)

CELTIC 2　　　　　　　　　**DUNDEE 1**
Gallacher, McGrory　　　　　McLean

SEASON 1925/26

10th April, 1926 at Hampden Park; Attendance 98,620;
Referee: Mr P. Craigmyle (Aberdeen)

ST. MIRREN 2　　　　　　**CELTIC 0**
McCrae, Howieson

SEASON 1926/27

16th April, 1927 at Hampden Park; Attendance 80,070;
Referee: Mr T. Dougray (Bellshill)

CELTIC 3　　　　　　　　　**EAST FIFE 1**
Robertson (o.g.), McLean, Connolly　Wood

SEASON 1927/28

14th April, 1928 at Hampden Park; Attendance 118,115;
Referee: Mr W. Bell (Motherwell)

RANGERS 4　　　　　　　　**CELTIC 0**
Meiklejohn (pen), McPhail, Archibald (2)

SEASON 1928/29

6th April, 1929 at Hampden Park; Attendance 114,708;
Referee: Mr T. Dougray (Bellshill)

KILMARNOCK 2　　　　　　**RANGERS 0**
Aitken, Williamson

SEASON 1929/30

12th April, 1930 at Hampden Park; Attendance 107,475;
Referee: Mr W. Bell (Motherwell)

RANGERS 0　　　　　　　　**PARTICK THISTLE 0**

REPLAY
16th April, 1930 at Hampden Park; Attendance 103,686;
Referee: Mr W. Bell (Motherwell)

RANGERS 2　　　　　　　　**PARTICK THISTLE 1**
Marshall, Craig　　　　　　　Torbet

SEASON 1930/31

11th April, 1931 at Hampden Park; Attendance 104,803;
Referee: Mr P. Craigmyle (Aberdeen)

CELTIC 2　　　　　　　　　**MOTHERWELL 2**
McGrory, Craig (o.g.)　　　　Stevenson, McMenemy

REPLAY
15th April, 1931 at Hampden Park; Attendance 98,579;
Referee: Mr P. Craigmyle (Aberdeen)

CELTIC 4　　　　　　　　　**MOTHERWELL 2**
R. Thomson (2), McGrory (2)　Murdoch, Stevenson

SEASON 1931/32

16th April, 1932 at Hampden Park; Attendance 111,982;
Referee: Mr P. Craigmyle (Aberdeen)

RANGERS 1　　　　　　　　**KILMARNOCK 1**
McPhail　　　　　　　　　　Maxwell

REPLAY
20th April, 1932 at Hampden Park; Attendance 110,695;
Referee: Mr P. Craigmyle (Aberdeen)

RANGERS 3　　　　　　　　**KILMARNOCK 0**
Fleming, McPhail, English

SEASON 1932/33

15th April, 1933 at Hampden Park; Attendance 102,339;
Referee: Mr T. Dougray (Bellshill)

CELTIC 1　　　　　　　　　**MOTHERWELL 0**
McGrory

SEASON 1933/34

21st April, 1934 at Hampden Park; Attendance 113,430;
Referee: Mr M. C. Hutton (Glasgow)

RANGERS 5　　　　　　　　**ST. MIRREN 0**
Nicholson (2), McPhail, Main, Smith

SEASON 1934/35

20th April, 1935 at Hampden Park; Attendance 87,286;
Referee: Mr H. Watson (Glasgow)

RANGERS 2　　　　　　　　**HAMILTON ACADEMICAL 1**
Smith (2)　　　　　　　　　　Harrison

SEASON 1935/36

18th April 1936 at Hampden Park; Attendance 88,859;
Referee: Mr J. M. Martin (Ladybank)

RANGERS 1　　　　　　　　**THIRD LANARK 0**
McPhail

SEASON 1936/37

24th April, 1937 at Hampden Park; Attendance 147,365;
Referee: Mr M. C. Hutton (Glasgow)

CELTIC 2　　　　　　　　　**ABERDEEN 1**
Crum, Buchan　　　　　　　　Armstrong

SEASON 1937/38

23rd April, 1938 at Hampden Park; Attendance 80,091;
Referee: Mr H. Watson (Glasgow)

EAST FIFE 1　　　　　　　**KILMARNOCK 1**
McLeod　　　　　　　　　　McAvoy

REPLAY
27th April, 1938 at Hampden Park; Attendance 92,716;
Referee: Mr H. Watson (Glasgow)

EAST FIFE 4　　　　　　　**KILMARNOCK 2**
McKerrell (2), McLeod, Miller　Thomson (pen), McGrogan
After extra-time

SEASON 1938/39

22nd April, 1939 at Hampden Park; Attendance 94,799;
Referee: Mr W. Webb (Glasgow)

CLYDE 4　　　　　　　　　**MOTHERWELL 0**
Wallace, Martin (2), Noble

SEASON 1946/47

19th April, 1947 at Hampden Park; Attendance 82,140;
Referee: Mr R. Calder (Glasgow)

ABERDEEN 2   **HIBERNIAN 1**
Hamilton, Williams   Cuthbertson

SEASON 1947/48

17th April, 1948 at Hampden Park; Attendance 129,176;
Referee: Mr J. M. Martin (Blairgowrie)

RANGERS 1   **MORTON 1**
Gillick   Whyte
After extra–time

REPLAY
21st April, 1948 at Hampden Park; Attendance 131,975;
Referee: Mr J. M. Martin (Blairgowrie)

RANGERS 1   **MORTON 0**
Williamson
After extra–time

SEASON 1948/49

23rd April, 1949 at Hampden Park; Attendance 108,435;
Referee: Mr R. G. Benzie (Irvine)

RANGERS 4   **CLYDE 1**
Young (2 (2 pens)),   Galletly
Williamson, Duncanson

SEASON 1949/50

22nd April, 1950 at Hampden Park; Attendance 118,262
Referee: Mr J. A. Mowat (Burnside)

RANGERS 3   **EAST FIFE 0**
Findlay, Thornton (2)

SEASON 1950/51

21st April, 1951 at Hampden Park; Attendance 131,943
Referee: Mr J. A. Mowat (Burnside)

CELTIC 1   **MOTHERWELL 0**
McPhail

SEASON 1951/52

19th April, 1952 at Hampden Park; Attendance 136,304;
Referee: Mr J. A. Mowat (Burnside)

MOTHERWELL 4   **DUNDEE 0**
Watson, Redpath, Humphries, Kelly

SEASON 1952/53

25th April, 1953 at Hampden Park; Attendance 129,861;
Referee: Mr J. A. Mowat (Burnside)

RANGERS 1   **ABERDEEN 1**
Prentice   Yorston

REPLAY
29th April, 1953 at Hampden Park; Attendance 112,619;
Referee: Mr J. A. Mowat (Burnside)

RANGERS 1   **ABERDEEN 0**
Simpson

SEASON 1953/54

24th April, 1954 at Hampden Park; Attendance 129,926;
Referee: Mr C. E. Faultless (Giffnock)

CELTIC 2   **ABERDEEN 1**
Young (o.g.), Fallon   Buckley

SEASON 1954/55

23rd April, 1955 at Hampden Park; Attendance 106,111;
Referee: Mr C. E. Faultless (Giffnock)

CLYDE 1   **CELTIC 1**
Robertson   Walsh

REPLAY
27th April, 1955 at Hampden Park; Attendance 68,735;
Referee: Mr C. E. Faultless (Giffnock)

CLYDE 1   **CELTIC 0**
Ring

SEASON 1955/56

21st April, 1956 at Hampden Park; Attendance 133,399;
Referee: Mr R. H. Davidson (Airdrie)

HEART OF MIDLOTHIAN 3   **CELTIC 1**
Crawford (2), Conn   Haughney

SEASON 1956/57

20th April, 1957 at Hampden Park; Attendance 81,057;
Referee: Mr J. A. Mowat (Burnside)

FALKIRK 1   **KILMARNOCK 1**
Prentice (pen)   Curlett

REPLAY
24th April, 1957 at Hampden Park; Attendance 79,785;
Referee: Mr J. A. Mowat (Burnside)

FALKIRK 2   **KILMARNOCK 1**
Merchant, Moran   Curlett
After extra–time

SEASON 1957/58

26th April, 1958 at Hampden Park; Attendance 95,123;
Referee: Mr J. A. Mowat (Burnside)

CLYDE 1   **HIBERNIAN 0**
Coyle

SEASON 1958/59

25th April 1959 at Hampden Park; Attendance 108,951;
Referee: Mr J. A. Mowat (Burnside)

ST. MIRREN 3   **ABERDEEN 1**
Bryceland, Miller, Baker Baird

SEASON 1959/60

23rd April, 1960 at Hampden Park; Attendance 108,017;
Referee: Mr R. H. Davidson (Airdrie)

RANGERS 2   **KILMARNOCK 0**
Millar (2)

SEASON 1960/61

22nd April, 1961 at Hampden Park; Attendance 113,618;
Referee: Mr H. Phillips (Wishaw)

DUNFERMLINE ATHLETIC 0   **CELTIC 0**

REPLAY
26th April, 1961 at Hampden Park; Attendance 87,866;
Referee: Mr H. Phillips (Wishaw)

DUNFERMLINE ATHLETIC 2   **CELTIC 0**
Thomson, Dickson

SEASON 1961/62

21st April, 1962 at Hampden Park; Attendance 126,930;
Referee: Mr T. Wharton (Clarkston)

RANGERS 2   **ST. MIRREN 0**
Brand, Wilson

SEASON 1962/63

4th May, 1963 at Hampden Park; Attendance 129,527;
Referee: Mr T. Wharton (Clarkston)

RANGERS 1   **CELTIC 1**
Brand   Murdoch

REPLAY
15th May, 1963 at Hampden Park; Attendance 120,263;
Referee: Mr T. Wharton (Clarkston)

RANGERS 3   **CELTIC 0**
Brand (2), Wilson

SEASON 1963/64

25th April, 1964 at Hampden Park; Attendance 120,982
Referee: Mr H. Phillips (Wishaw)

RANGERS 3   **DUNDEE 1**
Millar (2), Brand   Cameron

129

SEASON 1964/65

24th April, 1965 at Hampden Park; Attendance 108,800;
Referee: Mr H. Phillips (Wishaw)

CELTIC 3
Auld (2), McNeill

DUNFERMLINE ATHLETIC 2
Melrose, McLaughlin

SEASON 1965/66

23rd April, 1966 at Hampden Park; Attendance 126,559;
Referee: Mr T. Wharton (Clarkston)

RANGERS 0

CELTIC 0

REPLAY
27th April, 1966 at Hampden Park; Attendance 96,862;
Referee: Mr T. Wharton (Clarkston)

RANGERS 1
Johansen

CELTIC 0

SEASON 1966/67

29th April, 1967 at Hampden Park; Attendance 127,117;
Referee: Mr W. M. M. Syme (Glasgow)

CELTIC 2
Wallace (2)

ABERDEEN 0

SEASON 1967/68

27th April, 1968 at Hampden Park; Attendance 56,365;
Referee: Mr W. Anderson (East Kilbride)

DUNFERMLINE ATHLETIC 3
Gardner (2), Lister (pen)

HEART OF MIDLOTHIAN 1
Lunn (o.g.)

SEASON 1968/69

26th April, 1969 at Hampden Park; Attendance 132,870;
Referee: Mr J. Callaghan (Glasgow)

CELTIC 4
McNeill, Lennox, Connelly, Chalmers

RANGERS 0

SEASON 1969/70

11th April, 1970 at Hampden Park; Attendance 108,434;
Referee: Mr R. H. Davidson (Airdrie)

ABERDEEN 3
Harper (pen), McKay (2)

CELTIC 1
Lennox

SEASON 1970/71

8th May, 1971 at Hampden Park; Attendance 120,092;
Referee: Mr T. Wharton (Glasgow)

CELTIC 1
Lennox

RANGERS 1
D. Johnstone

REPLAY
12th May, 1971 at Hampden Park; Attendance 103,332;
Referee: Mr T. Wharton (Glasgow)

CELTIC 2
Macari, Hood (pen)

RANGERS 1
Callaghan (o.g.)

SEASON 1971/72

6th May, 1972 at Hampden Park; Attendance 106,102;
Referee: Mr A. MacKenzie (Larbert)

CELTIC 6
McNeill, Deans (3), Macari (2)

HIBERNIAN 1
Gordon

SEASON 1972/73

5th May, 1973 at Hampden Park; Attendance 122,714;
Referee: Mr J. R. P. Gordon (Newport-on-Tay)

RANGERS 3
Parlane, Conn, Forsyth

CELTIC 2
Dalglish, Connelly (pen)

SEASON 1973/74

4th May, 1974 at Hampden Park; Attendance 75,959;
Referee: Mr W. S. Black (Glasgow)

CELTIC 3
Hood, Murray, Deans

DUNDEE UNITED 0

SEASON 1974/75

3rd May, 1975 at Hampden Park; Attendance 75,457;
Referee: Mr I. M. D. Foote (Glasgow)

CELTIC 3
Wilson (2), McCluskey (pen)

AIRDRIEONIANS 1
McCann

SEASON 1975/76

1st May 1976 at Hampden Park; Attendance 85,354;
Referee: Mr R. H. Davidson (Airdrie)

RANGERS 3
Johnstone (2), MacDonald

HEART OF MIDLOTHIAN 1
Shaw

SEASON 1976/77

7th May, 1977 at Hampden Park; Attendance 54,252;
Referee: Mr R. B. Valentine (Dundee)

CELTIC 1
Lynch (pen)

RANGERS 0

SEASON 1977/78

6th May, 1978 at Hampden Park; Attendance 61,563;
Referee: Mr B. R. McGinlay (Glasgow)

RANGERS 2
MacDonald, Johnstone

ABERDEEN 1
Ritchie

SEASON 1978/79

12th May, 1979 at Hampden Park; Attendance 50,610;
Referee: Mr B. R. McGinlay (Glasgow)

RANGERS 0

HIBERNIAN 0

REPLAY
16th May, 1979 at Hampden Park; Attendance 33,504;
Referee: Mr B. R. McGinlay (Glasgow)

RANGERS 0
After extra–time

HIBERNIAN 0

SECOND REPLAY
28th May, 1979 at Hampden Park; Attendance 30,602;
Referee: Mr I. M. D. Foote (Glasgow)

RANGERS 3
Johnstone (2), Duncan (o.g.)
After extra–time – 2-2 After 90 Minutes

HIBERNIAN 2
Higgins, MacLeod (pen)

SEASON 1979/80

10th May, 1980 at Hampden Park; Attendance 70,303;
Referee: Mr G. B. Smith (Edinburgh)

CELTIC 1
McCluskey
After extra–time

RANGERS 0

SEASON 1980/81

9th May, 1981 at Hampden Park; Attendance 53,000;
Referee: Mr I. M. D. Foote (Glasgow)

RANGERS 0
After extra–time

DUNDEE UNITED 0

REPLAY
12th May, 1981 at Hampden Park; Attendance 43,099;
Referee: Mr I. M. D. Foote (Glasgow)

RANGERS 4
Cooper, Russell, MacDonald (2)

DUNDEE UNITED 1
Dodds

SEASON 1981/82

22nd May, 1982 at Hampden Park; Attendance 53,788;
Referee: Mr B. R. McGinlay (Balfron)

ABERDEEN 4
McLeish, McGhee, Strachan, Cooper
After extra–time – 1-1 after 90 minutes

RANGERS 1
MacDonald

SEASON 1982/83

21st May, 1983 at Hampden Park; Attendance 62,979;
Referee: Mr D. F. T. Syme (Rutherglen)

ABERDEEN 1   RANGERS 0
Black
After extra–time

SEASON 1983/84

19th May 1984 at Hampden Park; Attendance 58,900;
Referee: Mr R. B. Valentine (Dundee)

ABERDEEN 2   **CELTIC 1**
Black, McGhee   P. McStay
After extra–time – 1-1 after 90 minutes

SEASON 1984/85

18th May, 1985 at Hampden Park; Attendance 60,346;
Referee: Mr B. R. McGinlay (Balfron)

CELTIC 2   **DUNDEE UNITED 1**
Provan, McGarvey   Beedie

SEASON 1985/86

10th May, 1986 at Hampden Park; Attendance 62,841;
Referee: Mr H. Alexander (Irvine)

ABERDEEN 3   HEART OF MIDLOTHIAN 0
Hewitt (2), Stark

SEASON 1986/87

16th May, 1987 at Hampden Park; Attendance 51,782;
Referee: Mr K. J. Hope (Clarkston)

ST. MIRREN 1   DUNDEE UNITED 0
Ferguson
After extra–time

SEASON 1987/88

14th May, 1988 at Hampden Park; Attendance 74,000;
Referee: Mr G. B. Smith (Edinburgh)

CELTIC 2   **DUNDEE UNITED 1**
McAvennie (2)   Gallacher

SEASON 1988/89

20th May, 1989 at Hampden Park; Attendance 72,069;
Referee: Mr R. B. Valentine (Dundee)

CELTIC 1   RANGERS 0
Miller

SEASON 1989/90

12th May, 1990 at Hampden Park; Attendance 60,493;
Referee: Mr G. B. Smith (Edinburgh)

ABERDEEN 0   CELTIC 0
After extra–time. Aberdeen won 9–8 on Kicks from the Penalty Mark

SEASON 1990/91

18th May, 1991 at Hampden Park; Attendance 57,319;
Referee: Mr D. F. T. Syme (Rutherglen)

MOTHERWELL 4   **DUNDEE UNITED 3**
Ferguson, O'Donnell, Angus, Kirk Bowman, O'Neil, Jackson
After extra–time - 3-3 after 90 minutes

SEASON 1991/92

9th May 1992 at Hampden Park; Attendance 44,045;
Referee: Mr D. D. Hope (Erskine)

RANGERS 2   **AIRDRIEONIANS 1**
Hateley, McCoist   Smith

SEASON 1992/93

29th May, 1993 at Celtic Park; Attendance 50,715;
Referee: Mr J. McCluskey (Stewarton)

RANGERS 2   **ABERDEEN 1**
Murray, Hateley   Richardson

SEASON 1993/94

21st May, 1994 at Hampden Park; Attendance 37,709;
Referee: Mr D. D. Hope (Erskine)

DUNDEE UNITED 1   RANGERS 0
Brewster

SEASON 1994/95

27th May, 1995 at Hampden Park; Attendance 38,672;
Referee: Mr L. W. Mottram (Forth)

CELTIC 1   AIRDRIEONIANS 0
Van Hooijdonk

SEASON 1995/96

18th May, 1996 at Hampden Park; Attendance 37,760;
Referee: Mr H. Dallas (Motherwell)

RANGERS 5   **HEART OF MIDLOTHIAN 1**
Laudrup (2), Durie (3)   Colquhoun

SEASON 1996/97

24th May, 1997 at Ibrox Stadium; Attendance 48,953;
Referee: Mr H. Dallas (Motherwell)

KILMARNOCK 1   FALKIRK 0
Wright

SEASON 1997/98

16th May, 1998 at Celtic Park; Attendance 48,946;
Referee: Mr W. Young (Clarkston)

HEART OF MIDLOTHIAN 2   **RANGERS 1**
Cameron, Adam   McCoist

SEASON 1998/99

29th May, 1999 at The National Stadium, Hampden Park;
Attendance 51,746;
Referee: Mr H. Dallas (Motherwell)

RANGERS 1   CELTIC 0
Wallace

Scottish Football's Annual Report

JULY

- Rangers complete the £5 million signing of Dutch World Cup defender Arthur Numan from PSV Eindhoven. The Ibrox club also sign Gabriel Amato from Real Mallorca for £4.2 million, break the Scottish transfer record to sign Andrei Kanchelskis from Fiorentina for £5.5 million, pay Auxerre £1.2 million for goalkeeper Lionel Charbonnier and sign striker Rod Wallace under freedom of contract from Leeds United.

Arthur Numan

- Heart of Midlothian sign Steven Pressley and Rob McKinnon under freedom of contract from Dundee United and Twente Enschede respectively.

- Former Rangers manager Walter Smith is appointed boss of Everton.

- Aberdeen sign Craig Hignett, Mark Perry and Andy Dow under freedom of contract from Middlesbrough, Dundee United and Hibernian respectively.

- Stephen Wright joins Bradford City on a free transfer from Rangers.

- Roger Mitchell is appointed Chief Executive of The Scottish Premier League.

- Celtic appoint Dr Jozef Venglos as their Head Coach in succession to Wim Jansen.

- Kilmarnock complete the signing of Ian Durrant, who had been freed by Rangers.

- Brian McClair joins Motherwell from Manchester United.

- Dundee sign defender Willie Miller on a free transfer from Hibernian.

- Celtic beat St. Patrick's Athletic 2-0 on aggregate in the first qualifying round of the Champions League.

- Rangers, 3-0 down at one stage, defeat Shelbourne 7-3 in the first qualifying round of the UEFA Cup.

- Kilmarnock also progress in the UEFA Cup, beating Bosnian side Zeljeznicar 2-1 on aggregate.

- Other July transfers include: Roger Boli (Walsall to Dundee United), Brian O'Neil (Aberdeen to Wolfsburg), Dean Windass (Aberdeen to Oxford United), Daniel Prodan (Atletico Madrid to Rangers), Tommy Coyne (Motherwell to Dundee), Joe Miller (Aberdeen to Dundee United), Mark McNally (Stoke City to Dundee United), Goran Marklund (Vaslund to Dundee United), Darren Patterson (Luton Town to Dundee United), Tonny Mols (Lokeren to Dundee United), Derek Ferguson (Falkirk to Dunfermline Athletic), Gavin Johnson (Wigan Athletic to Dunfermline Athletic), Lee Butler (Wigan Athletic to Dunfermline Athletic), Richard Huxford (Burnley to Dunfermline Athletic), David Linighan (Blackpool to Dunfermline Athletic), Alan Mahood (Morton to Kilmarnock), Greg Miller (Livingston to Motherwell), Jered Stirling (Partick Thistle to Motherwell), Stephen Halliday (Hartlepool United to Motherwell), Mikko Kaven (HJK Helsinki to Motherwell), Michel Doesburg (AZ Alkmaar to Motherwell), Allan Ferguson (Hamilton Academical to St. Johnstone), Darren Dods (Hibernian to St. Johnstone), Ian Harty (Albion Rovers to Stranraer), James Loney (Forfar Athletic to Montrose), Craig Feroz (Brechin City to Livingston), Scott McArthur (Hamilton Academical to Partick Thistle), Iain Nicolson (Partick Thistle to St. Mirren) and Paul Holsgrove (Brighton & Hove Albion to Hibernian).

AUGUST

- Rangers sign Colin Hendry from Blackburn Rovers for £4 million on a four year contract.

- Ally McCoist signs a one-year contract with Kilmarnock after being released by Rangers.

- Celtic's preparations for their crucial Champions League qualifier against Croatia Zagreb are disrupted by an acrimonious row between the players and Managing Director Fergus McCann over bonus payments.

- Travel millionaire businessman John Boyle buys a controlling interest in Motherwell for £2.5 million.

- Airdrieonians spring a major surprise in the League Cup, knocking out holders Celtic 1-0 at the Shyberry Excelsior Stadium.

- St. Johnstone sign English striker Nathan Lowndes from Watford for £50,000.

- Christian Dailly becomes the most expensive Scottish footballer in history when he moves from Derby County to Blackburn Rovers for £5.35 million.

- Celtic are knocked out of the Champions League 3-1 on aggregate by Croatia Zagreb.

- Rangers progress in the UEFA Cup with a 2-0 aggregate win over PAOK Salonika of Greece.

- Kilmarnock's UEFA Cup campaign ends with a 4-0 aggregate defeat at the hands of Czech side Sigma Olomouc.

- Hearts win 6-0 on aggregate over Estonian side Lantana in the Cup Winners' Cup.

- Newcastle United part company with manager Kenny Dalglish.

- Former Rangers and England captain Terry Butcher joins the coaching staff at Dundee United.

- Ally McCoist is recalled to the Scotland squad when he scores a hat-trick in Kilmarnock's win over Hearts at the end of the month.

- Other August transfers include: Bernard Pascual (Le Havre to Dundee United), Shaun Teale (Happy Valley to Motherwell), Kai Nyyssonen (Cordoba to Motherwell), John Paul Dow (Celtic to Motherwell), Miguel Simao (Aves to St. Johnstone), Kevin McKeown (Ayr United to Newry Town), Peter Guggi (Rapid Vienna to Hibernian), Gordon Connelly (Airdrieonians to York City), Gareth Hutchison (Stenhousemuir to Falkirk), Graeme Davidson (Livingston to Stenhousemuir), Neil Alexander (Stenhousemuir to Livingston) and Peter Duffield (Morton to Falkirk).

SEPTEMBER

- Pat Nevin leaves Kilmarnock to join Motherwell as Player/Chief Executive.

- Paul Sturrock leaves St. Johnstone to become manager of Dundee United just hours after Tommy McLean leaves the Tannadice club.

- Scotland's Under-21 side open their European Under-21 Championship campaign with a 0-0 draw in Lithuania.

- Scotland's senior side start their Euro

2000 qualifying bid with a goalless draw against Lithuania 24 hours later.

- Sandy Clark is named the new manager of St. Johnstone.

- Former Rangers and Scotland goalkeeper Andy Goram joins Sheffield United on a short-term contract.

- Bobby Williamson signs a new five-year contract as manager of Kilmarnock.

- Hibs sign Finnish international striker Mixu Paatelainen from Wolves.

- Celtic general manager Jock Brown rejects calls for his resignation at the club's Annual General Meeting.

- Rangers draw 1-1 with Beitar Jerusalem in Israel in the first leg of their UEFA Cup tie.

- Hearts lose 1-0 at Tynecastle to Real Mallorca in the first leg of their Cup Winners' Cup tie.

- Dutch coach Vera Pauw is named Technical Director of the Scottish women's international side.

- Colin Miller is named Player/Manager of Hamilton Accies in succession to Sandy Clark.

- Billy Kirkwood is appointed assistant manager of St. Johnstone.

- Celtic sign Norwegian international Vidar Riseth from LASK Linz for £1.5 million.

- A Compensation Commission sets a compensation fee of £650,000 for Stephen Glass who moved to Newcastle United from Aberdeen.

- Celtic beat Portuguese side Vitoria Guimaraes 4-2 on aggregate to reach the Second Round proper of the UEFA Cup.

- Billy Dodds joins Dundee United from Aberdeen with Robbie Winters moving in the opposite direction.

- Other September transfers include: Derek Adams (Ross County to Motherwell), Malky Mackay (Celtic to Norwich City), Steve Welsh (Dunfermline Athletic to Ayr United),

Kevin Harper (Hibernian to Derby County), David Wylie (Morton to Clyde), Gary Higgins (Montrose to Ross County).

OCTOBER

- Rangers complete a 5-3 aggregate win over Beitar Jerusalem to reach the Second Round of the UEFA Cup.

- Hearts lose 2-1 on aggregate to Real Mallorca in the First Round of the Cup Winners' Cup but lodge a protest to UEFA over the height of the goals at the Spanish club's stadium.

- Hearts sign three players under freedom of contract - Vincent Guerin, Gary McSwegan and Juanjo from Paris St. Germain, Dundee United and Barcelona respectively.

- Scotland come from behind to beat Estonia 3-2 at Tynecastle in a Euro 2000 qualifier.

- Jim Leighton walks out of the Scotland squad after the Estonia match and announces his retirement from international football.

Billy Dodds celebrates scoring against Estonia

133

- Harri Kampman resigns as manager of Motherwell and is immediately replaced by Billy Davies.

- Scotland beat the Faroe Islands 2-1 in a Euro 2000 qualifier at Pittodrie.

- Scotland's Under-21's lose 2-0 to Belgium in Ghent in a European Under-21 Championship tie.

- Dundee United sign Alex Mathie from Ipswich Town for £400,000.

- Celtic draw 1-1 with FC Zurich at Parkhead in the first leg of their UEFA Cup Second Round Tie.

- Tommy Campbell resigns as manager of Montrose on health grounds.

- Dundee United sell striker Roger Boli to Bournemouth just three months after signing him.

- Rangers achieve one of Scotland's best results for several years in Europe when they beat Bayer Leverkusen 2-1 in Germany in the first leg of their UEFA Cup Second Round Tie.

- Motherwell sign Scotland international striker John Spencer on loan from Everton.

- Hibernian sign Trinidad and Tobago captain Russell Latapy from Porto.

- Kevin Drinkell is named new manager of Montrose.

- Rangers beat Airdrieonians 5-0 at Celtic Park and St. Johnstone defeat Heart of Midlothian 3-0 at Easter Road in the Semi-Finals of the League Cup.

- Celtic sign Slovakian midfielder Lubomir Moravcik from MSV Duisburg for £300,000.

- Other October transfers include: Jason De Vos (Darlington to Dundee United), Rino Gattuso (Rangers to Salernitana), Ged Brannan (Manchester City to Motherwell), Gary Teale (Clydebank to Ayr United), Colin McGlashan (Montrose to Arbroath), David Sinclair (Dundee United to Falkirk), Jim Hamilton (Forfar Athletic to Albion Rovers), John Hillcoat (Morton to Hamilton Academical), Allan McManus (Heart of Midlothian to Livingston), Paul Lovering (Clydebank to Hibernian).

Stephane Guivarc'h scores for Rangers in the League Cup Final.

NOVEMBER

- Celtic are knocked out of the UEFA Cup 5-3 on aggregate by FC Zurich.

- Rangers reach the Third Round of the UEFA Cup with a 3-2 aggregate win over Bayer Leverkusen.

- French World Cup striker Stephane Guivarc'h joins Rangers from Newcastle United for £3.5 million.

- Kenny Dalglish and Jim Kerr launch a takeover bid for Celtic which is rejected by the club's Managing Director Fergus McCann.

- Rangers' Chilean striker Sebastian Rozental returns to Universidad Catolica for an 18 month loan period as he recovers from his fourth knee operation.

- Celtic goalkeeper Jonathan Gould signs a new contract keeping him at the club until 2003.

- Dunfermline Athletic sign Brazilian striker Edinho on a three-month loan period from Bradford City.

- Goalkeeper Tony Warner joins Celtic on a short term deal from Liverpool and makes his debut in the 5-1 win over Rangers at Celtic Park.

- Scotland's Under-21 side draw 2-2 with Belgium at Love Street in a European Under-21 Championship qualifier.

- Celtic sign Swedish international

Johan Mjallby from AIK Stockholm for £1.5 million.

- Rangers draw 1-1 with Parma at Ibrox in the first leg of their UEFA Cup Third Round tie.

- Aberdeen sell Craig Hignett to Barnsley for £800,000 just four months after signing him.

- Dundee hand free transfers to defenders Eric Garcin and Gordon Hunter.

- Aberdeen sign midfielder Nigel Pepper from Bradford City for £300,000.

- Rangers beat St. Johnstone 2-1 at Celtic Park in the League Cup Final.

- Other November transfers include: Craig Moore (Rangers to Crystal Palace), Gordan Petric (Rangers to Crystal Palace), Mark Reilly (Reading to Kilmarnock), David Graham (Rangers to Dunfermline Athletic), Stephen McCormick (Dundee to Airdrieonians), Kevin Thomas (Heart of Midlothian to Morton), Keith Wright (Raith Rovers to Morton).

DECEMBER

- Celtic sign Mark Viduka from Croatia Zagreb for £3 million but the Australian striker leaves Glasgow and returns to Melbourne just a few days after joining the Parkhead club.

- Motherwell sign Tony Thomas from Everton for £150,000.

- Rangers make their exit from the UEFA Cup, losing 4-2 on aggregate to Parma in the Third Round.

- Alex Miller is dismissed as manager of Aberdeen. Paul Hegarty is named caretaker boss of the Pittodrie club.

- Rangers sign Scotland winger Neil McCann from Heart of Midlothian in a £2 million deal.

- Tony Fitzpatrick is dismissed as manager of St. Mirren. He is replaced by Tom Hendrie.

- Brian McClair leaves Motherwell to become assistant manager of Blackburn Rovers.

- Dundee sign former Hibernian defender Steven Tweed from Stoke City.

- Neale Cooper is given a new two-year contract as manager of Third Division pace setters Ross County.

- Rangers complete the signing of German goalkeeper Stefan Klos from Borussia Dortmund.

- Other December transfers include: Lee Sharp (Dumbarton to Dundee), Lee Feeney (Linfield to Rangers),

Mark Viduka

Leigh Jenkinson (Wigan Athletic to Heart of Midlothian), Paul McIllravey (Dundee United to Forfar Athletic), Grant McMartin (Livingston to Stranraer), Charles King (St. Johnstone to Livingston), Mike Reynolds (Emley to Ayr United), Derek Collins (Morton to Hibernian), Paul Hartley (Raith Rovers to Hibernian).

JANUARY

- Rangers and Celtic draw 2-2 in the New Year Old Firm derby.

- Bert Paton resigns as manager of Dunfermline Athletic. His assistant Dick Campbell takes over and is eventually given the job on a permanent basis.

- Hibernian sign Tom Smith from Clydebank as they pull clear in the First Division promotion race.

- Defender Kevin McGowne signs a new contract with Kilmarnock.

- Bob Brannan leaves his position of Chief Executive at Rangers.

- Mark Viduka returns to Celtic after six weeks in Australia.

- Scottish football has its first winter shutdown with The Scottish Premier League clubs having a three week break.

- Andy Goram signs for Motherwell for the rest of the season.

- Scotland's clubs again go out on a limb when they turn down the chance to take part in the UEFA Intertoto Cup.

- Paul Hegarty is told his contract as Aberdeen manager will be extended to the end of the season.

- Pittodrie is filled to capacity as Alex Ferguson returns with Manchester United for veteran trainer Teddy Scott's testimonial match.

- Scotland Under-21 striker Mark Burchill ends speculation over his future by signing a new four and a half year contract with Celtic.

- John Spencer signs a permanent deal with Motherwell after his successful loan period with the club.

- Aberdeen sign German midfielder Andreas Mayer from Norwegian Champions Rosenborg.

- Other January transfers include: Tony Rougier (Hibernian to Port Vale), Steven Laidlaw (Berwick Rangers to East Stirlingshire).

FEBRUARY

- St. Johnstone sign John Paul McBride from Celtic for £200,000.

- Motherwell give their backing to goalkeeper Andy Goram when he is the subject of allegations of sectarianism.

- Blackburn Rovers agree a deal to sign St. Mirren teenagers Burton O'Brien and David McNamee at the end of the season. The Paisley club will receive an initial payment of £600,000.

Burton O'Brien (back) and David McNamee

135

- Heart of Midlothian sell Scotland defender David Weir to Everton for £250,000.
- Andy Goram is left out of the Motherwell side to play Celtic at his own request.
- Rowan Alexander is dismissed as manager of Queen of the South.
- Dundee United sign midfielder John Eustace on loan from Coventry City for the rest of the season.
- Celtic sell midfielder David Hannah to Dundee United for £500,000 some two and a half years after he joined them from the Tannadice club.
- Hibs sign former French international midfielder Franck Sauzee under freedom of contract.
- Rangers and Scotland striker Gordon Durie is ruled out for the rest of the season by an achilles injury.
- Other February transfers include: Andy Kirk (Glentoran to Heart of Midlothian), Steven Boyack (Rangers to Dundee), Jason Dair (Raith Rovers to Dunfermline Athletic), Jamie Dolan (Dundee United to Dunfermline Athletic), Scott McCulloch (Dunfermline Athletic to Dundee United), Neil Murray (Lorient to Dundee United), Robert Mann (Forfar Athletic to Inverness Caledonian Thistle), Andrew Stewart (Dundee United to East Fife), Martin Glancy (Dumbarton to Inverness Caledonian Thistle), Alex Marinkov (Scarborough to Hibernian), Mark Campbell (Stranraer to Ayr United).

- Scottish Football Association Chief Executive Jim Farry is suspended during the course of a Tribunal into the transfer of Jorge Cadete from Sporting Lisbon to Celtic.
- John Inglis signs a three-month contract with Bulgarian side Levski

Sofia after being released by Aberdeen.
- The Scottish Football Association dismiss Jim Farry. Jack McGinn takes over as acting Chief Executive.
- Clydebank apply to The Scottish Football League to play their home games at Brunton Park in Carlisle. The application is rejected.
- Partick Thistle name John Lambie as their new manager after relieving Tommy Bryce of the post. Bryce is retained as a player but leaves the club to rejoin Queen of the South for the rest of the season.
- The Bank of Scotland announce a £2.25 million deal to sponsor The Scottish Premier League for the rest of the season and a further two seasons with a £1.5 million option for a further year.
- Motherwell sign midfielder Mark Gower on loan from Spurs for the rest of the season.
- Alex MacDonald resigns as manager of Airdrieonians after being told his contract will not be renewed in the summer. Gary Mackay takes over.
- Allan MacDonald is named the new Chief Executive of Celtic. He will officially take up the post on 1st July following the departure from the club of Fergus McCann.
- Celtic duo Simon Donnelly and Phil O'Donnell agree to join Sheffield Wednesday at the end of the season under freedom of contract.
- Rangers announce the £4 million signing of Dutch striker Michael Mols who will join them from Utrecht in the summer.
- Aberdeen sign striker Jim Hamilton from Heart of Midlothian for £250,000.
- Motherwell sign experienced English striker Don Goodman on a free transfer.
- Rangers midfielder Charlie Miller joins Leicester City on loan until the

end of the season.
- Scotland's Euro 2000 qualifier against Bosnia at Ibrox is postponed. The Bosnian team are unable to travel to Glasgow because of NATO air strikes in the Balkan region.
- Heart of Midlothian sign Scotland international Darren Jackson from Celtic for £450,000.
- Dundee United sell Andy McLaren to Reading for £150,000.
- Heart of Midlothian's French striker Stephane Adam ends speculation about his future by agreeing a new contract with the Tynecastle club.
- Scotland's Under-21 side lose 1-0 to the Czech Republic in a European Under-21 Championship qualifier at Fir Park.
- Scotland lose 2-1 to the Czech Republic in a Euro 2000 qualifier at Celtic Park.
- Former Scotland goalkeeper Bryan Gunn is forced to retire because of injury.
- Australian defender Craig Moore rejoins Rangers from Crystal Palace just four months after leaving Ibrox for the London club.
- Rangers sign USA international midfielder Claudio Reyna from German side Wolfsburg for £1.5 million.
- Other March transfers include: David Partridge (West Ham United to Dundee United), Owen Coyle (Motherwell to Dunfermline Athletic), Steven Nicholas (Stirling Albion to Motherwell), Mohamed Berthe (Bournemouth to Heart of Midlothian), Phil Scott (St. Johnstone to Sheffield Wednesday), Lars Zetterlund (Dundee United to Orebro), David Worrell (Blackburn Rovers to Dundee United), Kevin James (Falkirk to Heart of Midlothian), Brian McLaughlin (Celtic to Dundee United), Paul Kinnaird (Stranraer to Ross County), Colin McKinnon (Dumbarton to

Stenhousemuir), Gilbert Allan (East
Fife to Alloa Athletic), Ben
Honeyman (Forfar Athletic to East
Fife), Steven Ramsay (Alloa Athletic
to East Fife), David Murie (Heart of
Midlothian to Morton), Myles
Hogarth (Heart of Midlothian to
Falkirk), James Smith (East
Stirlingshire to Stranraer).

APRIL

- Livingston and Inverness Caledonian
  Thistle clinch promotion to the First
  Division.

- Hibernian win the First Division title
  with a 2-0 win over Hamilton
  Academical at Firhill.

- Ross County win the Third Division
  title with a 1-0 win over Brechin City
  at Victoria Park.

- Scotland captain Gary McAllister
  announces his retirement from
  international football. The Coventry
  player makes the decision in the wake
  of being booed by a section of the
  crowd during the 2-1 defeat by the
  Czech Republic the previous month.

- Celtic beat Dundee United 2-0 at
  Ibrox and Rangers defeat
  St. Johnstone 4-0 at Celtic Park in the
  Semi-Finals of the Tennents Scottish
  Cup.

- Henrik Larsson agrees a new four-year
  contract with Celtic. The Swedish
  striker is named Player of the Year by
  The Scottish Professional Footballers
  Association.

- Gary Mackay is confirmed as the new
  manager of Airdrieonians on a
  permanent basis.

- Swedish midfielder Jonas Thern admits
  defeat in his battle to overcome injury
  and announces he will be leaving
  Rangers to return home.

- Veteran goalkeeper John Martin
  announces he will be leaving

Hibernian – S.F.L. First Division Champions

Livingston – S.F.L. Second Division Champions

Ross County – S.F.L. Third Division Champions

Airdrieonians at the end of the season.

- Falkirk announce the signing of Kevin Christie from Motherwell under freedom of contract for next season. Striker Peter Duffield leaves the Brockville club to sign for Darlington.

- Scotland pull off a surprise 1-0 win over European Champions Germany in a friendly international in Bremen. Don Hutchison of Everton scores the goal.

- Ross County midfielder Neil Tarrant signs for Aston Villa.

MAY

- Rangers clinch the first SPL title and reclaim the Championship from Celtic with a 3-0 win over their Old Firm rivals at Celtic Park. The match is marred by crowd trouble while three players - Stephane Mahe and Vidar Riseth of Celtic and Rangers striker Rod Wallace - are sent off.

- Paul Hegarty is told he will not be retained as manager of Aberdeen beyond the end of the season.

Rangers captain Lorenzo Amoruso with The Scottish Premier League trophy

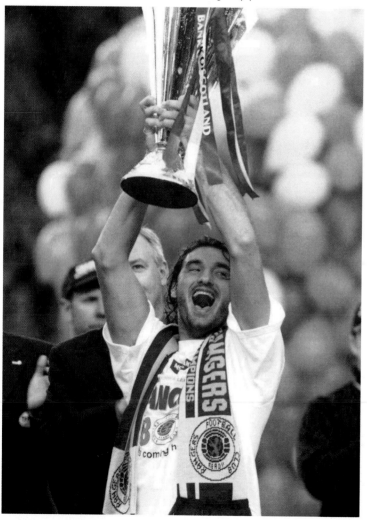

- Celtic beat Dundee 4-0 to win the BP Scottish Youth Cup.

- Dunfermline Athletic are relegated from the SPL when they lose 3-1 to Dundee.

- Kilmarnock announce the signing of English striker Mike Jeffrey from Dutch club Fortuna Sittard under freedom of contract. He will join them in the summer.

- Henrik Larsson is named Player of the Year by the Scottish Football Writers' Association.

- Campbell Money resigns as manager of Stranraer to take up a coaching position at Ayr United.

- St. Johnstone beat Dundee 1-0 on the final day of the SPL season to clinch third place in the table ahead of Kilmarnock and earn a UEFA Cup place. The Rugby Park club are later confirmed as Scotland's Fair Play representatives in the tournament.

- Dick Advocaat of Rangers is named Scotland's Manager of the Year.

- Aberdeen announce that Danish coach Ebbe Skovdahl of Brondby will become their new manager.

- Scotland's Under-21 side defeat the Republic of Ireland 1-0 at Elgin in the triangular Presidents Cup tournament.

- Rangers complete the domestic 'Treble' when they defeat Celtic 1-0 in the Tennents Scottish Cup Final at the newly refurbished Hampden Park.

JUNE

- Scotland's Under-21 side win the Presidents Cup with a 1-1 draw against Northern Ireland in Inverness.

- Former player Crawford Baptie is named as the new Chief Executive of Falkirk.

- Hibernian sign German striker Dirk Lehmann.

- Scotland draw 1-1 with the Faroe Islands in Toftir in a Euro 2000 qualifier. Leicester City defender Matt Elliott is sent off for the Scots who concede a late equaliser.

- Dunfermline Athletic sign former Morton and Rangers defender Brian Reid from Burnley.

- Scotland's Under-21 side lose 3-2 to the Czech Republic in Teplice in a European Under-21 Championship qualifier.

- Tommy Moller-Nielsen leaves the coaching staff of Rangers to become the new assistant manager of Aberdeen.

- Scotland let slip a 2-0 lead as they lose 3-2 to the Czech Republic in a Euro 2000 qualifier in Prague.

- Kenny Dalglish is named as the new Director of Football Operations of Celtic with John Barnes appointed as Head Coach in succession to Dr. Jozef Venglos.

- Raith Rovers dismiss their management team of Jimmy Nicholl and Alex Smith. They are replaced by John McVeigh and Peter Hetherston.

- Celtic announce the signing of Bulgarian midfielder Stilian Petrov subject to a work permit being granted.

- Russian international goalkeeper Dmitri Kharine joins Celtic from Chelsea under freedom of contract.

- Dundee United sign Portuguese striker Joaquim Ferraz under freedom of contract from Belenenses.

- Italian striker Marco Negri returns to Rangers after his loan spell with Venezia.

- Celtic defender Alan Stubbs undergoes successful surgery after a random drugs test following the Tennents Scottish Cup Final revealed he had testicular cancer.

STEPHEN HALLIDAY
(The Scottish Express)

Rod Wallace scores Rangers' winning goal in last season's Tennents Scottish Cup Final

Kenny Dalglish, Director of Football Operations at Celtic and John Barnes, Head Coach

THE SCOTTISH PREMIER LEAGUE

ABERDEEN

League Champions:
Division I: 1954/55
Premier Division: 1979/80,
1983/84, 1984/85
League Cup Winners:
1955/56, 1976/77, 1985/86,
1989/90, 1995/96
Scottish Cup Winners:
1947, 1970, 1982, 1983, 1984,
1986, 1990
European Cup Winners' Cup:
1982/83
European Super Cup:
1983
Drybrough Cup Winners:
1970/71, 1980/81

CELTIC

League Champions:
Division I: 1892/93, 1893/94,
1895/96, 1897/98, 1904/05,
1905/06, 1906/07, 1907/08,
1908/09, 1909/10, 1913/14,
1914/15, 1915/16, 1916/17,
1918/19, 1921/22, 1925/26,
1935/36, 1937/38, 1953/54,
1965/66, 1966/67, 1967/68,
1968/69, 1969/70, 1970/71,
1971/72, 1972/73, 1973/74
Premier Division: 1976/77,
1978/79, 1980/81, 1981/82,
1985/86, 1987/88, 1997/98
League Cup Winners:
1956/57, 1957/58, 1965/66,
1966/67, 1967/68, 1968/69,
1969/70, 1974/75, 1982/83,
1997/98
Scottish Cup Winners:
1892, 1899, 1900, 1904, 1907,
1908, 1911, 1912, 1914, 1923,
1925, 1927, 1931, 1933, 1937,
1951, 1954, 1965, 1967, 1969,
1971, 1972, 1974, 1975, 1977,
1980, 1985, 1988, 1989, 1995
European Cup Winners:
1966/67
Runners-up: 1969/70
Empire Exhibition Cup Winners:
1938
Coronation Cup Winners:
1953
Drybrough Cup Winners:
1974/75

DUNDEE

League Champions:
Division I: 1961/62
Division II: 1946/47
First Division: 1978/79,
1991/92, 1997/98
League Cup Winners:
1951/52, 1952/53, 1973/74
Scottish Cup Winners:
1910
B&Q Centenary Cup:
1990/91

DUNDEE UNITED

League Champions:
Division II: 1924/25, 1928/29
Premier Division: 1982/83
League Cup Winners:
1979/80, 1980/81
Scottish Cup Winners:
1993/94
UEFA Cup Runners-up:
1986/87

HEART OF MIDLOTHIAN

League Champions:
Division I: 1894/95, 1896/97,
1957/58, 1959/60
First Division: 1979/80
League Cup Winners:
1954/55, 1958/59, 1959/60,
1962/63
Scottish Cup Winners:
1891, 1896, 1901, 1906, 1956,
1998

HIBERNIAN

League Champions:
Division I: 1902/03, 1947/48,
1950/51, 1951/52
Division II: 1893/94, 1894/95,
1932/33
First Division: 1980/81, 1998/99
League Cup Winners:
1972/73, 1991/92
Scottish Cup Winners:
1887, 1902
Drybrough Cup Winners:
1972/73, 1973/74

KILMARNOCK

League Champions:
Division I: 1964/65
Division II: 1897/98, 1898/99
Scottish Cup Winners:
1920, 1929, 1997
**Scottish Qualifying Cup
Winners:**
1896/97

MOTHERWELL

League Champions:
Division I: 1931/32
First Division: 1981/82, 1984/85
Division II: 1953/54, 1968/69
League Cup Winners:
1950/51
Scottish Cup Winners:
1952, 1991

RANGERS

League Champions:
Division I: 1890/91 (shared),
1898/99, 1899/1900, 1900/01,
1901/02, 1910/11, 1911/12,
1912/13, 1917/18, 1919/20,
1920/21, 1922/23, 1923/24,
1924/25, 1926/27, 1927/28,
1928/29, 1929/30, 1930/31,
1932/33, 1933/34, 1934/35,
1936/37, 1938/39, 1946/47,
1948/49, 1949/50, 1952/53,
1955/56, 1956/57, 1958/59,
1960/61, 1962/63, 1963/64,
1974/75
Premier Division: 1975/76,
1977/78, 1986/87, 1988/89,
1989/90, 1990/91, 1991/92,
1992/93, 1993/94, 1994/95,
1995/96, 1996/97
SPL: 1998/99
League Cup Winners:
1946/47, 1948/49, 1960/61,
1961/62, 1963/64, 1964/65,
1970/71, 1975/76, 1977/78,
1978/79, 1981/82, 1983/84,
1984/85, 1986/87, 1987/88,
1988/89, 1990/91, 1992/93,
1993/94, 1996/97, 1998/99
Scottish Cup Winners:
1894, 1897, 1898, 1903, 1928,
1930, 1932, 1934, 1935, 1936,
1948, 1949, 1950, 1953, 1960,
1962, 1963, 1964, 1966, 1973,
1976, 1978, 1979, 1981, 1992,
1993, 1996, 1999
European Cup Winners' Cup:
1971/72
Runners-up: 1960/61, 1966/67
Drybrough Cup Winners:
1979/80

ST. JOHNSTONE

League Champions:
First Division: 1982/83,
1989/90, 1996/97
Division II: 1923/24, 1959/60,
1962/63

Club Honours

FIRST DIVISION

AIRDRIEONIANS
League Champions:
Division II: 1902/03, 1954/55,1973/74
Scottish Cup Winners: 1924
B&Q Cup Winners: 1994/95
Scottish Spring Cup Winners: 1976

AYR UNITED
League Champions:
Division II: 1911/12, 1912/13,
1927/28, 1936/37, 1958/59, 1965/66
Second Division: 1987/88, 1996/97

CLYDEBANK
League Champions:
Second Division: 1975/76

DUNFERMLINE ATHLETIC
League Champions:
Division II: 1925/26
First Division: 1988/89, 1995/96
Second Division: 1985/86
Scottish Cup Winners: 1961, 1968
Scottish Qualifying Cup: 1911/12

FALKIRK
League Champions:
First Division: 1990/91, 1993/94
Division II: 1935/36, 1969/70,1974/75
Second Division: 1979/80
Scottish Cup Winners: 1913, 1957
SFL Challenge Cup Winners:
1993/94 (known as B&Q Cup),
1997/98

INVERNESS CALEDONIAN THISTLE
League Champions:
Third Division: 1996/97

LIVINGSTON
League Champions:
Second Division: 1986/87, 1998/99
Third Division: 1995/96

MORTON
League Champions:
Division II: 1949/50, 1963/64,1966/67
First Division: 1977/78, 1983/84,
1986/87
Second Division: 1994/95
Scottish Cup Winners: 1922

RAITH ROVERS
League Champions:
First Division: 1992/93, 1994/95
Division II: 1907/08, 1909/10 (shared)
1937/38, 1948/49
League Cup Winners: 1994/95

ST. MIRREN
League Champions:
First Division: 1976/77
Division II: 1967/68
Scottish Cup Winners: 1926, 1959,
1987
Victory Cup: 1919
Anglo Scottish Cup Winners: 1979/80
Summer Cup: 1943

SECOND DIVISION

ALLOA ATHLETIC
League Champions:
Division II: 1921/22
Third Division: 1997/98

ARBROATH
Runners-up:
Division II: 1934/35, 1958/59,
1967/68, 1971/72,
Third Division: 1997/98

CLYDE
League Champions:
Division II: 1904/05, 1951/52,
1956/57, 1961/62, 1972/73,
Second Division:
1977/78, 1981/82, 1992/93
Scottish Cup Winners:
1939, 1955, 1958

HAMILTON ACADEMICAL
League Champions:
Division II: 1903/04
First Division: 1985/86, 1987/88
B&Q Cup Winners:
1991/92, 1992/93
Scottish Cup Runners-up:
1910/11, 1934/35
Second Division Runners-up:
1952/53, 1964/65, 1996/97
Lanarkshire Cup Winners:
10 Times

PARTICK THISTLE
League Champions:
First Division: 1975/76
Division II: 1896/97, 1899/1900,
1970/71
Runners-up: 1901/02,
League Cup Winners: 1971/72
Scottish Cup Winners: 1921

QUEEN OF THE SOUTH
League Champions:
Division II: 1950/51

ROSS COUNTY
League Champions:
Third Division: 1998/99

STENHOUSEMUIR
SFL Challenge Cup Winners:
1995/96

STIRLING ALBION
League Champions:
Division II: 1952/53, 1957/58,
1960/61, 1964/65,
Second Division: 1976/77, 1990/91,
1995/96

STRANRAER
League Champions:
Second Division: 1993/94, 1997/98
SFL Challenge Cup Winners:
1996/97

THIRD DIVISION

ALBION ROVERS
League Champions:
Division II: 1933/34
Second Division: 1988/89
Scottish Qualifying Cup:
1913/14

BERWICK RANGERS
League Champions:
Second Division: 1978/79
Runners-up: 1993/94

BRECHIN CITY
League Champions:
C Division: 1953/54
Second Division: 1982/83, 1989/90

COWDENBEATH
League Champions:
Division II: 1913/14, 1914/15,
1938/39

DUMBARTON
League Champions:
Division I: 1890/91 (shared with
Rangers), 1891/92
Division II: 1910/11, 1971/72
Second Division: 1991/92
Scottish Cup Winners: 1883

EAST FIFE
League Champions:
Division II: 1947/48
League Cup Winners:
1947/48, 1949/50, 1953/54
Scottish Cup Winners:
1938

EAST STIRLINGSHIRE
League Champions:
Division II: 1931/32

FORFAR ATHLETIC
League Champions:
C Division: 1948/49
Second Division: 1983/84
Third Division: 1994/95

MONTROSE
League Champions:
Second Division: 1984/85

QUEEN'S PARK
League Champions:
Division II: 1922/23
B Division 1955/56
Second Division: 1980/81
Scottish Cup Winners:
1874, 1875, 1876, 1880, 1881,
1882, 1884, 1886, 1890, 1893

The following section details the League Championship careers, appearances and goals of all players currently registered with each Scottish Premier League club for season 1999/2000 as at 14th September, 1999 that have played at senior first team level. It should be noted that all appearances include both full League appearances and substitute League appearances made by players. All club names shown in italics are for League appearances made when a player moved to a club on a Temporary Transfer basis with the player's registration subsequently reverting back to his original club.

SEASON	CLUB	LEAGUE APPEARANCES	GOALS
ADAM, Stephane Lucien			
Born : Lille 15/05/69			
1995-96	Metz	19	1
1996-97	Metz	21	3
1997-98	Heart of Midlothian	30	8
1998-99	Heart of Midlothian	29	10
ADAMCZUK, Dariusz			
Born : Stettin 20/10/69			
from Eintracht Frankfurt			
1993-94	Dundee	11	1
from Pogon Stettin			
1995-96	Dundee	13	-
1996-97	Dundee	30	1
1997-98	Dundee	33	1
1998-99	Dundee	26	6
ADAMS, Derek Watt			
Born : Glasgow 25/06/75			
1994-95	Burnley	-	-
1995-96	Burnley	2	-
1996-97	Ross County	34	22
1997-98	Ross County	34	16
1998-99	Ross County	4	3
1998-99	Motherwell	26	3
ALBERTZ, Jorg			
Born : Monchengladbach 29/01/71			
1990-91	Fortuna Dusseldorf	12	1
1991-92	Fortuna Dusseldorf	11	-
1992-93	Fortuna Dusseldorf	35	3
1993-94	Hamburger SV	31	4
1994-95	Hamburger SV	34	9
1995-96	Hamburger SV	34	9
1996-97	Rangers	32	10
1997-98	Rangers	31	10
1998-99	Rangers	34	11
AMATO, Gabriel Omar			
Born : Mar Del Plata 22/10/70			
1993-94	Huracan	15	6
1993-94	River Plate	9	-
1994-95	River Plate	24	5
1995-96	River Plate	34	8
1996-97	Hercules	36	2
1997-98	Real Mallorca	35	13
1998-99	Rangers	20	6
AMORUSO, Lorenzo			
Born : Bari 28/06/71			
1988-89	Bari	3	-
1989-90	Bari	3	-
1990-91	Bari	5	1
1991-92	Bari	-	-
1991-92	Mantova	13	1
1992-93	Bari	-	-
1992-93	Pescavo	19	1
1993-94	Bari	37	3
1994-95	Bari	27	4
1995-96	Fiorentina AC Spa	31	2
1996-97	Fiorentina AC Spa	23	1
1997-98	Rangers	4	-
1998-99	Rangers	33	1
ANDERSON, Russell			
Born : Aberdeen 25/10/78			
1996-97	Aberdeen	14	-
1997-98	Aberdeen	26	-
1998-99	Aberdeen	16	-
ANNAND, Edward			
Born : Glasgow 24/03/73			
1991-92	Partick Thistle	1	-
1992-93	Partick Thistle	-	-
from Sligo Rovers			
1995-96	Clyde	35	21
1996-97	Clyde	29	21
1996-97	Dundee	5	2
1997-98	Dundee	34	12
1998-99	Dundee	29	9

SEASON	CLUB	LEAGUE APPEARANCES	GOALS
BAGAN, David			
Born : Irvine 26/04/77			
1995-96	Kilmarnock	-	-
1996-97	Kilmarnock	17	-
1997-98	Kilmarnock	7	-
1998-99	Kilmarnock	5	-
BAKER, Martin			
Born : Govan 08/06/74			
1992-93	St. Mirren	29	-
1993-94	St. Mirren	38	1
1994-95	St. Mirren	26	2
1995-96	St. Mirren	26	-
1996-97	St. Mirren	31	-
1997-98	Kilmarnock	13	-
1998-99	Kilmarnock	23	-
BANNERMAN, Scott John			
Born : Edinburgh 21/03/79			
1995-96	Hibernian	-	-
1996-97	Hibernian	-	-
1997-98	Hibernian	1	-
1998-99	Hibernian	12	-
BAYNE, Graham			
Born : Kirkcaldy 22/08/79			
1997-98	Dundee	2	-
1998-99	Dundee	2	-
BERKOVIC, Eyal			
Born : Israel 02/04/72			
1992-93	Maccabi Haifa	32	7
1993-94	Maccabi Haifa	38	10
1994-95	Maccabi Haifa	29	5
1995-96	Maccabi Haifa	29	3
1996-97	Southampton	28	4
1997-98	West Ham United	35	7
1998-99	West Ham United	30	3
BERNARD, Paul			
Born : Edinburgh 30/12/72			
1990-91	Oldham Athletic	2	1
1991-92	Oldham Athletic	21	5
1992-93	Oldham Athletic	33	4
1993-94	Oldham Athletic	32	5
1994-95	Oldham Athletic	17	2
1995-96	Oldham Athletic	7	1
1995-96	Aberdeen	31	1
1996-97	Aberdeen	14	-
1997-98	Aberdeen	17	-
1998-99	Aberdeen	9	1
BETT, Baldur			
Born : Reykjavik 12/04/80			
1996-97	Aberdeen	-	-
1997-98	Aberdeen	-	-
1998-99	Aberdeen	1	-
BLINKER, Reginald Waldi			
Born : Surinam 04/06/69			
1986-87	Feyenoord	26	1
1987-88	Feyenoord	24	2
1988-89	Feyenoord	1	-
1988-89	Den Bosch	25	6
1989-90	Feyenoord	31	2
1990-91	Feyenoord	26	1
1991-92	Feyenoord	28	5
1992-93	Feyenoord	30	13
1993-94	Feyenoord	29	9
1994-95	Feyenoord	30	8
1995-96	Feyenoord	13	4
1995-96	Sheffield Wednesday	9	2
1996-97	Sheffield Wednesday	33	1
1997-98	Celtic	16	1
1998-99	Celtic	15	4
BOLLAN, Gary			
Born : Dundee 24/03/73			
1987-88	Celtic	-	-
1988-89	Celtic	-	-
1989-90	Celtic	-	-

SEASON	CLUB	LEAGUE APPEARANCES	GOALS
1990-91	Dundee United	2	-
1991-92	Dundee United	10	1
1992-93	Dundee United	15	3
1993-94	Dundee United	12	-
1994-95	Dundee United	7	-
1994-95	Rangers	6	-
1995-96	Rangers	4	-
1996-97	Rangers	-	-
1997-98	Rangers	1	-
1997-98	St. Johnstone	-	-
1998-99	St. Johnstone	33	4
BONNES, Stephane			
Born : France 26/02/78			
from FC Mulhouse			
BOTTIGLIERI, Emilio Hugh			
Born : Port Hardy 13/04/79			
1997-98	Hibernian	-	-
1998-99	Hibernian	1	-
1998-99	Albion Rovers	10	1
BOYACK, Steven			
Born : Edinburgh 04/09/76			
1993-94	Rangers	-	-
1994-95	Rangers	-	-
1995-96	Rangers	-	-
1996-97	Rangers	1	-
1997-98	Rangers	-	-
1997-98	Hull City	12	3
1998-99	Rangers	-	-
1998-99	Dundee	8	2
BOYD, Thomas			
Born : Glasgow 24/11/65			
1983-84	Motherwell	13	-
1984-85	Motherwell	36	-
1985-86	Motherwell	31	-
1986-87	Motherwell	31	-
1987-88	Motherwell	42	2
1988-89	Motherwell	36	1
1989-90	Motherwell	33	1
1990-91	Motherwell	30	2
1991-92	Chelsea	23	-
1991-92	Celtic	13	1
1992-93	Celtic	42	-
1993-94	Celtic	38	-
1994-95	Celtic	35	1
1995-96	Celtic	34	-
1996-97	Celtic	31	-
1997-98	Celtic	33	-
1998-99	Celtic	31	-
BRANNAN, Gerard Daniel			
Born : Liverpool 15/01/72			
1990-91	Tranmere Rovers	18	1
1991-92	Tranmere Rovers	18	1
1992-93	Tranmere Rovers	38	1
1993-94	Tranmere Rovers	45	9
1994-95	Tranmere Rovers	41	2
1995-96	Tranmere Rovers	44	-
1996-97	Tranmere Rovers	34	6
1996-97	Manchester City	11	1
1997-98	Manchester City	32	3
1998-99	Manchester City	-	-
1998-99	Norwich City	11	1
1998-99	Motherwell	25	5
BRATTBAKK, Harald Martin			
Born : Norway 01/02/71			
1990	Rosenborg BK	3	1
1991	Rosenborg BK	11	1
1992	Bodo Glimt	-	-
1993	Bodo Glimt	22	9
1994	Rosenborg BK	22	17
1995	Rosenborg BK	26	26
1996	Rosenborg BK	26	28
1997	Rosenborg BK	26	23
1997-98	Celtic	18	7
1998-99	Celtic	24	5

SEASON	CLUB	LEAGUE APPEARANCES	GOALS

BREBNER, Grant, Ian
Born : Edinburgh 06/12/77

SEASON	CLUB	APPEARANCES	GOALS
1994-95	Manchester United	-	-
1995-96	Manchester United	-	-
1996-97	Manchester United	-	-
1997-98	Manchester United	-	-
1997-98	*Cambridge United*	6	1
1997-98	*Hibernian*	9	1
1998-99	Reading	39	9

BUCHAN, Martin James
Born : Manchester 03/04/77

1994-95	Aberdeen	-	-
1995-96	Aberdeen	4	1
1996-97	Aberdeen	14	-
1997-98	Aberdeen	10	-
1998-99	Aberdeen	23	2

BURCHILL, Mark James
Born : Broxburn 18/08/80

| 1997-98 | Celtic | - | - |
| 1998-99 | Celtic | 21 | 9 |

BURKE, Alexander
Born : Glasgow 11/11/77

1995-96	Kilmarnock	-	-
1996-97	Kilmarnock	18	3
1997-98	Kilmarnock	19	3
1998-99	Kilmarnock	19	-

BURLEY, Craig William
Born : Ayr 24/09/71

1989-90	Chelsea	-	-
1990-91	Chelsea	1	-
1991-92	Chelsea	8	-
1992-93	Chelsea	3	-
1993-94	Chelsea	23	3
1994-95	Chelsea	25	2
1995-96	Chelsea	22	-
1996-97	Chelsea	31	2
1997-98	Celtic	35	10
1998-99	Celtic	21	9

Craig Burley

BYRNE, David
Born : Dublin 14/11/79
from Shelbourne

CAMERON, Colin
Born : Kirkcaldy 23/10/72

1990-91	Raith Rovers	-	-
1991-92	Sligo Rovers		
1992-93	Raith Rovers	16	1
1993-94	Raith Rovers	42	6
1994-95	Raith Rovers	34	7
1995-96	Raith Rovers	30	9
1995-96	Heart of Midlothian	4	2
1996-97	Heart of Midlothian	36	8
1997-98	Heart of Midlothian	31	8
1998-99	Heart of Midlothian	11	6

CHARBONNIER, Lionel
Born : Poitiers 25/10/66

1988-89	AJ Auxerre	1	-
1989-90	AJ Auxerre	-	-
1990-91	AJ Auxerre	-	-

SEASON	CLUB	LEAGUE APPEARANCES	GOALS
1991-92	AJ Auxerre	7	-
1992-93	AJ Auxerre	9	-
1993-94	AJ Auxerre	7	-
1994-95	AJ Auxerre	24	-
1995-96	AJ Auxerre	23	-
1996-97	AJ Auxerre	31	-
1997-98	AJ Auxerre	24	-
1998-99	Rangers	11	-

COLGAN, Nick
Born : Drogheda 19/09/73

1992-93	Chelsea	-	-
1993-94	Chelsea	-	-
1993-94	*Crewe Alexandra*	-	-
1994-95	Chelsea	-	-
1994-95	*Grimsby Town*	-	-
1995-96	Chelsea	-	-
1995-96	*Millwall*	-	-
1996-97	Chelsea	1	-
1997-98	Chelsea	-	-
1997-98	*Brentford*	5	-
1997-98	*Reading*	5	-
1998-99	Bournemouth	-	-

COLLINS, Derek Joseph
Born : Glasgow 15/04/69

1987-88	Morton	28	1
1988-89	Morton	35	1
1989-90	Morton	38	-
1990-91	Morton	37	2
1991-92	Morton	44	1
1992-93	Morton	41	-
1993-94	Morton	37	1
1994-95	Morton	33	1
1995-96	Morton	36	1
1996-97	Morton	35	-
1997-98	Morton	34	3
1998-99	Morton	18	-
1998-99	Hibernian	16	-

COMBE, Alan
Born : Edinburgh 03/04/74

1992-93	Cowdenbeath	18	-
1993-94	St. Mirren	16	-
1994-95	St. Mirren	21	-
1995-96	St. Mirren	21	-
1996-97	St. Mirren	36	-
1997-98	St. Mirren	30	-
1998-99	Dundee United	1	-

CONNOLLY, Patrick
Born : Glasgow 25/06/70

1986-87	Dundee United	-	-
1987-88	Dundee United	-	-
1988-89	Dundee United	2	-
1989-90	Dundee United	15	5
1990-91	Dundee United	10	2
1991-92	Dundee United	5	-
1992-93	Dundee United	42	16
1993-94	Dundee United	28	5
1994-95	Dundee United	6	-
1995-96	Dundee United	6	1
1995-96	Airdrieonians	6	3
1996-97	Airdrieonians	35	8
1997-98	Airdrieonians	23	8
1997-98	St. Johnstone	4	-
1998-99	St. Johnstone	9	1

CORR, Barry John
Born : Glasgow 13/01/81

| 1997-98 | Celtic | - | - |
| 1998-99 | Celtic | 1 | - |

COYNE, Thomas
Born : Glasgow 14/11/62

1981-82	Clydebank	31	9
1982-83	Clydebank	38	18
1983-84	Clydebank	11	10
1983-84	Dundee United	18	3
1984-85	Dundee United	21	3
1985-86	Dundee United	13	2
1986-87	Dundee	20	9
1987-88	Dundee	43	33
1988-89	Dundee	26	9
1988-89	Celtic	7	-
1989-90	Celtic	23	7
1990-91	Celtic	26	18
1991-92	Celtic	39	15
1992-93	Celtic	10	3

SEASON	CLUB	LEAGUE APPEARANCES	GOALS
1992-93	Tranmere Rovers	12	1
1993-94	Tranmere Rovers	-	-
1993-94	Motherwell	26	12
1994-95	Motherwell	31	16
1995-96	Motherwell	14	4
1996-97	Motherwell	27	11
1997-98	Motherwell	34	16
1998-99	Dundee	16	-

CRAIGAN, Stephen James
Born : Newtonards 29/10/76
from Bangor

1994-95	Motherwell	-	-
1995-96	Motherwell	-	-
1996-97	Motherwell	-	-
1997-98	Motherwell	14	-
1998-99	Motherwell	10	-

CRAWFORD, Stephen
Born : Dunfermline 09/01/74

1992-93	Raith Rovers	20	3
1993-94	Raith Rovers	36	5
1994-95	Raith Rovers	32	11
1995-96	Raith Rovers	28	3
1996-97	Millwall	42	11
1997-98	Hibernian	35	9
1998-99	Hibernian	35	14

DASOVIC, Nick Robert
Born : Vancouver 05/12/68
from Trelleborg

1996-97	St. Johnstone	14	-
1997-98	St. Johnstone	19	-
1998-99	St. Johnstone	31	1

DAVIES, William McIntosh
Born : Glasgow 31/05/64

1980-81	Rangers	-	-
1981-82	Rangers	4	-
1982-83	Rangers	4	-
1983-84	Rangers	3	1
1984-85	Rangers	-	-
1985-86	Rangers	-	-
1987-88	St. Mirren	18	-
1988-89	St. Mirren	27	4
1989-90	St. Mirren	29	1
1990-91	St. Mirren	-	-
1990-91	Leicester City	6	-
1990-91	Dunfermline Athletic	26	-
1991-92	Dunfermline Athletic	33	-
1992-93	Dunfermline Athletic	41	10
1993-94	Dunfermline Athletic	4	-
1993-94	Motherwell	10	-
1994-95	Motherwell	31	4
1995-96	Motherwell	33	2
1996-97	Motherwell	25	1
1997-98	Motherwell	17	2
1998-99	Motherwell	-	-

DE VOS, Jason Richard
Born : Ontario 02/01/74

1996-97	Darlington	8	-
1997-98	Darlington	24	3
1998-99	Darlington	12	2
1998-99	Dundee United	25	-

DELAUNAY, Jean Pierre
Born : Harfleur 17/01/66
from Le Havre

DEMPSIE, Mark William
Born : Bellshill 19/10/80

1996-97	Hibernian	-	-
1997-98	Hibernian	-	-
1998-99	Hibernian	8	-

DENHAM, Greig Paterson
Born : Glasgow 05/10/76

1993-94	Motherwell	-	-
1994-95	Motherwell	-	-
1995-96	Motherwell	13	-
1996-97	Motherwell	9	-
1997-98	Motherwell	18	-
1998-99	Motherwell	1	-

DENNIS, Shaun
Born : Kirkcaldy 20/12/69

SEASON	CLUB	LEAGUE APPEARANCES	GOALS
1988-89	Raith Rovers	10	-
1989-90	Raith Rovers	18	-
1990-91	Raith Rovers	35	1
1991-92	Raith Rovers	42	-
1992-93	Raith Rovers	31	1
1993-94	Raith Rovers	43	3
1994-95	Raith Rovers	26	1
1995-96	Raith Rovers	25	-
1996-97	Raith Rovers	16	-
1996-97	Hibernian	4	1
1997-98	Hibernian	5	-
1998-99	Hibernian	31	3

DINDELEUX, Frederic
Born : Lille 16/01/74
from Lille Olympic Sporting Club

DODDS, William
Born: New Cumnock 05/02/69

SEASON	CLUB	LEAGUE APPEARANCES	GOALS
1986-87	Chelsea	1	-
1987-88	Chelsea	-	-
1987-88	*Partick Thistle*	30	9
1988-89	Chelsea	2	-
1989-90	Dundee	30	13
1990-91	Dundee	37	15
1991-92	Dundee	42	19
1992-93	Dundee	41	16
1993-94	Dundee	24	6
1993-94	St. Johnstone	20	6
1994-95	Aberdeen	35	15
1995-96	Aberdeen	31	7
1996-97	Aberdeen	31	15
1997-98	Aberdeen	34	10
1998-99	Aberdeen	6	-
1998-99	Dundee United	30	17

DODS, Darren
Born : Edinburgh 07/06/75

SEASON	CLUB	LEAGUE APPEARANCES	GOALS
1992-93	Hibernian	-	-
1993-94	Hibernian	-	-
1994-95	Hibernian	1	-
1995-96	Hibernian	15	-
1996-97	Hibernian	20	-
1997-98	Hibernian	29	1
1998-99	St. Johnstone	34	2

DOESBURG, Michel
Born : Beverwyk 10/08/68

SEASON	CLUB	LEAGUE APPEARANCES	GOALS
1986-87	Haarlem	18	-
1987-88	Haarlem	8	-
1988-89	Haarlem	25	-
1989-90	Haarlem	23	-
1990-91	Wageningen	32	2
1991-92	Wageningen	33	1
1992-93	Heerenveen	31	2
1993-94	Heerenveen	29	-
1994-95	Heerenveen	30	-
1995-96	Heerenveen	21	-
1995-96	AZ Alkmaar	9	-
1996-97	AZ Alkmaar	24	-
1997-98	AZ Alkmaar	-	-
1998-99	Motherwell	30	-

DOUGLAS, Robert James
Born : Lanark 24/04/72

SEASON	CLUB	LEAGUE APPEARANCES	GOALS
1993-94	Meadowbank Thistle	4	-
1994-95	Meadowbank Thistle	8	-
1995-96	Livingston	24	-
1996-97	Livingston	36	-
1997-98	Dundee	36	-
1998-99	Dundee	35	-

DOW, Andrew James
Born : Dundee 07/02/73

SEASON	CLUB	LEAGUE APPEARANCES	GOALS
1990-91	Dundee	-	-
1991-92	Dundee	4	-
1992-93	Dundee	14	1
1993-94	Chelsea	14	-
1994-95	Chelsea	-	-
1994-95	*Bradford City*	5	-
1995-96	Chelsea	1	-
1995-96	Hibernian	8	1
1996-97	Hibernian	22	2

SEASON	CLUB	LEAGUE APPEARANCES	GOALS
1997-98	Hibernian	32	-
1998-99	Aberdeen	25	-

DURIE, Gordon Scott
Born : Paisley 06/12/65

SEASON	CLUB	LEAGUE APPEARANCES	GOALS
1981-82	East Fife	13	1
1982-83	East Fife	25	2
1983-84	East Fife	34	16
1984-85	East Fife	9	7
1984-85	Hibernian	22	8
1985-86	Hibernian	25	6
1985-86	Chelsea	1	-
1986-87	Chelsea	25	5
1987-88	Chelsea	26	12
1988-89	Chelsea	32	17
1989-90	Chelsea	15	5
1990-91	Chelsea	24	12
1991-92	Tottenham Hotspur	31	7
1992-93	Tottenham Hotspur	17	3
1993-94	Tottenham Hotspur	10	1
1993-94	Rangers	24	12
1994-95	Rangers	20	6
1995-96	Rangers	27	17
1996-97	Rangers	16	5
1997-98	Rangers	26	4
1998-99	Rangers	5	-

DURRANT, Ian
Born : Glasgow 29/10/66

SEASON	CLUB	LEAGUE APPEARANCES	GOALS
1984-85	Rangers	5	-
1985-86	Rangers	30	2
1986-87	Rangers	39	4
1987-88	Rangers	40	10
1988-89	Rangers	8	2
1989-90	Rangers	-	-
1990-91	Rangers	4	1
1991-92	Rangers	13	-
1992-93	Rangers	30	3
1993-94	Rangers	23	-
1994-95	Rangers	26	4
1995-96	Rangers	15	-
1996-97	Rangers	8	-
1997-98	Rangers	8	-
1998-99	Kilmarnock	36	4

Ian Durrant

EASTON, Craig
Born : Bellshill 26/02/79

SEASON	CLUB	LEAGUE APPEARANCES	GOALS
1995-96	Dundee United	-	-
1996-97	Dundee United	2	-
1997-98	Dundee United	29	1
1998-99	Dundee United	30	1

ELLIOT, Barry Robert
Born : Carlisle 24/10/78

SEASON	CLUB	LEAGUE APPEARANCES	GOALS
1995-96	Celtic	-	-
1996-97	Celtic	1	-
1997-98	Celtic	-	-
1998-99	Celtic	-	-
1998-99	*Clydebank*	4	2

ELLIOTT, John
Born : Edinburgh 04/07/80

SEASON	CLUB	LEAGUE APPEARANCES	GOALS
1996-97	Dundee	4	-
1997-98	Dundee	17	2

SEASON	CLUB	LEAGUE APPEARANCES	GOALS
1998-99	Dundee	-	-
1998-99	Arbroath	11	-

FALCONER, William Henry
Born : Aberdeen 05/04/66

SEASON	CLUB	LEAGUE APPEARANCES	GOALS
1982-83	Aberdeen	1	-
1983-84	Aberdeen	8	1
1984-85	Aberdeen	16	4
1985-86	Aberdeen	8	-
1986-87	Aberdeen	8	-
1987-88	Aberdeen	36	8
1988-89	Watford	33	5
1989-90	Watford	30	3
1990-91	Watford	35	4
1991-92	Middlesbrough	25	5
1992-93	Middlesbrough	28	5
1993-94	Middlesbrough	-	-
1993-94	Sheffield United	23	3
1993-94	Celtic	14	1
1994-95	Celtic	26	4
1995-96	Celtic	2	-
1995-96	Motherwell	15	5
1996-97	Motherwell	21	2
1997-98	Motherwell	22	3
1998-99	Dundee	33	4

FEENEY, Lee
Born : Newry 21/03/78

SEASON	CLUB	LEAGUE APPEARANCES	GOALS
1997-98	Linfield	18	3
1998-99	Rangers	1	-

FERGUSON, Allan Thomas
Born : Lanark 21/03/69

SEASON	CLUB	LEAGUE APPEARANCES	GOALS
1987-88	Hamilton Academical	6	-
1988-89	Hamilton Academical	31	-
1989-90	Hamilton Academical	34	-
1990-91	Hamilton Academical	37	-
1991-92	Hamilton Academical	16	-
1992-93	Hamilton Academical	36	-
1993-94	Hamilton Academical	40	-
1994-95	Hamilton Academical	24	-
1995-96	Hamilton Academical	26	-
1996-97	Hamilton Academical	27	-
1997-98	Hamilton Academical	25	-
1998-99	St. Johnstone	3	-

FERGUSON, Barry
Born : Glasgow 02/02/78

SEASON	CLUB	LEAGUE APPEARANCES	GOALS
1994-95	Rangers	-	-
1995-96	Rangers	-	-
1996-97	Rangers	1	-
1997-98	Rangers	7	-
1998-99	Rangers	23	1

FERGUSON, Ian
Born : Glasgow 15/03/67

SEASON	CLUB	LEAGUE APPEARANCES	GOALS
1984-85	Clyde	2	-
1985-86	Clyde	19	4
1986-87	Clyde	5	-
1986-87	St. Mirren	35	4
1987-88	St. Mirren	22	6
1987-88	Rangers	8	1
1988-89	Rangers	30	6
1989-90	Rangers	24	-
1990-91	Rangers	11	1
1991-92	Rangers	16	1
1992-93	Rangers	30	4
1993-94	Rangers	35	5
1994-95	Rangers	16	1
1995-96	Rangers	18	2
1996-97	Rangers	23	1
1997-98	Rangers	11	-
1998-99	Rangers	13	-

FERRAZ, Joaquim Miguel Leitao De Freitas
Born : Parades 16/05/74
from OS Belenenses

FITZGERALD, Darren
Born : Belfast 13/10/78

SEASON	CLUB	LEAGUE APPEARANCES	GOALS
1994-95	Rangers	-	-
1995-96	Rangers	-	-
1996-97	Rangers	1	-
1997-98	Rangers	-	-
1998-99	Rangers	-	-

FLÖGEL, THOMAS
Born : Vienna 07/06/71

SEASON	CLUB	LEAGUE APPEARANCES	GOALS
1989-90	Austria Vienna	16	1

SEASON	CLUB	LEAGUE APPEARANCES	GOALS
1990-91	Austria Vienna	28	5
1991-92	Austria Vienna	35	6
1992-93	Austria Vienna	35	10
1993-94	Austria Vienna	35	5
1994-95	Austria Vienna	36	7
1995-96	Austria Vienna	29	4
1996-97	Austria Vienna	34	4
1997-98	Heart of Midlothian	29	5
1998-99	Heart of Midlothian	20	2

FULTON, Stephen
Born: Greenock 10/08/70

SEASON	CLUB	LEAGUE APPEARANCES	GOALS
1986-87	Celtic	-	-
1987-88	Celtic	-	-
1988-89	Celtic	3	-
1989-90	Celtic	16	-
1990-91	Celtic	21	-
1991-92	Celtic	30	2
1992-93	Celtic	6	-
1993-94	Bolton Wanderers	4	-
1993-94	Peterborough United	3	-
1994-95	Falkirk	28	3
1995-96	Falkirk	5	-
1995-96	Heart of Midlothian	26	2
1996-97	Heart of Midlothian	29	1
1997-98	Heart of Midlothian	36	5
1998-99	Heart of Midlothian	27	2

GILLIES, Richard Charles
Born: Glasgow 24/08/76

SEASON	CLUB	LEAGUE APPEARANCES	GOALS
1992-93	St. Mirren	8	1
1993-94	St. Mirren	22	2
1994-95	St. Mirren	24	3
1995-96	St. Mirren	33	3
1996-97	St. Mirren	29	6
1997-98	St. Mirren	-	-
1997-98	Aberdeen	21	-
1998-99	Aberdeen	11	-

GOOD, Iain David
Born: Glasgow 09/08/77

SEASON	CLUB	LEAGUE APPEARANCES	GOALS
1995-96	Aberdeen	-	-
1996-97	Aberdeen	-	-
1997-98	Aberdeen-	-	-
1998-99	Aberdeen	1	-

GOODMAN, Donald Ralph
Born: Leeds 09/05/66

SEASON	CLUB	LEAGUE APPEARANCES	GOALS
1983-84	Bradford City	2	-
1984-85	Bradford City	25	5
1985-86	Bradford City	20	4
1986-87	Bradford City	23	5
1986-87	West Bromwich Albion	10	2
1987-88	West Bromwich Albion	40	7
1988-89	West Bromwich Albion	36	15
1989-90	West Bromwich Albion	39	21
1990-91	West Bromwich Albion	22	8
1991-92	West Bromwich Albion	11	7
1991-92	Sunderland	22	11
1992-93	Sunderland	41	16
1993-94	Sunderland	35	10
1994-95	Sunderland	18	3
1994-95	Wolverhampton Wanderers	24	3
1995-96	Wolverhampton Wanderers	44	16
1996-97	Wolverhampton Wanderers	27	6
1997-98	Wolverhampton Wanderers	30	8
from Hiroshima			
1998-99	Barnsley	8	-
1998-99	Motherwell	8	1

GORAM, Andrew Lewis
Born: Bury 13/04/64

SEASON	CLUB	LEAGUE APPEARANCES	GOALS
1981-82	Oldham Athletic	3	-
1982-83	Oldham Athletic	38	-
1983-84	Oldham Athletic	22	-
1984-85	Oldham Athletic	41	-
1985-86	Oldham Athletic	41	-
1986-87	Oldham Athletic	41	-
1987-88	Oldham Athletic	9	-
1987-88	Hibernian	33	1
1988-89	Hibernian	36	-
1989-90	Hibernian	34	-
1990-91	Hibernian	35	-
1991-92	Rangers	44	-
1992-93	Rangers	34	-
1993-94	Rangers	8	-
1994-95	Rangers	19	-
1995-96	Rangers	30	-
1996-97	Rangers	25	-
1997-98	Rangers	24	-
1998-99	Notts County	1	-
1998-99	Sheffield United	7	-
1998-99	Motherwell	13	-

GOTTSKALKSSON, Olafur
Born: Keflavik 12/03/68

SEASON	CLUB	LEAGUE APPEARANCES	GOALS
1988	IA Akranes	18	-
1989	IA Akranes	15	-
1990	KR	18	-
1991	KR	18	-
1992	KR	18	-
1993	KR	17	-
1994	Keflavik	18	-
1995	Keflavik	17	-
1996	Keflavik	18	-
1997	Keflavik	10	-
1997-98	Hibernian	16	-
1998-99	Hibernian	36	-

GOULD, Jonathan
Born: London 18/07/68

SEASON	CLUB	LEAGUE APPEARANCES	GOALS
1990-91	Halifax Town	23	-
1991-92	Halifax Town	9	-
1991-92	West Bromwich Albion	9	-
1992-93	Coventry City	9	-
1993-94	Coventry City	9	-
1994-95	Coventry City	7	-
1995-96	Coventry City	9	-
1995-96	Bradford City	9	-
1996-97	Bradford City	9	-
1996-97	Gillingham	3	-
1997-98	Celtic	35	-
1998-99	Celtic	28	-

GRADY, James
Born: Paisley 14/03/71

SEASON	CLUB	LEAGUE APPEARANCES	GOALS
1994-95	Clydebank	36	7
1995-96	Clydebank	36	10
1996-97	Clydebank	36	8
1997-98	Dundee	36	15
1998-99	Dundee	26	3

GRANT, Roderick John
Born: Gloucester 16/09/66

SEASON	CLUB	LEAGUE APPEARANCES	GOALS
1986-87	Cowdenbeath	24	14
1987-88	Cowdenbeath	32	11
1988-89	Cowdenbeath	8	2
1988-89	St. Johnstone	28	5
1989-90	St. Johnstone	37	19
1990-91	St. Johnstone	30	7
1991-92	St. Johnstone	25	2
1992-93	St. Johnstone	-	-
1992-93	Dunfermline Athletic	32	4
1993-94	Partick Thistle	37	13
1994-95	Partick Thistle	23	5
1995-96	St. Johnstone	27	5
1996-97	St. Johnstone	33	19
1997-98	St. Johnstone	34	6
1998-99	St. Johnstone	25	4

GRIFFIN, Daniel Joseph
Born: Belfast 10/08/77

SEASON	CLUB	LEAGUE APPEARANCES	GOALS
1993-94	St. Johnstone	-	-
1994-95	St. Johnstone	3	-
1995-96	St. Johnstone	31	1
1996-97	St. Johnstone	29	1
1997-98	St. Johnstone	13	-
1998-99	St. Johnstone	19	1

HALLIDAY, Stephen
Born: Sunderland 03/05/76

SEASON	CLUB	LEAGUE APPEARANCES	GOALS
1993-94	Hartlepool United	11	-
1994-95	Hartlepool United	28	5
1995-96	Hartlepool United	39	7
1996-97	Hartlepool United	31	8
1997-98	Hartlepool United	31	5
1998-99	Motherwell	4	-

HAMILTON, James
Born: Aberdeen 09/02/76

SEASON	CLUB	LEAGUE APPEARANCES	GOALS
1993-94	Dundee	1	-
1994-95	Dundee	28	12
1995-96	Dundee	33	14
1996-97	Dundee	12	1
1996-97	Heart of Midlothian	18	5
1997-98	Heart of Midlothian	32	14
1998-99	Heart of Midlothian	25	6
1998-99	Aberdeen	7	1

HANNAH, David
Born: Coatbridge 04/08/73

SEASON	CLUB	LEAGUE APPEARANCES	GOALS
1991-92	Dundee United	-	-
1992-93	Dundee United	5	-
1993-94	Dundee United	10	2
1994-95	Dundee United	32	2
1995-96	Dundee United	7	1
1996-97	Dundee United	12	2
1996-97	Celtic	18	-
1997-98	Celtic	15	-
1998-99	Celtic	9	-
1998-99	Dundee United	13	1

HART, Michael
Born: Bellshill 10/02/80

SEASON	CLUB	LEAGUE APPEARANCES	GOALS
1997-98	Aberdeen	-	-
1998-99	Aberdeen	14	-

HARTLEY, Paul
Born: Glasgow 19/10/76

SEASON	CLUB	LEAGUE APPEARANCES	GOALS
1994-95	Hamilton Academical	16	-
1995-96	Hamilton Academical	31	11
1996-97	Millwall	44	4
1997-98	Raith Rovers	30	10
1998-99	Raith Rovers	18	4
1998-99	Hibernian	13	5

HEALY, Colin
Born: Cork 14/03/80
from Wilton United

SEASON	CLUB	LEAGUE APPEARANCES	GOALS
1998-99	Celtic	3	-

HENDRY, Edward Colin James
Born: Keith 07/12/65

SEASON	CLUB	LEAGUE APPEARANCES	GOALS
1983-84	Dundee	4	-
1984-85	Dundee	4	-
1985-86	Dundee	20	-
1986-87	Dundee	13	2
1986-87	Blackburn Rovers	13	3
1987-88	Blackburn Rovers	44	12
1988-89	Blackburn Rovers	38	7
1989-90	Blackburn Rovers	7	-
1989-90	Manchester City	25	3
1990-91	Manchester City	32	1
1991-92	Manchester City	6	1
1991-92	Blackburn Rovers	30	4
1992-93	Blackburn Rovers	41	1
1993-94	Blackburn Rovers	23	-
1994-95	Blackburn Rovers	38	4
1995-96	Blackburn Rovers	33	1
1996-97	Blackburn Rovers	35	1
1997-98	Blackburn Rovers	34	1
1998-99	Rangers	19	-

HENRY, Fabrice
Born: Argenteuil 13/02/68
from FC Basel

HESSEY, Sean
Born: Liverpool 19/09/78

SEASON	CLUB	LEAGUE APPEARANCES	GOALS
1997-98	Wigan Athletic	-	-
1997-98	Leeds United	-	-
1997-98	Huddersfield Town	1	-
1998-99	Huddersfield Town	10	-

HOLMES, Derek
Born: Lanark 18/10/78

SEASON	CLUB	LEAGUE APPEARANCES	GOALS
1994-95	Heart of Midlothian	-	-
1995-96	Heart of Midlothian	-	-
1996-97	Heart of Midlothian	1	-
1997-98	Heart of Midlothian	1	1
1997-98	Cowdenbeath	13	5
1998-99	Heart of Midlothian	6	-
1998-99	Raith Rovers	14	6

HOLSGROVE, Paul
Born: Cosford 26/08/69

SEASON	CLUB	LEAGUE APPEARANCES	GOALS
1986-87	Aldershot	-	-
1987-88	Aldershot	2	-
1988-89	Aldershot	1	-
1988-89	Wimbledon	-	-
1989-90	Aldershot	-	-
1989-90	West Bromwich Albion	-	-
From Wokingham Town			
1990-91	Luton Town	1	-

SEASON	CLUB	LEAGUE APPEARANCES	GOALS
1991-92	Luton Town	1	-
From Heracles			
1992-93	Millwall	11	-
1993-94	Millwall	-	-
1994-95	Reading	24	3
1995-96	Reading	30	1
1996-97	Reading	14	2
1997-98	Reading	2	-
1997-98	*Grimsby Town*	10	-
1997-98	*Crewe Alexandra*	8	1
1997-98	Stoke City	12	1
1998-99	Stoke City	-	-
1998-99	Brighton & Hove Albion	-	-
1998-99	Hibernian	17	1

HOLT, Gary James
Born : Irvine 09/03/73

1994-95	Stoke City	-	-
1995-96	Kilmarnock	26	-
1996-97	Kilmarnock	12	1
1997-98	Kilmarnock	27	2
1998-99	Kilmarnock	33	3

HORN, Robert David
Born : Edinburgh 03/08/77

1994-95	Heart of Midlothian	-	-
1995-96	Heart of Midlothian	-	-
1996-97	Heart of Midlothian	1	-
1997-98	Heart of Midlothian	-	-
1998-99	Heart of Midlothian	-	-
1998-99	*Cowdenbeath*	8	-

HUGGON, Russel William
Born : Mapel Ridge 20/10/79

1996-97	Hibernian	-	-
1997-98	Hibernian	-	-
1998-99	Hibernian	-	-
1998-99	*Ross County*	-	-
1998-99	*Stenhousemuir*	2	1

HUGHES, John
Born : Edinburgh 09/09/64

1988-89	Berwick Rangers	27	10
1989-90	Berwick Rangers	14	4
1989-90	Swansea City	24	4
1990-91	Swansea City	-	-
1990-91	Falkirk	32	2
1991-92	Falkirk	38	2
1992-93	Falkirk	15	-
1993-94	Falkirk	29	3
1994-95	Falkirk	20	-
1995-96	Celtic	26	2
1996-97	Celtic	6	-
1996-97	Hibernian	4	-
1997-98	Hibernian	25	1
1998-99	Hibernian	23	3

INNES, Christopher
Born : Broxburn 13/07/76

1996-97	Stenhousemuir	24	1
1997-98	Stenhousemuir	30	2
1998-99	Kilmarnock	4	1
1998-99	*St. Mirren*	9	-

JACK, Matthias
Born : Leipzig 15/02/69
from Fortuna Dusseldorf

JACKSON, Darren
Born : Edinburgh 25/07/66

1985-86	Meadowbank Thistle	39	17
1986-87	Meadowbank Thistle	9	5
1986-87	Newcastle United	23	3
1987-88	Newcastle United	31	2
1988-89	Newcastle United	15	2
1988-89	Dundee United	1	-
1989-90	Dundee United	25	7
1990-91	Dundee United	33	12
1991-92	Dundee United	28	11
1992-93	Hibernian	36	13
1993-94	Hibernian	39	7
1994-95	Hibernian	31	10
1995-96	Hibernian	36	9
1996-97	Hibernian	30	11
1997-98	Celtic	23	3

SEASON	CLUB	LEAGUE APPEARANCES	GOALS
1998-99	Celtic	6	-
1998-99	*Coventry City*	3	-
1998-99	Heart of Midlothian	9	1

JAMES, Kevin Francis
Born : Edinburgh 03/12/75

1994-95	Falkirk	1	-
1995-96	Falkirk	14	2
1996-97	Falkirk	18	3
1997-98	Falkirk	17	4
1998-99	Falkirk	13	-
1998-99	Heart of Midlothian	4	-

JEFFREY, Michael
Born : Liverpool 11/08/71

1988-89	Bolton Wanderers	9	-
1989-90	Bolton Wanderers	4	-
1990-91	Bolton Wanderers	-	-
1991-92	Bolton Wanderers	2	-
1991-92	*Doncaster Rovers*	11	6
1992-93	Doncaster Rovers	30	12
1993-94	Doncaster Rovers	8	1
1993-94	Newcastle United	2	-
1994-95	Newcastle United	-	-
1995-96	Rotherham United	22	5
from Fortuna Sittard			

JENKINS, Iain
Born : Whiston 24/11/72

1990-91	Everton	1	-
1991-92	Everton	3	-
1992-93	Everton	1	-
1992-93	*Bradford City*	6	-
1993-94	Chester City	34	-
1994-95	Chester City	40	-
1995-96	Chester City	13	-
1996-97	Chester City	39	-
1997-98	Chester City	34	1
1997-98	Dundee United	7	-
1998-99	Dundee United	6	-

JENKINSON, Leigh
Born : Doncaster 09/07/69

1987-88	Hull City	3	1
1988-89	Hull City	11	-
1989-90	Hull City	22	-
1990-91	Hull City	26	-
1990-91	*Rotherham United*	7	-
1991-92	Hull City	42	8
1992-93	Hull City	26	4
1992-93	Coventry City	5	-
1993-94	Coventry City	16	-
1993-94	*Birmingham City*	3	-
1994-95	Coventry City	11	1
1995-96	St. Johnstone	18	2
1996-97	St. Johnstone	25	6
1997-98	St. Johnstone	24	3
1998-99	Wigan Athletic	7	-
1998-99	Heart of Midlothian	5	-

JESS, Eoin
Born : Aberdeen 13/12/70

| 1987-88 | Aberdeen | - | - |

Darren Jackson

SEASON	CLUB	LEAGUE APPEARANCES	GOALS
1988-89	Aberdeen	2	-
1989-90	Aberdeen	11	3
1990-91	Aberdeen	27	13
1991-92	Aberdeen	39	12
1992-93	Aberdeen	31	12
1993-94	Aberdeen	41	6
1994-95	Aberdeen	25	1
1995-96	Aberdeen	25	3
1995-96	Coventry City	12	1
1996-97	Coventry City	27	-
1997-98	Aberdeen	35	9
1998-99	Aberdeen	36	14

JOHANSSON, Jonatan
Born : Stockholm 16/08/75
from F.C. Flora

1997-98	Rangers	6	-
1998-99	Rangers	25	8

JOHNSON, Thomas
Born : Newcastle 15/01/71

1988-89	Notts County	10	4
1989-90	Notts County	40	18
1990-91	Notts County	37	16
1991-92	Notts County	31	9
1991-92	Derby County	12	2
1992-93	Derby County	35	8
1993-94	Derby County	37	13
1994-95	Derby County	14	7
1994-95	Aston Villa	14	4
1995-96	Aston Villa	23	5
1996-97	Aston Villa	20	4
1996-97	Celtic	4	1
1997-98	Celtic	2	-
1998-99	Celtic	3	3

JONSSON, Sigurdur
Born : Arkanes 27/09/66

1984-85	Sheffield Wednesday	3	-
1985-86	Sheffield Wednesday	10	2
1985-86	*Barnsley*	5	-
1986-87	Sheffield Wednesday	13	-
1987-88	Sheffield Wednesday	13	1
1988-89	Sheffield Wednesday	28	1
1989-90	Arsenal	6	1
1990-91	Arsenal	2	-
1991-92	Arsenal	-	-
1992	IA Akranes	11	-
1993	IA Akranes	16	1
1994	IA Akranes	13	3
1995	IA Akranes	16	2
1996	Orebro	20	-
1997	Orebro	22	2
1997-98	Dundee United	15	-
1998-99	Dundee United	14	1

KANCHELSKIS, Andrei
Born : Kirovograci 23/01/69

1988	Dynamo Kiev	7	1
1989	Dynamo Kiev	15	-
1990	Donetsk	16	2
1991	Donetsk	5	1
1990-91	Manchester United	1	-
1991-92	Manchester United	34	5
1992-93	Manchester United	27	3
1993-94	Manchester United	31	6
1994-95	Manchester United	30	14
1995-96	Everton	32	16
1996-97	Everton	20	4
1997-98	AC Fiorentina	17	2
1998-99	Rangers	30	8

KANE, Paul James
Born : Edinburgh 20/06/65

1982-83	Hibernian	-	-
1983-84	Hibernian	13	1
1984-85	Hibernian	34	8
1985-86	Hibernian	32	5
1986-87	Hibernian	37	1
1987-88	Hibernian	44	10
1988-89	Hibernian	35	5
1989-90	Hibernian	31	3
1990-91	Hibernian	21	-
1990-91	Oldham Athletic	17	-
1991-92	Oldham Athletic	4	-
1991-92	Aberdeen	25	2
1992-93	Aberdeen	27	4
1993-94	Aberdeen	39	3
1994-95	Aberdeen	27	2

SEASON	CLUB	LEAGUE APPEARANCES	GOALS
1995-96	*Barnsley*	4	-
1996	Viking Stavanger	15	3
1997-98	St. Johnstone	27	1
1998-99	St. Johnstone	34	3

KERNAGHAN, Alan Nigel
Born : Otley 25/04/67

SEASON	CLUB	LEAGUE APPEARANCES	GOALS
1984-85	Middlesbrough	8	1
1985-86	Middlesbrough	6	-
1986-87	Middlesbrough	13	-
1987-88	Middlesbrough	35	6
1988-89	Middlesbrough	23	-
1989-90	Middlesbrough	37	4
1990-91	Middlesbrough	24	-
1990-91	*Charlton Athletic*	13	-
1991-92	Middlesbrough	38	2
1992-93	Middlesbrough	22	2
1993-94	Middlesbrough	6	1
1993-94	Manchester City	24	-
1994-95	Manchester City	22	1
1995-96	*Bolton Wanderers*	11	-
1995-96	Manchester City	6	-
1995-96	*Bradford City*	5	-
1996-97	Manchester City	10	-
1997-98	Manchester City	1	-
1997-98	St. Johnstone	28	2
1998-99	St. Johnstone	26	3

KERR, Dylan
Born : Malta 14/01/67

SEASON	CLUB	LEAGUE APPEARANCES	GOALS
1988-89	Leeds United	3	-
1989-90	Leeds United	5	-
1990-91	Leeds United	2	-
1991-92	Leeds United	-	-
1991-92	*Doncaster Rovers*	7	1
1991-92	*Blackpool*	12	1
1992-93	Leeds United	5	-
1993-94	Reading	45	2
1994-95	Reading	36	1
1995-96	Reading	8	2
1996-97	Reading	-	-
1996-97	*Carlisle United*	1	-
1996-97	Kilmarnock	27	-
1997-98	Kilmarnock	20	-
1998-99	Kilmarnock	16	-

KERR, James Stewart Robert
Born : Bellshill 13/11/74

SEASON	CLUB	LEAGUE APPEARANCES	GOALS
1993-94	Celtic	-	-
1994-95	Celtic	-	-
1995-96	Celtic	-	-
1996-97	Celtic	26	-
1997-98	Celtic	-	-
1998-99	Celtic	4	-

KHARINE, Dmitri
Born : Moscow 16/08/68

SEASON	CLUB	LEAGUE APPEARANCES	GOALS
1984	Torpedo Moscow	1	-
1985	Torpedo Moscow	10	-
1986	Torpedo Moscow	25	-
1987	Torpedo Moscow	27	-
1988	Dynamo Moscow	19	-
1989	Dynamo Moscow	20	-
1990	Dynamo Moscow	1	-
1991	CSKA Moscow	11	-
1992	CSKA Moscow	23	-
1992-93	Chelsea	5	-
1993-94	Chelsea	40	-
1994-95	Chelsea	31	-
1995-96	Chelsea	26	-
1996-97	Chelsea	5	-
1997-98	Chelsea	10	-
1998-99	Chelsea	1	-

KIRIAKOV, Ilian
Born : Pavlikeni 04/08/67

SEASON	CLUB	LEAGUE APPEARANCES	GOALS
1991-92	La Coruna	36	3
1992-93	La Coruna	3	-
from Merida			
1994-95	CSKA Sofia	18	-
1994-95	Etur	8	3
1995-96	Anorthosis	19	8
1996-97	Aberdeen	27	1
1997-98	Aberdeen	15	-
1998-99	Aberdeen	22	-

KIRK, Andrew
Born : Belfast 29/05/79

SEASON	CLUB	LEAGUE APPEARANCES	GOALS
1995-96	Glentoran	1	1
1996-97	Glentoran	25	8
1997-98	Glentoran	25	9
1998-99	Heart of Midlothian	5	-

KLOS, Stefan
Born : Dortmund 16/08/71

SEASON	CLUB	LEAGUE APPEARANCES	GOALS
1990-91	Borussia Dortmund	2	-
1991-92	Borussia Dortmund	31	-
1992-93	Borussia Dortmund	34	-
1993-94	Borussia Dortmund	34	-
1994-95	Borussia Dortmund	34	-
1995-96	Borussia Dortmund	33	-
1996-97	Borussia Dortmund	34	-
1997-98	Borussia Dortmund	34	-
1998-99	Rangers	18	-

LAMBERT, Paul
Born : Paisley 07/08/69

SEASON	CLUB	LEAGUE APPEARANCES	GOALS
1985-86	St. Mirren	1	-
1986-87	St. Mirren	36	2
1987-88	St. Mirren	36	2
1988-89	St. Mirren	16	2
1989-90	St. Mirren	25	3
1990-91	St. Mirren	31	2
1991-92	St. Mirren	40	2
1992-93	St. Mirren	39	1
1993-94	St. Mirren	3	-
1993-94	Motherwell	32	3
1994-95	Motherwell	36	1
1995-96	Motherwell	35	2
1996-97	Borussia Dortmund	31	1
1997-98	Borussia Dortmund	13	-
1997-98	Celtic	26	2
1998-99	Celtic	33	1

LANGFIELD, James
Born : Paisley 22/12/79

SEASON	CLUB	LEAGUE APPEARANCES	GOALS
1996-97	Dundee	-	-
1997-98	Dundee	-	-
1998-99	Dundee	2	-

LARSSON, Henrik
Born : Sweden 20/09/71

SEASON	CLUB	LEAGUE APPEARANCES	GOALS
1993-94	Feyenoord	15	1
1994-95	Feyenoord	23	8
1995-96	Feyenoord	32	10
1996-97	Feyenoord	31	7
1997-98	Celtic	35	16
1998-99	Celtic	35	29

LATAPY, Russell Nigel
Born : Trinidad & Tobago 02/08/68

SEASON	CLUB	LEAGUE APPEARANCES	GOALS
1994-95	Porto	14	1
1995-96	Porto	26	5
1996-97	Boavista	21	-
1997-98	Boavista	19	1
1998-99	Hibernian	23	6

LAUCHLAN, James Harley
Born : Glasgow 02/02/77

SEASON	CLUB	LEAGUE APPEARANCES	GOALS
1994-95	Kilmarnock	2	-
1995-96	Kilmarnock	5	-
1996-97	Kilmarnock	9	1
1997-98	Kilmarnock	22	-
1998-99	Kilmarnock	14	-

LAUCHLAN, Martin Thomas
Born : Rutherglen 01/10/80

SEASON	CLUB	LEAGUE APPEARANCES	GOALS
1997-98	Partick Thistle	10	-
1998-99	Partick Thistle	27	5

LAVETY, Barry
Born : Paisley 21/08/74

SEASON	CLUB	LEAGUE APPEARANCES	GOALS
1991-92	St. Mirren	5	2
1992-93	St. Mirren	42	18
1993-94	St. Mirren	42	10
1994-95	St. Mirren	31	7
1995-96	St. Mirren	29	11
1996-97	Hibernian	10	-
1997-98	Hibernian	26	7
1998-99	Hibernian	27	2

LECLERCQ, Fabien Christain Rene
Born : Lille 19/10/72
from Lille Olympic Sporting Club

LEHMANN, Dirk
Born : Aachen 16/08/71

SEASON	CLUB	LEAGUE APPEARANCES	GOALS
1998-99	Fulham	26	2

LEIGHTON, James
Born : Johnstone 24/07/58

SEASON	CLUB	LEAGUE APPEARANCES	GOALS
1978-79	Aberdeen	11	-
1979-80	Aberdeen	1	-
1980-81	Aberdeen	35	-
1981-82	Aberdeen	36	-
1982-83	Aberdeen	35	-
1983-84	Aberdeen	36	-
1984-85	Aberdeen	34	-
1985-86	Aberdeen	26	-
1986-87	Aberdeen	42	-
1987-88	Aberdeen	44	-
1988-89	Manchester United	38	-
1989-90	Manchester United	35	-
1990-91	Manchester United	-	-
1990-91	*Arsenal*	-	-
1991-92	Manchester United	-	-
1991-92	*Reading*	8	-
1991-92	Dundee	13	-
1992-93	Dundee	8	-
1992-93	*Sheffield United*	-	-
1993-94	Hibernian	44	-
1994-95	Hibernian	36	-
1995-96	Hibernian	36	-
1996-97	Hibernian	35	-
1997-98	Aberdeen	34	-
1998-99	Aberdeen	22	-

LILLEY, David William
Born : Bellshill 31/10/77

SEASON	CLUB	LEAGUE APPEARANCES	GOALS
1995-96	Queen of the South	23	-
1996-97	Queen of the South	22	1
1997-98	Queen of the South	2	-
1998-99	Queen of the South	27	-

LOCKE, Gary
Born : Edinburgh 16/06/75

SEASON	CLUB	LEAGUE APPEARANCES	GOALS
1992-93	Heart of Midlothian	1	-
1993-94	Heart of Midlothian	33	-
1994-95	Heart of Midlothian	9	-
1995-96	Heart of Midlothian	29	4
1996-97	Heart of Midlothian	11	-
1997-98	Heart of Midlothian	21	-
1998-99	Heart of Midlothian	25	1

LOVELL, Stuart
Born : Sydney 09/01/72

SEASON	CLUB	LEAGUE APPEARANCES	GOALS
1990-91	Reading	30	2
1991-92	Reading	24	4
1992-93	Reading	22	8
1993-94	Reading	45	20
1994-95	Reading	30	11
1995-96	Reading	35	7
1996-97	Reading	26	5
1997-98	Reading	15	1
1998-99	Hibernian	31	11

LOVERING, Paul James
Born : Glasgow 25/11/75

SEASON	CLUB	LEAGUE APPEARANCES	GOALS
1994-95	Clydebank	3	-
1995-96	Clydebank	21	1
1996-97	Clydebank	26	-
1997-98	Clydebank	32	4
1998-99	Clydebank	12	-
1998-99	Hibernian	17	1

LOWNDES, Nathan
Born : Salford 02/06/77

SEASON	CLUB	LEAGUE APPEARANCES	GOALS
1994-95	Leeds United	-	-
1995-96	Leeds United	-	-
1995-96	Watford	-	-
1996-97	Watford	3	-
1997-98	Watford	4	-
1998-99	St. Johnstone	29	2

MacPHERSON, Angus Ian
Born : Glasgow 11/10/68

SEASON	CLUB	LEAGUE APPEARANCES	GOALS
1988-89	Rangers	-	-
1989-90	Rangers	-	-
1989-90	*Exeter City*	11	1
1990-91	Kilmarnock	11	-
1991-92	Kilmarnock	43	3
1992-93	Kilmarnock	40	5
1993-94	Kilmarnock	43	2
1994-95	Kilmarnock	33	1

SEASON	CLUB	LEAGUE APPEARANCES	GOALS
1995-96	Kilmarnock	35	1
1996-97	Kilmarnock	33	-
1997-98	Kilmarnock	25	-
1998-99	Kilmarnock	31	1

MADDISON, Lee Robert
Born : Bristol 05/10/72

1991-92	Bristol Rovers	10	-
1992-93	Bristol Rovers	12	-
1993-94	Bristol Rovers	37	-
1994-95	Bristol Rovers	14	-
1995-96	Bristol Rovers	-	-
1995-96	Northampton Town	21	-
1996-97	Northampton Town	34	-
1997-98	Dundee	24	1
1998-99	Dundee	21	-

MAHE, Stephane
Born : Puteaux 23/09/68

1988-89	Auxerre	1	-
1989-90	Auxerre	-	-
1990-91	Auxerre	6	-
1991-92	Auxerre	34	1
1992-93	Auxerre	21	-
1993-94	Auxerre	32	2
1994-95	Auxerre	29	-
1995-96	Paris St. Germain	23	-
1996-97	Stade Rennais	33	-
1997-98	Celtic	23	-
1998-99	Celtic	24	-

MAHOOD, Alan Scott
Born : Kilwinning 26/03/73

1990-91	Greenock Morton	8	-
1990-91	Nottingham Forest	-	-
1991-92	Nottingham Forest	-	-
1991-92	Greenock Morton	5	-
1992-93	Greenock Morton	17	6
1993-94	Greenock Morton	12	3
1994-95	Greenock Morton	21	1
1995-96	Greenock Morton	31	4
1996-97	Greenock Morton	27	3
1997-98	Greenock Morton	24	6
1998-99	Kilmarnock	28	2

MAIN, Alan David
Born : Elgin 05/12/67

1986-87	Dundee United	2	-
1987-88	Dundee United	8	-
1988-89	Dundee United	-	-
1988-89	Cowdenbeath	3	-
1988-89	East Stirlingshire	2	-
1989-90	Dundee United	27	-
1990-91	Dundee United	31	-
1991-92	Dundee United	17	-
1992-93	Dundee United	43	-
1993-94	Dundee United	18	-
1994-95	Dundee United	6	-
1994-95	St. Johnstone	17	-
1995-96	St. Johnstone	34	-
1996-97	St. Johnstone	34	-
1997-98	St. Johnstone	34	-
1998-99	St. Johnstone	34	-

MAKEL, Lee Robert
Born : Sunderland 11/01/73

1990-91	Newcastle United	3	-
1991-92	Newcastle United	9	1
1992-93	Blackburn Rovers	1	-
1993-94	Blackburn Rovers	2	-
1994-95	Blackburn Rovers	-	-
1995-96	Blackburn Rovers	3	-
1995-96	Huddersfield Town	33	2
1996-97	Huddersfield Town	19	3
1997-98	Huddersfield Town	13	-
1997-98	Heart of Midlothian	5	-
1998-99	Heart of Midlothian	14	1

MALCOLM, Stuart Ross
Born : Edinburgh 20/08/79

1996-97	St. Johnstone	-	-
1997-98	St. Johnstone	-	-
1998-99	St. Johnstone	-	-
1998-99	Cowdenbeath	4	-

SEASON	CLUB	LEAGUE APPEARANCES	GOALS
MALPAS, Maurice Daniel Robert			
Born : Dunfermline 03/08/62			
1979-80	Dundee United	-	-
1980-81	Dundee United	-	-
1981-82	Dundee United	19	-
1982-83	Dundee United	34	1
1983-84	Dundee United	34	2
1984-85	Dundee United	35	2
1985-86	Dundee United	36	2
1986-87	Dundee United	36	-
1987-88	Dundee United	44	-
1988-89	Dundee United	36	1
1989-90	Dundee United	30	2
1990-91	Dundee United	36	1
1991-92	Dundee United	44	3
1992-93	Dundee United	37	-
1993-94	Dundee United	35	-
1994-95	Dundee United	31	-
1995-96	Dundee United	30	2
1996-97	Dundee United	26	1
1997-98	Dundee United	31	1
1998-99	Dundee United	31	-

MARSHALL, Gordon George Banks
Born : Edinburgh 19/04/64

1980-81	Rangers	-	-
1981-82	Rangers	-	-
1982-83	Rangers	-	-
1982-83	East Stirlingshire	15	-
1982-83	East Fife	10	-
1983-84	East Fife	34	-
1984-85	East Fife	39	-
1985-86	East Fife	39	-
1986-87	East Fife	36	-
1986-87	Falkirk	10	-
1987-88	Falkirk	44	-
1988-89	Falkirk	39	-
1989-90	Falkirk	39	-
1990-91	Falkirk	39	-
1991-92	Celtic	25	-
1992-93	Celtic	11	-
1993-94	Celtic	1	-
1993-94	Stoke City	10	-
1994-95	Celtic	16	-
1995-96	Celtic	36	-
1996-97	Celtic	11	-
1997-98	Celtic	1	-
1997-98	St. Mirren	1	-
1997-98	Kilmarnock	12	-
1998-99	Kilmarnock	36	-

MATHIE, Alexander
Born : Bathgate 20/12/68

1987-88	Celtic	-	-
1988-89	Celtic	1	-
1989-90	Celtic	6	-
1990-91	Celtic	4	-
1991-92	Morton	42	18
1992-93	Morton	32	13
1992-93	Port Vale	3	-
1993-94	Newcastle United	16	3
1994-95	Newcastle United	9	1
1994-95	Ipswich Town	13	2
1995-96	Ipswich Town	39	18
1996-97	Ipswich Town	12	4
1997-98	Ipswich Town	37	13
1998-99	Ipswich Town	8	1
1998-99	Dundee United	22	1

MATTHAEI, Rob
Born : Duiven 20/09/66

1985-86	Haarlem	30	1
1986-87	Haarlem	31	3
1987-88	Haarlem	33	5
1988-89	Haarlem	32	2
1989-90	Haarlem	20	-
1990-91	Haarlem	-	-
1990-91	De Graffschap	12	1
1991-92	De Graffschap	25	-
1992-93	De Graffschap	32	-
1993-94	De Graffschap	29	1
1994-95	De Graffschap	30	1
1995-96	De Graffschap	26	-
1996-97	FC Volendam	22	-
1997-98	FC Volendam	29	-
1998-99	Motherwell	17	-

SEASON	CLUB	LEAGUE APPEARANCES	GOALS
MAYER, Andreas			
Born : Burgau 13/09/72			
1992-93	Bayern Munich	-	-
1993-94	St. Pauli	-	-
1994-95	St. Pauli	-	-
1995-96	St. Pauli	-	-
1995	Stabaek	7	1
1996	Stabaek	24	6
1997	Stabaek	12	1
1997	Rosenborg BK	7	-
1998-99	Aberdeen	13	2

McALLISTER, James Reynolds
Born : Glasgow 26/04/78

1995-96	Queen of the South	2	-
1996-97	Queen of the South	6	-
1997-98	Queen of the South	15	-
1998-99	Queen of the South	27	-

McANESPIE, Kieran Liam
Born : Gosport 11/09/79

1995-96	St. Johnstone	-	-
1996-97	St. Johnstone	9	2
1997-98	St. Johnstone	3	-
1998-99	St. Johnstone	18	2

McBRIDE, John Paul
Born : Hamilton 28/11/78

1995-96	Celtic	-	-
1996-97	Celtic	2	-
1997-98	Celtic	-	-
1998-99	Celtic	1	-
1998-99	St. Johnstone	3	-

McCAFFREY, Stuart Muir
Born : Glasgow 30/05/79

1996-97	Hibernian	-	-
1997-98	Hibernian	2	-
1998-99	Aberdeen	-	-

McCANN, Neil Docherty
Born : Greenock 11/08/74

1991-92	Dundee	-	-
1992-93	Dundee	3	-
1993-94	Dundee	22	1
1994-95	Dundee	32	2
1995-96	Dundee	22	2
1996-97	Heart of Midlothian	30	5
1997-98	Heart of Midlothian	35	10
1998-99	Heart of Midlothian	8	3
1998-99	Rangers	19	5

McCLUSKEY, Stuart Campbell
Born : Bellshill 29/10/77

1994-95	St. Johnstone	2	-
1995-96	St. Johnstone	2	-
1996-97	St. Johnstone	10	1
1997-98	St. Johnstone	18	1
1998-99	St. Johnstone	7	-

McCOIST, Alistair Murdoch
Born : Bellshill 24/09/62

1978-79	St. Johnstone	4	-
1979-80	St. Johnstone	15	-
1980-81	St. Johnstone	38	22
1981-82	Sunderland	28	2
1982-83	Sunderland	28	6
1983-84	Rangers	30	9
1984-85	Rangers	25	12
1985-86	Rangers	33	24
1986-87	Rangers	44	33
1987-88	Rangers	40	31
1988-89	Rangers	19	9
1989-90	Rangers	34	14
1990-91	Rangers	26	11
1991-92	Rangers	38	34
1992-93	Rangers	34	34
1993-94	Rangers	21	7
1994-95	Rangers	9	1
1995-96	Rangers	25	16
1996-97	Rangers	25	10
1997-98	Rangers	15	5
1998-99	Kilmarnock	26	7

McCONALOGUE, Stephen
Born : Glasgow 16/06/81

| 1997-98 | Dundee United | - | - |
| 1998-99 | Dundee United | 1 | - |

SEASON	CLUB	LEAGUE APPEARANCES	GOALS
McCULLOCH, Lee Henry			
Born : Bellshill 14/05/78			
1994-95	Motherwell	-	-
1995-96	Motherwell	1	-
1996-97	Motherwell	15	-
1997-98	Motherwell	25	2
1998-99	Motherwell	26	3
McCULLOCH, Scott Anderson James			
Born : Cumnock 29/11/75			
1992-93	Rangers	-	-
1993-94	Rangers	-	-
1994-95	Rangers	-	-
1994-95	Hamilton Academical	8	1
1995-96	Hamilton Academical	10	1
1996-97	Hamilton Academical	24	1
1997-98	Hamilton Academical	15	1
1997-98	Dunfermline Athletic	18	-
1998-99	Dunfermline Athletic	19	1
1998-99	Dundee United	9	-
McCULLOCH, Stephen George			
Born : Irvine 03/04/81			
1998-99	Dundee United	9	-
McCUTCHEON, Gary Kyle			
Born : Dumfries 08/10/78			
1995-96	Kilmarnock	-	-
1996-97	Kilmarnock	-	-
1997-98	Kilmarnock	1	-
1997-98	*Stenhousemuir*	20	7
1998-99	Kilmarnock	13	2
McGINLAY, Patrick David			
Born : Glasgow 30/05/67			
1985-86	Blackpool	-	-
1986-87	Blackpool	12	1
1987-88	Hibernian	-	-
1988-89	Hibernian	2	-
1989-90	Hibernian	28	3
1990-91	Hibernian	32	1
1991-92	Hibernian	43	9
1992-93	Hibernian	40	10
1993-94	Celtic	41	10
1994-95	Celtic	8	1
1994-95	Hibernian	24	7
1995-96	Hibernian	31	5
1996-97	Hibernian	29	6
1997-98	Hibernian	33	4
1998-99	Hibernian	30	12
McGOWAN, Jamie			
Born : Morecambe 05/12/70			
1992-93	Dundee	21	1
1993-94	Dundee	14	-
1993-94	Falkirk	9	2
1994-95	Falkirk	31	1
1995-96	Falkirk	29	1
1996-97	Falkirk	29	2
1997-98	Falkirk	33	2
1998-99	Motherwell	32	1
McGOWNE, Kevin			
Born : Kilmarnock 16/12/69			
1988-89	St. Mirren	-	-
1989-90	St. Mirren	2	-
1990-91	St. Mirren	10	-
1991-92	St. Mirren	36	-
1992-93	St. Johnstone	26	-
1993-94	St. Johnstone	41	-
1994-95	St. Johnstone	30	1
1995-96	St. Johnstone	23	2
1996-97	St. Johnstone	2	-
1996-97	Kilmarnock	31	-
1997-98	Kilmarnock	26	-
1998-99	Kilmarnock	32	4
McINNES, Derek John			
Born : Paisley 05/07/71			
1987-88	Greenock Morton	2	-
1988-89	Greenock Morton	29	1
1989-90	Greenock Morton	23	1
1990-91	Greenock Morton	31	3
1991-92	Greenock Morton	42	7
1992-93	Greenock Morton	40	2
1993-94	Greenock Morton	16	1
1994-95	Greenock Morton	26	3
1995-96	Greenock Morton	12	1
1995-96	Rangers	6	-

SEASON	CLUB	LEAGUE APPEARANCES	GOALS
1996-97	Rangers	21	1
1997-98	Rangers	-	-
1998-99	Rangers	7	-
1998-99	*Stockport County*	13	-
McKENZIE, Roderick			
Born : Bellshill 08/08/75			
1993-94	Heart of Midlothian	-	-
1994-95	Heart of Midlothian	-	-
1995-96	Stenhousemuir	36	-
1996-97	Heart of Midlothian	3	-
1997-98	Heart of Midlothian	4	-
1998-99	Heart of Midlothian	10	-
McKINLAY, Thomas Valley			
Born : Glasgow 03/12/64			
1981-82	Dundee	-	-
1982-83	Dundee	1	-
1983-84	Dundee	36	3
1984-85	Dundee	34	3
1985-86	Dundee	22	-
1986-87	Dundee	32	2
1987-88	Dundee	19	-
1988-89	Dundee	18	-
1988-89	Heart of Midlothian	17	1
1989-90	Heart of Midlothian	29	1
1990-91	Heart of Midlothian	33	2
1991-92	Heart of Midlothian	39	2
1992-93	Heart of Midlothian	34	-
1993-94	Heart of Midlothian	43	-
1994-95	Heart of Midlothian	11	-
1994-95	Celtic	17	-
1995-96	Celtic	32	-
1996-97	Celtic	27	-
1997-98	Celtic	5	-
1997-98	*Stoke City*	3	-
1998-99	Celtic	18	-
McKINNON, Robert			
Born : Glasgow 31/07/66			
1984-85	Newcastle United	-	-
1985-86	Newcastle United	1	-
1986-87	Hartlepool United	45	-
1987-88	Hartlepool United	42	2
1988-89	Hartlepool United	46	2
1989-90	Hartlepool United	46	1
1990-91	Hartlepool United	45	1
1990-91	*Manchester United*	-	-
1991-92	Hartlepool United	23	1
1991-92	Motherwell	16	1
1992-93	Motherwell	35	-
1993-94	Motherwell	42	4
1994-95	Motherwell	32	3
1995-96	Motherwell	27	-
1996-97	FC Twente	24	-
1997-98	FC Twente	26	1
1998-99	Heart of Midlothian	16	-
1998-99	*Hartlepool United*	7	-
McKNIGHT, Paul			
Born : Belfast 08/02/77			
1993-94	Rangers	-	-
1994-95	Rangers	1	-
1995-96	Rangers	-	-
1996-97	Rangers	-	-
1997-98	Rangers	-	-
1998-99	Rangers	-	-
McMAHON, Gerard Joseph			
Born : Belfast 29/12/73			
1992-93	Tottenham Hotspur	-	-
1993-94	Tottenham Hotspur	-	-
1994-95	Tottenham Hotspur	2	-
1994-95	*Barnet*	10	2
1995-96	Tottenham Hotspur	14	-
1996-97	Tottenham Hotspur	-	-
1996-97	Stoke City	35	3
1997-98	Stoke City	17	-
1997-98	St. Johnstone	10	-
1998-99	St. Johnstone	19	1
McMillan, Stephen			
Born : Edinburgh 19/01/76			
1993-94	Motherwell	1	-
1994-95	Motherwell	3	-
1995-96	Motherwell	12	-
1996-97	Motherwell	16	-
1997-98	Motherwell	34	1
1998-99	Motherwell	30	2

SEASON	CLUB	LEAGUE APPEARANCES	GOALS
McNALLY, Mark			
Born : Motherwell 10/03/71			
1987-88	Celtic	-	-
1988-89	Celtic	-	-
1989-90	Celtic	-	-
1990-91	Celtic	19	-
1991-92	Celtic	25	1
1992-93	Celtic	27	-
1993-94	Celtic	32	2
1994-95	Celtic	20	-
1995-96	Southend United	20	2
1996-97	Southend United	34	-
1996-97	Stoke City	3	-
1997-98	Stoke City	4	-
1998-99	Dundee United	5	-
McNAMARA, Jackie			
Born : Glasgow 24/10/73			
1991-92	Dunfermline Athletic	-	-
1992-93	Dunfermline Athletic	3	-
1993-94	Dunfermline Athletic	39	-
1994-95	Dunfermline Athletic	30	2
1995-96	Dunfermline Athletic	7	1
1995-96	Celtic	26	1
1996-97	Celtic	30	1
1997-98	Celtic	31	2
1998-99	Celtic	16	-
McQUILLAN, John			
Born : Stranraer 20/07/70			
1985-86	Stranraer	-	-
1986-87	Stranraer	-	-
1987-88	Dundee	-	-
1988-89	Dundee	-	-
1989-90	Dundee	2	-
1990-91	Dundee	14	1
1991-92	Dundee	40	3
1992-93	Dundee	29	-
1993-94	Dundee	34	-
1994-95	Dundee	32	-
1995-96	St. Johnstone	25	2
1996-97	St. Johnstone	32	-
1997-98	St. Johnstone	34	1
1998-99	St. Johnstone	28	1
McSKIMMING, Shaun Peter			
Born : Stranraer 29/05/70			
1986-87	Stranraer	-	-
1987-88	Dundee	-	-
1988-89	Dundee	-	-
1989-90	Dundee	7	-
1990-91	Dundee	16	3
1991-92	Kilmarnock	30	1
1992-93	Kilmarnock	35	5
1993-94	Kilmarnock	40	3
1994-95	Kilmarnock	8	-
1994-95	Motherwell	14	2
1995-96	Motherwell	15	1
1996-97	Motherwell	23	4
1997-98	Motherwell	12	-
1998-99	Dundee	29	2

Shaun McSkimming

SEASON	CLUB	LEAGUE APPEARANCES	GOALS
McSWEGAN, Gary			
Born : Glasgow 24/09/70			
1986-87	Rangers	-	-
1987-88	Rangers	1	-
1988-89	Rangers	1	-
1989-90	Rangers	-	-
1990-91	Rangers	3	-
1991-92	Rangers	4	-
1992-93	Rangers	9	4
1993-94	Notts County	37	15
1994-95	Notts County	22	6
1995-96	Notts County	3	-
1995-96	Dundee United	25	17
1996-97	Dundee United	31	7
1997-98	Dundee United	31	5
1998-99	Dundee United	5	3
1998-99	Heart of Midlothian	21	7
MELDRUM, Colin George			
Born : Kilmarnock 26/11/75			
1993-94	Kilmarnock	-	-
1994-95	Kilmarnock	4	-
1995-96	Kilmarnock	1	-
1996-97	Kilmarnock	6	-
1997-98	Kilmarnock	11	-
1998-99	Kilmarnock	-	-
1998-99	*Stranraer*	7	-
1998-99	*Ross County*	2	-
MILLER, Charles			
Born : Glasgow 18/03/76			
1992-93	Rangers	-	-
1993-94	Rangers	3	-
1994-95	Rangers	21	3
1995-96	Rangers	23	3
1996-97	Rangers	13	1
1997-98	Rangers	7	-
1998-99	Rangers	16	3
1998-99	*Leicester City*	4	-
MILLER, Kenneth			
Born : Edinburgh 23/12/79			
1996-97	Hibernian	-	-
1997-98	Hibernian	-	-
1998-99	Hibernian	7	1
1998-99	*Stenhousemuir*	11	8
MILLER, William Nisbit			
Born : Edinburgh 01/11/69			
1989-90	Hibernian	11	-
1990-91	Hibernian	25	1
1991-92	Hibernian	30	-
1992-93	Hibernian	34	-
1993-94	Hibernian	37	-
1994-95	Hibernian	34	-
1995-96	Hibernian	13	-
1996-97	Hibernian	31	-
1997-98	Hibernian	31	-
1998-99	Dundee	26	-
MILNE, Kenneth			
Born : Stirling 26/08/79			
1997-98	Heart of Mildothian	-	-
1998-99	Heart of Midlothian	-	-
1998-99	*Cowdenbeath*	23	6
MILNE, Steven			
Born : Dundee 05/05/80			
1997-98	Dundee	2	-
1998-99	Dundee	-	-
MITCHELL, Alistair Robert			
Born : Kirkcaldy 03/12/68			
1988-89	East Fife	18	4
1989-90	East Fife	35	12
1990-91	East Fife	34	7
1991-92	Kilmarnock	42	10
1992-93	Kilmarnock	32	6
1993-94	Kilmarnock	34	5
1994-95	Kilmarnock	35	4
1995-96	Kilmarnock	30	3
1996-97	Kilmarnock	30	2
1997-98	Kilmarnock	33	4
1998-99	Kilmarnock	32	4

SEASON	CLUB	LEAGUE APPEARANCES	GOALS
MJALLBY, Johan			
Born : Sweden 09/02/71			
1989	AIK Stockholm	1	-
1990	AIK Stockholm	14	-
1991	AIK Stockholm	26	-
1992	AIK Stockholm	-	-
1993	AIK Stockholm	7	-
1994	AIK Stockholm	23	-
1995	AIK Stockholm	19	-
1996	AIK Stockholm	23	5
1997	AIK Stockholm	7	1
1998-99	Celtic	17	1
MOLS, Michael			
Born : Amsterdam 17/12/70			
from FC Utrecht			
MOORE, Craig Andrew			
Born : Canterbury, Australia 12/12/75			
1993-94	Rangers	1	-
1994-95	Rangers	21	2
1995-96	Rangers	11	1
1996-97	Rangers	23	1
1997-98	Rangers	10	-
1998-99	Rangers	7	-
1998-99	Crystal Palace	23	3
1998-99	Rangers	1	1
MORAVCIK, Lubomir			
Born : Slovakia 22/06/65			
1990-91	St. Etienne	37	7
1991-92	St. Etienne	32	4
1992-93	St. Etienne	34	5
1993-94	St. Etienne	33	4
1994-95	St. Etienne	27	4
1995-96	St. Etienne	34	7
1996-97	Bastia	21	6
1997-98	Bastia	12	2
1998-99	Celtic	14	6
MURRAY, Grant Robert			
Born : Edinburgh 29/08/75			
1992-93	Heart of Midlothian	-	-
1993-94	Heart of Midlothian	-	-
1994-95	Heart of Midlothian	-	-
1995-96	Heart of Midlothian	-	-
1996-97	Heart of Midlothian	4	-
1997-98	Heart of Midlothian	10	-
1998-99	Heart of Midlothian	21	-
NAYSMITH, Gary Andrew			
Born : Edinburgh 16/11/78			
1995-96	Heart of Midlothian	1	-
1996-97	Heart of Midlothian	10	-
1997-98	Heart of Midlothian	16	2
1998-99	Heart of Midlothian	26	-
NEGRI, Marco			
Born : Milan 27/10/70			
1988-89	Udinese	3	-
1989-90	Novara	27	-
1990-91	Udinese	5	-
1991-92	Udinese	-	-
1991-92	Ternana	23	1
1992-93	Ternana	9	1
1992-93	Cosenza	25	4
1993-94	Cosenza	-	-
1993-94	Bologna	24	8
1994-95	Cosenza	34	19
1995-96	Perugia AC Spa	33	18
1996-97	Perugia AC Spa	27	15
1997-98	Rangers	29	32
1998-99	Rangers	-	-
NEVIN, Patrick			
Born : Glasgow 06/09/63			
1981-82	Clyde	34	12
1982-83	Clyde	39	5
1983-84	Chelsea	38	14
1984-85	Chelsea	41	4
1985-86	Chelsea	40	7
1986-87	Chelsea	37	5
1987-88	Chelsea	37	6
1988-89	Everton	25	2
1989-90	Everton	30	4
1990-91	Everton	37	8
1991-92	Everton	17	2
1991-92	*Tranmere Rovers*	8	-
1992-93	Tranmere Rovers	43	13

SEASON	CLUB	LEAGUE APPEARANCES	GOALS
1993-94	Tranmere Rovers	45	8
1994-95	Tranmere Rovers	44	4
1995-96	Tranmere Rovers	40	3
1996-97	Tranmere Rovers	21	2
1997-98	Kilmarnock	31	5
1998-99	Kilmarnock	3	1
1998-99	Motherwell	30	-
NICHOLAS, Steven Arthur			
Born : Stirling 08/07/81			
1997-98	Stirling Albion	7	-
1998-99	Stirling Albion	27	5
1998-99	Motherwell	7	1
NICHOLSON, Barry			
Born : Dumfries 24/08/78			
1995-96	Rangers	-	-
1996-97	Rangers	-	-
1997-98	Rangers	-	-
1998-99	Rangers	6	-
NIEMI, Antti			
Born : Oulu 31/05/72			
1991	HJK Helsinki	2	-
1992	HJK Helsinki	27	-
1993	HJK Helsinki	24	-
1994	HJK Helsinki	24	-
1995	HJK Helsinki	24	-
1995-96	FC Copenhagen A/S	17	-
1996-97	FC Copenhagen A/S	30	-
1997-98	Rangers	5	-
1998-99	Rangers	7	-
NUMAN, Arthur			
Born : Heemskerk 14/12/69			
1987-88	Haarlem	7	1
1988-89	Haarlem	32	-
1989-90	Haarlem	32	2
1990-91	Haarlem	20	2
1990-91	FC Twente	20	4
1991-92	FC Twente	29	3
1992-93	PSV Eindhoven	24	5
1993-94	PSV Eindhoven	34	10
1994-95	PSV Eindhoven	32	6
1995-96	PSV Eindhoven	27	2
1996-97	PSV Eindhoven	31	2
1997-98	PSV Eindhoven	31	2
1998-99	Rangers	10	-
O'BOYLE, George			
Born : Belfast 14/12/67			
1989-90	Dunfermline Athletic	28	3
1990-91	Dunfermline Athletic	16	6
1991-92	Dunfermline Athletic	16	1
1992-93	Dunfermline Athletic	3	2
1993-94	Dunfermline Athletic	32	17
1994-95	St. Johnstone	32	19
1995-96	St. Johnstone	35	21
1996-97	St. Johnstone	25	12
1997-98	St. Johnstone	33	10
1998-99	St. Johnstone	13	2
O'HALLORAN, Keith James			
Born : Dublin 27/03/77			
1994-95	Middlesbrough	1	-
1995-96	Middlesbrough	3	-
1995-96	*Scunthorpe United*	7	-
1996-97	Middlesbrough	-	-
1996-97	*Cardiff City*	8	-
1996-97	St. Johnstone	5	-
1997-98	St. Johnstone	22	1
1998-99	St. Johnstone	16	1
O'NEIL, John Thomas			
Born : Bellshill 06/07/71			
1988-89	Dundee United	1	-
1989-90	Dundee United	10	-
1990-91	Dundee United	15	-
1991-92	Dundee United	12	-
1992-93	Dundee United	28	3
1993-94	Dundee United	12	1
1994-95	St. Johnstone	27	3
1995-96	St. Johnstone	34	6
1996-97	St. Johnstone	29	3
1997-98	St. Johnstone	30	5
1998-99	St. Johnstone	33	2
O'NEILL, Kris			
Born : Edinburgh 29/09/80			
1998-99	Heart of Midlothian	3	-

SEASON	CLUB	LEAGUE APPEARANCES	GOALS

PAATELAINEN, Mika-Matti Petteri
Born : Helsinki 03/02/67
from Valkeokosken Haka

SEASON	CLUB	LEAGUE APPEARANCES	GOALS
1987-88	Dundee United	19	9
1988-89	Dundee United	33	10
1989-90	Dundee United	31	7
1990-91	Dundee United	20	1
1991-92	Dundee United	30	6
1991-92	Aberdeen	6	1
1992-93	Aberdeen	33	16
1993-94	Aberdeen	36	6
1994-95	Bolton Wanderers	44	12
1995-96	Bolton Wanderers	15	1
1996-97	Bolton Wanderers	10	2
1997-98	Wolverhampton Wanderers	23	-
1998-99	Wolverhampton Wanderers	-	-
1998-99	Hibernian	26	12

PARKER, Keigan
Born : Livingston 08/06/82

| 1998-99 | St. Johnstone | 2 | - |

PARTRIDGE, David William
Born : London 26/11/78

1997-98	West Ham United	-	-
1998-99	West Ham United	-	-
1998-99	Dundee United	1	-

PASCUAL, Bernard
Born : Aubervilliers 10/04/67

1993-94	Le Havre	32	-
1994-95	Le Havre	26	-
1995-96	Le Havre	36	-
1996-97	Le Havre	15	-
1997-98	Le Havre	6	-
1998-99	Dundee United	16	-

PATERSON, James Lee
Born : Bellshill 25/09/79

1996-97	Dundee United	-	-
1997-98	Dundee United	-	-
1998-99	Dundee United	15	-

PATTERSON, Darren James
Born : Belfast 15/10/69

1988-89	West Bromwich Albion	-	-
1989-90	Wigan Athletic	29	1
1990-91	Wigan Athletic	28	4
1991-92	Wigan Athletic	40	1
1992-93	Crystal Palace	-	-
1993-94	Crystal Palace	-	-
1994-95	Crystal Palace	22	1
1995-96	Luton Town	23	-
1996-97	Luton Town	10	-
1996-97	Preston North End	2	-
1997-98	Luton Town	23	-
1998-99	Dundee United	19	-

PEPPER, Colin Nigel
Born : Rotherham 25/04/68

1985-86	Rotherham United	7	-
1986-87	Rotherham United	2	-
1987-88	Rotherham United	15	-
1988-89	Rotherham United	2	-
1989-90	Rotherham United	19	1
1990-91	York City	39	3
1991-92	York City	35	4
1992-93	York City	34	8
1993-94	York City	23	-
1994-95	York City	35	4
1995-96	York City	40	8
1996-97	York City	29	12
1996-97	Bradford City	11	5
1997-98	Bradford City	32	5
1998-99	Bradford City	9	1
1998-99	Aberdeen	10	-

PEREZ, Juanjo Carricondo
Born : Barcelona 04/05/77

| 1997-98 | Barcelona B | 36 | 4 |
| 1998-99 | Heart of Midlothian | 11 | - |

PERRY, Mark George
Born : Aberdeen 07/02/71

1988-89	Dundee United	-	-
1989-90	Dundee United	-	-
1990-91	Dundee United	-	-
1991-92	Dundee United	-	-
1992-93	Dundee United	18	1

SEASON	CLUB	LEAGUE APPEARANCES	GOALS
1993-94	Dundee United	9	-
1994-95	Dundee United	9	-
1995-96	Dundee United	20	2
1996-97	Dundee United	35	-
1997-98	Dundee United	32	1
1998-99	Aberdeen	32	4

PETROV, Stilian
Born : Bulgaria 05/07/79
from CSKA Sofia

PETTA, Bobby Alfred Manuel
Born : Rotterdam 06/08/74

1996-97	Ipswich Town	6	-
1997-98	Ipswich Town	32	7
1998-99	Ipswich Town	32	2

PORRINI, Sergio
Born : Milan 08/11/68

1988-89	AC Milan	-	-
1989-90	Atalanta	8	1
1990-91	Atalanta	29	-
1991-92	Atalanta	30	-
1992-93	Atalanta	33	2
1993-94	Juventus	30	-
1994-95	Juventus	19	-
1995-96	Juventus	15	-
1996-97	Juventus	23	1
1997-98	Rangers	26	4
1998-99	Rangers	35	2

PREECE, David Douglas
Born : Darlington 26/08/76

1994-95	Sunderland	-	-
1995-96	Sunderland	-	-
1996-97	Sunderland	-	-
1997-98	Darlington	45	-
1998-99	Darlington	46	-

PRESSLEY, Steven John
Born : Elgin 11/10/73

1990-91	Rangers	-	-
1991-92	Rangers	1	-
1992-93	Rangers	8	-
1993-94	Rangers	23	1
1994-95	Rangers	2	1
1994-95	Coventry City	19	1
1995-96	Dundee United	35	2
1996-97	Dundee United	36	2
1997-98	Dundee United	29	2
1998-99	Heart of Midlothian	30	1

PRESTON, Allan
Born : Edinburgh 16/08/69

1985-86	Dundee United	-	-
1986-87	Dundee United	-	-
1987-88	Dundee United	2	-
1988-89	Dundee United	9	1
1989-90	Dundee United	8	-
1990-91	Dundee United	3	-
1991-92	Dundee United	2	-
1992-93	Dundee United	-	-
1992-93	Heart of Midlothian	21	2
1993-94	Dunfermline Athletic	26	5
1993-94	St. Johnstone	9	-
1994-95	St. Johnstone	26	2
1995-96	St. Johnstone	27	2
1996-97	St. Johnstone	32	1
1997-98	St. Johnstone	35	1
1998-99	St. Johnstone	15	1

PRODAN, Daniel
Born : Satu Mare 23/03/72
from Atletico De Madrid

| 1998-99 | Rangers | - | - |

QUITONGO, Jose Manuel
Born : Luanda 18/11/74

1995-96	Darlington	1	-
1995-96	Hamilton Academical	22	4
1996-97	Hamilton Academical	34	3
1997-98	Hamilton Academical	6	2
1997-98	Heart of Midlothian	17	3
1998-99	Heart of Midlothian	12	-

RAE, Gavin
Born : Aberdeen 28/11/77

| 1995-96 | Dundee | 6 | - |
| 1996-97 | Dundee | 17 | 2 |

SEASON	CLUB	LEAGUE APPEARANCES	GOALS
1997-98	Dundee	6	-
1998-99	Dundee	30	1

RAESIDE, Robert
Born : South Africa 07/07/72

1990-91	Raith Rovers	14	-
1991-92	Raith Rovers	13	-
1992-93	Raith Rovers	10	-
1993-94	Raith Rovers	-	-
1994-95	Raith Rovers	10	-
1995-96	Raith Rovers	8	1
1996-97	Dundee	34	4
1997-98	Dundee	11	-
1998-99	Dundee	21	-

RAMSAY, Douglas
Born : Irvine 26/04/79

| 1997-98 | Motherwell | - | - |
| 1998-99 | Motherwell | 4 | 1 |

REILLY, Mark Francis
Born : Bellshill 30/03/69

1988-89	Motherwell	-	-
1989-90	Motherwell	4	-
1990-91	Motherwell	-	-
1991-92	Kilmarnock	19	-
1992-93	Kilmarnock	19	3
1993-94	Kilmarnock	38	-
1994-95	Kilmarnock	32	-
1995-96	Kilmarnock	28	-
1996-97	Kilmarnock	33	2
1997-98	Kilmarnock	36	3
1998-99	Reading	6	-
1998-99	Kilmarnock	18	-

RENWICK, Michael
Born : Edinburgh 29/02/76

1992-93	Hibernian	-	-
1993-94	Hibernian	-	-
1994-95	Hibernian	1	-
1995-96	Hibernian	2	-
1996-97	Hibernian	9	-
1997-98	Hibernian	6	-
1998-99	Hibernian	16	-

REYNA, Claudio
Born : Livingston, New Jersey 20/07/73

1996-97	Bayer Leverkusen	5	-
1997-98	Wolfsburg	28	4
1998-99	Wolfsburg	20	2
1998-99	Rangers	6	-

RIEPER, Marc Jensen
Born : Copenhagen 05/06/68

1992-93	Brondby	32	2
1993-94	Brondby	31	-
1994-95	Brondby	18	1
1994-95	West Ham United	21	1
1995-96	West Ham United	36	2
1996-97	West Ham United	28	1
1997-98	West Ham United	5	1
1997-98	Celtic	30	2
1998-99	Celtic	7	-

RISETH, Vidar
Born : Levanger 21/04/72

1992	Rosenborg BK	1	-
1993	Rosenborg BK	10	2
1994	Kongsvinger	18	3
1995	Kongsvinger	24	12
1996	Kongsvinger	14	5
1996-97	LASK Linz	33	7
1997-98	LASK Linz	29	4
1998-99	Celtic	27	3

RITCHIE, Paul Simon
Born : Kirkcaldy 21/08/75

1992-93	Heart of Midlothian	-	-
1993-94	Heart of Midlothian	-	-
1994-95	Heart of Midlothian	-	-
1995-96	Heart of Midlothian	28	1
1996-97	Heart of Midlothian	28	3
1997-98	Heart of Midlothian	34	-
1998-99	Heart of Midlothian	29	1

SEASON	CLUB	LEAGUE APPEARANCES	GOALS
ROBERTS, Mark Kingsley			
Born : Irvine 29/10/75			
1991-92	Kilmarnock	1	-
1992-93	Kilmarnock	5	-
1993-94	Kilmarnock	13	2
1994-95	Kilmarnock	4	1
1995-96	Kilmarnock	11	-
1996-97	Kilmarnock	11	2
1997-98	Kilmarnock	32	7
1998-99	Kilmarnock	22	3
ROBERTSON, Hugh Scott			
Born : Aberdeen 19/03/75			
1993-94	Aberdeen	8	-
1994-95	Aberdeen	3	2
1995-96	Aberdeen	11	-
1996-97	Aberdeen	-	-
1996-97	Dundee	15	1
1997-98	Dundee	-	-
1997-98	*Brechin City*	7	-
1998-99	Dundee	10	-
1998-99	*Inverness Caledonian Thistle*	12	1
ROBERTSON, Stephen			
Born : Glasgow 16/03/77			
1993-94	St. Johnstone	-	-
1994-95	St. Johnstone	-	-
1995-96	St. Johnstone	2	-
1996-97	St. Johnstone	2	-
1997-98	St. Johnstone	2	-
1998-99	St. Johnstone	-	-
1998-99	*Hamilton Academical*	6	-
ROUSSET, Gilles			
Born : Hyeres 22/08/63			
from Rennes			
1995-96	Heart of Midlothian	25	-
1996-97	Heart of Midlothian	33	-
1997-98	Heart of Midlothian	32	-
1998-99	Heart of Midlothian	26	-
ROWSON, David Andrew			
Born : Aberdeen 14/09/76			
1994-95	Aberdeen	-	-
1995-96	Aberdeen	9	-
1996-97	Aberdeen	34	2
1997-98	Aberdeen	30	5
1998-99	Aberdeen	22	-
SALVATORI, Stefano			
Born : Rome 29/12/67			
1986-87	AC Milan	-	-
1987-88	Virescit	32	-
1988-89	Parma	7	-
1988-89	Fiorentina AC Spa	23	1
1989-90	AC Milan	10	-
1990-91	AC Milan	-	-
1990-91	Fiorentina AC Spa	18	1
1991-92	Fiorentina AC Spa	27	-
1992-93	Fiorentina AC Spa	-	-
1992-93	Spal	22	-
1993-94	Spal	8	-
1994-95	Atalanta	23	-
1995-96	Atalanta	22	-
1996-97	Heart of Midlothian	14	-
1997-98	Heart of Midlothian	32	1
1998-99	Heart of Midlothian	12	-
SAUZEE, Franck Gaston Henri			
Born : Aubenas 28/10/65			
1983-84	Sochaux	19	1
1984-85	Sochaux	37	8
1985-86	Sochaux	27	7
1986-87	Sochaux	37	8
1987-88	Sochaux	30	16
1988-89	Marseille	32	4
1989-90	Marseille	36	5
1990-91	Monaco	28	7
1991-92	Marseille	22	2
1992-93	Marseille	35	12
1993-94	Atalanta	16	1
1994-95	Strasbourg	30	5
1995-96	Strasbourg	27	4
1996-97	Montpellier	27	7
1997-98	Montpellier	12	-
1998-99	Hibernian	9	2

SEASON	CLUB	LEAGUE APPEARANCES	GOALS
SEVERIN, Scott Derek			
Born : Stirling 15/02/79			
1996-97	Heart of Midlothian	-	-
1997-98	Heart of Midlothian	-	-
1998-99	Heart of Midlothian	7	-
SHARP, Lee			
Born : Glasgow 22/05/75			
1995-96	Dumbarton	15	1
1996-97	Dumbarton	35	5
1997-98	Dumbarton	34	7
1998-99	Dumbarton	17	2
1998-99	Dundee	6	1
SIMAO, Miguel Angelo Da Cruz			
Born : Oporto 26/02/73			
from Clube Desportivo Das Aves			
1998-99	St. Johnstone	26	4
SKOLDMARK, Magnus			
Born : Langsele 22/09/68			
from Dalian Wanda			
1997-98	Dundee United	19	-
1998-99	Dundee United	25	-
SMITH, Barry Martin			
Born : Paisley 19/02/74			
1991-92	Celtic	3	-
1992-93	Celtic	6	-
1993-94	Celtic	7	-
1994-95	Celtic	3	-
1995-96	Celtic	-	-
1995-96	Dundee	20	-
1996-97	Dundee	36	-
1997-98	Dundee	34	1
1998-99	Dundee	33	-
SMITH, Gary			
Born : Glasgow 25/03/71			
1988-89	Falkirk	3	-
1989-90	Falkirk	36	-
1990-91	Falkirk	31	-
1991-92	Aberdeen	16	1
1992-93	Aberdeen	40	-
1993-94	Aberdeen	21	-
1994-95	Aberdeen	31	-
1995-96	Aberdeen	33	-
1996-97	Stade Rennais	14	-
1997-98	Aberdeen	31	1
1998-99	Aberdeen	30	-
SMITH, James Anthony			
Born : Bellshill 28/10/73			
1990-91	Heart of Midlothian	-	-
1991-92	Heart of Midlothian	-	-
1992-93	Heart of Midlothian	-	-
1993-94	Airdrieonians	6	1
1994-95	Airdrieonians	27	2
1995-96	Airdrieonians	31	3
1996-97	Airdrieonians	28	2
1997-98	Airdrieonians	30	1
1998-99	Airdrieonians	25	-
SMITH, Thomas William			
Born : Glasgow 12/10/73			
1990-91	Partick Thistle	1	-
1991-92	Partick Thistle	-	-
1992-93	Partick Thistle	2	-
1992-93	Cork City	1	-
1993-94	Partick Thistle	8	1
1994-95	Partick Thistle	14	1
1994-95	Portadown	4	-
1995-96	Partick Thistle	25	2
1996-97	Partick Thistle	1	-
1996-97	Ayr United	21	4
1997-98	Ayr United	18	1
1998-99	Clydebank	21	3
1998-99	Hibernian	5	-
SOLBERG, Thomas			
Born : Oslo 25/01/70			
from Viking Stavanger			
SPENCER, John			
Born : Glasgow 11/09/70			
1986-87	Rangers	-	-
1987-88	Rangers	-	-
1988-89	Rangers	-	-
1988-89	*Morton*	4	1
from Lai Sun			
1990-91	Rangers	5	1
1991-92	Rangers	8	1

SEASON	CLUB	LEAGUE APPEARANCES	GOALS
1992-93	Chelsea	23	7
1993-94	Chelsea	19	5
1994-95	Chelsea	29	11
1995-96	Chelsea	28	13
1996-97	Chelsea	4	-
1996-97	Queens Park Rangers	25	17
1997-98	Queens Park Rangers	23	5
1997-98	Everton	6	-
1998-99	Everton	3	-
1998-99	Motherwell	21	7
STENSAAS, Stale			
Born : Trondheim 07/07/71			
1992	Rosenborg BK	1	-
1993	Rosenborg BK	6	-
1994	Rosenborg BK	20	-
1995	Rosenborg BK	24	1
1996	Rosenborg BK	25	1
1997	Rosenborg BK	9	-
1997-98	Rangers	20	1
1998-99	Rangers	1	-
1998-99	*Nottingham Forest*	7	-
STUBBS, Alan			
Born : Kirkby 06/10/71			
1990-91	Bolton Wanderers	23	-
1991-92	Bolton Wanderers	32	1
1992-93	Bolton Wanderers	42	2
1993-94	Bolton Wanderers	41	1
1994-95	Bolton Wanderers	39	1
1995-96	Bolton Wanderers	25	4
1996-97	Celtic	20	-
1997-98	Celtic	29	1
1998-99	Celtic	23	1
TEALE, Shaun			
Born : Southport 10/03/64			
1988-89	Bournemouth	20	-
1989-90	Bournemouth	34	-
1990-91	Bournemouth	46	4
1991-92	Aston Villa	42	-
1992-93	Aston Villa	39	1
1993-94	Aston Villa	38	1
1994-95	Aston Villa	28	-
1995-96	Tranmere Rovers	29	-
1996-97	Tranmere Rovers	25	-
1996-97	*Preston North End*	5	-
from Happy Valley			
1998-99	Motherwell	29	1
TEBILY, Olivier			
Born : Abidjan 19/12/75			
1998-99	Sheffield United	8	-
TELESNIKOV, Jan			
Born : Torinsk 11/12/72			
from Beiter Jerusalem			
THOMAS, Kevin Roderick			
Born : Edinburgh 25/04/75			
1992-93	Heart of Midlothian	4	2
1993-94	Heart of Midlothian	12	-
1994-95	Heart of Midlothian	18	5
1995-96	Heart of Midlothian	3	-
1996-97	Heart of Midlothian	13	-
1997-98	Heart of Midlothian	1	-
1997-98	*Stirling Albion*	6	-
1998-99	Heart of Midlothian	-	-
1998-99	Greenock Morton	22	9
THOMAS, Tony			
Born : Liverpool 12/07/71			
1988-89	Tranmere Rovers	9	2
1989-90	Tranmere Rovers	42	2
1990-91	Tranmere Rovers	33	3
1991-92	Tranmere Rovers	30	3
1992-93	Tranmere Rovers	16	-
1993-94	Tranmere Rovers	40	2
1994-95	Tranmere Rovers	26	-
1995-96	Tranmere Rovers	31	-
1996-97	Tranmere Rovers	30	-
1997-98	Everton	7	-
1998-99	Everton	1	-
1998-99	Motherwell	10	-
THOMPSON, Steven			
Born : Paisley 14/10/78			
1996-97	Dundee United	1	-
1997-98	Dundee United	8	-
1998-99	Dundee United	15	1
TOWNSLEY, Derek			
Born : Carlisle 21/03/73			
1996-97	Queen of the South	31	2

SEASON	CLUB	LEAGUE APPEARANCES	GOALS
1997-98	Queen of the South	29	7
1998-99	Queen of the South	27	10

TWADDLE, Kevin
Born : Edinburgh 31/10/71

1994-95	St. Johnstone	25	6
1995-96	St. Johnstone	26	4
1996-97	Raith Rovers	28	4
1997-98	Raith Rovers	10	-
1997-98	Morton	14	2
1998-99	Morton	31	5

TWEED, Steven
Born : Edinburgh 08/08/72

1991-92	Hibernian	1	-
1992-93	Hibernian	14	-
1993-94	Hibernian	29	3
1994-95	Hibernian	33	-
1995-96	Hibernian	31	-
1996-97	Ionikos	2	-
1997-98	Stoke City	38	-
1998-99	Stoke City	1	-
1998-99	Dundee	10	1

VALAKARI, Simo Johannes
Born : Helsinki 28/04/73

1995	Finn PA	22	3
1996	Finn PA	26	2
1996-97	Motherwell	11	-
1997-98	Motherwell	28	-
1998-99	Motherwell	35	-

VAN BRONCKHORST, Giovanni
Born : Rotterdam 05/02/75

1993-94	FC Feyenoord	-	-
1993-94	RKC	12	2
1994-95	FC Feyenoord	10	1
1995-96	FC Feyenoord	27	9
1996-97	FC Feyenoord	34	4
1997-98	FC Feyenoord	32	8
1998-99	Rangers	35	7

Giovanni Van Bronckhorst

VAN EIJS, Frank
Born : Geleen 02/11/71
from FC Vinkenslag

VAREILLE, Jerome
Born : Vernoux 01/06/74
from F.C. Mulhouse

1997-98	Kilmarnock	34	4
1998-99	Kilmarnock	23	5

VENETIS, Anastasios
Born : Larissa 24/03/80
from Larissa

VIDMAR, Antony
Born : Adelaide 04/07/70

1992-93	Ekeren	9	1

from Adelaide City

1995-96	NAC Breda	30	2
1996-97	NAC Breda	31	2
1997-98	Rangers	12	-
1998-99	Rangers	28	1

VIDUKA, Mark Anthony
Born : Australia 09/10/75
from Croatia Zagreb

1998-99	Celtic	9	5

WALES, Gary
Born : East Calder 04/01/79

1997-98	Hamilton Academical	3	-
1998-99	Hamilton Academical	30	11

WALLACE, Rodney
Born : Lewisham 02/10/69

1987-88	Southampton	15	1
1988-89	Southampton	38	12
1989-90	Southampton	38	18
1990-91	Southampton	37	14
1991-92	Leeds United	34	11
1992-93	Leeds United	32	7
1993-94	Leeds United	37	17
1994-95	Leeds United	32	4
1995-96	Leeds United	24	1
1996-97	Leeds United	22	3
1997-98	Leeds United	31	10
1998-99	Rangers	34	18

WATT, Michael
Born : Aberdeen 27/11/70

1989-90	Aberdeen	7	-
1990-91	Aberdeen	10	-
1991-92	Aberdeen	2	-
1992-93	Aberdeen	3	-
1993-94	Aberdeen	4	-
1994-95	Aberdeen	14	-
1995-96	Aberdeen	30	-
1996-97	Aberdeen	9	-
1997-98	Aberdeen	-	-
1997-98	*Blackburn Rovers*	-	-
1998-99	Norwich City	8	-

WEIR, James McIntosh
Born : Motherwell 15/06/69

1986-87	Hamilton Academical	3	-
1987-88	Hamilton Academical	6	-
1988-89	Hamilton Academical	29	-
1989-90	Hamilton Academical	30	1
1990-91	Hamilton Academical	39	2
1991-92	Hamilton Academical	40	1
1992-93	Hamilton Academical	37	1
1993-94	Hamilton Academical	2	-
1993-94	Heart of Midlothian	26	-
1994-95	Heart of Midlothian	2	-
1994-95	St. Johnstone	17	-
1995-96	St. Johnstone	29	-
1996-97	St. Johnstone	32	3
1997-98	St. Johnstone	25	-
1998-99	St. Johnstone	7	1

WHITEFORD, Andrew
Born : Bellshill 22/08/77

1994-95	St. Johnstone	-	-
1995-96	St. Johnstone	4	-
1996-97	St. Johnstone	11	-
1997-98	St. Johnstone	1	-
1998-99	St. Johnstone	1	-

WHYTE, Derek
Born : Glasgow 31/08/68

1985-86	Celtic	11	-
1986-87	Celtic	42	-
1987-88	Celtic	41	3
1988-89	Celtic	22	-
1989-90	Celtic	35	1
1990-91	Celtic	24	2
1991-92	Celtic	40	1
1992-93	Celtic	1	-
1992-93	Middlesbrough	35	-
1993-94	Middlesbrough	42	1
1994-95	Middlesbrough	36	1
1995-96	Middlesbrough	25	-
1996-97	Middlesbrough	21	-
1997-98	Middlesbrough	8	-
1997-98	Aberdeen	19	-
1998-99	Aberdeen	35	-

WIEGHORST, Morten
Born : Glostrup 25/02/71
From Lyngby

1992-93	Dundee	23	2
1993-94	Dundee	24	2
1994-95	Dundee	29	3
1995-96	Dundee	14	4
1995-96	Celtic	11	1
1996-97	Celtic	17	2

SEASON	CLUB		
1997-98	Celtic	31	4
1998-99	Celtic	7	-

WILSON, Scott
Born : Edinburgh 19/03/77

1993-94	Rangers	-	-
1994-95	Rangers	-	-
1995-96	Rangers	-	-
1996-97	Rangers	1	-
1997-98	Rangers	-	-
1998-99	Rangers	12	1

WINTERS, Robert
Born : East Kilbride 04/11/74

1991-92	Dundee United	-	-
1992-93	Dundee United	-	-
1993-94	Dundee United	-	-
1994-95	Dundee United	13	2
1995-96	Dundee United	35	7
1996-97	Dundee United	36	8
1997-98	Dundee United	30	8
1998-99	Dundee United	3	1
1998-99	Aberdeen	28	12

WOODS, Stephen Gerard
Born : Glasgow 23/02/70

1989-90	Hibernian	-	-
1990-91	Hibernian	-	-
1991-92	Hibernian	-	-
1991-92	Clydebank	5	-
1992-93	Clydebank	42	-
1993-94	Clydebank	10	-
1993-94	Preston North End	20	-
1994-95	Motherwell	33	-
1995-96	Motherwell	-	-
1996-97	Motherwell	6	-
1997-98	Motherwell	35	-
1998-99	Motherwell	7	-

WORRELL, David
Born : Dublin 12/01/78

1994-95	Blackburn Rovers	-	-
1995-96	Blackburn Rovers	-	-
1996-97	Blackburn Rovers	-	-
1997-98	Blackburn Rovers	-	-
1998-99	Blackburn Rovers	-	-
1998-99	Dundee United	4	-

WRIGHT, Paul Hamilton
Born : East Kilbride 17/08/67

1983-84	Aberdeen	1	-
1984-85	Aberdeen	-	-
1985-86	Aberdeen	10	2
1986-87	Aberdeen	25	4
1987-88	Aberdeen	9	4
1988-89	Aberdeen	23	6
1989-90	Queens Park Rangers	15	5
1989-90	Hibernian	3	1
1990-91	Hibernian	33	6
1991-92	St. Johnstone	41	18
1992-93	St. Johnstone	42	14
1993-94	St. Johnstone	17	7
1994-95	St. Johnstone	12	1
1994-95	Kilmarnock	7	1
1995-96	Kilmarnock	36	13
1996-97	Kilmarnock	31	15
1997-98	Kilmarnock	28	10
1998-99	Kilmarnock	33	6

WYNESS, Dennis Middleton
Born : Aberdeen 22/03/77

1994-95	Aberdeen	-	-
1995-96	Aberdeen	-	-
1996-97	Aberdeen	7	-
1997-98	Aberdeen	-	-
1998-99	Aberdeen	14	1

YOUNG, Darren
Born : Glasgow 13/10/78

1995-96	Aberdeen	-	-
1996-97	Aberdeen	26	1
1997-98	Aberdeen	5	-
1998-99	Aberdeen	11	-

YOUNG, Derek
Born : Glasgow 27/05/80

1996-97	Aberdeen	-	-
1997-98	Aberdeen	-	-
1998-99	Aberdeen	4	-

Scottish Professional Footballers' Association

1992/93

Premier Division	Andy Goram (Rangers)
First Division	Gordon Dalziel (Raith Rovers)
Second Division	Alexander Ross (Brechin City)
Young Player of the Year	Eoin Jess (Aberdeen)

1993/94

Premier Division	Mark Hateley (Rangers)
First Division	Richard Cadette (Falkirk)
Second Division	Andrew Thomson (Queen of the South)
Young Player of the Year	Philip O'Donnell (Motherwell)

1994/95

Premier Division	Brian Laudrup (Rangers)
First Division	Stephen Crawford (Raith Rovers)
Second Division	Derek McInnes (Greenock Morton)
Third Division	David Bingham (Forfar Athletic)
Young Player of the Year	Charlie Miller (Rangers)

1995/96

Premier Division	Paul Gascoigne (Rangers)
First Division	George O'Boyle (St. Johnstone)
Second Division	Stephen McCormick (Stirling Albion)
Third Division	Jason Young (Livingston)
Young Player of the Year	Jackie McNamara (Celtic)

1996/97

Premier Division	Paolo Di Canio (Celtic)
First Division	Roddy Grant (St. Johnstone)
Second Division	Paul Ritchie (Hamilton Academical)
Third Division	Iain Stewart (Inverness Cal. Thistle)
Young Player of the Year	Robbie Winters (Dundee United)

1997/98

Premier Division	Jackie McNamara (Celtic)
First Division	James Grady (Dundee)
Second Division	Paul Lovering (Clydebank)
Third Division	Willie Irvine (Alloa Athletic)
Young Player of the Year	Gary Naysmith (Heart of Midlothian)

1998/99

Scottish Premier League	Henrik Larsson (Celtic)
First Division	Russell Latapy (Hibernian)
Second Division	David Bingham (Livingston)
Third Division	Neil Tarrant (Ross County)
Young Player of the Year	Barry Ferguson (Rangers)

Scottish Football Writers' Association

1965	Billy McNeill (Celtic)
1966	John Greig (Rangers)
1967	Ronnie Simpson (Celtic)
1968	Gordon Wallace (Raith Rovers)
1969	Bobby Murdoch (Celtic)
1970	Pat Stanton (Hibernian)
1971	Martin Buchan (Aberdeen)
1972	Dave Smith (Rangers)
1973	George Connelly (Celtic)
1974	World Cup Squad
1975	Sandy Jardine (Rangers)
1976	John Greig (Rangers)
1977	Danny McGrain (Celtic)
1978	Derek Johnstone (Rangers)
1979	Andy Ritchie (Morton)
1980	Gordon Strachan (Aberdeen)
1981	Alan Rough (Partick Thistle)
1982	Paul Sturrock (Dundee United)
1983	Charlie Nicholas (Celtic)
1984	Willie Miller (Aberdeen)
1985	Hamish McAlpine (Dundee United)
1986	Sandy Jardine (Heart of Midlothian)
1987	Brian McClair (Celtic)
1988	Paul McStay (Celtic)
1989	Richard Gough (Rangers)
1990	Alex McLeish (Aberdeen)
1991	Maurice Malpas (Dundee United)
1992	Alistair McCoist (Rangers)
1993	Andy Goram (Rangers)
1994	Mark Hateley (Rangers)
1995	Brian Laudrup (Rangers)
1996	Paul Gascoigne (Rangers)
1997	Brian Laudrup (Rangers)
1998	Craig Burley (Celtic)
1999	Henrik Larsson (Celtic)

S.F.W.A. and S.P.F.A. Player of the Year 1998/99, Henrik Larsson (Celtic)

S.P.F.A. Young Player of the Year 1998/99, Barry Ferguson (Rangers)

S.P.F.A. First Division Player of the Year 1998/99, Russell Latapy (Hibernian)

The first S.F.W.A. Player of the Year, Billy McNeill (Celtic)

S·F·L

TENNENT'S LAGER · SINCE 1885 · *JVR Tennent*

1995/96

Premier Division
26 P. Van Hooijdonk (Celtic)
17 G. Durie (Rangers)
16 A. McCoist (Rangers)
14 P. Gascoigne (Rangers)
13 P. Wright (Kilmarnock)
11 C. Cameron (9 for Raith Rovers, 2 for Heart of Midlothian)
   J. Collins (Celtic)
   J. Robertson (Heart of Midlothian)
9 S. Booth (Aberdeen)
   D. Jackson (Hibernian)
   A. Johnston (Heart of Midlothian)
   J. Miller (Aberdeen)
   K. Wright (Hibernian)

First Division
21 G. O'Boyle (St. Johnstone)
17 C. Brewster (Dundee United)
   G. McSwegan (Dundee United)
14 J. Hamilton (Dundee)
   D. Lilley (Greenock Morton)
13 W. Hawke (Greenock Morton)
   S. Petrie (Dunfermline Athletic)
12 G. Shaw (Dunfermline Athletic)
11 J. Grady (Clydebank)
   P. Hartley (Hamilton Academical)
   B. Lavety (St. Mirren)
   M. Rajamaki (Greenock Morton)

Second Division
25 S. McCormick (Stirling Albion)
21 E. Annand (Clyde)
19 A. Bone (18 for Stirling Albion, 1 for St. Mirren)
16 C. McGlashan (Montrose)
13 W. Irvine (Berwick Rangers)
12 G. Higgins (Forfar Athletic)
   S. Mallan (Queen of the South)
11 R. Scott (East Fife)
10 P. Forrester (Berwick Rangers)
   M. Mathieson (Stenhousemuir)

Third Division
23 I. Stewart (Caledonian Thistle)
21 P. Dwyer (East Stirlingshire)
18 J. Young (Livingston)
15 C. Milne (Ross County)
12 C. Christie (Caledonian Thistle)
   J. MacPherson (Ross County)
   G. Young (Albion Rovers)
11 B. Grant (Ross County)
   D. Scott (Cowdenbeath)
10 A. Hercher (Caledonian Thistle)

1996/97

Premier Division
25 J. Cadete (Celtic)
16 B. Laudrup (Rangers)
15 W. Dodds (Aberdeen)
   P. Wright (Kilmarnock)
14 J. Robertson (Heart of Midlothian)
13 G. Britton (Dunfermline Athletic)
   P. Gascoigne (Rangers)
12 P. Di Canio (Celtic)
   K. Olofsson (Dundee United)
11 T. Coyne (Motherwell)
   D. Jackson (Hibernian)
10 J. Albertz (Rangers)
   A. McCoist (Rangers)
   A. Smith (Dunfermline Athletic)
   D. Windass (Aberdeen)

First Division
19 R. Grant (St. Johnstone)
15 D. Lilley (Greenock Morton)
   M. Yardley (St. Mirren)
12 G. O'Boyle (St. Johnstone)
   P. Scott (St. Johnstone)
11 D. Moss (Partick Thistle)
10 J. O'Driscoll (Dundee)
9 A. Bone (Stirling Albion)
   G. Evans (Partick Thistle)
8 C. Adams (Partick Thistle)
   P. Connolly (Airdrieonians)
   S. Cooper (Airdrieonians)
   J. Grady (Clydebank)
   S. McCormick (Stirling Albion)
   M. McGraw (Clydebank)
   B. McPhee (Airdrieonians)

Second Division
31 P. Ritchie (Hamilton Academical)
21 E. Annand (Clyde)
15 G. Harvey (Livingston)
14 S. Kerrigan (Ayr United)
   J. Little (Stenhousemuir)
13 S. Mallan (Queen of the South)
12 T. Bryce (Queen of the South)
11 C. Flannigan (Queen of the South)
10 L. Haddow (Stenhousemuir)
9 P. Smith (Ayr United)

Third Division
27 I. Stewart (Inverness Caledonian Thistle)
22 D. Adams (Ross County)
17 B. Honeyman (Forfar Athletic)
15 A. Morgan (Forfar Athletic)
   W. Watters (Albion Rovers (4 for Arbroath)
12 W. Irvine (Alloa)
11 P. Dwyer (Alloa)
   C. McGlashan (Montrose)
10 B. Thomson (Inverness Caledonian Thistle)
9 G. Inglis (East Stirlingshire)
   A. Ross (Ross County)
   S. Taylor (Montrose)

1997/98

Premier Division
32 M. Negri (Rangers)
18 K. Olofsson (Dundee United)
16 H. Larsson (Celtic)
   A. Smith (Dunfermline Athletic)
15 T. Coyne (Motherwell)
14 J. Hamilton (Heart of Midlothian)
10 J. Albertz (Rangers)
   C. Burley (Celtic)
   O. Coyle (Motherwell)
   W. Dodds (Aberdeen)
   S. Donnelly (Celtic)
   N. McCann (Heart of Midlothian)
   G. O'Boyle (St. Johnstone)
   P. Wright (Kilmarnock)

First Division
15 J. Grady (Dundee)
13 A. Bone (Stirling Albion)
12 E. Annand (Dundee)
   B. McPhee (Airdrieonians)
   D. Moss (Falkirk)
11 S. Cooper (Airdrieonians)
10 L. D'Jaffo (Ayr United)
   P. Hartley (Raith Rovers)
   W. Hawke (Greenock Morton)
   M. Keith (Falkirk)
   K. Wright (Raith Rovers)

Second Division
16 I. Stewart (Inverness Caledonian Thistle)
15 G. Harvey (Livingston)
   I. Little (Stenhousemuir)
14 M. McLauchlan (Forfar Athletic)
13 C. McDonald (Clydebank)
   B. Thomson (Inverness Caledonian Thistle)
12 B. Honeyman (Forfar Athletic)
   T. Bryce (Queen of the South)
   M. Dyer (East Fife)
   G. Young (Stranraer)

Third Division
20 C. McGlashan (Montrose)
18 W. Irvine (Alloa Athletic)
16 D. Adams (Ross County)
   W. Spence (Arbroath)
13 D. Watt (East Stirlingshire)
   W. Watters (Albion Rovers)
10 P. Forrester (Berwick Rangers)
   R.L. Gardner (Albion Rovers)
   B. Grant (Arbroath)
   C. McKinnon (Dumbarton)

1998/99

Scottish Premier League
29 H. Larsson (Celtic)
18 R. Wallace (Rangers)
17 W. Dodds (Dundee United)
14 E. Jess (Aberdeen)
13 R. Winters (12 for Aberdeen, 1 for Dundee United)
11 J. Albertz (Rangers)
10 S. Adam (Heart of Midlothian)
9 E. Annand (Dundee)
   M. Burchill (Celtic)
   C. Burley (Celtic)

First Division
18 G. Hurst (Ayr United)
17 M. Keith (Falkirk)
15 A. Walker (Ayr United)
14 S. Crawford (Hibernian)
12 P. McGinlay (Hibernian)
   M-M. Paatelainen (Hibernian)
11 S. Lovell (Hibernian)
   G. Wales (Hamilton Academical)
   M. Yardley (St. Mirren)
10 S. Crabbe (Falkirk)

Second Division
21 A. Bone (Stirling Albion)
19 S. McLean (Inverness Caledonian Thistle)
15 M. Cameron (Alloa Athletic)
   W. Irvine (Alloa Athletic)
   S. Mallan (Queen of the South)
14 B. Wilson (Inverness Caledonian Thistle)
13 B. Moffat (East Fife)
12 S. Convery (Clyde)
   C. McGlashan (Arbroath)
   J. Robertson (Livingston)
   D. Shearer (Inverness Caledonian Thistle)

Third Division
17 S. Ferguson (Ross County)
   P. Flannery (Dumbarton)
   N. Tarrant (Ross County)
15 J. Dickson (Brechin City)
12 M. Leask (Berwick Rangers)
   S. Sorbie (Brechin City)
   G. Wood (Ross County)
11 R. Hamilton (Stenhousemuir)
10 D. Lorimer (Albion Rovers)
9 P. Forrester (Berwick Rangers)
   W. Watters (Stenhousemuir)

Leading Goalscorers – Club By Club Since 1984/85

ABERDEEN

Season	Div	No. of Goals	Player
1984-85	P	22	F. McDougall
1985-86	P	14	F. McDougall
1986-87	P	12	W. Stark
1987-88	P	10	J. Bett
1988-89	P	16	C. Nicholas
1989-90	P	11	C. Nicholas
1990-91	P	14	H. Gillhaus
1991-92	P	12	E. Jess
1992-93	P	22	D. Shearer
1993-94	P	17	D. Shearer
1994-95	P	15	W. Dodds
1995-96	P	9	S. Booth
			J. Miller
1996-97	P	15	W. Dodds
1997-98	P	10	W.Dodds
1998-99	P	14	E. Jess

AIRDRIEONIANS

Season	Div	No. of Goals	Player
1984-85	F	21	D. MacCabe
1985-86	F	11	J. Flood
1986-87	F	13	D. MacCabe
1987-88	F	20	D. MacCabe
1988-89	F	22	K. Macdonald
1989-90	F	10	O. Coyle
1990-91	F	20	O. Coyle
1991-92	P	11	O. Coyle
1992-93	P	9	O. Coyle
1993-94	F	10	D. Kirkwood
1994-95	F	12	Andrew Smith
1995-96	F	9	J. McIntyre
1996-97	F	8	P. Connolly
			S. Cooper
			B. McPhee
1997-98	F	12	B. McPhee
1998-99	F	8	S. Cooper

ALBION ROVERS

Season	Div	No. of Goals	Player
1984-85	S	27	B. Slaven
1985-86	S	6	S. Conn
			V. Kasule
			A. Rodgers
1986-87	S	11	C. Wilson
1987-88	S	10	A. Graham
1988-89	S	15	J. Chapman
			A. Graham
1989-90	F	10	M. McAnenay
1990-91	S	12	M. McAnenay
1991-92	S	11	G. McCoy
1992-93	S	16	M. Scott
1993-94	S	17	M. Scott
1994-95	T	7	M. Scott
1995-96	T	12	G. Young
1996-97	T	11	W. Watters
1997-98	T	13	W. Watters
1998-99	T	10	D. Lorimer

ALLOA ATHLETIC

Season	Div	No. of Goals	Player
1984-85	S	16	D. Lloyd
1985-86	F	11	M. Jamieson
			S. Sorbie
1986-87	S	14	S. Sorbie
1987-88	S	14	P. Rutherford
1988-89	S	23	C. Lytwyn
1989-90	F	9	P. Lamont
1990-91	S	11	J. Irvine
1991-92	S	12	M. Hendry
1992-93	S	19	B. Moffat
1993-94	S	7	W. Newbigging
1994-95	T	13	B. Moffat
1995-96	T	5	B. Moffat
			S. Rixon
1996-97	T	12	W. Irvine
1997-98	T	18	W. Irvine
1998-99	S	15	M. Cameron
			W. Irvine

ARBROATH

Season	Div	No. of Goals	Player
1984-85	S	6	R. Brown
1985-86	S	14	M. McWalter
1986-87	S	14	J. Fotheringham
1987-88	S	13	A. McKenna
1988-89	S	11	J. Fotheringham
1989-90	S	12	J. Marshall
1990-91	S	10	M. Bennett
			S. Sorbie
1991-92	S	12	S. Sorbie
1992-93	S	19	S. Sorbie
1993-94	S	10	D. Diver
1994-95	T	11	S. Tosh
1995-96	T	8	S. McCormick
			D. Pew
1996-97	T	5	B. Grant
1997-98	T	10	W. Spence
1998-99	S	12	C. McGlashan

AYR UNITED

Season	Div	No. of Goals	Player
1984-85	F	8	G. Collins
			J. McNiven
1985-86	F	6	D. Irons
1986-87	F	26	J. Sludden
1987-88	F	31	J. Sludden
1988-89	F	17	H. Templeton
1989-90	F	10	T. Bryce
1990-91	F	11	T. Bryce
1991-92	F	14	A. Graham
1992-93	F	9	A. Graham
1993-94	F	12	S. McGivern
1994-95	F	4	J. Jackson
1995-96	F	5	B. Bilsland
			I. English
1996-97	S	14	S. Kerrigan
1997-98	F	10	L. D'Jaffo
1998-99	F	18	G. Hurst

BERWICK RANGERS

Season	Div	No. of Goals	Player
1984-85	S	9	P. Davidson
1985-86	S	12	J. Sokoluk
1986-87	S	8	E. Tait
1987-88	S	3	M. Cameron
			H. Douglas
			T. Graham
			G. Leitch
			C. Lytwyn
			M. Thompson
1988-89	S	10	J. Hughes
1989-90	S	16	S. Sloan
1990-91	S	14	K. Todd
1991-92	S	12	S. Bickmore
1992-93	S	11	D. Scott
1993-94	S	15	W. Irvine
1994-95	S	16	W. Hawke
1995-96	S	13	W. Irvine
1996-97	S	6	P. Forrester
1997-98	T	10	P. Forrester
1998-99	T	12	M. Leask

BRECHIN CITY

Season	Div	No. of Goals	Player
1984-85	F	17	K. Eadie
1985-86	F	22	K. Eadie
1986-87	F	12	C. Adam
1987-88	S	15	G. Buckley
1988-89	S	15	C. Adam
1989-90	S	12	G. Lees
1990-91	F	14	P. Ritchie
1991-92	S	12	P. Ritchie
1992-93	S	23	A. Ross
1993-94	F	10	M. Miller
1994-95	S	6	G. Price
			R. Smith
1995-96	T	8	A. Ross
1996-97	S	7	S. Kerrigan
1997-98	S	7	C. Feroz
1998-99	T	15	J. Dickson

CELTIC

Season	Div	No. of Goals	Player
©1984-85	P	19	B. McClair
1985-86	P	22	B. McClair
1986-87	P	35	B. McClair
1987-88	P	26	A. Walker
1988-89	P	16	M. McGhee
1989-90	P	8	D. Dziekanowski
1990-91	P	18	T. Coyne
1991-92	P	21	C. Nicholas
1992-93	P	13	A. Payton
1993-94	P	10	P. McGinlay
1994-95	P	8	J. Collins
1995-96	P	26	P. Van Hooijdonk
1996-97	P	25	J. Cadete
1997-98	P	16	H. Larsson
1998-99	P	29	H. Larsson

CLYDE

Season	Div	No. of Goals	Player
1984-85	F	19	J. F. Frye
1985-86	F	12	J. F. Frye
1986-87	F	12	J. Murphy
1987-88	F	16	C. McGlashan
			D. Walker
1988-89	F	16	C. McGlashan
1989-90	F	11	C. McGlashan
1990-91	F	8	S. Mallan
1991-92	S	16	D. Thompson
1992-93	S	16	F. McGarvey
1993-94	F	5	I. McConnell
			G. Parks
1994-95	S	10	J. Dickson
1995-96	S	21	E. Annand
1996-97	S	21	E. Annand
1997-98	S	8	P. Brownlie
1998-99	S	12	S. Convery

CLYDEBANK

Season	Div	No. of Goals	Player
1984-85	F	11	M. Conroy
1985-86	P	7	M. Conroy
			D. Lloyd
1986-87	P	9	M. Conroy
			S. Gordon
1987-88	F	11	M. Conroy
1988-89	F	21	K. Eadie
1989-90	F	21	K. Eadie
1990-91	F	29	K. Eadie
1991-92	F	22	K. Eadie
1992-93	F	21	C. Flannigan
1993-94	F	11	K. Eadie
			C. Flannigan
1994-95	F	9	K. Eadie
1995-96	F	11	J. Grady
1996-97	F	8	J. Grady
1997-98	S	13	C. McDonald
1998-99	F	9	C. McDonald

COWDENBEATH

Season	Div	No. of Goals	Player
1984-85	S	16	K. Ward
1985-86	S	15	C. McGlashan
1986-87	S	14	W. Blackie
			R. Grant
1987-88	S	11	R. Grant
1988-89	S	8	A. McGonigal
1989-90	S	16	A. Ross
1990-91	S	15	A. MacKenzie
1991-92	S	26	G. Buckley
1992-93	F	9	W. Callaghan
1993-94	S	11	W. Callaghan
1994-95	T	23	M. Yardley
1995-96	T	11	D. Scott
1996-97	T	6	G. Wood
1997-98	T	6	W. Stewart
1998-99	T	7	W. Stewart

DUMBARTON

Season	Div	No. of Goals	Player
1984-85	P	7	J. Coyle
1985-86	F	13	G. McCoy
1986-87	F	21	G. McCoy
1987-88	F	14	O. Coyle
1988-89	S	13	S. MacIver
1989-90	S	20	C. Gibson
1990-91	S	14	J. McQuade
1991-92	S	19	J. Gilmour
1992-93	F	15	J. McQuade
1993-94	F	13	C. Gibson
1994-95	S	17	M. Mooney
1995-96	F	5	M. Mooney
1996-97	S	7	H. Ward
1997-98	T	10	C. McKinnon
1998-99	T	17	P. Flannery

DUNDEE

Season	Div	No. of Goals	Player
1984-85	P	8	R. Stephen
1985-86	P	14	R. Stephen
1986-87	P	12	G. Harvey
1987-88	P	33	T. Coyne
1988-89	P	9	T. Coyne
1989-90	P	13	W. Dodds
1990-91	F	18	K. Wright
1991-92	F	19	W. Dodds
1992-93	P	16	W. Dodds
1993-94	P	6	D. Ristic
1994-95	F	16	G. Shaw
1995-96	F	14	J. Hamilton
1996-97	F	10	J. O'Driscoll
1997-98	F	15	J. Grady
1998-99	P	9	E. Annand

DUNDEE UNITED

Season	Div	No. of Goals	Player
1984-85	P	14	P. Sturrock
1985-86	P	12	D. Dodds
1986-87	P	16	I. Ferguson
1987-88	P	11	I. Ferguson
1988-89	P	10	M-M. Paatelainen
1989-90	P	7	D. Jackson
			M-M. Paatelainen
1990-91	P	12	D. Jackson
1991-92	P	17	D. Ferguson
1992-93	P	16	P. Connolly
1993-94	P	16	C. Brewster
1994-95	P	7	C. Brewster
1995-96	F	17	C. Brewster
			G. McSwegan
1996-97	P	12	K. Olofsson
1997-98	P	18	K. Olofsson
1998-99	P	17	W. Dodds

DUNFERMLINE ATHLETIC

Season	Div	No. of Goals	Player
1984-85	S	15	J. Watson
1985-86	S	24	J. Watson
1986-87	F	13	J. Watson
1987-88	P	13	C. Robertson
1988-89	F	18	R. Jack
1989-90	P	16	R. Jack
1990-91	P	8	R. Jack
1991-92	P	6	D. Moyes
1992-93	F	12	H. French
1993-94	F	17	G. O'Boyle
1994-95	F	14	S. Petrie
1995-96	F	13	S. Petrie
1996-97	P	13	G. Britton
1997-98	P	16	A. Smith
1998-99	P	8	A. Smith

EAST FIFE

Season	Div	No. of Goals	Player
1984-85	F	12	G. Murray
1985-86	S	14	S. Kirk
1986-87	F	15	B. McNaughton
1987-88	F	17	P. Hunter
1988-89	S	9	P. Hunter
1989-90	S	14	P. Hunter
1990-91	S	10	W. Brown
			R. Scott
1991-92	S	21	J. Sludden
1992-93	S	16	R. Scott
1993-94	S	10	R. Scott
1994-95	S	14	R. Scott
1995-96	S	11	R. Scott
1996-97	F	4	M. Dyer
			P. Ronald
1997-98	S	11	M. Dyer
1998-99	S	13	B. Moffat

EAST STIRLINGSHIRE

Season	Div	No. of Goals	Player
1984-85	S	12	S. Maskrey
1985-86	S	12	S. Maskrey
1986-87	S	5	A. McGonigal
			J. Paisley
1987-88	S	9	G. Murray
1988-89	S	16	W. McNeill
1989-90	S	4	W. McNeill
			D. Wilcox
			C. Wilson
1990-91	S	10	C. Lytwyn
			Dk. Walker
1991-92	S	18	D. Diver
1992-93	S	9	P. Roberts
1993-94	S	12	M. McCallum
1994-95	T	16	M. Geraghty
1995-96	T	21	P. Dwyer
1996-97	T	9	G. Inglis
1997-98	T	13	D. Watt
1998-99	T	8	W. McNeill

FALKIRK

Season	Div	No. of Goals	Player
1984-85	F	22	G. McCoy
1985-86	F	15	J. Gilmour
1986-87	P	6	K. Eadie
1987-88	P	9	C. Baptie
1988-89	F	12	A. Rae
1989-90	F	17	D. McWilliams
1990-91	F	16	S. Stainrod
1991-92	P	9	K. McAllister
			E. May
1992-93	P	8	R. Cadette
1993-94	F	18	R. Cadette
1994-95	P	9	C. McDonald
1995-96	P	6	P. McGrillen
1996-97	F	8	M. McGraw
1997-98	F	12	D. Moss
1998-99	F	17	M. Keith

FORFAR ATHLETIC

Season	Div	No. of Goals	Player
1984-85	F	14	K. Macdonald
1985-86	F	10	J. Clark
1986-87	F	17	K. Macdonald
1987-88	F	20	K. Macdonald
1988-89	F	12	K. Ward
1989-90	F	8	C. Brewster
1990-91	F	12	G. Whyte
1991-92	F	8	G. Winter
1992-93	S	21	S. Petrie
1993-94	S	13	D. Bingham
1994-95	T	22	D. Bingham
1995-96	S	12	G. Higgins
1996-97	T	17	B. Honeyman
1997-98	S	14	M. McLauchlan
1998-99	S	10	R. Brand

HAMILTON ACADEMICAL

Season	Div	No. of Goals	Player
1984-85	F	8	J. Brogan
			J. McGachie
1985-86	F	23	J. Brogan
1986-87	F	6	J. Brogan
1987-88	F	10	M. Caughey
1988-89	P	5	S. Gordon
			C. Harris
1989-90	F	9	C. Harris
1990-91	F	14	G. McCluskey
1991-92	F	14	G. Clark
1992-93	F	11	P. McDonald
1993-94	F	19	P. Duffield
1994-95	F	20	P. Duffield
1995-96	F	11	P. Hartley
1996-97	S	31	P. Ritchie
1997-98	F	7	P. Ritchie
1998-99	F	11	G. Wales

HEART OF MIDLOTHIAN

Season	Div	No. of Goals	Player
1984-85	P	8	A. Clark
			J. Robertson
1985-86	P	20	J. Robertson
1986-87	P	16	J. Robertson
1987-88	P	26	J. Robertson
1988-89	P	5	J. Colquhoun
			I. Ferguson
1989-90	P	17	J Robertson
1990-91	P	12	J. Robertson
1991-92	P	15	S. Crabbe
1992-93	P	11	J. Robertson
1993-94	P	10	J. Robertson
1994-95	P	10	J. Robertson
1995-96	P	11	J. Robertson
1996-97	P	14	J. Robertson
1997-98	P	14	J. Hamilton
1998-99	P	10	S. Adam

HIBERNIAN

Season	Div	No. of Goals	Player
1984-85	P	8	G. Durie
			P. Kane
1985-86	P	19	S. Cowan
1986-87	P	9	G. McCluskey
1987-88	P	10	P. Kane
1988-89	P	13	S. Archibald
1989-90	P	8	K. Houchen
1990-91	P	6	P. Wright
1991-92	P	11	M. Weir
1992-93	P	13	D. Jackson
1993-94	P	16	K. Wright
1994-95	P	10	D. Jackson
			M. O'Neill
			K. Wright
1995-96	P	9	D. Jackson
			K. Wright
1996-97	P	11	D. Jackson
1997-98	P	9	S. Crawford
1998-99	F	14	S. Crawford

INVERNESS CALEDONIAN THISTLE

Season	Div	No. of Goals	Player
1994-95	T	6	C. Christie
			A. Hercher
1995-96	T	23	I. Stewart
1996-97	T	27	I. Stewart
1997-98	S	16	I. Stewart
1998-99	S	20	S. McLean

KILMARNOCK

Season	Div	No. of Goals	Player
1984-85	F	12	B. Millar
1985-86	F	14	I. Bryson
1986-87	F	10	I. Bryson
1987-88	F	16	C. Harkness
1988-89	F	12	W. Watters
1989-90	S	23	W. Watters
1990-91	F	14	R. Williamson
1991-92	F	10	C. Campbell
			A. Mitchell
1992-93	F	11	G. McCluskey
1993-94	F	7	R. Williamson
1994-95	P	6	C. McKee
1995-96	P	13	P. Wright
1996-97	P	15	P. Wright
1997-98	P	10	P. Wright
1998-99	P	7	A. McCoist

LIVINGSTON

FORMERLY MEADOWBANK THISTLE

Season	Div	No. of Goals	Player
1984-85	F	14	A. Sprott
1985-86	S	17	D. Jackson
			A. Lawrence
1986-87	S	21	J. McGachie
1987-88	F	14	J. McGachie
1988-89	F	6	D. Roseburgh
1989-90	F	8	B. McNaughton
1990-91	F	15	D. Roseburgh
1991-92	F	8	D. Roseburgh
1992-93	F	9	R. Rutherford
1993-94	S	12	I. Little
1994-95	S	6	L. Bailey
1995-96	S	18	J. Young
1996-97	S	15	G. Harvey
1997-98	S	15	G. Harvey
1998-99	S	12	J. Robertson

MONTROSE

Season	Div	No. of Goals	Player
1984-85	S	12	D. Somner
1985-86	F	6	M. Allan
1986-87	F	10	I. Paterson
1987-88	S	11	H. Mackay
1988-89	S	21	G. S. Murray
1989-90	S	11	D. Powell
1990-91	S	11	G. Murray
1991-92	F	9	J. McGachie
1992-93	S	10	D. Grant
1993-94	S	12	D. Grant
1994-95	T	19	C. McGlashan
1995-96	S	16	C. McGlashan
1996-97	T	11	C. McGlashan
1997-98	T	20	C. McGlashan
1998-99	T	7	S. Taylor

MORTON

Season	Div	No. of Goals	Player
1984-85	P	5	J. Gillespie
1985-86	F	14	J. McNeil
1986-87	F	23	R. Alexander
1987-88	P	8	Jim Boag
1988-89	F	11	R. Alexander
1989-90	F	11	R. Alexander
1990-91	F	21	D. MacCabe
1991-92	F	18	A. Mathie
1992-93	F	13	A. Mathie
1993-94	F	11	R. Alexander
1994-95	S	16	D. Lilley
1995-96	F	14	D. Lilley
1996-97	F	15	D. Lilley
1997-98	F	10	W. Hawke
1998-99	F	9	K. Thomas

MOTHERWELL

Season	Div	No. of Goals	Player
1984-85	F	9	A. Harrow
			R. Stewart
1985-86	P	9	J. Reilly
1986-87	P	10	S. Kirk
			A. Walker
1987-88	P	9	S. Cowan
1988-89	P	14	S. Kirk
1989-90	P	11	N. Cusack
1990-91	P	14	D. Arnott
1991-92	P	8	D. Arnott
1992-93	P	10	S. Kirk
1993-94	P	12	T. Coyne
1994-95	P	16	T. Coyne
1995-96	P	5	W. Falconer
1996-97	P	11	T. Coyne
1997-98	P	15	T. Coyne
1998-99	P	7	O. Coyle
			J. Spencer

PARTICK THISTLE

Season	Div	No. of Goals	Player
1984-85	F	12	A. Logan
1985-86	F	11	G. Smith
1986-87	F	10	C. West
1987-88	F	13	E. Gallagher
1988-89	F	19	G. McCoy
1989-90	F	18	C. Campbell
1990-91	F	13	D. Elliot
1991-92	F	18	C. McGlashan
1992-93	F	12	G. Britton
1993-94	F	14	A. Craig
1994-95	P	7	W. Foster
1995-96	P	5	A. Lyons
			R. McDonald
1996-97	F	11	D. Moss
1997-98	F	6	J. Stirling
1998-99	S	10	R. Dunn

QUEEN OF THE SOUTH

Season	Div	No. of Goals	Player
1984-85	S	9	G. Cloy
1985-86	S	15	T. Bryce
			S. Cochrane
1986-87	F	20	T. Bryce
1987-88	F	17	J. Hughes
1988-89	F	7	G. Fraser
1989-90	S	8	S. Gordon
1990-91	S	11	A. Thomson
1991-92	S	26	A. Thomson
1992-93	S	21	A. Thomson
1993-94	S	29	A. Thomson
1994-95	S	9	D. Campbell
			S. Mallan
1995-96	S	12	S. Mallan
1996-97	S	13	S. Mallan
1997-98	S	11	T. Bryce
1998-99	S	15	S. Mallan

QUEEN'S PARK

Season	Div	No. of Goals	Player
1984-85	S	18	J. Nicholson
1985-86	S	11	G. Fraser
1986-87	S	13	R. Caven
1987-88	S	17	P. O'Brien
1988-89	S	9	M. Hendry
1989-90	S	10	M. Hendry
1990-91	S	17	M. Hendry
1991-92	S	17	S. McCormick
1992-93	S	11	R. Caven
1993-94	S	18	J. O'Neill
1994-95	T	8	S. McCormick
1995-96	T	6	S. Edgar
			K. McGoldrick
1996-97	T	7	D. Ferry
1997-98	T	8	S. Edgar
			J. Mercer
1998-99	T	7	S. Edgar

RAITH ROVERS

Season	Div	No. of Goals	Player
1984-85	S	22	K. Wright
1985-86	S	21	P. Smith
			K. Wright
1986-87	S	22	C. Harris
1987-88	F	25	G. Dalziel
1988-89	F	11	G. Dalziel
1989-90	F	20	G. Dalziel
1990-91	F	25	G. Dalziel
1991-92	F	26	G. Dalziel
1992-93	F	32	G. Dalziel
1993-94	P	8	G. Dalziel
1994-95	F	15	G. Dalziel
1995-96	P	9	C. Cameron
1996-97	P	5	P. Duffield
			D. Lennon
1997-98	F	10	P. Hartley
			K. Wright
1998-99	F	8	C. Dargo

RANGERS

Season	Div	No. of Goals	Player
1984-85	P	12	A. McCoist
1985-86	P	24	A. McCoist
1986-87	P	33	A. McCoist
1987-88	P	31	A. McCoist
1988-89	P	12	K. Drinkell
1989-90	P	15	M. Johnston
1990-91	P	12	M. Walters
1991-92	P	34	A. McCoist
1992-93	P	34	A. McCoist
1993-94	P	22	M. Hateley
1994-95	P	13	M. Hateley
1995-96	P	17	G. Durie
1996-97	P	16	B. Laudrup
1997-98	P	32	M. Negri
1998-99	P	18	R. Wallace

ROSS COUNTY

Season	Div	No. of Goals	Player
1994-95	T	12	B. Grant
1995-96	T	15	C. Milne
1996-97	T	22	D. Adams
1997-98	T	16	D. Adams
1998-99	T	17	S. Ferguson
			N. Tarrant

ST. JOHNSTONE

Season	Div	No. of Goals	Player
1984-85	F	9	J. Reid
1985-86	S	11	W. Brown
1986-87	S	25	W. Brown
1987-88	S	16	W. Watters
1988-89	F	12	S. Maskrey
1989-90	F	19	R. Grant
1990-91	P	9	H. Curran
1991-92	P	18	P. Wright
1992-93	P	14	P. Wright
1993-94	P	7	P. Wright
1994-95	F	19	G. O'Boyle
1995-96	F	21	G. O'Boyle
1996-97	F	19	R. Grant
1997-98	P	10	G. O'Boyle
1998-99	P	4	G. Bollan
			R. Grant
			M. Simao

ST. MIRREN

Season	Div	No. of Goals	Player
1984-85	P	16	F. McAvennie
1985-86	P	7	G. Speirs
1986-87	P	10	F. McGarvey
1987-88	P	10	P. Chalmers
1988-89	P	11	P. Chalmers
1989-90	P	12	G. Torfason
1990-91	P	4	P. Kinnaird
			K. McDowall
			G. Torfason
1991-92	P	8	G. Torfason
1992-93	F	18	B. Lavety
1993-94	F	10	B. Lavety
1994-95	F	5	B. Lavety
1995-96	F	11	B. Lavety
1996-97	F	15	M. Yardley
1997-98	F	9	J. Mendes
1998-99	F	11	M. Yardley

STENHOUSEMUIR

Season	Div	No. of Goals	Player
1984-85	S	6	H. Erwin
			A. McNaughton
1985-86	S	11	J. Sinnet
1986-87	S	5	A. Bateman
			P. Russell
1987-88	S	10	T. Condie
1988-89	S	9	C. Walker
1989-90	S	15	S. McCormick
1990-91	S	17	A. Speirs
1991-92	S	6	M. Mathieson
1992-93	S	26	M. Mathieson
1993-94	S	14	M. Mathieson
1994-95	S	10	G. Hutchison
1995-96	S	10	M. Mathieson
1996-97	S	14	I. Little
1997-98	S	15	I. Little
1998-99	F	11	R. Hamilton

STIRLING ALBION

Season	Div	No. of Goals	Player
1984-85	S	21	W. Irvine
1985-86	S	17	W. Irvine
1986-87	S	7	S. Gavin
			C. Gibson
1987-88	S	23	J. Brogan
1988-89	S	18	C. Gibson
1989-90	S	16	J. Reid
1990-91	S	14	D. Lloyd
1991-92	F	17	W. Watters
1992-93	F	11	W. Watters
1993-94	F	13	W. Watters
1994-95	S	15	W. Watters
1995-96	S	25	S. McCormick
1996-97	F	9	A. Bone
1997-98	F	13	A. Bone
1998-99	S	20	A. Bone

STRANRAER

Season	Div	No. of Goals	Player
1984-85	S	10	J. Sweeney
1985-86	S	8	J. McGuire
			S. Mauchlen
1986-87	S	13	B. Cleland
1987-88	S	8	B. Cleland
1988-89	S	11	D. Lloyd
1989-90	S	13	C. Harkness
1990-91	S	14	C. Harkness
1991-92	S	14	T. Sloan
1992-93	S	19	T. Sloan
1993-94	S	16	T. Sloan
1994-95	F	4	D. Henderson
			T. Sloan
1995-96	S	6	A. Grant
1996-97	S	7	P. McIntyre
1997-98	S	11	G. Young
1998-99	S	5	P. Ronald
			G. Young

Bully Wee for Clyde in the Programme Championship

There are few opportunities in the modern game for David to get the better of Goliath ; shock results in the League Cup and Scottish Cup may occur on an annual basis, but it's rarely the wee chap with the sling who prevails when the winners' medals are being distributed at the end of these, and League Championship competitions.

Not so in the case of football programmes, where Second Division Clyde have been ruling the roost for the last four seasons. Their "Clyde View" matchday magazine has been judged to be better than all others in Scotland by those who should know... the programme editors themselves. The Bully Wee have shrugged off limited sales (their average attendance is about 1% of two of their former Glasgow rivals) and poured a great deal of work and attention-to-detail into their 32 page programme, proving that such qualities can

overcome small crowds, official indifference and the hundred-and-one other obstacles which are placed in the path of a programme editor as he toils towards a fortnightly deadline.

The recent successes of the Clyde

programme, in the annual awards organised by "Programme Monthly" magazine and judged from a poll of every programme editor in Scotland, has reversed the trend of the previous 15 years, when the then "big four" of Scottish football, Rangers, Celtic, Aberdeen and Dundee United, passed the award amongst themselves. Before that, winners came from the ranks of the smaller clubs, which is precisely where the development of match programmes into the substantial, glossy, colourful issues that we recognise today, originated.

Ayr United, Berwick Rangers and, most frequently, Hamilton Academical, were amongst the earliest winners of the awards as enthusiastic young programme editors looked over the border, admired what they saw at some of the pioneering English clubs, and attempted to emulate

Programme sellers at last season's Tennents Scottish Cup Final

within their limited budgets. Full colour printing was out due to high cost, although it should be noted that Albion Rovers had the first four-colour match programme cover in Scotland, but imaginitive features, greater use of photographs, authoritative historical articles and a refreshingly candid style of writing soon gave supporters a compelling reason to buy them.

The revival came not a moment too soon ; the traditional reasons for purchasing a programme - team lines and half-time scoreboard - were disappearing with the legendary inaccuracy of the former and the replacement of the latter by transistor radios and improved public address announcements. However, this revolution was not without its casualties; with readability came some controversy as the new editors threw blandness - and caution - to the wind and betrayed their terracing roots with some injudicious comments on officialdom and rival clubs and players. Previously little used paragraphs of The Scottish Football Association and The Scottish Football League Rule books were dusted down and contrite young men were hauled before the appropriate committees for such misdeed as referring to a rival club as "that paltry little oufit", disclosing certain players' wayward lifestyles and condemning opponents' dirty play.

Such publicity only served to make the programmes more popular, of course, and persuaded recalcitrant clubs to jump on the better-programme bandwagon, while club officials began to take note that the matchday scraps of paper were a valuable means of imparting information to supporters, and, not least, a significant money-earner.

This late 1970's revolution, a full decade behind England, transformed programmes from the penny-

dreadfuls of the first thirty post-war years. Only a handful of clubs - Heart of Midlothian, Hibernian, St. Bernards, Partick Thistle, Queen of the South and belatedly Celtic - issued regular programmes before the war, although most produced for special occasions such as big cup ties, grandstand openings and benefit matches. After the war, few clubs took any notice when paper rationing was lifted and continued, for 30 years, to produce programmes which showed little or no signs of improvement.

Exceptions were in Edinburgh, where Hearts, and particularly Hibs, produced programmes full of interesting features and photographs and which were amongst the best in Britain. Elsewhere, the modestly produced, advert laden, perfunctorily written glorified team sheets were poor value even for the modest 3d (1.2p) cover price.

The revival of the late 1970's, kicked off by the smaller clubs in the Scottish League, changed the face of football programmes for ever. Faced with the outlay of £1 or £1.50 for a matchday programme today, supporters of "a certain age" no doubt wistfully recall the splendid programmes of their youth, which cost 5p or 10p (or even 3d, 6d and 1/- for those with longer memories). In truth, the programmes of twenty years ago stand little comparison to the 32 or more pages of colour, gloss, entertainment and information provided today.

More commercially aware clubs now realise that value-for-money has to be provided, otherwise sales will fall. Increasingly image-conscious clubs and sponsors welcome the opportunity of the official matchday programme to attract supporters to their market and have harnessed advances in printing, typesetting and design techniques to improve the standard, and value-for-money of their

matchday programme.

Further down the League ladder, advances in quality are very much dependent upon the endurance of programme editors who are prepared to work extremely hard to produce entertaining, informative and sometimes innovative programmes for, at times, fewer than one hundred readers.

It is not only in the quality of match production that football programmes have improved beyond all recognition over the last two decades. The programme industry itself has mushroomed, with a mature and sophisticated infrastructure servicing the growing hobby of programme collecting. Major auction houses such as Christies, Bonhams, Sotheby's and Phillips organise regular sales at which prices of over £1,000 for a single pre-war rarity are regularly achieved. "Programme Monthly" sends over 2,000 copies around the world each month and programme fairs organised throughout the country retain the interest of hundreds of collectors.

The pioneering programme editors of 25 years ago are now within positions of authority in the game; Club Secretaries, Directors, at least one Club Chairman, all started

their involvement with their clubs as programme editors and that gives a clue as to the secret of a successful club programme. Somehow, a love of the club and its heritage has to be conveyed within the pages, to strike a chord with the paying spectators, and to remind readers of the non-monetary richness of our national game. The team that produces the award-winning Clyde programme have hit upon, and stuck with, that very formula. Huge sales and a massive production budget are not the recipe for a successful programme ; time devoted to planning, writing, imagining new features and imparting the essence of the game in words and pictures is what makes the best match programmes. Given the right choice of editorial team, that is within the scope of every club, no matter how large or small.

JOHN LITSTER
(Editor of "Programme Monthly & Football Collectable" Magazine)

A copy of the current edition of Programme Monthly & Football Collectable may be obtained by sending 7 x 1st class stamps to 46 Milton Road, Kirkcaldy, KY1 1TL.

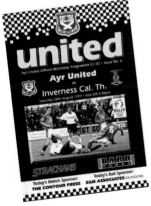

SCOTTISH PROGRAMME AWARDS

SCOTTISH PROGRAMME OF THE YEAR AWARDS 1998/99

SCOTTISH PREMIER LEAGUE
1. Dundee United
2. Rangers
3. Kilmarnock
4. Dunfermline Athletic
5. Celtic
6= Heart of Midlothian
6= St. Johnstone
8. Motherwell
9. Aberdeen
10. Dundee

S.F.L. FIRST DIVISION
1. Hibernian
2. St. Mirren
3. Greenock Morton
4. Ayr United
5. Falkirk
6. Raith Rovers
7. Airdrieonians
8. Hamilton Academical
9. Stranraer
10. Clydebank

S.F.L. SECOND DIVISION
1. Clyde
2. Partick Thistle
3. Stirling Albion
4. Livingston
5. Inverness Caledonian Thistle
6. Queen of the South
7. Alloa Athletic
8. Forfar Athletic
9. East Fife
10. Arbroath

S.F.L. THIRD DIVISION
1. Queen's Park
2. Montrose
3. Albion Rovers
4. Ross County
5. Berwick Rangers
6. Brechin City
7. Cowdenbeath
8. Stenhousemuir
9. Dumbarton
10. East Stirlingshire

SCOTTISH PROGRAMMES OF THE YEAR - PREVIOUS WINNERS

1973/74	Ayr United
1974/75	Hamilton Academical
1975/76	Heart of Midlothian
1976/77	Motherwell
1977/78	Hamilton Academical
1978/79	Hamilton Academical
1979/80	Berwick Rangers
1980/81	Aberdeen
1981/82	Hamilton Academical
1982/83	Dundee
1983/84	Dundee United
1984/85	Aberdeen
1985/86	Celtic
1986/87	Rangers
1987/88	Rangers
1988/89	Rangers
1989/90	Aberdeen
1990/91	Celtic
1991/92	Aberdeen
1992/93	Rangers
1993/94	Rangers
1994/95	Rangers
1995/96	Clyde
1996/97	Clyde
1997/98	Clyde
1998/99	Clyde

PREMIER LEAGUE PROGRAMME OF THE YEAR
(as above except...)

1974/75	Motherwell (old Div. One)
1975/76	Heart of Midlothian
1976/77	Motherwell
1977/78	Rangers
1978/79	Morton
1979/80	Morton
1995/96	Kilmarnock
1996/97	Dundee United
1997/98	Dundee United
1998/99	Dundee United

FIRST DIVISION PROGRAMME OF THE YEAR

1975/76	Hamilton Academical
1976/77	Hamilton Academical
1977/78	Hamilton Academical
1978/79	Hamilton Academical
1979/80	Berwick Rangers
1980/81	Hamilton Academical
1981/82	Hamilton Academical
1982/83	Queen's Park
1983/84	Hamilton Academical

1984/85	Clyde
1985/86	Clyde
1986/87	Clyde
1987/88	Hamilton Acad. & Clydebank
1988/89	Dunfermline Athletic
1989/90	Airdrieonians
1990/91	Dundee
1991/92	Partick Thistle
1992/93	Kilmarnock
1993/94	Dunfermline Athletic
1994/95	Dunfermline Athletic
1995/96	Dundee United
1996/97	Partick Thistle
1997/98	St. Mirren
1998/99	Hibernian

SECOND DIVISION PROGRAMME OF THE YEAR

1973/74	Hamilton Academical
1974/75	Hamilton Academical
1975/76	Berwick Rangers
1976/77	Albion Rovers
1977/78	Meadowbank Thistle
1978/79	Berwick Rangers
1979/80	Albion Rovers
1980/81	Clyde
1981/82	Clyde
1982/83	Stirling Albion
1983/84	Stirling Albion
1984/85	Stirling Abion
1985/86	Stirling Albion
1986/87	Raith Rovers
1987/88	Stirling Albion
1988/89	Stirling Albion
1989/90	Kilmarnock
1990/91	Stirling Albion
1991/92	Clyde
1992/93	Clyde
1993/94	Forfar Athletic
1994/95	Clyde
1995/96	Clyde
1996/97	Clyde
1997/98	Clyde
1998/99	Clyde

THIRD DIVISION PROGRAMME OF THE YEAR

1994/95	Forfar Athletic
1995/96	Livingston
1996/97	Inverness Caledonian Thistle
1997/98	Montrose
1998/99	Queen's Park

THE SCOTTISH PREMIER LEAGUE

ABERDEEN
EBBE SKOVDAHL
Player: Van Loes, Brondby, Hvalsoe
Manager: Hvalsoe, Glostrop BC,
Bronshoi, Brondby IF, Benfica,
Brondby IF, Vejle, Brondby IF, Aberdeen

CELTIC
JOHN BARNES
Player: Watford, Liverpool, Newcastle United,
Charlton Athletic, England
Head Coach: Celtic

DUNDEE
JOCKY SCOTT
Player: Chelsea, Aberdeen, Dundee
Manager: Dundee, Aberdeen (Co-Manager),
Dunfermline Athletic, Arbroath,
Hibernian (Caretaker Manager), Dundee

DUNDEE UNITED
PAUL STURROCK
Player: Dundee United, Scotland
Manager: St. Johnstone, Dundee United

HEART OF MIDLOTHIAN
JIM JEFFERIES
Player: Heart of Midlothian, Berwick Rangers
Manager: Berwick Rangers, Falkirk, Heart of Midlothian

HIBERNIAN
ALEX McLEISH
Player: Aberdeen, Motherwell, Scotland
Manager: Motherwell, Hibernian

KILMARNOCK
BOBBY WILLIAMSON
Player: Clydebank, Rangers, West Bromwich Albion,
Rotherham United, Kilmarnock
Manager: Kilmarnock

MOTHERWELL
BILLY DAVIES
Player: Rangers, St. Mirren, Leicester City,
Dunfermline Athletic, Motherwell
Manager: Motherwell

RANGERS
DICK ADVOCAAT
Player: Den Haag, Breda Kerkrod, Berlow, Chicago Sting
Manager: Haarlem, Dordrecht, Holland,
PSV Eindhoven, Rangers

ST. JOHNSTONE
SANDY CLARK
Player: Airdrieonians, West Ham United, Rangers,
Heart of Midlothian, Partick Thistle,
Dunfermline Athletic, Heart of Midlothian
Manager: Partick Thistle, Heart of Midlothian,
Hamilton Academical, St. Johnstone

FIRST DIVISION

AIRDRIEONIANS
GARY MACKAY
Player: Heart of Midlothian, Airdrieonians, Scotland
Manager: Airdrieonians

AYR UNITED
GORDON DALZIEL
Player: Rangers, Manchester City, Partick Thistle,
East Stirlingshire, Raith Rovers, Ayr United
Manager: Ayr United

CLYDEBANK
IAN McCALL
Player: Queen's Park, Dunfermline Athletic, Rangers,
Bradford City, Dunfermline Athletic, Dundee, Falkirk,
Hamilton Academical, Happy Valley (Hong Kong),
Hamilton Academical, Partick Thistle
Manager: Clydebank

DUNFERMLINE ATHLETIC
DICK CAMPBELL
Player: Brechin City, East Stirlingshire
Manager: Dunfermline Athletic

FALKIRK
ALEX TOTTEN
Player: Liverpool, Dundee, Dunfermline Athletic,
Falkirk, Queen of the South, Alloa Athletic
Manager: Alloa Athletic, Falkirk, Dumbarton,
St. Johnstone, East Fife, Kilmarnock, Falkirk

INVERNESS CALEDONIAN THISTLE
STEVE PATERSON
Player: Manchester United, Sheffield United,
Hong Kong Rangers, Sydney Olympic,
Yorniuri Tokyo
Manager: Inverness Caledonian Thistle

LIVINGSTON
RAY STEWART
Player: Dundee United, West Ham United,
St. Johnstone, Stirling Albion, Scotland
Manager: Livingston

MORTON
BILLY STARK
Player: St. Mirren, Aberdeen, Celtic, Kilmarnock,
Hamilton Academical, Kilmarnock, Celtic
Manager: Morton

RAITH ROVERS
JOHN McVEIGH
Player: Airdrieonians, Clyde, Hamilton Academical,
Kilmarnock, Falkirk
Manager: Partick Thistle, Raith Rovers

ST. MIRREN
TOM HENDRIE
Player: Meadowbank Thistle, Berwick Rangers
Manager: Berwick Rangers, Alloa Athletic, St. Mirren

SECOND DIVISION

ALLOA ATHLETIC
TERRY CHRISTIE
Player: Dundee, Raith Rovers, Stirling Albion
Manager: Meadowbank Thistle, Stenhousemuir,
Alloa Athletic

ARBROATH
DAVID BAIKIE
Player: Did Not Play at Senior Level.
Manager: Arbroath

CLYDE
ALLAN MAITLAND
Player: Did not play at senior level
Manager: Clyde

HAMILTON ACADEMICAL
ALLY DAWSON
Player: Rangers, Blackburn Rovers, Airdrieonians,
St. Andrews (Malta)
Manager: St. Andrews (Malta), Hamilton Academical

PARTICK THISTLE
JOHN LAMBIE
Player: Falkirk, St. Johnstone
Manager: Hamilton Academical, Partick Thistle,
Hamilton Academical, Partick Thistle, Falkirk,
Partick Thistle

QUEEN OF THE SOUTH
CO-MANAGERS:
GEORGE ROWE & KEN EADIE
GEORGE ROWE
Player: Clydebank, Queen of the South
Manager: Queen of the South
KEN EADIE
Player: Kilmarnock, Brechin City, Falkirk, Clydebank,
Airdrieonians, Queen of the South
Manager: Queen of the South

ROSS COUNTY
NEALE COOPER
Player: Aberdeen, Aston Villa,
Rangers, Reading,
Dunfermline Athletic, Ross County
Manager: Ross County

STENHOUSEMUIR
GRAEME ARMSTRONG
Player: Stirling Albion, Berwick Rangers,
Meadowbank Thistle, Stenhousemuir
Manager: Stenhousemuir

STIRLING ALBION
JOHN PHILLIBEN
Player: Stirling Albion, Doncaster Rovers, Motherwell,
Stirling Albion
Manager: Stirling Albion

STRANRAER
BILLY McLAREN
Player: Queen of the South (twice), Morton (twice),
East Fife, Cowdenbeath, Dunfermline Athletic,
Hibernian, Partick Thistle
Manager: Queen of the South, Hamilton Academical,
Albion Rovers, Queen of the South, Albion Rovers,
Stranraer

THIRD DIVISION

ALBION ROVERS
MARK SHANKS
Player: Ayr United, Dumbarton, Queen of the South
Manager: Queen of the South, Albion Rovers

BERWICK RANGERS
PAUL SMITH
Player: Dundee, Dundee United, Raith Rovers,
Motherwell, Dunfermline Athletic, Falkirk,
Dunfermline Athletic, Heart of Midlothian, Ayr United,
Berwick Rangers
Manager: Berwick Rangers

BRECHIN CITY
JOHN YOUNG
Player: St. Mirren, Brechin City, Arbroath
Manager: Brechin City

COWDENBEATH
CRAIG LEVEIN
Player: Cowdenbeath, Heart of Midlothian, Scotland
Manager: Cowdenbeath

DUMBARTON
JIMMY BROWN
Player: Partick Thistle, Dumbarton, Oxford United
Manager: Dumbarton

EAST FIFE
STEPHEN KIRK
Player: East Fife, Stoke City, Partick Thistle, East Fife,
Motherwell, Falkirk, Raith Rovers, East Fife
Manager: East Fife

EAST STIRLINGSHIRE
HUGH McCANN
Player: Celtic, Alloa Athletic, Berwick Rangers,
East Stirlingshire
Manager: Alloa Athletic, Queen's Park (Coach),
East Stirlingshire

FORFAR ATHLETIC
IAN McPHEE
Player: Forfar Athletic, Dundee United, Airdrieonians,
Forfar Athletic
Manager: Forfar Athletic

MONTROSE
KEVIN DRINKELL
Player: Grimsby Town, Norwich City, Rangers,
Coventry City, Falkirk, Stirling Albion
Manager: Stirling Albion, Montrose

QUEEN'S PARK
JOHN McCORMACK
Player: Clydebank, St. Mirren, Dundee, Airdrieonians,
Partick Thistle
Coach: Dundee (Manager), Queen's Park

INFORMATION COMPILED BY JIM JEFFREY

EUROPEAN CHAMPIONS LEAGUE

First Qualifying Round - First Leg

Wednesday, 22nd July, 1998

CELTIC 0   ST. PATRICK'S 0

Celtic: Gould, Boyd, Mahe, McNamara, (Donnelly), Rieper, (Annoni), Stubbs, Larsson, Burley, Lambert, Blinker, Brattbakk, (Jackson)
Substitutes not used: McKinlay, Mackay, Kerr, McBride
St. Patrick's: Wood, Clarke, Campbell, Lynch, Hawkins, Osam, Gormley, Russell, Molloy, (Reilly), Braithwaite, (Crolly), Gilzean
Substitutes not used: Byrne, Devereux, Long, Morgan, McKenna
Referee: B. Benedik (Slovakia)
Attendance: 56,864

First Qualifying Round - Second Leg

Wednesday, 29th July, 1998

ST. PATRICK'S 0   CELTIC 2
                           Brattbakk, Larsson

Aggregate: 0-2
St. Patrick's: Wood, Clarke, Campbell, (Doyle), Lynch, Hawkins, Osam, Gormley, Morgan, (Russell), Braithwaite, Gilzean, (Reilly), Molloy
Substitutes not used: Moody, Devereux, Crolly, McKenna
Celtic: Gould, Boyd, McNamara, Stubbs, Larsson, Burley, Brattbakk, Lambert, Jackson, (Donnelly), Mackay, Blinker, (McKinlay)
Substitutes not used: Annoni, Kerr, McBride, Burchill, Elliot
Referee: M. Vuorola (Finland)
Attendance: 9,500

Second Qualifying Round - First Leg

Wednesday, 12th August, 1998

CELTIC 1   CROATIA ZAGREB 0
Jackson

Celtic: Gould, Boyd, McNamara, Rieper, Stubbs, Larsson, Burley, Brattbakk, (Jackson), Donnelly, Lambert, Blinker
Substitutes not used: O'Donnell, Hannah, Annoni, McKinlay, Mackay, Kerr
Croatia Zagreb: Ladic, Tokic, Maric, (J. Simic), Juric, Prosinecki, Viduka, Rukavina, D. Simic, Cvitanovic, Jelicic, (Mujcin), Jurcic
Substitutes not used: Maldinic, Savic, Butina, Mikic, Saric
Referee: J.M. Garcia Aranda (Spain)
Attendance: 51,397

Second Qualifying Round - Second Leg

Wednesday, 26th August, 1998

CROATIA ZAGREB 3   CELTIC 0
Maric, Prosinecki (2)

Aggregate: 3-1
Croatia Zagreb: Ladic, Tokic, Maric, (Saric), Juric, Prosinecki, Viduka, (Sokota), Rukavina, D. Simic, Cvitanovic, Jelicic, (Mujcin), Jurcic
Substitutes not used: Maldinic, Savic, Butina, Mikic
Celtic: Gould, Boyd, Mahe, McNamara, Rieper, Stubbs, Larsson, Burley, Lambert, Jackson, (Donnelly), Blinker, (Brattbakk)
Substitutes not used: Hannah, Annoni, McKinlay, Burchill, Kerr
Referee: P. Collina (Italy)
Attendance: 27,000

EUROPEAN CUP WINNERS' CUP

Qualifying Round - First Leg

Thursday, 13th August, 1998

FC LANTANA 0   HEART OF MIDLOTHIAN 1
                         Makel

FC Lantana: Ussoltsev, Krasnopgrov, Kalimullin, Kolotsei, Bahmatski, Mitjunov, Borissov, Leitan, (Tselnokov), Valuiski, Gorjatsov, (Kulikov),Koulitchenko
Substitutes not used: Kiseljov, Jersov
Heart of Midlothian: Rousset, Naysmith, Weir, Salvatori, Ritchie, McCann, Adam, (Murray), Hamilton, (Quitongo), Locke, Flögel, Makel
Substitutes not used: McKenzie, McKinnon, Pressley, Murie, Holmes
Referee: M. Benes (Czech Republic)
Attendance: 1,300

Qualifying Round - Second Leg

Thursday, 27th August, 1998

HEART OF MIDLOTHIAN 5   FC LANTANA 0
McCann, Fulton, Hamilton,
Flögel, Holmes

Aggregate: 6-0
Heart of Midlothian: Rousset, Pressley, McKinnon, Weir, Locke, Ritchie, McCann, Fulton, Adam, (Quitongo),Makel, (Holmes), Hamilton, (Flögel)
Substitutes not used: Salvatori, Murray, Murie, Hogarth
FC Lantana: Ussoltsev, Kransnopgorov, Kolotsei, Bahmatski, Mitjunov, Leitan, Valuiski, (Tselenkov), Gorjatsov, Koulitchenko, Tjunin, Kulikov
Substitutes not used: Kalimullin, Kiseljov, Jersov
Referee: J. Wegeree (Holland)
Attendance: 15,053

First Round - First Leg

Thursday, 17th September, 1998

HEART OF MIDLOTHIAN 0   REAL MALLORCA 1
                         Marcelino

Heart of Midlothian: Rousset, McPherson, Naysmith, Weir, Salvatori, Ritchie, McCann, Adam, Hamilton, (Holmes), Locke, Pressley
Substitutes not used: McKenzie, Makel, Murray, Murie, Horn, Severin
Real Mallorca: Roa, M. Soler, Siviero, Marcelino, Dani, Stankovic, (Carreras), Lauren, Olaizola, Arpon, (Nino), Engonga, Lopez, (Dominguez)
Substitutes not used: Galvez, F. Soler, Pavnovic, Biagini
Referee: A. Prentalange (Italy)
Attendance: 13,573

First Round - Second Leg

Thursday, 1st October, 1998

REAL MALLORCA 1   HEART OF MIDLOTHIAN 1
Lopez   Hamilton

Aggregate: 2-1
Real Mallorca: Galvez, M. Soler, Siviero, Marcelino, Dani, (Nino), Stankovic, Lauren, F. Soler, (Carreras), Arpon, Lopez, (Biagini)
Substitutes not used: Franco, Dominguez, Rufete, Pavnovic
Heart of Midlothian: Rousset, Naysmith, Weir, Salvatori, Ritchie, McCann, (Holmes), Adam, Hamilton, Locke, Makel, (McPherson), Pressley
Substitutes not used: McKenzie, Murray, Murie, Horn, Severin
Referee: A. Albrecht (Germany)
Attendance: 11,912

UEFA CUP

First Qualifying Round - First Leg
Wednesday, 22nd July, 1998

SHELBOURNE 3   **RANGERS 5**
Porrini (o.g.),   Albertz (2), Amato (2),
Rutherford, Morley   Van Bronckhorst
Match Played at Prenton Park, Birkenhead
Shelbourne: Gough, Geoghegan, McCartney, Scully, D. Baker, Rutherford, Smith, Fenlon, Fitzgerald, Morley, (Sheridan), Kelly
Substitutes not used: Campbell, Neville, Flood, Gifford, R. Baker, O'Brien
Rangers: Niemi, Porrini, Amoruso, Petric, Van Bronckhorst, Gattuso, (Amato), B. Ferguson, Thern, (I. Ferguson), Albertz, Graham, (Johansson), Durie
Substitutes not used: Wilson, Charbonnier, Moore, Vidmar
Referee: V. Anghelinei (Romania)
Attendance: 6,047

ZELJEZNICAR 1   **KILMARNOCK 1**
Vazola   McGowne
Zeljeznicar: Guso, Biocevic, Mulmuic, Kunic, (Pehliranovic), Greolic, (Ceman), Falic, Vazola, Muharemonic, Mulaosmanovic, Burek, Zeric, (Selinonic)
Substitutes not used: Kruzik, Kozic, Jahic, Sopovic
Kilmarnock: Marshall, MacPherson, Montgomerie, McGowne, Baker, Holt, Wright, (Roberts), Durrant, Mitchell, Mahood, Lauchlan
Substitutes not used: Henry, Nevin, Meldrum, Hamilton, Bagan, Burke
Referee: S. Braa (France)
Attendance: 17,000

First Qualifying Round - Second Leg
Wednesday, 29th July, 1998

KILMARNOCK 1   **ZELJEZNICAR 0**
Mahood
Aggregate: 2-1
Kilmarnock: Marshall, MacPherson, McGowne, Holt, Wright, Durrant, Mitchell, Mahood, Baker, Lauchlan, Burke, (Roberts)
Substitutes not used: Montgomerie, Henry, Nevin, Meldrum, Hamilton, Bagan
Zeljeznicar: Guso, Biocevic, Mulaosmanovic, Kunic, Mulmuic, Burek, Fulimovic, Greolic, (Zeric), Muharemonic, Vazola, Satic, (Edin)
Substitutes not used: Kruzik, Jahic, Pehliranovic, Kozic, Ceman
Referee: M. Tokat (Turkey)
Attendance: 14,512

RANGERS 2   **SHELBOURNE 0**
Johansson (2)
Aggregate: 7-3
Rangers: Niemi, Porrini, Moore, Amoruso, Numan, Kanchelskis, (Amato), B. Ferguson, Van Bronckhorst, (I. Ferguson), Albertz, Durie, (Gattuso), Johansson
Substitutes not used: Brown, Thern, Petric, Graham
Shelbourne: Gough, Geoghegan, McCartney, Scully, D. Baker, Rutherford, Smith, Fenlon, Fitzgerald, Morley, (Sheridan), Kelly
Substitutes not used: O'Brien, Neville, Gifford, Byrne, R. Baker, Campbell
Referee: M. Milewski (Poland)

Attendance: 46,906

Second Qualifying Round - First Leg
Tuesday, 11th August, 1998

RANGERS 2   **PAOK SALONIKA 0**
Kanchelskis, Wallace
Rangers: Niemi, Porrini, Moore, Amoruso, Numan, Kanchelskis, B. Ferguson, (Albertz), I. Ferguson, Van Bronckhorst, (Gattuso), Wallace, Durie, (Amato)
Substitutes not used: Charbonnier, Petric, Johansson, Miller
PAOK Salonika: Mihopoulos, Bancovic, Olivares, Kapetanopoulos, Vrizas, (Cominges), Toursounidis, (Zafseiriou), Srdatzeskos, Nagre, Katisabis, Konstanpinibis, Macheridis
Substitutes not used: Koulakiotis, Balis, Argyriou, Merisaoies, Uafes
Referee: K.M. Nielsen (Denmark)
Attendance: 35,392

SIGMA OLOMOUC 2   **KILMARNOCK 0**
Krohmer, Konig
Sigma Olomouc: Skacel, Kovar, Ujfalusi, Krohmer, Mucha, (Steska), Barborik, (Ryska), Drulak, (Cupak), Machala, Konig, Kotulek, Heinz
Substitutes not used: Vivek, Kovac, Kucera, Pizanowski
Kilmarnock: Marshall, MacPherson, Montgomerie, McGowne, Lauchlan, Baker, Holt, Durrant, Mahood, (Burke), Mitchell, Wright, (Vareille)
Substitutes not used: Meldrum, Hamilton, O'Neill, Roberts, Bagan
Referee: E. Ersoy (Turkey)
Attendance: 4,200

Second Qualifying Round - Second Leg
Tuesday, 25th August, 1998

KILMARNOCK 0   **SIGMA OLOMOUC 2**
                           Heinz, Mucha
Aggregate: 0-4
Kilmarnock: Marshall, MacPherson, Kerr, McGowne, Lauchlan, Nevin, (McCutcheon), Holt, Mahood, Durrant, Burke, Wright, (Roberts), Vareille
Substitutes not used: Mitchell, Meldrum, Baker, Bagan
Sigma Olomouc: Skacel, Kovar, Ujfalusi, Mucha, (Ryska), Barborik, (Steska), Machala, Balcarek, Konig, Kucera, Kotulek, Heinz, (Vivek)
Substitutes not used: Krohmer, Drulak, Kovac, Pizanowski
Referee: L. Baptista (Portugal)
Attendance: 11,140

PAOK SALONIKA 0   **RANGERS 0**
Aggregate: 0-2
PAOK Salonika: Mihopoulos, Bancovic, Olivares, Zafseiriou, (Uafes), Kapetanopoulos, Srdatzeskos, Vrizas, Toursounidis, Nagre, Koulakiotis, Katisabis
Substitutes not used: Argyriou, Velis, Samaras, Marifaliev, Cominges, Mastos
Rangers: Charbonnier, Porrini, Amoruso, (Petric), Numan, B. Ferguson, Kanchelskis, (Gattuso), Van Bronckhorst, Albertz, (Amato), I. Ferguson, Wallace, Moore
Substitutes not used: Niemi, Johansson, Vidmar, Miller
Referee: M. Merk (Germany)
Attendance: 36,000

First Round - First Leg
Tuesday, 15th September, 1998

VITORIA GUIMARAES 1   **CELTIC 2**
Geraldo   Larsson, Donnelly
Vitoria Guimaraes: Espinha, Carlos, Alexandre, Auri, Berto, Paneira, Costa, (Riva), Rocha, Geraldo, Edmilson, (Milovanovic), Gilmar
Substitutes not used: Neno, Soderstrom, Gomes, Arley, Kasongo
Celtic: Gould, Boyd, (Annoni), Mahe, Rieper, Stubbs, Larsson, Burley, O'Donnell, Donnelly, Lambert, Jackson, (Hannah)
Substitutes not used: McKinlay, Mackay, Kerr, McLaughlin, McBride
Referee: M. Frohlich (Germany)
Attendance: 10,750

BIETAR JERUSALEM 1 **RANGERS** 1
Abukasis Albertz

Beitar Jerusalem: Kornfein, Domb, Dery, Levy, Abukasis, Telesnikov, Shelah, Shitrit, Hamar, Sandor, Rehuben, (Raythman)
Substitutes not used: Mizrahi, Grif, Ohama, Yaacobi
Rangers: Charbonnier, Porrini, Amoruso, B. Ferguson, Kanchelskis, Van Bronckhorst, I. Ferguson, Wallace, (Graham), Moore, Johansson, (Albertz), Vidmar, (Stensaas)
Substitutes not used: Niemi, Petric, Gattuso, Miller
Referee: B. Souse (France)
Attendance: 14,000

First Round - Second Leg
Tuesday, 29th September, 1998

CELTIC 2 **VITORIA GUIMARAES** 1
Stubbs, Larsson Soderstrom
Aggregate: 4-2
Celtic: Gould, Mahe, Rieper, Stubbs, Larsson, Burley, Brattbakk, (Jackson), Donnelly, Lambert, Hannah, McKinlay
Substitutes not used: Kerr, McLaughlin, Healy, McBride, Burchill, Elliot
Vitoria Guimaraes: Espinha, Arley, Alexandre, Berto, Costa, Gilmar, (Basilio), Milovanovic (Edmilson), Soderstrom, Kabve, Riva, Geraldo
Substitutes not used: Paneira, Carlos, Auri, Gomes, Paiva
Referee: O. Sarvan (Turkey)
Attendance: 38,583

Thursday, 2nd October, 1998

RANGERS 4 **BIETAR JERUSALEM** 2
Gattuso, Porrini, Salloi, Ohama
Johansson, Wallace
Aggregate: 5-3
Rangers: Charbonnier, Porrini, Moore, (Hendry), Amoruso, Vidmar, Gattuso, B. Ferguson, Van Bronckhorst, Albertz, Wallace, Johansson, (Miller)
Substitutes not used: Niemi, Petric, Stensaas, Graham, Rozental
Beitar Jerusalem: Kornfein, Levy, (Ohama), Shelah, Dery, Telesnikov, Abukasis, Mizrahi, Salloi, Hamar, Sandor, Shitrit
Substitutes not used: Grif, Raythman, Tretiak, Yaacobi
Referee: S. Khussainov (Russia)
Attendance: 45,610

Second Round - First Leg
Tuesday, 20th October, 1998

CELTIC 1 **ZURICH** 1
Brattbakk Fischer
Celtic: Gould, Boyd, Mahe, McNamara, Larsson, Burley, Brattbakk, (Jackson), O'Donnell, Donnelly, Lambert, McKinlay
Substitutes not used: Hannah, Kerr, McLaughlin, McBride, Burchill, Vaugh
Zurich: Pascolo, Hodel, Santanna, (Castillo), Bartlett, Lima, Nixon, (Wiederkeher), Signore, Chassot, Fischer, Di Jorio, Taroni
Substitutes not used: Huber, Djordjevic, Iodice, Tronbini
Referee: V. Melnichuk (Ukraine)
Attendance: 44,121

Thursday, 22nd October, 1998

BAYER LEVERKUSEN 1 **RANGERS** 2
Reichenberger Van Bronckhorst, Johansson
Bayer Leverkusen: Matysek, R. Kovac, Happe, (Reichenberger), Reeb, Nowotny, Ze Roberto, Emerson, (N. Kovac), Meijer, Rink, Beinlich, Ramelow, (Heintze)
Substitutes not used: Vollborn, Zivkovic, Lehnhoff, Mamic
Rangers: Charbonnier, Porrini, B. Ferguson, Kanchelskis, Van Bronckhorst, Albertz, Wallace, (Durie), Johansson, (I. Ferguson), Wilson, Vidmar, Hendry
Substitutes not used: Niemi, Amato, Petric, Stensaas, Miller
Referee: K. Bo Larsen (Denmark)
Attendance: 22,000

Second Round - Second Leg
Tuesday, 3rd November, 1998

ZURICH 4 **CELTIC** 2
Del Signore, Chassot, O'Donnell, Larsson
Bartlett, Santanna
Aggregate: 5-3
Zurich: Pascolo, Hodel, Wiederkeher, (Opengo), Santanna, Bartlett, Lima, Signore, (Nixon), Chassot, (Castillo), Fischer, Di Jorio, Taroni
Substitutes not used: Tronbini, Huber, Iodice,
Celtic: Gould, (Kerr), Mahe, McNamara, Larsson, Brattbakk, O'Donnell, Donnelly, Lambert, Jackson, Hannah, McKinlay
Substitutes not used: McLaughlin, Healy, McBride, Burchill, Crossley, Vaugh
Referee: L. Sundell (Sweden)
Attendance: 14,500

Thursday, 5th November, 1998

RANGERS 1 **BAYER LEVERKUSEN** 1
Johansson Kirsten
Aggregate: 3-2
Rangers: Charbonnier, (Niemi), Porrini, Hendry, Amoruso, Numan, Kanchelskis, (I. Ferguson), B. Ferguson, (Wilson), Van Bronckhorst, Albertz, Wallace, Johansson
Substitutes not used: Amato, Petric, Vidmar, Miller
Bayer Leverkusen: Matysek, R. Kovac, (Emerson), Happe, Reeb, Nowotny, Ze Roberto, Kirsten, Meijer, (N. Kovac), Heintze, Beinlich, Ramelow
Substitutes not used: Zivkovic, Rink, Mamic, Reichenberger, Vollborn
Referee: L. Batista (Portugal)
Attendance: 50,012

Third Round - First Leg
Tuesday, 24th November, 1998

RANGERS 1 **PARMA** 1
Wallace Balbo
Rangers: Niemi, Porrini, (Durie), Amoruso, Hendry, Numan, B. Ferguson, Kanchelskis, Albertz, I. Ferguson, Wallace, Johansson, (Amato)
Substitutes not used: Stensaas, Wilson, Vidmar, Miller, Brown
Parma: Buffon, Bennarivo, Sartor, Baggio, Crespo, (Orlandini), Veron, (Fiore), Stanic, Boghossian, Cannavaro, Balbo, Thuram
Substitutes not used: Guardalden, Pedros, Giunti, Sensini, Vanoi
Referee: A. Sars (France)
Attendance: 49,514

Third Round - Second Leg
Tuesday, 8th December, 1998

PARMA 3 **RANGERS** 1
Balbo, Fiore, Chiesa Albertz
Aggregate: 4-2
Parma: Buffon, Thuram, Sensini, Cannavaro, Fuser, (Mussi), Baggio, Boghossian, (Fiore), Bennarivo, Veron, Balbo, Chiesa, (Crespo)
Substitutes not used: Nista, Vanoli, Orlandini, Giunti
Rangers: Niemi, Porrini, Hendry, Amoruso, Numan, Albertz, B. Ferguson, (Miller), I. Ferguson, Van Bonckhorst, Wallace, (Amato), Durie, (Vidmar)
Substitutes not used: Brown, Stensaas, Wilson, Kanchelskis
Referee: T. Hauge (Norway)
Attendance: 17,000

A Record of European Championship and International Friendly Matches played by Scotland during Season 1998/99

EUROPEAN CHAMPIONSHIP

Saturday, 5th September, 1998 - Zalgiris Stadium, Vilnius

LITHUANIA 0   **SCOTLAND 0**

Lithuania: Stauce, Sugzda, (Butrus), Semberas, R. Zutautas, Baltus, Zvirgzdauskas, Mikulenas, (Slekys), Fugzda, Preiksaitis, Skarbalius, Jankauskas

Substitutes not used: V. Zutautas, Stumbrys, Gleveckas, Razanauskas, D. Zutautas

Scotland: J. Leighton, C. Dailly, T. Boyd, M. Elliott, C. Hendry, C. Calderwood, (C. Davidson), P. Lambert, K. Gallacher, A. McCoist, (N. McCann), D. Jackson, (B. Ferguson), J. Collins

Substitutes not used: N. Sullivan, D. Weir, S. Fulton, D. Whyte

Referee: C.D. Zotta (Romania)

Attendance: 4,800

Saturday, 10th October, 1998 - Tynecastle Stadium, Edinburgh

SCOTLAND 3   **ESTONIA 2**

Dodds (2),   Hohlov-Simson, Smirnov

Hohlov-Simson (o.g.)

Scotland: J. Leighton, D. Weir, C. Davidson, C. Calderwood, (S. Donnelly), C. Hendry, T. Boyd, W. McKinlay, I. Durrant, A. McCoist, (W. Dodds), K. Gallacher, (D. Jackson), A. Johnston

Substitutes not used: N. Sullivan, D. Whyte, M. Elliott, S. Glass

Estonia: Poom, Smirnov, Kirs, Hohlov-Simson, Rooba, M. Alonen, Terehhov, Oper, Kristal, Reim, Zelinski, (Viikmae)

Substitutes not used: Tohvrr, Allas, O'Konnell-Bronin, Annishe, Meet

Referee: J.J.B. Marques (Portugal)

Attendance: 16,930

Wednesday, 14th October, 1998 - Pittodrie Stadium, Aberdeen

SCOTLAND 2   **FAROE ISLANDS 1**

Burley, Dodds   J.K. Hansen

Scotland: N. Sullivan, D. Weir, C. Davidson, M. Elliott, C. Hendry, T. Boyd, W. McKinlay, (I. Durrant), S. Donnelly, W. Dodds, C. Burley, A. Johnston, (S. Glass)

Substitutes not used: J. Gould, C. Calderwood, D. Jackson, A. McCoist, D. Whyte

Faroe Islands: Mikkelsen, Johannsen, J.K. Hansen, Thorsteinsson, H. Hansen, Jonsson, Jarnskor, J. Johnsson, Arge, Petersen, S. Johnsson

Substitutes not used: Dam, Jan Joensen, Johannus Joensen, Eliasen, Knudsen, Borg, John Hansen

Referee: C. Kapitanis (Cyprus)

Attendance: 18,517

Wednesday, 31st March, 1999 - Celtic Park, Glasgow

SCOTLAND 1   **CZECH REPUBLIC 2**

E. Jess   M. Elliott (o.g.), Smicer

Scotland: N. Sullivan, D. Hopkin, C. Davidson, (A. Johnston), M. Elliott, T. Boyd, D. Weir, C. Burley, P. Lambert, N. McCann, G. McAllister, (D. Hutchison), E. Jess

Substitutes not used: J. Gould, D. Whyte, J. McNamara, I. Durrant, P. Ritchie

Czech Republic: Srnicek, Votava, Suchoparek, Nedved, Hornak, Hasek, Nemec, Poborsky, (Rada), Lokvenc, (Kuka), Smicer, (Baranek), Berger

Substitutes not used: Vlcek, Koller, Cizek, Postulka

Referee: K.M. Nielsen (Denmark)

Attendance: 44,515

Saturday, 5th June, 1999 - Toftir Stadium, Toftir

FAROE ISLANDS 1   **SCOTLAND 1**

H. Hansen   A. Johnston

Faroe Islands: Mikkelsen, Johannsen, H. Hansen, Thorsteinsson, O. Hansen, (J. Hansen), Johnsson, J. Joensen, (Borg), S. Joenson, Moerkore, Jonsson, Petersen, (Arge)

Substitutes not used: Knudsen, Benjaminsen, Dam

Scotland: N. Sullivan, D. Weir, M. Elliott, C. Davidson, C. Calderwood, T. Boyd, I. Durrant, (C. Cameron), K. Gallacher, (E. Jess), W. Dodds, P. Lambert, A. Johnston, (S. Gemmill)

Substitutes not used: J. Gould, D. Whyte, P. Ritchie, R. Winters

Referee: P. Kalt (France)

Attendance: 1,500

Wednesday, 9th June, 1999 - AC Sparta Prague Stadium, Prague

CZECH REPUBLIC 3   **SCOTLAND 2**

Repka, Kuka, Koller   Ritchie, Johnston

Czech Republic: Srnicek, Repka, Suchoparek, Nedved, Hornak, Hasek, (Baranek), Nemec, Poborsky, (Koller), Lokvenc, (Kuka), Smicer, Berger

Substitutes not used: Galasek, Nikl, Horvath, Maier

Scotland: N. Sullivan, D. Weir, C. Davidson, T. Boyd, P. Ritchie, C. Calderwood, A. Johnston, P. Lambert, W. Dodds, I. Durrant, (E. Jess), K. Gallacher

Substitutes not used: J. Gould, D. Whyte, P. O'Donnell, S. Gemmill, C. Cameron, R. Winters

Referee: H. Krug (Germany)

Attendance: 22,086

GROUP NINE TABLE

	P	W	D	L	F	A	PTS
CZECH REPUBLIC	7	7	0	0	17	5	21
SCOTLAND	6	2	2	2	9	9	8
LITHUANIA	7	2	3	7	9	8	8
BOSNIA HERZEGOVINA	6	2	2	2	9	10	8
ESTONIA	7	2	1	4	12	13	7
FAROE ISLANDS	7	0	3	4	4	12	3

FULL INTERNATIONAL FRIENDLY MATCH

Wednesday, 28th April, 1999 - Weserstadion, Bremen

GERMANY 0   **SCOTLAND 1**

       D. Hutchison

Germany: Lehmann, Nowotny, Heinrich, Worns, Strunz, (Janker), Jeremies, (Ramelow), Neuville, Hamann, (Ballack), Bierhoff, (Kirsten), Matthaus, Heldt

Substitutes not used: Butt, Preetz, Rehmer

Scotland: N. Sullivan, D. Weir, C. Davidson, (D. Whyte), T. Boyd, C. Hendry, (P. Ritchie), P. Lambert, (C. Cameron), S. Gemmill, (E. Jess), I. Durrant, (R. Winters), W. Dodds, D. Hutchison, A. Johnston, (B. O'Neil)

Substitute not used: A. Main

Referee: U. Meier (Switzerland)

Attendance: 27,000

Don Hutchison scores Scotland's winner against Germany

UEFA
EURO
2000
Belgium - The Netherlands

Billy Dodds scores Scotland's second goal against Estonia

"UNDER 21" - EUROPEAN CHAMPIONSHIP
1998/2000 QUALIFYING MATCHES
GROUP NINE

Friday, 4th September, 1998 - Vingis Stadium, Vilnius

LITHUANIA 0   **SCOTLAND 0**

Lithuania: Leus, Joksas, Gleveckas, (Sonajovas), Zutautas, (Laurisas), Dziaukstas, Gardzijauskas, Cikas, (Cepas), Kauspadas, Danilevicius, Fomenko, Graziunas
Substitutes not used: Balius, Alunveris
Scotland: N. Alexander, C. McEwan, S. McCluskey, A. Archibald, M.J. Buchan, C. Easton, G. Brebner, G. Strachan, (G. Mason), S. Campbell, M. Burchill, (A. Notman), D. Graham, (B. Elliot)
Substitutes not used: S. Robertson, R. Horn, P. Dalglish, J.P. McBride
Referee: K. Vassaras (Greece)
Attendance: 400

Friday, 9th October, 1998 - Excelsior Stadium, Airdrie

SCOTLAND 2   **ESTONIA 0**
C. Dargo, P. Dalglish

Scotland: N. Alexander, R. Anderson, (C. McEwan), M.J. Buchan, S. Wilson, G. Naysmith, S. Campbell, (M. Burchill), C. Easton, G. Strachan, G. Brebner, P. Dalglish, C. Dargo, (A. Notman)
Estonia: Kaalma, Piiroja, Anis, Nommik, Kurjanov, Anniste, Haavistu, Allas, Saviauk, Stepanov, Oun
Substitutes not used: Treiel, Jurisson, Taan, Vink, Mae
Referee: K. Guerguinov (Bulgaria)
Attendance: 5,676

Wednesday, 14th October, 1998 - AA Gent Stadium, Ghent

BELGIUM 2   **SCOTLAND 0**
Morhaye (2)

Belgium: Gillet, Verlinden, Van Dender, Hoeskens, De Coninck, Remacle, (Baseggio), Van Handenoven, (Delorde), Somers, (Daems), Morhaye, Vanderpaar, Roussel
Substitutes not used: Delwarte, Cavens, Collen, Schockart
Scotland: N. Alexander, C. McEwan, M.J. Buchan, S. Wilson, G. Naysmith, S. Campbell, (C. Dargo), C. Easton, (J. Paterson), G. Strachan, G. Brebner, P. Dalglish, (A. Notman), M. Burchill
Substitutes not used: S. Robertson, A. Archibald, G. Mason, J.P. McBride
Referee: M. Peltola (Finland)
Attendance: 1,000

Wednesday, 18th November, 1998 - St. Mirren Park, Paisley

SCOTLAND 2   **BELGIUM 2**
C. Dargo (2)   Somers, Vanderpaar

Scotland: N. Alexander, C. McEwan, R. Anderson, S. Wilson, G. Naysmith, G. Strachan, (J. Paterson), B. Ferguson, (C. Easton), S. Campbell, (A. Notman), G. Brebner, C. Dargo, M. Burchill
Substitutes not used: P. Gallacher, G. Mason, S. McGarry, I. Anderson
Belgium: Gillet, Verlinden, Van Dender, (Daems), Smet, Hoeskens, Remacle, Van Handenoven, Somers, Morhaye, Vanderpaar, Roussel, (Cavens)
Substitutes not used: Renard, Barbe, De Coninck, Delorge, Schockart
Referee: E. Ersoy (Turkey)
Attendance: 5,087

Tuesday, 30th March, 1999 - Fir Park Stadium, Motherwell

SCOTLAND 0   **CZECH REPUBLIC 1**
                          Sionko

Scotland: N. Alexander, C. McEwan, (G. Teale), G. Naysmith, R. Hughes, J. Lauchlan, M.J. Buchan, S. Campbell, (D. Young), P. Dalglish, L. McCulloch, (C. Dargo), G. Brebner, M. Burchill
Substitutes not used: P. Gallacher, R. Anderson, B. Nicholson, G. Mason
Czech Republic: Skacel, Dosek, Petrous, Sedlacek, (Jarosk), Lengvel, Plesko, (Simak), Sionko,Ujfalusi, Pacanda, (Lukes), Heinz, Brabec
Substitutes not used: Licka, Chvalovsky, Kovac
Referee: M. Boukhtir (Tunisia)
Attendance: 3,681

Tuesday, 8th June, 1999 - FK Teplice Stadium, Teplice

CZECH REPUBLIC 3   **SCOTLAND 2**
Dosek, Heinz, Sionko   S. Thompson, R. Hughes

Czech Republic: Skacel, Dosek, Brabec, (Sedlacek), Licka, (Simak), Lengvel, Tyce, Sionko, Polak, (Garosik), Jankulevski, Vosek, Heinz,
Substitutes not used: Kovac, Plesko, Chvalovsky, Petrous
Scotland: P. Gallacher, R. Anderson, (B. Nicholson), G. Naysmith, (B. O'Brien), G. Rae, S. Wilson, J. Lauchlan, R. Hughes, M. Burchill, S. Thompson, G. Brebner, I. Anderson, (S. Campbell)
Substitutes not used: D. Mathieson, G. Teale, C. Dargo, N. Tarrant
Referee: J. Larsen (Denmark)
Attendance: 3,141

GROUP NINE TABLE

	P	W	D	L	F	A	PTS
CZECH REPUBLIC	7	6	1	0	13	2	19
LITHUANIA	7	4	1	2	12	4	13
BELGIUM	5	3	1	1	9	4	10
SCOTLAND	6	1	2	3	6	8	5
BOSNIA HERZEGOVINA	5	1	1	3	4	12	4
ESTONIA	6	0	0	6	3	17	0

"UNDER-21" INTERNATIONAL FRIENDLY MATCH

Tuesday, 27th April, 1999 - Emslandstadion, Meppen

GERMANY 2   **SCOTLAND 1**
Nehrbauer, Reich   S. Thompson

Germany: Enke, Maltritz, Klitzpera, Hertzsch, Ernst, Keidel, Schindzielorz, Bugera, Reich, Nehrbauer, Rosler
Substitutes: Borel, Sherbe, Voigt, Dabrowski, Rost, Frommer, Villa
Scotland: N. Alexander, (D. Mathieson), B. Nicholson, (D. Young), G.Naysmith, R. Anderson, S. Wilson, J. Lauchlan, (K. McAnespie), S. Campbell, (G. Teale), M.J. Buchan, (C. McEwan), C. Dargo, (I. Anderson), G. Brebner, L. McCulloch, (S. Thompson)
Referee: R. Lajuks (Latvia)
Attendance: 1,500

MEN AND WOMEN IN BLACK

Everyone is aware of how football has changed over the years - tactics, TV coverage, sponsorship, stadia and many other changes make the game almost unrecognisable from its earlier days.

The game has also changed over the years for the referee and for the Laws of the Game. Over 100 years ago in the 1880's, you would never have heard the spectators criticising the referee for not giving a penalty kick for the simple reason that the penalty kick was not introduced into the Laws until 1891.

It was only when the penalty kick was introduced that the field markings were changed to include the penalty area.

An interesting rule was found in the 1860's - hacking was allowed. Hacking was clearly defined as kicking an opponent below the knee. If you kicked him above the knee it was a foul but kicking him below the knee was within the Laws. Times have changed a bit - or have they!

In the 1880's you would never hear the spectators shout to the referee to keep up with play. He would have found this very difficult as he stood at the side of the field with his top hat, coat and walking stick.

In this period the referee's role was exactly what his name suggested. He was referred to by the two umpires - one from each team - when they could not agree on a decision. It was only in 1891 again that the decision was taken by the International Football Association Board to place a referee in the centre of the field with the two umpires becoming linesmen.

Referees are fitter than they have ever been and the results of the FIFA Fitness Test for Scottish Referees over the years prove this.

Any time spectators criticise the referee for being unfit they should ask the question whether they could pass the fitness test that he has to pass three times each year.

Test 1   50 Metre Run—7.5 seconds
Test 2   200 Metre Run—32 seconds
Test 3   50 Metre Run—7.5 seconds
Test 4   200 Metre Run—32 seconds
Test 5   12 Minute Run—Minimum distance to be covered 2,700 metres

During the match, the referee will cover a greater distance than any player - more than 10 km - so all aspects of fitness are very important.

Class 1 referees recently had a Fitness Master Class taken by Tommy Boyle, a top International Athletics Coach responsible for athletes such as Yvonne Murray and Tom McKean.

His message was very simple - regular training and a fitness programme to develop speed, stamina and strength. A sensible diet with pasta, white meat and fish is essential. Pre-match the referee must drink plenty of isotonic fluid and also at half time. Post-match a gentle warm-down, more fluid, a couple of bananas and carbohydrates such as raisins, jelly babies or wine gums.

Definitely a case for buying some shares in sweet manufacturers!

There are many other changes in Scottish refereeing today. Just as clubs are organising Youth Academies and Schools of Excellence to encourage the skills of young players, so the SFA Referee Development Academies have been started to develop the refereeing skills of young referees all over Scotland.

There is no transfer system in refereeing, unlike in clubs, so home grown talent must be developed. Hugh Dallas, Jim McCluskey, Willie Young and the other top Scottish referees all learned their trade on the public parks and junior fields in Scotland. This new development will ensure that the next generation will have the ability to reach similar heights.

Women's football is the fastest growing sport in the world and The Scottish Football Association recognises that it is also necessary to encourage more women to take up refereeing. At present, there are less

Stuart Dougal

than 50 registered women referees in Scotland but it is hoped that this number will increase dramatically in the next few years.

The target is to have a woman referee officiating as an Assistant Referee in Senior football in Scotland by the year 2006. There is no reason why this cannot be achieved and the Youth Development Academies will play an important part.

Teams have coaches who give advice to players and referees have coaches who also give advice on performance and ways of improving their game.

SFA Supervisors and Match Assessors will cover almost every Senior match in Scotland this year giving both written and verbal advice to referees. In the lower levels, Referee Development Advisors attend Junior and amateur matches all over the country identifying young talent and developing their refereeing skills.

The S.F.L. Youth Development Initiative is a major project for the future of Scottish football and the SFA is closely involved in the refereeing development which forms part of the Initiative.

Young referees from the Referee Development Academies are appointed to these matches and have the ideal opportunity to develop aspects of their game such as positioning, movement and signals in this football development environment.

The Youth Development Initiative has great potential for everyone involved - coaches, players and referees.

Refereeing is an important part of the game and can give great enjoyment to those involved at all levels.

Fancy trying it?

GEORGE CUMMING
(S.F.A. Development Director)

John Rowbotham keeps the play flowing

Official List of Referees 1999/2000

CLASS 1 REFEREES		CLASS 1 ASSISTANT REFEREES		
Kevin Bisset	David Somers	John McElhinney	David Davidson	Eddie Mack
Tom Brown	Kevin Toner	Derek Mason	Willie Dishington	Craig Marshall
Brian Cassidy	John Underhill	Tom Murphy	Jamie Downie	Brian Martin
Kenny Clark	Willie Young	Peter Peace	Mark Doyle	Gordon Middleton
Martin Clark		Stewart Shearer	George Drummond	Michael Monaghan
George Clyde	**CLASS 1 SPECIALIST**	Rod Williamson	Steven Duff	Ricky Mooney
Hugh Dallas	**ASSISTANT REFEREES**		Jack Fenton	Alan Muir
Stuart Dougal	Graeme Alison	**CLASS 1 ASSISTANT**	Graham Ferguson	Billy Murray
Ian Elmslie	Neil Brand	**REFEREES**	Stephen Finnie	Calum Murray
John Fleming	Roddy Cobb	Crawford Allan	Andrew Gault	Willie Murray
Alan Freeland	Peter Crilley	Francis Andrews	John Gilmour	Stevie O'Reilly
Ian Frickleton	Alan Cunningham	James Bee	John Gover	Charlie Richmond
Ian Fyfe	Graeme Curr	Stuart Bennett	Keith Hadden	Eric Robertson
Alan Gemmill	Andy Davis	John Bicknell	Joe Heggie	Scott Robertson
Colin Hardie	David Doig	Alan Boyd	David Hodgson	Brian Rooney
Jim Herald	Martin Doran	Jim Boyd	Derek Horan	Andrew Seymour
Steve Kaney	Jim Dunne	Christopher Boyle	Willie Hornby	Ricky Smith
Jim McCluskey	Bob Gunn	David Boyle	Andrew Hunter	Martin Sproule
Michael McCurry	Gordon Hunter	John Brady	Robert Hunter	Gary Sweeney
Douglas McDonald	Wilson Irvine	Iain Brines	Steve Jolly	Craig Thomson
Brian McGarry	Robert Johnston	Harry Brodie	Lawrence Kerrigan	George Thomson
Craig MacKay	Stuart Logan	Colin Brown	Raymond King	Allen Thurston
Eric Martindale	John Love	Scott Brown	Derek Lithgow	Steve Todd
Cammy Melville	Derek Lowe	John Campbell	Scott MacDonald	Mike Tumilty
Garry Mitchell	Jim Lyon	Campbell Carson	Stephen McGeouch	Jim Walker
Bobby Orr	Stuart Macaulay	Kevin Carter	Mike MacGregor	Paul Watson
Mike Ritchie	Gordon McBride	Derek Clark	Gordon Mackay	Willie Weir
John Rowbotham	Jim McBride	Frank Cole	Robert McKendry	Brian Winter
George Simpson	Ross McCluskie	Steve Conroy	Willie McKnight	Ewan Young
Dougie Smith	Joe McDowall	Martin Cryans		
	Brian McDuffie	Hugh Dalgetty		

COMPLETE FIXTURE LISTS FOR
THE SCOTTISH PREMIER LEAGUE
& THE SCOTTISH FOOTBALL LEAGUE

Saturday, July 31st, 1999
BANK OF SCOTLAND SCOTTISH PREMIER LEAGUE
Dundee United v. Dundee
Hibernian v.Motherwell
Rangers v. Kilmarnock
St. Johnstone v. Heart of Midlothian

Sunday, August 1st, 1999
BANK OF SCOTLAND SCOTTISH PREMIER LEAGUE
Aberdeen v. Celtic

Saturday, August 7th, 1999
BANK OF SCOTLAND SCOTTISH PREMIER LEAGUE
Celtic v. St. Johnstone
Heart of Midlothian v. Rangers
Kilmarnock v.Aberdeen
Motherwell v.Dundee United

Saturday, August 7th, 1999
BELL'S SCOTTISH LEAGUE FIRST DIVISION
Clydebank v. Airdrieonians
Dunfermline Athletic v. Inverness Cal. Th.
Falkirk v. Morton
Livingston v. Raith Rovers
St. Mirren v. Ayr United
BELL'S SCOTTISH LEAGUE SECOND DIVISION
Clyde v. Alloa Athletic
Partick Thistle v. Stenhousemuir
Queen of the South v. Arbroath
Ross County v. Hamilton Academical
Stirling Albion v. Stranraer
BELL'S SCOTTISH LEAGUE THIRD DIVISION
Albion Rovers v. Dumbarton
East Fife v. Berwick Rangers
Forfar Athletic v. Brechin City
Montrose v. Cowdenbeath
Queen's Park v. East Stirlingshire

Sunday, August 8th, 1999
BANK OF SCOTLAND SCOTTISH PREMIER LEAGUE
Dundee v. Hibernian

Saturday, August 14th, 1999
BANK OF SCOTLAND SCOTTISH PREMIER LEAGUE
Aberdeen v. Dundee
Hibernian v.Heart of Midlothian

Saturday, August 14th, 1999
BELL'S SCOTTISH LEAGUE FIRST DIVISION
Airdrieonians v. Dunfermline Athletic
Ayr United v. Livingston
Inverness Cal. Th. v. Falkirk
Morton v. Clydebank
Raith Rovers v. St. Mirren
BELL'S SCOTTISH LEAGUE SECOND DIVISION
Alloa Athletic v. Partick Thistle
Arbroath v. Clyde
Hamilton Academical v. Queen of the South
Stenhousemuir v. Stirling Albion
Stranraer v. Ross County
BELL'S SCOTTISH LEAGUE THIRD DIVISION
Berwick Rangers v. Albion Rovers
Brechin City v. Queen's Park
Cowdenbeath v. Forfar Athletic
Dumbarton v. Montrose
East Stirlingshire v. East Fife

Sunday, August 15th, 1999
BANK OF SCOTLAND SCOTTISH PREMIER LEAGUE
Dundee United v.Celtic
Rangers v.Motherwell
St. Johnstone v. Kilmarnock

Saturday, August 21st, 1999
BANK OF SCOTLAND SCOTTISH PREMIER LEAGUE
Dundee v. Celtic
Kilmarnock v. Motherwell
Rangers v. Dundee United
St. Johnstone v. Hibernian
BELL'S SCOTTISH LEAGUE FIRST DIVISION
Clydebank v. Raith Rovers
Dunfermline Athletic v. Morton
Falkirk v. Ayr United
Livingston v. Airdrieonians
St. Mirren v. Inverness Cal. Th.
BELL'S SCOTTISH LEAGUE SECOND DIVISION
Clyde v. Stranraer
Partick Thistle v. Arbroath
Queen of the South v. Alloa Athletic
Ross County v. Stenhousemuir
Stirling Albion v. Hamilton Academical
BELL'S SCOTTISH LEAGUE THIRD DIVISION
Albion Rovers v. Brechin City
East Fife v. Dumbarton
Forfar Athletic v. East Stirlingshire
Montrose v. Berwick Rangers
Queen's Park v. Cowdenbeath

Sunday, August 22nd, 1999
BANK OF SCOTLAND SCOTTISH PREMIER LEAGUE
Heart of Midlothian v. Aberdeen

Saturday, August 28th, 1999
BANK OF SCOTLAND SCOTTISH PREMIER LEAGUE
Hibernian v. Rangers
Motherwell v. Dundee
BELL'S SCOTTISH LEAGUE FIRST DIVISION
Airdrieonians v. Raith Rovers
Ayr United v. Inverness Cal. Th.
Dunfermline Athletic v. Falkirk
Morton v. Livingston
BELL'S SCOTTISH LEAGUE SECOND DIVISION
Alloa Athletic v. Hamilton Academical
Clyde v. Stirling Albion
Partick Thistle v. Queen of the South
Ross County v. Arbroath
Stenhousemuir v. Stranraer
BELL'S SCOTTISH LEAGUE THIRD DIVISION
Berwick Rangers v. Queen's Park
Brechin City v. Dumbarton
East Fife v. Montrose
East Stirlingshire v. Cowdenbeath
Forfar Athletic v. Albion Rovers

Sunday, August 29th, 1999
BANK OF SCOTLAND SCOTTISH PREMIER LEAGUE
Aberdeen v. St. Johnstone
Celtic v. Heart of Midlothian
Dundee United v. Kilmarnock
BELL'S SCOTTISH LEAGUE FIRST DIVISION
Clydebank v. St. Mirren

Saturday, September 4th, 1999
BELL'S SCOTTISH LEAGUE FIRST DIVISION
Falkirk v. Clydebank
Inverness Cal. Th. v. Morton
Livingston v. Dunfermline Athletic
Raith Rovers v. Ayr United
St. Mirren v. Airdrieonians
BELL'S SCOTTISH LEAGUE SECOND DIVISION
Arbroath v. Alloa Athletic
Queen of the South v. Clyde
Stirling Albion v. Ross County
Stranraer v. Partick Thistle
BELL'S SCOTTISH LEAGUE THIRD DIVISION
Albion Rovers v. East Fife

Cowdenbeath v. Brechin City
Dumbarton v. Berwick Rangers
Montrose v. East Stirlingshire
Queen's Park v. Forfar Athletic

Sunday, September 5th, 1999
BELL'S SCOTTISH LEAGUE SECOND DIVISION
Hamilton Academical v. Stenhousemuir

Saturday, September 11th, 1999
BANK OF SCOTLAND SCOTTISH PREMIER LEAGUE
Dundee United v. Hibernian
Heart of Midlothian v. Dundee
Rangers v. Aberdeen
St. Johnstone v. Motherwell
BELL'S SCOTTISH LEAGUE FIRST DIVISION
Ayr United v. Airdrieonians
Dunfermline Athletic v. St. Mirren
Falkirk v. Livingston
Inverness Cal. Th. v. Clydebank
Morton v. Raith Rovers
BELL'S SCOTTISH LEAGUE SECOND DIVISION
Alloa Athletic v. Ross County
Arbroath v. Stirling Albion
Clyde v. Partick Thistle
Hamilton Academical v. Stranraer
Queen of the South v. Stenhousemuir
BELL'S SCOTTISH LEAGUE THIRD DIVISION
Albion Rovers v. Montrose
Berwick Rangers v. Cowdenbeath
Brechin City v. East Stirlingshire
Dumbarton v. Queen's Park
East Fife v. Forfar Athletic

Sunday, September, 12th, 1999
BANK OF SCOTLAND SCOTTISH PREMIER LEAGUE
Kilmarnock v. Celtic

Saturday, September 18th, 1999
BANK OF SCOTLAND SCOTTISH PREMIER LEAGUE
Aberdeen v. Dundee United
Celtic v. Rangers
BELL'S SCOTTISH LEAGUE FIRST DIVISION
Airdrieonians v. Falkirk
Clydebank v. Ayr United
Livingston v. Inverness Cal. Th.
Raith Rovers v. Dunfermline Athletic
St. Mirren v. Morton
BELL'S SCOTTISH LEAGUE SECOND DIVISION
Partick Thistle v. Hamilton Academical
Ross County v. Clyde
Stenhousemuir v. Arbroath
Stirling Albion v. Alloa Athletic
Stranraer v. Queen of the South
BELL'S SCOTTISH LEAGUE THIRD DIVISION
Cowdenbeath v. East Fife
East Stirlingshire v. Dumbarton
Forfar Athletic v. Berwick Rangers
Montrose v. Brechin City
Queen's Park v. Albion Rovers

Sunday, September 19th, 1999
BANK OF SCOTLAND SCOTTISH PREMIER LEAGUE
Dundee v. St. Johnstone
Hibernian v. Kilmarnock

Monday, September 20th, 1999
BANK OF SCOTLAND SCOTTISH PREMIER LEAGUE
Motherwell v.Heart of Midlothian

Saturday, September 25th, 1999
BANK OF SCOTLAND SCOTTISH PREMIER LEAGUE
Dundee United v. Heart of Midlothian

Hibernian v. Celtic
Kilmarnock v. Dundee
Motherwell v. Aberdeen
Rangers v. St. Johnstone
BELL'S SCOTTISH LEAGUE FIRST DIVISION
Dunfermline Athletic v. Ayr United
Falkirk v. St. Mirren
Inverness Cal. Th. v. Raith Rovers
Livingston v. Clydebank
Morton v. Airdrieonians
BELL'S SCOTTISH LEAGUE SECOND DIVISION
Alloa Athletic v. Stenhousemuir
Arbroath v. Stranraer
Clyde v. Hamilton Academical
Partick Thistle v. Ross County
Queen of the South v. Stirling Albion
BELL'S SCOTTISH LEAGUE THIRD DIVISION
Albion Rovers v. East Stirlingshire
Berwick Rangers v. Brechin City
Dumbarton v. Cowdenbeath
East Fife v. Queen's Park
Montrose v. Forfar Athletic

Saturday, October 2nd, 1999
BANK OF SCOTLAND SCOTTISH PREMIER LEAGUE
Aberdeen v. Hibernian
Dundee v. Rangers
BELL'S SCOTTISH LEAGUE FIRST DIVISION
Airdrieonians v. Inverness Cal. Th.
Ayr United v. Morton
Clydebank v. Dunfermline Athletic
Raith Rovers v. Falkirk
St. Mirren v. Livingston
BELL'S SCOTTISH LEAGUE SECOND DIVISION
Hamilton Academical v. Arbroath
Ross County v. Queen of the South
Stenhousemuir v. Clyde
Stirling Albion v. Partick Thistle
Stranraer v. Alloa Athletic
BELL'S SCOTTISH LEAGUE THIRD DIVISION
Brechin City v. East Fife
Cowdenbeath v. Albion Rovers
East Stirlingshire v. Berwick Rangers
Forfar Athletic v. Dumbarton
Queen's Park v. Montrose

Sunday, October 3rd, 1999
BANK OF SCOTLAND SCOTTISH PREMIER LEAGUE
Celtic v. Motherwell
Heart of Midlothian v.Kilmarnock
St. Johnstone v.Dundee United

Saturday, October 9th, 1999
BELL'S SCOTTISH LEAGUE SECOND DIVISION
Hamilton Academical v. Ross County

Saturday, October 16th, 1999
BANK OF SCOTLAND SCOTTISH PREMIER LEAGUE
Celtic v. Aberdeen
Heart of Midlothian v. St. Johnstone
Kilmarnock v. Rangers
Motherwell v. Hibernian
BELL'S SCOTTISH LEAGUE FIRST DIVISION
Clydebank v. Morton
Dunfermline Athletic v. Airdrieonians
Falkirk v. Inverness Cal. Th.
Livingston v. Ayr United
St. Mirren v. Raith Rovers
BELL'S SCOTTISH LEAGUE SECOND DIVISION
Clyde v. Arbroath
Partick Thistle v. Alloa Athletic
Queen of the South v. Hamilton Academical

Ross County v. Stranraer
Stirling Albion v. Stenhousemuir
BELL'S SCOTTISH LEAGUE THIRD DIVISION
Albion Rovers v. Berwick Rangers
East Fife v. East Stirlingshire
Forfar Athletic v. Cowdenbeath
Montrose v. Dumbarton
Queen's Park v. Brechin City

Sunday, October 17th, 1999
BANK OF SCOTLAND SCOTTISH PREMIER LEAGUE
Dundee v. Dundee United

Saturday, October 23rd, 1999
BANK OF SCOTLAND SCOTTISH PREMIER LEAGUE
Aberdeen v. Kilmarnock
Dundee United v. Motherwell
Hibernian v. Dundee
Rangers v. Heart of Midlothian
BELL'S SCOTTISH LEAGUE FIRST DIVISION
Airdrieonians v. Clydebank
Ayr United v. St. Mirren
Inverness Cal.Th. v. Dunfermline Athletic
Morton v. Falkirk
Raith Rovers v. Livingston
BELL'S SCOTTISH LEAGUE SECOND DIVISION
Alloa Athletic v. Clyde
Arbroath v. Queen of the South
Stenhousemuir v. Partick Thistle
Stranraer v. Stirling Albion
BELL'S SCOTTISH LEAGUE THIRD DIVISION
Berwick Rangers v. East Fife
Brechin City v. Forfar Athletic
Cowdenbeath v. Montrose
Dumbarton v. Albion Rovers
East Stirlingshire v. Queen's Park

Sunday, October 24th, 1999
BANK OF SCOTLAND SCOTTISH PREMIER LEAGUE
St. Johnstone v. Celtic

Saturday, October 30th, 1999
BANK OF SCOTLAND SCOTTISH PREMIER LEAGUE
Aberdeen v. Rangers
Celtic v. Kilmarnock
Dundee v. Heart of Midlothian
Motherwell v. St. Johnstone
BELL'S SCOTTISH LEAGUE FIRST DIVISION
Airdrieonians v. Ayr United
Clydebank v. Inverness Cal. Th.
Livingston v. Falkirk
Raith Rovers v. Morton
St. Mirren v. Dunfermline Athletic
BELL'S SCOTTISH LEAGUE SECOND DIVISION
Partick Thistle v. Clyde
Ross County v. Alloa Athletic
Stenhousemuir v. Queen of the South
Stirling Albion v. Arbroath
Stranraer v. Hamilton Academical
BELL'S SCOTTISH LEAGUE THIRD DIVISION
Cowdenbeath v. Berwick Rangers
East Stirlingshire v. Brechin City
Forfar Athletic v. East Fife
Montrose v. Albion Rovers
Queen's Park v. Dumbarton

Sunday, October 31st, 1999
BANK OF SCOTLAND SCOTTISH PREMIER LEAGUE
Hibernian v. Dundee United

Saturday, November 6th, 1999
BANK OF SCOTLAND SCOTTISH PREMIER LEAGUE
Dundee United v. Aberdeen

Heart of Midlothian v. Motherwell
Kilmarnock v. Hibernian
St. Johnstone v.Dundee
BELL'S SCOTTISH LEAGUE FIRST DIVISION
Ayr United v. Clydebank
Dunfermline Athletic v. Raith Rovers
Falkirk v. Airdrieonians
Inverness Cal. Th. v. Livingston
Morton v. St. Mirren
BELL'S SCOTTISH LEAGUE SECOND DIVISION
Alloa Athletic v. Stirling Albion
Arbroath v. Stenhousemuir
Clyde v. Ross County
Hamilton Academical v. Partick Thistle
Queen of the South v. Stranraer
BELL'S SCOTTISH LEAGUE THIRD DIVISION
Albion Rovers v. Queen's Park
Berwick Rangers v. Forfar Athletic
Brechin City v. Montrose
Dumbarton v. East Stirlingshire
East Fife v. Cowdenbeath

Sunday, November 7th, 1999
BANK OF SCOTLAND SCOTTISH PREMIER LEAGUE
Rangers v.Celtic

Saturday, November 13th, 1999
BANK OF SCOTLAND SCOTTISH PREMIER LEAGUE
Aberdeen v. Heart of Midlothian
Celtic v. Dundee
Dundee United v. Rangers
Hibernian v. St. Johnstone
Motherwell v. Kilmarnock
BELL'S SCOTTISH LEAGUE FIRST DIVISION
Airdrieonians v. St. Mirren
Ayr United v. Raith Rovers
Clydebank v. Falkirk
Dunfermline Athletic v. Livingston
Morton v. Inverness Cal. Th.
BELL'S SCOTTISH LEAGUE SECOND DIVISION
Alloa Athletic v. Arbroath
Clyde v. Queen of the South
Partick Thistle v. Stranraer
Ross County v. Stirling Albion
Stenhousemuir v. Hamilton Academical
BELL'S SCOTTISH LEAGUE THIRD DIVISION
Berwick Rangers v. Dumbarton
Brechin City v. Cowdenbeath
East Fife v. Albion Rovers
East Stirlingshire v. Montrose
Forfar Athletic v. Queen's Park

Saturday, November 20th, 1999
BANK OF SCOTLAND SCOTTISH PREMIER LEAGUE
Dundee v. Motherwell
Heart of Midlothian v. Celtic
Kilmarnock v. Dundee United
Rangers v. Hibernian
St. Johnstone v. Aberdeen
BELL'S SCOTTISH LEAGUE FIRST DIVISION
Falkirk v. Dunfermline Athletic
Inverness Cal. Th. v. Ayr United
Livingston v. Morton
Raith Rovers v. Airdrieonians
St. Mirren v. Clydebank
BELL'S SCOTTISH LEAGUE SECOND DIVISION
Arbroath v. Ross County
Hamilton Academical v. Alloa Athletic
Queen of the South v. Partick Thistle
Stirling Albion v. Clyde
Stranraer v. Stenhousemuir

BELL'S
SCOTTISH
FOOTBALL
LEAGUE

BELL'S SCOTTISH LEAGUE THIRD DIVISION
Albion Rovers v. Forfar Athletic
Cowdenbeath v. East Stirlingshire
Dumbarton v. Brechin City
Montrose v. East Fife
Queen's Park v. Berwick Rangers

Saturday, November 27th, 1999
BANK OF SCOTLAND SCOTTISH PREMIER LEAGUE
Dundee United v.St. Johnstone
Hibernian v. Aberdeen
Kilmarnock v. Heart of Midlothian
Motherwell v. Celtic
Rangers v. Dundee
BELL'S SCOTTISH LEAGUE FIRST DIVISION
Dunfermline Athletic v. Clydebank
Falkirk v. Raith Rovers
Inverness Cal. Th. v. Airdrieonians
Livingston v. St. Mirren
Morton v. Ayr United
BELL'S SCOTTISH LEAGUE SECOND DIVISION
Alloa Athletic v. Stranraer
Arbroath v. Hamilton Academical
Clyde v. Stenhousemuir
Partick Thistle v. Stirling Albion
Queen of the South v. Ross County
BELL'S SCOTTISH LEAGUE THIRD DIVISION
Albion Rovers v. Cowdenbeath
Berwick Rangers v. East Stirlingshire
Dumbarton v. Forfar Athletic
East Fife v. Brechin City
Montrose v. Queen's Park

Saturday, December 4th, 1999
BANK OF SCOTLAND SCOTTISH PREMIER LEAGUE
Aberdeen v. Motherwell
Celtic v. Hibernian
Dundee v. Kilmarnock
Heart of Midlothian v. Dundee United
St. Johnstone v. Rangers
BELL'S SCOTTISH LEAGUE FIRST DIVISION
Airdrieonians v. Morton
Ayr United v. Dunfermline Athletic
Clydebank v. Livingston
Raith Rovers v. Inverness Cal. Th.
St. Mirren v. Falkirk
BELL'S SCOTTISH LEAGUE SECOND DIVISION
Hamilton Academical v. Clyde
Ross County v. Partick Thistle
Stenhousemuir v. Alloa Athletic
Stirling Albion v. Queen of the South
Stranraer v. Arbroath
BELL'S SCOTTISH LEAGUE THIRD DIVISION
Brechin City v. Berwick Rangers
Cowdenbeath v. Dumbarton
East Stirlingshire v. Albion Rovers
Forfar Athletic v. Montrose
Queen's Park v. East Fife

Saturday, December 11th, 1999
BANK OF SCOTLAND SCOTTISH PREMIER LEAGUE
Aberdeen v. Celtic
Dundee United v. Dundee
Hibernian v. Motherwell
Rangers v. Kilmarnock
St. Johnstone v. Heart of Midlothian
BELL'S SCOTTISH LEAGUE FIRST DIVISION
Airdrieonians v. Livingston
Ayr United v. Falkirk
Inverness Cal. Th. v. St. Mirren
Morton v. Dunfermline Athletic
Raith Rovers v. Clydebank

Saturday, December 18th, 1999
BANK OF SCOTLAND SCOTTISH PREMIER LEAGUE
Celtic v. Dundee United
Dundee v. Aberdeen
Heart of Midlothian v. Hibernian
Kilmarnock v. St. Johnstone
Motherwell v. Rangers
BELL'S SCOTTISH LEAGUE FIRST DIVISION
Clydebank v. Airdrieonians
Dunfermline Athletic v. Inverness Cal. Th.
Falkirk v. Morton
Livingston v. Raith Rovers
St. Mirren v. Ayr United
BELL'S SCOTTISH LEAGUE SECOND DIVISION
Clyde v. Alloa Athletic
Partick Thistle v. Stenhousemuir
Queen of the South v. Arbroath
Ross County v. Hamilton Academical
Stirling Albion v. Stranraer
BELL'S SCOTTISH LEAGUE THIRD DIVISION
Albion Rovers v. Dumbarton
East Fife v. Berwick Rangers
Forfar Athletic v. Brechin City
Montrose v. Cowdenbeath
Queen's Park v. East Stirlingshire

Monday, December 27th, 1999
BANK OF SCOTLAND SCOTTISH PREMIER LEAGUE
Aberdeen v. Dundee United
Celtic v. Rangers
Dundee v. St. Johnstone
Hibernian v. Kilmarnock
Motherwell v. Heart of Midlothian
BELL'S SCOTTISH LEAGUE FIRST DIVISION
Ayr United v. Airdrieonians
Dunfermline Athletic v. St. Mirren
Falkirk v. Livingston
Inverness Cal. Th. v. Clydebank
Morton v. Raith Rovers
BELL'S SCOTTISH LEAGUE SECOND DIVISION
Alloa Athletic v. Queen of the South
Arbroath v. Partick Thistle
Hamilton Academical v. Stirling Albion
Stenhousemuir v. Ross County
Stranraer v. Clyde
BELL'S SCOTTISH LEAGUE THIRD DIVISION
Berwick Rangers v. Montrose
Brechin City v. Albion Rovers
Cowdenbeath v. Queen's Park
Dumbarton v. East Fife
East Stirlingshire v. Forfar Athletic

Monday, January 3rd, 2000
BELL'S SCOTTISH LEAGUE FIRST DIVISION
Airdrieonians v. Falkirk
Clydebank v. Ayr United
Livingston v. Inverness Cal. Th.
Raith Rovers v. Dunfermline Athletic
St. Mirren v. Morton
BELL'S SCOTTISH LEAGUE SECOND DIVISION
Partick Thistle v. Hamilton Academical
Ross County v. Clyde
Stenhousemuir v. Arbroath
Stirling Albion v. Alloa Athletic
Stranraer v. Queen of the South
BELL'S SCOTTISH LEAGUE THIRD DIVISION
Cowdenbeath v. East Fife
East Stirlingshire v. Dumbarton
Forfar Athletic v. Berwick Rangers
Montrose v. Brechin City
Queen's Park v. Albion Rovers

Saturday, January 8th, 2000
BELL'S SCOTTISH LEAGUE FIRST DIVISION
Falkirk v. Clydebank
Inverness Cal. Th. v. Morton
Livingston v. Dunfermline Athletic
Raith Rovers v. Ayr United
St. Mirren v. Airdrieonians

Saturday, January 15th, 2000
BELL'S SCOTTISH LEAGUE FIRST DIVISION
Airdrieonians v. Raith Rovers
Ayr United v. Inverness Cal. Th.
Clydebank v. St. Mirren
Dunfermline Athletic v. Falkirk
Morton v. Livingston
BELL'S SCOTTISH LEAGUE SECOND DIVISION
Alloa Athletic v. Ross County
Arbroath v. Stirling Albion
Clyde v. Partick Thistle
Hamilton Academical v. Stranraer
Queen of the South v. Stenhousemuir
BELL'S SCOTTISH LEAGUE THIRD DIVISION
Albion Rovers v. Montrose
Berwick Rangers v. Cowdenbeath
Brechin City v. East Stirlingshire
Dumbarton v. Queen's Park
East Fife v. Forfar Athletic

Saturday, January 22nd, 2000
BANK OF SCOTLAND SCOTTISH PREMIER LEAGUE
Dundee United v. Hibernian
Heart of Midlothian v. Dundee
Kilmarnock v. Celtic
Rangers v. Aberdeen
St. Johnstone v. Motherwell
BELL'S SCOTTISH LEAGUE FIRST DIVISION
Dunfermline Athletic v. Ayr United
Falkirk v. St. Mirren
Inverness Cal. Th. v. Raith Rovers
Livingston v. Clydebank
Morton v. Airdrieonians
BELL'S SCOTTISH LEAGUE SECOND DIVISION
Alloa Athletic v. Stenhousemuir
Arbroath v. Stranraer
Clyde v. Hamilton Academical
Partick Thistle v. Ross County
Queen of the South v. Stirling Albion
BELL'S SCOTTISH LEAGUE THIRD DIVISION
Albion Rovers v. East Stirlingshire
Berwick Rangers v. Brechin City
Dumbarton v. Cowdenbeath
East Fife v. Queen's Park
Montrose v. Forfar Athletic

Saturday, February 5th, 2000
BANK OF SCOTLAND SCOTTISH PREMIER LEAGUE
Aberdeen v. St. Johnstone
Celtic v. Heart of Midlothian
Dundee United v. Kilmarnock
Hibernian v. Rangers
Motherwell v. Dundee
BELL'S SCOTTISH LEAGUE FIRST DIVISION
Airdrieonians v. Inverness Cal. Th.
Ayr United v. Morton
Clydebank v. Dunfermline Athletic
Raith Rovers v. Falkirk
St. Mirren v. Livingston
BELL'S SCOTTISH LEAGUE SECOND DIVISION
Hamilton Academical v. Arbroath
Ross County v. Queen of the South
Stenhousemuir v. Clyde
Stirling Albion v. Partick Thistle
Stranraer v. Alloa Athletic
BELL'S SCOTTISH LEAGUE THIRD DIVISION
Brechin City v. East Fife
Cowdenbeath v. Albion Rovers
East Stirlingshire v. Berwick Rangers
Forfar Athletic v. Dumbarton
Queen's Park v. Montrose

Saturday, February 12th, 2000
BANK OF SCOTLAND SCOTTISH PREMIER LEAGUE
Dundee v. Celtic
Heart of Midlothian v. Aberdeen
Kilmarnock v. Motherwell
Rangers v. Dundee United
St. Johnstone v. Hibernian

Saturday, January 15th, 2000
BELL'S SCOTTISH LEAGUE FIRST DIVISION
Clydebank v. Raith Rovers
Dunfermline Athletic v. Morton
Falkirk v. Ayr United
Livingston v. Airdrieonians
St. Mirren v. Inverness Cal. Th.
BELL'S SCOTTISH LEAGUE SECOND DIVISION
Alloa Athletic v. Hamilton Academical
Clyde v. Stirling Albion
Partick Thistle v. Queen of the South
Ross County v. Arbroath
Stenhousemuir v. Stranraer
BELL'S SCOTTISH LEAGUE THIRD DIVISION
Berwick Rangers v. Queen's Park
Brechin City v. Dumbarton
East Fife v. Montrose
East Stirlingshire v. Cowdenbeath
Forfar Athletic v. Albion Rovers

Saturday, February 19th, 2000
BELL'S SCOTTISH LEAGUE SECOND DIVISION
Arbroath v. Alloa Athletic
Hamilton Academical v. Stenhousemuir
Queen of the South v. Clyde
Stirling Albion v. Ross County
Stranraer v. Partick Thistle
BELL'S SCOTTISH LEAGUE THIRD DIVISION
Albion Rovers v. East Fife
Cowdenbeath v. Brechin City
Dumbarton v. Berwick Rangers
Montrose v. East Stirlingshire
Queen's Park v. Forfar Athletic

Saturday, February 26th, 2000
BANK OF SCOTLAND SCOTTISH PREMIER LEAGUE
Aberdeen v. Hibernian
Celtic v. Motherwell
Dundee v. Rangers
Heart of Midlothian v. Kilmarnock
St. Johnstone v. Dundee United
BELL'S SCOTTISH LEAGUE FIRST DIVISION
Airdrieonians v. Dunfermline Athletic
Ayr United v. Livingston
Inverness Cal. Th. v. Falkirk
Morton v. Clydebank
Raith Rovers v. St. Mirren
BELL'S SCOTTISH LEAGUE SECOND DIVISION
Alloa Athletic v. Partick Thistle
Arbroath v. Clyde
Hamilton Academical v. Queen of the South
Stenhousemuir v. Stirling Albion
Stranraer v. Ross County
BELL'S SCOTTISH LEAGUE THIRD DIVISION
Berwick Rangers v. Albion Rovers
Brechin City v. Queen's Park
Cowdenbeath v. Forfar Athletic
Dumbarton v. Montrose
East Stirlingshire v. East Fife

Saturday, March 4th, 2000
BANK OF SCOTLAND SCOTTISH PREMIER LEAGUE
Dundee United v. Heart of Midlothian
Hibernian v. Celtic
Kilmarnock v. Dundee
Motherwell v. Aberdeen
Rangers v. St. Johnstone
BELL'S SCOTTISH LEAGUE FIRST DIVISION
Airdrieonians v. Ayr United
Clydebank v. Inverness Cal. Th.
Livingston v. Falkirk
Raith Rovers v. Morton
St. Mirren v. Dunfermline Athletic

BELL'S SCOTTISH LEAGUE SECOND DIVISION
Clyde v. Stranraer
Partick Thistle v. Arbroath
Queen of the South v. Alloa Athletic
Ross County v. Stenhousemuir
Stirling Albion v. Hamilton Academical

BELL'S SCOTTISH LEAGUE THIRD DIVISION
Albion Rovers v. Brechin City
East Fife v. Dumbarton
Forfar Athletic v. East Stirlingshire
Montrose v. Berwick Rangers
Queen's Park v. Cowdenbeath

Saturday, March 11th, 2000
BANK OF SCOTLAND SCOTTISH PREMIER LEAGUE
Celtic v. St. Johnstone
Dundee v. Hibernian
Heart of Midlothian v. Rangers
Kilmarnock v. Aberdeen
Motherwell v. Dundee United

BELL'S SCOTTISH LEAGUE SECOND DIVISION
Partick Thistle v. Clyde
Ross County v. Alloa Athletic
Stenhousemuir v. Queen of the South
Stirling Albion v. Arbroath
Stranraer v. Hamilton Academical

BELL'S SCOTTISH LEAGUE THIRD DIVISION
Cowdenbeath v. Berwick Rangers
East Stirlingshire v. Brechin City
Forfar Athletic v. East Fife
Montrose v. Albion Rovers
Queen's Park v. Dumbarton

Saturday, March 18th, 2000
BANK OF SCOTLAND SCOTTISH PREMIER LEAGUE
Aberdeen v. Dundee
Dundee United v. Celtic
Hibernian v. Heart of Midlothian
Rangers v. Motherwell
St. Johnstone v. Kilmarnock

BELL'S SCOTTISH LEAGUE FIRST DIVISION
Ayr United v. Clydebank
Dunfermline Athletic v. Raith Rovers
Falkirk v. Airdrieonians
Inverness Cal. Th. v. Livingston
Morton v. St. Mirren

BELL'S SCOTTISH LEAGUE SECOND DIVISION
Alloa Athletic v. Stirling Albion
Arbroath v. Stenhousemuir
Clyde v. Ross County
Hamilton Academical v. Partick Thistle
Queen of the South v. Stranraer

BELL'S SCOTTISH LEAGUE THIRD DIVISION
Albion Rovers v. Queen's Park
Berwick Rangers v. Forfar Athletic
Brechin City v. Montrose
Dumbarton v. East Stirlingshire
East Fife v. Cowdenbeath

Saturday, March 25th, 2000
BANK OF SCOTLAND SCOTTISH PREMIER LEAGUE
Dundee United v. Aberdeen
Heart of Midlothian v. Motherwell
Kilmarnock v. Hibernian
St. Johnstone v. Dundee

BELL'S SCOTTISH LEAGUE FIRST DIVISION
Falkirk v. Dunfermline Athletic
Inverness Cal. Th. v. Ayr United

Livingston v. Morton
Raith Rovers v. Airdrieonians
St. Mirren v. Clydebank

BELL'S SCOTTISH LEAGUE SECOND DIVISION
Arbroath v. Ross County
Hamilton Academical v. Alloa Athletic
Queen of the South v. Partick Thistle
Stirling Albion v. Clyde
Stranraer v. Stenhousemuir

BELL'S SCOTTISH LEAGUE THIRD DIVISION
Albion Rovers v. Forfar Athletic
Cowdenbeath v. East Stirlingshire
Dumbarton v. Brechin City
Montrose v. East Fife
Queen's Park v. Berwick Rangers

Sunday, March 26th, 2000
BANK OF SCOTLAND SCOTTISH PREMIER LEAGUE
Rangers v. Celtic

Saturday, April 1st, 2000
BANK OF SCOTLAND SCOTTISH PREMIER LEAGUE
Aberdeen v. Rangers
Celtic v. Kilmarnock
Dundee v. Heart of Midlothian
Hibernian v. Dundee United
Motherwell v. St. Johnstone

BELL'S SCOTTISH LEAGUE FIRST DIVISION
Airdrieonians v. St. Mirren
Ayr United v. Raith Rovers
Clydebank v. Falkirk
Dunfermline Athletic v. Livingston
Morton v. Inverness Cal. Th.

BELL'S SCOTTISH LEAGUE SECOND DIVISION
Alloa Athletic v. Arbroath
Clyde v. Queen of the South
Partick Thistle v. Stranraer
Ross County v. Stirling Albion
Stenhousemuir v. Hamilton Academical

BELL'S SCOTTISH LEAGUE THIRD DIVISION
Berwick Rangers v. Dumbarton
Brechin City v. Cowdenbeath
East Fife v. Albion Rovers
East Stirlingshire v. Montrose
Forfar Athletic v. Queen's Park

Saturday, April 8th, 2000
BANK OF SCOTLAND SCOTTISH PREMIER LEAGUE
Dundee v. Motherwell
Heart of Midlothian v. Celtic
Kilmarnock v. Dundee United
Rangers v. Hibernian
St. Johnstone v. Aberdeen

BELL'S SCOTTISH LEAGUE FIRST DIVISION
Airdrieonians v. Morton
Ayr United v. Dunfermline Athletic
Clydebank v. Livingston
Raith Rovers v. Inverness Cal. Th.
St. Mirren v. Falkirk

BELL'S SCOTTISH LEAGUE SECOND DIVISION
Hamilton Academical v. Clyde
Ross County v. Partick Thistle
Stenhousemuir v. Alloa Athletic
Stirling Albion v. Queen of the South
Stranraer v. Arbroath

BELL'S SCOTTISH LEAGUE THIRD DIVISION
Brechin City v. Berwick Rangers

Cowdenbeath v. Dumbarton
East Stirlingshire v. Albion Rovers
Forfar Athletic v. Montrose
Queen's Park v. East Fife

Saturday, April 15th, 2000
BANK OF SCOTLAND SCOTTISH PREMIER LEAGUE
Aberdeen v. Heart of Midlothian
Celtic v. Dundee
Dundee United v. Rangers
Hibernian v. St. Johnstone
Motherwell v.Kilmarnock

BELL'S SCOTTISH LEAGUE FIRST DIVISION
Dunfermline Athletic v. Clydebank
Falkirk v. Raith Rovers
Inverness Cal. Th. v. Airdrieonians
Livingston v. St. Mirren
Morton v. Ayr United

BELL'S SCOTTISH LEAGUE SECOND DIVISION
Alloa Athletic v. Stranraer
Arbroath v. Hamilton Academical
Clyde v. Stenhousemuir
Partick Thistle v. Stirling Albion
Queen of the South v. Ross County

BELL'S SCOTTISH LEAGUE THIRD DIVISION
Albion Rovers v. Cowdenbeath
Berwick Rangers v. East Stirlingshire
Dumbarton v. Forfar Athletic
East Fife v. Brechin City
Montrose v. Queen's Park

Saturday, April 22nd, 2000
BANK OF SCOTLAND SCOTTISH PREMIER LEAGUE
Aberdeen v. Motherwell
Celtic v. Hibernian
Dundee v. Kilmarnock
Heart of Midlothian v. Dundee United
St. Johnstone v. Rangers

BELL'S SCOTTISH LEAGUE FIRST DIVISION
Airdrieonians v. Clydebank
Ayr United v. St. Mirren
Inverness Cal. Th. v. Dunfermline Athletic
Morton v. Falkirk
Raith Rovers v. Livingston

BELL'S SCOTTISH LEAGUE SECOND DIVISION
Alloa Athletic v. Clyde
Arbroath v. Queen of the South
Hamilton Academical v. Ross County
Stenhousemuir v. Partick Thistle
Stranraer v. Stirling Albion

BELL'S SCOTTISH LEAGUE THIRD DIVISION
Berwick Rangers v. East Fife
Brechin City v. Forfar Athletic
Cowdenbeath v. Montrose
Dumbarton v. Albion Rovers
East Stirlingshire v. Queen's Park

Saturday, April 29th, 2000
BANK OF SCOTLAND SCOTTISH PREMIER LEAGUE
Dundee United v. St. Johnstone
Hibernian v. Aberdeen
Kilmarnock v. Heart of Midlothian
Motherwell v. Celtic
Rangers v. Dundee

BELL'S SCOTTISH LEAGUE FIRST DIVISION
Clydebank v. Morton
Dunfermline Athletic v. Airdrieonians
Falkirk v. Inverness Cal. Th.

Livingston v. Ayr United
St. Mirren v. Raith Rovers

BELL'S SCOTTISH LEAGUE SECOND DIVISION
Clyde v. Arbroath
Partick Thistle v. Alloa Athletic
Queen of the South v. Hamilton Academical
Ross County v. Stranraer
Stirling Albion v. Stenhousemuir

BELL'S SCOTTISH LEAGUE THIRD DIVISION
Albion Rovers v. Berwick Rangers
East Fife v. East Stirlingshire
Forfar Athletic v. Cowdenbeath
Montrose v. Dumbarton
Queen's Park v. Brechin City

Saturday, May 6th, 2000
BANK OF SCOTLAND SCOTTISH PREMIER LEAGUE
Celtic v. Aberdeen
Dundee v. Dundee United
Heart of Midlothian v. St. Johnstone
Kilmarnock v. Rangers
Motherwell v. Hibernian

BELL'S SCOTTISH LEAGUE FIRST DIVISION
Airdrieonians v. Livingston
Ayr United v. Falkirk
Inverness Cal. Th. v. St. Mirren
Morton v. Dunfermline Athletic
Raith Rovers v. Clydebank

BELL'S SCOTTISH LEAGUE SECOND DIVISION
Alloa Athletic v. Queen of the South
Arbroath v. Partick Thistle
Hamilton Academical v. Stirling Albion
Stenhousemuir v. Ross County
Stranraer v. Clyde

BELL'S SCOTTISH LEAGUE THIRD DIVISION
Berwick Rangers v. Montrose
Brechin City v. Albion Rovers
Cowdenbeath v. Queen's Park
Dumbarton v. East Fife
East Stirlingshire v. Forfar Athletic

Saturday, May 13th, 2000
BANK OF SCOTLAND SCOTTISH PREMIER LEAGUE
Aberdeen v. Kilmarnock
Dundee United v. Motherwell
Hibernian v. Dundee
Rangers v. Heart of Midlothian
St. Johnstone v. Celtic

Sunday, May 21st, 2000
BANK OF SCOTLAND SCOTTISH PREMIER LEAGUE
Celtic v. Dundee United
Dundee v. Aberdeen
Heart of Midlothian v. Hibernian
Kilmarnock v. St. Johnstone
Motherwell v. Rangers

1st Round

East Fife   -v-   Stirling Albion
Partick Thistle   -v-   Alloa Athletic
Brechin City   -v-   Dumbarton
Ross County   -v-   Forfar Athletic
Stranraer   -v-   Raith Rovers
Queen of the South -v-   Arbroath
Albion Rovers   -v-   Clyde
Clydebank   -v-   East Stirlingshire
Cowdenbeath   -v-   Livingston
Stenhousemuir   -v-   Inverness Cal. Th.
Queen's Park   -v-   Berwick Rangers
Montrose   -v-   Hamilton Academical

Above ties to be played on Saturday, 31st July, 1999

2nd Round

Dundee   -v-   Dumbarton
Inverness Cal. Th.   -v-   St. Mirren
Ayr United   -v-   Hamilton Academical
East Fife   -v-   Airdrieonians
Aberdeen   -v-   Livingston
Clyde   -v-   Hibernian
Morton   -v-   Alloa Athletic

Above ties to be played on Tuesday, 17th August, 1999

Raith Rovers   -v-   Motherwell
Dundee United   -v-   Ross County
Queen of the South   -v-   Heart of Midlothian
Dunfermline Athletic   -v-   Queen's Park
East Stirlingshire   -v-   Falkirk

Above ties to be played on Wednesday, 18th August, 1999

3rd Round

-v-
-v-
-v-
-v-
-v-
-v-
-v-
-v-

*Ties to be played on Tuesday, 12th or
Wednesday, 13th October, 1999*

4th Round

-v-
-v-
-v-
-v-

*Ties to be played on Tuesday 30th November or
Wednesday, 1st December, 1999*

Semi–Finals

-v-
-v-

*Ties to be played on Sunday, 13th February, and
Tuesday, 15th or Wednesday 16th February, 2000*

THE CIS INSURANCE CUP FINAL

-v-

To be played on Sunday, 19th March, 2000

In the event of a draw after normal time in all rounds, extra-time of 30 minutes (i.e. 15 minutes each way) will take place and thereafter, if necessary, Kicks from the Penalty Mark in accordance with the rules laid down by The International Football Association Board will be taken.

The CIS Insurance Cup

*CIS General Manager, Marketing, Martin Clarke with Duncan Shearer
(Inverness Caledonian Thistle) and Colin Cameron (Heart of Midlothian)
at the launch of The CIS Insurance Cup*

1st Round

Berwick Rangers	-v-	Queen of the South
Airdrieonians	-v-	Dumbarton
Clyde	-v-	Ross County
Montrose	-v-	Hamilton Academical
Ayr United	-v-	Raith Rovers
Arbroath	-v-	East Fife
Brechin City	-v-	Queen's Park
Cowdenbeath	-v-	Alloa Athletic
Dunfermline Athletic	-v-	Morton
East Stirlingshire	-v-	Clydebank
Inverness Cal. Th.	-v-	St. Mirren
Stranraer	-v-	Falkirk
Stirling Albion	-v-	Stenhousemuir
Partick Thistle	-v-	Albion Rovers

Byes: Livingston and Forfar Athletic

Above ties to be played on Tuesday, 10th August, 1999

2nd Round

-v-
-v-
-v-
-v-
-v-
-v-
-v-
-v-

Ties to be played on Tuesday, 24th August, 1999

3rd Round

-v-
-v-
-v-
-v-

Ties to be played on Tuesday, 14th September, 1999

Semi-Finals

-v-
-v-

Ties to be played on Tuesday, 28th September, 1999

THE BELL'S CHALLENGE CUP FINAL

-v-

To be played on Sunday, 21st November, 1999

In the event of a draw after normal time in all rounds, extra-time of 30 minutes (i.e. 15 minutes each way) will take place and thereafter, if necessary, Kicks from the Penalty Mark in accordance with the rules laid down by The International Football Association Board will be taken.

BREAKDOWN OF HOW ALL THE SCOTTISH FOOTBALL LEAGUE SPONSORSHIP MONIES WILL BE ALLOCATED DURING SEASON 1999/2000

DISTRIBUTION OF BELL'S SCOTTISH FOOTBALL LEAGUE CHAMPIONSHIP MONIES

First Division	£17,000 per club
Second Division	£10,000 per club
Third Division	£8,500 per club

DISTRIBUTION OF CIS INSURANCE CUP MONIES

1st Round Losers	12 x £6,000
2nd Round Losers	12 x £8,500
3rd Round Losers	8 x £15,000
4th Round Losers	4 x £20,000
Semi-Final Losers	2 x £30,000
Runner-up	£60,000
Winner	£80,000

DISTRIBUTION OF BELL'S CHALLENGE CUP MONIES

1st Round Losers	14 x £3,000
2nd Round Losers	8 x £4,000
3rd Round Losers	4 x £5,000
Semi-Final Losers	2 x £6,000
Runner-up	£12,000
Winner	£16,000

TENNENTS SCOTTISH CUP 1999/2000

First Round ....11th December, 1999
Second Round ....8th January, 2000
Third Round ....29th January, 2000
Fourth Round ....19th February, 2000
Fifth Round ....11th March, 2000
Semi-Finals ....8th April, 2000
Final ....27th May, 2000

EUROPEAN CHAMPIONSHIP - EURO 2000 QUALIFYING COMPETITION - GROUP 9

Bosnia Herzegovina -v- Scotland........Saturday, 4th September, 1999
Estonia -v- Scotland ....Wednesday, 8th September, 1999
Scotland -v- Bosnia Herzegovina........Tuesday, 5th October, 1999
Scotland -v- Lithuania......................Saturday, 9th October, 1999

EUROPEAN "UNDER-21" CHAMPIONSHIP, 1998/2000 QUALIFYING MATCHES - GROUP 9

Bosnia Herzegovina -v- Scotland........Saturday, 4th September, 1999
Estonia -v- Scotland ....Tuesday, 7th September, 1999
Scotland -v- Bosnia Herzegovina........Tuesday, 5th October, 1999
Scotland -v- Lithuania......................Friday, 8th October, 1999

EUROPEAN "UNDER 18" CHAMPIONSHIP 1999/2000 QUALIFYING GROUP - MINI TOURNAMENT
To be played in France

France -v- Scotland............................Monday, 25th October, 1999
Armenia -v- Scotland ....Wednesday, 27th October, 1999

THREE NATIONS "UNDER 17" INTERNATIONAL TOURNAMENT
To be played in Scotland

Scotland -v- Belgium ....Monday, 27th September, 1999
Belgium -v- Denmark ....Wednesday, 29th September, 1999
Scotland -v- Denmark.......................Friday, 1st October, 1999

EUROPEAN "UNDER 16" CHAMPIONSHIP 1999/2000 QUALIFYING MATCHES - MINI TOURNAMENT
To be played in Portugal

Austria -v- Scotland...........................Tuesday, 14th March, 2000
Portugal -v- Scotland ....Saturday, 18th March, 2000

"UNDER 16" INTERNATIONAL CHALLENGE MATCHES

Malta -v- Scotland ....Saturday, 4th September, 1999
Malta -v- Scotland ....Monday, 6th September, 1999

UEFA CHAMPIONS LEAGUE

Qualifying Round 1
First-Leg matches ....Wednesday, 14th July, 1999
Second-Leg matches..........................Wednesday, 21st July, 1999
Qualifying Round 2
First-Leg matches ....Wednesday, 28th July, 1999
Second-Leg matches..........................Wednesday, 4th August, 1999
Qualifying Round 3
First-Leg matches ....Wednesday, 11th August, 1999
Second-Leg matches..........................Wednesday, 25th August, 1999
First Group Stage:
1st Match Days: ....Tuesday, 14th September and
....Wednesday, 15th September, 1999
2nd Match Days: ....Tuesday, 21st September and
....Wednesday, 22nd September, 1999

3rd Match Days:................................Tuesday, 28th September and
....Wednesday, 29th September, 1999
4th Match Days:................................Tuesday, 19th October and
....Wednesday, 20th October, 1999
5th Match Days: ....Tuesday, 26th October and
....Wednesday, 27th October, 1999
6th Match Days: ....Tuesday, 2nd November and
....Wednesday, 3rd November, 1999
Second Group Stage:
1st Match Days: ....Tuesday, 23rd November and
....Wednesday, 24th November, 1999
2nd Match Days: ....Tuesday 7th December and
....Wednesday, 8th December, 1999
3rd Match Days:................................Tuesday, 29th February and
....Wednesday, 1st March, 2000
4th Match Days:................................Tuesday, 7th March and
....Wednesday, 8th March, 2000
5th Match Days: ....Tuesday, 14th March and
....Wednesday, 15th March, 2000
6th Match Days: ....Tuesday, 21st March and
....Wednesday, 22nd March, 2000
Quarter Finals:
First-Leg:..Tuesday, 4th April and
....Wednesday, 5th April, 2000
Second-Leg: ....Tuesday, 18th April and
....Wednesday, 19th April, 2000
Semi-Finals:
First-Leg:..Tuesday, 2nd May and
....Wednesday, 3rd May, 2000
Second-Leg: ....Tuesday, 9th May and
....Wednesday, 10th May, 2000
Final: ....Wednesday, 24th May, 2000

U.E.F.A. CUP

Qualifying Round:
First-Leg matches:.............................Thursday, 12th August, 1999
Second-Leg matches: ....Thursday, 26th August, 1999
First Round:
First-Leg matches:.............................Thursday, 16th September, 1999
Second-Leg matches: ....Thursday, 30th September, 1999
Second Round:
First-Leg matches:.............................Thursday, 21st October, 1999
Second-Leg matches: ....Thursday, 4th November, 1999
Third Round:
First-Leg matches:.............................Thursday, 25th November, 1999
Second-Leg matches: ....Thursday, 9th December, 1999
Fourth Round:
First-Leg matches:.............................Thursday, 2nd March, 2000
Second-Leg matches: ....Thursday, 9th March, 2000
Quarter Finals:
First-Leg matches:.............................Thursday, 16th March, 2000
Second-Leg matches: ....Thursday, 23rd March, 2000
Semi-Finals:
First-Leg matches:.............................Thursday, 6th April, 2000
Second-Leg matches: ....Thursday, 20th April, 2000
Final: ....Wednesday, 17th May, 2000

EUROPEAN CHAMPIONSHIP - FINAL COMPETITION EURO 2000 - THE LOW COUNTRIES

Group Matches: Saturday, 10th- Wednesday, 21st June, 2000 inclusive
(Group Matches Played Each Day)
Quarter Finals: Saturday, 24th & Sunday, 25th June, 2000
Semi-Finals: Wednesday, 28th & Thursday, 29th June, 2000
Final: Sunday, 2nd July, 2000